Political Modernization
in Japan and Turkey

STUDIES IN
POLITICAL DEVELOPMENT

1. Communications and Political Development
Edited by Lucian W. Pye

2. Bureaucracy and Political Development
Edited by Joseph LaPalombara

3. Political Modernization in Japan and Turkey
Edited by Robert E. Ward and Dankwart A. Rustow

❖

Sponsored by the Committee on
Comparative Politics of the Social
Science Research Council

Gabriel A. Almond, *Chairman*

Leonard Binder
R. Taylor Cole
James S. Coleman
Herbert Hyman
Joseph LaPalombara
Sigmund Neumann
Lucian W. Pye
Sidney Verba
Robert E. Ward
Myron Weiner

Bryce Wood, *staff*

Political Modernization in Japan and Turkey

Edited by Robert E. Ward
& Dankwart A. Rustow

CONTRIBUTORS

JOHN WHITNEY HALL   FREDERICK W. FREY
HALİL İNALCIK   SHŪICHI KATŌ
ROBERT A. SCALAPINO   KEMAL H. KARPAT
RODERIC H. DAVISON   MASAMICHI INOKI
WILLIAM W. LOCKWOOD   RICHARD L. CHAMBERS
PETER F. SUGAR   ROGER F. HACKETT
R. P. DORE   NOBUTAKA IKE
ARİF T. PAYASLIOĞLU

PRINCETON, NEW JERSEY
PRINCETON UNIVERSITY PRESS

1964

FOREWORD

THIS volume is the third in a series of Studies in Political Development sponsored by the Committee on Comparative Politics of the Social Science Research Council under a grant from the Ford Foundation. In turning to the theme of political change and modernization, the Committee hopes to make a contribution to political theory as well as to enhance our understanding of the national and political "explosion" of our time. The distinctive phenomenon of contemporary politics is the new or rapidly changing nation, testing out political forms, processes, and policies in its efforts to find its place in the modern world. The Committee's program seeks to develop concepts, insights, and theories which will improve our capacity to understand these experiments and to evaluate their prospects.

The present volume follows a different tack than that employed in other volumes in the series. It takes two of the non-Western countries which have gone farthest in the direction of modernization—Japan and Turkey—and then searches systematically in the historical experiences of these countries for answers to two questions: First, how can we account for their relative success in modernization? Second, how can we account for the differences in their rates and patterns of modernization?

The method is complementary to that of the other Studies in Political Development. The volumes treating the media of communication, bureaucracy (already published as Vols. 1 and 2) education, and political parties (forthcoming) are concerned with the significance of these institutions for political change in different national and cultural contexts. Our aim here is to improve our understanding of how specific institutions may affect particular political outcomes. *Political Modernization in Japan and Turkey* examines these and other institutions in historical perspective and in connection with their premodern cultures, in an effort to improve our understanding of the interrelationships of the various components of the process of modernization. Used together, these methods may advance our thinking about two fundamental problems in the theory of political change: First, are there necessary and recurrent sequences in political and social change which have to be respected in all planning for political development? Second, how can we "invest" most effectively in the "growth" of particular institutions in order to produce the political outcomes which we prefer?

The papers which appear in this volume were prepared for the Conference on Political Modernization in Japan and Turkey which was held from September 10 to 14, 1962, at Gould House, Dobbs Ferry, New York, under the direction of Robert E. Ward and Dankwart A. Rustow. The papers have been revised since that time and the editors have provided an introduction which presents an analytical framework and a concluding chapter which systematically draws together the findings of the study.

The conference was attended by members of the Committee on Comparative Politics, and by the authors of the papers published in the volume. Others who participated were: Richard K. Beardsley, Center for Japanese Studies, University of Michigan; Wolfram Eberhard, Department of Sociology, University of California, Berkeley; Charles Frankel, Department of Philosophy, Columbia University; Haruhiro Fukui, University of Michigan; Manfred Halpern, Department of Politics, Princeton University; Pendleton Herring, Social Science Research Council; Bert F. Hoselitz, Research Center in Economic Development and Cultural Change, University of Chicago; Samuel P. Huntington, Institute of War and Peace Studies, Columbia University; Takeshi Ishida, Institute for Social Research, Tokyo University; Akdes Nimet Kurat, Dil ve Tarih Coğrafya Fakültesi, University of Ankara; James Morley, East Asian Institute, Columbia University; Herbert Passin, East Asian Institute, Columbia University; James Perkins, Carnegie Corporation of New York; Gustave von Grunebaum, Center for Middle Eastern Studies, University of California, Los Angeles; Walter F. Weiker, Department of Political Science, Rutgers University; and Bryce Wood, Social Science Research Council.

The authors would like to express their indebtedness and gratitude to all of the foregoing participants. They also take pleasure in acknowledging the invaluable assistance of Dr. Alexander W. Allison, who edited all of the papers. Finally, Dr. Ward would like to thank the Carnegie Corporation of New York for support which was of material assistance to the preparation and editing of this volume.

Gabriel A. Almond

CONTENTS

CONTENTS

Political Modernization
in Japan and Turkey

CHAPTER 1

INTRODUCTION

DANKWART A. RUSTOW AND ROBERT E. WARD

I. Modernization and Politics

THE present volume seeks to compare, in a series of parallel essays, the political modernization of Japan and Turkey. To introduce the reader to it, three explanations seem in order: of our choice of topic, of our choice of locales, and of our manner of comparison.

The term "modernization" has found increasing acceptance among social scientists and historians to refer to the grand transformation that began in Western Europe at the end of the Middle Ages and that in our own day has engulfed the remotest countries. Like any term describing a broad historical phenomenon, such as "feudalism," "enlightenment," "industrial revolution," or "nationalism," it must reconcile the precision of conceptual logic with the diffuseness of recorded human experience.

In logic and in etymology, modernization denotes a process of long-range cultural and social change accepted by members of the changing society as beneficial, inevitable, or on balance desirable. Modernization, therefore, is in conflict with any view of human history as moving in periodic cycles from perfection to decay and regeneration, or as a continual decline, or as a predicament escapable only in a hereafter. When Voltaire extolled "Ah, le bon temps que ce siècle de fer,"[1] and in the following verses proceeded to ridicule the Greek myth of the Golden Age and the Christian myth of the Garden of Eden, he was speaking as a proud modernizer. As the age of iron and steel has evolved into the age of atomic bombs and space missiles, this earlier optimism has become tinged with considerable apprehension. Yet such apprehension has not given rise to any serious efforts to return to the economic and social patterns of earlier ages.

Modernization as a historical concept includes such specific aspects of change as industrialization of the economy or secularization of ideas, but it is not limited to these. It involves a marked increase in geographic and social mobility, a spread of secular, scientific, and tech-

---

[1] Voltaire, "Le mondain."

3

nical education, a transition from ascribed to achieved status, an increase in material standards of living, and many related and subsidiary phenomena. Rough numerical measures of modernization are provided, in our century, by the ratio of inanimate to animate energy used in the economy, the proportion of the working force employed in secondary and tertiary rather than primary production (that is, in manufacturing and services, as opposed to agriculture and fishing), the degree of urbanization, the extent of literacy, the circulation of mass media, the gross national product per capita, and the length of life expectancy at birth.

Perhaps the central aspect of modernization as a historical phenomenon, as Cyril Black has suggested,[2] is man's rapidly increasing control over the forces of nature—or rather society's control, for it is achieved not by any individual in isolation, but rather by men in a complex division of labor. Hence growing control over the physical environment is accompanied by growing social interdependence. Man becomes master of nature and servant to other men. Even as it confers unprecedented benefits, modernization brings with it inevitable costs and hazards. Fewer men in modernized society are killed by lightning and more in traffic accidents. The electric current that lets us read late at night, that keeps our food from spoiling, that permits us to hear music at the flick of a switch, also makes us impotent victims of the power failure and the utility strike. Every day we pay for the comforts of technology with sacrifices of privacy, of intimacy, of leisure. Although a society as a whole cannot engage in modernization without accepting it, on balance, as beneficial, the student of modernization need not for himself concur in this evaluation. His study is amply justified if modernization, for good or for ill, is recognized as one of the most potent and significant forces of the age.

In the political sphere, it is advisable not to link the broad historical concept of modernization with any particular regime or ideology. The growth of representative and democratic institutions has accompanied modernization in many of the countries of Western Europe and their overseas offshoots. Most other countries of the world, including even totalitarian regimes, have embraced at least some of the outward forms of representative and democratic government, such as elections, parliaments, and written constitutions. Often this amounts to little more than a fashionable acceptance of customs endowed with the political-economic-cultural prestige of the West—

[2] Cyril E. Black, *Modernization: Essays in Comparative History* (forthcoming).

4

comparable to the adoption, say, of trousers and brimmed hats. At other times it has been a more organic and meaningful response to popular expectations and demands aroused by social and economic modernization. It is quite conceivable that similar expectations and demands will arise in still other countries as they proceed along their paths of modernization. The precise relationship between modernity and democracy is therefore a legitimate and important subject for scholarly enquiry.

But nothing is to be gained by foreclosing such empirical study with a mere verbal equation. Democracy and representative government are not implied in our definition of modernization. Czar Peter of Russia, Sultan Mahmud of Turkey, and Emperor Meiji of Japan were modernizers, but decidedly not democrats or conscious forerunners of democracy. Germany was more modern in the 1930's than in the 1880's, though its government was less representative and less liberal. Classical Marxists believed that all societies move along a single path, though not at equal pace, toward one preordained goal. This artless and simplistic notion does not gain in validity as we change the sign at the finish line from "Communism" to "Democracy."

There are nonetheless certain definite political characteristics that modernizing societies share. Commonly modernization begins under autocracy or oligarchy and proceeds toward some form of mass society —democratic or authoritarian. Under whatever regime, the hallmarks of the modern state are a vastly expanded set of functions and demands. Public services come to include education, social security, and public works while civic duties involve new forms of loyalty, tax payment and, in a world of warring states, military service.[3] The very concepts of public service and civic duty, indeed, are among the vital prerequisites of modern politics.

The tendency, moreover, is for services and obligations to become universal: schooling for all children, a road into every village, conscription for all men, and a tax out of every pay envelope. Hence political modernization clearly has egalitarian tendencies. The performances of all the new or expanded services usually means a vast increase in public employment, just as the more intensive interaction among citizens is accompanied by a vast expansion in the network of communications.

[3] For an elaboration of these themes see William Kornhauser, *The Politics of Mass Society*, Glencoe, Ill., 1959, and Ernest Barker, *The Development of Public Services in Western Europe, 1660-1930*, London, 1944.

The public services and civic duties of the modern polity and the division of labor in a modern economy require a stable geographic context. Nomadic tribalism, feudalism, and any system such as the Ottoman *millets*, whereby the individual carries his law from place to place, are incompatible with modernization. The modern state is a territorial state.

Frequently, however, modernization involves a change in the size of the effective political unit. The vast traditional realms of the Holy Roman Emperors, of the Mughals, Habsburgs, and Ottomans proved too unwieldy and their populations too heterogeneous to permit modernization. The more limited traditional units of village and tribe proved too small. In the history of Europe since the fifteenth century and of Asia and Africa in the twentieth, political modernization has been closely associated with nationalism. But here, as earlier with democracy, the empirical relationship should not be prejudged by an act of definition. Western European countries that established their national identities at an early stage, such as Britain, France, and the Netherlands, became the leaders in the industrial revolution and other aspects of modernization. Yet in our own century, the highest levels of economic production and political effectiveness can be attained only in larger entities—witness the drive toward European integration. And the two leading Communist states are carrying out their modernization programs within the vast boundaries of the former Romanov and Manchu empires. Nationalism in the historic sense may yet cease to be a normal concomitant of the political modernization process.

Certain psychological attitudes are also of prime importance for political modernization. Modernization, as Charles Frankel has observed, changes the concept of "social time."[4] Modern people are impatient people: they want change now or, at the latest, within their generation; they firmly believe that today's society and tomorrow's technology can produce changes unthinkable in bygone days. The modern citizen also joins a political association or supports a political group for the sake of specified aims and concrete benefits. Even the case for conservatism tends to be argued on instrumental, utilitarian grounds. The modern political spirit is thus secular and pragmatic, and bargaining is its most favored technique.

In more technical language, then, a modern polity may be said to be characterized by:

[4] See Charles Frankel, *The Democratic Prospect*, New York, 1962, pp. 13-20.

1. A highly differentiated and functionally specific system of governmental organization;
2. A high degree of integration within this governmental structure;
3. The prevalence of rational and secular procedures for the making of political decisions;
4. The large volume, wide range, and high efficacy of its political and administrative decisions;
5. A widespread and effective sense of popular identification with the history, territory, and national identity of the state;
6. Widespread popular interest and involvement in the political system, though not necessarily in the decision-making aspects thereof;
7. The allocation of political roles by achievement rather than ascription; and
8. Judicial and regulatory techniques based upon a predominantly secular and impersonal system of law.

No society, of course, displays all of the qualities or traits here suggested in pure, complete, or exclusive form. Even the most modern society retains some pre-modern or traditional elements. The monarchical institutions of Britain and Japan are good illustrations. At the other extreme, no states survive in the mid-twentieth century that are untouched by modernization. In a strict sense, therefore, all societies may be said to offer a mixture of modern and traditional traits; yet there are obvious and vast differences in the proportions and interrelations of the ingredients. In some countries the mixture approximates pure "tradition," as in Ethiopia or Afghanistan; in others, it represents a pattern as innovational, as "modern," as the United States or the Soviet Union. In this sense evaluations of development are more concerned with the central tendency of societies than with any search for uniform or undiluted "traditionality" or "modernity."

II. Japan and Turkey

In the early planning of this volume, the possibility was considered of including a larger number of political systems in the comparative analysis. A wider and more representative sample might have increased the persuasiveness and utility of many findings. The decision to limit the study to only two countries stemmed from the conviction that in this early and highly experimental phase of comparative developmental

7

analysis an examination in some detail of only two political systems would prove more useful than would more generalized and dilute information about the development of four or five systems.

Of the two countries selected, Turkey is twice as large in area and Japan three times as large in population. The countries differ considerably in their specific mixtures of modernity and tradition. In present levels of economic and social attainment, the disparity is striking. The standard of living of the average Japanese today is nearly twice as high as that of his Turkish contemporary. In Japan, 98 per cent of the population is literate and only 37 per cent are engaged in agriculture or other forms of primary production. In Turkey, the ratios are 39 and 77 per cent. Japan is the only country outside of Europe and without a European-descended population that has joined the foremost ranks of industrialized nations. Turkey, by contrast, displays most of the problems typical of "underdeveloped" economies, and while Turkey has, for well over a decade, been an eager recipient of foreign aid, Japan now has joined the "advanced" donor countries.

In their recent political history and in their programs of modernization, however, Japan and Turkey offer some remarkable parallels. Modernization began in Western and Central Europe in the fifteenth and sixteenth centuries, and it spread mainly by virtue of the superior technology and the greater economic, military, and political power attained by the early modernizing nations. Specifically the spread took three forms: the settlement of solid European populations in overseas colonial territories such as North America, Australia, or New Zealand; the establishment of European colonial rule over native populations in Africa, South and Southeast Asia, and Latin America; and the threat of European invasion or conquest in countries (such as Russia, China, Japan, Turkey, Iran, and Thailand) that retained their traditional cultural and political identities. In these latter countries, the first impulse to modernize came as the conscious decision of an indigenous ruler or an indigenous elite bent on preserving their political power and traditions against the military threat from the West. In Russia that decision was made in the early eighteenth century. Other countries in this non-colonial, non-Western category, such as Yemen, Afghanistan, Thailand, Nepal, and Ethiopia, are only now on the verge of intensive modernization programs. In Japan and Turkey, the initial programs of defensive modernization[5] came in the mid-nineteenth century: the Tanzimat in 1839, the Meiji Restoration in 1868, al-

[5] For this concept see Black, *op.cit.*

though many might prefer to date the Ottoman reforms from the New Order of Selim III in the 1790's. To be sure, the subsequent political experience of Turkey, characterized as it was by the gradual decline and final collapse of the Ottoman Empire and the emergence of a new national state after 1908, contains many elements which diverge widely from the Japanese case. But, if one looks to such essential criteria of political modernization as secularization, functional differentiation of governmental organization, or the creation of a professionalized, achievement-oriented bureaucracy, it will be seen that below the surface of a dramatically different political history there flowed a strong sub-current of modernizing experience which Turkey shares with Japan and other developing societies.

Besides this question of the timing and duration of exposure to the modernizing process, the extent of the social and political changes to which this exposure gave rise is also of interest. In this respect, there is probably no question about the extent of modernizing change which has occurred in Japan, but there are several other Asian countries which might have been considered as alternatives to Turkey. Israel by most tests would probably rank as the most developed society in Asia. But present-day Israel lacks the roots in Asian history and culture which were thought desirable for our study. China in many respects would have made a particularly interesting partner to compare with Japan, but the sparsity of accurate or reliable data on recent developments and the unique aspects of her totalitarian experience argued against this. A long colonial history and special polyethnic and linguistic problems made India seem a somewhat less attractive choice than Turkey.

Such considerations aside, however, strong positive support for the selection of Turkey was afforded by the following considerations. Turkey was, like Japan, a society of Asian background and culture. It had never been subject to outright colonial rule but had maintained its independence throughout the period of our concern. Its government had since 1908 at least—and, more markedly, since 1919—been engaged in a systematic and persistent attempt to modernize the country's social and political structure, attitudes, and behavior. By 1960 these efforts had borne fruit. If one examines the common statistical indicators which relate to the socio-political development of all major Asian states as of 1960-1961, it will be seen that the performance characteristics of Turkey compare very favorably to those of any other

9

Asian state, except Israel and Japan.[6] This is true in an averaged sense with respect to demographic data, literacy, life expectation, newspaper circulation, radio ownership, volume of domestic mail, industrial working force, production of electric energy, steel and concrete production and consumption, the origins of gross domestic product, and per capita distribution of gross national product. Turkey does not lead Asia in any of these respects, but, by current Asian standards, she performs very respectably in all of them. By such criteria, Turkey undoubtedly stands high in the ranks of the most developed states in Asia. Despite recent difficulties, it was felt that this was also true of Turkish political structure and performance.

It is this combination of similarities and contrasts in the political, economic, social, and cultural aspects of modernization that suggested Japan and Turkey as fruitful examples for more detailed comparison. We have been impressed by both the similarities of impulsion, direction, and pattern that characterized the modernization process in both countries and by the differential results obtained. Throughout, we have primarily been concerned with political modernization as a process embedded in a wider social and cultural transformation that extends over a century or more.

III. Political Statics and Political Dynamics

It seems to us that most studies to date in the field of comparative government or politics (when they have been concerned with comparison at all) have tended to concentrate on the static aspects of comparison. The search generally has been for categories of comparison which would be applicable to political systems as they are, whether these categories have been sought in institutions, in groups, or in functions.[7] There is a great need for studies of this kind, and the many theoretical problems which they suggest constitute a fruitful field for further systematic investigation. Yet the type of comparison these studies embody is static: they analyze and compare political systems viewed in cross-section at a given point of time, and they conceive of these systems as existing essentially in a state of equilibrium.

Another dimension of comparison is possible and, we would argue, equally essential to a mature and comprehensive theory of politics.

[6] For a more detailed statistical survey, see Robert E. Ward and Roy C. Macridis, eds., *Modern Political Systems: Asia*, Englewood-Cliffs, N.J., 1963, pp. 459-468.

[7] The most comprehensive and illuminating recent study of this type combines the group and functional categories. See Gabriel Almond and James S. Coleman, eds., *The Politics of the Developing Areas*, Princeton, 1960.

This is the dynamic or developmental dimension. Political systems change over time—and not only in accidents but in essentials. History, indeed, is in large part a loose-knit chronicle of the seemingly endless variety of changes to which human politics has been subject. The theoretical questions posed by such changes are ancient: is there any pattern or patterns in the developmental experience of particular societies and their politics and, if so, can one discover common features of sufficient importance to justify comparison and allow generalization? To put the question more sharply: can categories be found that would permit the comparison of the political development of the United States with that of Britain or the USSR, or, as in our present venture, that of Japan with that of Turkey? If so, one could add a dynamic dimension to what has been the essentially static preoccupation of theory and methodology in the field of comparative politics.

If further weight were needed, it is obviously given by the practical political involvements and needs of the moment. One of the great themes of twentieth-century political history is the emergence or re-emergence of former colonial or "backward" societies as claimants of more independent and positive roles on the world stage. At the moment this means that practically all of them are immersed in protean struggles for "modernization" or "development"—economic, social, psychological, and political. They are not alone in these struggles. A considerable number of the so-called "developed" societies are also committing very sizeable amounts of capital and other forms of assistance in an effort to shorten, meliorate, and direct this process of "development" among the "underdeveloped" nations. Both sides are eagerly seeking guide-lines calculated to simplify their problems and inject some greater element of predictability and certainty into the overall process. It would help enormously in this endeavor if we had a larger measure of understanding of how societies which are, in a relative sense at least, considered "advanced" came to achieve their present levels of economic, social, and political "development." Are there regularities to be found among their several developmental experiences? Are there discernible stages or sequences of change through which all or some tend to pass? Or, at least, do they face similar problems or crises and do these occur in some regular sort of sequence? A positive, documented answer to any of these questions, based upon a comparative analysis of developmental patterns in several societies, would be of great assistance along both theoretical and practical lines. This is the type of information which the developmental sort of comparative study hopes gradually to build up.

A useful distinction in such a comparative and dynamic study is that between factors that are mostly or entirely beyond the control of a society's leaders and factors that are more amenable to conscious choice and direction. The first category includes a country's cultural heritage and its international environment throughout the various stages of the modernization process; the second includes its political institutions and a wide range of patterns of political and social organization. Nor is the sequence of problems that present themselves for solution entirely arbitrary or accidental. A feeling of national identity and a minimum of external security, for example, must be established before other aspects of political and economic development can be tackled in earnest. The first four essays of this volume will be devoted largely to the historical and environmental factors that are the "givens" for the modernization process. The remaining dozen essays focus on various instrumentalities and patterns of leadership, and the processes of organized choice. As we sum up our major findings in the conclusion, we shall return both to this distinction between "givens" and "variables" and to the various crises and problems that have to be faced in the course of political modernization.[8]

The plan we have adopted is simple. Under each of eight chapters there is one essay on Japan and one on Turkey. Although no rigid uniformity has been sought in outlook or organization, the treatment is broadly parallel. The first two pairs of essays take up the nature of traditional society in the period preceding modernization, and the environmental and foreign factors that stimulated subsequent political, social, and cultural changes of a modernizing sort. The importance of foreign and environmental factors is obvious in the Japanese and Turkish cases. Some explicit treatment of relevant aspects of the traditional society, including the forces for political and social change implicit within the tradition, has seemed to us essential in order to avoid the widespread illusion that traditional society is some sort of *tabula rasa,* an inert and plastic mass ready to be activated and shaped by the modernizing impact of the West.

A third pair of papers deals with the relationship between economic and political aspects of modernization. Further sections take up some of the major instrumentalities and social groups that have been involved in the process of political modernization: education, the mass

[8] See the list of such crises and problems on pp. 465-466 below.

media, the civil bureaucracies, the military establishments, and political parties and leadership. Finally, the editors have attempted in a concluding chapter to draw certain general conclusions about the process of political modernization in Japan and Turkey, and to suggest the relevance of these to further work in the field of comparative developmental studies.

This selection, no doubt, leaves some gaps. Separate chapters might well have been devoted to the role of religious ideas and institutions in the process of modernization. Interesting comparisons could also have been made between the development of literature and art in Japan and Turkey as they reflect social and political changes. But our purpose was to study the more specifically political aspects of modernization, our space was limited, and our coverage, therefore, has had to be selective.

CHAPTER 2

THE NATURE OF TRADITIONAL SOCIETY

~~~~~~

A. JAPAN[1]

JOHN WHITNEY HALL

~~~~~~

THE "traditional past" from which "modern" Japan is acknowledged to have emerged during the last hundred years is usually identified with the Tokugawa period (1603-1868). But if "tradition" is to have the particular meaning which the student of political modernization intends, it must refer to a system of institutions and values both peculiar to the past and somehow comprising the enduring qualities of an historic Japanese culture. It must refer, that is, to an abstraction which is both more and less than the attitudes and practices of the Tokugawa period.

This qualification might not have been thought necessary a few years ago when the Tokugawa age was conceived as wholly feudal or Oriental and Japan's emergence from it a miracle of sudden transformation under Western influence. But a number of scholars have lately reflected on the degree to which the startling changes which occurred after 1868 were anticipated in the preceding century, and have concluded that Tokugawa society may not have been so "traditional" as was once supposed.

This recent change in perspective illustrates the hazards of generalizing about Japanese society prior to 1868. The evaluation of that society varies according to the particular problem with which the scholar is preoccupied and according to his personal and professional interests. Nakamura Kichiji, who asked why sixteenth-century Japan did not follow out trends towards urbanization and social mobility, looked upon Tokugawa society as returning somewhat artificially to feudal strictures. Araki Mansho, claiming that the Tokugawa cultivator was the first real serf in Japan, classified the same society as representing feudalism in its mature state. Yet Asakawa Kan'ichi, who traced the evolution of village administration, was struck by the

[1] The author would like to express his appreciation for support received from the Carnegie Corporation of New York in connection with the preparation of this essay.

14

"public" and hence non-feudal character of Tokugawa government. Again, a Western scholar believing Japan "successful" in her modernization will scan the pre-Meiji years for anticipations of desirable change. A Japanese scholar recalling wartime suffering and ideological regimentation will look askance at this same period for having laid the basis of "imperial absolutism." For some, judgment may rest upon whether Japan's escape from Communism is taken as the final gauge of achievement, or whether the sorry years of nationalist hysteria and wartime defeat are more vivid in memory. For others, differences are taken from whether Japanese achievements are measured against the history of Western Europe or that of other parts of Asia.

Evaluation tends ultimately to be tied to expectation: to what changes one expects of the modernization process and in what order. What happened after 1868 is judged against what should or might have happened. And who is to determine what that may be? Japan was in fact eminently successful in the development of national consciousness, in the creation of an efficient bureaucratic government, in controlling social disintegration, and in competing as a power among other powers. Yet she was comparatively slow in granting civil liberties to the people and in creating a government responsive to popular wishes. Could she have attained both goals at once? We cannot ask of history that it rerun the course of the last hundred years to provide an alternative course of development in which democratic principles might everywhere have triumphed over nationalist and statist concerns. And we should not be seduced into special pleading.

The description of Tokugawa society which follows is intended to serve as a basis for the study of subsequent political change and not as an effort to isolate that elusive entity "traditional Japan." The description is of necessity selective. The criteria for political modernization suggested by the Committee on Comparative Politics provide one standard of selection. The assumption that Japan made a relatively orderly and successful transition from the Tokugawa period into more recent times is also accepted. Finally, the discussion is somewhat arbitrarily confined to the political sector of Tokugawa society.

I. Tokugawa Concepts of Sovereignty and Authority

Tokugawa Japan had no supreme law or constitution which defined the locus and prerogatives of sovereignty or the manner of the exercise of supreme authority. Yet the Tokugawa system left little room for confusion regarding the institutional basis of that authority. The first Tokugawa shogun had gained power by force of arms, but he did not rest until his hegemony had acquired legitimacy, and his status been dignified, by inclusion into the ceremonial structure of the imperial order.

Though we may belittle the actual power of the imperial house in the sixteenth century, there is no denying that the Tokugawa regime accepted the premise of a sovereign emperor (*tennō*). The shogun's authority over his peers, the daimyo, was justified in the name of the emperor, whom the shogun both controlled and served. Scholars and officials in his service found a justification for his regime in Chinese political theory, and elaborated the historical traditions of imperial rule. Hayashi Razan, the Confucian advisor of the first shogun, converted the sacred regalia of the imperial house (the mirror, the precious stones, and the sword) into symbols of the moral principles supporting sovereign power in Japan, so that the shogun could claim to have received his authority over the people of Japan as a "trust from Heaven."[2]

Throughout the succeeding centuries of the Tokugawa era, the repertory of Shinto rituals and court ceremonials, and the hierarchy of titles which had served the dignity of the imperial system during its heyday in the eighth century, continued to confess the ancient order. The emperor was of particular importance to those aristocratic houses close enough to the apex of the social and political hierarchy to have their status defined by court ranks. During this period Japanese practice and Confucian theory merged to create a vision of a hierarchy of conditions or estates each bearing its own relationship to the source of authority. Under the sovereign, Japan was separated into five main strata: the court nobility, the military nobility, the priesthood, the peasantry, and the urban artisans and merchants. Each estate lived by its own laws and precedents. The court nobility, which included the imperial house, was presided over by the Fujiwara lines, which customarily filled the post of imperial regent (*sesshō*). The military nobility exercised authority over their own and all other estates, including farmers, merchants, and priests, by virtue of having gained control of the land patents of the entire country. They further justified their authority as a delegation from the emperor.

[2] J. W. Hall, "The Confucian Teacher in Tokugawa Japan," in *Confucianism in Action*, ed. by David S. Nivison and Arthur F. Wright, Stanford, 1959, p. 274.

Sansom's apt statement that in Tokugawa Japan "the emperor was an absolute ruler in theory and the shogun an absolute ruler in practice"[3] should be complemented by the awareness that there was no necessary conflict of interest between emperor and shogun. Even when, in the latter days of the Tokugawa regime, the shogun's opponents spoke of his "usurping" authority, they were seeking only to share in the powers delegated him, or, as it turned out, to replace him in "the emperor's service."

The authority of the Tokugawa shogun had very specific precedents. In 1192 the emperor had granted to Minamoto-no-Yoritomo, through the title of shogun, supreme authority over all military affairs and military houses. Later, during the fighting in the sixteenth century, all but a fraction of the land rights in Japan had come into the possession of the military houses. And finally, in the battles of 1600 and 1614-1615, the Tokugawa shogun was able to gain ultimate powers of investiture over the daimyo houses. Hence the office of shogun, and the court titles and precedents which went with it, conferred on the head of the Tokugawa house ultimate power over the entire administrative apparatus of the country. His titles, supported by the power of his own armies and those of his allies, were a sufficient basis for his rule.

The shogun's exercise of authority was nevertheless not indiscriminate. In ideal theory, he continued to serve the emperor as a loyal official. As a philosopher of the Mito school wrote: "If the Bakufu reveres the imperial house, then all the feudal lords will respect the Bakufu. If the feudal lords respect the Bakufu, the ministers and officials will respect the feudal lords. Thus high and low protect each other. The entire country is in accord. What is it that unites the country at the hands of the Bakufu? Above it is its reverent attitude toward the emperor; below it is its protective treatment of the feudal lords. This rulership, however, is merely the exercise of imperial sovereignty."[4]

More specifically, the shogun's titles restricted his overall powers to those of chief of the military houses and his land rights to tenure as defined by the term *chigyō*. He possessed, and could redistribute under his red or black seals, the right of public tenure of land, as well as the rights of taxation and manpower recruitment and the responsibilities of governance. The tenure of both the shogun and the daimyo

[3] G. B. Sansom, *The Western World and Japan*, New York, 1950, p. 182.
[4] Herschel F. Webb, "The Mito Theory of the State," *Researches in the Social Sciences on Japan*, Columbia University, East Asian Studies No. 4, 1952, p. 43.

nevertheless remained conditional, in theory residing in a delegation from emperor to shogun.

The actual exercise of political authority in Tokugawa Japan, though rigorous and absolute, was increasingly specified by law. Because of the hierarchical nature of the society, the exercise of authority inevitably involved both social and legal coercion. Assertions of social privilege were most blatant when the exercise of authority crossed class lines. The military aristocracy (*buke*) as a class acknowledged the superior breeding and prestige of the courtiers (*kuge*), though they found themselves under no institutional compulsion to yield to this superiority. The military aristocracy asserted both social and legal prerogatives when they carried out their political duties. Their badges of distinction—their court ranks and surnames, the long and short swords which they wore—had once of themselves conferred on them the authority to govern the peasantry and service class. But whereas prior to Tokugawa times power was predominantly personal and exercised directly by the lord over the fief and its inhabitants, it was thereafter increasingly subsumed into the impersonal bureaucratic apparatus authorized by shogunal and daimyo law. Though the individual military official might still in fact display arrogance toward the inferior estates or claim the right to draw his sword against an offender, the precedents supporting his superior status also limited his sphere of action, and the precepts of Confucianism constantly reminded him that power was to be used justly and humanely.

Within the estates, the exercise of authority was determined by the pattern of administrative or communal association, hence differing considerably from estate to estate. The internal organization of the military class was originally dependent upon feudal ties. During the sixteenth century, when the military houses were fighting for ultimate control over the land and its government, they had formed tight military bands consisting of lords and vassals. When the process of military consolidation was extended after the middle of the century, these small local bands were absorbed as sub-units (*kumi*) into the larger organization of great lords (daimyo). Eventually all military men in the service of a daimyo came to be considered his vassals (*kashin*). With the establishment of the Tokugawa shogunate, the shogun claimed as his superior retainers the 266 daimyo and as his lesser housemen some 23,000 enfeoffed and stipended retainers known as *hatamoto* and *gokenin*. At the outset of the Tokugawa period, this entire structure had been tightly bound together by oaths of loyalty and reciprocal grants of fief or hereditary stipend certificates. In later years the personal bond was transmuted into less personal but no less potent sentiments of loyalty to the system.

No such systems of internal pledges bound together the peasant and merchant communities. Both of these estates were provided with headmen who customarily possessed superior social distinction by virtue of long residence, wealth, or former possession of title or rank, but whose authority came from the daimyo or shogun and was vested in the laws and precedents of superior government. When families within the rural and urban estates became bound or indentured to other families, this relationship derived from the conditions of tenancy or from the extension of family ties; it was not a function of the political hierarchy.

The primacy of authority over the freedom of action of all persons and groups was one of the outstanding features of the Tokugawa political system. The emphasis on authority derived in large part from the attitudes of the military class, which traditionally exacted unquestioning obedience. It derived also from the overwhelming force possessed by the military authorities. In such a system the hardiest might defy authority only by resort to assassination or insurrection and with the sure expectation of a death penalty.

Such an exercise of authority engendered in the Tokugawa Japanese a spirit of profound obedience. Expressions of respect for superiors within the official hierarchy were frequently demanded. The Tokugawa Japanese could not, as did the Chinese, put family above government. The samurai was expected to be loyal to his official superior first, his family second. In mores generally the primacy of the organization over the person was constantly reiterated. The inferior member, in particular, was kept perpetually aware of his debt of obligation (*on*) toward the system which in paternalistic fashion both nurtured and disciplined him, and the debt naturally weighed heaviest upon the estates at the bottom of the social scale.

Yet, despite the authoritarian and even ruthless nature of military rule, the exercise of authority could be meliorated in practice. The distance between ruler and ruled in Japan was perhaps not so great as in most such systems, even when a superior encountered a subordinate far beneath him in class. The lesser members of the daimyo's military officialdom, the local intendants, were not sharply distinguished either by the possession of arbitrary authority or by a superior way of life from the village headmen with whom they had to deal.

The room in which the headman billeted his samurai superiors was merely a special wing of his own residence. He could obtain by distinguished service the privilege of bearing a surname and wearing a sword (*myōji-taitō*), and he often clung secretly to a genealogy reminding him that the only difference between himself and the daimyo's local agents was the turn of fate in a battle lost before 1600.

The exercise of authority was softened by Confucian theory as well. Though in their fighting days the daimyo had exercised harsh martial law, under the peaceful Tokugawa regime rulers sought to justify their actions in terms of the public good. As the daimyo Ikeda Mitsumasa said, "If one person within my domain is without his place, this reflects discredit upon the shogun."[5] The brutal remark ascribed to Tokugawa Ieyasu, the first shogun, that peasants should be handled so that they would "neither die nor live," does not describe the actual lot of the people. The records show that the "good ruler" was expected to turn his attention to improving agricultural conditions and alleviating distress from crop failure or famine in the interest not only of good economics but of good statecraft.

II. The Political Structure of Tokugawa Japan

Government entered into the lives of the people of Tokugawa Japan through four main institutions: the imperial court, the shogunate, the daimyo domains, and the religious houses. The first and the last of these institutions involved only a fraction of the population, for the administration of government was the responsibility almost wholly of the military estate. The extent to which military administration dominated the country is revealed by figures on the distribution of land rights (*chigyō-ken*) at the end of the seventeenth century:

	Koku	Per Cent
Imperial lands	141,000	.5
Shogunal lands	6,800,000	25.8
Daimyo lands	19,100,000	72.5
Temple and shrine lands	316,000	1.2
Total	26,357,000	100.0[6]

Of the registered territory of Japan, that is, over 98 per cent was administered by the military estate.

[5] J. W. Hall, "Confucian Teacher," p. 275.
[6] Kanai Madoka, "Bakuhan taisei no shomondai," *Nihon rekishi*, 118, 16.

The imperial court was obviously of little significance as an entity within the administrative system. The emperor and the court families resident in Kyoto maintained a thin and conventionalized form of the administrative ritual which had obtained since the days when the emperor actually governed through his appointed officials. But the import of this ritual was hardly felt beyond the confines of the court itself. The courtiers somehow took their functions seriously, appointing themselves to ministries of state and maintaining a certain noble elegance in their lives. But, besides helping to support the institutions of imperial sovereignty, they contributed to government at large only by making appointments and granting court honors which defined the status of the upper echelons of the military elite.

The only rulers whom most of the people of Tokugawa Japan knew were the shogun and the daimyo. The administrative apparatus of the military estate, generally referred to by Japanese historians as the *baku-han* system, had evolved when the practices prevailing at the headquarters of the shogun (the *bakufu*) had been imposed upon the system of local administration devised by the newly emergent daimyo in their domains (the *han*). It was characteristic of this style of government that, at all reaches above the relatively autonomous politics of villages and towns, military authority appropriated all superior rights and administration was entirely in the hands of the samurai class. Being warriors by profession, all samurai stood ready, in theory, to draw their swords on call. In peacetime they fulfilled tasks as civil officials under the shogun or daimyo. The convertibility of Tokugawa government from civil to military functions was symbolized in the roles of the shogun, who was the commander-in-chief of all Japan, and of the daimyo, who as his military agents were accountable to him for putting armies into the field on command. Tokugawa government amounted quite literally to the conversion of military rule to the uses of peace.

Originally, the Tokugawa house had been merely the largest of the daimyo, the first among equals. During the period of widespread civil warfare in the sixteenth century, the daimyo themselves were no more than local military lords organized to protect their territories from the encroachments of their neighbors. Each daimyo led a hierarchy of retainers, his *kashindan*, who were organized into fighting bands, or *kumi*. These bands were of two general types, some consisting of fighting samurai who were themselves organized under independently enfeoffed commanders of castles, and others consisting of the daimyo's own immediate retainers who served as his private army and administrative staff.

Under the hegemony imposed by the Tokugawa house, in the first decades of the seventeenth century, the daimyo domains were stripped of their primary military functions and converted more and more into units of local administration. Each daimyo was permitted only one castle or garrison headquarters, former castellans taking their places around him as advisory retainers (*karō* or *bangashira*). Though the shogun required each daimyo to maintain a certain minimum military establishment, he required also that it be kept rather small. Increasingly the daimyo's retainers became occupied in peaceful pursuits.

As a unit of local administration the daimyo domain acquired certain common features. The territory of the domain, as defined by shogunal grant, was under the direct rule of the daimyo. The highest ranks of the daimyo's retainers, the *karō* and *bangashira*, staffed a policy-making council and high court. Members of these ranks further served as heads of guard groups or standing army units, as chiefs of police and financial affairs and as liaison agents between the daimyo and the shogunate. The intermediate ranks of retainers served in more specifically bureaucratic posts. Under the generic title of superintendent (*bugyō*) they undertook such various civil functions as the administration of the castle town, the collection of taxes, military procurement, and the management of civil engineering, education, and religious affairs. Under the general title of captain (*kumigashira*) they headed various lesser units of the standing army. The lower levels of the daimyo's retainers staffed the agencies of the daimyo's private and public bureaucracy or served as low-ranking military officers.

Among the inhabitants of his domain, the daimyo recognized two types. His own samurai, who had freely chosen to serve him and were accountable to his house laws, were in a special sense "his men." The "people" (*tami*) were his wards, given him in "trust from the shogun."[7] They were to be governed with compassion,[8] but impersonally, unlike the household samurai. Over members of non-military estates, of course, he exercised all of the usual prerogatives of civil administration. Within the domain, a superintendent of temples and

[7] Ikeda Archives, Hōreishū, kan 7.
[8] Ikeda Archives, Hōkōgaki, Tenna 1, 12, 27.

shrines oversaw Buddhist and Shinto establishments. A superintendent of village affairs was responsible for administration and tax
collection in the local villages (*mura*). A magistrate of the castle
town exercised authority over the town's several wards (*machi*). At
the lowest levels of communal organization there existed what was
euphemistically called self-government.

The *mura* became relatively autonomous units when the samurai
class was gradually separated from the land and organized into a superior military and civil establishment. At the outset of the sixteenth
century most samurai still lived in or near their fiefs, which they both
protected as warriors and managed as stewards. But as the daimyo drew
their vassals to the center of their domains and obliged them to live
in the castle towns, the actual administration of the peasant village
fell into the hands of village headmen. Then, to bridge the gap
between himself and the villages, the daimyo created an impersonal
administrative apparatus staffed with his own retainers. A rural staff
of this kind consisted typically of a superintendent drawn from the
highest rank of retainers, county administrators of intermediate condition, and a rather large body of local intendants. This body of officials exercised general supervision over civil administration, tax
collection, police surveillance, and judicial affairs. Assistants and
clerks performed specialized fiscal, administrative, and constabulary
tasks.

So-called village self-government came into being after the completion of the nationwide cadastral survey begun by Hideyoshi in
1582. According to Hideyoshi's plan each piece of arable land was
surveyed, graded, and recorded against the name of a cultivator
(*hyakushō*) who was responsible for paying taxes on it. Taxpaying
cultivators were secure in their tenures but were bound by the cadastral register and could not freely dispose of their land. The land registers of each area, brought together in the name of a single village,
defined the territory and the present and prospective inhabitants of a
new legal unit, the *mura*. In Tokugawa times each *mura* generally
comprised several natural agricultural communities.

Village or *mura* administration was the responsibility of the headman (*nanushi* or *shōya*), whose appointment from some influential
household of the community was confirmed by the daimyo. The
village population as a whole was divided into mutually responsible
units of about ten families (*goningumi*), each with its own head. The
village headmen kept the tax and land registers, copies of laws and

petitions, and other records. They were responsible to the daimyo's rural staff for the maintenance of law and order and the collection of taxes. At the same time, being themselves *hyakushō*, they were expected to represent the interests of their villages before the higher daimyo authority.

The administration of the towns or *machi* was handled in essentially the same manner as that of the *mura*. The daimyo's castle town was organized into self-administered blocks or wards under the jurisdiction of elders (*toshiyori*) selected from among the richest and most highly respected households in the block. Frequently a group of senior elders, also of merchant status, served as a town council. Within the wards the responsibilities of civil administration, including tax collection, registration for census and religious preference and the enforcement of civil and criminal laws, devolved on officials appointed from within the commercial estate.

Although the peasant and commercial estates were thus given wide areas of self-regulation, their members were scrupulously restricted from attaining positions of real political influence. The social order was rigidly adhered to, and the division between ruler and ruled accepted without reference to natural rights. As a result, the lower orders rarely sought to gain legal or political concessions from the daimyo or shogun. Efforts to secure more explicit legal protection of existing rights were made by the commercial class, which found itself in a position to exploit the samurai; but the class as a whole had to remain content with its service status. Influential members of the peasant and commercial estates could hope to gain no more than immunity from interference into their private financial enterprises.

Politically, then, Tokugawa society was divided into discrete compartments under the single control of the shogun. The shogun, as first among the daimyo, both governed his own territories and exercised control over the imperial court and the other daimyo. The headquarters of the Tokugawa house, known as the *bakufu*, served substantially as "the government of Japan," assuming full national authority over military and foreign affairs, and civil and religious administration. The shogunate might, of course, exert authority directly, as in the shogun's own lands, or indirectly through the daimyo; it often made little practical difference, for, in their general principles of governance, their basic laws, and their political and social institutions, the daimyo domains were usually more like the shogun's territories than not.

We can perhaps gain better insight into the shogunal administration if we conceive of the shogun as a super-daimyo, administering the country through what was essentially his own body of retainers (*kashin-dan*). The chief difference between shogunal administration and that of the daimyo lay in the fact that the shogun's castellan retainers (daimyo in this case) continued in the field as semi-independent great vassals. While the daimyo had withdrawn their retainers from the countryside into their garrison headquarters, the shogun had not fully done so. Yet the shogun did achieve powerful authority over his vassal daimyo, and through the *sankin-kōtai* system he literally required the residence of his vassals at his castle on a half-time basis.

Shogunal administration radiated outward from the great castle of Edo. The palaces and guarded keeps of that castle served both as a residence for the Tokugawa household and as the headquarters of the shogun's bureaucracy. This bureaucracy served the regime in three essential ways. First, it controlled the imperial court and access to imperial honors. Second, it provided the machinery through which the shogun could exercise his supreme military and civil authority over lesser lords. Third, it administered the shogun's personal territories.

Control of the imperial court was secured in straightforward fashion. A shogunal deputy (*shoshidai*) in Kyoto commanded a substantial military force garrisoned at Nijō castle. The shogun's wishes were communicated directly through this deputy to special liaison officers in the court. The court communicated with the lesser military houses through this same chain of command. The access of these latter houses to the court was carefully guarded, although nearly all of the larger *tozama* daimyo maintained discreet relations, assumed to be purely social, with one or another of the noble families.

Since the daimyo were technically the shogun's peers, the machinery of control over them was necessarily complex and involved with the military power balance between the *bakufu* and the *han*. The shogun's hegemony over the country rested on military victories in which a coalition of daimyo loyal to his house had successively defeated a series of opposing coalitions. After each of these battles, the Tokugawa house had accepted the defeated daimyo as vassals, variously trusted and confessing varying degrees of subordination. The Tokugawa house, in sum, had imposed on all Japan an order not unlike that achieved by the daimyo in their own domains. But the process of military conquest was never pushed to its logical end, and that of national consolidation was discontinued before anything resembling

25

complete centralization was attained. The shogunal system hence contained within itself many unresolved tensions between central and local interests.

The Tokugawa ascendancy rested upon a dynamic balance among three main groups of daimyo. Collateral branches of the Tokugawa house, known as *shimpan,* were assumed to be absolutely loyal. Daimyo known as *fudai* who had been created by the Tokugawa house formed the backbone of the shogun's administration and military service. These daimyo who had first held allegiance to non-Tokugawa overlords, such as Nobunaga and Hideyoshi, and had subsequently sworn allegiance to the Tokugawa house, were called *tozama* and regarded as uncertain allies. One of the policies of the Tokugawa house was to keep a strategic balance between the shogun's own territories and the three types of daimyo. The tensions inhering in the original balance of power were by this means perpetuated, and, while most of the *tozama* daimyo forgot their old enmities, others, such as Chōshū, kept alive the thought of striking again when the moment was right.

That moment eventually came, of course, as a result of the dramatic intervention of foreign powers in Japanese affairs. There is little indication that the shogun's hold over the daimyo could have been broken otherwise. His control of the rights of investiture and the daimyo's reciprocal oath of loyalty to him bound the *baku-han* system together in a union which was long indissoluble because it was direct and personal. Just how personal it was is exemplified in the provision of the daimyo code that each daimyo maintain a residence in Edo and domicile his private family there as hostages. By oath the daimyo were committed to obey the shogun's code, which governed the military houses. This document explicitly or by implication spelled out the daimyo's responsibility to the shogun and to his status as a local ruler. The daimyo was expected to provide military and civil service at the request of the shogun and to assure the peaceful administration of his territory. While the daimyo was not burdened with regular national taxes, he was from time to time obliged to contribute toward various shogunal building projects and national public works. Given the economic and technological premises of Tokugawa society, the shogunal system was remarkably stable.

For his public administration the shogun relied exclusively on the *fudai* daimyo and the *hatamoto* and *gokenin.* At the apex of the *bakufu* bureaucracy were two policy councils. Five or six of the largest *fudai* were appointed senior councillors (*rōjū*) and assigned responsibilities of national scope. Six junior councillors (*wakadoshi-yori*), selected from among the lesser *fudai*, handled the shogun's private affairs, including control of his private retainers. The administrative functions of the *bakufu* were distributed between these two councils. Under the senior councillors were such officers as keepers of Edo castle, chamberlains, inspectors-general, magistrates of the great cities, magistrates of religious affairs, finance officers, civil engineers, and shogunal secretaries. The junior councillors were in charge of the shogunal guard groups and the common police. Unique to the shogunal administration were the large areas of "the shogun's lands" which were governed by district commissioners. Many of these local officials administered territories equal in size to large daimyo domains, yet they performed their duties with a minimum of staff and armed forces. It was in this commissioner system that shogunal administration most closely approximated a strictly centralized method of field administration.

The combination of *bakufu* and *han* bureaucracies provided Tokugawa Japan with an elaborate and functionally diverse machinery of government which was remarkably durable. Few regimes have managed to hold together a population of over thirty million for a period of 250 years with so little evidence of administrative breakdown. These, of course, were relatively tranquil years in the west Pacific. But isolation from the stream of world events had not been a guarantee of internal peace in the past. The secret of the Tokugawa "great peace" lay in the density of government functions and the balance which they created in favor of authority. Few people in pre-modern times have lived under such a heavy load of official regulation and supervision as the Tokugawa Japanese. Since every mature male samurai was considered a potential military or civil officer, government in the person of the two-sworded *bushi* was visible everywhere. In the daimyo domains, one might often have found more than one officer for every fifty or a hundred members of the *chōnin* and *hyakushō* classes. Outside the samurai class, the Tokugawa system managed to identify the upper strata of both farmers and merchants with the system. The Tokugawa Japanese lived out his life with his head constantly lowered to higher authority.

III. The Political Process in Tokugawa Japan

Because of the authoritarian nature of Tokugawa government the political process was confined largely to the sphere of administration proper. Authority flowed downward through the appropriate channels, leaving to the general run of subjects the alternative of compliance or at most petition or remonstrance. The factors which most significantly influenced the operation of such government, then, were the recruitment of officials, their performance in office, and their manner of making decisions.

While the bureaucratic features of the *baku-han* system of administration eventually became predominant, it should be remembered that Tokugawa government grew out of a feudal environment and drew its high officials exclusively from the samurai class. From the first, therefore, both access to government and accountability to government depended in large measure on status. The distinctive quality of the Tokugawa political process was its ability to reconcile a feudal inheritance with the demands of bureaucratic practice.

The system of recruitment prevailing in Tokugawa government effected an ingenious compromise between considerations of heredity and merit. A great many offices were filled only by the members of certain hereditary classes. Daimyo houses, for instance, were limited in number and tended to perpetuate themselves throughout the Tokugawa era, relying on adoption to assure continuity if necessary. Within the daimyo's band of retainers, also, the senior (*karo*) families served their lord generation after generation. Village government drew its officials from the highest ranking families of the peasant estates and these too exhibited a remarkable continuity. But if we look at individual government posts, the hereditary limitations become less apparent. In Tokugawa society generally it was not office which was inherited but family rank or status (*mibun* or *kakaku*).

In the *mibun* system families inherited military rank and a base stipend but not official posts. Lower ranks of the samurai class were not accorded even this degree of hereditary privilege, for the members of some of these inherited a rank one step below that of their fathers. In origin the *mibun* system derived from the military organizations of the daimyo during the pre-Tokugawa years of civil warfare. Names and types of ranks thus varied somewhat from domain to domain, but the Okayama example will serve as an illustration. The Okayama daimyo's retinue was divided into ten basic ranks (*see table on p. 29*).

As the *mibun* system became stabilized, so also did the administrative hierarchy. In time it became the standard practice to equate government posts with military grades and to fill them only from those

Rank	Number of Families	Salary Range
Elder (karō)	6	10,000-33,000 koku
Divisional commander (bangashira)	14-22	500-5,000 koku
Task commander (monogashira)	25-28	below 500 koku
Captain (kinju-kashirabun)	20	
Divisional captain (kumigashira)	20-30	
Officer (heishi)	730-840	40 bales or more
Musketeer officer (shideppō)	70	4 rations
Senior petty officer (kachi)	450-490	3 rations
Junior petty officer (keihai)	550	2 rations
Footsoldier (ashigaru)	1,900-2,600	1 ration[9]

grades. But for every office there were always a number of candidates of appropriate official status, and the selection among these could, at least in theory, be made on the basis of ability alone.

Within the reaches of government staffed by samurai, candidacy for office was sometimes explicitly contingent on the income which a certain rank conferred. In the *bakufu* system, for instance, the candidates for the office of senior councillor had to possess a rank assuring them of at least 25,000 *koku*; candidates for junior councillor and master of shogunal ceremony had to possess an income of 10,000 *koku*; candidates for chamberlain of 5,000 *koku*; and candidates for city magistrate and superintendent of finance of 3,000 *koku*.[10] These minimum salary qualifications were based on the twin presumption that a daimyo or *hatamoto* would tend to have "stature" and "experience" commensurate with his rank and that he needed a certain income to fulfill the requirements of office. Yet while mobility between ranks was infrequent, especially at the higher levels, mobility within a given stratum was a matter of course. There was a variety of offices to which each samurai could aspire, and a young family head tended to come into government a step or two below the highest office which his father had attained, so that he could gain experience as he worked up the ladder of preferment.[11]

Ability was a commodity constantly sought. Both shogun and daimyo were given to expostulating on the need to play down rank to secure ability. At the end of the Tokugawa period, in particular, we find a considerable body of protest against the practice of filling offices on hereditary principles. "Why is it," wrote Ogyū Sorai, "that during a period of prolonged peace men of ability are only found among the

[9] Taniguchi Sumio, "Han kashindan no keisei to kōzō," *Shigaku zasshi*, 66.6, June 1957, p. 607.
[10] J. W. Hall, *Tanuma Okitsugu*, Cambridge, 1955, p. 32.
[11] Ikeda Archives, On tazune shinajina no kakiage, Meiwa 1.

lower classes, while men of the upper class grow increasingly stupid?"[12] Such complaints were answered in part by the actual career patterns of fast-rising officials in the service of the shogun or daimyo. Some officials rose through favoritism, or so it was claimed, thereby proving to detractors the inadequacy of the whole system. But here and there as we probe the service records of Tokugawa government we find men like the following financier, who rose in the service of the House of Ikeda apparently on the basis of particular ability:

Takagi Jin'uemon

1763	inherited father's status as divisional captain (*kumi-gashira*) with 200 *koku* base salary
1789	appointed *han* recorder (*tomegata*)
1791	named to additional duty, superintendent of spears (*yari-bugyō*)
1793	promoted to superintendent of taxes
1794	promoted to chief inspector (*ōmetsuke*)
1795	promoted to chief financial accountant and privy seal (*hangyō*)
1798	received an additional 200 *koku* base salary
1800	received an additional 100 *koku* and named superintendent of rural affairs (*kori-bugyō*)
1807	received an additional 100 *koku* and the rank of provisional divisional commander (*bangashira-kaku*)
1812	named acting junior councillor (*kojioki-kaku*)
1820	achieved 1,000 *koku* and full rank of commander with duties of junior councillor in charge of finance (*sakumaigata*)
1825	retired[13]

A less apparent source of mobility was the unusual system of adoption practiced during the Tokugawa period. The individual Japanese was identified primarily as a member of a household. The family, not the individual, inherited rank or property, and the highly competitive nature of Tokugawa society made it essential that the family produce able male heirs in order to perpetuate itself. Laws of inheritance were so contrived, therefore, that samurai families in particular could make adoptions almost at will. This fresh blood kept the families of the ruling class from petering out or becoming debilitated and frequently put men of high capacity into government office.

The mechanics of selection for office itself differed considerably among the sectors of the bureaucracy. In the relatively stable villages, the post of headman was normally held for life. The same was true of specialized posts in the daimyo's bureaucracies, such as court physi-

[12] *Sources of the Japanese Tradition*, Ryusaku Tsunoda, Wm. Theodore de Bary, Donald Keene, comps., New York, 1958, p. 432.
[13] Ikeda Archives, Hōkōgaki.

cian or Confucian teacher. If several families in the village were of approximately equal status, then villagers sometimes balloted for headman and communicated their preference to the authorities for action.

Posts in the higher samurai service were filled more flexibly—by nomination or sometimes by a vote among peers. Each samurai entering the service of a lord was enrolled at a designated rank and salary and placed within a certain group (*kumi*). The *kumi,* the samurai's primary disciplinary unit, served as a personnel group, and the head of that group would recommend individual samurai for office. The samurai then entered the service command of a bureaucratic superior. The practice of separating the personnel or disciplinary function of the bureaucracy from the line or service command made for impersonality in recruitment. The system was, of course, easily abused; we find complaints of "improper" recommendations made through bribery or family pull. But we should not judge the system merely by its abuses.

Despite the accusations of stupidity in high places and of slothful performance among those protected by hereditary rank, the Tokugawa system appears to have obtained much loyal and conscientious service from its officers. Such service, though in part coerced, was in part the voluntary response to competition within the samurai class. Once withdrawn from the land and herded into assigned quarters in the daimyo's castle headquarters, that class found itself exposed to public view and unalterably committed to administrative or military service. Though the highborn retainer, secure in a tenured inheritance, could abuse his privileges and spend his days in comparative idleness, the head of the average samurai house who did not strive for distinction in his lord's service was not assured of his son's tenure or even his own. The downward drift of families who lost out in the competition and were disinherited was constantly visible, especially among the lower reaches of the official scale. In the service of the Ikeda House of Okayama, 1,102 families of a total of 3,935 recorded to have served as retainers between 1630 and 1868 died out during the interval.[14]

Finally the formal education and the entire environment of the samurai were saturated with inducements to performance and reminders that he was the leader of his society, the bulwark of his state. The remarkable thing about him was the degree to which he took his indoctrination to heart. Even when thousands of idle samurai overstaffed the atrophied organs of Tokugawa government at the end

[14] Taniguchi, "Han kashindan," p. 596.

of the regime, competition was still keen within the system itself. A substantial number of retainers broke under the strain, either physically or mentally. The most common type of defection recorded in the personnel records of the shogun and daimyo was running amok.

As a bureaucratic type the Tokugawa samurai was surely unique in Asia. A cross between a feudal warrior and a man of letters, he somehow reconciled the rough heritage of qualities required in the field with the humane values of the Confucian system. He was confined throughout his life to official service. He could not own rice fields or participate in commercial ventures. His sole rewards were favors from his lord; his sole temptation, the abuse of political power.

As if these personal and social pressures were not enough, the Tokugawa administrative system was liberally supplied with devices for the reinforcement of loyalty. Historically, of course, the samurai had been organized into tight bands united by personal oaths of allegiance. Every samurai at some time swore an oath to "serve his lord singly and without reservation," in the presence of an imposing host of Buddhist and Shinto deities such as the Daigongen of the three Kumano shrines and the Daibosatsu of Nitta Hachiman.[15] In addition, the network of marriage alliances, the taking of hostages, and the rigorous enforcement of regulations against subversive conduct wrapped the samurai in an almost inescapable net of obligation and responsibility. By the eighteenth century the ties of loyalty to the lord had become somewhat conventional, though not necessarily weaker. Constantly, shogun and daimyo, through regular ceremonies of audience, inspection, and ritual dedication to the spirits of departed ancestors, confirmed the loyalties of the samurai class collectively. In the annual probe of religious preference each family head swore before the chief of his personnel unit that no Christian existed in his family. Loyalty was increasingly owed to the "system" as a matter of abstract principle.

In the bureaucracy itself many means of assuring obedience and honesty in office had been developed. The separation of personnel and line functions mentioned earlier made for impersonal and disinterested recruitment and supervision. Salaries were determined routinely on the basis of rank. While a man in an influential office could count on "gifts" from subordinates and petitioners, Tokugawa officials rarely had the opportunity to acquire permanent sources of income or to practice corruption on a grand scale. A general concept of what

[15] K. Asakawa, *The Documents of Iriki*, Tokyo, 1955, p. 294.

the highly placed civil servant owed to his lord—shogun or daimyo—may be gleaned from this characteristically explicit oath of office, sworn in 1642 and after by the four chief inspectors of Okayama *han*:

1. We shall not neglect the lord's interest.
2. As chief inspectors we agree to report all breaches of the laws and any failures to execute the lord's commands. If we learn of anything affecting the lord's interests, whether great or small, whether it concerns our own parents, children, relatives, or subordinates, we will report the details immediately.
3. Official secrets or any other official information however minor, if its revelation should be detrimental to the lord's interests, will be divulged to no one. We shall undertake no public duty while harboring private interests.
4. We shall see to it that the inspectors appointed under us perform their duties without negligence.
5. As officials of our lord, we shall speak no ill of each other.[16]

The *metsuke* (inspectorate) system here referred to was a further potent device for assuring loyalty. While not properly a spy system (the name given to it by Murdoch and others), it did provide the Tokugawa government with an efficient means of policing its civil service. *Ōmetsuke* kept the eyes of the shogun on the daimyo, while *metsuke* or *yokome* served up and down the *bakufu* and *han* bureaucratic systems. Most important administrative transactions were performed in the presence of members of this independent inspectorate. In sensitive government posts the practices of appointing several persons to hold an office in rotation and of paralleling fiscal services with systems of audit were common. In the shogunal staff there were four or five inspectors-general, two magistrates of Edo, four superintendents of finance, three magistrates of Nagasaki, four superintendents of temples and shrines.

The whole system of association and communication within the Tokugawa bureaucracy made for honesty and loyalty. The *baku-han* administration was so arranged that central authority was everywhere within easy reach of its decentralized branches. In the shogunal and daimyo administration, links in the chain of command tended to be short and to be constantly reinforced by personal encounters. The *sankin-kōtai* system brought the daimyo to Edo, where they attended shogunal functions several times monthly. In their own domains the

16 Kibi Gunshoshūsei Kankōkai, *Kibi gunsho shūsei*, Tokyo, 1932, V, 10, 255.

daimyo housed most of their offices within their castle walls. Even field administrators—with the exception of the *gōshi*—usually resided at the center of authority, going out to their distant offices if their duties required it. Except for the shogunal territories, daimyo domains were small enough so that an official might travel from the castle town to the most remote outposts in two days at most.

The *baku-han* system provided an administration which was efficient in its supervisory and regulatory features though relatively inflexible in policy. Once the shogunal and daimyo bureaucracies had taken shape (roughly between 1630 and 1690) it was generally assumed that the system had been very nearly perfected. The traditions had been set, the admonitions of the early leaders (Ieyasu, Iemitsu, and the daimyo who served them) had been enshrined in memory, and the basic laws and regulations had been assembled. The spirit of government after the turn into the eighteenth century is well illustrated in the admonition given by Lord Asano of Hiroshima to his retainers in 1713:

1. Administration of this province will rest upon the respectful adherence to the laws of the previous generation and to their elaboration. Primary attention must be given to rewards and punishments. When the principle is in doubt be liberal in reward and light in punishment. Use leniency and strictness to induce the diligence of the cultivators. . . . Treat farmers with consideration; give your full attention to agriculture; let no season be missed. Strive to make all within the province, old and young, male and female, high and low, secure and free from suffering. . . . If you do not govern filled with the spirit of benevolence, distress will inevitably come to the people. Ponder these principles well.

2. Though it is accepted that all matters will be governed by precedent, since there will be circumstances in which old usages do not fit, precedent should not be applied automatically. Each problem should be handled justly in accordance with the circumstances once the underlying principles have been determined. But basic laws and important precedents shall not be put aside.[17]

An administrative process accommodated to regulations and precedents of this sort can well be imagined. Regulations flowed down to subordinates, memorials and petitions worked their way upward to

[17] Hayashi Yasutaka, Comp., *Geihan shūyō*, Hiroshima, 1933, II, 105.

superior officials. The endorsement of a memorial for action was the common procedure whereby the request or suggestion of a subordinate was acknowledged. The routine business, though voluminous, was handled conscientiously and systematically. Few bureaucratic systems at a comparable stage of national development have exercised such remarkable documentary control of affairs. There were rank and income registers, land registers, tax records, budgets, financial records, personnel records, religious inspection records, dossiers on adjudication of disputes, diaries of petitions, diaries of decisions—almost every conceivable administrative document. Every individual, whether of samurai status or lower, was known to the government and registered on some official roster.

Within this government, as in others of the same sort, decisions were made routinely in the course of administrative conferences. Administrative decisions followed established procedure whenever possible. A staff decision normally consisted in a consensus attained if necessary in the presence of superior authorities. Both the political and judicial process placed a premium on mutual agreement or compromise. The system had no place for a loyal opposition or for legal adjudications. Since the style and philosophy of administration depended largely upon the nature of the men in office, major changes of policy came only with the resignation, removal, or death of officials. Acknowledging this fact, the samurai administrator would not infrequently resort to assassination or suicide when his views were rejected by the system. The pressure for obedience and consensus drove often to exasperation and sometimes to violence.

IV. *Political Conditions on the Eve of Japan's Modernization*

To say that the political conditions of the Tokugawa regime provided the base from which Japan began its political modernization says little about the manner in which pre-modern society related to the Restoration of 1868, or to the modernizing reforms which followed. Some would minimize the importance of the "indigenous base." The images of the "knock on the door," the "opening," and the "awakening" of Japan all play down the significance of what was happening in Japan as opposed to what was about to befall it from outside. The temptation of historians has been to equate the emergent features of modern Japan with creative forces generated outside the Tokugawa system, either in pockets of internal resistance or on foreign soil. But granted the importance of the Western impact on Japan, there is still no adequate explanation of what happened after 1850 without taking into account the influence of Japan's domestic political culture upon the process of political modernization.

Traditional society can influence the course of institutional change in two fundamental ways: first, there are what historians have called trends or processes which can carry their momentum beyond the traditional base into the period of modernization; second, there is the basic institutional structure which by its patterns of resistance and receptivity can channel the flow of change. What can we say of the process and structure of the political life of the Japanese in 1850 as these affected the subsequent process of modernization?

The difficulty in giving a clear answer to this question stems in part from the fact that the political history of Tokugawa Japan is so flat. There are no major turning points or crises, no battles from which one can date declining vigor, no dramatic evidence of institutional senility. The elements of process are rather more subtle and the evidence of their existence spread out over a long span of time. But if one places the Tokugawa political structure as it attained its maturity towards the middle of the seventeenth century alongside what it had become on the eve of modernization in 1850, comparisons become more easily discernible. There were clear-cut changes in the operation of government, some towards increased bureaucratic efficiency, others of a degenerative nature. The samurai as administrators were more civilian-oriented and better attuned to bureaucratic service; the application of government to the governed had become increasingly impersonal and legally defined. At the same time many features of the original system had begun to lose relevance for the new social and economic problems which the Japanese government had to face in 1850. This interplay between processes which portended modernization and the obvious features of dynastic decline requires careful balance in any assessment of the 1850 political scene.

In 1650 the samurai who could read and write easily was a rarity; by 1850 virtually no samurai were illiterate and few would confess to an inability to turn a Confucian phrase. Samurai of 1850 were generally better trained for government than their predecessors; their knowledge of philosophy, history, and politics was far richer. The ethical and political literature produced by men like Ogyū Sorai, Satō Nobuhiro, or Rai Sanyō was incomparably more sophisticated in both style and content than the early works of the Hayashi family scholars. The writings of the late Tokugawa period realists were far more pertinent to the political, moral, or social problems of their age than those of their predecessors. By 1850 Japan had produced a host of able scholar-officials whose apt criticism and advice, though too seldom taken to heart, had been published and widely circulated. The samurai officials of the late Tokugawa period were not generically ignorant or careless of the shortcomings of their system.

By the same tokens, government had by that time become almost completely civilian. Up through the seventeenth century most of the daimyo continued to keep their military establishments in active readiness and to hold large-scale maneuvers from time to time. Thereafter the military branches of service in the domains, though continuing to command prestige, suffered increasingly from want of money and want of purpose. There is little record of what the some fifty per cent of retainers remaining in the military branch actually did after the middle of the Tokugawa period. They appeared to have been used, as Kaempfer noted when he entered Edo castle, "more for state than defense."[18] Meanwhile military technology not only failed to improve but began to deteriorate. The traditional military arts, increasingly ineffective in the field, became the means of physical training and mental discipline only. The forces which won the balance of power in 1868 were already the products of a recruitment and training learned from the West.

Meanwhile the civil organs of administration were gaining in diversity and impartiality. The mid-seventeenth century had been a period of very active diversification of the shogunal and daimyo bureaucracies; the nineteenth century witnessed a further surge of specialization, chiefly in the educational and fiscal branches of government. The shift from enfeoffment to salaried service was completed in the middle of the eighteenth century, the samurai class having by then almost wholly been withdrawn from the land. Only the senior vassals of a very few of the *tozama* daimyo remained enfeoffed.

In the shogunal and *han* bureaucracies the hold of the *mibun* system on personnel recruitment was being weakened. Salary increments (*tashidaka*) for certain offices, initiated by the eighth shogun Yoshimune, could bring the actual income of a meritorious but low-ranking retainer up to that of a putative superior. At the same time offices which had once required incumbents to use their own staff and salaries in the line of duty began to acquire separate budgets. In Okayama, for example, senior councillors received 200 bales of rice and the services

[18] Engelbert Kaempfer, *The History of Japan*, New York, 1906, V, III, 86.

of three men; chief auditors, 100 bales of rice and three men; inspectors general, 90 bales and three men; superintendents of ships, 90 bales and two men.[19] Quantities of paper, record books, brushes, and ink were also supplied. Meanwhile there had been a steady tendency to move offices out of the homes of officials into public quarters within the castle or castle town. Although a senior official might still rely on his private retainers to perform some of the functions of his office, the administrative branches of the shogunal and daimyo bureaucracies had adopted, in the main, a fairly impersonal mode of operation.

In the country, similar practices were being adopted among the villages. During the early years of the Tokugawa regime village headmen often took advantage of their position within the village and exercised an extra-legal political influence. The corvée system and the headman's practice of taking his salary out of the village tax payment were frequently abused. Increasingly, however, the authorities were able to abolish the corvée and to require the headmen to draw their salaries directly from the daimyo's treasury.

Furthermore, while the mere recordings of regulations and precedents does not of itself assure government by law, there is evidence that Tokugawa officials did come to understand the role of the law and the necessity of subordinating certain aspects of government to it. By the end of the Tokugawa period officials or scholars in the shogunate and in the major domains were at work collecting, codifying, and disseminating the basic laws of the realm. Insofar as was possible in a land lacking an independent tradition of jurisprudence and a specialized legal profession, efforts were made to compile the legal regulations and precedents necessary for official usage and even, as we see in Tosa, to clarify and simplify them.

Such evidence of increased sophistication in Tokugawa Japan is matched, however, by obvious signs of decline. Other functions of government than those involving the military had lost their original significance. In most domains there were a great many surplus retainers who often carried out quite meaningless routines.

The system with its sacred precedents was ceasing to bear much relationship to the state of affairs in the country at large. No aspect of late Tokugawa history has been more exhaustively and cheerfully described by historians than the indices of dynastic decline and of "worsening social and economic conditions." Economic and techno-

[19] *Kibi gunsho shūsei,* pp. 213-216.

logical problems had vexed Tokugawa administrators from the start. By the mid-eighteenth century the depletion of shogunal and daimyo treasuries and the impoverishment of the samurai were added to signs of rather general peasant distress. The political effect of this deterioration was a growing tension among various sectors in the power balance. The daimyo were becoming alienated from the shogunate, higher retainers from lower, samurai officialdom from the other estates, and village headmen from taxpaying villagers.

Peasant uprisings and mob demonstrations in the cities were dramatic signs of the impending breakdown. Yet Tokugawa Japan saw no infringement of lower orders upon the political rights of their superiors—no revolts of distressed samurai against their daimyo, no demands of merchants for political immunities, no agitation of the sort customary in a parliamentary society. Not even the few "forerunners of the Restoration" who harbored ideas subversive to the Tokugawa shogunate had plans for mass action. Perhaps the most significant political portents were the signs of leakage in the administrative hierarchies, as frustrated officials began to pull out of line to make their views known to their superiors. In the domains, lesser officials remonstrated with their daimyo, and even among the cadet daimyo of the Tokugawa house there was talk of a higher loyalty to the national good and the emperor.

These elements of "process" in the Tokugawa base were not, of course, the triggering elements in the Restoration movement. The Restoration itself was precipitated by the foreign crisis. But the historical circumstances of the Restoration, the fact that a threat from abroad could have the effect it did, that political leadership should have driven in the direction it did—these were in large part influenced by the political structure of the time. In following the course of political change in Japan from 1850 past 1868, one cannot help but be struck by the remarkable smoothness of the transfer of power and of the reform of political institutions. For a Japanese living through these years, the smoothness would hardly be apparent. For him these were momentous times when the entire world was revolving under him. Yet by comparison with other Asian countries undergoing modern revolutions, Japan managed to avoid the most destructive consequences of civil war and national disunity. The new was built upon the foundations of the old.

The outstanding general legacy of the Tokugawa political system to the Restoration years was a confidence in authoritarian procedure and in the primacy of an elite class. Despite radical changes in the composition of the group wielding power after 1853, that power remained in the hands of the samurai estate. Nor was the ultimate source of authority ever challenged. Appealing to the transcendent sovereignty of the emperor, the reformers were able to liquidate the shogunate without wholly or avowedly disrupting political tradition. The emperor, who had wielded little power in the old political order, was salvaged from the ruin of that order and made a symbol around which the nation, and particularly the samurai estate, could rally in time of foreign crisis.

At the crucial moment when the emperor provided a single focus of national loyalty, the daimyo domains provided multiple paths of political action. During the 1850's the *han,* for all their seeming dispersal of talent and national purpose, formed the breeding ground and training school of that able and versatile group of revolutionary leaders, the *shishi.* What distinguished the *shishi* as a group was their remarkable capacity for finding revolutionary goals within the existing system. Having devoted their early careers to their own domains, they were persuaded, at least until the Restoration, that they could fulfill their aspirations by asserting the vested interests of their domains against those of the shogunate. Transferring their loyalty to the nation, they became patriots but not class revolutionaries.

The final assault on the shogunate, made in the name of the emperor and in the national interest, did not destroy the social hierarchy within which the court nobility and daimyo had lived. We may contemplate what would probably have happened had the daimyo been threatened with violent overthrow or the samurai with the specter of mob uprisings in their castle towns. Would they not have drawn together to defend their status and prerogatives, by civil war if necessary? As it turned out, the last shogun could capitulate and the daimyo surrender their domains in the name of the emperor, secure in the knowledge that these acts would find favor under the new dispensation. The absence of social-revolutionary elements in the late Tokugawa scene had a profound bearing on the course of political action up to 1868 and on the success of the reforms which followed.

But in the final analysis the successful transfer of power would have been of little avail if the machinery of government had not been capable at once of maintaining political discipline and of incorporating appropriate reforms. The Tokugawa system of administration proved sufficiently stable on the one hand and adaptable on the other primarily because it was a very good system of its sort. The Restoration leaders, who placed no value upon change for its own sake, safely and wisely permitted that system to carry much of the burden of government during the crucial reform years. Many local administrative practices were retained almost intact for many years beyond 1868. Domain administration, little changed until after 1871, was then rather easily translated into prefectural administration. Except that the villages were combined into larger units, village administration remained virtually untouched, even under the laws of 1889 governing local autonomy. Behind the rapidly changing façade of government and the new faces of the Meiji state, the institutions and even, for a number of years, the persons of the Tokugawa regime remained specifically visible. The brave new world of the Meiji regime may have been quite as brave as it has been represented. It was not, however, quite so new.

B. TURKEY

BY HALİL İNALCIK

We can best describe the original features of the Ottoman-Turkish traditional society by going back to the time of Süleyman I (1520-1566). In the period immediately before the political modernization of the nineteenth century, we find only more or less degenerate forms of the original Ottoman institutions, and new social and political developments threatening the basis of those institutions. The generation of reformers confronting the period of decline after the sixteenth century avowedly sought to restore the Golden Age of Süleyman I. Under the impact of the defeats in Hungary between 1683 and 1699 the Ottoman Turks first became aware of the superiority of the West; the reforms thereafter increasingly acknowledged Western influences, first in the military field and then, in the nineteenth century, in administration. The decisive modernization movement, accompanied by a basic change in the concept of state and society, began with the national revolution after the First World War.

The hesitations and delays in the Turkish modernization process were due to the fact that, until the twentieth century, Turkey was an empire comprising nations of different cultures and that the dynasty became at a certain time the only focus of common loyalty. On the other hand, the political and social superstructure of the empire was still based on the *shari'ah* (Turkish: *şeriat*), the unalterable religious law of Islam, and this politico-religious structure culminated in the office of the sultan-caliph.

The position of this Ottoman ruler and the developments which reduced his power and ultimately led to modernization will constitute the main theme of this essay.

I. The Ottoman Ruler and Ottoman Society

Tursun Beg, Ottoman statesman and historian of the late fifteenth century, stressed that harmony among men living in society was achieved only by statecraft, which kept each individual in his proper place as determined by his ability. As the instrument of social order, statecraft possessed two aspects or sanctions: the authority and power of the ruler and the divine reason or *shari'ah*. Insofar as the rules instituted by the ruler did not have a perpetual character, he should always be present in a human society. He should have absolute power to determine the place of each man in the social scheme. Always seeking to strengthen his position by expanding his revenues and his armies, he should serve society as a whole by consolidating public security and order. Tursun Beg's rational arguments were manifestly designed to prove that every society must have one ruler with absolute power and with the authority of issuing regulations and laws outside the religious law. The values which this ruler was to conserve were social order and security under justice. These ideas constituted the basic political philosophy of the Ottomans.

The absolute power of the Ottoman ruler found further support in the old Oriental maxim that a ruler can have no power without soldiers, no soldiers without money, no money without the well-being of his subjects, and no popular well-being without justice. Repeated in Turkish political literature from *Kutadgu Bilik* in the eleventh century to the Gülhane Rescript of 1839, this formula was regarded as the summation of practical statesmanship. Kâtib Çelebi in the seventeenth century particularly stressed the central position of the sultan in the state. Though absolute power was ascribed to the caliph in the Islamic community, the theorists stressed that absolute power was simply a means of implementing the religious law.

The Ottoman rulers first made this theoretical absolutism a reality by establishing a type of administration that concentrated power in their persons. This they achieved notably by eliminating all kinds of aristocracies in the conquered lands, by entrusting executive functions only to slaves trained in the court (*kuls*), and by enlisting the *ulema* in their service. The sultan's slaves were entrusted with executive power and the *ulema* with the administration of law, including the supervision of all legal and financial matters. Both of these branches of administration were attached to the central government but each was independent of the other. A governor had no authority to give orders to a local judge (*kadı*) appointed by the sultan. If a conflict arose between the branches, it was appealed directly to the central government. The same judges administered both the *sharī'ah* and the subsidiary laws and regulations directly issued by the sultan. On the other hand, the *şeyhülislâm*, the highest authority in formulating opinions on points concerning the *sharī'ah*, had no right to interfere directly in the government or in legal administration. Once, when Şeyhülislâm Ali Cemali came over to the seat of the government to protest against a decision of Sultan Selim I (1512-1520) which he thought contrary to the *sharī'ah*, the sultan denounced him as interfering in state affairs. But in the eighteenth century it became established practice to seek the *şeyhülislâm's* opinion on every governmental matter of importance. The limitations so imposed on the government by the *sharī'ah* and by religious authority in the period of decline made the application of reforms especially difficult. The all-embracing *sharī'ah* became the stronghold of traditionalism in Ottoman government and society— introducing, as we may note in passing, a major difference between the Turkish and the Japanese modernization processes.

Ottoman social policy conformed closely to the traditional view that for the sake of social peace and order the state should keep each man in his appropriate social position. In the first place, Ottoman society was divided into two major classes. The first one, called *askerî*, literally the "military," included those to whom the sultan had delegated religious or executive power through an imperial diploma, namely, officers of the court and the army, civil servants, and *ulema*. The second included the *reaya*, comprising all Muslim and non-Muslim subjects who paid taxes but who had no part in the government. It was a fundamental rule of the empire to exclude its subjects from the privileges of the "military." Only those among them who were actual fighters on the frontiers and those who had entered the *ulema* class after a regular course of study in a religious seminary could obtain the sultan's diploma and thus become members of the "military" class. It was, in fine, the sultan's will alone that decided a man's status in society. In the period of decline, Koçi Beg and others asserted that a major cause of the disorganization of the empire was the abandonment of this fundamental rule in favor of letting subjects become Janissaries or fief (*tımar*) holders.

The subjects in turn were divided into Muslims and non-Muslims, townspeople and peasants, sedentaries and nomads, each with a different status, as reflected in their tax obligations. Taxation was indeed the most important factor in determining the subject's status. Those who were granted certain tax immunities in return for public service actually constituted an intermediate group between the simple subjects and the "military," who were wholly tax-exempt. Living for the most part on state-owned lands as tenants, the peasantry were subject to special taxes and were divided into groups according to the taxes they paid, the status of each being individually recorded at regular intervals. Peasants were not allowed to leave their lands, nor could they settle in towns.

These laws reflect a rigid social organization imposed by the will of the Ottoman ruler. But in the late sixteenth century a profound transformation took place which may be attributed ultimately to economic and military changes in Western Europe. During this period, for example, in order to resist German infantrymen, the Ottomans discarded their *tımar* cavalry in the provinces and increased the force of Janissaries, who were by this time equipped with firearms. This neglect of the fief holders within the army was followed by the disorganization of the land and taxation system upon which their status had been based. Simultaneously, the shift of international trade routes to the Atlantic Ocean and the invasion of the markets of the Levant by American silver resulted in the disorganization of the rigid Ottoman fiscal and economic structure.

Already during this period of decline, the sultan and his bureaucracy, who sensed immediate danger to the state from outside, adopted the idea of reform, although they thought of it as a reform along traditional lines. The Japanese, at a much later date, experienced the same challenge from outside and their emperor too personified the idea of reform. But the Japanese reform movement found national support at least among some leading classes in the society, while in the Ottoman Empire the major ruling classes took a reactionary stance. In the Ottoman Empire reform remained a concern of the sultan and his immediate collaborators alone. *Ulema* and a rising semi-feudal landed aristocracy in the provinces, called the *âyan,* resisted any innovation that might disturb their vested interests.

II. The Decline of the Sultan's Power; The Janissaries, the Ulema, and the Rise of the Âyan

In the capital of the empire the politically influential groups were the military corps at the sultan's Porte, particularly the Janissaries, constituting the "military" proper, and the *ulema,* the learned in Islamic sciences, who were vested with authority to express and apply the commands of the *sharī'ah.* In the provinces, too, the *ulema* and the Janissaries at one time possessed commanding power, but in the eighteenth century the *âyan,* a group of provincial magnates, came to be the most powerful class throughout the empire.

The Janissary corps constituted the original foundation of the centralist government and the principal support of the sultan's absolute power. It formed a standing army at the Porte, which was directly attached to the person of the sultan and which he could use at any time to strike at an internal or external foe. In addition, Janissary garrisons were stationed in the main strongholds in the provinces. In the large cities they occupied the forts, which no one else, not even a governor, was allowed to enter. In the period when central authority grew weaker, these Janissaries took over the actual control of the government in such distant parts of the empire as North Africa, Baghdad, and Belgrade. In the capital they determined who would wield control. As early as 1446, Murad II had accepted the throne only after obtaining their consent in a public meeting. In the first half of the seventeenth century they strengthened their grip on the government. In 1628 for the first time a former commander of the Janissary corps was appointed Grand Vezir with the support of the *şeyhül-islâm*, the head of the *ulema*. In the 1630's Koçi Beg complained that the balance established earlier between the power of the Janissaries and that of the provincial forces was gone and that the Janissaries invaded all sectors of the empire. The vezirs, courtiers, and heirs to the throne all sought their aid to attain power. The Janissaries furthermore obtained for themselves additional privileges, among them that of engaging in trade. Hence many of them joined the class of small shopkeepers and were thus affected by the government's financial policy as was the rest of the Istanbul population.

Let us observe also how the *âyan*, a powerful class of magnates, rose in the provinces. Traditionally the Ottomans granted the craftsmen and merchants in the towns a distinct and honorable status and recognized the most influential and wealthy among them as their natural leaders. Organized in so-called *ahi* unions, the craftsmen had played a major social and political role in Anatolia from the thirteenth century onward; their leaders, the *ahi*'s, acquired control of the administration in many Anatolian towns. Under the centralist government of the Ottomans, they were gradually reduced to simple guilds, but each guild continued to elect its own master, called *kâhya*, to supervise the application of the guild's rules and to act as its representative before the authorities.

Above the guildmasters were the *âyan* (notables) and the *eşraf*, the most influential residents of the city whom the government always addressed on matters directly concerning the town population. We find these *âyan* and *eşraf* present even in fourteenth-century Ottoman cities. Whenever an imperial order was to be communicated to the townsmen, the local judge convoked the *âyan*, *eşraf*, guildmasters, and *imams* (district clerics) of the town, because "these were," our source adds, "the agents and representatives of the people, who did what they said to do." Among the population, *kâhya*'s were elected as representatives of each district of the town and, from very early times, a mayor or town *kâhya*, representing the whole municipality. The local *eşraf* included the head of the descendants of the Prophet in the town, the head of the local *ulema*, and the mufti, the local agent of the *şeyhülislâm*. Though their influence derived originally from religious services, the *eşraf* were usually among the well-to-do citizens.

The *âyan* were the most influential and wealthy citizens in a town except for the *eşraf*. Most of them came from humble origins, many being minor local officials or Janissary officers who had risen by exploiting their official position.

As pointed out earlier, the tax and land-tenure system of the empire underwent a transformation during the upheavals between 1595 and 1610. The new conditions enabled the *âyan* to become feudal lords in the provinces, replacing the fief holders in the state-owned lands as lessees or tax collectors. In the meetings of *âyan* and *eşraf* under the judge, the most important issue was usually the distribution among the people of the total tax assessment of the district. After the decline of the earlier army, the central government, in increasing need of money to support the enlarged Janissary army, resorted more and more to extraordinary assessments, which were allotted to the counties. These special taxes and the assessments for local expenses were farmed out to individual persons by the council of *âyan* and *eşraf*, who often used these responsibilities to increase their own wealth and influence. They usually added to the assessment books items for themselves, or collected additional dues for their services. They often neglected to send the assessment books to the central government for inspection, and thus levied taxes without government control. In 1705 in Manisa, a city in western Anatolia, the populace became outraged by such abuses, and invaded the judge's court where the *âyan* and *eşraf* were sitting.

But usually the *âyan* managed to show themselves to the people as their protectors. They occasionally sent the sultan petitions for tax exemptions, which bore their own signatures though they were confirmed by the judge. They contended with oppressive government officials sent by the sultan. They were so influential in their areas, all in all, that the sultan's governor and judge often became simple tools in their hands. Without their cooperation, the authorities could not collect taxes, levy troops, or maintain public security.

The *âyan* gained their wealth and power through leasing state-owned lands as well as by tax farming. The larger part of such lands ceased to be assigned to fief holders and were leased by the state to local notables, *âyan* and *ağa's* (*âyan* usually had the title of *ağa's*, but *ağa's* mentioned together with *âyan* meant lesser *âyan* in the provinces), and more than fifty per cent of agricultural lands in the empire were state-owned leaseholds. Large areas of endowed land and land assigned to officials and favorites were similarly exploited. The *âyan's* influence on, and close cooperation with, local authorities favored them in these leasing operations. Later, in the eighteenth century, the leases were made for lifetime and prior rights to the leases were granted to the sons of lessees.

Tax farming, too, was extended after the dissolution of the old *timar* system near the end of the sixteenth century, and local notables benefited from their involvement in this profitable business.

In the period of decline, the sultan's governors themselves employed the *âyan* as their local agents in financial and administrative matters under such various titles as *mütesellim, voyvoda,* and *subaşı.* Increasingly in need of new troops for its prolonged wars, furthermore, the state encouraged the *âyan* to equip at their own expense the forces under their direct command. Thus in the eighteenth century the ground work had been laid for the rise of a powerful semi-feudal aristocracy in the provinces of Anatolia and in the Balkans. Many of the *âyan* families were able to maintain their position for several generations and founded local dynasties. Actual clashes sometimes occurred among rival *âyan* seeking to extend the area of their leasehold. Some of the most powerful among them even forced the government to confer upon them the official titles of vezir or pasha, thereby consolidating their control of the provinces in which they held their estates and becoming able in time to challenge the sultan's authority. The latter tried in his weakness to play one *âyan* against another, but often only with the result of making his ally excessively powerful. Tepedelenli Ali Pasha, actual ruler of southern Albania and northern Greece, was the most famous example of a pasha of *âyan* origin.

III. The Revolutions of 1807 and 1808: The Struggle for Power Among Janissaries, Ulema, *and* Âyan

A brief account of the revolutions of 1807 and 1808 will illustrate the part which the Janissaries, *ulema,* and *âyan* played in political developments in the Ottoman Empire at the turn of the nineteenth century.

Selim III (1789-1807) has been regarded as the father of Ottoman-Turkish Westernization and as an exponent of general reform in the state. He was indeed interested in Western civilization in its various aspects. Ebu Bekir Ratib, his envoy to Vienna in 1791, brought him a detailed report not only of the military and administrative establishments but also of technology and social advances as embodied in such institutions as postal systems and hospitals. Selim gave positive instructions to his newly appointed ambassadors to Western capitals to study the administrative as well as the military institutions of those states and encouraged the staffs at the embassies to learn Western languages and observe all the things that they considered useful. At home before he began his reform he invited the principal officials in his service, among whom was a French officer in the Ottoman army, to submit appropriate reform proposals. But Selim's main motive for reform was his determination to restore the military power of the empire and throw back the Russians, who had recently conquered the Muslim-inhabited land north of the Black Sea and now threatened Istanbul itself. His state philosophy was not very different from that of his predecessors. He reasoned, that is, that there could be no power without an army, no army without sufficient sources of revenue, and no revenue without justice and prosperity among his subjects. In his decrees introducing military reforms he pointed out that his ancestors had given him an example and that the *sharī'ah* permitted Muslims to use "the enemies' tricks to overcome them." What was new and anti-traditional in his measures was the introduction not only of European weapons but also of the sciences, training procedures and uniforms of Europe. For Western scientific thought challenged traditional Muslim thought, and the European uniforms challenged traditional symbols.

He also issued reform decrees on governorship, *âyan* leases of the domains, currency, and the status of the *ulema,* but all these followed absolutely traditional lines.

Despite his personal conservatism, Selim III created in Ottoman society a trend toward Westernization and a sense of the necessity for rapid and progressive change. The *ulema*, representing religiously sanctioned traditions, opposed him for the most part. The reforms found support only among some of the higher *ulema* who either sought the favor of the sultan or considered the reforms necessary to the ultimate interests of Islam and caliphate. These supporters too appealed to the *sharī'ah* to justify their position.

The true reasons for the opposition to Selim were to be found in the social situation. His efforts to create a regular army under his direct command threatened the dominant position in the state of the Janissaries, on the one hand, and of the *âyan*, on the other. In addition, his financial measures created widespread discontent in the country and turned public opinion and the *ulema* against him.

To finance the new army, Selim created a treasury of the "New Order" and allotted to it the revenues of an important part of the domain leaseholds. To find additional resources he also raised the rates of the various dues. Since the dues paid for the imperial diplomas conferring an office, immunity, or fief were among these, he thereby alienated a number of influential people. The first reaction came from the *âyan*. When the sultan in 1806 planned to extend the military reform to the Balkans by a transfer of "new troops" from Anatolia, the *âyan* in the Balkans gathered together in Edirne and opposed his further advance. Selim retreated, and this marked the beginning of his fall. The conservatives at once seized power under the leadership of Hilmi Pasha, the new Grand Vezir who had once been the commander of the Janissaries, and *Şeyhülislâm* Ata'ullah, a fanatic supported by the reactionaries. The opposition of the Janissaries to the New Order was understandable enough: it was no less than an instrument of their own destruction. They also rallied the populace of Istanbul, who were afflicted by the new taxes and by the inflation following Selim's debasing of the currency. The sultan's price-fixing and terrible threats against profiteers had proved useless. The abolition of Janissary pensions in the possession of non-military persons had also affected a number of people in the capital. Finally, Selim had let a group of favorites draw up his reform plans and control their application. Exploiting his ambition to restore the power of the sultanate, many of these favorites in fact set out to gain wealth and power for themselves. The responsible government officials hated them and in time turned against the sultan himself. In their eyes the reformist sultan had merely brought back the arbitrary rule of a handful of favorites. Under his successors the same accusation was made.

In brief, the population of Istanbul was, as our analyst says, split into two camps, partisans of the New Order, and its enemies. Finally in 1807 the Janissary *yamak*'s rose against the reformist sultan. All the Janissaries, *ulema*, and the populace of Istanbul joined them, seeking the abolition of the New Order and of the treasury created for it, and the execution of the favorites. The head of the *ulema*, Ata'ullah, gave a formal opinion (*fetva*) for the deposition of Selim III, in which he said that Selim was unfit for the caliphate because he had let irresponsible men usurp power and use it against the Muslim population. The rebels made an agreement with the new sultan, Mustafa IV, providing that they would not be prosecuted for their past actions; in return they themselves promised not to interfere in state affairs any more. Our analyst notes that such a pledge on the part of the sultan was unheard of in Ottoman history. The Janissaries and their conservative allies were now in control of the whole government and busy with the purge of Selim's partisans. Mustafa's authority was not heeded outside the walls of his court.

The *âyan* were quick to seize power from the hands of the Janissaries. The *âyan* of Rumelia under the leadership of Alemdar Mustafa Pasha, formerly an *âyan* of Rusçuk (Russe), marched against the capital together with the imperial army then on the Danube. Alemdar seized Istanbul, suppressed the Janissary leaders, and demanded Selim's restoration to the throne. When it turned out that Selim had been put to death in the meantime, Alemdar made Mahmud II sultan and became himself Grand Vezir and dictator. In his diploma of appointment to the Grand Vezirate it was stressed that he should be most careful to act in accordance with the *sharī'ah* in all state affairs, to cooperate with the Janissary corps and *ulema*, and enforce the ancient laws of the Ottoman sultans. Under Alemdar, nevertheless, there was a violent reaction against the enemies of the New Order, about one thousand of whom were executed in two months.

Previously the *âyan* had not made a united front against the Janissary corps. In 1806 those in Rumelia had cooperated with the Janissaries while some powerful *âyan* in Anatolia supported Selim's New Order. But now the *âyan* of Rumelia and Anatolia united against the reactionaries, less out of sympathy for the reforms than from a desire to control the central government and guarantee their position in the provinces. Soon the joint forces of the *âyan* flocked into the capital with their armies, terrifying the Janissaries and the court.

Following the example of the Janissaries, they too made the sultan sign an agreement called *Sened-i Ittifak* (Covenant of Union). In the introduction of this document, it was emphasized that the division and conflicts within the government and among the *âyan* in the provinces were the main causes of the desperate situation of the empire and that this covenant proposed to revive it. The main provisions were as follows: Vezirs, *ulema*, high officials, "dynasties" of major *âyan* in the provinces, and military corps in the capital promised always to respect the sovereign authority of the sultan and the orders of the Grand Vezir, who represented in his person the sultan's absolute power, and to take united action against any rebellion. The important article 5 declared that, just as the signatories promised collectively to safeguard the person and authority of the sultan and the order and security of the state, so the security of the provincial "dynasties" was to be protected by joint action of the signatories in the event that any law-abiding "dynasty" was assailed by the "state" or by vezirs in the provinces. The "dynasties" further undertook not to punish any lesser *âyan* under their own authority without first consulting the central government. Each "dynasty" was to respect the boundaries of the other's area of control, and all were to take joint action against any transgressor. In article 2, the "dynasties" and lesser provincial notables sanctioned a state army and promised to conscript soldiers for it in the face of any opposition, including opposition from the military corps in the capital. In the same article, they promised to cooperate in the collection of state taxes for the sultan in the provinces. They further pledged themselves to protect the population under their authority and observe carefully the tax regulations agreed upon among the state, ministers, and provincial *âyan* (article 7).

The document was drawn up in the form of a regular contract according to the *sharī'ah*, the parties being the state and its officials, *ulema*, generals of the military corps in the capital, and representatives of the provincial "dynasties." It will be noted that the "state" but not the sultan himself was mentioned as a party in the document. He took no oath as the others did, but for confirmation put his imperial seal upon the covenant, even though he had been warned by his closest advisers that it would severely limit his absolute power. The several "dynasties" stood surety for each other. In the postscript it was made clear that the covenant was to be the perpetual and unalterable basis for the regeneration of the empire. As such it was to be signed by every Grand Vezir and *şeyhülislâm* upon his accession to office, and these were to see that it was observed in every detail. A copy of it was also to be deposited with the sultan, who would see in person that it remained in force forever.

This important document has been interpreted in very different ways, often without sufficient recognition of its historical meaning and background. Like Magna Carta, it was a limitation upon the king's power imposed by local magnates; it was not, like Magna Carta of popular conception, a preparation for liberal-democratic development. It clearly indicates the diminution of the sultan's power and the rise of the provincial magnates. In it the "dynasties" acknowledged many traditional rights of the sultanate: the supreme authority of the sultan, the independence of his government, and the rights of the state to conscript soldiers and collect taxes directly in the provinces (articles 1-4). At the same time it clearly stated that as long as the "dynasties" did not infringe upon the central authority, the government had to respect their status and their established rights. The "dynasties" and grandees of the empire, furthermore, were arrogating the right to take common action against anyone, including members of the sultan's government, who violated the provisions of the document. Article 4 provided that if the Grand Vezir violated the laws and fell into corrupt practices, it was the duty of all to sue him and check the abuses. But the document did not constitute any special organization which might carry out such a suit. What the "dynasties" wanted, in fact, was precisely to assure themselves of a degree of autonomy incompatible with a centralist and progressive government.

IV. The Restoration of the Sultan's Power in the Empire: His Bureaucracy Takes the Lead in Modernizing the State

The rule of the *âyan* did not last long. The court and members of Ottoman bureaucracy as well as the population of Istanbul were in a state of terror and rather welcomed the counter-attack of the Janissaries which put an end to *âyan* rule. To reestablish his authority in the provinces, Mahmud II (1808-1839) could only rely on the Janissaries, who now became more disobedient than ever. In 1812, nevertheless, immediately after the conclusion of the peace treaty with Russia, Mahmud began to suppress the principal *âyan* in the provinces. He crushed some of those who resisted him by sending into their territories troops commanded by the neighboring governors. Others he was able directly to deprive of their titles and leases so that they themselves were forced to submit and their sons to accept humbler positions. But in 1821 Tepedelenli Ali Pasha, the most powerful among the pashas of *âyan* origin, raised truly massive resistance. The Greek insurrection followed his revolt.

Mahmud's war against the refractory *âyan* resulted in the dispossession of many of them and restored much of the sultan's authority in the provinces. Yet hundreds of these notables remained at the head of local administrations and in possession of large leaseholds. Still constituting the most influential class in the provinces, they often appeared to the passive local populations in the guise of protectors against oppressive governors and an arbitrary central authority. Later, when the masses were given the opportunity to participate in political life, men of this class were to play a major part in political leadership.

In 1826, during the most critical period of the Greek insurrection, Mahmud II at last made the fateful decision to get rid of the Janissaries. Having done away with these as well as the rebellious *âyan* in the provinces, he would then possess unlimited power to reorganize the empire as the conditions of the time required.

Before the destruction of the Janissaries, Hâlet Efendi, a favorite whom they had supported, had been virtual master of the state. Thereafter, Hüsrev, a reformer left over from Selim's time, was given the task of creating a new army and became the major force in the empire for fifteen years. He was a product of the old Ottoman *kul* (imperial slave) system. This institution, established to provide wholly reliable instruments for the exercise of the sultan's absolute power, had been clearly defined by Kemal Pasha-zâde at the beginning of the sixteenth century. Hüsrev, its last great representative, had himself trained many slaves who became generals and governors of the empire. It would remain, of course, for westernized diplomat-bureaucrats to introduce truly modern reforms in the Ottoman state.

Muhammad Ali, who had become pasha of Egypt in the manner of pashas of *âyan* origin, proved more dangerous than Tepedelenli. From 1833 on, he threatened to extend his power to all Asiatic provinces of the empire. His influence was felt even in Anatolia, where the *âyan* and conservative masses hostile to Mahmud's reforms were sympathetic to him. He defeated Mahmud's new armies in 1833 and 1839. It was during this critical period that a new generation of reformers, of whom Mustafa Reşid Pasha was typical, emerged to save the empire from total destruction. Differing wholly from the military reformers like Hüsrev, these men were chiefly diplomats who had become acquainted with international conditions and with the structure of Western states during service in European capitals. They came out of the age-old bureaucracy which formed the third class of Ottoman state functionaries, the other classes being the *ulema* and the military. Their training was a practical one in the state bureaus, differing from that of the military, who were mostly trained under the *kul* system, and more markedly still from that of the *ulema*, who came from the rigidly formal religious seminaries. Thanks to their services in diplomacy and finance, the bureaucrats gained an increasing influence in the administration from the eighteenth century on. Devoted exclusively to the secular interests of the state and free from formalism and the bonds of tradition, they were ready to become faithful instruments of radical administrative reform. In 1821 when the Ottoman government had to replace the Greek interpreters with Turks, a Translation Office was created at the Sublime Porte, and Western languages were taught there, the first teacher being a professor from the military engineering school. This Translation Office, like the embassies which Selim III had established in Western capitals, became an educational center for a new generation of Westernized administrators and intellectuals. Âli Pasha, future Grand Vezir and reformer, and Fuad Pasha, collaborator of Reşid, received their first education in these centers.

Confronted with the disaster at Navarino in 1827 and Muhammad Ali's startling successes, Mahmud II heeded the advice of his reformist diplomats who saw the necessity of gaining the sympathy and confidence of Western powers and modernizing the Ottoman administration. Accordingly he introduced, between 1831 and 1838, some administrative and social reforms which can be regarded as the first decisive steps toward Westernization. Principal among these were the creation of state departments and of a council of ministers with a prime minister, the establishment of two high councils for military and civil reform, the use in the administration of civil servants with fixed salaries, the founding of a modern postal service and of secular professional schools, and modernization in clothing and state protocol. But Mahmud's most significant achievement remained the restoration of the sultan's power in the provinces and in all branches of administration.

After his success on a diplomatic mission to London in 1838, when war was pending with Muhammad Ali of Egypt, Reşid Pasha gained an increasing influence over Mahmud II and was able to persuade him that the disposition of Egypt would finally be decided in Western capitals. The very survival of the Ottoman state, in his view, was dependent on a modernization of its administration which would enable it to enter the concert of European states. The Ottoman defeat at Nezib in 1839 was followed by the death of Mahmud II, and thereafter everyone, including his great opponent Hüsrev, looked to Reşid for salvation and became receptive to his reform projects. The most radical Turkish decisions to reform, we observe, were almost always made in time of crisis.

On November 3, 1839, an imperial rescript, read by Reşid Pasha at Gülhane, initiated the era of reform called Tanzimat in Turkish history. That document said in summary: The empire had been declining for one hundred and fifty years because the religious law and imperial laws had been disregarded. In order to restore its prosperity and strength, new legislation was required which should be based on the principle of securing the life, honor, and property of all subjects. Taxation and conscription laws would be revised in accordance with the demands of justice. The tax farming system would be abolished and each citizen taxed in proportion to his means. Every accused person should be publicly judged. These guarantees should be extended to all subjects of whatever religion or sect.

A high council of reforms (*Meclis-i Vâlâ-yı Ahkâm-ı Adliye*) would devise, after free debate, bills fulfilling the purposes agreed upon, and those in turn would be submitted to the sultan to be confirmed and published. Since all the bills would be drawn up for the sake of resuscitating Islam, the state, and the empire, the sultan promised to take an oath not to disregard them. The *ulema* and grandees of the empire were to take oaths to the same effect, and those who broke their word were to be punished without respect of rank and position according to the provisions of a penal code. These dispositions, finally, were to be made public throughout the empire and communicated officially to all the ambassadors of friendly powers resident at Istanbul.

In this rescript the main features of the European constitutions of the 1830's are quite skillfully combined with traditional Ottoman institutions and with practical necessities. A number of references to the *sharī'ah* obscured from conservatives the revolutionary content of the document, and indeed the traditional state philosophy was genuinely apparent in it: The rescript said that the state needed armed forces which in turn required money, that state finances could remain

56

in good order only if the subjects were protected against injustices, and so on. The basic principle of legislation, also, was discovered not in natural rights but in the practical necessity of resuscitating the empire. In brief, state power remained the ultimate goal as before; the people were still regarded as mere subjects of the state.

It should be remembered that in classical Islamic thought no principles of law could exist apart from the *sharī'ah*. But with the Ottomans there had always in fact been an independent category of laws called imperial laws or *kanun*'s which were derived directly from the sovereign will of the ruler. For their justification it was asserted that, though applying to situations not covered by the *sharī'ah*, they were necessary for the well-being of the Islamic community. The Ottoman sultans had promulgated hundreds of such *kanun*'s concerning public law, state finances, taxation, economic life, and criminal law. The Gülhane rescript was promulgated on the same principle, the legislation which it envisaged being thought necessary to regenerate the state. The document itself was rendered in the form of a decree.

When all this is said, it remains nevertheless clear that the rescript introduced revolutionary ideas and institutions into Ottoman society. Among them was the sultan's promise, confirmed by an oath, to respect the laws to be made pursuant to its principles and the establishment of a council for legislative activities with the guarantee of freedom of debate.

When he composed the decree, Reşid had intended to impose limits on the despotic power of the sultan. In his letter to Palmerston, dated August 12, 1839, he confessed this intention: "Les puissances de l'Europe," he wrote, "savent à quel dégré était progressivement parvenue la tyrannie des Empereurs ottomans depuis la destruction des Janissaires. . . . Lorsque malgré la considération, si forte du voisinage, l'Autriche et la Russie, quelqu'en soit le motif, permettent à la Walachie et à la Servie, d'adopter une constitution, aucune puissance ne saurait-elle jamais vouloir empêcher que les populations musulmans obtiennent rien que de simples sûretés pour leur [sic] vies et pour leur fortune."[1]

A further revolutionary element in the document was the extension of the guarantees in it to all subjects. Later, in 1846, the sultan could confirm these principles in a speech saying: "The differences of religion and sect among the subjects is something concerning only their

---

[1] F. E. Bailey, *British Policy and the Turkish Reform Movement*, Cambridge, Mass., 1942, p. 275.

persons and not affecting their rights of citizenship. As we are living all in the same country under the same government, it is wrong to make discriminations among us." The revolt of the Greeks and the European crusade for Greek independence had taught a severe lesson to the Ottomans. Now, possessing equality before the law, the non-Muslim subjects would, it was expected, no longer feel that they were a segregated and oppressed element in the state and would no longer strive for independence from it. The Western powers, too, would appreciate this change in favor of the Christians in the empire. It must be noted that with their demands for equality, freedom, home rule, reforms in taxation, and land ownership the non-Muslim subjects were contributing to the Westernization of the Ottoman-Turkish state. Perceiving their peculiar position and the intervention of the West on their behalf, the sultan was moved increasingly to secularize public institutions. As sultan-caliph, he began to distinguish as best he could between his offices as ruler of all Ottoman citizens equally and his office as caliph of only the Muslims in accordance with the *sharī'ah*. The significant concession to the non-Muslims caused apprehensions among the Muslims in general, who regarded it as the destruction of the caliphate and denounced the Westernization movement as a whole. The fanatical ones stigmatized it as apostasy. The division thereby brought into focus between Westernizers with chiefly secular views and conservatives attached to the rule of the *sharī'ah* remained for many years the principal schism in Turkish political life.

In brief, equality before the law and the securing of life, honor, and property for all subjects were the revolutionary ideas in the rescript. Reşid himself asserted that the Tanzimat, the reforms introduced with the rescript, would change the imperial regime completely. The change in the concept of the state was further visible in the various decrees in which the sultan announced that the laws were made solely for the subjects' benefit.

We can ascertain the sincerity of Reşid's professions when we study the measures by which he undertook to put into effect the principles proclaimed in the rescript. Reşid showed his zeal to make the rule of law a reality by the haste with which he published a penal code.

In the provinces, administrative councils were established, the members of which were the governor, his two secretaries, the local judge, the mufti, the local military commander, four notables, and, if there was a Christian community in the province, the *metropolit* and two Christian notables. The notables were to be elected by the people.

The provincial councils and smaller councils in the dependent towns were freely to discuss all administrative matters and were to sit as criminal courts. The High Council of Reforms in the capital constituted a court of appeal for them. With the establishment of the provincial councils, Ottoman subjects, non-Muslims in particular, may be said to have received for the first time a voice in the local administration, though in actual fact these councils were composed of the local high officials, *ulema*, and notables, and differed little from the old councils of notables under the judge. Sometimes, paradoxically enough, the local *âyan* and *eşraf* used their new positions in local administration to obstruct the Tanzimat and incite the conservative masses against it.

Introduced with the intention of protecting both the peasants and the public treasury, financial reforms followed hard upon the proclamation of the rescript. To secure greater justice in taxation Reşid abolished the tax immunities and exemptions affecting such influential groups as *âyan, ağa*'s, *ulema,* and the military, as well as the exemptions connected with religious endowments. The affected groups started an intense propaganda campaign against the reforms. The survey and census embarked upon for purposes of the reform gave them an opportunity to incite the conservative masses, and they spread rumors variously that the government had determined to double the taxes or to abolish them altogether. The abolition of tax farming affected the large group of tax farmers and credit agents and the substantial number of officials profiting from it in dubious ways. It must be recalled that most of the tax farmers were local notables who had gained wealth and influence through this activity. Again in order to extend the state's protection over the peasantry, Reşid abolished forced labor and usury. One of the first decisions of the High Council of Reforms read: "In the Balkans most of the notables used to think that the peasants were their serfs, and employed them for their own services without any compensation. Also they did not permit them to leave their estates to work elsewhere and they interfered even in their marriages. Now the sultan has never accepted such abuses, and those who oppose this order [abolishing them] will be punished according to the provisions of the penal code recently published." Another decree pointed out that the usurers were getting twenty per cent per month for the money they lent to the peasants. Never able to pay their debts, these were eventually deprived of all their possessions. The usurers also used to appropriate the peasants' crops at below market prices. Now the government reduced the rates of interest and permitted the peasantry to pay their accumulated debts in installments.

The government had ordered the officials in the provinces to explain to the people in mass meetings the principles embodied in the Rescript of Gülhane. In some areas in the Balkans the peasants became so impatient to see the results of the reforms that they attempted desperate actions. Seeing that the Tanzimat had not brought any immediate relief in their tax burden, for example, and that they were still subject to forced labor, the Bulgarian peasants around Nish rose up under their own lesser notables. Further uprisings in 1849 and 1850 in the Vidin area were even more serious. Most of the agricultural lands in this area were originally state-owned. But local Muslim *ağa*'s had the exclusive rights to lease them and in fact possessed them as their own estates. Rejecting the popular demands and organizing a local militia (*başıbozuk*'s), the *ağa*'s fell upon the rebels, and it required regular government forces to end the struggle. The High Council of Reforms in Istanbul decided first to abolish the existing administrative council and granted the Christian peasants the right to lease the state-owned lands themselves. These radical decisions proved impracticable, however, and the situation did not change much subsequently. Similar reactions occurred in Anatolia. The *âyan* of Bala near Ankara, for example, was prosecuted before the High Council of Reforms for evading tax payments, subjecting the peasants to forced labor, inciting people to rise against the government. The difference here was that the Muslim population, under the influence of the local *ulema* and *âyan*, were extremely conservative, whereas the Christian subjects in the Balkans, under the influence of nationalist leaders, were in a mood to rebel.

These examples indicate how difficult it was for Reşid to effect his reforms and how various were the social forces arrayed against him. The privileged classes of the old regime, especially *ağa*'s in collaboration with the *ulema*, were asserting that the grant of civil equality to the non-Muslims and the "infidel" disregard of the *sharī'ah* would ruin the state and religion. To control them, Reşid had hastily published his penal code so that he might legally prosecute offenders against the government's reform measures. Many reactionaries in the capital as well as in the provinces, including even old Hüsrev, were punished. In Ankara a mufti, a member of the administrative council, was condemned for inciting people to rebel against the reforms.

In line with his efforts to introduce a Western system of administration, Reşid decided to entrust public service in the provinces exclusively to salaried civil servants appointed by the central government and to abolish all the forms of dues and bribes which the *âyan* and officials of all degrees had been accustomed to accept. In seeking to create a corps of civil servants to implement the reforms, Reşid was directly threatening the position of the provincial *âyan* who, as agents of the governors-general, then occupied most of the local administrative posts in Anatolia. Reşid was intent on changing those features of the organization of the empire which were inherited from feudalism. His administrative reform meant, in the last analysis, profound social reform. One of his radical measures after the abolition of tax farming was to appoint revenue collectors (*muhassıl's*) in the provinces who were attached directly to the central government. But he failed to find enough civil servants trained for the job and was forced after all to employ local notables, who often followed the old practices.

It was later decided to found special secular schools to supply the civil servants so urgently needed. In these schools and in the military academies a body of Westernized officials were trained who were destined to play a decisive part in the modernization of Turkey. The resistance to Reşid's reforms caused his fall in 1841 (he was then foreign minister). The newly introduced institutions had not worked well; the new system of tax collection in especial was a failure. Reşid had relied solely on the sultan's favor, which he had gained through his services in solving the Egyptian question. His successor in power was Rıza Pasha, the Minister of War, who like many old-type reformers believed chiefly in military reorganization as a means of resuscitating the empire. Tax farming came back with him, and radical reforms in the administration generally were judged ill-timed. When in 1845 Reşid came back to power he gave priority to training the bureaucrats needed to implement his reforms; to this end he created a High Council of Public Education and projected the foundation of a university.

In the same year the government took the bold step of asking each province to elect two delegates and send them to Istanbul to consult on the reforms to be undertaken. These delegates were "elected from among the prominent and respected people." The assembly seemed in concert to be simply an extension of the provincial administrative councils. Yet it remains the first representative assembly ever convoked in the Ottoman capital. Though the *âyan* who appeared at the sultan's Porte were timid enough and soon returned home, the conservatives were appalled. Serasker Said Pasha went so far as to denounce Reşid for intending to proclaim a republic. Perhaps more significant in its consequence was the promulgation of a commercial code borrowed from France which established tribunals of commerce, the first secular tribunals of the Ottoman state.

For two principal reasons the bold steps taken by Reşid remained without effect. In the first place, the current severe economic depression was identified in the popular mind with the West and its ways—not improperly, since the cheap and plentiful products of Western industry, invading the Turkish market under the capitulary regime, were ruining the native industries. Of these happenings the contemporary consular reports give us vivid descriptions. In the second place, disgruntled persons were accusing the reformist Sultan Abdülmecid (1839-1861) of letting Reşid abuse the power of the sultanate. The highly centralist and authoritarian system of government espoused by Reşid and his followers became the particular target of the rising Ottoman-Turkish intelligentsia, who saw in it a despotism harmful to the empire. Organized as the secret society of the Young Ottomans in 1867, these intellectuals embraced the romantic nationalism then prevalent in Europe and advocated a constitutional regime which would introduce elements of Western civilization while preserving traditional Islamic-Turkish culture. For the first time we find a group of progressives acting independently of the government and opposing the official reform program. The Young Ottomans were the real forerunners of the nationalist and democratic movement in Turkey.

The major characteristics of modernization in this early period can be succinctly summarized.

A program of modernization was first adopted by the state as a measure of self-defense against an aggressive and imperialistic Europe. The superiority of European military techniques and organization was recognized as early as the end of the seventeenth century. This perception was a necessary psychological preparation for the later cultural borrowings from the West.

Second, systematic modernization started with military reforms in the eighteenth century, especially under Selim III. From 1830 on, the process was extended to administration and public institutions, a trend which culminated in the proclamation of the Ottoman constitution of 1876.

Third, in the modernization movement the state was the initiator, and changes were imposed from above, the sultan using his absolute power to create the bureaucratic machinery necessary to effect changes.

Fourth, the masses, the great majority of whom were living in a closed rural economy, were generally dependent on the *âyan*, *ağa's*, and clerics, who were vitally interested in keeping them attached to the traditional institutions. Even in the period between 1800 and 1850 these groups actively resisted the reforms imposed by the state; the Turkish-Muslim population of the empire remained in general indifferent or even refractory in the face of change.

Fifth, a desire to satisfy non-Muslim subjects and the Western powers definitely encouraged the Ottoman state to adopt secular laws and institutions. The Western powers were interested in furnishing the empire with liberal institutions, which they thought would guarantee at once the integrity of that state and their own economic interests in it.

Sixth, around 1860 a small group of Turkish patriots with Western outlook emerged and carried out, in the newly introduced press and in a number of literary periodicals, a vigorous campaign against the sultan's absolutism. His reform measures were, they believed, both arbitrary and contrary to the real interests of the Turkish-Muslim population.

In the Turkish modernization movement, finally, the principal difficulties stemmed from the religious basis of the traditional society and state. In general, the Tanzimat reformers and intellectuals, though wanting to Westernize the administration and to borrow modern techniques, believed it desirable to preserve such basic traditional institutions as the *sharī'ah*, the religious courts, and the religious schools. It was thought that these might be taken out of public affairs and relegated to their own sphere. Later, radicals who wanted wholesale Westernization and a national sovereignty like that of European states were to blame the failure of the Tanzimat upon this dualism. But no concept of the nation-state was in fact realized until Atatürk called the Turkish republic into being after the dissolution of the empire in 1919.

CHAPTER 3

ENVIRONMENTAL AND FOREIGN CONTRIBUTIONS

A. JAPAN

ROBERT A. SCALAPINO

"MODERNIZATION" is now a term with which any aspiring social scientist must contend. Today almost everyone reads—or writes— about the movement of various societies from "traditionalism" toward "modernity." An intensive search is underway to discover the requisites for effective or rapid change. In part, this is the result of urgent policy needs both at home and abroad. In part, it is an intellectual aspect of the progressive American discovery of the world that has developed since 1945.

Whether "modernization" is an entirely satisfactory term might be debated. It is difficult to use this word without thinking in Western-value-oriented terms, envisaging a process whereby "backward" societies move toward predetermined goals in difficult but relatively unambiguous fashion, and follow the Western model. As in many theories, there is enough truth in such a formulation to make it potent, if considerably less useful than may appear at first glance. Above all, it is important to realize that "modernization" is an ongoing process, significantly different from era to era, and society to society, despite certain broad common denominators which must be identified and defined with the greatest care. Who can foretell the nature or goals of "modernization" in the twenty-first century? And who yet understands the significant differences between nineteenth and twentieth century "modernization"?

It seems clear that Marx, for example, generalizing from the experience of nineteenth-century Europe, was wrong in assuming that the rest of the world would follow the specific European pattern and that a given set of economic circumstances would automatically produce a given set of political institutions. Industrialization does not necessarily produce Western-style democracy or the same dominant ideology. Nor does the "advanced" West provide the only model for moderniza-

64

tion at present. We cannot even assume that democracy as we have known it has a healthy future in the present democratic societies.

The normal criteria of modernization in the mid-twentieth century are economic diversification within an advanced industrial technology; heightened social mobility and the movement toward impersonal and rationalized social relationships; a concentration of the population in cities and in more comprehensive social units generally; and the mobilization of persons en masse through popular education, organization, and communications.

Mass mobilization is not to be confused with democracy. Since he has been discovered, the common man has perhaps made fewer of the major decisions affecting his life than before. Certainly he has had less chance to govern himself in the classical Western sense. At this point the modernization process militates against democracy. Nor is it certain that man is more rational today, despite the homage paid to science, the advancement of knowledge in a variety of fields, and the defeat of many superstitions. Though the movement toward impersonal relations provides, in some measure, for greater rationality, the tempo and complexity of modern life frequently impose tensions beyond those which reason can master. The quotient of irrationality in the modern world may hence be higher than in the past; certainly, given the advance of science, it is more dangerous. Even the equation of modernity with social mobility is only partly valid. It is evident that a goodly measure of hierarchy—a fairly high degree of social immobility—is an asset in economic development.

In the final analysis, "modernization" in its broadest contemporary form represents a series of complex, unresolved paradoxes. Economic diversification promises higher living standards, yet the pressures within a highly complex economy are destructive of personal well-being. Economic concentration and urbanization are centripetal forces of awesome proportions, yet family and clan ties are loosened and anonymity and loneliness enhanced. Communication, made technically easy, becomes more difficult as specialists go their several ways and eventually cease to understand each other.

I. Basic Factors in Japanese Political Modernization

Modernization involves these paradoxes and others. We are concerned here specifically with the political modernization of Japan, however. What did that modernization process, which for our purposes began in the mid-nineteenth century, involve?

It involved the creation of a nation-state, and the successful adjustment of loyalties to that state; the substantial increase of centralized political power.

It involved the replacement of an hereditary officialdom, recruited out of the military class and fixed in status by birth or adoption, with a differentiated civil and military officialdom, the former recruited via the civil service system after higher education, and the latter given technical training in specialized institutions, with merit playing an increasing role in selection and promotion for both groups.

It involved the establishment of a comprehensive legal system, capped by a national constitution; the universalization and standardization of law and procedures, with the abolition of legally privileged classes, and the movement toward equal rights under the law for all citizens of the state.

It involved participation of the citizen in the political process through the mechanism of elections, and the gradual development of political parties and interest-group associations attuned to this system.

It should be noted that the initial process of political modernization in Japan was complicated, even while it was aided, by the fact of cultural borrowing. The overwhelming majority of Japanese equated modernization with Westernization. Certain traditional biases were reenforced and emotional obstacles established because of the extensive "foreign" element in the modernization program.

It is also doubtful whether the political modernizers of Japan avoided many mistakes as a result of the experiences—the lessons—of earlier modernizers. Certainly there were advantages in being able to observe and borrow from others. One could take the latest inventions and technology. But the process of modernization is vastly more complex than the mere copying of a textile machine or the employment of a foreign technician. In the political field particularly, the mechanical borrowing of foreign institutions and procedures nearly always ended in failure, and produced a sharp reaction against such practices. In the final analysis, Japanese modernizers in the political field learned by their own experiences through a process of trial and error. They made many mistakes, but it was the willingness to experiment, the essential pragmatism characterizing the leadership, that gave the political modernization of Japan its most progressive qualities, especially in the Meiji era.

If one seeks keys to the effectiveness of modernization in Japan, three interrelated factors stand out: selective geopolitical-cultural features of this society conducive to modernization; advantages of timing in comparison with the rest of the world; and the fact that, by a combination of accident and design, the modernization program was harnessed to available resources with a minimum of destruction and waste. This latter point is supremely important although it has bequeathed massive problems as well as major progress. But it is the combination of these three factors that shaped the character and results of Japanese modernization.

At the outset, let us suggest some of the ways in which geography affected Japanese modernization. In the search for intricate factors, sometimes obvious factors are minimized or overlooked. Japan was located close enough to the Asian continental mass to have intensive and relatively continuous cultural intercourse. Yet its physical separation permitted the society to develop in relatively homogeneous fashion and to become possessed of a sense of identity and a quality of uniqueness.

It is possible, of course, to exaggerate these advantages. The unification of the Japanese islands required a thousand years and more after a relatively advanced civilization was implanted on Honshū. Cultural variations within the society continued to exist, and provincialism remained a powerful force within the modern era. In these and many other respects, Japan resembled Great Britain, and like Britain, its great historical dilemma was the issue of continental involvement versus isolation.

Geography also played a significant part in determining the timing of Japanese modernization. Located on the periphery of Northeast Asia, the country was largely secluded from early Western contacts. The penetration of missionaries in the sixteenth century was temporary. When the more formidable Western expansion of the eighteenth and nineteenth centuries occurred, Japan was not in the main path of the initial thrust. Southern Asia and China had already felt the force of Western power when the Perry Expedition succeeded in "opening" Japan. And, Japan became economically important only when the northern Pacific route began to be used extensively and when northern Chinese ports became available to Western trade. By that time, Japanese leaders were in a position to understand something of the West and its ways.

67

Can one generalize about the significance of timing, more precisely, the advantages accruing to Japan as the result of the particular timing of her own modernization? She was the first Afro-Asian nation consciously to undertake a program of rapid modernization, and there are some disadvantages in being a pioneer. Yet in the late nineteenth century, it was still possible to pursue a national goal with some degree of leisure. Neither the ideology nor the technique of the one-generation revolution had yet been perfected. Thus the tempo of change was less frenetic than it was to become a century later. There was also a single basic model to follow: the classically liberal, "advanced" Western society.

Japan turned to Germany and especially Prussia for many ideas, because Germany shared a common timing of emergence with Japan, and hence certain common problems of development. There were perhaps also some complex cultural similarities between the two nations. In any instance, Japan and Germany accepted the same basic Western model and with the same imperfect success. In both societies, parliamentary government failed signally in the era before 1945. Further examination would indicate that Japan and Germany in terms of their modernization represented transitional societies in the great world continuum that may be said to have started with Britain and its Glorious Revolution and come at this point to Communist China, and its "Great Leap Forward." As in-between societies, these two nations were destined neither to fall wholly into the classical liberal mold nor, until very late, to embrace totalitarian patterns of change.

Contrast the situation of nineteenth-century Japan with that of the Afro-Asian societies emerging today into the world stream. Today, the classical Western model has substantial competition. "Backward" societies of the mid-twentieth century are frequently attracted to more "efficient" methods of modernization. At the very least, they are disposed to pick and choose among diverse models, seeking a synthesis that will fit the contours of their own society. The crucial, initial stages of Japanese modernization occurred in a simpler era, and the history of modern Japan bears eloquent testimony to this fact.

It is further significant that Japan first sought a place among modern nations at a time when she could limit her external commitments and concentrate upon the task of internal consolidation. Today, most emergent nations are forced to shoulder regional and international obligations while they are still struggling to establish themselves as independent states. In the mid-twentieth century, isolation is no longer possible. The new nations must share their precariously limited resources of wealth and talent with agencies so remote as the United Nations.

The circumstances of the contemporary world diffuse also the loyalties of individual citizens. Nationalism can no longer have an exclusive right of way. Even as the assault against provincialism or tribalism within the nation-state is undertaken, certain commitments to the supranational community must be cultivated. For Japan, world involvement came more gradually, as a natural consequence of developing power and maturity. Long after she had entered into economic and cultural commerce with the West, Japan was still able to limit her external commitments largely to Northeast Asia.

Finally, as noted above, the modernization of Japan was effected by the maximum use of indigenous resources, and with minimal waste and destruction. Japan is one of the few examples of a "late developing" society that was transformed under the leadership of an essentially conservative elite. In Japan "enlightened conservatism," while subject to many qualifications, was a real entity, not, as so often, a mere notion or slogan. The ruling elite wanted to make the minimum number of changes necessary to enable Japan to survive, or perhaps more accurately, to flourish. Their goal was evolution, not revolution. Like such great Western conservatives as Edmund Burke, they did not want to see the Japanese cultural legacy swept away in some revolutionary flash flood.

Under these conditions, the use of existing values and institutions was greatly facilitated. Long-standing traditions were pressed into service on behalf of change. And though some institutions, like those of the military, had to be radically altered, others remained virtually the same. The overall bias of the political elite was toward conservation, yet without the rigidity characterizing the majority of traditionally oriented ruling classes.

The quite general preservation of tradition by the Japanese modernizers was not an unmixed blessing. Ultimately, a revolution of sorts was required—one conducted primarily by Americans. Even now, Japanese society abounds with paradoxes and "backward" elements. What can be said unequivocally on behalf of the Japanese way is that it was vastly efficient. The nation as a whole did not waste its energies or resources in the mass liquidation of persons and institutions.

II. The Creation of the Modern Japanese State

To the process of creating a modern state, then, Japan brought whatever she could husband from her own past. One of her most valuable assets was a system of *political* loyalty such as much of the non-Western world still lacks. During her feudal period Japan had established a system of obligation and rights transcending ties of family and clan and involving entire communities. The lord had enjoyed primary loyalty, not the parents; the state had triumphed over the family. It remained only to broaden the scope of existing political concepts: to transform the *han* into the nation, and loyalty to the lord into reverence for the emperor. We have only to contrast feudal Japan with traditional China, where blood ties were supreme, to perceive how early the nation had cultivated a political consciousness anticipating the modern. In considerable measure, the supremacy of *public politics* had already been established in traditional Japan.

Nor was Japanese political organization before Perry's advent confined to the fief. That society had had extensive experience with larger-scale political organization.[1] The Tokugawa era has been commonly called an era of "centralized feudalism." The power of the Edo shogunate was substantial, especially over the *fudai daimyō*, the lords with whom it had most intimate contact. Its methods of exercising authority, moreover, were highly sophisticated, involving tactics such as conferring legitimacy via imperial investiture and compelling each feudal lord to spend a certain amount of time in the capital, properly watched and indoctrinated.

But in this era, the Japanese system of authority was inseparable from the class structure, to the perpetuation of which it was dedicated. Hierarchy, minutely defined and rigidly enforced, underlay the political ethics of traditional Japan. The exalted reaches of this hierarchy provided an elite that could wield authority easily because it was trained to that task, and because it was accepted by the governed. Such acceptance did not depend upon the plebiscite in Japan until long after parliamentary institutions had been formally established and the elite had become accustomed to fulfilling the tasks characteristic of modern government.

In Japan, paternalism was a deeply engrained part of the culture,

---

[1] See the essay by John W. Hall in this volume, and also his *Tanuma Okitsugu, 1719-1788: Forerunner of Modern Japan*, Cambridge, 1955.

having a powerful effect upon governed and governing alike. To those whose value system is based upon modern democracy, who cherish egalitarianism and maximum social mobility, hierarchy and paternalism are not satisfactory substitutes. It remains true, however, that paternalism is one method, and perhaps the most effective method, of producing a type of elitist "enlightenment" that, in the early stages of political modernization, serves to minimize abuse, regularize rights and obligations, and preserve human relationships with minimum violence even in an era of major social change. Later, paternalism can give way gradually to an "enlightenment" based upon an appreciation of the importance of meeting mass needs, at least in minimal respects, in order to obtain the necessary votes to stay in power; or an "enlightenment" based upon more skillful manipulation of mass media and political controls.

In sum, Japan could approach political modernization having in her possession the concept of political loyalty, the acceptance of the supremacy of the state over the individual or private association; experience with large-scale organization involving fairly advanced political techniques; and a disciplined, committed, and reasonably efficient political elite. In all of these respects, Japan in the mid-nineteenth century possessed many of the attributes of Great Britain in the late feudal period.

Granting these indigenous qualities, what were the foreign contributions to the creation of the nation-state, and a successful adjustment of loyalties to that body? In the broadest sense, there were both positive and negative contributions from abroad, both conscious and unconscious stimuli. In confronting the Western challenge, a challenge inescapable by the early nineteenth century, Asia went through three basic responses: first, total rejection; second, the attempt to distinguish between values and general culture which would continue to be drawn from tradition, and "technology" which would be borrowed from the West; and finally, the quest for some workable, comprehensive synthesis between indigenous and foreign elements at all levels, a quest that is still continuing.

Japan, like other Asian societies, displayed these reactions. Japanese nationalism in its modern form was from the first a response to the Western challenge,[2] arising out of the struggle to survive in the

[2] For four significant English language works on Japanese nationalism, see Delmer Brown, *Nationalism in Japan*, Berkeley, 1955; D. C. Holtom, *Modern Japan and Shinto Nationalism*, Chicago, 1943; Ivan I. Morris, *Nationalism and the Right*

face of real and imagined Western threats. Like modern nationalism elsewhere in the Afro-Asian world, it has always incorporated some fear and hatred of the West.[3] Merely by posing a lively external danger, the West contributed mightily to the cohesion of the people and their acceptance of centralized power. Nor is it appropriate to minimize this contribution—if it can be called that—as sheerly negative. It is still very often the negations of our times—the appeals against foreign races, religions, and moves—that produce the most deeply felt political cohesion.

The West goaded the nation into the awareness of being threatened, and then suggested to the discerning how that threat might be overcome. The nation-state as we now conceive it had been created by a few of the peoples of Western Europe in areas of such size and character as to make national defense and political integrity possible. When Japan entered into contact with it, this portion of the West had already had considerable experience in administering and defending such states and was quite willing to share its expertise with admiring latecomers.

At first, the young Meiji leaders borrowed Western institutions eagerly and with a certain lack of discrimination. After experiencing a few failures, they gradually became more cautious. Still, Western influence infiltrated the Japanese body politic at many levels. Even the terms describing the new politics were largely foreign. Words like "political party," "constitution," "sovereignty," and "nationalism" had to be created by building new Chinese-character compounds[4]—into which, incidentally, some old connotations were carried by the constituent characters. The political vocabulary of modern Japan has been composed, symbolically enough, of terms initially foreign, but incorporating traditional elements from the first and now saturated with distinctively Japanese associations.

Wing in Japan, New York, 1960; and Richard Storry, *The Double Patriots*, Boston, 1957. In Japanese, the writings of Maruyama Masao are of great interest.

[3] For some intelligent eyewitness accounts by Westerners of Japanese attitudes toward the West in the *bakufu* and early Meiji eras, see William E. Griffis, *The Mikado's Empire*, 2 vols., New York, 1876, and Sir Ernest Satow, *A Diplomat in Japan*, London, 1921. For Japanese observations of the Western impact in English, see Inazo Nitobe, *Japanese Traits and Foreign Influences*, London, 1927, and Nitobe et al., *Western Influences in Modern Japan*, Chicago, 1931.

[4] See Osatake Takeshi, *Nihon kensei shi taiko* (An Outline of Japanese Constitutional History), Tokyo, 1939, II, 446.

As with words, so it was with ideas. In developing systems of national defense and of political authority, modern Japan borrowed heavily from Western ideology. As in all "late-developing" societies, however, the Western ideas were borrowed out of context, and not necessarily in the order in which they were originally developed. In the consciousness of persons or nations first coming to a knowledge of the West, Mill can come before Rousseau, and Bluntschli before both. The intellectual apprehension of political ideas, moreover, is almost certain to outrun the capacity of the society to realize them; there may, indeed, be no relationship at all between the ideas and the current proclivities of the society.

Ideas so laid hold of are not necessarily the outgrowth of present social processes, nor even of prophetic vision. Thus, the elite of emergent societies faces the problem of how to be creative on the one hand, and how to avoid permanent utopianism on the other. Nowhere does this dilemma bear down more harshly than upon the intelligentsia of such societies, as Japan illustrates so magnificently.

In the course of adapting novel ideas to the character and needs of their society, political leaders will inevitably emphasize certain themes and discard or minimize others. The original ideas will be drastically altered in the process, even when an undying fealty is pledged to them. As it is with Marx-Leninism in Asia today, so it was with the theories of Mill, Rousseau, and Burke in Meiji Japan.[5] Western liberalism in that era was invoked by a small Japanese *avant-garde,* many of them anxious to come to power and hopeful that this new weapon would prove more effective than shot and shell. But implicit in the times and the needs of Japanese society were the themes that liberalism would provide greater state power and cohesion through an enlightened, committed people; that liberalism was in no basic conflict with the Emperor system, since the Emperor wanted what was best for his people, and was being prevented from coming close to them by the interference of those around him. The triumph of nationalism affected every institution and ideology implanted in modern Japan, once again, a fact with great contemporary significance in the Afro-Asian world.

The reformed Japanese state, however, could not be sustained by ideology alone. Concrete instruments of coercion and persuasion were

[5] One recent and thorough work relating to Western ideology in Japan is *Japanese Thought in the Meiji Era,* the Centenary Culture Council Series, edited by Masaaki Kosaka and translated by David Abosch, Tokyo, 1958.

essential to it. These too the West in part supplied, furnishing in particular blueprints for the weapons and modern military establishment so necessary to the early precarious years of the Meiji government. It enabled that government to acquire physical power at a rate that swiftly outdistanced all actual or potential rebellion. Within a few decades, the Western example induced a revolution in the official Japanese concept of the military and of such security agencies as the police. An uncomfortable parallel exists in the influence which the Communist example has had upon groups like the Viet Minh and Pathet Lao in contemporary Asia. The Asian dissidents of the mid-twentieth century are borrowing guerrilla warfare, the concept of the mobilized countryside, and popular front tactics to resist the growth of state power. In the late nineteenth century, Asian modernists borrowed modern weaponry and mass organization to confront the older concepts of an elitist, hereditary military force.

Military power alone cannot sustain even a totalitarian state if the overwhelming majority of the people steadfastly oppose it. Hence every modern elite has sought to possess itself of instruments of persuasion along with those of coercion. Once again, the West was able to supply the modern Japanese state with appropriate techniques. And as in the case of its military contribution, the West contributed most by illustrating the importance of the *mass*, in word and in deed. Following Western examples, the Meiji leaders quickly cultivated education, religion, and the press as means of explaining state goals and enlisting public support. Within a generation, the Japanese state was secure from all internal enemies. Patriotism had been implanted in the consciousness of every citizen, and only a few peripheral elements of the society were disposed to question state values and institutions.

Any precise distribution of credit for this fact, however, involves complex issues. For example, no institution was utilized more effectively in creating an indissoluble link between people and government than the imperial court, perhaps the most indigenous institution in modern Japan. The mythology that surrounded the Emperor system came from the Japanese agrarian past, deeply rooted in the traditional culture. The techniques of propagating it had been radically changed, but the substance of the myth, with only minor alterations, was serviceable for the (early) modern era. So it was also with many other aspects of Japanese traditionalism. It must be reiterated that the capacity to utilize selective elements of the past—to employ to the maximum, certain built-in resources—for the purpose of modernization, is a major factor in accounting for the relatively rapid and smooth process of modernization in this society.

Japanese nationalism, the great unifier, came essentially from traditional sources in the prewar era. It was a mixture of Confucianism, feudal thought, and the remote, primitive beliefs of an ancient agrarian society. This amalgam was projected into modern times because, with some reshaping, it could serve modern needs, especially when to it were added the dynamic concepts of progress and the mass man derived from the West.

III. The Creation of a Modern Bureaucracy

The extensive use of the state for purposes of modernization came naturally to Japan. Traditionally, public government had been an important aspect of Japanese life, and the public official had had the highest status in society. To him, all bowed low. His role was that of inspector, supervisor, arbiter. His function was not to legislate—or innovate; it was rather to interpret and transmit. And in theory, at least, he ruled by example.

From time immemorial, heredity and hierarchy shaped the structure and character of the Japanese bureaucracy. One's class, and one's rank within that class, determined one's official position, or, indeed, the question of whether one had the right to hold any position. The Chinese examination system was known and even tried on occasion, but it was never effective in Japan because of the vastly different nature of Japanese society. From the earliest recorded Japanese sources, it seems clear that certain clans or families were designated for specific governmental or public functions, and these responsibilities (rights) were transmitted from generation to generation. In ancient Japan, indeed, it would appear that the Imperial clan shared its power with other clans who were nearly equal in prestige and power.

The unique quality of Japanese politics lay in oligarchy, not in personal authoritarianism. The individual was always blended into the group; the basis of decisions—and power—was always collective. It should be noted that no system as rigid as that of the Japanese "ideal" could have long survived without certain adjustments to reality. Thus adoption supplemented birth as a method of transmitting family lineage. And ability was rewarded by making a distinction between office and power. But perhaps the most important indigenous contribution of Japan to the science of government lay in the highly developed system of discussion, adjustment of difference, consensus, and joint responsibility that characterized its historic political process. The techniques of negotiation, the art of compromise, the diffusion of responsibility—these were basic to the political procedures of traditional Japan, and they have become an inextricable part of modern Japan as well.

Of further significance to traditional Japanese politics was the belief that the functions of government were held in trust by the elite. Despite its differences from China, Japan partook of the same Confucian philosophy. While Confucianism, unlike Taoism, preached the doctrine of participation in politics, of man *in* society, it also acknowledged the dangers of the will to power and sought to define authority in terms of responsibility rather than of rights. The exercise of authority was a painful if necessary burden for those whose abilities and status fitted them for the task. It could and should be abjured when the welfare of society permitted. The cultured man valued the arts over politics, and always refused office twice before reluctantly accepting. He never clung to power, and he accepted full responsibility for all acts occurring under his jurisdiction, including those not under his control. When mishaps occurred, he either committed suicide or resigned.

To these doctrines designed to curb the individual will to power were added doctrines advancing the role of the state. Confucianism is famous for its concept of the educative state, the state with a responsibility for every aspect of the subject's life. To Confucius as to Plato, the authority of the state extended to art, music and literature as it did to politics in the narrow sense. The function of the state was to tutor the people, to make of them better men, and government ideally was rule not by law, but by wise men, who should serve as examples of the right path.

The high status conferred upon officialdom belied the myth that power was altogether a painful burden. Painful though it often is, power is a coveted object for most men, and there is no indication that men in the classical Confucian societies proved exceptional. Certain limitations upon power were implicit—and important—products of the Confucian way, but there was also, in practice, a high level of officiousness. The phrase *kanson mimpi* (officials honored, people despised) is a Japanese saying of venerable age. In their rigidly hierarchical society, the rule was humility before superiors, imperiousness before inferiors.

76

In sum, Japanese tradition, including the earlier borrowing from China, did much to shape the modern Japanese official. First, it provided him with a set of values: authority was not a personal or individual prerogative, but a legacy which one inherited, would hold in trust with others, and pass on to others. In general, moreover, the Japanese elite rather severely limited their material desires. Japanese culture, particularly as expressed through the military ethic, placed a premium on the simple and even the spartan life. But the same ethic bequeathed officiousness as the symbol of the politics of inequality and perhaps as the recompense for meager material rewards.

The modern Japanese official must be viewed against that background.[6] He combined discipline, dedication to his task, and relative honesty with an imperious quality that would have been inappropriate in any culture regarding the official as "civil *servant*," but that accorded well with the tutelage he was required to supply to an emergent society. Tutelage is the one ideology embracing the whole of the "backward" world, the one concept inextricably connected with the modernization process. To Japan, it came naturally and easily.

One final attribute of the modern political elite of Japan was derived from the past traditions of that society. The men who sought to make that nation over were not reluctant to borrow foreign ideas. Despite a struggle, the forces of blind xenophobia and ethnocentrism were early subdued. Though continuing to exist, they remained generally subordinated to a flexible and pragmatic view of the rest of the world.

Japan, we may recall, had existed on the peripheries of a major civilization, to which it had freely paid tribute and from which it had as freely borrowed. The Japanese elite, unlike their Chinese counterparts, did not generally possess a sense of superiority or a certainty that theirs was the only way. At the time when Japan was forced into intimate contact with the West, moreover, internal changes were breeding dissatisfaction among certain elements of the elite and enhancing their receptivity to change. The fact that a rising proportion of the samurai class conceived of themselves as restoring a mythical ancient regime is perhaps less significant than their willingness to depart radically from the present condition of things.

The political leaders of modern Japan came to their task, then,

---

[6] Studies on the Japanese bureaucracy are still very limited, and most of the general works are not satisfactory. For the best insights, it is desirable to study the biographies of such leaders as Ito, Yamagata, Saionji, and Hara.

equipped with a psychology, an authority, and a system of values, as appropriate to their task as those of any non-Western leaders. Certain foreign influences further shaped the character of these officials, though without translating them into popular leaders of the democratic Western persuasion. The first notable change induced by foreign example was the movement away from appointment to public office upon the basis of class affiliations and personal connections alone. For a brief time, the old feudal aristocracy filled the new offices, the daimyo, for example, being made governors of their former *han*. But this expedient was designed only to ensure a peaceful transition. The favoritism shown men from Chōshū and Satsuma lasted longer, since the leaders of the modernization movement came largely from these two areas. Personal connections have continued to be supremely important in Japanese politics, as in every other facet of this society. Supplementing personal relations, however, a civil service system was established only two decades after the Restoration, borrowed largely from the German model. From this point, the cream of the Japanese bureaucracy went through a rigorous program of training, with the final stop generally being Tokyo University, or some "finishing work" overseas.

Initially, the old values were not discarded but supplemented, the German model being consciously selected to provide a maximum of "progress" with a minimum of "change." German legalism and German techniques of administration were added to the curriculum. Science, and in cautious measure, social science, especially the science of social policy," were also provided for the aspiring official.

As previously suggested, the extensive political influence of Germany, and especially of Prussia, upon prewar Japan was no accident. Despite their different cultural heritages, Japan and Germany had similar problems and proclivities as a result of their common timing of development. When the Japanese political leaders looked for examples or models, they found in Germany a political system that they could appreciate and understand, a set of goals that they could emulate. In the aggregate, cultural borrowing is never random. Accident plays a role, even a vital role on occasion, but the broadest patterns of cultural diffusion are connected with capacities for absorption and use, which in turn relate to stages of development.

For this reason, American influence upon Japanese modernization was minimal until after World War II. In the earlier era, our influence was much greater upon a radical *avant-garde* than upon the main political stream of Japanese society. The American occupation of Japan after 1945 can be considered an accident, a product of a war that might not have been. But current American influence upon the main stream of Japanese politics and upon the nature of the contemporary Japanese official, in particular, is not an accident. It is the product of the natural interaction between two societies that have in the course of their respective drives toward modernity increased greatly in their capacity to communicate with each other. Thus, if the chief foreign influence upon the Japanese official was once German legalism, it is today American pragmatism. Slowly, in conformity with the needs and nature of his society, an altered official is emerging; one whose training is more varied as to place and type. The movement toward specialization naturally attends the present stage of national development, and the essentially pragmatic approach of American social science—its insistence upon a working relationship between theory and action—is necessary to current processes of adaptation.

Legalism, however, remains entrenched in the Japanese psychology generally, and especially in that of certain groups. A portion of its strength is shown in the continuing vigor of Marxism among some of the intelligentsia. As it has developed in Japan, Marxism is a form of legalism: a rigid set of doctrines and rules, debated by means of endless, detailed textual analyses and appeals to previously established authority. And this type of legalism can prevail in certain intellectual circles at present because these circles play the role of social critics, not policy scientists; they are concerned with pure "theory," not practice; they are largely separated from the process of change itself. Meanwhile the persons actually involved in social change, and the younger generation of scholars influenced by the new social science literature, are challenging all of the definitions of "science" and "truth" derived from the various types of Western legalism. The influence of the West remains fluid as always; as the recipient society itself changes, it becomes permeable to different elements in the Western tradition.

Beyond that last generalization one cannot safely go. One can detail the fact of extensive German influence upon Japanese politics in the period before 1945, and the fact of extensive American influence since World War II. One can in part explain these facts. One can further indicate, in general, the cyclical nature of foreign borrowing—the waves of importation, followed by periods of accommodation and reaction. But one cannot quantify with any degree of accuracy the

79

proportions of foreign and indigenous influence upon the process of political modernization at any given time. The receptivity to external ideas and influences is inextricably connected with the on-going process (itself an accumulation of mixed external and internal forces) of modernization.

We can predict that the present accelerated rate of Japanese modernization, placing that society into increasing contact with other societies in similar or more advanced stages of development is likely to expand foreign influence—of the "advanced, industrial society" type—in Japan, at least for the immediate future. In this respect, it will be instructive to watch trends within Japanese officialdom, and among the political elite at large, particularly to note their adjustment to mass power, real and potential.

IV. Government by Law

A third aspect of Japanese political modernization was the establishment of a uniform and comprehensive legal system, written into a constitution which defined both new institutions and, in some measure, the rights and duties of each citizen. Whatever the strictures of traditional theory, political modernization has generally served to substitute the rule of law for the rule of man. Perhaps it would be more accurate to say that modernization has meant the supplementation of man by law, since man has always emerged supreme over law when the two have come into fundamental conflict. It is man who interprets and enforces the law. No law can stop a political elite possessing the power to enforce its will. Nor can any law check, of itself, a revolutionary group determined to overthrow the existing social and political order.

The rule of law is nevertheless rightly regarded as a part of the process of political modernization. The erection of impersonal rules of conduct applicable to the whole of the citizenry is one of the first acts of any group who would establish a modern state. The Meiji leaders of Japan soon discovered the importance of law. In no area was the West more scornful of Japanese "backwardness," more insistent upon change as the price for conceding her a degree of equality. A far-flung search for workable legal models was undertaken at once. A "constitution" that took many of its ideas from the American system was experimentally adopted, but disillusionment was swift. The early Meiji experience was like that of the Southeast Asian societies after World War II: the attempt to borrow Western political institutions issued first in failure, then in reexamination and the quest for suitable adaptations. In Japan, a period of retreat began as early as 1872 and became pronounced in the 1880's. The final Meiji Constitution was not a hastily conceived or naïvely imitative document; it might be said to have prescribed guided democracy, Japanese style.

In this era, however, the alternate routes to political modernity were not so numerous and so varied. The forced march, underwritten by a totalitarian-mass society, was still a full generation away. Hence, Japan chose the model nearest to her needs and nature, as noted earlier: Germany. Other European nations also contributed to the modern Japanese legal structure. France, for example, was used as a model for the civil code, and British and American influences are also to be found. But the Meiji Constitution, and much of the law that supported that Constitution was derivative from Prussia, and the constitutional theories of men like Gneist and Stein.[7]

Rapidly advancing societies of the late nineteenth century and afterward have found constitutionalism both a promise and a problem. Constitutions promise to provide stability by permanently fixing the institutions and values of a society. Having a special ritual quality, they tend to be or to become "immutable law" subject to major change only under extraordinary conditions. By contrast with unwritten "constitutions," which develop only over exceedingly long periods of time, written constitutions seem a short-cut to political permanence.

Yet, given the conditions of rapid social change now prevailing in the world, constitutions often bear little relationship to the actual political processes of the society for which they were written. Perhaps the constitution has set down a vision of the future which circumstances never permit the nation to realize. Or perhaps, though bearing some relation to the society when first enacted, it becomes outmoded through social and economic change. The latter experience was that of Japan. The Meiji Constitution of 1889 was appropriate for Meiji society and was even in some degree in advance of that society, although certainly it was no blueprint for Western-style democracy. To the extent that it froze political institutions and procedures, however, it provided stability at a special cost: it helped to retard the political change so necessary to keep pace with the total modernization process.

[7] On Meiji constitutionalism, see George M. Beckman, *The Making of the Meiji Constitution*, Lawrence, 1957; Nobutaka Ike, *The Beginnings of Political Democracy in Japan*, Baltimore, 1950; Robert A. Scalapino, *Democracy and the Party Movement in Prewar Japan*, Berkeley, 1953; and Robert A. Wilson, *Genesis of the Meiji Government in Japan*, Berkeley, 1957.

As a result, in the 1920's, Japan was ahead of Meiji constitutionalism, just as in the 1880's, she had been behind it. As the gap between Constitution and society grew, tensions mounted and political instability increased.

Once again, in 1947, a constitution was promulgated in Japan.[8] This time, the inspiration came from the United States, and the underlying principles were Anglo-American. Clearly, the nature of Japanese society did not fully answer to the premises of that constitution. Nor was there any assurance that the nation could or would "catch up" with a document embodying some wholly alien elements.

Let us be more specific. The Meiji Constitution was foreign in form, but derived much of its content from indigenous sources. Even the fact that the oligarchs caused the emperor to "give" the constitution to his people was significant. Japan did not witness that struggle for power between the monarchy and the "people" which was characteristic of the political evolution of Western Europe. The brief struggle for "civil rights," launched in about 1872, did not involve the throne. In one sense, the emperor did *give* the people a constitution, though in doing so he raised the ancient question whether he himself was subject to constitutional restraints.

The Meiji Constitution was attuned in other respects to the premises of its society. It was based upon the principles of the organic state. It could work only if consensus were obtained among the civil bureaucracy, the military, and the elected representatives in the Diet. Until after World War I, an organic state did exist in Japan in some measure; indeed, it proved desirable to create an extra-constitutional body, the *Genrō*, or senior councillors, to serve as final arbiters. In this period, there was a relatively high degree of harmony between the premises of the constitution and the disposition of the society. However strong the German influence upon it, this constitution was responsive to Japanese conditions.

After 1920, however, the processes of change carried Japanese society beyond the Meiji Constitution. New centrifugal tendencies were in operation, and conflicts arose which the old institutions were inadequate to resolve. The institution of the *Genrō* faded away, and efforts to supplant it with a new body were not very successful. In

[8] For postwar constitutional trends, see Ardath W. Burks, *The Government of Japan*, New York, 1961; Kazuo Kawai, *Japan's American Interlude*, Chicago, 1960; John M. Maki, *Government and Politics in Japan*, New York, 1961; and Robert E. Ward, "The Origins of the Present Japanese Constitution," *American Political Science Review*, Vol. L, No. 4, December 1956.

the competition for power which ensued, the military at length gained supremacy. Without altering the constitution, they ruled in the name of the emperor, having first either subordinated or combined with the civil bureaucracy and the political parties. Once again, an organic state had been established, with all of its subjects united at the foot of the throne.

It may nevertheless be doubted whether the military regime as constituted in the 1930's could long have survived, even had Japan avoided the war or won it. The senior military men who then controlled the state were too traditionalist, too out-of-step with the times. Authoritarianism might well have been the order of the day, but it would have had to have found more dynamic forms.

One kind of continuity, however, would have existed in all probability. Whatever political institutions she indigenously developed, modern Japan would have retained the basic forms of organization and decision-making that were implicit in her society. Consensus would have triumphed over majoritarianism; oligarchy would have prevailed over individual leadership; and the small leader-follower group that represents the primary unit of Japanese politics would have continued. It cannot be denied that Meiji Constitutionalism was attuned to these forces in considerable degree.

Whether the present constitution can sufficiently cope with such forces remains to be seen. Indigenous forms of political organization remain exceedingly strong in modern Japan, and are sometimes incompatible with the constitutional and legal framework within which they exist. It is not certain that Japanese society can accommodate such incompatibility, or that the contradictions will diminish with the passage of time.

Even the most fundamental Japanese attitudes toward law pose a problem. In the United States, *the law* is something to be applied to present circumstance with as much precision as possible; in Japan, it is an ideal toward which one should aim. In the United States, *the law*, especially fundamental law, is accorded a special position in society; in Japan, the combination of man and custom continues to be more formidable than any statutes. The struggle on the one hand for the supremacy of law in modern Japanese society, and on the other for the integration of law and custom in that society remains an absorbing drama. In the "American era," the drama has become even more exciting.

83

V. Politics and the Masses

The involvement of the masses in Japanese politics began at an early point in the modern era, and followed somewhat diverse lines thereafter. The class distinctions imbedded in the feudal law had first to be removed. By means of a leveling process, rendering every citizen equal before the law and endowing him with obligations and rights, a mass foundation for loyalty and service to the state was established. This foundation was further solidified by the conscription system, by universal primary education, by advances made in communications, and, indeed, by virtually every species of standardization that is characteristic of the modern state. Gradually, provincialism declined in significance, although it has not yet lost all of its import to the political scene. By the end of the First World War, however, most Japanese thought of themselves as citizens of Japan, not of their respective prefectures as in feudal days; they spoke a language relatively standardized, and generally intelligible; they celebrated the same holidays, visited the same shrines, studied the same texts, and received the same military indoctrination.

Once again, Western influence must be accorded a very high position. It was the "advanced" West that had set the pace in rendering all men equal before the law; providing them with certain common obligations and rights; advancing a standardized language, set of values, culture. This was the centripetal aspect of the modernization process, one not to be minimized. And Japanese leadership was quick to seize upon it, in their efforts to unify their nation during perilous times. But as we have previously noted, if the techniques of unification were largely foreign derived, the substantive issues—the value system —around which the drive for unity gravitated were strongly indigenous.

It is important, moreover, to make the obvious distinction between legal and actual equality. The Japanese citizen has had legal equality for nearly a century, but even today, Japan is far from being an egalitarian society. No legislation could possibly have obliterated the deep sense of class distinction that pervades that society. In the political field, as in others, Japan is dominated by small elites who have known each other long and well, whose families intermarry and perform certain familial-political functions for each other, and who in general perpetuate the distinction between the ruling and the ruled.

It is questionable whether the limited social mobility that has characterized twentieth-century Japan has served as a barrier to modernization, especially in its early and middle stages. The principle of hierarchy conserved the traditions of a committed and well-qualified elite on the one hand, and a disciplined and malleable people on the other. In a society so ordered, there is little waste through violence and there is a heightened capacity for sacrifice. We again recall that Great Britain and Japan, two societies with a notable capacity for peaceful change, have both been societies in which the principle of hierarchy persisted. Both societies provided the legal basis for a mass-oriented state on the one hand, while at the same time they possessed a social structure well tailored to a form of elitist tutelage, a guidance of the mass toward "purposeful," "efficient" goals.

Among the particular products of legal equality in Japan were a conscript army that was the equal of many Western forces; a peasantry free to move and in fact flowing into the urban factories; and a traditional elite retaining its cohesiveness and morale and yet able to adjust quickly to the new industrial era. There have been few parasites in modern Japan. Legal equality was translated into progress and power rather than dissipated in social disorder.

In sum, all citizens, though not rendered socially equal, were required to participate in the political process. The Japanese leadership first invited this involvement with grave misgivings. Yet the external pressures exerted on the nation in the years from 1880 to 1932 obviated any other course. It is important to reiterate, moreover, that during the first part of these decades the only available Western model was the classic democratic state. The model of the one-party state, wherein citizens march regularly to the poll to cast their votes for the regime, had not yet come into being. Hence public participation in politics could only represent a certain hazard to those in power.

It was natural that the political elite should seek to devise as many safeguards as possible. The Meiji Constitution, as we have noted, placed strict limitations upon the popularly elected branch of government. Initially, moreover, suffrage itself was limited, and the struggle for its expansion was a lengthy one, with only partial success being attained in the era before World War II. Though universal manhood suffrage was first exercised in the general election of 1928, Japanese women were given the franchise only in 1946. Despite these and other legal obstacles, public participation in politics steadily increased between 1880 and 1930, and in accordance with the general process of a parliamentary society. The rise of political parties and of politically oriented interest groups, and the increase in the number and variety of mass media attuned to politics betokened the advent of "democratic Japan."

Especially in the period after World War I, Japan appeared to be following rather precisely the political example of the "advanced" West. Men like Woodrow Wilson had a deep influence upon the wartime generation of young Japanese liberals. Already, however, the West was beginning to furnish another example, that of a "new democracy" possessing a more insistent appeal than the classic type. The success of the Bolshevik Revolution raised questions in the minds of the intellectuals, especially since the Japanese parliamentary system was faced with serious problems. Japan in this era did not escape the vices characteristic of contemporaneous Western democratic states: corruption was rampant, the sense of responsibility of elected officials was deficient, and the line between debate and violence was ill-defined. All of these problems were perhaps indicative of one basic problem: the low level of political consciousness and political sophistication among the Japanese electorate. And thus, for some there was an appeal in the new, dynamic concept of an elitist tutelage that made use of all of the democratic symbolism "on behalf of the proletariat," but that did not actually depend upon the political wisdom of the mass, nor wait for it to develop. Now, the "advanced" world projected two images to Japan, and the struggle between these became relatively tense in the late 1920's, especially in intellectual-labor circles.

In fact, the "advanced" world projected three images. By this era, Fascism was beginning to develop as a significant political force on the world scene. And once again, Japan drew major stimulus from Germany. German Fascism could appeal because it combined a fervent nationalism, a welfare-state concept, and a dedication to state power via mass mobilization. The forms of Fascist massification were in many respects closer to the proclivities of Japanese society than the forms of the parliamentary societies which were too "advanced" or those of Communist societies which were too "backward"! The idea of mobilizing the people to serve the state, of fostering a myth of racial superiority, and creating a messianic world mission—these were aspects of massification that had roots in the Japanese past and present.

While the decade and a half after 1930 represented a sharp divergence from the previous course of Japanese politics, there was no retreat from the encouragement of mass participation in political life.

On the contrary, during those years the Japanese citizen became more intimately involved in the political process than ever before. The first truly mass organizations in Japan were then constructed: organizations like *Sampō*, the "patriotic" labor movement to which each worker belonged; the Imperial Rule Assistance Association, an ersatz political party with mass membership, intended to "assist" the emperor; and the neighborhood associations encompassing every citizen. The capacity of Japan after 1945 to adopt new forms of mass organization was due partly to her wartime experiences.

Notwithstanding German influence, this was a period when indigenous forms of mass organization took precedence over foreign forms. German Fascism supplied only a very general model. The era of Japanese militarism was distinguished from the comparable period in German history by the absence of a *fuehrer*, the continuance of traditional groupings which resisted subsumption into a truly monolithic state, and some old-fashioned Confucian elements imbedded in the military ideology. During this period the society as a whole experienced a nostalgia for the past even while it was being propelled disastrously into the future.

After her military defeat Japan returned to the parliamentary path under the new tutelage of Americans. Once again, the nation accepted the model of an open, pluralistic society. Perhaps the most impressive feature of this new democratic era has been the development of far more substantial social and economic interest groups than any which had previously existed. In increasing measure, these have provided channels of political expression for all segments of Japanese society. The powerful agrarian cooperative societies, the large-scale unions, and the expanded business and commercial pressure groups betokened new stages of political development, wherein the diversities of a maturing society are acknowledged. These associations supplement the political parties and not infrequently exercise a stronger influence than the parties themselves. At the same time, the periodic plebiscite wherein all citizens cast their ballots for candidates and for parties has now become critical to the political process. Parliamentary supremacy has been written into Japanese law, and Japanese politics are becoming attuned to this fact. The political parties have become vastly more powerful than at any time before 1945, and they now operate in an atmosphere of complete freedom.

These facts clearly indicate the enormous influence of foreign, predominantly American political mores and institutions. Yet once again, the impact of the United States has been directly related to changes within Japanese society that make this impact possible. But we must also acknowledge the strength of other indigenous forces hostile to the new foreign influences. A considerable gap exists today between *politics* and *society* in Japan, if we make a distinction that is perhaps dubious. Public politics is now based upon the principles of majoritarianism derivative from the historic doctrines of the majority right to rule and the minority right to oppose—within the framework of certain rules. Unless these concepts are accepted, the effective operation of Western-style parliamentarism becomes exceedingly difficult, if not impossible. But how does Japanese society operate? In considerable measure, it denies the moral validity of majoritarianism, and operates on the basis of consensus, insisting upon a process of accommodation and compromise. Thus the right of the majority to govern is not accepted by all, nor is the right of the minority to oppose. Indeed, with respect to the latter point, if the rights of the minority are not clearly staked out on the one hand, neither are their responsibilities. The interaction between violence and suppression continues in some measure. The Socialist minority gravitate toward "parliamentarism-plus," the plus representing a willingness to go beyond parliamentarism if it appears politically profitable. The majority, on the other hand, often ignore or deal contemptuously with the minority, unless forced to take action against them. There is a one-and-one-half party system in Japan: one party that knows only how to govern and a half party that knows only how to oppose. Despite the existence of a full-fledged parliamentary system, Japan has not yet had a change of political administration by way of national elections. Nor is it clear that any such change will occur in the foreseeable future. The question whether democracy can live with one party permanently in power and another or others permanently out, is a serious one for Japan and for a number of other democratic societies, both "advanced" and "backward."

A further vexatious problem inheres in the paradox that contemporary Japan represents: it is an open society composed of closed units. The most basic political unit of Japan remains the leader-follower group, held together by an intricate system of favors and obligations. Such units divide all organizations, including even the Communist party of Japan, into factions on the one hand, and close them to "outsiders" on the other hand. These groups reflect the continuing vitality of Japanese-style organization and decision-making.

VI. A Summing Up

What conclusion can we finally draw? First, foreign influence has contributed immeasurably to the political modernization of Japan. Two sources have predominated: Germany—as a society that developed at approximately the same time as Japan and hence faced similar problems and had similar political affinities; and the Anglo-American societies where a combination of certain cultural points of relationship (relating to Great Britain) and increasingly similar "advanced" developmental conditions have resulted in a growing Japanese capacity for political interaction.

In broadest terms, the type and degree of foreign influence have been closely related to two factors: the internal conditions and proclivities of Japanese society and the major currents flowing in the world scene.

The susceptibility at different times to the example of such countries as Germany, Great Britain, the Soviet Union, and the United States has been directly related to changes in these two factors. Undoubtedly, this principle will operate in the future as in the past.

It is natural that foreign influences upon Japanese politics should be discernible most clearly in institutions, indigenous influences most clearly in political behavior. A continuing conflict between institutional demands and functional capacities characterizes Japanese politics today, symbolizing the incomplete synthesis between foreign and indigenous elements.

In general, foreign influence has *increased* rather than decreased as the modernization process has gathered momentum, for new avenues of communication have thereby been opened up. At the same time, some purely indigenous forms and uses have gained a new vitality as they have been accommodated to the changed conditions and needs of the society. One cannot naively conceive of "indigenous influences" as static, "foreign influences" as dynamic. Both have elements of dynamism just as both incorporate obsolescent elements.

Successful modification of the political structure as of the economic structure is made vastly easier by a maximum use of existing resources. Foreign ideas and institutions must be adopted *in degree* so that they appear to supplement and enrich the society rather than challenge and defy it, and *in kind* so that they are meshed with the capacities and proclivities of the particular stage of development in which the society finds itself.

The ideology that must support this process is one of tutelage; the methods those of experimentation, of a high degree of pragmatism; the goal that of "catching up" in developmental terms with other "advanced" societies, so that all can plunge ahead into the unknown as equals. This is the great egalitarian drive of the mid-twentieth century in whose name all manner of inequity is justified and maintained.

B. TURKEY

RODERIC H. DAVISON

On December 2, 1922, Baron Hayashi had some advice on political modernization for İsmet Pasha. Each was representing his country at Lausanne in the peace negotiation following the Turkish victory over the Greeks. Sitting in a meeting of the Second Commission to discuss the regime of foreigners, they and other diplomats were considering the capitulations and a possible transitional regime which might replace them. Hayashi proclaimed his sympathy for the Turks, since Japan also had once had a capitulatory regime. "He would, however, like to point out for the kind consideration of İsmet Pasha that Japan had taken twenty years or more to prepare for herself a complete juridical system. It was only after hard work by Japan, lasting more than twenty years, that the Powers were able to agree to the Capitulations being brought to an end."[1] He counselled similar slow haste on the part of the Turks.

İsmet was unmoved by this appeal. Reviewing past history, he declared that the modernization of jurisprudence in his country had begun before the Crimean War, and that, since the Congress of Paris in 1856, "Turkey has worked feverishly at the perfection of her judicial system." He cited commercial, penal, and procedural law codes fashioned on the European model, and the recent "very important reform in the civil law, by which our judicial institutions have been completely secularized." Furthermore, he said, a European-model law faculty had for forty years been training judges and advocates. Turkey therefore needed no transitional regime of law. After adducing many other arguments, İsmet concluded that "the Government of the Grand National Assembly of Turkey can in no wise agree to the reestablishment of the Capitulations."[2]

At a second meeting of the commission six days later its president, Marquis Garroni of Italy, reminded İsmet that there were colonies of foreigners in Turkey possessing interests and rights, that these persons needed guarantees of justice, and that this end might be achieved under Turkish law if the Ankara government would appoint to its

[1] Great Britain, Turkey No. 1 (1923), *Lausanne Conference on Near Eastern Affairs, 1922-1923* (Cmd. 1814), p. 470. Cf. p. 493.
[2] *Ibid.*, p. 479.

courts some foreign judges on recommendation of the Hague International Tribunal. "I am convinced," said Garroni, "that Turkey will succeed within a short time in creating a system of laws and a bench of judges which will fulfill all modern requirements; but it must be recognized that even under the new regime Turkish justice has not yet been able to give proof of its worth, and also that Turkey is still subject today to laws some of which are based on religious laws." A transitional regime was thus indispensable, and Garroni referred back to Japan, "a country which is making brilliant advance on the path of progress," and to Hayashi's statement that twenty years were required to pass from capitulations to the "regime of freedom." İsmet replied that Garroni's proposals, especially as regarded foreign judges, were "clearly incompatible with the independence and sovereignty of Turkey," and that the Turkish civil code, from whatever sources it might be derived, "had no religious or theocratic character; . . . there was no appreciable difference between it and the codes of foreign countries as regards the fundamental principles and rules of law enshrined in it."[3]

Lord Curzon made a masterful rejoinder to İsmet. İsmet had talked again and again of sovereignty. "Cannot the Turks realize that theirs is not the only sovereignty in the world?" Curzon too found the Turkish civil code "based in the last resort on Muslim religious law." Finally, taxing İsmet with asserting that "the judicial system of Turkey is excellent and indeed almost perfect," he himself bleakly asserted, "Everybody knows that this is not the case." Nor, he added, would İsmet's repetitions make it so, even though he might have deluded himself. Turkey's dependence on foreign trade conducted by Europeans, Armenians, and Greeks made sound judicial procedures vital for the nation's own welfare.[4]

İsmet's replies at a meeting on January 6 contained no concessions. He stated once again that "the Turkish Civil Code has no religious character at all." Further, "the reason why we have frequently spoken of our sovereignty is that we have been compelled to do so owing to the proposals made to us, which were calculated to injure that sovereignty."[5]

This episode at Lausanne derives its relevance to this study of political modernization not only from the fortuitous confrontation of Japanese and Turkish experience. It also sums up many of the major foreign contributions to Turkey's political condition. Among these are

[3] *Ibid.*, pp. 482-483, 489.   [4] *Ibid.*, pp. 496-497.   [5] *Ibid.*, pp. 510, 514.

some basic impulsions or stimuli to modernization which were implicit in the situation leading to the Lausanne conference. Turkey had been defeated in the Great War, had been shorn of much of her territory, and had been subjected to foreign occupation. She had then been the victor in a nationalist war against the occupation forces, particularly those of the Greeks. At the conference itself she was subjected by the European powers to heavy diplomatic pressure, of which the prodding on capitulations and judicial reform is but one instance. These incitements to political reform, moreover—military defeat, the loss of territory, the revival of national energies, and diplomatic pressure—have all been felt in Turkish political life more than once in modern times. They have repeatedly urged on the struggle of the Ottoman Empire before 1918, and of the emerging Turkish Republic from 1919 on, for survival as a sovereign state an equal among equals: *Cet animal est très méchant; quand on l'attaque, il se défend.* The Turks have sought to preserve themselves not only through military rejuvenation, but through political modernization.

İsmet's emphasis on undiluted sovereignty exhibited, however, not only a desire for survival, but also the adoption of a foreign political concept that had for some time been working its way into the Turkish consciousness. That is the concept of sovereignty attached to a particular territory and to the people who live in it. Such a sacrosanct territorial sovereignty, a product of recent European thought, replaced the earlier concept of a sovereign monarch who could win, lose, or trade territory without impairing his right to rule, and without thought of the people involved or of the sanctity of boundaries. Among other foreign concepts evident in İsmet's discourse was his acceptance of secularism as a test of progress. He was willing and even anxious to declare that the Turkish civil code had nothing religious about it. And he made explicit his acceptance of European models, repeatedly asserting that for decades the Turks had been patterning law codes after those in the West.

The arguments at Lausanne touched finally on some of the channels through which foreign contributions were made to the Turkish culture: the new Turkish schools with Westernized curricula, the contacts of foreign "colonies" of businessmen and diplomats, and the activity of Greeks and Armenians.

As İsmet pointed out, Turkey had been embarked on a path of political modernization since the Crimean War. He could have gone back to the eighteenth century, when the Ottoman Turks began to suffer the recurring military defeats which persuaded them of the need for change. The pattern of Ottoman military retreat and cession of territory that began with the treaty of Karlowitz in 1699 was never permanently broken until 1922. Particular military defeats were suffered in 1718, 1774, 1792, 1799, 1812, 1829, 1878, 1912, 1913, and 1918. In virtually every case the victors were European powers. European military science hence very naturally became the example for Ottoman sultans and vezirs, and the desire for military reform opened channels of communication with Europe through which a flood of influences was eventually to pass. Beginning with the mission of Yirmisekiz Çelebi Mehmed, who, after the defeat of 1718, was sent to Paris to report on those aspects of Western knowledge from which the Ottoman Empire might profit, there was sporadic contact of individual Turks with Europe. The military, naval, and engineering schools established in the eighteenth century with the help of European instructors gave some acquaintance with the French language and with European "progress," and produced graduates who were not infrequently advocates of political change.

By the end of the eighteenth century, significant efforts toward political modernization were visible in Turkey. From the time of Selim III (1789-1807), and more especially the time of Mahmud II (1808-1839), the foreign influences on Turkish political life became so manifold that a chronological account alone could exceed the bounds of this essay. It is possible in shorter compass to review analytically the last century and a half of Turkish political development and the influence of foreign nations upon it. The three topics already referred to—the immediate stimulus of international encounter, the concepts supplied by European political theory and practice, and the channels through which these and other influences flowed—will supply a sufficient framework. A fact which may normally be taken for granted is that, from the time of Mahmud II, political reform in Turkey was almost always modernization, and modernization was almost always Westernization.

I. Foreign Stimuli to Political Modernization

There are certain periods when political reform in Turkey took on a new élan, or became concentrated and comparatively rapid, and we might inquire what external stimuli were present on each occasion. These periods were the latter years of Mahmud II's reign, especially from 1833 to 1838; two periods early in the reign of Abdülmecid, from 1839 to 1841 and from 1845 to 1850; the stretch of time from the Crimean War to the death of Āli Pasha, from 1854 to 1871; the time of Midhat's constitution and the first years of Abdülhamid II's reign, from 1876 to 1882; the Young Turk and World War I era, from 1908 to 1918; the period of the establishment of the Turkish Republic, from 1919 to 1926; and the half decade in which the two-party system grew up, from 1945 to 1950.

When he first came to the throne, Sultan Mahmud II could exercise little authority outside his own capital. The governors of many provinces paid scant attention to the central administration, *derebeyis*, or lords of the valley, being established in many sections of Anatolia and Rumelia almost by hereditary right. Furthermore, there was a revolt in Serbia; the Wahhabi power was growing in Arabia; and Egypt was launched on the path toward autonomy. In addition, the Janissaries, who had deposed Selim III, were an ever-present danger. To this list of troubles must be added the Greek revolt, breaking out in 1821 and continuing for a decade, and the war launched by Muhammad Ali of Egypt in 1832. In the first twenty or so years of his reign, therefore, Mahmud undertook chiefly to quell insurrection or rival authority within the empire, so that he might become master in his own house. But this work of destruction made easier any political reform that might follow, weakening the vested interests that might oppose it and concentrating power in the hands of the sultan, who, with his group of advisers, was the necessary instrument of change.

The events of Mahmud's reign also provided some foreign stimuli to change. The military superiority of Europe was several times demonstrated. In 1812 and 1829, Mahmud's armies were defeated by the Russians, Russia winning Balkan territory from Turkey on each occasion. In the latter war the Russians came as close as ever in history to taking Istanbul. In 1830 France began the conquest of Algeria. The Serb revolt, which in 1829 issued in semi-autonomy for the Serbian principality, had foreign support. The Greek revolt was able to succeed because of European naval aid, which destroyed the Turkish fleet at Navarino, and the Russo-Turkish war of 1828-1829. The Egyptian attack of 1832-1833, which also threatened Istanbul, was met only with timely help from the Russians. The Egyptians themselves were so nearly successful because their army had been reorganized on European lines. This war resulted in the cession to them of Syria and of the administration of Cilicia.

To these negative stimuli of military defeat and territorial loss in the face of European power was added the positive prodding of Europe, especially of England, toward political reform. Mahmud II had vainly sought British help in the face of Egyptian attack. The British cabinet was much more interested in current crises over Belgium and Portugal, and realized too late the seriousness of the Near Eastern situation. Palmerston, the foreign minister, later found this inaction "a tremendous blunder,"[6] however, and set about encouraging Mahmud in the rejuvenation of the Ottoman Empire. Ponsonby, the British ambassador, was ordered to impress upon him the need for naval, military, economic, financial, and administrative progress. In the same interest, the British pursued a policy which today would go by the name of trade and aid. The Turks were moved to accept the British offers to escape overtures from Russia. The Russian aid against Muhammad Ali in 1833 had resulted in the Russo-Turkish treaty of Hünkâr İskelesi, an eight-year defensive alliance which made Turkey a junior partner to Russia and provided for consultation on all matters concerning "their respective tranquillity and safety."[7] The ultimate Russian aim, however, as the Turks well knew, was to keep the Ottoman Empire itself weak and Russian influence strong within it. To escape this unwanted embrace, the Turks would have to progress as fast as possible.

These were the external stimuli which prompted Mahmud II's measures of political modernization. In addition he was faced with internal revolt and needed to bolster his domestic position. He abolished a number of the traditional offices of state, and created new ones dependent on his own fiat. The new bureaucracy he began to build was relatively European and modern both in organization and in the type of personnel appointed to it. Though Mahmud himself had no experience of the West and knew no Western language, he presided over the period in which Turkish institutions were genuinely started on the path of Westernization.

The external stimulus to the next period of rapid modernization is obvious. Mahmud II died and Abdülmecid ascended the throne at a most critical period, when Turkish-Egyptian warfare again threatened the integrity of the Ottoman Empire. After the Egyptian victory at the battle of Nezib, and the surrender to the Egyptians of much of

[6] C. K. Webster, *The Foreign Policy of Palmerston, 1830-1841*, London, 1951, I, 283.

[7] Art. I. Text in J. C. Hurewitz, *Diplomacy in the Near and Middle East, A Documentary Record: 1535-1914*, Princeton, 1956, p. 105.

the Turkish fleet, the Turks sought foreign help. They succeeded in gaining, in 1839, diplomatic support from all the great powers except France, and, in 1840, military support from Britain and Austria. As a token that the Ottoman Empire was at least as progressive, and as well worth saving, as Egypt, the dramatic proclamation of the Hatt-i Şerif of Gülhane was issued on November 3, 1839. Its promises— greater security of life and property, tax reform, the reform of military conscription, and the equal treatment of all Ottoman subjects in these matters—were precisely such as would attract European approval. The author of this edict was Reşid Pasha, the energetic foreign minister, who was himself a product of embassies to London and Paris and who genuinely admired the West. "M. Thiers transformed into a pasha and with a fez on his head," a French journalist said of him.[8] Reşid was also interested in safeguarding the bureaucracy from the arbitrary power of the sultan which Mahmud II's reforms had so vastly increased. The promises in the edict about security of life and property took on a special meaning for civil servants. The periods of intensive reform effort, 1839 to 1841, and 1845 to 1850, coincide roughly with Reşid's tenure of office as foreign minister and as Grand Vezir, before his reforming *élan* seemed to wane. When Lord Palmerston had written in 1839 to his ambassador Ponsonby, "Your Hatti Sheriff was a grand stroke of policy,"[9] he was under a misconception —the imperial rescript of reform was Reşid's, not Ponsonby's. But Palmerston's very error shows that the British pushed Reşid and other Turkish ministers as hard as they could. Especially was this so after Stratford Canning in 1842 became ambassador to the Porte.

It is usual to think of the next phase of Turkish reform as opening with a new imperial rescript, the Hatt-i Hümayun of February 18, 1856. The beginnings of the later phase of the Tanzimat may as plausibly be found in 1854, the year in which the British and French became the allies of Turkey against Russia. Though most of the foreign troops went on to fronts first in Bulgaria and then in the Crimea, the Turkish capital was host to a kind of foreign occupation from 1854 to 1856, at about the same period when Commodore Perry's ships appeared in Edo Bay. Turkish ministers could not easily avoid the diplomatic pressures exerted on them by the ambassadors of their military allies. A series of measures in 1854 and 1855 designed to promote administrative reform and to bring Christians into parity

---

[8] C. Hippolyte Castille, *Réchid-pacha*, Paris, 1857, p. 23.
[9] Webster, *op.cit.*, II, 657.

with Muslims before the law and in the army was undoubtedly the result of allied pressure. The Hatt-i Hümayun itself was the product of conferences which the British, French, and Austrian ambassadors held with Âli and Fuad Pashas, and its proclamation was hastened by the approach of the Paris Peace Conference. In order to keep in their own hands as much initiative as possible at that conference, the Turkish ministers agreed in advance to the fairly sweeping terms of the edict. At the same time, as the chief Muslim dignitary (*şeyhül-islâm*) wryly observed, English and French naval vessels, as well as land forces of both nations, were in the environs of Istanbul. Some negative reactions to their presence were soon observable.

During the succeeding years of political reform, which lasted until Âli Pasha's death in 1871, foreign influences were intermittently felt. In some cases the stimulus was conveyed by direct diplomatic representation, as in 1859 and 1867, when collective or nearly simultaneous notes by the great powers urged the Turks to faster action on the pledges of the Hatt-i Hümayun. Foreign occupation—the disembarkation of a French force in 1860 with the sanction of all the powers —helped to bring about revision of the administrative statute of the Lebanon. In 1867, pressure from the great powers to have all Turkish troops withdrawn from Belgrade, coupled with European interest in the cause of the Cretan rebels, stimulated new Turkish reform, this time by revulsion against the pressure. In this period a distaste for Western interference worked in a curious way to keep in power in the Ottoman government the two statesmen who were the most consistent Westernizers, Âli and Fuad. During most of the decade from 1861 to 1871, one or the other of these men was Grand Vezir, and his colleague foreign minister. These accomplished statesmen, with their knowledge of the French language and of Europe, were better equipped to ward off further intervention than were any of their contemporaries. Within the confines of Turkey, meanwhile, a series of uprisings in various provinces, some of them influenced by a foreign "ism"—nationalism—gave impetus to the drive for a more efficient administration. And the personal ambition of Âli and Fuad made them anxious so to organize the government as to preserve the ruling administrative bureaucracy from the sultan and his palace officials.

The next period of rapid modernization was again the product of various forces, some of which were exerted from abroad. In 1875 and 1876 domestic risings in Bosnia and Herzegovina, followed by revolts on the part of Bulgars, Serbs, and Montenegrins, took their source both from local discontent and from a nationalism tinged with Pan-Slavism. The threat of forceful Russian intervention on the side of the Balkan rebels and the prospect of a conference of the great powers on Turkish affairs triggered a major political reform, the proclamation of the constitution of December 23, 1876. European loans to the Ottoman Empire that had piled up since 1854 and the default on bond interest that ensued in 1875-1876 were an immediate source of pressure. Among the more purely indigenous forces simultaneously felt were the driving energy of Midhat Pasha, the constitution's chief advocate, and the growth of a small but influential public opinion, voiced by certain New Ottoman writers, in favor of a parliament consistent with Islamic tradition. Midhat was joined by statesmen desiring to curb the extravagance and caprice of the sultan's government and to restore administrative and economic order after five years of chaos. The military and diplomatic crisis of the mid-1870's gave these men occasion to act.

Though the parliament was prorogued in early 1878, the period of reform to which it gave birth may logically be extended until 1882, in Sultan Abdülhamid II's reign. Some of the Tanzimat reforms, especially of the judiciary, culminated in these years. There were the further bitter incentives of defeat by Russia in the war of 1877-1878, of the loss of Serbia, Roumania, and Montenegro, and of the occupation of Bosnia and Herzegovina by Austria-Hungary. The British forced the Turks to accept British administration of Cyprus in 1878, and occupied Egypt in 1882. The French took Tunis in 1881. In that year the powers forced the cession of additional Turkish territory to Greece. These events stimulated Abdülhamid II less to political modernization than to the reform of the army and of Turkish education. His emphasis on Islam as a means of holding the empire together was a step into the political past, and the appointment of eight British military consuls to cooperate with two commissions of the Porte to improve administration in the "Armenian" vilayets served only to make Abdülhamid more wary of the great powers. The continuing Ottoman financial crisis did, however, lead to the establishment of the Ottoman Public Debt Administration under the supervision of foreign bond holders. In effect, a separate administrative system was set up to control a large proportion of Ottoman revenues; it was efficiently run and had a beneficial effect on the Ottoman economy and on Ottoman bureaucratic practices, even while opening the door to further

99

financial imperialism. Throughout the rest of Abdülhamid's reign there was intermittent European diplomatic pressure for administrative reform in Turkey, most notably in 1895-1896 over the Armenian question, and in 1903-1904 over the Macedonian question. In the first instance, largely because the powers failed to agree among themselves, the results were nil. In the second instance the gendarmerie and parts of the civil administration were somewhat improved. But foreign intervention generally elicited a negative response from Abdülhamid.

The threat of still further great-power pressure and the possibility of the further loss of Balkan territory explain in part the revolt of the Young Turk officers in 1908. Their basic motive, like that of earlier reformers, was to preserve the empire. Abdülhamid's autocratic and spy-ridden rule was their aversion, and his efforts to investigate military insubordination in Macedonia provided the occasion for their uprising. The Reval meeting of Edward VII and Tsar Nicholas II, renewing the threat of foreign support for separatist movements within the empire, provided another stimulus, however. And perhaps the Japanese defeat of Russia in 1905 encouraged Near Eastern officers to believe that they too could resist European power. No sooner had the Young Turks achieved, in 1908, the restoration of the Constitution of 1876 than they were confronted by the foreign danger anew: Bulgaria declared her independence, and Austria-Hungary annexed Bosnia and Herzegovina. In the ten years before the Turkish collapse of 1918, the Young Turk regime was constantly faced with domestic revolt or foreign war, or both together. The Italians defeated the Turks and took Tripoli from them in 1912; the Balkan League defeated them and took almost all their remaining European possessions in 1913; and in the Great War, despite their victories at Gallipoli and in the Caucasus, the Turks faced defeat by the summer of 1918. Much of the political modernization in this era undoubtedly came by way of reaction against defeat; some, especially after 1914, came because a period even of victorious war tends to speed up social change.

When the Turkish military effort collapsed in 1918 and the Allies occupied the country, there seems at first to have been a feeling of lassitude and even of relief among the population. What might have happened had the occupation been brief and benevolent, the peace treaty lenient, and the government of Sultan Mehmed VI firm in upholding the national dignity, it is impossible to say. The sultan almost eagerly collaborated with the occupation authorities. Four specific acts of the victorious Allies, from 1919 to 1922, spurred the development of a vigorous nationalist movement which was eventually to inaugurate swift and drastic political change. The first act of provocation was the landing of Greek troops in İzmir on May 15, 1919, which aroused Turkish opinion to the point where Mustafa Kemal could hope to weld the resistance into an organized movement. The second was the British occupation of Istanbul on March 16, 1920, accompanied by the arrest of prominent nationalist deputies to the parliament. This event spurred Kemal to convert the movement into the Government of the Grand National Assembly at Ankara—the one which İsmet represented at Lausanne. The third act was the imposition of the extremely harsh treaty of Sèvres, of which the terms, revealed to the Turks on May 11, were perforce signed by Mehmed VI's government on August 10, 1920. Thereafter the Kemalists felt that they had nothing to lose in all-out opposition to the powers and the Greek invaders. Two years later, after the Turks had won their war against the Greeks, the Allies perpetrated a fourth act, the invitation of both the Istanbul and the Ankara governments to attend the peace conference at Lausanne, in the face of which the Grand National Assembly declared the sultanate abolished, leaving only a member of the house of Osman as caliph. Within two years he too was gone, partly because of the interest shown in him by Muslims abroad. It was as if the European nations were deliberately driving Turkey precisely where Mustafa Kemal was seeking to head her. They were contributing unwittingly to the will and purpose personified by İsmet at Lausanne: to make Turkey a sovereign national state, equal to other sovereign states, and progressive enough to hold her own among them.

Since 1922, Turkey has known no military defeat. She has participated in no foreign war except the United Nations action in Korea. But World War II put her for a time in a very delicate position between the warring nations, and left her at the end confronted with Russian demands for partial control of the Straits and for the cession of eastern territory. From 1945 on, Turkey found shelter in a close association with the Western powers, especially the United States. This association in turn contributed to the rapid political change occurring in the years from 1945 to 1950, which saw the establishment of an effective opposition party and its victory in a free election. How much of a stimulus to change the association with the Western democracies provided it is hard to say, for economic and political discontent within Turkey itself made at least some change inevitable. Nevertheless, the Turkish adherence to the United Nations charter in 1945, the Western and particularly American diplomatic support in 1945-1946 against Russia, the beginning of military and economic aid to Turkey under the Truman Doctrine in 1947, and American criticism of *étatism* must have had some effect. The influence felt was not like that of 1856, when direct pressure from Turkey's allies dictated a charter of reform; it was more like that of 1839, when Reşid sought to show the Western powers that Turkey was progressive and was worth helping.

The foregoing historical review allows two generalizations. One is that throughout the last century of its existence, the Ottoman Empire was confronted constantly with the challenge of increasing power in the hands of European states, and that the efforts to meet their challenge by way of political and military modernization proved insufficient. In apparent exception to this rule, victory in the Crimean War was in fact a triumph only for Turkey's allies. Minor victories like those over Greece in 1897 and over Bulgaria in 1913 were not enough to obliterate the reality of recurring defeat. Nor was the reality of diplomatic inferiority affected by the theoretical admission of Turkey to the concert of the European powers in 1856. In sum, until 1922, when military victory gave a final *élan* to reformism, the rest of the world contributed to the development of modern institutions in Turkey very largely by convicting the Turks of past and present inadequacy.

It is evident, secondly, that there was no period of concentrated political reform which did not begin with one or more specific stimuli from without. This is true of 1833, 1839, 1854-1856, 1876, 1908, 1919-1922, and 1945. Though in no case was the external stimulus a sufficient explanation or cause for the reforms which ensued, it presented at least an opportunity which could be seized and a warning to conservatives that change was necessary. The Hatt-i Şerif of 1839, the Constitution of 1876, and the establishment of the Ankara government and elimination of the sultanate in the years from 1920 to 1922 furnish cogent examples.

Two additional observations may be offered. The periods of reform here cited are cut from the fabric of Turkish history to serve as clinical examples. Historically, each built on its predecessors. There is a cumulative effect of reform which the successive consideration of isolated periods will not show. The process of modernization, once well started, was not easy to arrest; after a certain point it probably became irreversible even without further external stimuli. After 1839 there was at any rate no possibility of return, as some would-be reformers still wished, to the good old days.

It should also be noted that Turkish reaction to external pressure was sometimes negative. Such, in particular, was the response to diplomatic pressure, which often amounted to intervention and was never disinterested. The Constantinople Conference of 1876, for example, the recommendations of which were rejected in toto by the Turks despite the pressure of all six powers, had a result exactly opposite to that which the powers intended: it aroused a patriotic Muslim reaction. There was considerable truth in Fuad Pasha's bitter jest to a European statesman: "Our state is the strongest state. For you are trying to cause its collapse from without, and we from within, but still it does not collapse."[10] Diplomatic pressure, unless delicately used, could also render Turkish statesmen hateful in the eyes of their Muslim Turkish subjects, and lower their prestige. Âli Pasha complained of such use by Lord Stratford, the British ambassador, who had in many ways helped the Ottoman Empire greatly. Fuad complained similarly of a friendly French ambassador, M. Bourée, that "the French will never be satisfied with giving advice in an unassuming way; . . . whatever good thing was done must be advertised as a benefit conferred by France. . . ."[11] A similar sensitivity existed under the republic. Joseph Grew, the American ambassador, observed in one period of tension that even "friendly contact would inevitably be interpreted as intervention."[12] The natural fear was, of course, that Turkey's sovereignty would be impaired, and the effectiveness of her government weakened, if she gave in to foreign diplomatic pressures. This was the issue when İsmet Pasha at Lausanne absolutely rejected a transitional judicial regime, or anything resembling the capitulations. He preferred to declare categorically that the Turkish civil law had no religious character, and was adequate to modern life. He was willing to break up the conference on this issue. It is sufficient commentary on his remarks to note that, less than four years after he presented his brief, the Kemalist republic abandoned its existing civil code for a new one modelled on the Swiss.

[10] Abdurrahman Şeref, *Tarih Musahabeleri*, Istanbul, A.H. 1339, p. 104.
[11] Elliot (Constantinople), No. 68 confidential, 17 December 1867, F.O. 78/1965, Public Record Office, London.
[12] Joseph C. Grew, *Turbulent Era*, New York, 1952, II, 758.

II. Foreign Concepts and Models

Much of the foreign contribution to Turkish political modernization came in the form of ideas and institutions, concepts and models, which the Turks could make their own by adoption or adaptation. The first infusion of European ideas came in the late eighteenth and early nineteenth centuries, as a result of the changing position of the Ottoman Empire in a world increasingly ordered by European power. First, of course, was the series of military reforms that partly Westernized the organization, dress, drill, and specialized education of the army and navy. Then came changes in Ottoman diplomatic procedure. When the fiction of the superiority of the Ottoman sultan to all other rulers had perforce been abandoned and he had to deal with European powers on their own terms, the sultan began to send regular diplomatic missions instead of *ad hoc* envoys to the major Western capitals. Selim III began the practice, which became fully established in the reign of Mahmud II—the Turks recapitulating at that late date the transition made by Western Europe in the Renaissance. Further, to take care of diplomatic business in his own capital, Mahmud II, after the Greek revolt, gave up his reliance on Greek interpreters and replaced them with Muslims. Soon thereafter, he established a Translation Bureau in which young Turks might master French. The exigencies of war and diplomacy had thus persuaded the Turks to create new institutions in two fields, each serving to educate an official elite that knew French and something of Western ways. The diplomatic establishment may be counted the first concrete step toward modernization in Ottoman political organization.

From this point on, foreign concepts and models adapted by the Turks became so numerous that only general categories can be treated in an essay of this scope. The categories I have chosen, corresponding approximately to those which Robert Scalapino employs in his discussion of Japanese politics, are the administrative machinery of the state, equal individual citizenship under secular law, representative government, and modern nationalism.

Mahmud II, as has been noted, abolished a good many traditional offices and created new ones more directly dependent on his will. Some of these bore European titles, and exemplified a relatively modern allocation of functions among officials. Before the end of his reign there were ministers of foreign affairs, finance, and interior; the title of grand vezir even was briefly changed to that of prime minister. Such titles often meant that the mere trappings of European government were being approximated. But in the course of time new ministries were created, genuinely reflecting the European belief that modern government should acknowledge wide public responsibilities. For example, a ministry of education was established in 1847, and under its aegis a scheme of state-supported education from the primary school to the university was drawn up in 1869. Another foreign institution adopted was the Council of State, which developed through several permutations out of a deliberative committee set up by Mahmud II. As reorganized in 1868 this Council of State had much in common with that of Napoleon III. Provincial government also was reorganized with the vilayet law of 1867, again very close to the French pattern. In this and subsequent Ottoman legislation the modern principle of the separation of administrative and judicial powers was incorporated. The corporate municipality, a concept quite foreign to Islamic law, first appeared in embryo in Turkey in 1858 as the *sixième cercle* of Istanbul—answering to the desires of Europeans and Levantines living there.

Every one of these developments in administrative machinery answered to some foreign model, whether or not the Turkish imitation was altogether faithful. One need not catalogue all the organs of Turkish government of which this may eventually be said. Under the modern republic it may be said of them all, with the solitary exception of the Directorate of Religious Affairs.

In lesser ways, too, the administrative machinery has become more European. Midhat Pasha was unable, when president of the Council of State in 1868, to carry through the reforms in filing procedures that he wanted. But gradually the traditional sack, or *torba*, was replaced by the folder, the box, and the filing cabinet. Ahmed Vefik Pasha was a radical when, as director-general of indirect taxation in 1871, he ordered all employees to be in their offices by nine a.m., on pain of dismissal; but punctuality has greatly increased. The statute of 1855—that "in the future, the *nizamat* laws or ordinances will no longer be written in obscure or ambiguous words, they shall be stated and explained in clear, easy, and concise terms"[13]—was not uniformly observed thereafter. Yet, allowing for some peculiar experimentation with official vocabulary, the clarity of ordinances has been much improved over the past century. The first "modern" census of 1831

[13] Quoted from the *Takvim-i vekayi*, the official gazette, in T. X. Bianchi, *Khaththy Humaioun*, Paris, 1856, p. viii.

yielded at length to the first really modern census of 1927, which availed itself of expert Belgian advice. In a multitude of such particulars Turkey owes much to European bureaucratic example.

Beyond the fairly mechanical aspect of administration, Europe supplied philosophical concepts of far-reaching significance. One of these was the concept of the secular state. The realization of this concept involved abandonment of any official state religion and a shift in the legal basis for individual rights and personal status. Traditionally such status had derived from the individual's membership in a millet —Muslim, Christian, or Jewish. The modern European concept, which slowly worked its way into Turkish political life, was that an individual's rights and duties were grounded rather in his political status as subject of a ruler—or, in a later period, as citizen of a state.

The first secular political ideas came to the Ottoman Empire during the French Revolution, although these were roundly condemned as godlessness in some quarters. Âtıf Efendi, the foreign minister (*reisül-küttab*), wrote that the revolution was a product of atheists like Voltaire and Rousseau, and that the Declaration of the Rights of Man and the Citizen was a means of reducing them to the level of animals.[14] Nevertheless, such ideas spread among a few young Turks of the elite, providing Selim III with supporters for his attempted reforms. Although reaction wiped out a number of the reformers, Mahmud II himself began to speak of equal treatment for all his subjects. By 1839 the Hatt-i Şerif of Gülhane reflected some of the major principles of eighteenth-century liberal thought. Security of life, honor (rather than "liberty"), and property were promised in that document, together with equal justice for the great and the small; and these promises were made to all the sultan's subjects, "of whatever religion or sect." Thus the doctrine of Ottomanism (*Osmanlılık*) was solemnly pronounced. It meant, if carried to its logical conclusion, that millet boundaries would be wiped out. Phrases promising equality without distinction as to religion recur like a *leitmotif* throughout the period from 1839 to 1876. Though in part an answer to European criticism and minority separatism, equality of all subjects before the law was sincerely espoused by a growing number of Ottoman statesmen as the way of salvation for the heterogeneous empire. In the Constitution of 1876, all subjects were considered "Osmanlı, whatever religion or

---

[14] Cited by Abdülhak Adnan-Adıvar, *Osmanlı Türklerinde ilim* (Istanbul, 1943), p. 192. Cf. translation of part of the document in Bernard Lewis, *The Emergence of Modern Turkey*, London, 1961, pp. 65-66.

creed they hold," and their legal equality was reaffirmed. It was again reaffirmed when the constitution was restored in 1908.

Never during the last century of the Ottoman Empire was full equality in fact conferred on the adherents of all religions. Even the reforming statesmen who enunciated the principle tended to retain an instinctive belief in Muslim superiority. Yet, from 1850 on, secular law patterned on European codes was increasingly accepted. The ideal of equality persisted, to be supplemented early in this century by the belief of a few Turkish *philosophes* in the ideal of a secular state. Finally, with the adoption of the Swiss-based civil code in 1926, came the official triumph of secular law guaranteeing equal rights to adherents of all religions. In 1928, the second article of the 1924 Constitution was altered to eliminate the statement "The religion of the Turkish state is Islam." In 1937, the principle of secularity, or laicism, was positively written into the constitution. This foreign contribution to Turkish polity has nevertheless failed to win complete popular acceptance. The state itself, furthermore, still maintains certain official connections with Islam and some of its institutions, despite the victory of secular law over religious.

Parliamentary and representative government, and the sovereignty of the people, represent a third complex of ideas imported into Turkey from abroad. It can be argued that the sultans were in a fashion "elected" by the military and civil elite. It can also be argued, and was in fact argued by the New Ottoman propagandists of the 1860's and 1870's, that Islam is fundamentally democratic, enjoining that the ruler heed counsels other than his own. Ottoman sultans and Grand Vezirs did sometimes convene general assemblies of high officials, ex-officials, and notables to discuss important public issues. Yet there was more color than substance to the argument that representative government was indigenous to Turkey. Its adoption there came historically as the result of Western influences.

The process of its adoption was a curious inversion of Western expectations. Parliamentary procedure was first used in a deliberative assembly which was neither representative nor elected. This was the Supreme Council of Judicial Ordinances, a body created by Mahmud II at the end of his reign to discuss possible new regulations. As of 1839, this body was charged with writing into Turkish law the promises of the Hatt-i Şerif. Its procedural rules included free speech for all members, acknowledged in the order of their inscription; the interpellation of ministers; the keeping of minutes; and decision by majority vote. All these practices were borrowed from the West. Next —in the 1840's—came a recognition of the principle of representation, when the newly created advisory councils attached to each provincial governor incorporated a few non-Muslim members. The same representative principle, though still without elections, was first applied to a national body in 1856, when some non-Muslims were designated to sit with the Supreme Council.

The electoral principle was first recognized—apart from its inclusion in the reformed non-Muslim millet structures of the early 1860's—in the vilayet laws of 1864 and 1867. Under these laws the administrative councils of the province (vilayet) and its subdivisions contained members elected by the local population, though by a complex and indirect process. Each vilayet also had an elected general assembly, though with powers essentially advisory. Finally the Constitution of 1876 created an elected chamber of deputies. This constitution was fashioned upon a number of foreign models. Popular sovereignty was not achieved by it, for the sultan retained great powers, and the ministers were ultimately responsible to him rather than to the chamber—as in the Prussian Constitution of 1850 or the German Constitution of 1871. Ministerial responsibility was broadened after the restoration of the Constitution in 1908, however, and in 1920 the Grand National Assembly, newly convened in Ankara, firmly proclaimed the sovereignty of the people. In somewhat later debate on the deposition of the sultan, Kemal succinctly said: "Sovereignty and Sultanate are not given to anyone by anyone because scholarship says so. . . . The Turkish nation . . . has rebelled and taken the sovereignty into its own hands."[15] Though expression of popular sovereignty in a completely free multi-party election had to wait until 1950, İsmet already spoke at Lausanne in the name of an elected parliament representing the Turkish people. Nearly a century of Western-inspired change lay behind his claim; further changes were to follow.

Bound up with the concept of popular sovereignty is the peculiarly Western spirit of nationalism. This consciousness of the unity and individuality of a people possessing common cultural traits and a common homeland has spread rapidly since the days of the French Revolution. Together with modern industrialism, it is probably the major European contribution to the world at large. Certainly it is the major political contribution of Europe to Turkey's modernization.

Such a concept was foreign to the Ottoman Empire, where, as gen-

[15] Quoted in G. L. Lewis, *Turkey*, New York, 1955, p. 70.

erally in the world of Islam, distinctions among peoples followed religious lines. But together with the concept of the secular state, it slowly entered the national consciousness over the course of a century. Ottoman leaders traditionally served faith and state, but had no sense of solidarity with the people they ruled. "Turk" was a term of opprobrium, denoting an uncultivated boor. To conceive of serving fatherland and nation (*vatan ve millet*) rather than faith and state (*din ve devlet*), and of being basically a Turk rather than a Muslim or an Osmanlı, was extremely difficult for them. All who know modern Turkey realize that it is still difficult for most Turks to conceive of a non-Muslim Turk.

The idea of fatherland began to be expressed as *vatan* about the middle of the nineteenth century. The growing familiarity of Osmanlı intellectuals with the French *patrie*, in fact and in literature, called into being a companion concept in Turkey. For a long time, however, *vatan* connoted not a true and fervent nationalism but a spirit of patriotism, the older and milder European antecedent of the modern sentiment. It viewed with distress the shrinking boundaries of the Ottoman Empire, and promoted the desire to defend those boundaries; it sought also to promote Osmanlılık among the various peoples and creeds of the imperial state. The Hatt-i Hümayun of 1856 coined a word, *vatandaş*, meaning patriotism or perhaps "compatriotism," the common bond among all Turkish subjects.[16] The spirit, first of patriotism and later of nationalism, was nurtured also by revulsion against European attacks and pressures, and by reaction against the nationalism of the rebellious Balkan peoples. By 1873, when the journalist and poet Namık Kemal produced his drama entitled *Vatan*, the fatherland concept was charged with emotional content. This fatherland was not yet fully Turkish; it was still Ottoman. The emotional content was Islamic as well as patriotic. *Vatan* freed itself from such ambivalence and became clearly nationalist in the twentieth century. The term *millet* underwent a similar gradual metamorphosis from its older meaning of "religious community" to its modern meaning of "nation." The patriotic spirit, however defined, grew steadily more secular and national. In the Russo-Turkish war period of 1877-1878 it was Islamic. By 1908, when the Young Turks boycotted Austrian goods in retaliation for Austrian annexation of Bosnia and Herzegovina, it was perhaps predominantly political rather than religious.

[16] Bianchi, *op.cit.*, p. 4, n.1. Later the word came to mean simply "compatriot."

Meanwhile, helped along by Russian Turks and by European writers like Léon Cahun, the concept of Turkishness grew during the late nineteenth and earlier twentieth centuries to the point where it displaced Ottoman sentiment and vied only with Islam for primary allegiance. The loss of the non-Turkish territories of the empire, especially as the result of the Balkan Wars and the Great War, hastened this transfer of loyalties. The eventual acceptance of the Turkish state as a small, relatively homogeneous republic allowed Mustafa Kemal to emphasize purely national virtues and to point out the burden that imperial and Islamic responsibilities had imposed on Turks in the past. Today it is possible to speak not only of a Turkish patriotism (the successor to Ottoman patriotism), but of a Turkish nationalism, at least among the educated and Westernized citizens of the country. The European diplomats who faced the stubborn Ismet at Lausanne felt that they were already in the presence of such a force.

III. Channels for Foreign Contributions

It remains for us to identify the channels through which foreign contributions to the modern Turkish polity chiefly flowed. There were many such channels, and they entered the Turkish national life at such a diversity of points that generalizations concerning them are difficult. But a skeletal treatment of them may be attempted.

There had always existed contacts between the Ottoman Empire and the West. Almost from its inception, that empire was physically and politically oriented toward Europe more than toward Asia. Nor was the empire ever closed to foreign visitors as was Japan. Not only the contacts provided by military campaigns, but those with Western diplomats, merchants, refugees, renegades, and travellers within the empire, and with minorities among the sultan's subjects, brought knowledge of the West to Turkey. It is true, however, that until the nineteenth century few Turks had themselves travelled in Europe beyond the Ottoman boundaries. It is also true that, though the Ottoman Empire was not a physically closed domain, the Ottoman or Islamic mind was generally closed to Western influences. This mind opened only very gradually.

The first obvious channel of communication was the European diplomat. Many able and intelligent diplomats of the great powers served in the Ottoman capital. Though they associated almost exclusively with European or Levantine circles, or with Turkish officials, they were seldom backward in giving advice on political reforms. Such advice was as often resented as not, especially when it was accompanied by pressure. Yet some changes with important consequences for political modernization were effected by it. The *lycée* of Galatasaray, for example, was established upon the advice of an expert from Napoleon III's ministry of education after the French ambassador to the Porte had urgently proposed that action. There were also foreign diplomats who gave the Turks a sympathetic ear and perhaps friendly unofficial advice in periods of crisis; among these were Sir Henry Elliott, British ambassador in 1875-1876, and Admiral Mark Bristol, American High Commissioner after the Great War. In all, however, the Turks learned less than they might have from foreign diplomats. The foreign consul, lord in a small domain, was often obnoxious to them.

The much larger group of foreigners in Turkey were private citizens —merchants, adventurers, concession-hunters, travellers, missionaries, and teachers. Individual Turks, and sometimes Turkish statesmen, gained a sympathetic knowledge of European ways from them. Ahmed Vefik Pasha, for instance, used to discuss a variety of questions with Americans on the Robert College faculty. Especially after 1908, the number of Turkish graduates of foreign schools in Turkey increased rapidly. Of these graduates—the late Adnan Menderes was one— some attained high positions in government.

Before the republican period, and even to some extent during it, the foreign "colonies" usually had more associations with Greeks, Armenians, Jews, and Levantines than they did with the Turks. The merchants tended to live apart, although their desires and interests, especially after the Crimean War, helped to bring Westernized commercial law into Turkish courts. Colonies of foreign workers, like the Swiss factory hands at Amasya or the British dockyard employees at Hasköy, seem to have had little influence on their Turkish neighbors. The adventurers and concession-hunters, and the dubious or even criminal European rabble that operated under the protection of the capitulations, made anything but a good impression on Turks. The missionaries, usually exemplary in character, worked almost entirely among the Christian minorities. When their evangelical enthusiasm touched Muslim Turks, a violent reaction was likely to ensue—even, as the Bursa incident of 1928 shows, under the "secular" republic. The total impact of such groups on Turkish political modernization is hard to assess. So also is the impact of American military men in Turkey in recent years. The effect of foreign cultures on Turkish social and economic aspirations is easier to see. The Turkish reaction to the foreign "colonies" in their midst has, at best, been mixed.

Among the foreigners in Turkey have been some, however, directly employed for specific purposes, who have had an undoubted national influence. The list of foreign military instructors and advisers, from Bonneval and Tott through Moltke, Goltz, and Liman von Sanders down to the Americans of today, is long and distinguished. During the period of the French Revolution and the Napoleonic era the French influence was predominant. Mahmud II introduced a diversity of foreign technicians and advisers. Mahmud employed a Frenchman to start a medical school, a Spaniard at the head of the naval academy, a Scotsman to run his steamboat, a Cornishman to set up a tannery, an Italian to instruct army bandsmen, Americans to build ships, English officers to train the navy, and Prussian officers to improve the army. In the 1870's the empire employed De Salve to head Galatasaray, Count Szechenyi to set up a model fire brigade, and the German or Austrian renegade Emin Efendi, who had been a teacher in the Translation Bureau, to head the law school. In the Young Turk period, the state had Crawford to reorganize the customs, Baumann for the gendarmerie, Ostrorog as legal adviser. Turkish reactions to these men were normally favorable among the upper administrative echelons, otherwise mixed. To measure the impact such advisers and technicians had, individually and collectively, on political modernization, is difficult. Some such impact must perforce have existed.

Perhaps even more influential as a channel for the communication of Western concepts, at least in the mid-nineteenth century, were the Polish and Hungarian refugees who found asylum in the Ottoman Empire after the revolutions of 1830, 1848, and 1863. Some turned Turk, adopting Islam and marrying Turkish wives. Since they served no great power and were uniformly anti-Russian, they were more likely to be trusted than were Europeans generally. They served the Turks as doctors, engineers, and army officers, and helped to staff the administrations of several vilayets. They introduced ideas of nationalism, political liberty, and constitutionalism.

Another channel of communication that cannot be disregarded was provided by the non-Muslim minorities of the empire. The educated among the Greeks, Armenians, and Jews were closer to European ways and ideas than the Turks. As middlemen in business and as translators they constituted in part a buffer between Turks and Europeans. As second-class citizens of the empire, they were not collectively influential; yet, as individuals, some undoubtedly were. Many an Ottoman statesman had as his *homme d'affaires* a Greek or Armenian banker who could play a political role behind the scenes. Odian Efendi, one of the leading Armenians, was for years a close adviser of Midhat Pasha, and influenced the latter's constitutional ideas. It is possible even that the revised constitution of the Armenian millet provided a model for some provisions in the vilayet law of 1867 and the constitution of 1876.

Those portions of the Ottoman Empire which were breaking away from the control of Istanbul also reacted upon the Turkish nation in some significant ways. Balkan nationalism served to arouse Turkish nationalism, though by revulsion rather than by contagion. The development of parliaments in Serbia and Roumania influenced Namık Kemal's thinking about parliaments. Even more influential was Egypt. Muhammad Ali's advances were a stimulus to Turkish modernization, and both his regime and that of his successors contributed political ideas to the Ottoman Empire. A number of Ottoman statesmen had their early education or professional training in the Egyptian service. The persons and influences passing between Egypt and Turkey in the nineteenth century might be the object of an independent study. For example, though European manners and Parisian modes came to Istanbul via the Levantines and during the Crimean War via an influx of Europeans, free-spending members of the Egyptian ruling family were exemplifying such fashions in Istanbul at an early date. To take a more significant example from political history: Âli Pasha evidently got some of his ideas about introducing parts of the French *code civil* into Turkey from his knowledge of an Arabic translation of that work made in Egypt. Hayreddin Pasha, who became Grand Vezir under Abdülhamid II, brought with him from Tunis ideas based on his knowledge of French civilization.

Muslims from outside the confines of the Ottoman Empire, and the later Republic, brought still further ideas to Istanbul and Ankara. Some of these were archaic enough—like those emanating from Bokhara or Kashgar in the 1870's; or, later on, from the Senussi brotherhood of Libya; or, most recently, from the North Africa-centered Ticani order. Other Muslim visitors, like Djemaleddin el-Afghani, encouraged a defensive modernization. The most important among the progressive Muslim visitors were certain Russian Turks. Often well educated, proponents of new departures in writing, eager for a Turkish

113

renaissance, familiar with pan-Slavism, and advocates of Turkish nationalism or of Pan-Turkism, these men—Yusuf Akçura, for example—channeled new ideas into Turkey in the late nineteenth and early twentieth centuries. Some came as immigrants or exiles to spend their lives in Turkey.

When all such visitors from abroad are considered together, however, they appear to have contributed less to political modernization than did the education variously obtained by members of the Ottoman, and later the republican, elite. This education was sometimes secured on the job—through service in the Translation Bureau, or in diplomatic posts in the West. Sometimes it was supplied by formal study abroad—in the *Mekteb-i Osmanî* maintained in Paris from about 1855 to 1874, or in one of the European universities or military academies. Sometimes it was gained in exile, as in the case of some of the New Ottomans and of the later Young Turks. Most often, especially in more recent times, it was gained in one of the higher schools established in Turkey—the military and naval schools, the military and civilian medical schools, the various schools set up to train administrative personnel, and the universities. The curricula of these schools became progressively Westernized, from the time of Selim III on. Those schools designed especially to train government clerks and administrators—the *Mekteb-i Maarif-i Adliye* (1838), the *Mekteb-i Mülkiye* (1859), and others—developed a curriculum which today would be called "public and international affairs."

The common denominator of education gained from these several sources was a knowledge of French, which opened up new vistas on the modern world, and numbers of Turks piled one educational experience upon another. Fuad Pasha studied at the military medical school, worked in the Translation Bureau, and then held major diplomatic posts. Ahmed Vefik Pasha was a product of the Lycée St. Louis, the military engineers' school, the Translation Bureau, and diplomatic service; in addition, he came from a family that had already provided two generations of dragomans. The bilingual elite began to dominate the government toward mid-century, gradually eclipsing those with the traditional Islamic education. And as army officers, after the *coups d'état* of 1876 and 1908, entered more deeply into politics, the Westernized education received in the military schools had an increasingly important effect on Turkish political life.

Westernized education, even for a comparatively large number of the elite, was no total guarantee that the Ottoman Empire would

114

turn modern. There was always opposition from the people as a whole, who were steadfastly opposed to innovation. There was further opposition from vested interests. Many a modernizing statesman was called the *gâvur paşa*, the "unbeliever of a pasha." Nor was there any guarantee that a Western education would produce a Westernizer. Some products of this education became cynical, others acquired more vices than virtues. Some, like Ahmed Vefik, became modernizers but without accepting the Western political example. Namık Kemal, admitting Ahmed Vefik's great learning, said that he understood nothing of parliamentary procedure,[17] and others who knew him thought Ahmed Vefik would have made a good Grand Vezir for Mahmud II or even Süleyman the Law Giver. Many bureaucrats came to possess only a superficial veneer of Western education. "The result of a half-baked Frank education is depressing," wrote Mark Sykes of a young *kaymakam* he met in 1906. "His idea of reform was the regular payment of Kaimakams, the provision of free illustrated newspapers for Kaimakams to read, the building of railways for Kaimakams to travel by, and eventually the restoration of all Kaimakams to Constantinople, where they would be given places as highly-paid deputies in a Parliament of Kaimakams, who would collect and control the expenditure."[18]

Yet, when all these weaknesses are taken into account, the foreign contribution to Turkish politics by way of Western education was tremendous. Most of the modernizers have come from the civilian and military bureaucracies. Most have had a Western education. Many have known French. Modern Turkey could not have come into being except through their labors. In the end, they came to serve not as the channel of transmission for foreign influences but as the self-reliant political leaders and philosophers of a changing nation-state. "Past a critical threshold," as William Schorger wrote in a paper presented in 1961, "the impetus for modernization of the society derives from modernized indigenous elements as much as, or more than, from external sources."[19] The Turkish experience bears this out.

At the Lausanne conference, Signor Montagna, one of the Italian plenipotentiaries, was very dubious about Turkey's political growth.

[17] Fevziye A. Tansel, *Namık Kemal ve Abdülhak Hâmid, hususî mektuplarına göre*, Ankara, 1949, p. 52.
[18] Mark Sykes, *The Caliphs' Last Heritage*, London, 1915, p. 365.
[19] "The Social Community in the Contemporary Middle East," mimeographed, 1961, p. 6.

He talked about this to the American observer, Joseph Grew. "In his own mind," said Grew, "he compares Turkey to a mummy which so long as it remains sealed in its tomb retains its normal state but as soon as the tomb is opened and it comes into contact with the outside air it immediately begins to decompose and to crumble away. Turkey's contact with the outside nations would make her crumble away because she was not content to make the transition gradually as Japan had done, but must bring it about all at once."[20]

Turkey of course did not crumble. What Montagna failed to realize was that she had for more than a century been in contact with the outside air. Foreign nations had provided the harsh stimulus of military defeat. Foreign contacts had planted in the Turkish consciousness the seeds of such vital concepts as nationalism and the sovereignty of the people. And they had made possible an education, the principal advantage of which was usually knowledge of the French language, whereby Turkish leaders might inform themselves of the new state of the world and of expedients for adapting to it.

[20] Grew, *op.cit.*, I, 568.

CHAPTER 4

ECONOMIC AND POLITICAL MODERNIZATION

A. JAPAN

WILLIAM W. LOCKWOOD

THE influence of Japan's economic development upon her political institutions is visible in three striking features of her modern history: (1) the forging of a powerful nation-state after 1868; (2) the subsequent military expansion into East Asia; and (3) the tardier but persistent growth at home of a more open, competitive politics, interrupted by the great crisis of 1931-1945.

The analogies among emerging nations of the non-Western world today need no emphasis. The Age of Self-Determination has called into being regimes in Africa, South Asia, and the Near East that lack all too plainly the strength either to maintain order at home or to defend themselves abroad. Can economic development of any sort suffice to consolidate their authority? Or will their economic problems inevitably render them unstable and demoralize them?

Again, what does an industrial revolution do to the war-making capabilities and propensities of developing nations? Liberals are inclined to identify world peace with economic progress in "underdeveloped" areas. Yet for half a century the peace of the Pacific was troubled by the one Far Eastern nation that industrialized itself on a massive scale. The outcome was a disastrous war. What was the role of economic forces in Japan's imperialist career? What inference may be drawn concerning Japan's future in Asia?

Finally, democracy stands, together with political stability and national security, in the forefront of nation-building goals. Even the "people's republics" of the Communist world pay it lip service. The Western democracies extend aid to uncommitted nations in the hope that economic development will not only shore up their defenses against immediate subversive pressures but help them eventually to build an enduring order based on free institutions. While such hopes are plausible, no coherent theory of the relation of economic progress to political change now exists.

117

No one will suppose that the experience of any nation will be paralleled in a different age or society. Japan is *sui generis*, to an unusual degree. And the world in which she began to modernize was a Victorian world that has vanished. Yet, as the only Asian nation yet to modernize conclusively, her response to the great contemporary forces of nationalism, industrialism, and democracy may help us to understand the working of these forces elsewhere.

I. Economic Development and Political Stability

SINEWS OF NATIONAL POWER

The forcing of Japan's Closed Door by the Western Powers after 1850 presented a multiple challenge to her political leaders. They confronted a threat to national independence from an altered structure of world power that was steadily bringing Asia under Western subjection. They became cognizant of the power of modern industrial technology, with all of the gains it conferred on those who could master its secrets. And they faced the ideological challenge of democracy, soon to demonstrate its potency in subverting the authority structures of the traditional East. The Meiji Renovation represents the first comprehensive Japanese reaction to these forces.

Initially, technology was selectively borrowed to meet certain immediate needs of the Meiji regime. The most presssing requirement of the government was military strength, needed at once to check malcontents at home and as quickly as possible to deter hostile moves from abroad. A military establishment meant arms and modern communications, the keys to central power and national security. But armament and transport themselves required the administrative apparatus of a modern state, tax revenues to put a stop to the printing of paper money, exports to pay for imports and stem the drain of specie, shipyards, machine shops, technical schools, and many other innovations.

The early efforts of the Meiji rulers to supply these underlying needs of a modern state form a well-known story. Possessing few general blueprints, the new ministries moved a step at a time. The *han* were demolished in 1871 in favor of centralized political authority in Tokyo. A far-reaching reform of land taxes in 1873 stabilized revenue from agriculture at a level that largely supported the government for forty years. Experimentation in the field of banking and currency led finally to the Matsukata reforms of the eighties, paving the way for more orderly growth. A score of industries were introduced, with Western equipment and the advice of Western technical experts. After a dubious beginning, marred by the military rebellions of 1874-1877 and recurrent financial crises, the results of these efforts began to appear.

Meanwhile the new security and freedom formed an atmosphere in which private enterprise, too, was able to develop. New constellations of private financiers, the nascent *zaibatsu*, emerged to take over more and more of the managerial responsibilities of the modern industries pioneered by the state. After 1880, needing funds for naval expansion, the government sold off most of its unprofitable industrial properties. Later it built the big Yawata Iron Works and nationalized the railways, telephones, and telegraph; it further retained certain arsenals and dockyards and became the biggest stockholder in the South Manchuria Railway; finally, it reserved certain powers of maintaining and directing the flow of capital, mostly private, into industrial development. Beyond that it contented itself with surveillance and subsidy in those sectors of industry, trade, and colonial enterprise deemed strategic to the national security. To exercise the necessary control it relied on the usual instrumentalities of tariffs and taxes and buying preferences, on its postal savings system, and on a number of big quasi-public banks that it had formed jointly with private capital.

Thus emerged that mutually beneficial alliance of bureaucrat and businessman that built the country's industrial potential over the next half century and that eventually brought about far-reaching changes in the political center of gravity.

Yet economic growth was by no means confined to large-scale modern enterprises. These formed the basic overhead structures, and provided many of the essential instruments of growth. But the overall gains in national output came largely from the host of smaller entrepreneurs in industry, the services, and agriculture. These sectors, too, responded to the stimuli of widening markets and new technology. Agricultural output increased by two thirds or more from 1880 to 1913, with only a slight increase in the amount of land cultivated. Industrial output rose five-fold, and national income more than doubled. Meanwhile the country's population grew only from 37 to 52 millions. Over half of all the families still derived their livelihood from agriculture but substantial changes in economic structure were clearly taking place.

These developments had major political consequences. At home they enhanced the range and efficiency of state power as exercised not only through the army and the police but through the whole apparatus for mobilizing resources in a political interest. Slowly foundations were built for the national circulation of goods, capital, and even labor of the more mobile types. This new mobility cut away at the parochialism of village society, and drew people increasingly into a national economy and polity. After the 1870's there was no further question of armed rebellion from any quarter.

In foreign affairs, too, industrial progress gave authority to the new order by adding steadily to its military capabilities. Soon fears of foreign subjection abated, and a clamor arose to terminate the unequal treaties that limited tariffs and conferred extraterritorial privileges on the foreigner. This goal was achieved shortly after Japan's victory over China in 1895. In a brief encounter her new armed forces had decisively defeated the moribund armies of Li Hung-chang in Manchuria and had sent his fleet to the bottom of the Yellow Sea.

Japan's debut in world politics was achieved almost wholly by her own financial resources. She borrowed virtually nothing in Western money markets until the turn of the century. Nor did she welcome Western business enterprise within Japan, except in trade and pursuits auxiliary to it; she guarded her economic independence from the beginning. In this regard she presents a striking contrast to regions like the Ottoman Empire and China, in which, during the nineteenth century, Western business enterprise played a major role, the government became heavily indebted to foreign lenders, and the national sovereignty was seriously compromised.

In rendering these judgments one should not let the lapse of a hundred years foreshorten perspectives unduly. The Japanese policy succeeded in over twenty-five years, not in five or ten. Civil war and inflation nearly bankrupted the new government before it found its feet. There was far less coherent long-range planning than any regime today would regard as the fig-leaf of respectability. The interesting thing, nevertheless, is the way in which the government drew back from mistakes when it discovered them, and groped its way towards institutions that could undergird the necessary growth and stability.

The Meiji improvisations managed, all in all, to move in a consistent direction. They never took the country off on tangents like reckless overseas ventures that were beyond her capabilities. Nor did they contradict one another, as do too many policies of those modern nations simultaneously pursuing the goals of welfare and of power. The aptest parallel is perhaps with mercantilism in seventeenth-century Europe. Then, too, the political consequence of commercial and industrial advance was to consolidate the central authority of the nation-state and to arm it against its foreign rivals. The principal motives of growth were a blend of patriotism and profit-seeking foreshadowing the Japanese alliance of "Yen and Sword."

THE WIDENING OF OLIGARCHY

Industrialization equipped the state to exercise its authority with growing efficiency. It further attracted the support of persons in the political elite and the rising business and professional classes whose participation in development was essential. The new order was for the most part accepted not only by aristocrats from the old order who retained influence in the new, but by persons rising from commoner ranks to new positions of power. Displaced samurai were a nagging problem, and the government tried none too successfully to find new employment for them. Once it had weathered the first decade's unrest, however, it faced no further serious danger from this quarter.

Initially power was narrowly monopolized, especially by the Sat-Cho clansmen. This gave rise to political intrigue and disaffection on the part of both outsiders who wanted in and of liberals who objected on principle. But the growth of the economy served to reduce dissatisfaction, slowly widening the scope of personal opportunity in both public and private life as more and more persons climbed the new ladders of influence and wealth. Manifest gains in national power were also a source of gratification to all.

Control of the new industry was highly authoritarian, yet not narrowly exclusive except at the top. A slowly widening elite competed vigorously for status, power, and wealth while preserving an underlying consistency of purpose. The state was absolute, but not monolithic. Political and economic power were both closely held, but not in identical hands. A perennial contest went on within government and business, and sometimes between them as well. An appearance of agreement between them often concealed, in the best Japanese tradition, a struggle in which every interest seemed represented except that of the public.

National loyalties were strong, being sedulously cultivated and invested with the sanctity of the "imperial myth." They united Japan as they were then dividing the Ottoman Empire. But patriotism alone will hardly explain the vitality of the Meiji enterprise in business and politics. Public decisions were bound up with private goals. Like all successful organizations, the Meiji regime stabilized itself partly by giving scope to personal initiative. Its spirit was pragmatic, even to the point of refurbishing traditional symbols of authority to legitimize modernization. In economic affairs particularly it encouraged the rise of a leadership based on achievement. It preserved order because it was at once authoritarian and committed to change.

ENTERPRISE AND POWER

A similar attempt elsewhere, or in another day, might have produced quite different results. Economic growth in Meiji Japan proceeded rather efficiently and served to widen rather than narrow the range of freedom for two quite particular reasons.

First, the whole conjuncture of circumstance made for coincidence between national needs and the personal ambitions of soldiers, bureaucrats, and businessmen seeking to exploit the new technology. Many interests, such as those of the tenant farmer or the child laborer, were poorly served. Yet if a certain priority may be conceded to minimum levels of national strength and rates of economic growth, it happened more often at that time than in later decades that what was good for Mitsui or the army General Staff was good for Japan.

Second, the emergence of modern business enterprise with its political allies created new foundations on which to construct an equilibrium of diverse interests no major element of which could be wholly ignored by a cabinet without risk of overthrow. If this sometimes invited stalemate, especially as the old clan oligarchs departed from the scene, it also protected the government from errors to which authoritarian regimes are prone. Until the disaster of the 1930's, Japan was less seriously handicapped by military leaders unable to calculate power abroad or make intelligent judgments at home than many other states in which armies have more largely monopolized the initiative in modernization.

The role of the professional military in Meiji Japan was relatively restricted outside their own realm, both because of the strength of countervailing civil forces in the oligarchy and because of the weakness of revolutionary threats from below. Civil elements could compete with increasing success for a share in power, provided they did not challenge the fundamentals of national policy. When this challenge did come, in the twenties and thirties, the Japanese military acted as their counterparts have acted elsewhere. Meanwhile, however, the consolidation both of economic growth and of political stability owed much to the dual processes of conflict and consensus that developed among the groups competing for leadership.

Japan thus avoided both the stagnation characterizing so many despotisms and the disasters that an unrestrained totalitarianism can inflict on its people. She was sufficiently united and disciplined, furthermore, so that she could avoid that other horn of the dilemma confronting many modernizing states, namely the internal cleavages that break down civil order and cut the thread of legitimacy. Except for occasional assassinations by fire-eating ultranationalists, she was singularly free of *putsches* or attempts to determine political succession by open violence from 1877 to 1931.

THE COMMON PEOPLE

The common people shared only tardily in the fruits of progress. The majority remained peasants, like their forefathers, on family holdings of from one to three acres. The techniques of rice cultivation combined with population growth to preclude any reorganization of agriculture such as attended the Industrial Revolution in Europe. Farmers now found their feudal dues exchanged for a heavy tax on land which furnished over half the national revenues until 1888. Many were driven into debt and tenancy despite substantial gains in farm productivity and income. By the turn of the century the growth of population was applying relentless pressure. Some 45 per cent of farmlands were now tenanted, and one cultivator in every four owned no land at all.[1]

Thereafter additions to the labor force were siphoned off into industry and the services, which were both rapidly growing. In the cities these people mostly eked out a precarious living in small-scale trades that mushroomed along with modern factories. In the countryside, too, manufacturing and other by-employments—notably silkworm-raising—began to spread under the leadership of rural merchants and landlords. Though the farm population remained stationary at about 5½ million families, these supplementary employments added a growing increment of cash income to farm livelihood.

Politically it was significant that industrialization could thus absorb the swelling labor force, leaving the rural society and rural politics relatively stable. Many developing nations today, with populations

[1] Asahi Shimbun-sha, *Nihon Keizai Tōkei Sōkan* (General Economic Statistics of Japan), Tokyo, 1930, pp. 682, 689.

growing at two or three times Japan's pre-war annual rate of 1.2 per cent seem fated to herd even more people together on densely crowded farmlands before they bring fertility under control. For three generations, it is true, the gains in human well-being were meager for most Japanese. Yet famines were a thing of the past. Personal freedom and legal equality were written into the law. Slow improvements appeared in the supply of essentials; real industrial wages, for example, probably rose about one third from 1897 to 1914.[2] Furthermore, the spread of popular education and the growth of cities slowly lifted the horizon of opportunity for the youth of each succeeding generation.

It was equally significant that no revolution in popular expectations arose to plague the Meiji rulers or complicate their decisions. "Creative obedience" was the public mood. The reasons are familiar: the discipline and solidarity of society within a long-standing authoritarian tradition; the absence of popular contacts with more advanced industrial societies; the firmness with which the oligarchs maintained control; and the overall facts that this was the world of 1880-1910, not of 1960. The peasant, in E. H. Norman's words, was Atlas patiently bearing the burden of industrialization on his back. The very stability of the political system revealed its accommodation to the general framework within which authority was exercised at the time. Not until after World War I did Japan's industrial revolution give rise to proletarian movements.

GRADUALISM AND LEGITIMACY

Two further observations should be added. "There is no subtler, surer way of overturning the existing basis of society," Lord Keynes once said, "than to debauch the currency." In Japan monetary disorders were kept within tolerable bounds, after the inflation of 1877-1881 and the deflation of 1881-1885. Except for the short-lived boom of World War I, masses of people were not again impoverished by that debasement of the currency which sets one class against another, until the exigencies of World War II. Governments financed themselves mainly by taxes, regressive as these were. The monetary mechanism was used with reasonable success to furnish one essential of good government.

[2] William W. Lockwood, *The Economic Development of Japan*, Princeton, 1959, p. 144. Real wages rose 58% from 1875 to 1910, according to data cited by M. Umemura, in Tsuru Shigeto and Ohkawa Kazushi, eds., *Nihon Keizai No Bunseki* (Analysis of the Japanese Economy), Vol. 1, Tokyo, 1954, p. 247.

More broadly, if Meiji statesmen paid little heed to the peasant's welfare except to offer him modest technical services, they at least gave him civil order and political security. And they did not uproot him from his cherished way of life in order to force industrialization on him in the modern totalitarian fashion. Though the gradualism of agricultural policy long denied the peasant his democratic due, it preserved the continuity and stability of the Japanese village, the conservative base of Japanese society even today.

The same thing may be said, in fact, of the whole process of development in Japan. Politically, of course, the Restoration constituted a radical break with the past, transferring power to an emergent wing of the ruling class invigorated with new goals and capacities. It ushered in structural reforms that provided the framework of modernization. Thereafter, however, policies of development were incremental. They confirmed the rights of private property rather than eroding them. Though governments did not hesitate to employ the resources of the state to foster industrial progress, they proceeded for the most part in accordance with established conventions. In philosophy, too, the governing authority conserved long-standing traditions and practices. Because it was successful in inducing growth, it discouraged rising demands for more drastic departures from national tradition such as began to appear in China after the turn of the century. It thereby won the adherence of groups both old and new. In uniting technological progressiveness with social conservatism, the Japanese displayed their genius for effecting massive changes with no breakdown in social order.

In summary, sustained economic development served to strengthen the political order. First, it achieved the growth needed to preserve the nation from external threats and to provide stability at home. Second, it followed a pattern of economic sponsorship that evoked fresh initiatives, both political and economic. Third, it contributed to producing an elite that slowly became more numerous and diverse, yet remained coherent enough to resolve conflicts within itself. Finally, the benefits it diffused among the masses, though long failing to endow them with a capability for political action, were real enough to strengthen the traditional sanctions upholding the structure of authority.

In short, Japan's early strategy of nation building sought stability through change and growth while preserving resolute safeguards against social disorder.

II. Economic Development and Political Expansion

Though industrialization served initially to stabilize the new political order at home, it soon had profoundly disruptive effects on the international politics of the Pacific.

Entering a predatory world, Japan proved a ready pupil of Western imperialism. Her first major encroachment was upon Korea, where incidents offered provocation and China's weakness the opportunity. Patriotic societies, abetted by the General Staff, fanned the imperialistic flame. War came in 1894, and yielded easy victories to the emperor's new forces. When the Triple Intervention forced Japan to disgorge her territorial gains on the Liaotung Peninsula, she turned her attention to Russia. For ten years tension mounted over China's northeastern provinces, again fostered by the army and patriotic groups. Reassured by her new alliance with Britain, Japan took on her continental rival in 1904. Again she emerged victorious, the master of Korea and possessor of a foothold in Manchuria. By 1914 she was already an imperial power, with an overseas realm matching the home islands in extent.

Europe's fratricidal war opened fresh avenues for expansion. Three continental forays—the Shantung seizure, the Twenty One Demands, and the Siberian expedition—attested the restless urge of the military.

Soon opportunity knocked again, as depression and disillusionment undermined the liberal forces of the twenties. The young military radicals struck in Manchuria and committed Tokyo step by step to the seizure of China's eastern provinces. After that, events moved in steady sequence to the Pacific war. The empire stretched briefly from Sakhalin to Sumatra before it collapsed.

So dominant a feature of national policy extending over four generations could hardly fail to be involved with economic development. But what was the precise nature of their relationships?

WAR AND ECONOMIC GROWTH

The relationships most clearly evident are the influences on economic development exerted by the whole syndrome of war and preparation for war. The building up of armaments, the seizure and development of colonies, the moves and countermoves of international rivalries and their repercussions in domestic politics—all these contributed to shaping Japanese industrial growth from the beginning.

First, the building of a military machine assured the nation of political freedom from Western control. This initial achievement profoundly affected her future.

Second, the military introduced Western technology and organization, bringing indirect gains to civil industries and occupations. They supplied motives for modernization and a new ladder of social mobility; through conscription, also, the army gave generations of peasant boys their first glimpse of the modern world and its ways.

Third, international tensions determined in good part the political atmosphere in which development proceeded. In Meiji times, the sense of an external threat reinforced unity and authoritarian leadership, probably with beneficial effects on economic growth. After 1918 it had a contrary tendency. The divergence of opinions on foreign policy intensified domestic strife. Militarism, always on the side of autocracy, bred division in politics and dyarchy in administration. Economic growth faltered in the twenties, partly because of drift and deadlock in high political circles and the resulting failure of the government to grapple with the problems of agriculture and of other lagging sectors of the economy.

Finally, militarism and imperialism had direct effects on the economy, some beneficial and others not. The manufacture of arms was a major factor in the rise of the metallurgical and engineering industries. It also stimulated fuller use of the country's resources generally, particularly in the 1900's and during the reflation of 1932-1936. On one occasion victory on the battlefield won a sizable bonanza—the £38 million indemnity wrung from China in 1895. Again, Korea and Formosa, and later Manchuria, supplied the nation with food and other essentials. They also constituted protected markets for Japanese manufactures. By the mid-thirties Japan was selling nearly 40 per cent of her exports within the empire and buying there about 30 per cent of her imports, including a fifth of all her food. Besides the occupying armies, two million resident nationals found a livelihood in the overseas territories, most of them in business and the professions.

The losses were formidable too. Arms outlays absorbed 40 per cent of the national budget year after year from 1895 to 1935, in a country pressed for development capital. Resources and skills were dissipated in expensive colonial enterprises, in subsidies to uneconomic industries, and in intrigues like the Nishihara loans to venal Chinese politicians in 1915. The Siberian intervention alone wasted a billion yen to no purpose. In the protected strategic industries, monopoly and corruption were prevalent, with baneful effects on parliamentary politics.

Among the wars themselves, it was World War I that profited Japan most, for then she was a bystander, capitalizing as an exporter and shipper on the needs of belligerents and neutrals alike. But the earlier limited wars with China and Russia likewise imposed no excessive drain on her resources. The early empire was cheaply enough acquired.

After 1931, however, Japan dissipated immense wealth in a vain effort to build a self-contained realm in East Asia. It is hard to believe that her economic interest would have been served even had she succeeded, or that her prospects in peaceful foreign trade were so bleak as to leave her no alternative. As it turned out, the war laid waste her economy, detroyed her great continental neighbor's resistance to Communist totalitarianism, and played havoc with structures of world trade and world power that were peculiarly important to the exposed and dependent Japanese nation.[3]

INDUSTRIAL MEANS TO EXPANSION

The role of purely economic forces in fostering such political expansion is problematical. One should nevertheless distinguish (a) industrialism as the *means* to securing national and imperial power from (b) industrialism as the creator of interests which are subsequently served by war and imperialism—i.e., as a *propelling force.*

Modern industrial technology, as is commonly said, brings the nations of the world into increasingly close contact. It also creates wide disparities of power. Japan provided a conspicuous illustration of both these generalizations during the era in which she became the preponderant industrial nation of Asia.

At home, industrialization was turned at once to the manufacture of arms, and of exports to pay for the purchase of arms abroad. Through the decades it also built supporting structures of heavy industry, and of public administration, taxation, banking, and communications. Uniting businessmen and bureaucrats in a close alliance, it fostered public acquiescence in their leadership. Finally, it created wealth rapidly enough to make empire building possible without an excessive drain on the national standard of living.

Abroad, too, industrialization provided both instrumentalities and opportunities for extending political control. On the one hand, it made

[3] Supporting evidence for these assertions will be found in *The Economic Development of Japan,* cited, pp. 50-53, 290-291, 378-404, 533-539, 577-578. Some authorities, it should be noted, ascribe a greater economic importance to Japan's colonies than is given them here.

potential antagonists increasingly wary of the rising power of Japan. By 1919 she had a formidable fleet in the Western Pacific. Foreign business interests also acquired a stake in Japanese trade that handicapped retaliatory moves against her. One recalls the equivocal position even of Chinese business interests in the face of Japanese aggression during the thirties. And American firms continued to sell Japan oil and scrap and aircraft designs long after the hostile purposes of the Japanese army in China were manifest.

Economic instruments of penetration in East Asia lay at hand in the spreading net of Japanese business interests. The South Manchuria Railway, the Bank of Taiwan, and the Oriental Development Company were employed as agencies of intelligence and influence. The Bank of Chosen served after 1931 as financial agent of the Kwantung Army; it helped smuggle opium and silver into North China; it put up funds for bribing puppets; it made itself available as the right arm of the militarists. Purely private companies also developed intimate ties with officials, politicians, and patriotic societies pushing expansion abroad. Such concerted action was made the easier by the close relation generally prevailing between the bureaucracy and big business. In all these ways industrialism was the servant of empire.

ECONOMIC DRIVES TO IMPERIALISM

The economics of imperialism embraces motives and goals as well as means. It may be asked specifically whether the economic interests of various Japanese groups and classes were present in armament and empire building, and, if so, whether they were the primary force behind military expansion.[4]

The first question is readily answered in the affirmative. Reversing a long tradition, Meiji governments made the search for commercial opportunity abroad their special concern from the beginning. By 1910 the overseas empire accounted already for 10 per cent of Japan's overseas trade. Thereafter the colonies grew steadily as markets and as sources of supply, until a generation later they accounted for about one third of that trade. Through semi-official companies like the South Manchuria Railway the government cooperated with private interests in the growing exploitation of the colonies. The whole process of exploitation reaching a crescendo in the inflationary boom of the thirties.

[4] This phrasing of the question is borrowed from Joseph A. Schumpeter's classic, *Imperialism and Social Classes*, Oxford, 1951, pp. 4-5.

Placed on the defensive after 1931 by criticism abroad and at home, official spokesmen stressed increasingly the doctrine of *lebensraum*. Japan was a poor country, with a growing population. She came late on the world scene, only to find the choice opportunities appropriated. Barred from emigration overseas, her people now also faced rising tariff barriers against peaceful trade. Extremist elements did not hesitate to draw what seemed to them the logical conclusion: Japan must conquer or perish.

One may question both the details of this argument and its conclusion. Ironically, it gained currency only on the crest of an unprecedented boom in Japanese trade. From 1930 to 1936 exports doubled in volume, raising the gross national product 50 per cent. Yet it was in the summer of 1936, following the military uprising of February 26, that those moves began which took Japan down the road to war. For decades the Japanese economy had been growing in an expanding world market. Her industrialization owed little to empire building; rather, the debt was the other way. There is nevertheless no reason to doubt the sincerity of those Japanese who came to view the "East Asia Co-prosperity Sphere" as an urgent economic need, for by 1936 they included not only firebrands like Colonel Hashimoto Kingorō but many a liberal businessman and scholar.[5]

Whatever their precise view of the national interest, various groups now found ther own personal fortunes bound up with arms and the empire. To be sure, imperialism was not a class interest in any coherent, inclusive sense. Certain business interests benefited, mainly those engaged in the munitions business or in colonial trade and investment. Urban workers in general came to have a stake in cheap Korean and Formosan rice. Other groups were unaffected or even adversely affected by the growth of the empire, as the imperialistic ventures drained tax resources and savings otherwise available for domestic uses. Yet once the process gathered headway, overseas expansion was clearly economic imperialism in the general meaning of the term. "One can hardly go into any corner of the Japanese Empire," wrote a veteran American journalist, W. H. Chamberlain, in 1937, without finding one of the big capitalist combines firmly entrenched and skimming the cream of whatever profits are made."

Whether Japanese imperialism found its principal motor force in such material interests is more doubtful. The history of Japanese

[5] See, for example, Takao Tsuchiya, "Sensō to Nihon Shihonshugi" (War and Japanese Capitalism), *Kaizō*, Vol. 20, No. 1, January 1958, pp. 41-57.

imperialism does not suit the Marxist-Leninist dogma, or the emphasis on economic motivation in the works of Harold Laski, Parker T. Moon, and others. It set in before there was any serious industrial urge to expand abroad. Agitation over Korea, the war with China, the acquisition of Formosa, the victory over Russia, the early moves into Manchuria, and the Shantung seizure were none of them motivated primarily by calculations of business gain or national economic interest, though these factors were not absent.

After World War I business gained a greater voice in politics, through its influence with bureaucrats and party politicians. Significantly the twenties were also marked by greater international cooperation and serious efforts at disarmament. Business leaders now had sizable stakes in the colonies that Japan had won by the sword, and in her special position in China. But they also had major trading relations with the West that were imperilled by conflict. They calculated risks with an attention to the balance sheet such as their military compatriots scorned. And they resented the tax burdens of heavy armament. On the other hand, they were still dependent on official patronage, subordinate in social status, and divided in their calculations of immediate advantage. While they were disposed to follow rather than lead, they yet stood ready to profit from any opportunities won by force, especially when the government underwrote the risks.

In the crucial decisions after 1931 the *zaibatsu* were thrust increasingly into the background. The older financial combines like Mitsui were reluctant to follow the army into Manchuria. Profits seemed dubious, especially while army bureaucrats retained a tight grip on development. The planners only overcame their handicap by joining hands with combines like the Aikawa and Kuhara groups, newly built on armament. By 1936 most Japanese business leaders were increasingly alarmed over the impasse in China. They feared growing isolation abroad and military terrorism at home. They were discreetly urging a settlement south of the Great Wall at the very time when the army struck at Lukouchiao in July 1937. Thereafter the big trusts went along with war mobilization; their cooperation was indispensable. Ironically they built huge fortunes in the process, then lost them in the final military disaster they had helped to bring about.[6]

[6] The role of the capitalists in Shōwa imperialism remains a controversial topic among Japanese scholars. Some cling to orthodox Marxist-Leninist interpretations of the war in China as the consequence of capitalist needs and rivalries. Others

FEAR, FACE, FRUSTRATION

Other elements in the equation of Japanese imperialism have already been suggested. These are clearly distinguishable, even if one cannot assign them magnitudes.

First is the inner logic, not of capitalism, but of an unstable power balance among rival sovereign states. Militant nationalism in Japan was given a powerful thrust at the outset of the modern period by the perils to which she was exposed. Before 1910 national security appears to have been the dominant motive, reinforced increasingly by considerations of prestige as Japan entered the family of Great Powers.

Security is an elusive concept. Its pursuit may commit a nation to action that increasingly threatens the security of other peoples, thereby creating the very danger it was supposed to avert. It is no apology for Japan's attempt to conquer East Asia to note her natural anxiety as she confronted her great continental neighbors. Japanese policy in China long felt "the weight of the future on the present." What would happen when China got on her feet and resumed her historic role in East Asia? As for Russia, even the distinguished liberal Takagi Yasaka wrote in 1932 of "the gigantic Russian bear squatting on Manchuria." All Japanese, from the time of the Triple Intervention on, he said, knew that their "manifest destiny" in Manchuria would require them to fight Russia. Today, with the Soviet Union in the Habomai, the United States in the Ryukus, and a resurgent China dominating the Asiatic continent, this anxiety remains a dominant note in Japanese politics.

Yet other nations which have been similarly exposed to danger abroad and have similarly been industrializing their economies have managed to live at peace with their neighbors. Japanese imperialism reflects other elements in her tradition and environment, above all the psychological dispositions of the military and their place in Japanese society. For though a powerful military does not of itself commit a nation to territorial expansion, in Japan it intensified other forces working to that end. The search for security bred an appetite for national power and prestige, values that are prized among status-conscious nations no less than among similarly disposed individuals. Her rela-

---

assign the predominant role to the Japanese military, against whose policies the *zaibatsu* are found with some equivocation to be in opposition. These respective positions are illustrated respectively in the essays of Professors Takahashi Yūji and Muramatsu Yūji in Nihon Gaikō Gakkai, *Taiheiyō Sensō Gen-in Ron* (On the Causes of the Pacific War), Tokyo, 1953, pp. 179-230, 515-571.

tively early industrialization gave her an advantage over her neighbors and supplied her with economic incentives to use her power. Conscious of their strength, the military developed a strong propensity to the aggrandizement both of the nation and of their own role within it. Their special position under the constitution assured them an ample military establishment and the power to use it. The feudal substance of Japan thus lived on in the psychology and status of the military bureaucrat, supporting autocracy at home and aggression abroad.

While the military were the self-appointed guardians of the national polity, other classes became pervaded by a strong national consciousness. Repeatedly democratic movements were confused and dispersed when nationalist appeals were invoked in behalf of bureaucratic despotism. Meanwhile patriotic societies like the *Genyōsha* and *Kokuryūkai* stoked the fires of extremism, supported by the General Staff on the one hand and interested businessmen on the other.

One further economic fact is relevant. Japanese imperialism, said Thorstein Veblen in his famous 1919 essay on "The Opportunity of Japan," was a passing phenomenon.[7] It resulted from joining industrial technology with a "high-wrought spirit of feudalistic fealty and chivalric honor." As a relic of feudal militarism, it would inevitably be overborne by the more rational, more tolerant, more materialistic values of modern industrial society.

Veblen's forecast was in error, of course. In retrospect it is not difficult to see why. He underestimated the survival power of what he called "the spiritual landmarks of feudalism" and the extent to which these could fuse with modern nationalism. And he failed to anticipate how industrialism itself would breed tensions and anxieties in Japanese society that could be diverted into imperialism.

Let us briefly consider this role of industrialization, not in arming the nation or in creating desires for markets abroad, but in breeding more pervasive disturbances within Japanese society.

By the 1920's Japan was beginning to experience the characteristic malaise of a modern industrial state. New values had begun to erode old loyalties and solidarities, especially in the cities. A new class consciousness bred social unrest, and called into doubt the old authoritarian concept of order. Such internal disorders were the more disturbing to guardians of Japanese tradition because they were paralleled by the appearance of Communist movements on the continent of Asia and

[7] *Essays in Our Changing Order*, New York, 1934, pp. 248-266.

by the reassertion of Russian power in the Far East under Bolshevik rule.

Meanwhile, World War I had left a heritage of inflationary maladjustments that plagued the Japanese economy for a decade. Agriculture in particular ceased to grow as rapidly as before. Industry failed lamentably to provide jobs for the swelling labor market. The worldwide depression struck Japan very heavily indeed. It bankrupted the countryside, reducing farm income by one half. And it discredited party government, with its plutocratic alliances among the *zaibatsu*.

Members of the military, first fanatic young lieutenant-colonels and later their more conservative seniors, capitalized on these frustrations and discontents and seized the helm of state. The military expansion that followed had its industrial motives and instruments, as noted earlier. Yet in its way it represented a nostalgic repudiation of Japan's industrial revolution and the changes it was bringing into Japanese society.

We need not suppose that the majority of citizens accepted literally such slogans as "bury the traitor millionaires," and "nationalize the land." They were aware, chiefly, that the army had the guns. In the end the slogans served hardly at all for economic or social reform. Even the state of Manchoukuo, where the military planners had a relatively free hand to develop state socialism, remained a jerry-built affair, little more than an adjunct of the Japanese war economy.

The disastrous ineptitude of the political leadership during this crisis was manifested not only by the zenophobia of its moving spirits, but by their almost universal irresponsibility. Even those high civil and military officials who did not share the illusions of the hotheads allowed themselves to be borne along toward war. In later self-justification, they could only plead resignation and helplessness. Professor Maruyama Masao, reflecting on the war crimes testimony, contrasts the Japanese leaders with the German Nazi leaders, who at least knew what they were doing and made no bones about it.[8] Once again, as in the Meiji Renovation, the decisive motives are found primarily in the sphere of political ideology and structure, only secondarily in the economic sphere. But the "double patriots" of the thirties, unhappily, while modeling themselves on their forebears,

[8] "Gunkoku Shihaisha no Seishin Keitai" (The Mentality of the Military Rulers), *Chōryū*, Vol. 4, No. 5, May 1949, pp. 15-37.

lacked entirely the Meiji quality of cool and calculating pragmatism. Bravado was no substitute for judgment, and they led their nation to disaster.

III. Economic Development and Political Democracy

It is a commonplace of history thus far that modern democracy has only established itself in societies that have shared the cultural heritage of Hebraic-Christian ideals and Greco-Roman thought, as mediated by the Renaissance, the Reformation, and the political revolutions of Western Europe.

Yet it is equally commonplace that economic progress in modern times tends to create social conditions favorable to the rise of an open, competitive political system, at least wherever it proceeds under non-totalitarian auspices. This is the assumption underlying the current hope that massive economic aid from the Western democracies will foster the spread of democratic institutions among the uncommitted nations, despite their authoritarian traditions.

As it happens, Japan is the only non-Western nation thus far to pass through an industrial revolution. Moreover, her experience now stretches back over nearly a century. It may therefore prove illuminating to ask whether the above propositions are substantiated by recent Japanese history.

RISE AND ECLIPSE OF LIBERALISM

The bare facts of Japanese political history since 1868 offer no conclusive evidence either way. For half a century she followed broadly the pattern of evolution already familiar in Western Europe. From the ruins of feudalism, a centralized nation-state was built by an autocratic bureaucracy invoking the quasi-religious sanctions of the throne. Almost at once there arose a political opposition which was styled liberal but was led mainly by ex-samurai demanding a share in power. Business interests played a humbler role at first than in Western Europe. But soon they too began to assert their interests through political alliances of one sort or another.

Before long the oligarchs were compelled to grant a series of concessions, culminating in the Constitution of 1889. Thereafter the new parliament, enjoying a qualified legislative power, was able increasingly to impose constitutional restraints on autocracy. Eventually, as the franchise broadened, it summoned the strength to institute more or less responsible cabinet government. There was nothing peculiarly

Japanese in all this, except that the pace of the developments was faster than it had been in the West.

At its heyday in the late twenties, constitutional government in Japan represented a shifting equilibrium of elitist elements. These vied for power in a cabinet still largely independent of popular control. At the top it was a pluralistic, even headless structure of power, now admitting limited representation of business interests, the professions, and agriculture, along with the military and civil bureaucrats and aristocrats around the throne. Universal manhood suffrage was enacted in 1925, and for six years the majority party in the Diet largely controlled the cabinet. Usually, though, it was not the verdict of the polls that made or unmade governments but the balance of forces within the oligarchy. When the crisis came in the wake of world depression, Japanese liberalism lacked the mass support which would have enabled it to withstand the counter-revolutionary assault of the militarists.

The continuity of events was violently interrupted for a generation. First there was the war regime, then the disaster of defeat, then the postwar Occupation. The Allied reforms of 1945-1952 sought forcibly to clear away immediate obstacles to the return to parliamentary rule, while introducing changes to democratize the underlying structure of power. These reforms set the stage for a decade of unexampled economic progress and political stability, following the end of the Occupation in 1952. Being imposed from the outside and from above, however, they were an exogenous force in politics. It is difficult now to say how far Japanese democracy in the fifties can be taken as a fulfillment of the twenties, or how durable it will prove in the sixties.

ECONOMIC REQUISITES OF POLITICAL PARTICIPATION

The bearing of economic development on the political process during the past century may be summarized in three propositions:

1. Rapid industrialization first strengthened authoritarian rule by providing new instruments for concentrating power. Then, as it went ahead under non-totalitarian auspices, it set in motion tendencies for a once narrow and autonomous elite to admit new elements to a share in government and to grow increasingly responsive to wider and more diverse interests.

2. Inasmuch as other circumstances have helped to shape the course of political development, however, no linear relation can be found between industrial progress and advances towards political de-

mocracy. Industrialization itself, while serving to reduce inequalities inherited from the old order, tended to build new concentrations of wealth and power.

3. A period of political instability set in after the early dominance of a narrow oligarchy began to be undermined by the demands and capabilities of new groups entering politics, but before the more affluent, pluralistic, and egalitarian society which was then emerging could attain unity by democratic means. Analogous periods of instability occur among modernizing nations today—usually at an earlier stage of national development than in Japan. Asoka Mehta suggests that nations enter this critical era when their incomes rise to perhaps $150 per year, and emerge from it only when they pass $300. To carry the argument this far, however, implies a degree of economic determinism for which there is no warrant in history.

Let us consider more closely the Japanese record.

As has been observed, the industrial revolution in Japan served to consolidate the Meiji state. A vigorous political elite sought first to strengthen the sinews of state power in order to defend the regime from threats both at home and abroad. Some of the new instruments of command, such as the armed forces, were held securely by the government itself. Others, like the banks and shipping companies, came increasingly to be controlled by financial magnates of the rising business class as the government gained confidence in the aims and capacities of these men. The new autocracy won acceptance among them by virtue of its manifest contributions to national power and to their economic and social opportunity. So much is familiar.

There followed in the natural course a process of development in which an increasing number of persons came to possess the economic and social prerequisites for participation in politics. This process is still under way as industrialization continues to work its transformation of society. As the decades have passed, indeed, the scale of economic development has exceeded the most extravagant anticipations of the Meiji elite. Per capita income increased at least three-fold from 1875 to 1935, and another 80 per cent by 1961. In half a century the Japanese have raised themselves well above the traditional poverty of the Orient, despite population growth and the wastes of armament, and despite gross inequalities in the distribution of wealth.

Today, as the Affluent Society of the East, Japan's consumption level approaches that of Italy, say, a decade ago. It is well above that of Turkey or Mexico. At current exchange rates, per capita income in 1961 was $399, and not far below $600 in real purchasing power; it is thus very nearly one quarter of the U.S. income level of $2,400.[9]

Other consequences of industrialization are equally visible. The percentage of the labor force employed mainly outside agriculture rose to 45 per cent by 1930, and 75 per cent by 1962. Urbanization, too, proceeded apace after 1900; as Clapham says of Germany, "the figures suggest a whole nation rushing to town." The rural population failed to grow at all after 1920. Today two out of three Japanese live in cities of 20,000 or more, and most farmers live within 50 miles of an industrial center with which they have easy communications. Japan offers a sharp contrast with countries like Turkey, and especially with great continental nations like India and China with their half-million villages remote from urban influence.

The resulting social changes spread unevenly and haltingly throughout the nation. The new impulses radiated out from the cities, especially from their industries and professions. The lagging response of agriculture and indigenous trades, especially in the remote areas to the north and south, gave rise to a pronounced dualism in Japanese life. Nevertheless, the processes of change have seeped slowly through the countryside. In central Honshū, along the coastal plains, industrialization has progressed to a point where the rural population itself might be called an urban peasantry. Here one is never long out of sight of a factory chimney, a power line, or a schoolhouse, and here a rising occupational and social mobility has spread new skills and aspirations and narrowed traditional gaps. In inter-personal relations the consequence is a gradual abandonment of ascriptive standards inherited from a hierarchic past in favor of a regard for individual achievement.

The spread of education has hastened this transition. By 1890 50 per cent of all young children had access to some schooling, thanks to the government's early commitment to universal public education. In 1908 six years of schooling became free as well as compulsory, at which point attendance rose above 90 per cent.[10] On this foundation an extensive pyramid of middle and higher education was reared. And, though education was long employed to instill political orthodoxy, it

[9] Based on rough estimates by the Economic Planning Agency, which put the yen's consumer purchasing-power parity in 1959 at 204 to the dollar, by comparison with the official exchange rate of 360. *Economic Survey of Japan (1959-1960)*, Tokyo, 1960, p. 205.

[10] Mombushō, *Gakusei Hachijō Nen Shi* (Eighty-Year History of the Educational System), Tokyo, 1954, pp. 1,036-1,037, Table 1.

served also to foster growth and change by diffusing initiative, skills, and property ownership among millions of small businessmen and farmers. Today virtually all Japanese over 25 have had some schooling; 28 per cent have finished junior high school. Outside the Western world only Israel can match this educational achievement.

Meanwhile the several mass media supply a network of communications exceptional among non-Western societies. In rural Japan, as in no other rural area in the East, the home radio has long since lost any novelty, and farmers subscribe to printed journals as a matter of course; by 1961 half of them also had television sets. Japanese newspapers have a gross circulation of 26 million, a ratio to total population (1/4) above that of the United States. The early spread of literacy is another reason why modernization has created less of a gulf between the urban elite and the common people in Japan than in so many developing countries today. Facilitating the emergence of leaders of middle rank, like prosperous peasants, tradesmen, foremen, and teachers, it has made communication between classes possible and thereby added tensile strength to a social structure that has had to bear a considerable strain.

These social concomitants of industrialization make for the democratization of politics except in systems ruthlessly despotic. The old order of things becomes less rigid. More and more people acquire the disposition, the skills, and the economic margin to take part in politics. Voluntary associations give expression to the varied interests of an industrialized community. Political competition arising from these interests calls parties and parliaments into being. The old lower classes at length gain a stake in the political order, and the former privileged classes grow less fearful of conceding them political power, especially if they themselves are permitted to retain certain symbols of status.[11]

All these tendencies are observable in Japanese society. The modern business elite was given a share in political power after 1890; a generation later came "Taishō democracy." The electorate was enlarged from 450,000 well-to-do taxpayers in 1890 to three million persons in 1919 and to all adult men in 1925. More significantly, the oligarchy governing Japan became more diverse and more sensitive to public needs and attitudes. Throughout Japanese society there was, in

[11] See S. M. Lipset, "Some Social Requisites of Democracy: Economic Development and Political Legitimacy," *American Political Science Review*, Vol. LIII, No. 1, March 1959, pp. 69-105.

R. P. Dore's phrase, "a general loss of submissiveness on the part of 'the lower orders'" that had deep-seated political implications.

THE INTERWAR CRISIS

Yet no arithmetical correlation exists between progress towards political democracy and such industrial and social changes. Economic well-being is usually a necessary condition of successful democracy but does not automatically engender it.

Two facts of modern Japanese history are noteworthy. In many modernizing nations today, the masses are demanding, and have commonly been granted, the right to participate in politics at an early stage in the national development. These demands arose much later in Japan.

Second, populist movements had hardly attained significant force before they were suppressed or perverted in the counter-revolution of the thirties. History teaches that great social issues are best resolved singly if the thread of legitimacy is to be preserved. In the years after the First World War three great issues arose simultaneously to divide Japanese society. Any one might perhaps have been handled peacefully, but in combination they proved too much.

The first of these was the crisis in relations between civil and military authority that came to a head in the late twenties. The Japanese constitution had somewhat evasively lodged ultimate power over both the army and the civil regime in the emperor. At the critical moment, the senior statesmen lacked the power and the courage to control the military themselves, and they advised the emperor not to involve his prestige in the struggle. The issue was hence left to force, which the army abundantly possessed.

A second issue coming insistently to the fore was the problem of a capitalist society generating inequalities in wealth and well-being. Giant combines towered over the hard-pressed small businessmen. Affluent landlords invoked police support to put down struggling tenant farmers. A new plutocracy that dominated the *Minseitō* and *Seiyūkai* in the Diet set its face against efforts to ameliorate the lot of slum dwellers and factory laborers. To feed social discontent still more, financial disorders inherited from World War I set in motion a wave of industrial mergers that further concentrated economic controls. The rationalization of industry limited further gains in urban job opportunities even before the Great Depression struck in 1929. And just at this time the long-sustained growth of agriculture slackened its pace.

The two issues mentioned were brought to a crisis by a third happening: the demand of the masses for a voice in politics. Following the rice riots of 1918, conservative politicians came reluctantly to consent to universal suffrage in the hope of staving off more radical demands. Popular forces were now to be reckoned with in a way that the Meiji oligarchs would never have understood and their successors were reluctant to concede.

The question of who should take part in politics was on its way to being resolved in the Western democracies before a proletarian demand for social justice became very urgent. Typically, too, the principle of civil supremacy over feudal military power then had long been established. In Japan these several contests coincided, or at least overlapped. And together they weakened the supports of constitutional government just when the military radicals—themselves influenced by these discontents—determined to assert themselves. Following their assassination of Premier Inukai in 1932, they attained power with remarkable ease. Once in the saddle they set all other issues aside with appeals to national security that ended by plunging the country into war.

POST-WAR EQUILIBRIUM: ECONOMIC PROGRESS AND POLITICAL CONSENSUS

Whether the subsequent decades have resolved these conflicts remains to be seen. Devastation and defeat are likely to break down the social fabric. In our time they have characteristically bred totalitarianism. Yet Japan's first decade following the conclusion of the Occupation in 1952 offers striking promise that she may prove an exception to the rule.

The war itself, with its disastrous outcome, discredited military ambition and military leadership for at least a generation. Yet it brought about no radical overthrow of the existing social and political order. Defeat also stripped away the preoccupation with a costly overseas empire, and unburdened the nation of heavy armament, leaving her free to devote her public funds to education, social security, and economic growth.

Finally, the war greatly reduced the large private fortunes, initiating a process continued by post-war inflation and taxation. Rent and interest paid to individuals amounted to only 8 per cent of national income in 1954-1959, as compared to 18 per cent before the war. Since property income is the chief source of inequality in a capitalistic society, this reduction testifies to a marked equalizing of wealth during the post-war generation.

In the second place, the Allied Occupation sought deliberately to introduce new standards of equality and a wider dispersal of initiative and responsibility in the whole society. The democratic Constitution of 1947, the political purges, and the other measures designed to create an unambiguous setting for free and responsible rule shifted political authority indisputably to the Diet, and lodged it specifically in the leaders of the majority party.

No less important to the new democracy were the series of economic and social reforms. The land-reform measure virtually expropriated landowners who were not themselves farmers in favor of their tenants. Tenanted land was reduced from 46 per cent to 9 per cent of the cultivated area. A "Wagner Act" legalized trade unions. Eight million workers are now organized to bargain collectively and to press their political demands with some vehemence. An attempt to break up the business monopolies, meeting with scanty support from the Japanese themselves, was left incomplete, but it proceeded far enough to make the Japanese economy more open and competitive. The growing scale and complexity of industry today preclude a return to the tight power concentrations of pre-war years, unless the authority of the government is invoked to compel it.

The retreat from these Occupation reforms since 1952 is surprisingly slight, despite modifications in such fields as local government, education, and industrial competition. The longer the innovations survive, the more fully they become domesticated. It may turn out that the Occupation accomplished at one stroke what could otherwise have been achieved only by long and bitter struggle.

The new political order has been enormously strengthened, in the third place, by the recent unexampled economic progress.[12] National income doubled during the years 1952-1961, repairing the lag of the previous decade. Living standards, rising by 6 per cent a year, attained levels 40 per cent higher than before the war. With this growth has come a marked equalization of personal opportunity. The business world is more diverse and flexible. Social security benefits, though still grossly inadequate, have been extended in some form to 48 million workers. Long-standing inequalities and inefficiencies in small-scale industry are being reduced by the upward pressure on sub-

[12] See the author's "Japan's 'New Capitalism,'" in a forthcoming volume, *The State and Economic Enterprise in Japan*, to be published by the Princeton University Press.

standard wages.[13] And the new affluence of the farming class, thanks to land reform, price supports, technical progress, and the passage of younger people out of agriculture into industrial life, is very striking. Today the distribution of household income in Japan is rather like that in the United States. Even worker families save 8-9 per cent of their income, and invest it widely in bank deposits and securities.

In politics, prosperity makes for a general complacency among the mass of voters. Election after election returns the conservative Liberal Democratic Party to power with comfortable majorities. It is hard to defeat a party that campaigns on a pledge to double the national income in ten years and that can point to the previous decade's record to support its promise.

More fundamentally, however, a diversity of organized interests now make their demands heard in politics. Unions, left and center, support chiefly the Socialist parties in the Diet, though some workers continue to vote conservative in company with most businessmen and farmers. Small business is becoming aware of its power as the parties compete for its vote. Farm sentiment, expressed through cooperatives and other associations, compels respect on issues like the price of rice or fertilizer. Even housewives and P.T.A.'s organize to protest the costs of living, a salary grab by local assemblymen, or traffic accidents to children. On specific issues of this kind, the citizenry is more articulate than ever before. Confronting major national problems like foreign policy or minimum wages, however, the general public still relegates decisions to the interests involved or to ideologists of the left and right. And little countervailing power is yet at the disposal of groups that remain at a political disadvantage.

The military having been displaced, and the civil service rendered more responsive to the Diet, the business community has become the most powerful class in Japanese affairs through its influence in party politics and the ministries. Though it does not always have its way, and is internally divided, it is the mainstay of the Liberal Democrats, who in turn have a two-thirds majority in the Diet, and exercises a preponderant influence especially on economic policies.

[13] While a general wage disparity remains, young workers entering the job market in 1962 can command as much from small enterprises as from large. Regional disparities in income, however, are being widened by the industrial boom in the favored areas. The result is a surge of people toward these areas that reduced the population of seven low-income prefectures by 2.5 million people from 1955 to 1960. Tokyo alone absorbed a million, adding still further to its acute congestion. Economic Planning Agency, *Economic Survey of Japan (1960-1961)*, Tokyo, 1961, pp. 51, 315.

143

The Liberal Democratic Party supplies the means of cooperation between the business community and the bureaucratic elite. Many of its leaders are former career officials who turned to party politics after the war. Yet, while dominated by this conservative alliance at the top, the party has sponsored a wide range of socialistic welfare measures as the condition of its supremacy. It is under pressure today as never before to justify itself in the face of attacks from a vigilant left.

The Socialists, for their part, remain thus far a minority. In election after election they have failed to win more than about one-third of the seats in the Diet. Factionalism and a lack of money hamper them; and so, very decisively, does their refusal to abandon the ideological battles of classical Marxism in favor of a more conciliatory appeal to the middle class. Though furnishing no effective counterweight to the conservatives, they manage, in their somewhat rowdy way, to exert an influence on legislation beyond their voting strength. And they draw confidence from the thought that the generation now growing up, though it aspires less to revolution than to middle-class affluence, votes well to the left of its elders.

Three issues worry thoughtful Japanese when they view the future. One is the economic prospect. Will growth continue in such a way as to ease the tensions of industrial conflict, to secure a greater degree of consensus between the two parties, and to fulfill the rising material expectations of young Japanese? Or will the great interest groups become locked in legislative combat and increasingly throw off the restraints of reason and conscience, inviting the return of authoritarian rule?

Conditioning the economic outlook is international insecurity, political as well as economic. Among the issues dividing right and left nothing provokes more violence than foreign policy. It was the U.S. Security Treaty that brought on the riots of 1960. It is Article IX of the Constitution renouncing an armed force that lends fervor to the struggle over constitutional revision. The principal anxieties of the Japanese as a nation reside today, as during most of the past century, in the realm of foreign relations.

Finally, one must ask whether the formal subscription to democracy is yet more than superficial. When the Socialist party readily repudiates parliamentary process and retaliatory violence bursts out among ultra-nationalists, the general public stands apathetically by. One suspects that the average citizen has only a fleeting concept of his responsibility to the democratic state. The instigators of the recent "mass struggles" hail them as tokens of democracy coming of age. Others see in them a portent of totalitarianism. Many members of the older generation lament the departure of the oligarchs "who knew what was good for the country" and settled matters without unseemly riots or even majority votes.

The issues, in short, have not changed. They are the same ones that parliamentary government once failed to resolve in pre-war Japan. Yet the forces of democracy have clearly advanced far beyond where they were a generation ago. We may hope that political stability, achieved in Meiji times by autocracy, will in this industrial age become firmly rooted in the responsible consent of the governed. To attain this end, Japan will need to live in a world order that encourages her to preserve the integrity of civil rule and the supremacy of peaceful pursuits.

B. TURKEY

PETER F. SUGAR

I. Introduction

Since 1946 many excellent studies have been devoted to the political and economic problems of "underdeveloped" countries. In these works, words like "Westernization" and "modernization" are used repeatedly, always carrying the connotation of progress. In economics, the additional concepts of growth and industrialization are frequently appealed to, and they too stand for progress. Sometimes several terms, like industrialization, Westernization, and modernization, are treated as synonyms.

There is nothing wrong with these terms themselves. The works in which they are used and the theories based on them have made valuable contributions to our knowledge of the process of change in society. Yet a great many questions remain. How do we define and measure modernization, Westernization, and progress? The criteria of persons who have confronted these and other such questions are normally derived from the values and historical experience of the Western world. Yet, with a relatively few exceptions—like Latin America, Eastern Europe, Spain, and Portugal—"underdeveloped" countries are the heirs of other traditions, and many positively reject Western values. And even if developing societies become disposed to measure progress in some part by Western economic and ideological standards, they are not necessarily right. If we could compute the price sometimes paid for economic progress in cultural values and social stability, we might easily wind up with an unfavorable balance sheet. It is possible, even, that quantitative (technological) progress quite normally entails qualitative (cultural) regression.

For the reasons indicated "development" is a more satisfactory word for social change than "progress." Any change, of whatever sort and in whatever period of history, represents a "development." The word is therefore happily neutral.

Observing economic and political developments in several parts of the world, we can easily distinguish some countries in which development occurred "organically" and others in which it was "induced." The nations in these two categories have changed for different reasons, at different times, and in different manners.

146

In Western Europe, a so-called modern or Western society developed "organically." The process began in the late Middle Ages with the disintegration of feudal society and the revival of trade and of town life, and early involved the growth of manufacture. This development created a new force in society, the citizen or urban dweller, who derived such political power as he possessed from his economic pursuits. The bourgeois needed freedom and security to carry on his commerce, and he therefore lent his support to the man best able to grant them, the ruler. Out of this alliance the modern state was born. The relationship of rulers and citizenry thereafter became subject to certain tensions which culminated in the great revolutions at the end of the eighteenth century and in the final triumph of the bourgeoisie. This organic development began then, with (1) a change in economic activities leading first to (2) the emergence of a new force in society, the bourgeoisie, and then, through the cooperation of this new interest with the ruler, to (3) the establishment of the centralized state. While the ruler's aims were not identical with those of the urban merchants and craftsmen, he would have been feeble indeed without their support, and he purchased this by consenting to charters and privileges guaranteeing freedom of person and of economic activity. Centuries later, when the bourgeoisie wanted to extend its power still further at the expense of the ruler and successfully carried out the revolutions already mentioned, there at length occurred (4) the establishment of constitutional government. Such government conformed to the final middle-class desideratum: a well-regulated but individualistic society.

This entire development took centuries. Western Europe, left largely to its own devices after the last waves of the Great Migration had broken over it, took advantage of the long respite to develop wholly in its own way. The other parts of the world either did not have a sufficiently long respite from outside intervention to develop independent and distinctive polities or developed in directions which were better suited to local conditions, but which failed to attain a political power and ideological assurance comparable to those of the Western world. The resulting disparity of power between societies and regions grew steadily after the fifteenth century until at length the non-Western societies decided that they must imitate the West in order to survive.

All recent "induced" developments—from the time of Peter the Great to that of Nasser, Mao, and Nkrumah—have had as their immediate purpose the attainment of power comparable to that of the Western world. Viewed in this light, all Westernizers are in a manner anti-Western: they hope to eliminate all real or imaginary manifestations of Western power from their countries or regions.

We find other common features when we look at the numerous "induced" developments. Westernization always implies some departure from social, economic, and political patterns of life which the great majority of the people are accustomed to and in some measure cherish. The development has to be induced, therefore, by a "leader" or "leaders" who both perceive the powerlessness of their society and are able to force that society to change against its will. Before such leaders begin their work, furthermore, they must possess themselves of means for enforcing their will. The usual instrument is a bureaucracy which has few roots in earlier administrative structures and which is therefore amenable to change.

In sum, the development of countries hastily catching up, unlike the "organic" growth of Western Europe, must begin with the transformation of the political structure. Political power will first shift internally in such countries, without altering their power position in relation to nations or other regions. To achieve this, a second and much more thorough change is required. This further development begins with the leaders' upsetting, with the help of the new bureaucracy, the political stability of the region; this, be it noted, is what happens even when the new political masters claim that economic change alone is their goal. They may even claim that their reforms are designed to conserve the old values of the society. That was the customary cry in the Ottoman Empire in the late eighteenth and early nineteenth centuries, and it is the rationalization used by the Arab leadership today. The characteristic modern result of such rationalization is a new economic nationalism dressed up in a traditional garb.

When we investigate developments artificially fostered we find again that economic change follows political change and is initiated at least in part by the government. The time that elapses before this new economy becomes an "organic" part of the society into which it was introduced depends both on the technical and economic competence of those holding political power, and on the capacity of the population at large for making significant economic decisions. An important although not necessarily numerous middle class emerges either simultaneously with the "naturalization" of the new economy or just a few years before it. Depending on circumstances too complex to analyze here, the next phase of the national development will vary greatly. We have already had examples, including that of Turkey during the last years of the Menderes regime, of this new middle class opposing the government. But we have not yet seen enough of these conflicts fully resolved to generalize concerning their outcome.

We need not here consider the differences that, within this general framework, give the several developmental efforts their individual character. That these exist becomes evident when we think of such diverse men as Nasser, Mao, and Nkrumah. Let us generalize merely, that a period of "induced" development requires, in order of time, (1) an outside stimulus, usually in the form of overwhelming power; (2) the emergence of a leader (or leaders) who seek to elevate their nation to a position of like power; (3) the creation of a new bureaucracy and a change in the political structure; (4) economic change, planned and in part executed by the central government; and (5) the emergence of a middle class followed by a variety of further expressions of collective economic interest.

This sequence is on its face radically different from that detailed for societies developing organically.

We may now proceed to the specific history of development in the Ottoman Empire and Republican Turkey—a history which began with the reign of Sultan Selim III (1789-1807) and is far from terminated. In reviewing the component periods of this history we shall briefly note the elements they have in common with comparable periods elsewhere, but shall leave detailed analogies to occur to the reader.

II. Ottoman Reforms, 1789-1877

The Ottoman Empire is an excellent example of a state that first undertook reforms in order to reverse an unfavorable balance of power. The Ottoman state, which grew and prospered by the sword, could shrug off the difficulties it faced in the late sixteenth and seventeenth centuries because they did not presage ultimate military disaster. It is a sign of the conservatism of the Ottoman state that the first reformer, Selim III, emerged a full ninety years after the conclusion of the Peace of Karlowitz (1699), in which, for the first time since the battle of Ankara in 1402, the Ottomans had had to acknowledge military defeat.

Selim III was an unexceptionable ruler of the old school. His intention was to restore the military supremacy of his country so that it might reoccupy lost territories and conquer new ones for the Muslim cause; he sought to borrow military know-how from the West only to turn it against the Occident. He was intelligent enough to see, however, that this borrowing could not be limited to the purchase of arms and the hiring of a few drillmasters. Armorers, armament works, and some specialized schools[1] were included in his plans. He sought to achieve, at least for the military, the largest possible measure of independence. But Ottoman society at the turn of the eighteenth century found even this relatively minor innovation intolerable, and he himself paid with his life for his ventures in reform.

When we speak of Ottoman society we refer to the small upper layer of the population which by virtue of its culture, education, or position constituted the Ottoman elite. These men formed the palace advisors, served in the bureaucracy or the military, or belonged to the *ulema* (the learned men) who staffed the imperial religious-legal-educational institutions of the empire. Their education, values, and way of life made them in their own esteem the only persons in the empire deserving the name of Ottoman.[2]

It was the fact and the sense of their community as Ottomans which qualified the members of this class for entrance into one of the branches of the imperial administration. Advancement thereafter followed in accordance with rather rigidly established, although unwritten, rules. Each administrative branch had its rights and privileges

---

[1] The first school established to aid military reform was the School of Geometry, the Hendeshane, organized by the French Count de Bonneval in 1734 during the reign of Sultan Mahmud I (1730-1754). Under Mustafa III (1757-1774) a school of mathematics for naval officers was organized by another Frenchman, Baron de Tott. Thus when he established special schools for the military, Selim III could already point to some precedents. For his and Mahmud II's schools see Bernard Lewis, *The Emergence of Modern Turkey*, London-New York-Toronto, 1961, pp. 58, 82-85.

[2] I shall refer to this group in this essay as the professional Ottomans. Muslims, but not necessarily Turkish in origin, this very small group of men, born or recruited into the group from the Muslim or non-Muslim population, was the only politically significant element in the empire. Whether holding office or not, its members were bound together by their specific education, their knowledge of the artificial bureaucratic language, Muslim orthodoxy, loyalty to the sultan, and many other similar factors adding up to a specific and characteristic *Weltanschauung*. Other expressions which will be used—Old Ottoman, Young Ottoman, and Young Turk—denote increasing degrees of deviation from the old *Weltanschauung* of the professional Ottoman. The Old Ottomans served Mahmud II and were prominent in the early Tanzimat period as reforming bureaucrats. They represent a transition between the professional Ottomans' conservatism and the Young Ottomans' radicalism. The latter, a rather well-known group, the left wing of the bureaucracy, was responsible for the 1876 Constitution and fathered the even better known Young Turkish movement which came to power in 1908. All these groups will be discussed at some length later in this essay.

which, despite his theoretical omnipotence, the sultan could not violate. If in the empire as a whole these Ottomans represented a small oligarchy, within their ranks we find something like checks and balances —a limited constitutionalism, very nearly, in which everyone's functional and corporate, although not private, rights were respected even by the sultan.

Selim's reforms violated the rights of the military and the *ulema* in particular, but an insult to one element of the old order was an insult to all. When Selim turned to the West for models he admitted, in spite of his professed orthodoxy, that Ottoman values were not perfect. This admission no self-respecting Ottoman could tolerate, for it reflected on his whole style of life, including his religion.

Selim suffered from a lack of any machinery to protect him and to carry out his reform. His successor, Mahmud II (1808-1839), would have shared Selim's fate but for two circumstances. He was the last living male member of the ruling family, and he had both good political sense and much patience. His aim was that of his cousin and teacher: to regain the position of power which the empire had lost. But he learned from Selim's fate and realized that in seeking that end he could not employ the existing state machinery. It had to be destroyed and replaced by instruments of government which he himself controlled. In technical terms, he had to replace oligarchic constitutionalism with absolutism. He had, in particular, to organize his own bureaucratic and military followers, to place them in key positions, and to dissolve the internal ties that gave the ruling institutions their traditional autonomy.

Mahmud spent the major portion of his reign building up a personal following and devoted to straightforward reform only the years from 1826-1839, after the destruction of the Janissaries. For the Janissaries, once the backbone of the Ottoman army, had become, by the end of the eighteenth century, a hereditary armed band, closely allied with various ultra-conservative elements and able to terrorize both the capital and the provinces. Arnold Toynbee has described Mustafa Kemal's work as an effort "to extricate the Turkish nation from the ruins of the Ottoman Empire, and to set this nation on its feet again by putting it through a 'totalitarian' conversion from a hereditary Islamic to a newfangled way of life."[3] In this brief evaluation of Atatürk, Toynbee further provides us with an evaluation of that entire development that began with Mahmud II. Selim

[3] *The Spectator*, Vol. CLXI, No. 5760, November 18, 1939, p. 580.

fell victim to an Islamic-Ottoman tradition embodied in a theoretically absolute but practically limited monarchy. Mahmud II destroyed the political framework of this society, but was unable to establish total power. In the last ninety years, the seeds which Mahmud had sown at length bore fruit, and the Turks lived under absolute masters, Abdülhamid II and Mustafa Kemal.

The period of Turkish history from 1789 to the fall of the Janissaries represents the first two phases of "induced" modernization: the appearance first of an external threat and then of a leader preparing to meet it. In 1826 began a second period, corresponding to the third and fourth phases of development, which entail revisions first of the national polity and then of the economy. There was not immediately the complex interaction we expect between economic and political change. The political changes—chiefly devoted to supplying the necessary civil and military servants of the state—had to come first.

The death of Mahmud II was followed by the Tanzimat period, extending until the Russo-Ottoman War of 1877-1878. It was in 1878 that Abdülhamid II, then in the second year of his reign, suspended the Constitution of 1876, which, in one sense, was the culmination of the Tanzimat period. Historians have debated whether the Tanzimat reforms represented a sincere attempt to improve the condition of the state and its people, or were mere window-dressing designed to please the Western powers on whom the Ottomans relied as a counterweight to Russia. Most authorities incline to the latter view. Enough changes were nevertheless effected to make a return to the past impossible. The old empire was gone forever. It is here significant that, during those nearly forty years, the government became increasingly centralized, with power concentrated in the hand of a steadily decreasing number of people within a steadily growing bureaucracy.

This bureaucracy was very different from the one Mahmud had destroyed. It did not enjoy the same position and privileges, and the former avenues of advancement within it had also been eliminated. The surest road to advancement had become a Westernized education or at least the knowledge of French or some other Western language. Yet the members of this bureaucracy were drawn from the Ottoman class and retained the values of that class. The name given to the period which this new bureaucracy dominated—Tanzimat, renovation or reordering—itself testifies to a nostalgia for the past. The empire was to be recreated in its pristine form, though admittedly with the help of new means; it was not to be remolded in the image of Europe. Even Ahmed Cevdet Pasha (1822-1895), the legal and educational reformer whose work did more to Westernize the Ottoman Empire than did the efforts of the various politicians, was an old-fashioned Ottoman trained as an *alim* (a member of the *ulema*).

The first generation of Tanzimat bureaucracy had sought legal and educational as well as military and political reforms, but the problem of economic growth did not attract official attention before the middle of the nineteenth century. Even among the second generation of Tanzimat men we cannot find a single one who really had a clear understanding of economic issues or a sincere interest in them. Economic affairs did not enter into the traditional education of the Ottoman and were entrusted mainly to the Christian and Jewish subjects of the state—to second-class citizens, that is, whose modes of livelihood were incompatible with the Ottoman way of life. There were millions of Muslims, it is true, who tilled the soil, raised animals, and worked as artisans. But the elite looked down on these too. And not even the lower-class Muslims exercised much commercial initiative in the nineteenth century. There did not arise from any quarter a Muslim bourgeoisie from which economists could have been recruited for the bureaucracy. The absence of a Muslim-Ottoman and later a Turkish middle class earning its livelihood in trade, manufacture, communications, or even the professions was a serious barrier to economic growth as late as during the early days of the republic.

The occupations named were the domain of the minorities, who performed many services but could not conceivably be admitted to power in the central government. We may also safely assume that by the middle of the nineteenth century members of this economically important segment of these minorities would have refused administrative appointments in any event. By then they had escaped from the jurisdiction of the state in which they lived and formed a discrete group, the "Levantines."

The emergence of the Levantines was one of the results of the Capitulations. We need not trace the history of those treaties at length here. The first Capitulations significant to this study were those granted to France in 1740 by Mahmud I, upon which the provisions of subsequent treaties with France and other powers were based. The most important privileges granted to foreign powers in these treaties were freedom of religion and movement, inviolability of person and domicile, exemption from taxes, consular jurisdiction, and the limitation of customs duties to 3 per cent ad valorem on goods imported into the Ottoman Empire. The only important subsequent change was introduced in the British Capitulations of 1838 (aimed mainly at Muhammad Ali of Egypt), which granted tax exemptions not only from levies imposed by the sultan but also from those imposed by the various provincial governors.

When Mehmed II and Süleyman I signed Capitulations with Western states, they entered into agreements accommodating both Western and Ottoman practices. European feudal law was personal law and not territorial, whereas Ottoman practice gave each millet its own specific law. The minorities of the Ottoman Empire, originally defined solely as adherents of minority religions, were organized in millets with broad powers to regulate their own affairs. For the early sultans the Capitulations represented merely the extension of the millet system to foreigners. By the eighteenth century the legal situation had changed drastically in Western Europe, but not in the Ottoman Empire. The Ottoman reverence for precedent, as well as the weakened condition of the Ottoman government, enabled the Western powers to obtain as unilateral rights in the modern treaties what had been reciprocal privileges in the earlier ones. By sheer virtue of their power the Western states were further able to extend their privileges beyond those granted them by the Capitulations. We can find, for example, no provision in these agreements establishing the various foreign post offices, nor any anticipating the creation of the Levantine group.

The Levantines came into being because the Ottomans were helpless to prevent the Great Powers from extending their privileges arbitrarily. Originally the Capitulations covered only citizens of foreign states. Then the privileges and immunities which they conferred were expanded to cover, first, non-Muslim Ottoman subjects working for foreign embassies and consulates, then a number of monasteries and religious communities, and finally those native protégés of ambassadors and consuls known as *berat* holders. The *berats* were the documents issued by diplomats to their clients certifying that they were under foreign diplomatic protection. When the immunities conferred by the *berats* became hereditary, the Levantine class was born. The extent of *berat*-granting can be indicated by one example. By the end of the 1700's Austria had 200,000 subjects in Moldavia and 60,000 in Wallachia, all of whom exchanged their Austrian *berats* for Russian when Russian influence became predominant in the principalities.

The Capitulations have been justly blamed for many of the empire's economic problems. Even the republic suffered from them. But one early effect of the Capitulations is seldom stressed strongly enough. Up to at least the middle of the nineteenth century they hardly hampered economic growth, for those interested in commerce or finance—foreigners and members of the minority groups—merely performed under the Capitulations functions which they would have performed anyway. Coupling economic and extraterritorial privileges, these treaties transformed the economically active segment of the minorities into the protégés of foreign nations, who owned no loyalty to the government of the empire and shared none of their economic knowledge and experience with it. In sum, Capitulations alienated whatever middle class had been developing in the empire.

The first Ottoman attack directed against the Capitulations was hence very reasonably aimed less at the economic clauses of those agreements than at the abuse of berat-granting. In 1863 the Great Powers finally agreed to refrain from issuing any more of these letters of protection but insisted that families already subject to their jurisdiction retain their rights. Abuses must have occurred even after that date, however, for in 1869 the government issued a decree stipulating that Ottoman subjects who wanted to change their nationality had to leave the country and would not be permitted to return. While this restriction of the power of the foreign states must have given the Ottomans some satisfaction, it by no means helped Ottoman subjects to compete with berat holders—the most desirable consummation.

Even though the authorities began to realize the importance of economic progress during the second half of the Tanzimat period, actual economic development in the empire was negligible and was limited either to foreign enterprises or to those of the government. In Turkey proper, progress was limited largely to public utilities in Istanbul, which were foreign creations and cost the government rather dearly in concessions and privileges granted to the entrepreneurs. As a result of the increasing needs of the reforming state, inept fiscal administration, an archaic tax structure, and the irresponsible spending of the Sultan Abdülaziz (1861-1876), the Ottoman state soon found financial difficulties further hampering its economic activities.

These difficulties, as is well known, led to a series of foreign loans, increasing indebtedness, and finally, in 1881, to the establishment of the Council of Administration of the Ottoman Public Debt. On the

ECONOMIC AND POLITICAL MODERNIZATION

eve of World War I this administration managed a debt of 716 million dollars. France was the largest creditor (with claims to about 60 per cent of this amount), followed by Germany (20 per cent), and Britain (15 per cent). During the 1911-1912 fiscal year 30.7 per cent of the Ottoman Empire's budget was earmarked for payments to the Administration of the Public Debt. Despite these payments, the debt increased steadily, new loans being required to cover budgetary deficits which, during the reign of Abdülhamid II (1876-1909), averaged 13 million dollars yearly.

Even these few figures indicate the magnitude of the financial problems confronting the Ottoman government and explain why economic progress, depending as it did on government investment, was extremely slow. The government's main task, even before the establishment of the Public Debt Administration and increasingly after 1881, was to find new sources of income to balance the budget and pay its debts. The introduction of various state monopolies and the attempt to secure from the capitulary powers a revision of the customs tariffs were directed to this end. We might generalize that the Capitulations, the creation of the Levantine group, and the public debt collectively represented the barrier to economic development which the Tanzimat statesmen and their successors could not surmount. Nor did Ottoman officials attack that problem directly. They secured the abolition of berat-granting chiefly to gratify an incipient nationalistic prejudice against the Levantines: their request for higher customs rates was dictated merely by fiscal considerations.

The professional Ottomans, in power until 1826, had no interest in or understanding of economic issues. The rulers of Turkey from 1826 to 1877, however, had at least some understanding of economics as a factor in the total power of a nation. In 1831 Mahmud II abolished the timars, the old feudal holdings, and after the destruction of the Janissaries placed the evkaf estates (property of the Muslim religious institutions) under the management of the government. These reforms were designed chiefly to weaken the power of the sultan's main opponents, the landowners, and the ulema. Yet the income which they made available was unfortunately not used for economic reform. The peasants continued to live and work as they had for centuries, though paying their taxes and dues to tax-farmers instead of to ecclesiastical or lay landlords.

The economic views of the Young Ottomans were far more progressive. These men, though the sons and grandsons of the professional Ottomans, had received Western educations and were ready to transform the empire into a European state. They possessed a real measure of power only during the short and troubled months (1876-1877) when Midhat Pasha served as Grand Vezir, however, and are here interesting primarily as a segment of the upper class possessing a rather clear view of economic matters and anticipating some of the ideas of the Young Turks.

III. The Hamidian and Young Turk Periods

The development occurring between the accession of Selim III and the close of the Tanzimat period set the pattern for the remaining years of the empire and to a certain extent for the republic. The expanding bureaucracy became increasingly centralized, its power being wielded by a steadily diminishing number of persons within it. The influence of this shrinking power elite spread throughout the life of the state. It was nevertheless unable to cope with economic and fiscal problems, being hampered—though increasingly less as time passed—by its traditional value system and by the difficulties growing out of the Capitulations. The government suffered, finally, from a lack of economic leadership, and the Muslim-Ottoman population failed to produce a class of entrepreneurs. These conditions persisted throughout the Hamidian and Young Turk periods, to which, therefore, we need devote less attention than we did to the preceding era.

The revision of the customs rates may be taken to usher in the period following the Tanzimat. The tariffs were increased from 3 per cent to 5 per cent, then to 8 per cent, and finally, in 1907, to 11 per cent. But the increased revenue did not help lessen the financial embarrassment of the government, because customs revenues together with those of the imperial monopolies (salt in 1862, tobacco in 1874, and gunpowder in 1875), were collected by the Administration of the Public Debt. As the introduction of the monopolies indicates, the Ottoman Empire borrowed some European fiscal practices. It could not, however, imitate the West in tax reforms, which might have increased revenues more than did all the other measures together. Most of the evkaf and agricultural income was already state-controlled. The taxable enterprises paid higher taxes already, often more than they could afford to pay without impairing their future usefulness as tax sources, and the creation of further such enterprises was not possible in a state in which economic activity was at best stagnant. The capital formed in the Ottoman Empire, whether by foreigners, Levantines, or Muslim landlords, was exported either directly or through the purchase of foreign goods. Such of it as remained in the empire went for the construction of homes or villas in the capital or the surrounding countryside. And if, in spite of all its difficulties, the state managed to increase its revenues, these were absorbed by the expenses of the increasingly complex Hamidian absolutist machinery.

Some economic development did take place during Abdülhamid's reign. In addition to public utilities, harbor facilities and railroads were constructed. But the railroads, except for the economically insignificant Hijaz line, were built and operated by foreign concessionaires,[4] who exacted a heavy price from the Ottoman treasury for every kilometer constructed, and often artificially lengthened the track mileage by selecting circuitous routes. The building companies also acquired exploitation rights along the lines. And the profit which the railroads finally made once again left the country.

Of all the economic developments taking place during the reign of Abdülhamid II only the construction of the railroads had real

[4] According to "Nos Nouvelles Voies Ferrées," *La Turquie Kemaliste*, Ankara, October 1934, p. 11, the republic inherited 2,455 miles (4,083 kms.) of track. The following are specifically identified in G. B. Ravndal, *Turkey, A Commercial and Industrial Handbook*, U.S. Department of Commerce, Bureau of Foreign and Domestic Commerce, Trade Promotion Series, No. 28, Washington, 1926, pp. 46-53.

1. Ottoman construction		
Haydarpaşa-İzmit*	56 miles opened in 1871	
2. British built and managed		
İzmir-Aydın	" " 1866	
İsmir-Kasaba	" " 1866	
Kasaba-Alaşehir	664 " " " 1875	
Mersin-Adana**	" " 1886	
Manisa-Afyonkarahisar	" " stages, 1890-1912	
3. French built and managed		
Mudanya-Bursa	26 miles opened in 1892	
4. German built and managed†		
Konya-Aleppo (mainly in Turkey)	650 " " " stages, 1904-1918	
5. International companies‡		
(mainly French capital)		
Istanbul-Lüleburgaz	174 " " " 1888	
İzmit-Ankara	303 " " " 1892	
Eskişehir-Konya	276 " " " 1896	

* Placed under British management in 1880.
** Management transferred to the French in 1896 and then, in 1908, to the Germans.
† In this construction French capital also participated.
‡ The companies involved were: in European Turkey the S. A. des Chemins de Fer Orientaux and in Anatolia La Société des Chemins de Fer Ottomans d'Anatolie.

importance. The political innovations during the same years were more significant. In Abdülhamid II the Ottoman Empire acquired an absolute ruler, who brought to a culmination the long centralizing process which had begun in the days of Selim III. Abdülhamid was a patriot in that he sought to improve the international position of his state, but he disliked the modes of change embraced during the Tanzimat period and those later advocated by the Young Ottomans and still later the Young Turks. Even the tradition-bound old Ottomans deplored his one-man rule; they had in any case abdicated political power and lived in the nostalgic retirement described so well by Harrison G. Dwight in *Stamboul Nights*.[5] The Young Ottomans lived in exile. The number of persons opportunistic enough to work for the sultan was finally very small.

The opportunists shared the administration with a new group, not necessarily Turkish although Muslim, which executed the orders of Abdülhamid, but did not make policy. The people of this rootless and isolated group, lacking contact even with the numerically small upper class, were as much prisoners in their offices as Abdülhamid was in Yıldız Palace. The statesmen of the Tanzimat period, though often unpopular because of their innovations, were at least respected by virtue of the prestige attaching to their origin, position, or personality. Abdülhamid's bureaucrats were simply detested. And the wily sultan must have evaluated the popularity of his servants correctly, for he very quickly capitulated before the Young Turks in 1908. In Abdülhamid's police state the centuries-old Ottoman administration finally collapsed, clearing the way for new experiments under the Young Turks and the Republic.

The Young Turks were a new class of leaders. The work "Turk" had for them the nationalistic connotations we associate with "Englishman" or "Frenchman." While they were dedicated to building a modern Turkish state, they were Westernized enough to advocate, at least until 1911, equal rights for the minorities. But the Western garb in which they paraded did not quite fit, and under the stress of Abdülhamid's machinations, war with Italy, and the Balkan wars, a part of it was exchanged for old Ottoman and Hamidian dress. Abdülhamid's dictatorship was replaced by that of the Young Turk triumvirate of Enver, Cemal, and Talât Pashas, and the minorities were once again excluded from power, although in the name of Pan-

---

[5] Garden City, 1922.

Turanism rather than of Pan-Islam. The bureaucracy continued passively to execute orders.

If in politics the Young Turks soon reverted to "Ottoman" or "Hamidian" ways, their economic outlook differed from that of their predecessors. They understood the economic foundations of national power and realized that the state, which should have taken the lead in economic development, was in no financial position to do so. When they looked to the private sector of the economy they realized that the industrial products imported from Europe had deprived native craftsmen of their livelihood and forced them to revert to agriculture. The few remaining industrial establishments, almost entirely foreign-owned, processed chiefly agricultural products and raw materials for export. The foreign banks operating in the Ottoman Empire invested almost exclusively in utilities and in the operations of the Public Debt Administration.

The Young Turks began to plan and to execute economic projects on a respectable scale. To stimulate economic enterprise they passed in 1909, and revised in 1915, a Law for the Encouragement of Industry. By 1915 the seven largest cities boasted 282 industrial establishments employing more than five workers each and a total of 14,060 laborers. Of these enterprises 55 per cent were in Istanbul and 81 per cent were privately owned. Although the war permitted the government to replace the capitulary custom tariffs with differentiated and specific rates, industrial production (with the exception of alcoholic beverages and fish canning) decreased sharply during the war because "any mention of economic considerations was looked upon by them [the country's leaders during the war] as a sort of dangerous sentimentalism."[6] Within the government, however, an important development occurred. The governmental machinery for economic planning and control—which became so important in the days of the republic—was perfected during the war years.

That the Young Turks reverted so easily to absolutism is not astonishing. Though they were not old-fashioned Ottomans themselves, they were trained in schools in which some of the old values were still conserved. During their ten years in power they confronted a revolution and four wars, all demanding strong centralized leadership. This leadership the Young Turks—themselves mainly soldiers and possessing an instinct for discipline—consented to supply. And their record, though poor overall, is not without achievements. They were the first

[6] Ahmed Emin (Yalman), *Turkey in the World War*, New Haven, 1930, p. 107.

rulers of the Ottoman Empire to issue industrial legislation and to recognize the political importance of economic considerations. And they made the all-important decision to abandon an Ottoman-Islamic approach to politics and adopted Turkish nationalism in its place. Their conscientious and not ineffectual labors certainly made easier the later monumental task of Atatürk, one of their number.

IV. From Empire to Republic

Let us summarily skip the years that elapsed between the signing of the armistice at Mudros, on October 30, 1918, and that of the Peace Treaty of Lausanne on July 24, 1923. In times of war, civil war, and competing governments, we are unlikely to find—and in Turkey we do not find—significant economic development.

In the political realm, as we know, important changes occurred during that period. In January of 1921 the revolutionary National Assembly declared the nation sovereign, and in November of 1922 proclaimed the end of the sultanate. Some three months after the signing of the Treaty of Lausanne, which readmitted the country into the international family, the Assembly proclaimed the republic. These events we should remember, but need not dwell upon.

The remnants of the old Ottoman society, which sided with the sultan between 1918 and 1922, either left with their sovereign or disappeared from public life. Yet when the new administration replaced the old, a good number of the same men sat behind the desks in the various offices. To the simple Anatolian, the government as a whole must have looked rather familiar. It was led by a hero, even if not an hereditary one. Surrounding him, the peasant saw men not unlike those he was used to finding about his leader: members of the *ulema*, bureaucrats, and soldiers.[7] The simple men, the majority of citizens, could feel almost at home in the new state.

In one sense such persons were right; in another they were wrong. They were right in perceiving that the structure and composition of the republican government were not altogether novel, and that the government remained monolithic and arbitrary in spirit. They were wrong in equating the new absolutism with the old and in identifying

[7] In the National Assembly which met in April 1920 we find among the deputies 92 who were members of the just dissolved last Ottoman parliament. Of the deputies 125 were civil servants, 13 municipal officials, 53 soldiers, 53 who belonged to the *ulema*, and 5 tribal chiefs. Together they made up two-thirds of the assembly's membership. Quoted by Lewis, *op.cit.*, p. 360 from Tarık Tunaya, *Türkiye Büyük Millet Meclisi Hükümetinin Kuruluşu ve Siyasî Karakteri*, Istanbul, n.d., p. 5.

the new military-bureaucratic elite with their predecessors, for the government of the republic sought not defensive revision but a total transformation of the social, political, and economic life of the nation —including the liquidation of arbitrary power itself. This change in aims, which is the truly significant political development of the time, indicates also the changed character of the ruling elite. We have discussed how the nature and background of the bureaucracy gradually changed in accordance with the new tasks it had to perform in the empire. The years of Young Turkish rule and war accelerated this transformation, for the Young Turks were chiefly military officers, and once in power—after 1908 but especially after 1922—they forced their own values on the bureaucrats too.

In the empire the best schools, teachers, and equipment had been provided for the officers. The officers' corps had hence become Westernized early. Each new reform weakened the hold on the military of those who traditionally controlled it; the expansion of the army's size and the addition of new, specialized services created a need for more men than the old military classes could or would supply; despite its prestige the profession was one which ambitious young men not born into the "right" families could join with relative ease. Mustafa Kemal himself, the son of a petty official turned timber merchant and the grandson of a schoolteacher, is a good example of the first-generation officer rising to eminence in the Ottoman Empire. Such men had no loyalties except those of their profession and those few inherited values that were still current in the schools which they attended. When, in the years between 1908 and 1924, they became possessed of political power, they effected a general social revolution among the ruling elite. And if they continued to manifest some of the old sense of superiority of the Turkish official, they had a more rational justification for their pride than most of their predecessors.

Changes occurred in all social groups, not only in the elite. During the Western occupation of Istanbul the minorities in that city took good advantage of their first opportunity since 1863 to become citizens of foreign countries. Those who lived in regions occupied by the Greeks sided with the invaders in great numbers and vented their pent-up animus against the Turkish population. The actions of these people made all minorities appear unreliable and potentially dangerous in the eyes of the men of Ankara, and account for the population exchange which occurred between 1923 and 1930 and the restrictions placed on those who stayed behind.

If the Muslim population of the country could misjudge the character of its new leaders, the leaders had no illusions concerning their fellow citizens. Mustafa Kemal, who in his speeches exalted the Turks, especially the Anatolian peasants, had in fact no illusion about them. And he gauged the selfishness of the wealthy landowners as correctly as the conservatism of the peasants. One does not know what to admire more: his restraint in using the almost unlimited power that was his from 1924 to his death, or his ability to push his reforms at exactly the speed that peasants could be forced to accept. He early realized that his only potentially serious opposition, the *ulema*, had to be eliminated—a task in its way more difficult than the abolition of the monarchy, for the sultan's position had already been weakened by the Young Turk parliamentarianism, by the war, and by his spineless behavior after the war and the abrogation of his office was made more palatable to the population by the retention of the caliphate.

The influence of the *ulema* could not be broken unless the caliphate was abolished. Many of Mustafa Kemal's own followers opposed such a move for reasons both religious and political. The government had committed itself to preserving the caliphate when it had expelled the sultan. That institution, moreover, had enjoyed a virtually undiminished prestige during a century of change because it attracted the religious loyalty of the people. The timing of the future Atatürk was excellent. He acted while the "traitorous" behavior of the caliph and his *şeyhülislâm* (the chief religious dignitary of the empire) during the Greek war were still fresh in the popular memory and could serve to justify his action. The Assembly, acting on Mustafa Kemal's request, deposed the last caliph on March 3, 1924. The blow was softened by the retention of Islam as the state religion and of "reorganized" religious establishments. The office of *şeyhülislâm* and the Ministry of Religious Affairs were replaced by a Religious Affairs Presidency (*Diyanet İşleri Reisliği*) and the Pious Foundation were entrusted to the General Directorate of Pious Foundations (*Evkaf Umum Müdürlüğü*). All religious affairs so came under government control. In 1928, the concept of a state religion was stricken from the constitution although not from the minds of the people. The religious revolution, when it finally came, was much swifter than the political.

By 1924, then, virtually all of the traditional objects of loyalty were gone. Mustafa Kemal, universally known and almost as generally respected and feared, was the inevitable cynosure. And he took command of the foundering country with the same determination with which, during the war, he had accepted leadership of the demoralized armies. Except that it is too early to judge the newly established Gürsel-İnönü regime, we might generalize that personal rule—that of the president or prime minister—has existed *de facto* in Turkey ever since.

V. *The Turkish Republic*

The government of the new republic displayed some characteristics of the old empire, including an ignorance of economic matters. Yet the republican regime of soldiers and bureaucrats was sincerely resolved to create an independent and progressive state, strong enough in all respects to withstand foreign intervention in its affairs. The sultanate and the caliphate having been abolished, together with everything these institutions stood for, those who made policy for the state no longer needed to justify their goals as means to somewhat extraneous ends, but might pursue political strength, economic growth, and autarky for their own sake. That these might be mutually exclusive was something Mustafa Kemal and his friends did not realize.

The Kemalists' mistrust of the Great Powers extended to economics. The experience of the Capitulations and the unfavorable customs tariffs, persisting until 1928, justified the desire of the new Turkish leadership for economic self-sufficiency as well as political independence. Although possessing only the vaguest economic notions, the Kemalists realized that without modern industrialized economy Turkey could not become a fully independent state. Economic growth was one of their main aims from the beginning.

The economic situation in Turkey in 1924 was bleak. After thirteen years of almost uninterrupted warfare, the country was disorganized and practically bankrupt. It had to pay for the utilities it had nationalized in 1916. Private capital was chiefly in the hands of uncooperative Muslim landlords, Levantines, and foreigners. Many experienced traders, merchants, and artisans were on the list of people whose forced emigration, through the population exchange agreement, just had begun. The Anatolian Turk was ignorant, uneducated, and often lazy in his way. When he discovered what industry and commerce entailed, he turned away from them as occupations unbecoming a true believer. Even if the government had not been disposed to extend its field of activity, it would have had to concern itself with economics. But the government too was in a very difficult situation.

We have seen how limited Turkish communications and the Turkish industrial establishment were. The tax system, which remains unreformed to the present, yielded very little, being "based on no principle except the ability to collect, . . . the remnants of every successful device for extracting revenue from a reluctant population."[8] Customs revenues were limited for another four years in accordance with the Lausanne Treaty. Though her revenues were meager, Turkey had to carry a heavy debt load. According to the decision rendered in April of 1926 by the Board of Arbitration at Lausanne, she had to pay off $401,195,247, or 62.25 per cent of the old Ottoman public debt. She was further saddled with outstanding internal loans of about 9.25 million dollars, a floating debt of almost 48 million dollars, and a paper currency of 82.5 million dollars in circulation. When we consider that until 1947, when the Ottoman public debt was finally cancelled, Turkey poured an average yearly sum of 10.25 million dollars into the old imperial debt alone while the government's income in 1928 amounted to only 105.5 million dollars, we begin to see the financial difficulties of the government in a true light.

Capital was almost unobtainable. The country had only one important domestic bank, the Ziraat (Agricultural) Bank, established in 1889 as the result of an experiment started by Midhat Pasha as a provincial governor in 1863. This bank had never served as a commercial bank. All other financial establishments included the Banque Ottomane (est. 1856) and the Banque de Salonique (est. 1888) were foreign-controlled, and were as suspicious of the republican government as it was of them. Finding capital for its various projects became one of the greatest problems of the Kemalist government. Unlike its Soviet neighbors, it was unwilling to force the needed amounts out of the peasantry, and the method adopted—extremely large profits on finished goods, mainly textiles produced in government enterprises—never yielded enough. The problem of capital formation was never solved satisfactorily in the Turkish republic.

Though Turkey is a potentially rich country, her resources were hardly even known when the republican government took power. Agriculture supported some 82 per cent of the population, but only 13.8 per cent of the land was under cultivation. While the population density was 17.9 people per square kilometer for the entire country, it was 175 for each square kilometer of cultivated land.

It was under these unfavorable circumstances that the government first sought to create conditions favoring economic growth. In 1925

[8] Max Weston Thornburg, et al., *Turkey: An Economic Appraisal*, New York, 1949, p. 174.

it abolished the tithe (the basis for agricultural taxation since the early Ottoman days); in 1926 it modernized the regulations governing land tenure; and in 1927 and 1929 it issued laws prescribing the distribution of land to the peasantry. Additional land-reform measures followed in 1945 and 1950 (and still others are under discussion today), but the distribution of holdings was never pushed in earnest. A first step toward industrial growth was the establishment, in 1924, of the İş (Work or Labor) Bank, a putatively private commercial bank that became the country's largest. This measure was followed in 1927 by a law that offered tax advantages and other inducements to industries which would establish new plants. It is interesting to note that under this law only 342 factories—out of a total of 59,245 listed as engaged in the production of goods in the 1927 census—qualified as "industries"; these employed some 17,000 workers. By 1933 the number of "industrial" establishments had risen to 1,473, having a total capital of 34.8 million dollars and employing 62,000 workers. The new establishments, employing on the average about forty people, were hardly of a size to satisfy a government trying to industrialize rapidly. The state's main contribution to economic growth prior to the introduction of *étatisme* were railroad construction and the establishment of the Merkez (Central) Bank in 1930. By 1933, 897 miles (1,405 kms.) of railroad had been completed and 483 miles (778 kms.) were under construction. By the end of 1949 the total railroad mileage reached 4,723 miles (7,600 kms.).

The year 1929, the first in which Turkey was fully master of her own economic house, was also the year of the Great Depression. All over the world the predominantly agricultural countries, whose economies were not diversified, suffered most severely. Turkey was no exception. As the economic and financial crisis deepened, the Turkish government assumed a general responsibility for economic conditions and worked out a policy dictated by economic necessities. And since that government traditionally considered every phase of the nation's life its own domain, its intervention in the economic life of the people was much more thorough and radical than that of most governments reacting to the depression.

The decision of the Kemalists was logical though naïve. They saw only that the local business community was not very cooperative, that economic growth was slow, and that the same system of free enterprise which had seemingly failed to work in Turkey had produced a worldwide crisis.

On the other hand, the Soviet Union with its state-planned and controlled economy had made remarkable progress and was unaffected by the depression. It seemed logical to suppose that the Soviet Union had found a proved method to achieve both growth and a large measure of autarky. In 1930, an early hint of the coming change was included in a speech by Prime Minister İsmet (İnönü), who stressed the need for state economic activity. Mustafa Kemal himself spelled out what this activity was to be when, on April 21 of 1931, he included among the "basic and eternal" principles of his party and state that of *devletçilik,* usually translated *étatisme.* He defined this as the duty of the state to participate in the economic life of the nation in order to guide it to prosperity in the shortest possible time.

Under these circumstances it was not surprising that Turkey tried to improve her relations with the Soviet Union. Visits between Moscow and Ankara increased in frequency, and in 1932 Premier İsmet returned from the USSR with the republic's first foreign loan of 8 million dollars. By the time the Kayseri textile kombinat, based on Russian plans, was finished, Turkey owed the Soviet 18 million dollars. In January of 1934 the first Turkish five-year plan was launched, involving the state yet more deeply in economic activities. The first five-year plan placed under state management or supervision those plants either (1) producing goods for the domestic markets from Turkish raw materials, (2) manufacturing finished and semi-finished products from domestic raw materials for export, or (3) utilizing imported raw materials to satisfy essential needs of the home market. The chemical, ceramics, iron and steel, paper and cellulose, sulphur and copper mining, cotton, woolen, hemp and sponge industries were the first ones placed under state control.

To carry out the five-year plan, two great banks were established, which could best be described as state-owned holding companies. The Sümer Bank, which promoted industry, was established in 1934 with a 34 million (Turkish) pound capital. It took over several armament industries formerly controlled by the treasury and later established a great variety of other industrial plants. The Eti Bank, the mining company, became established in 1935 with a 20 million (Turkish) pound capital and operated all mines the state owned and all those subsequently opened up or nationalized. Together with the Ziraat and İş Banks, these financial institutions became the executors of the state's economic plans. If we add up the state monopolies (salt, tobacco, alcoholic products, matches and explosives), the government-owned power plants and railroads, and the forests which, in 1937, were placed under the management of the State Forestry Exploitation Office, we begin to see how thoroughly the government regulated the economy.

We must additionally note that the Turkish labor force has been strictly supervised by the government. A law of 1936 provided some standard safeguards and rights for labor. It was not until 1952 that a national labor federation was organized: before that time the legalized union movement had remained ineffectual. When these lines were written, strikes were still not legal although the question was under discussion.

In agriculture, state intervention was less prominent. Village institutes to train peasants were established, and storage and distribution facilities were somewhat improved. But except on the large-scale state-owned model farms, production methods and tools were allowed to remain primitive.

The literature on Turkish *étatisme* is quite extensive. The results which it has achieved can be evaluated with the help of numerous and moderately reliable statistics published by the Turks and made available in many Western publications. But we are now interested less in these data than in the nature of *étatisme*—the specific Turkish contribution to planning economies—and its connection with politics.

It was characteristic of Turkey that, in establishing the state banks, she did not slavishly imitate the Soviet model. Nor did she copy Nazi Germany, which, after 1935, replaced the Soviet Union as her main supplier of plans and experts. While some of the banks' capital was furnished from the budget, some by loans from the Merkez bank, and some by temporary treasury deposits, they relied more and more on their own and their enterprises' profits for additional resources. "The financial provisions applied to the Sumerbank and Etibank are most significant because they have permitted state economic enterprises to determine their own investment programs. Allowed to retain their net earnings for additional investment, the holding company banks have been able largely to finance their own expansion."[9] This situation placed heavy responsibility on bank and plant managers and soon produced a small class of Turkish executives, managers, and entrepreneurs, many of whom subsequently left state employment and started enterprises of their own. These men played and still

[9] Robert W. Kerwin, "Etatism in Turkey," in Aitken, Hugh G. J., ed., *The State and Economic Growth*, New York, 1959, p. 242.

PETER F. SUGAR

play an important role in the slowly growing Turkish middle class. When he incorporated *devletçilik* into his principles, Mustafa Kemal did not deviate from his original aim—a strong, modern state modeled on the West but independent of it. He did not wish to create a monolithic state. State ownership and control of industries and distribution facilities was not the goal, only the means. Private enterprise was therefore not interfered with, although it fared badly in competition with state-owned factories and plants.

Both the public and private sectors of the economy continued to suffer from a shortage of capital as Atatürk held to his original decision to exclude foreign capital from the country. In addition to the Soviet loan already mentioned, he accepted only an English loan of 13 million sterling to modernize the army and construct the Karabük iron and steel works, and, just before his death, a 150 million Reichsmark loan from Germany to finance mineral exploitation projects. The result, says Max W. Thornburg, "looks not like a planned economy but like a poorly managed capitalist economy in which most of the capital happens to be supplied by the government."[10] That the management was poor cannot be denied. The railroad lines never added up to a well-planned network. A serious highway building program did not get under way until the 1950's. The Karabük plant is the most spectacular single example of bad planning. Built on top of a 4,000 foot range, which the army selected for security reasons, it is separated from the sea and from the Zonguldak coal mines by 45 miles. The iron mines at Divrigi are 600 miles away. Turkey needs rails, construction steel, and small sections, yet the plant produced only large section, heavy plates, and rods ½" and over in diameter. Nor do the components of the complex match. When the plant opened it was able to produce 350,000 tons of pig iron, but the steel furnaces had only a 150,000 ton capacity, while the rolling mill could produce only 40-50,000 tons of finished steel products. "Since there are no other steel mills in the country, the result is that even if the rolling mill could operate at capacity, the steel furnaces could operate at only one-third capacity, and the blast furnaces at only one-sixth. Such a waste of capital would be serious for any country; to Turkey it represents a tragic diversion of scanty resources."[11]

Other examples of bad planning could be listed to justify Thornburg's opinion of the wastefulness of *étatisme*. But it did represent a serious effort to induce economic growth which was badly needed.

[10] Thornburg, *op.cit.*, p. 39.   [11] *Ibid.*, p. 107ff.

169

A study published by the International Bank for Reconstruction and Development states that "under *étatisme* Turkey had made substantial progress. It is doubtful whether comparable accomplishment would have taken place in this period under domestic private enterprise with the handicap of the Ottoman heritage."[12] This judgment should complement Thornburg's hard verdict. While errors would have been less frequent if the work had been carried out by experienced businessmen or economic planners rather than by soldiers and bureaucrats preoccupied with political and military power, progress would have been slower. From the Kemalist viewpoint agricultural reform was not a prime necessity while the food supply remained satisfactory, and heavy steel plates, strategic railroad lines, and industrial power plants were more important than T-bars, an economically sound railroad network, or rural electrification. *Étatisme* was and is a curious mixture of private and state enterprise invented by people who understood the importance of economic growth but only as a factor in national power, and who had no grasp of the technical aspects of economic planning. Given the philosophy of the entire reform period beginning with Selim III and especially the goal of Atatürk, this emphasis is perfectly intelligible and explains why, in a slightly modified form, *étatisme* is still with us today.

There was some speculation at the end of the Second World War and in the early 1950's concerning a new approach to economics by the Turkish government. Economic controls had been tightened during the war, in Turkey as elsewhere. Even the *Varlık Vergisi* (capital levy) of November 1942 was in theory justified by the government's effort to maintain its defenses and its neutral status with an almost empty treasury. When the levy turned out in fact to be an anti-minority measure in the late Ottoman tradition, responsible Turks and their foreign friends explained it as an atavistic measure perpetrated by some ex-pashas cornered by something they did not understand: a serious economic crisis. Some eight years later, at the time of the first really free national elections, often attributed to the pressure of the United States and other Western democracies, these same people found the origin of the "miracle" of 1950 in the *Varlık Vergisi*. That levy had been revoked under strong foreign pressure, they pointed out—the first such pressure successfully exerted since the

<hr />

[12] International Bank for Reconstruction and Development, *The Economy of Turkey; An Analysis and Recommendations for a Development Program*, Baltimore, 1951, p. 9, also quoted by Lewis, *op.cit.*, p. 282.

establishment of the republic—and, being a desperate response to an economic and fiscal crisis, it had proved in the first place that something was wrong with the country's planned economy. Did not the same foreign pressure conduce toward economic reforms, and were there not other signs of economic change? As early as 1946 the government began to return to private control some of the activities placed under governmental management during the war, beginning with flour milling and wheat sales. Two years later the press was permitted to report both American criticism and the condemnation of *étatisme* by the National Economic Congress meeting in Istanbul. With the institution of Point Four and the Marshall Plan, American pressure increased steadily. Finally, in 1950, the government created the Industrial Development Bank of Turkey, with the specific aim of making industrial credits available to private enterprise. And the ruling Republican People's Party promised that, if it should win the national elections of the same year, it would end *étatisme*, keeping under state control only mining, electrical power generation, heavy and defense industries, transportation and communications, meat packing, and sugar refining. The party further invited both domestic and foreign capitalists and entrepreneurs to enter the economic sectors vacated.

It nevertheless appears now that the seeming drift away from *étatisme* was temporary and partial, arising from the desire to please a single element of the Turkish population. Professor Bernard Lewis says of this element: "Another and quite different element in the pro-Democrat camp was the new commercial and industrial middle class that had grown up in Turkey during the previous decades. These were increasingly restive under the *étatist* policies of the People's Party, against which they now revolted in the name of democracy and free enterprise. In a sense, the revolt against *étatisme* was the measure of its success, for it was the *étatist* impulse, supplemented by the opportunities afforded by six years of neutrality in a world war, that led to the emergence of this new Turkish class."[13]

The emergence of this new class, which in 1946 already supported the opposition party and whose votes the Republican group wanted to regain, explains the economic measures and promises of the years 1946-1950. The laws passed by the new Democratic government in 1951 and 1954 served the interest of this group and also of foreign investors (reversing Atatürk's policy on foreign capital). The provision im-

[13] B. Lewis, *op.cit.*, p. 311.

portant to foreign investors guaranteed them the right to withdraw, in the currency of the original investment, everything they brought to the country as capital together with their earnings. Investments were defined as (1) capital imported in foreign currency, (2) the value of installations and equipment, (3) the value of trademarks, patents, and protected processes.

At the same time, the Bayar-Menderes regime, which soon became at least as arbitrary as the regime it had ousted, continued *étatist* practices, although it shifted the emphasis to sectors previously neglected (highway construction, agricultural mechanization, etc.) for the sake of bringing the economy into better balance. Unfortunately the plans of the Democratic government were too ambitious, its fiscal policy careless, its spending of both foreign and domestic capital reckless. The result was a new economic crisis preparing the revolt that finally ousted it.

Nobody expected sweeping economic reforms from the military regime that came to power in the spring of 1960. And evidently the recently-inaugurated new civilian government does not intend to give up *étatisme* either. We were informed by *News from Turkey*,[14] early in 1962 that "Premier İnönü stressed the importance of detailed economic planning and said that every government agency was giving priority attention to the preparation of the five-year-development plan which will be ready this year. He termed the State Planning Organization 'an invaluable inheritance from the interim military government,' and added that its resources would be used to the utmost. . . . Turning to industry Premier İnönü declared that state and private industries must be developed together in a coordinated plan. . . ." This statement could as well have been issued in 1934. Even private industries must fit into a "coordinated plan" or, by implication, they will not be encouraged. *Étatisme*, government control of the economy, is still the policy of the Turkish authorities.

Yet the impression lingers that this principle—at least in the form in which we have known it since Turkey's first five-year plan was introduced—will not much longer be embraced. Turkey has reached the fifth stage of the developmental scheme we presented at the beginning of this study. The new Turkish bourgeoisie, to which Professor Lewis referred, will not permit its establishments to be treated with less consideration than the state enterprises or those businesses founded by foreigners taking advantage of the guarantees

[14] Vol. xv, No. 4, January 24, 1962.

of the law of 1954. The Turkish middle class knows how powerful it already is. It won a peaceful victory in 1950 and a less orderly one ten years later. It will not permit the man it ousted from power in 1950 (Prime Minister İnönü) and the one it brought to power in 1960 (President Gürsel) to take its gains away from it.

We must end our investigation with a short look at this new element in Turkish society. The word "bourgeoisie" is not inclusive enough to describe this group, which is known in Turkey as *gençlik* (youth). The Turkish expression is also misleading, unless youth denotes recency of origin alone. It includes young and old, irrespective of profession or place of residence—even the well-to-do farmers slowly emerging into political consciousness. Although its leaders are members of the small but closely knit middle class proper—professional people, merchants and manufacturers, students and young army officers—it includes virtually every Turk who possesses any form of education, or even any form of enlightening experience.

The "education" of the individual citizen could have originated in the state banks and industrial plants, in the *Halk Evleri* or *Halk Odaları* (People's Houses and People's Rooms) which served as information and indoctrination centers all over the country; in the steadily expanding Turkish school system; in a peasant's trips to the nearest city; in small but successful business ventures or in the "wisdom" imparted by an American N.C.O. to Turkish recruits; more broadly, it could be the product of the war years, when all segments of the population worked harder and relied more on their own abilities than before; or it could simply signify the final success of the Kemalist effort to instill self-confidence and self-reliance into a demoralized people. Whatever it is that makes Turks conceive of themselves as a part of the *gençlik*, they all have one thing in common: a steadily diminishing reliance on the traditional values of their class and an increasing awareness of what is new or "Western" in Turkey.

This new Turk, though still naïve by most Western standards, demands the consideration and freedom of action that the Westerner enjoys. One-party rule under a powerful leader has been thrown off twice in one decade. Turkey has a new constitution, a new multi-party government and legislature. We do not have to go back to Selim III or even to Abdülhamid to realize how swift and important the political changes in the country have been.

The government's economic policy has been less responsive to current changes and still very largely follows the 1931 principles of *étatisme.* Given the emergence of the *gençlik* since the beginning of the Second World War and the remarkable economic growth since 1934, however, it is reasonable to expect that the government will modify its policy. When it does, political development will become more responsive to economic and social change, reversing a casual relation that has persisted throughout modern Turkish history.

VI. Conclusion

We have followed the development of one country in which changes had been "induced" or brought about largely by forces other than "organic." We have seen how an outside stimulus produced first of all political change; how, in the Tanzimat period, economic considerations began to enter the consciousness of the elite, and how, with the Young Turks economics assumed an importance nearly equal to that of politics in the mind of policy makers. We have further observed how under the influence of the depression the Republican government introduced *étatisme* and from that time on intimately involved itself in the economic life of the nation. During this same period a considerable urban middle class grew up, which, in the 1950's, began to make its voice heard. The overthrow of the Menderes regime introduces the final stage of our developmental history.

We cannot predict in which of the many possible directions the country will now turn. But wherever she will go, Turkey starts from a sounder economic basis than the one from which Mustafa Kemal set out. The economic progress of that country has been described ably and in detail by Z. Y. Hershlag, *Turkey, An Economy in Transition,*[15] to which the following summary is indebted.

The economy, in spite of *étatisme,* was not managed in the interest of the state. While national income increased 44 per cent (in 1938 prices) between 1929 and 1938, and another 71 per cent (in 1948 prices) between 1938 and 1955, the budgetary deficit grew by 807.9 per cent and 346.6 per cent respectively during the same periods. In this way the government "bought" increases of the per capita income of 30.1 per cent in the first of the two periods and 20.3 in the second. Mining production increased under *étatist* management by 132 per cent by 1938 and by an additional 42.6 per cent between that year and 1955. Industry made even more impressive progress.

The country is still predominantly agricultural, but the pressure on the land has greatly diminished. The area under cultivation has

[15] The Hague, 1958.

been raised by 62.4 per cent. As a result, the number of inhabitants per arable square kilometer diminished by 53.2 per cent (from 175 to 82), even though the total population density of the country rose by 70.3 per cent (from 17.9 to 30.5). Furthermore, the yields of industrial crops per hectare also increased in roughly the same period (1936-1956). The yield per hectare of sugar beets, for example, increased 44.1 per cent; of cotton (lint) 17.7 per cent; of potatoes 220.5 per cent; and of onions 123.5 per cent. The buying power of the peasantry has therefore increased and Turkish industry can count on an expanding domestic market.

These figures indicate that Turkey is in a much better economic position than ever before. The new power of the middle class, and the independent spirit which it has manifested since the end of the last war, are signs also of political health. A final token of the general national advance is an increasingly intimate and complex interrelation between Turkish economics and Turkish politics—arguing that the nation has in a manner come of age and that future changes within it will be primarily organic.

CHAPTER 5

EDUCATION

·∿·∿·∿·∿·∿·∿·∿·∿·∿·∿·∿·∿·∿·∿·∿·

A. JAPAN

R. P. DORE

·∿·∿·∿·∿·∿·∿·∿·∿·∿·∿·∿·∿·∿·∿·∿·

WE MAY have lost some of the optimism of Henry Brougham; it is no longer as self-evident that "education makes a people easy to lead but difficult to drive; easy to govern but impossible to enslave," and we may well support our skepticism by pointing to the modern history of Japan. We nevertheless can be as certain as Brougham was that a society's school and university system affects its political institutions and processes (and *vice versa*). This essay will consider some specific ways in which educational institutions have influenced political institutions in Japan in the last century. My particular topics are the legacy of the Tokugawa schools, the education of political leaders, and the relationship of education to popular political attitudes and to national unity.

I. The Tokugawa Legacy

The question of the "base-line" is important. To what extent did the pre-existing educational institutions of the Tokugawa period lay the basis for the political changes which followed the Meiji Restoration? How did they mould the ideas of the leaders who initiated those changes, and who remained in control of national policy for the next three decades? What presuppositions concerning the functions of schools did they embody which influenced the evolution of the educational system in Meiji Japan?

Tokugawa Japan had, of course, no organized national educational system, but it had a great many schools. These were of two kinds. There were, first of all, many thousands of small private establishments which taught children to read and write and count. Although some schools, catering to samurai children, received public support from the governments of the fiefs, most of them were unsubsidized private schools which catered to commoner parents willing to pay fees to have their children made literate. Feudal governments rarely interfered in the operations of these latter schools; literacy on the part of the masses was not thought of as a threat, and where control was exercised it was usually to ensure that the moral injunctions of the copy-books inculcated qualities appropriate to the lower orders in a feudal society—obedience to superiors, submission to family and community; in the current Confucian terms, the due observance of the five basic social relationships. These preoccupations with "ethics of political consequence" were inherited by later framers of educational policy and lie at the root of some controversial issues of educational policy even today.

These reading and writing schools disseminated a literacy which was of itself politically significant. They ensured that, by 1870, perhaps as many as half the male population could read and write simple Japanese,[1] were capable of being reached by written public notices and even newspapers, could understand the documentary instruments of a modern administrative system, and could keep accounts. The schools further provided the generation whose members were to be the first to adapt to industry with a training in being trained— in the business of acquiring new skills. They betokened, finally, that growing popular demand for education which enabled the Meiji government to establish a national school system at first relying in part on the collection of fees.

The second kind of school taught Chinese, or rather a curious form of Japanese which made it possible to "construe" Chinese texts. Their pupils being mainly samurai, most such schools were maintained by the governments of the fiefs. The education they gave was based on the Confucian classics, the basic texts of which all pupils learned to read and the more intelligent came to understand. Those among the latter who were lucky enough to find an inspiring teacher or had enough native curiosity of their own read more widely in non-Confucian Chinese philosophy, in the Chinese and Japanese belles-lettres, in the legal codes of China and Japan, and above all in Chinese and Japanese history.

The most gifted among them emerged with a good deal of *technical* political sophistication: an awareness of the difficulties of administering distant territories from a single center and of possible means to that end, of the contrasting forms of organization in a feudal and a centralized system, of the relative advantages of an hereditary

[1] For a muster of the relevant evidence, see my forthcoming *Education in Tokugawa Japan*.

and a merit-appointed governing elite, and of the desirability in principle of rational consistency in administration and in the operations of the law.

Even more explicitly formed were their assumptions about the *moral* basis and aims of politics. Society consisted of the rulers and the ruled: the former endowed with breeding, learning, and morality; the latter ignorant and ignoble, prone to laziness, extravagance, and immorality—responsive, nevertheless, to moral exhortation and example and amenable to good treatment. A good society was one in which proper hierarchical distinctions were observed and expressed in sharply differentiated living standards, though benevolence and prudence both required that the rulers should not so exploit the ruled as to engender disobedience or a loss of productivity. Ostentatious luxury on the part of rulers was in any case improper since it showed a concern with the privileges rather than with the duties of office, a concern with "private" as opposed to "public" interest. Good government, devotion to the "public" interest, meant, in effect, government which would benefit the *whole* of society. There was no place in this scheme for the politics of compromise—for accommodations among persons with unavoidably conflicting aims and interests. Every situation had a *just* solution which would be apparent to a ruler sincerely devoted to the interests of the whole society.

These were some of the basic elements of the Confucian ideology as, having been adapted by samurai teachers to the more distinctively Japanese and less well-codified martial traditions of the samurai class, it was absorbed in the Tokugawa schools by the small group of young samurai who seized power in 1868 and carried through the Meiji reforms. Its basic assumption that the path of honor lay exclusively in political and military leadership, rather than in, say, scholarship, or holiness, or wealth, provided a direction for their ambitions. It further provided a moral framework for nationalism as soon as dangerous contact with foreign powers induced a consciousness of "Japan" as a new and larger whole possessing clearly defined common interests to which private interests should be subordinated. (What had been the "public" interests of the fief as opposed to the "private" interests of individuals became the "private" interests of the fief as opposed to the "public" interests of the nation. And in Japan, the facts of geography and history left no doubt where the geographical, ethnic, or class boundaries of the nation should lie.) The samurai leaders' claim to promote that public interest and hence to serve the emperor, the symbol of the nation, was the source of their assured conviction of their own right to usurp power. Nor was it merely claim; the purposes of "enriching the country and strengthening the army," to use the contemporaneous slogan, were real objects of policy as well as excuses for self-aggrandisement.

The fact, too, that they had been educated in a Chinese rather than an indigenous tradition may have made it easier for them to abandon that very tradition in favor of Western models. Their own history provided them with precedents for the deliberate importation of foreign institutions as a means of improving their own society. Also, before they took power in 1868, many of the new leaders already had at least a distant knowledge of some of those Western institutions from which they might profitably learn. For this knowledge too they were partly indebted to the Tokugawa schools. In the last two decades of the period many of the fief schools added new departments of "Western learning" which taught the Dutch and later the French and English languages, Western science and technology, and eventually an elementary knowledge of Western political and economic institutions. Thanks to these schools and a few private academies, knowledge which had formerly been the preserve of coteries of scholars became diffused among the samurai population and laid the basis for the enthusiastic cultural borrowing of the Meiji period.

In all these ways the education developed in the samurai schools of the Tokugawa period had political relevance. It was an elite education, "learning appropriate to the world of rulers," as Fukuzawa Yukichi said in explaining why it had ceased to bear the same relevance to the Japan of the 1870's. As the feudal authorities reiterated when laying down educational policy, the schools were to "produce men of talent who can be useful to the fief." With the substitution of nation for fief, and with a broadening of the meaning of "useful" to include not only political leadership but all kinds of administrative and technical skills, these aims continued to characterize Japanese educational policy throughout the modern period. Education in Japan was not, in contrast to many other countries, thought of primarily as the road to a fuller, holier, or more prosperous life for the individual.

So much, then, for the legacy from the Tokugawa period. In what follows, the modern educational system which was built on these foundations can most conveniently be followed through its political consequences if we consider in turn: the established leadership and the political opposition, the education of the masses and the creation of national unity.

II. Education and Political Leaderhip

The role of Japanese high schools and universities in training the leaders of the political establishment is rather generally recognized and is considered in another essay in this volume.[2] Hence it need only be briefly summarized here.

The first generation of political leaders in the modern era was the product of the Confucian schools described above. The men of the succeeding generation were predominantly Western-trained—either abroad, or in Japan with Western-language texts, and sometimes by Western teachers. The third and subsequent generations, beginning their higher education after Mori's university reforms of 1885, were predominantly graduates of the law departments of the imperial universities who had undergone a training more formal, more authoritarian, and more fully indigenous. (The classics of Western philosophy and jurisprudence were now available in Japanese translation and their principles were in some degree embodied in the legal codes and institutions of the new *Japanese* state.) These universities have never ceased to provide the majority of all Japanese higher civil servants and an even greater majority of these in the upper grades. Ever since the admission of political parties to a share in political power, ex-bureaucrats have dominated the major parties. The imperial universities' graduates have lost political control only temporarily—to the products of the military schools.

But they have never been without civil opponents. The bureaucracy always faced an opposition which attacked its policies and demanded a part in the governing process. As soon as the demands of one group were partially met, furthermore, and they were in some way admitted to a share in power, a widening political consciousness would call into being a new layer of opposition which would have to be accommodated in turn. The opportunities for popular involvement in politics have thus been widened largely as a result of pressure from an opposition. It can even be argued that the reforms of the Occupation period, themselves an exception to the rule, have been preserved chiefly as a result of opposition pressure. The educational origins of that opposition and its leaders are therefore worth consideration.

The first generation of opposition leaders were samurai like the members of the Restoration government, and were trained like them for the samurai's governing role. But the new centralized state ap-

[2] See Chapter 7, Masamichi Inoki, on the civil bureaucracy in Japan.

paratus did not have room for all those who had read the standard histories and commentaries, and who, claiming to know the moral principles on which government should be based, asserted their right to raise their voices—and, if need arose, their swords—in defense of those principles. Japan did not have to await the emergence of an urban middle class seeking political confirmation and reinforcement of its economic power for politics as we know it to commence. Important segments of the nation outside the establishment were already politically conscious and demanding a share in the making of decisions.

When, among the fractional opposition groups, there developed in the Popular Rights Movement the beginnings of organized non-violent opposition, the original Confucian ideology was already laced with a strong admixture of foreign ideas. European doctrines of the rights of man were combined in the Movement's polemics with the argument that popular participation in government was necessary to solidify the Japanese state and to enhance its military and economic power. But apart from the scholars of the Popular Rights Movement who provided the knowledge of European parliamentary institutions, most of the early opposition leaders were in education and basic attitudes not greatly different from the first-generation government leaders—some of them being, in fact, former members of the ruling group who had resigned after policy disputes and found themselves "outs" instead of "ins."

It is further partly true that the members of the second generation —the largely foreign-trained or foreign-language-trained generation —who joined the opposition, resembled their contemporaries who joined the government and worked their way into leadership positions. But there was a difference. Strains of French radicalism and English liberalism appeared in the opposition, whereas the government, in its political, educational, military, and administrative reforms in the eighties increasingly embraced German models. A German background was less likely to lead one into opposition than a period of education in Britain or France or America. "French learning" still had its uses to the establishment—the new legal codes were largely based on French models—and British traditions continued to dominate the navy. But a thorough acquaintance with the state-centered ideology of Bismarck's Germany was the background securing the warmest welcome in government circles.

As the opposition gained the status of a movement and began to form political parties, it developed institutional strongholds in the press and in the private universities. The early private schools, such as Fukuzawa's Keio Gijuku, were not primarily organs of opposition. Fukuzawa's utilitarian individualism, for instance, was by no means a subversive doctrine in the seventies; it inspired the government's early educational policy, and graduates from his school were eagerly sought for posts in government and in the new teacher-training colleges. With his stress on "independence and self-respect" Fukuzawa did seek to counter the current assumption that government service was the only honorable occupation, but he encouraged his young men to carve out careers in business rather than in political opposition (though later a good number of them did in fact enter opposition politics). Others of the private schools, notably the law schools which have grown into the present Senshū, Meiji, Hōsei, and Nippon universities, were primarily concerned with training aspirants for official careers.

It was otherwise with Waseda University, founded in 1882 by Okuma and his group of supporters within a year after they had left the government and moved into opposition. Waseda was intended as the breeding ground of future opposition politicians. Its core departments were those of politics and economics, and of law, and the character of the new school was sufficiently clear for the government to take the precaution of enlisting spies among its students. The first president's foundation address was a plea for academic freedom and the need to make education independent of government restriction. It is significant of the nationalism of the time, however—the opposition being usually holier than the Pope in this respect and constantly accusing the government of weakness in protecting the national interest—that he found academic independence important chiefly as a condition for national independence.[3]

The School of English Law founded three years later in 1885, the embryo from which grew the present Chūō University, was another institution with an opposition streak. Its main purpose was to promote a knowledge of English law as opposed to the French legal tradition which dominated government circles, and its teachers were active in the movement which secured the postponement and eventual revision of the new civil code.[4] Pioneering in correspondence and evening courses for poorer students, it sought to diffuse legal knowledge more widely in preparation for the inauguration of parliamentary govern-

---

[3] Nagai Michio, "Chishikijin no seisan-ruuto," in *Kindai Nihon Shisōshi Kōza*, Vol. 4, 1959, p. 220.
[4] *Ibid.*, p. 225.

ment. An ideologically independent school of a different complexion was the Tetsugakkan, founded in 1889 on the wave of the new Japanism, in reaction against what its founder considered the excessive Westernization of Japanese learning and culture. Japanese and Chinese literature, Buddhism and Confucianism were to be the core studies at this school—the Oriental University, as it later became.

The fate of the opposition educational institutions paralleled the fate of the political parties. Just as the parties entered the first Diet in a mood of uncompromising opposition and then gradually allowed their cooperation to be bought for a small share in the power and emoluments of the oligarchy, so the private universities adapted themselves to the increasingly firmly established status quo. The School of English Law became more and more concerned with students hoping for an official career. Many of its lecturers were officials teaching on the side, and in 1903 it established a special preparatory school for students wishing to enter state universities.[5] The founder of the Oriental University abjectly apologized to the Ministry of Education and dismissed a professor its inspectors had suspected of dangerous thoughts in order to retain the school's privilege of licensing teachers for middle schools and training colleges.[6] The new university regulations of 1918, which extended the coveted title of university to any institution accepting a greater measure of government supervision and meeting certain standards, finally brought all private universities into compliance.

Waseda remained identified with Okuma until his death, and its nonconformity was modified as Okuma became a grand old man of Japanese politics and was readmitted to the inner ranks of the oligarchy. But a Waseda education, then journalism, then politics, a route followed by a number of the men at present sitting in the Diet, continued to be a common career pattern for party politicians. It was a background somewhat different from that of the typical bureaucrat from the imperial universities. It was not a direct apprenticeship for the dutiful and cautious exercise of power; it was more catholic in scope, less authoritarian in manner, less formalistic in content. The story of the Shakespearean scholar at Waseda lecturing on the constitution while the constitutional lawyer lectured on Shakespeare is indicative of a freer spirit than prevailed at the state universities, where the sovereignty of academic specialties was jealously guarded.

[5] *Ibid.*, p. 226.
[6] *Ibid.*, p. 224.

The original Meiji opposition movement became incorporated into the establishment; the samurai outsiders, the landlords, and the new urban middle classes were allowed some share in the exercise of power. Then, with the turn of the century, ferment began in a new stratum of political consciousness. We shall concern ourselves here with the leaders of the twentieth-century opposition movements and in the next section with the sources of rank and file support.

The founders of the early Socialist societies, the editors of the first People's Daily, the members of the anarchist movement whose growth was stunted by the executions following the amateurish plot to assassinate the emperor in 1910, were men of diverse backgrounds and origins. Some, like Yamakawa Kin and Arahata Kanson, were largely self-educated men from lower middle-class families. Some were products of the non-governmental liberal schools, Kinoshita Naoe and Kishimoto Nobuta from Waseda, Abe Isō, the Christian from the Christian foundation of Dōshisha, Sugiura Kotarō and Ishikawa Sanshirō from the School of English Law. At least four (Katayama Sen, Murai Tomoyoshi, Tazoe Tetsuji, and Kaneko Kiichi) had studied for a period in the United States.

These men brought something new to Japanese politics. They were not, like the earlier members of the opposition, men who disagreed with the oligarchy merely over the policy implications of a common nationalist outlook. These were men who preached the rejection of the existing order of society in the name of foreign ideologies, and espoused the right of the "common people" to a measure of political power.

By the end of the First World War it became clear that they had to be taken seriously. The summary executions of 1910 had had a dampening effect on the new movements, but the acceleration of industrialization which followed the beginning of the World War led to an equally rapid rise in the number of labor disputes and strikes. Tenants began to organize collective demands for the reduction of rents. The news of the Russian Revolution gave immediacy to the threat—and the promise—of Socialist and Communist ideas. The Rice Riots of 1918, though not the product of deliberate political organization, made clear the potential explosiveness of class divisions in Japanese society.

At this point the intellectual center of disaffection moved from the private to the imperial universities, the heartland of the ruling bureaucracy. The new academic elite had already begun to develop the professional pride and independence which enabled it gradually to free itself of some irksome forms of government control; in 1917 Kyoto University, and shortly thereafter Tokyo University, won the right to elect their own presidents. It was Yoshino Sakuzō, a professor of politics at Tokyo University, who, also in 1917, stated the case against the existing order in a famous magazine article. His *mimponshugi*—democentrism, as one might translate it—was an unrevolutionary demand for liberal democracy, manhood suffrage, and popular welfare, and the first student society of radical leanings—the Society of New Men founded in Tokyo University in 1918—at first followed his leadership. But progressive thought in the universities gradually took on a more radical color, particularly at Tokyo and Waseda universities. The first general students' organization was formed (in 1922) to organize famine relief for Russia. After the disruption which followed the earthquake, the organization was revived in 1924 as a result of student support of striking Osaka tram workers. By this time Marxism was replacing democentrism as the favorite doctrine of the student societies, and was beginning to find its way into departments of economics and politics. Young assistant professors taking their normal two years' study leave were returning from the Weimar Republic with ideas rather different from those their predecessors had found in Imperial Germany.

The movement was periodically repressed. The first arrests of students came in 1925. Others followed, on a large scale in 1928 and 1929. The Student Department (later the Thought Department) of the Ministry of Education grew in size and importance and in the intensity of its counter-measures. Political societies were banned in the universities, sports were encouraged instead, and the puritanical restrictions on high-school love affairs were relaxed in an effort to divert student energies to less dangerous channels. Military training was intensified and with it instruction in the martial traditions of Japan; rebuttals of Marxism were commissioned and imprisoned students were patiently, and usually successfully, reeducated. Professors of undesirable left-wing tendencies were gradually dismissed from their posts, and by the conclusion of the Minobe witch-hunt in 1935 —when a professor emeritus of law, whose thesis that the throne was an "organ" of the state had in fact been long accepted, was hounded from the House of Peers—the universities had been brought into conformity.

At least into open conformity. Japanese scholarship in the social sciences had by this time become heavily Germanic and, a premium being placed on pompous obscurity of expression, it was not always easy to discern whether scholarly works were critical of established authority or not. Some former intellectuals satisfied an inner sense of rebellion with scholarly innuendoes. Others, despairing that a dictatorship of the proletariat would ever curb the predations of the capitalist bourgeoisie, settled for the dictatorship of a Fascist military clique as the next best thing and entered into wholehearted cooperation with the army. Although many members of the government continued until the end of the war to fear the hidden hand of Communism among Japanese intellectuals (Konoe in particular becoming obsessed with the fear of revolution), a casual observer of Japan in 1940 might have said that Japanese Marxism was dead.

He would have been wrong. The seeds sown in the twenties and thirties bore fruit in the forties and fifties. In the post-war universities, Marxism swept the departments of economics and politics, capturing at least those more articulate teachers whose journalistic activities made the ideological running. The latter, once again, were predominantly men in the state—the former imperial—universities.

The situation is now more complicated. The courses in "modern" economics in most universities claim more students than the parallel courses in "Marxist" economics. The solidarity of the "progressive intellectual" camp has been broken and Japan's leading political scientists, economists, and sociologists take a variety of public positions. Still, the center of gravity of the Japanese academic world is well to the left, and—continuing the trend begun by Yoshino in 1917—further to the left in the state than in the private universities. It was the president of Tokyo University who was pushed by his faculty into a public statement blaming the government rather than the demonstrating students for the riots of June 1960. The government's academic defenders were to be found almost exclusively in the private universities. It is still Tokyo University (together with Waseda) which is the home of the Trotskyite student organization, the Zengakuren. The private Keiō University, on the other hand, the school of some of the Meiji oligarchs' first opponents, is noted for the apolitical and well-behaved nature of its students.

The pattern of evolution may be simply—somewhat over-simply—summarized. In the latter half of the Meiji period the political conflict was between the samurai oligarchy and its favored industrialists on the one hand and the rising individualistic middle class on the other.

The state universities were identified with the former, the private universities with the latter. Today, the industrial middle class, grown corporate and bureaucratic rather than individualistic, has achieved political dominance, and the private universities, supported by it and retaining their allegiance to it, are well satisfied with the status quo. The state universities, on the other hand, have preserved the "devotion-to-high-principle" strain in the Confucian scholar-ruler tradition of the oligarchy and remain the home of the politically minded intellectual —now typically "alienated" and forming the nucleus of political opposition.

The ideological disposition of the universities has been worth considering in some detail since they have provided the intellectual inspiration for opposition movements. (And their importance has been enhanced by the fact that Japan has few outstanding journalists. The Lippmanns and Kingsley Martins of Japan are found in the universities, writing their influential articles at scholarly length in the political monthlies—though unlike, say, a Laski or a Schlesinger, they remain apart from the rough-and-tumble of active politics.) To dwell exclusively on the universities would however be to ignore the actual organizers of opposition: the leaders of the proletarian parties, the trade unions and tenant unions of the thirties and of the Socialist movement since the war require separate consideration.

Concerning the origins of these more active leaders it is difficult to generalize. In the twenties and thirties some were students, others were unemployed intellectuals, victims of the overproduction of university graduates in the stagnant late twenties. (Most of the latter were absorbed after 1931 in the bureaucracy and the research organizations of the new Manchuria.) Still others were lawyers or schoolteachers or graduates of the technical schools which expanded rapidly after the First World War. It is difficult to discern a consistent pattern. What does seem fairly clear from the meager data summarized in Table 1 is that the rank-and-file participants in working-class movements have not produced leaders in sufficient numbers to much reduce the dominance of the middle-class intellectuals—a fact for which both the tendency for leadership to perpetuate itself in an authoritarian society and the traditional popular respect for learning may be responsible. It is also clear that the state universities as well as the private have played an important part in training the political leadership of the opposition.

TABLE 1: EDUCATIONAL BACKGROUND OF DIET MEMBERS IN LOWER HOUSE

	Proletarian Parties		Socialist Party
	1937	1947	1958
Elementary education	3 (8%)		
Secondary, higher, technical (below university standard)	5 (14%)	38 (27%)	69 (41%)
Waseda University	5 (14%)	7 (5%)	12 (7%)
Other private universities	6 (17%)	15 (11%)	27 (16%)
State universities	10 (28%)	39 (28%)	41 (24%)
Not available	7 (19%)		
Not reported, probably elementary		40 (29%)	19 (12%)
Total	36(100%)	139(100%)	168(100%)

Sources: For 1937, biographical dictionaries. For 1947 and 1958, *Shūgiin yōran* for relevant years.

III. Popular Education: Subjects become Electors

To the Tokugawa Confucian ruler, education was a good thing for the lower orders since it helped to keep them moral and obedient. To the leaders of the new Meiji regime who drew their inspiration from new sages in the West, it was necessary because an educated man was more likely to be a useful and patriotic citizen, better able to contribute to the economic and military strength of Japan. They had few doubts about the early perfectibility of man, at least of Japanese man, and few doubts about the importance of trying to perfect him. Unlike Turkey, where secondary education has expanded at the expense of popular education, Japan strove initially for mass literacy. (See Table 2.) There is no mistaking the confident enthusiasm of the declaration of 1872, which formed the preamble to the new school regulations: "Henceforth, throughout the land, without distinctions of class and sex, in no village shall there be a house without learning, in no house an ignorant individual."[7] The figures of Table 3 show how, eventually, this promise was translated into fact.

A remarkable feature of the 1872 declaration is the total (though temporary) abandonment of the collectivist assumptions which under-

[7] This preamble is translated in full in D. Kikuchi, *Japanese Education*, London, Murray, 1909, pp. 68-69.

TABLE 2: PUPILS IN SCHOOLS OF DIFFERENT GRADES PER
10,000 POPULATION

	JAPAN			TURKEY	
Year	Primary Schools	Middle and High Schools, Academic & Vocational	Year	Primary Schools	Middle Schools and Lycée
1885	808	9	1927-1928	312	12
1895	882	11	1945-1946	716	37
1905	1147	38			

Sources: For Japanese figures, Mombushō, *Meiji ikō kyōiku seidō hattatsushi*, 1938.
Turkish figures calculated from those given by Frey, p. 219.

lay traditional education and which seemed in other spheres of policy
to inspire the new emphasis on "enriching the nation and strengthening the army." Education is no longer a means of learning to fulfill
one's duty according to one's station; such a view is explicitly repudi-
ated as the product of "bad customs of long standing." The object
dwelt upon is to enable each citizen to "raise himself, manage his
property and prosper in his business." One's learning is one's "capital"
for worldly success.

Presumably the authors of this declaration knew enough of classical liberal doctrine to feel certain that a vigorous individualism *would*
ultimately promote the national welfare but, perhaps for the purposes
of arousing enthusiasm for the new education, the emphasis was all
on individual ambition. This was, however, an aberrant interlude in
Japan's educational history. Nothing in it was more aberrant than
the perfunctory treatment of the subject of moral training—the core
of traditional Confucian schooling—in elementary schools; such training was relegated to a place, and a minor place, in the curriculum only

TABLE 3: PRIMARY SCHOOL ATTENDANCE

Year	Registered Pupils Aged 6-13 as Proportion of Total Population Aged 6-13	Proportion of Girls among Registered Pupils	Average Daily Attendance as Proportion of Registered Pupils
1880	41%	25%	71%
1890	49	30	73
1900	82	45	83
1910	98	—	93

Source: Mombushō, *Meiji ikō kyōiku seidō hattatsushi*, vols. 1-5.

of the first two grades.[8] The most common textbook for the course was a straight translation of a French original published in 1867 and designed to plant a decent respect for God and the laws of the Second Empire in the hearts of little Frenchmen. Enterprising teachers were allowed to substitute instruction in contemporary Japanese police regulations.[9]

It was not long before a reaction set in. The equation of morality with fear of penal consequences shocked a good many people, as did the total abandonment of Japanese traditions implied by the inculcation of French Catholic sentiments. The first rallying call of the resurgent forces of Confucianism came in a pamphlet by the emperor's Confucian tutor, Motoda Eifu. It had all the greater authority in that Motoda had secured the emperor's permission to attribute the authorship to the emperor himself: "It has always been the understanding of all classes of our nation, the teaching of our ancestors and the doctrine of our national classics that the fundamental purpose of education is to cultivate the virtues of benevolence, righteousness, loyalty and filial piety, to develop knowledge and skills and so enable each to fulfil the duty of man. In recent years, however, only knowledge and skill have been valued; in reckless pursuit of so-called 'civilization and enlightenment' too often damage has been done to public morals and ordinary behaviour has suffered."[10]

Except that "benevolence and righteousness" (the emphasis on which has prompted some of the more politically liberating or "protestant" strains of Confucianism) were later to be overshadowed by "loyalty and filial piety," Motoda set the tone which dominated Japanese elementary education up to 1945. From the time of the revised regulations of 1881, "morals" occupies pride of place in any list of subjects to be taught in primary schools, and by 1891 the new version of these regulations defines "the development of moral character" as the most important objective of primary education.

Another crucial event in this process of "moralizing" and "nationalizing" popular education was the promulgation in 1890 of the Imperial Rescript on Education, the final product of Motoda's attempts to make the imperial institution the fount and origin of all morality. All the virtues which the rescript enumerates—loyalty and filial piety

[8] Mombushō, *Kyōiku gojūnenshi*, 1922, p. 39.
[9] Aizawa Akira, *Kyōiku hyakunen-shi-dan*, 1953, p. 64.
[10] Aizawa, *Hyakunen*, p. 74. See also D. H. Shively, "Motoda Eifu; Confucian Lecturer to the Meiji Emperor," in D. S. Nivison and A. F. Wright, *Confucianism in Action*, Stanford, 1959.

(which are one and indivisible inasmuch as the emperor is father to his people), brotherly affection, marital harmony, charity, diligence, public spirit, respect for the laws, willingness to die for the emperor in battle—are identified as part of the "Way . . . bequeathed by Our Imperial Ancestors" of which the emperor is the guardian and embodiment. Thus all the private virtues were subsumed under the general virtue of patriotic loyalty, and the rescript became until 1945 the basic sacred text of the new religion of patriotism. Memorized by all school children and subjected to endless exegesis in school ethics courses, its ceremonial incantation on all national holidays became a feature of school rituals conducted in an atmosphere of impressive solemnity.

The saturation of the schools with the reformulated national morality was the more easily achieved because central control over the school system—particularly over teacher training and textbook production— was gradually tightened. The prefectural normal schools, brought under direct ministry control by Mori's reforms of 1886, provided substantial scholarship assistance to recruit the able children of poor parents, and subjected all students to a fiercely disciplined boarding-school regime calculated to inculcate in them the military virtues of "obedience, dignity, and comradely trust."[11] The production in 1904 of the first government textbook for compulsory use in all primary schools—significantly an ethics text—was both an immediate reaction to the textbook scandal of 1903 and the culmination of a gradual process of tightening control. Thereafter, until 1945, all primary texts and a good proportion of secondary were standard ministry productions.

Thus by the early twentieth century the pattern of Japanese ideological education was fairly firmly set. The instruments of this education were the Imperial Rescript, the ethics course (working up from the homely virtues to the civic duties of loyal subjects), the Japanese language readers (designed, according to their editors, "to develop a taste for things traditionally Japanese . . . to nurture maritime and rural interests, strengthen the spirit of constitutional self-government, create pride in citizenship of a great nation . . . and as a consistent and constant theme develop a spirit of loyalty to the Emperor and love of country"),[12] and finally, in the upper years, the history course

---

[11] See especially Aizawa, *Hyakunen*, p. 116, and Kikuchi, *Japanese Education*, p. 283.
[12] Teito Kyōiku Kenkyūkai, ed., *(Kokutei Kyōkasho) Hensen shuisho shūsei*, 1932, Kokugo section, p. 32.

designed to develop a "consciousness of the national polity" by "special attention to the dignity [*awesome dignity* might be a better translation] of the Imperial Throne and to the distinction between loyal and disloyal ministers, between obedience and revolt."[13] In the latter course, orthodoxy was so delicately and rigidly balanced between ascertainable facts and the necessity of glorifying the imperial institution that an attempt to alter the accepted version of the locus of legitimacy in the wars of the fourteenth century set off a crisis which almost resulted in the cabinet's resignation.[14]

This, however, was not the end of the evolution of popular political education. The growth of working-class and Socialist movements after the turn of the century has already been mentioned. Universal education was beginning to have unintended as well as intended consequences. The workers and farmers who could now read did not confine themselves to morally improving textbooks. They began increasingly to read newspapers and by 1903 there was already, though circulating in editions of only two or three thousand copies, a radical left-wing weekly—the *Heimin Shimbun* (Common People's Newspaper)—for them to read.

As long as the developing political consciousness of the newly literate masses was primarily a *national* consciousness, there had been no cause for alarm; the Tokyo mobs, led by jingoistic demagogues, which demonstrated against the government's "weakness" in 1896 and in 1905, could be managed easily enough. But the new class-conscious movements were a different matter—as the *Heimin Shimbun*'s anti-war stand in 1904 made clear.

As soon as Katsura, the "front" leader of Yamagata's army faction, resumed power as prime minister in 1908, he gave evidence of his concern with what was now coming to be called the "ideological problem," a concern sharpened by the bloodiest of the labor disputes of the period at Ashio in the previous year. Three months after taking office, he secured a new imperial proclamation exhorting the people to greater diligence, frugality, and loyalty. At the same time a revision of the ethics texts was put in hand. The new version was completed in 1911 and, though professing to be "no different from the earlier version" in the desire to "develop the spirit of loyalty and filial piety which is the core of our national morality," it put "additional emphasis on these ideals, placed sections on the imperial shrine

[13] *Ibid.*, Rekishi section, p. 3.
[14] Aizawa, *Hyakunen*, pp. 259-262.

at Ise and on ancestor worship already in the second year and increased the number of such sections in the third and later years."[15]

In the process the texts were made somewhat more indigenously Japanese, the number of illustrative anecdotes which portrayed exemplary foreigners being reduced from 13 to 5—perhaps still a cosmopolitan selection by current international standards. At the same time there was a subtle change in the kind of patriotism which the texts sought to promote. From "love of country" the emphasis moved to "loyalty to the emperor"; the new texts dwelt not on every individual's membership in the nation and the need for individual initiatives to promote the nation's material welfare, but on the need for spiritual solidarity within a nation-family loyal to the emperor. Ishida Takeshi, who has analyzed this development of the "family-state ideology," cites the following two passages, the first of which disappeared from the early version of the ethics text, the second of which appeared for the first time in the revised version:[16]

"Farmers, merchants and artisans, each following their own professions have a duty to work diligently at their tasks and so increase the wealth and strength of our country; those who are engaged in scholarship and the arts must ever study and improve themselves and thus strive to advance our national culture. Compared with the great powers of Europe and America conditions in our country still leave much to be desired. We should all be conscious of this and do our very best to increase our national strength.

"Our country is based on the family system, and indeed our whole country is one vast family; the Imperial Family our founding family, the stem family from which we are all descended. With the same sense of loving respect as the child bears towards its parents, we Japanese revere the Imperial Throne, descended in direct line through ages eternal. It is in this sense that loyalty and filial piety are one and indivisible."

With the growing disorder of the closing years of the First World War, the demand again arose for efforts to teach not merely patriotism but the loyal self-abnegation which would help the lower orders to remain satisfied with their ample opportunities to serve society and unmoved by such materialistic considerations as the effects of inflation on their living standards. Particularly influential were a pair of resolutions passed (outside of its terms of reference) by the Emergency Edu-

---

[15] Teito Kyōiku Kenkyūkai, *Shuisho*, Shūshin section, p. 40.
[16] Ishida Takeshi, *Kindai Nihon seiji kōzō no kenkyū*, 1956, pp. 21-23.

cation Committee formed to consider questions of school organization in 1916. The drafter of these resolutions was Baron Hiranuma, the Home Office bureaucrat whose conservatism typified the "bureaucratic Fascism" which was to gain control in the thirties. The first resolution spoke of the excessive Europeanization of Japanese society, the growing materialism, the ideological disunity which attended the importation of Western ideas and institutions and outweighed the acknowledged advantages they conferred. It advocated a more strenuous effort to diffuse an understanding of the national policy and the sacred position of the imperial family, and to insure a return to the traditional "frugality and honesty" of Japan, "where sympathy and trust, mutual compassion and mutual sacrifice, governed relations between noble and base, rich and poor, so that the nation was a united family." In this way, by educational measures, by legislative reinforcement of the authority within the family of the head of the household, by improvement of official morality, and by some attempts to equalize incomes and "harmonize" the interests of capital and labor, the nation might be able to reverse current tendencies for "the rich to wallow in vain luxury and for the poor to abandon moderation."[17]

The second resolution suggested the introduction of military drill into primary schools in order to cultivate "good habits of discipline and obedience" and "a sincere spirit . . . on which the practical application of the virtues taught in the ethics course depends."[18]

The first resolution inspired attempts to revise the provisions of the civil code relating to the family, the foundation of the Conciliation Society (*Kyōchōkai*) to "harmonize" the interests of capital and labor, and a still further revision of the ethics textbooks, begun in 1918 and completed in 1923. The second resolution was partly put into effect in 1925 when military officers were attached to every middle and high school to drill pupils for two hours a week.

The cure was not entirely adequate to the disease, however, and the dose had to be made stronger. Yet another revision of the ethics courses, begun in 1933, further strengthened their nationalistic content, and, as the nation finally prepared for a total war, new civics texts, the *Kokutai no Hongi* (Essence of the National Polity), 1937[19] and the *Shimmin no Michi* (Way of the Subject), 1941, carried patriotism to

[17] Mombushō, *Meiji ikō*, vol. 5, pp. 1,197-1,203.
[18] *Ibid.*, p. 1,196.
[19] A translation of this work is available, R. K. Hall, ed., *Kokutai no Hongi: Cardinal Principles of the National Entity of Japan*, Cambridge, 1949.

a degree of fervor and metaphysical obscurity which the authors of Meiji ethics texts might have found it difficult to imagine.

Intensified indoctrination was not, of course, the only solution Japanese governments adopted to meet the problem posed by a literate, increasingly politically conscious and by no means contented populace. The logical consequence of universal primary education—and universal conscription—was finally accepted; the working classes were admitted as voters to the political community. It was a measure of the country's readiness for the manhood suffrage act of 1925 that 80 per cent of the electorate voted in the next elections three years later. Most of the new voters had ties with landlords or employers which integrated them into the existing middle-class parties; some supported the new "proletarian" parties which, finding parliamentary representation possible at the very time when intensified police repression was further discouraging revolutionary aspiration, came more and more to content themselves with demanding fair shares for the underprivileged within the existing political system. Sometimes, allying themselves with radical elements in the army against the middle-class parties, they showed an impeccably patriotic nationalism.

When Veblen wrote in 1915 that the "opera bouffe mythology" of emperor-centered Shinto and "the medieval spirit of servile solidarity" of the people was bound sooner or later to be eaten away by the rationalism and individualism which the processes of industrialization and urbanization inevitably brought in their train[20] there were signs enough that he might be right. But he underestimated the efficiency of the educational system. Continuously fortified, until 1942, with the real successes of Japanese arms in keeping the national image ever more refulgent, the sacredness of the complex of imperial and national symbols hardly needed the protection of stringent laws against lèse-majesté. So oppressive was the orthodoxy of the national myths that even those who promoted them for the sake of expediency ceased to be able to question them. In the closing months of the war, when the peace party was seeking ways of extricating Japan from an impossible position, none of its members could openly hint that it might be worth sacrificing the imperial institution in order to do so.[21]

The year 1945 marked the end of the ethics course and of attempts to achieve standard production of loyal and obedient patriots in the

[20] "The Opportunity of Japan," in *Essays in Our Changing Order*, New York, 1943.
[21] See R. Butow, *Japan's Decision to Surrender*, Stanford, 1954.

elementary schools. But after half a century in which these had been central concerns, it was impossible that primary education should lose its political significance. The schools have continued to be a major source of political conflict to the present day.

The changes introduced under the Occupation regime were radical. Textbook production was turned over to free enterprise with only loose certification by a central authority. Locally elected education committees assumed powers over staff, curriculum, and textbook choice which had formerly been concentrated in the ministry. Ethics disappeared from the curriculum along with history and geography, and the social studies course which took their place was supposed to teach an objective and critical knowledge of the nature and history of Japanese institutions. History was written to make students mindful not of the glorious reigns of former emperors but of class divisions, of economic exploitation, and of struggles for freedom and equality in the face of oppression and despotism. The teachers became organized in a powerful trade union dominated by radical left-wing leaders, and were able in many districts to secure sympathetic majorities on local education committees.

The decade since the ending of the Occupation has seen steady pressure by the conservative parties controlling the government to "correct the excesses" of these reforms, and legislation seeking that end has been responsible for some of the tensest political crises of the period. Particular sources of controversy have been the bills to prevent teachers from joining political parties and to prohibit their union from disseminating political literature, the bill to replace elected by nominated education committees, an abortive bill to restore central control over textbooks, the institution of a new course of moral instruction, and the introduction of a merit-rating system increasing the teachers' liability to discipline on political as well as on other grounds. Perhaps no other educational system in the world is so continuously and so earnestly fought over.[22] In part the struggles have been struggles for power between the government and a union fighting to retain its organizational cohesion and the privileges of its members. It is much more, however, than a mere dependence on that union's funds and organization which has prompted the Socialist party to resist these measures with every constitutional and unconstitutional means at its disposal. Socialists have seen in these measures a

[22] For an excellent analysis see M. B. Jansen, "Education, Values and Politics in Japan," *Foreign Affairs*, July 1957.

196

conscious attempt by the conservatives to restore thought-control of the pre-war sort, and university intellectuals even of moderate political views have shared their fears—as witness the public protest by a group of university presidents against the abolition of education committee elections in 1956. It is true enough that a good many conservative politicians look back with nostalgia to the days when their patriotic oratory evoked tears rather than cynical smiles and when the nation really seemed a united family thrilling to the exploits of its heroic soldiery. But this is nostalgia rather than a basis for policy, if for no other reason than that the world now provides no arena for Japanese soldiers. It would be hard to find even a conservative politician who truly believed in the possibility of resurrecting the pre-war "national polity" with its imperial rescript and sacred rituals. These men are striving rather, more modestly, for a world in which children will once again sing the national anthem with enthusiasm, show a proper respect for their elders, and cease to imagine that the critical application of ideas from books can compete with the accumulated wisdom of men of character: a world above all in which children will grow up into patriotic and respectful adults disposed to vote for the Liberal-Democratic Party.

The "reverse-course" has proceeded slowly, if steadily, perhaps most effectively by means which have not required legislation and so have not attracted much attention. The gradual tightening of central ministry control by fiscal and other measures has now given the advisory circulars of that ministry the authority of directives, and the system of textbook certification has been slowly tightened. Thanks to the latter expedient, the more single-minded interpretations of Japanese history in the light of class warfare have now been expunged from the textbooks, but the Japanese child still gets a version of his country's past much less partisan and much closer to the canons of academic historians than his counterpart in most industrial countries. The new morals course reminds children of the duties as well as the rights of democratic citizens, but in terms which would have counted as pernicious and subversively individualistic before the war.[23] If it is no longer as certain now as it

[23] The general intention of the course is defined as follows: "While consistently inculcating a respect for human dignity, to show how that respect is expressed in practice within the family, the school and other groups to which the individual belongs, and to train Japanese who will strive for the creation of a rich and distinctive culture and the development of a democratic state and society, and so make a positive contribution to a peaceful international society." The topics range from "developing a respect for life and health" and "learning that dress, speech, and gesture should be appropriate to place and occasion" in the early elementary years, to a final section in the last middle-school year on patriotism, the short outline of

197

was ten years ago that an overwhelming proportion of the rising generation will cast their first votes for the Socialist party, it is by no means certain, either, that they would fall easy victims to mass totalitarian appeals of any complexion. The content of education apart, there seems to have been a considerable change in the atmosphere of post-war schools. There is greater freedom of classroom discussion and less disposition on the part of teachers to maintain an aloof dignity. The more subtle forms of value transmission between teachers and pupils may not have changed so very radically—it is easy to imagine the implications a graduate of a pre-war normal school could give to the theme in the new morals course that "dress, language, and gesture should be appropriate to place and occasion"—but it seems safe to say that the products of post-war schools, as compared with their fathers, are *more* like citizens rather than subjects, are *better* capable of forming political opinions which they at least imagine are their own, and are *more* certain of their right to hold and express such opinions.

Whether they are more *likely* to hold such opinions is a different matter. Quite apart from the enervating effects of intensified competition for higher education and a career, the political neutralization of post-war education may well have made the new generation as a whole less politically conscious than its parents. The young man who left an upper elementary school in 1935 may not have thought himself entitled to an opinion about what Japan's foreign policy should be, but at least he thought he ought to read the newspapers with care and concern. The modern young man may well be more concerned to get a transistor television set. It is as difficult to find conclusive evidence for trends towards "apathy," "privatization," "mass-media hypnosis," or "consumption orientation" in Japanese as in Western societies, and the evidence of polling statistics is ambiguous.[24] The

which runs: "As citizens of our country it is natural for us to feel an affection for our land and our fellow-countrymen and to respect and admire our cultural traditions. We should foster this natural sentiment and strive to build an even better country. However, we should not forget that a spirit of patriotism can only too easily develop into racial prejudice and narrow self-sufficiency. We should be on our guard against this and strive to get a full appreciation of the national cultures of other countries and to develop a general love of humanity, while at the same time, each in our own country, trying to create a distinctive culture which can be a source of pride to us as members of international society." (*Teikoku Chihō Gyōsei Gakkai, Dōtoku kyōiku jisshi yoko*, 1958, pp. 3, 4, 30.)

[24] A public opinion poll suggests that the voting ratio for 20-29-year-olds in the 1955 elections was no lower than for older age groups. (Jichichō, Senkyobu, *Shōwa 30-nen 2-gatsu shikkō Shūgiin sōsenkyo kekka shirabe*, 1955, p. 173.) A survey of voters in Nara prefecture in the 1958 elections, however, shows considerable dif-

point is that in these respects Japan now differs little from Western societies.

One final point deserves mention. Since the war, women have been given the vote and all higher education has become coeducational in principle, even though the majority of female university students still in fact attend segregated women's colleges. The proportion of women voters has climbed steadily with each post-war election—the female voting ratio being 15 per cent lower than the male in 1946, only 7 per cent lower in 1958—and there is evidence to suggest that the female vote is not simply part of a family vote. The fact that civics and morals courses at all levels are now taught in a coeducational context should further promote the integration of women into the active political community. In a country where there has been a sharp divergence between the values and personalities of men and women, politics are likely to change as they become less exclusively an all-male preserve.

IV. National Unity and Class Division

Whether a society like Britain in which political party organization reflects class divisions is more or less "modern" than a society like America where it does not, is a topic which may be safely left to those who think "modernization" a useful concept for political science. It is nevertheless worth pointing out in any discussion of the relation between education and politics that, whether making in this regard for greater modernity or for less, the modern Japanese educational system has worked in a number of ways to prevent the development of class consciousness in Japan.

The most obvious and direct way—the propagation of the family-state ideology—has already been treated at length. Second, the almost total state monopoly of provisions for primary and secondary schooling, with the attendant national uniformity of curricula, produced a great homogeneity of sentiment and knowledge. Third, the school system made possible quite high rates of social mobility from one generation to the next.

---

ferences between age groups. Abstentions for each age between 20 and 29 ranged between 22.5% and 29.9% compared with averages of 16.1% for those aged 37-41 and 13.7% for those aged 42-46. A survey of voters in Nakano-ku, Tokyo, is said to have shown similar results. (Sakurazawa Tohei, "Chikagoro no tōhyō keikō," *Senkyo Jihō*, Vol. 9, No. 5, May 1960, p. 4.) It is impossible, however, to discount the effect of the greater mobility of the unmarried younger age groups.

The small part played by private schools in primary education is clear from the first column of Table 4. Since Japanese cities (and *a fortiori* rural areas) tend to show less clear patterns of residential segregation by social class than most Western cities, the public monopoly alone ensures a considerable mixing of social classes in school.

TABLE 4: STUDENTS PER TEN THOUSAND POPULATION AND PROPORTION IN PRIVATE SCHOOLS

A. Number of students per 10,000 population
B. Proportion of students enrolled in private foundations (per cent)

Year	Primary Schools[1] B	Boys Academic Middle Schools[2] A	B	Vocational & Technical Middle Schools[3] A	B	Vocational & Technical High Schools[4] A	B	Academic High Schools[5] A	B	Universities A	B
1890	1.9	3	14.1	incl. in ➡		3	69.8	1	0.0	0.3	0.
1915	0.3	27	22.3	17	13.0	6	78.0	1	0.0	1.9	0.
1940	0.3	61	(17?)	87	(35?)	20	70.3	3	11.4	11.5	61

Year	Lower Secondary Schools[1] B	Higher Secondary Schools[7] A	B	Junior Colleges[8] A	B	Universities A	B
1959	0.3	3.3	339	26.3	9	78.5	54.5	64.

[1] Attendance compulsory. (For 4 years in 1890, 6 in 1915 and 1940, 9 in 1959.)
[2] Ages 13 to 17.
[3] A variety of schools usually classified as *jitsugyō-gakkō*, with courses of one to five years falling between the ages 13 and 17. A variety of other short-course trade schools and continuation schools are excluded from these figures.
[4] A variety of schools usually classified as *semmon-gakkō*, with courses of one to five years falling between the ages 16 and 20.
[5] Three-year courses usually at ages 18 to 20.
[6] Usually entered at ages 20 plus to 1940, 18 plus in 1959.
[7] Including both academic and vocational courses, ages 16 to 18.
[8] Usually two-year courses, ages 19 to 20.
Sources: Mombushō, *Meiji ikō kyōiku seidō hattatsushi*, 1938 (for 1890 and 1915). Sōrifu, Tōkeikyoku, *Nihon tōkei nenkan* No. 1 (for 1949), No. 11 (for 1959).

Private schools have contributed more to secondary education. These schools, however, have been of three kinds: Christian foundations, which made up the majority in the early period; progressive schools, founded mostly in the twenties by adherents of particular educational philosophies; and preparatory schools whose main *raison d'être* is that they provide for those whose parents can afford it a better preparation for *state* schools of the next higher grade. Though each of these types of schools drew its pupils predominantly (the last two types almost exclusively) from the middle class, they never attracted all, or even a large proportion, of middle class children. At no time did the pre-war private middle schools absorb as much as 2 per cent of an age group. Finally, at the top of the system the state universities have never ceased to enjoy a prestige superior to that even of Keio and Waseda, the "best" private universities. Hence private university education has always been a second-best alternative, its graduates commanding lower starting salaries in the big firms before the war and inferior employment chances since, and private pre-university education has generally been geared to the requirements of state university entrance.

As a consequence, one does not find in Japanese society the cultural differences which separate the Etonian from the graduate of Little-puddle Grammar School or the product of a New England private school from an Oklahoma country high-school graduate. The whole-sale reordering of the class system brought about by the land and fiscal reforms of early Meiji considerably blurred such differentiations according to status in any case, and the educational system has operated further to homogenize its products rather than to promote new differences among them. Until 1945 almost every Japanese had spent the first six years of his school life in the same kind of school reading the same textbooks. Landlord and tenant, judge and prison warder, prime minister and carpenter all knew the same stories about Benjamin Franklin and his kite-flying, Florence Nightingale and her lamp-carrying, the faithful dog Hachiko and his mourning of his master's death; they all had the same image of London as wrapped in perpetual fog, had learned the same poems about cherry blossoms, and could sing the same words to "Coming through the Rye."[25] A large store of shared sentiment and knowledge has political implications. First, it minimizes the extent to which cultural differences carrying resented implications of "upper" and "lower" add to antagonism arising from economic inequalities. Second, it makes for ease of communication between political leaders and their electorate, between officials and citizens. In this century, for example, Japanese agrarian administration, and its extension services in particular, have been more efficient than those of India or Southern Italy, where cultural divisions create a wider gulf between administrators and peasants.

---

[25] Some evidence of this cultural homogeneity may be seen in a Tokyo study of manual and non-manual workers' wives. Tominaga Kenichi, "Toshi kazoku no shufu ni okeru kaisonai doshitsusei to kaisokan ishitsusei," *Shakaigaku Hyōron*, No. 38, 1960.

Finally, there is the complex relationship between education, social mobility, and political structure. It seems reasonable enough to suppose that, whatever other kinds of conflict it may engender and whatever its effect in heightening awareness of class divisions, a high rate of social mobility tends to weaken conscious class solidarity and diminish the probability of class conflict—because so many people change their class position within their lifetime, because potential leaders of lower class groups become absorbed into the class above them, and because the prospect of higher status for oneself or one's children offers a personal solution for the frustrations of class inferiority as an alternative to a collective solution through class-conscious political activity. Such personal solace depends, of course, not on whether the opportunities for upward mobility are in fact great but on whether they are believed to be great.

Fundamentally, the high rate of upward mobility in Japan in the last century has been the result of economic development. "Upper" occupational groups have been expanding faster than the occupational groups of lower prestige. That education itself has contributed much to this economic development, a glance at the figures for technical and vocational education given below will suggest.

It follows from the importance of the contribution of vocational education to economic development that such education has become a chief instrument of upward mobility, especially in modernized sectors of industry where the rates of labor turnover are low. At the same time, academic education has provided the path to prestige positions of a more general administrative and managerial kind. The figures quoted by Inoki elsewhere in this volume[26] indicate the importance of a university training for entry into the higher civil service, and comparable evidence reveals its importance for business leaders. Whereas a sample of business men in a *Who's Who* of 1915 contained only 8 per cent who had received higher education, the proportion was 69 per cent for a similar sample drawn from the 1955 edition.[27] At more modest levels of life the relationship between educational level and job destination is shown by a survey of national scope conducted in 1955. The proportion of managerial and professional workers with an education beyond the upper elementary was 77 per cent. For all other clerical workers the figure was 66 per cent, for all manual

[26] See p. 296.
[27] Asō Makato, "Kindai Nihon ni okeru eriito-kōsei no hensen," *Kyōiku Shakai-gaku Nempō*, 15, p. 159.

workers, excluding farmers with an even lower percentage, 16 per cent.[28]

Granted the importance of the school system in advancing personal careers, whether or not the system worked to increase mobility between the generations depends on how equally distributed the opportunities for access to education were. Some relevant evidence may be seen in the published figures of applicants and entrants in pre-war schools. At no time after 1896 were more than 71 per cent of those who sought to enter the academic middle schools successful in the competitive entrance examinations, and in periods when the competition was keenest that ratio fell as low as 45 per cent. For the academic high school, where selection was still more rigorous, the ratio of acceptances fell steadily from 56 per cent in 1896 to 15 per cent in 1937.[29] Since the entrance tests have almost always been objectively fair, a certain measure of academic ability has clearly been required of entrants to the schools conferring the greatest advantages. One consequence of this is that rates of downward mobility—a useful measure for comparing the permeability of class barriers in different countries since it discounts the effect of differing rates of economic expansion—have been fairly high by international standards.[30]

But if ability was a necessary criterion, it was not a sufficient one. Secondary schools and universities have always charged fees, and there have been very few scholarship allowances to compensate for earnings foregone. Hence, although fees were modest, particularly in state schools, children of the poorest families have been excluded from academic higher education and have been able to secure secondary vocational training only at a sacrifice. One of the most striking differences between the recruitment of contemporary business leaders in Japan and America, according to a recent statistical comparison, lies in the total absence in the Japanese sample of the sons of manual laborers and tenant farmers.[31]

It still remains true that vocational and academic secondary and higher education has been provided in sufficient variety and at sufficiently low cost for most parents to have realistic hopes of advancing a

[28] Nihon Shakai Gakkai Chōsa Iinkai, *Nihon shakkai no kaiso-teki kōzō*, 1958, p. 152.

[29] Mombushō, *Meiji ikō*, Vol. 4, and Shimizu Yoshihiro, *Shiken*, 1957, p. 9.

[30] S. M. Miller, *Comparative Social Mobility*, *Current Sociology*, Vol. ix, No. 1, 1960, esp. the summary table, p. 56.

[31] J. C. Abegglen and H. Mannari, "Leaders of Modern Japan: Social Origins and Mobility," *Economic Development and Cultural Change*, Vol. 9, No. 1, Part 2, October 1960, p. 128.

brighter-than-average child at least one step higher than his parents in the hierarchy of occupations. If failure in an entrance examination disappointed these hopes, at least the system had a certain impartiality which served to blunt resentment. Evidence that the chances of "getting on" seem to most Japanese real enough and fairly enough distributed may be seen in the policy declarations of the Socialist party. For all its preoccupation with educational questions in recent years, the demand for scholarships to equalize educational opportunities receives bare mention in its policy documents and almost no attention in its electioneering.[32]

V. Summary

The Confucian education of the period which preceded the drive to modernity provided in many respects a solid foundation for that drive.

The bureaucracy rather quickly and effectively established its own academies for training its successors, and the products of these institutions have continued until the present time to dominate the elite groups of the Japanese nation.

The non-official higher schools, early associated with opposition movements, eventually became reconciled to the status quo, and the ideological center of nonconformity moved to the state universities. The graduates of private universities, however, having less easy access to positions of power have continued to be active in opposition movements.

Elementary education was skillfully used to inculcate nationalism and the incentive to put it to such uses was strengthened by the need to heal social divisions which universal education itself had inevitably helped to bring to articulate political expression—an inevitability which was recognized in the granting of universal suffrage.

The predominance of public over private education, the uniform control over public education, and the wide diffusion of opportunities for some kind of secondary or higher education served to minimize class divisions.

[32] See, e.g., Nihon Shakaitō, *Shakaitō no shinrosen (Dai-20-kai taikai ketteishū)*, 1961, p. 119.

B. TURKEY

FREDERICK W. FREY

I. Introduction

In this essay we shall interpret "education" as referring to the legally sanctioned public and private *school system* in Turkey. And we shall confine our treatment of "political development" to modern changes in the structure of *power*. Hence our topic becomes the relationship between the Turkish school system and the distribution of power in Turkish society in comparatively modern times.

In all industrial societies the citizenry is highly organized. Potent armies are maintained. Taxes are regularly collected from masses of people. Detailed laws are enforced over a wide area. Industrial enterprises command the labor of tens of thousands. Highways are built, railroads laid, tele-communications are established, and complex voluntary associations formed—all involving the interrelated efforts of great numbers of people. One of the hallmarks of a "modern" nation, in fact, is its ability continuously to mobilize the efforts of a large percentage of its citizens. Conversely, one of the salient characteristics of a "traditional" society is its relative inability to do so. Traditional societies tend to be fragmented and to lack the massive institutions distinguishing the modern powers they so often wish to emulate. Behavior in these societies tends to be concerted only irregularly, on a small scale, and for limited ends.

The high degree of organization in "advanced" states is necessarily produced by power, by consensus, or by some combination of the two. People act in concert either spontaneously because they possess similar attitudes or because they are acted upon by other people. The description of the forces making for coordination is one of the basic tasks confronting current social science.

Most well-established modern societies, totalitarian as well as democratic, work quite hard at securing consensus on matters deemed important by guiding elements in the society. Many emerging nations, Turkey among them, labor even harder to create consensus among an awakening populace. It is in the long run cheaper and surer to unite a nation through persuasion than through establishing effective power relations. If a man can be made to want to act in concert with his fellows, he will cooperate more efficiently and more certainly than if he must forever be prodded by someone else.

THE EDUCATIONAL SYSTEM AS A SOCIALIZING AGENCY

In many developing nations the school system is a major agency for inducing the consensus so urgently sought. Since it is difficult to reach into the sanctum of the family, the school will normally provide the state with its first opportunity to mold the ideas and opinions of its citizens. A comprehensive school system, even when it fails to make its students agree consciously among themselves, will impart some of the same values and modes of cognition to them all. It is in school, for example, that the child usually gets his first intensive experience of peer relationships. In the family he occupies a unique position—as the oldest boy, for instance, or the youngest girl, or the third of five sons. No other family member is in an identical position. In school, he is one student among many, in a position of virtual power equality with his classmates vis-à-vis the teacher.[1]

In school, also, the child may encounter for the first time the concept of power invested in a role rather than in a specific person. In the family, the notion of paternal authority is hardly separable from the distinctive personality of the father. But in school the child usually encounters a new teacher each year, and perceives that, while their personalities may differ, each one wields a similar power. The concept of legitimate power invested in a role regardless of personality—i.e., of authority—is inevitably impressed on the child through these experiences.

Finally, in most school systems the child is taught certain specific values, explicitly or implicitly, and he also forms certain intellectual habits which will color his subsequent thinking about politics. He becomes distinguishable from persons in the same society who have had no schooling or different schooling. He is exposed, moreover, to values and attitudes different from those of his family, and he must come to terms with them. His means of accomplishing this initial reconciliation may well influence how he will resolve value conflicts and face social pressures throughout his life.

In general, certainly, schools are able to produce a considerable degree of consensus in a society and to facilitate that organization of

---

[1] Many stimulating suggestions about the role of the school system in American society are contained in Talcott Parsons, "The School Class as a Social System: Some of Its Functions in American Society," reprinted in A. H. Halsey, Jean Flood, and C. Arnold Anderson, eds., *Education, Economy and Society*, New York, 1961, pp. 434-455.

masses of people in the society which is necessary to national economic and political power.

EDUCATION AND SOCIAL PLACEMENT

School experiences directly affect an individual's subsequent political attitudes; they also change his subsequent position in the society, for the mere awareness that he has attended certain schools will cause other people to react differently to him. In most societies, people tend to defer to the man with formal education. The decisions made in a society about who will secure an education hence go far toward determining future patterns of power in that society.

The ability of education to determine the place of a person in his society also implies the ability to raise him to a higher class. In many societies the educational system is one of the main avenues of social mobility. In traditional societies it may be virtually the only such avenue. The greater the social rewards which education can offer, the more crucial the popular evaluation of access to the educational system will become. In most emergent nations, education offers great rewards and hence looms large in the popular consciousness.

Education further alters a man's behavior in that it places him in certain circles of friendship or acquaintance. The bonds formed between classmates, particularly in elite secondary schools, often endure throughout life. There is ample evidence of the significance of these bonds among political leaders in many countries.

We have not, unfortunately, enough data at hand to study the social and political positions of samples of the graduates of Turkish schools at every level. Only limited information from a few schools is available. Starting from the other end of the scale, however, we can call upon a detailed study of the social backgrounds of Turkish political leaders.[2] Using these materials, we shall try to ascertain the bearing of Turkish education on Turkish political careers.

THE EDUCATIONAL INSTITUTION AS POLITICAL ACTOR AND POLITICAL ISSUE

We have been looking upon the school system as a training and socializing institution. But that is not all it is. The school system in most countries is also a large-scale organization, serving its own interests and vying with other organizations in the society for power and

[2] Frederick W. Frey, *The Turkish Political Elite*, Cambridge, Mass., 1964.

resources. Attempting to sway governmental policy, it affects even non-educational decisions of government. The Minister of Education is usually a cabinet official who actively seeks greater budgetary appropriations and specific changes in policy and personnel. Teachers often organize as an occupational group and ask politicians to attend to their grievances. Private schools frequently attempt to further their interests by political action. Students stage demonstrations which often have momentous political repercussions. In these activities, the component parts of the educational system become "interest groups," striving to affect policy without assuming formal power, and all such activities tend to alter the distribution of power in the society.

Among non-academic interests in the society, meanwhile, a simultaneous struggle may well go on over the educational system and its performance. Education is usually a prominent political issue. Political parties commonly wrangle about the degree of state influence to be exercised over the schools, the role of religion in the schools, the costs of education, the types of instruction to be given, the recruitment of teachers, and so on. The press regularly comments on educational matters, criticizing specific practices, or proposing new policies. Voluntary associations and often the schools themselves may be drawn into the melee. Inasmuch as the elements in an educational system become political agents as well as objects of political conflict, we shall further consider the educational system in Turkey as an active element in the Turkish political system.

For the reasons given, this examination of education and political development in Turkey will have four main parts. The first will supply the historical background of the present Turkish school system. The next will deal with the impact of the school system on the "political culture" of the nation, much of the evidence in this section being drawn from a national survey of the values of secondary-school students in Turkey conducted in 1959.[3] The third part will discuss the social position of the educated person in Turkish society and will analyze the educational backgrounds of Turkish political leaders. In the fourth and concluding section, the educational institution will be examined as a direct actor in politics.

[3] This survey (involving 1,847 respondents) was directed by Frederick W. Frey, George W. Angell, Jr., and Abdurrahman Ş. Sanay, and accomplished with the co-operation of the Test and Research Bureau of the Turkish Ministry of Education. Detailed analyses of the results are currently being prepared and will be published for specific topics in article form as they are completed.

II. A Brief Sketch of the Development of the Modern Turkish Educational System[4]

By the end of the nineteenth century, Turkish society was rent into two parts: the "ruling elite" and the peasant masses. The *passe partout* for entry into the governing class was education as manifested in a minimal literary competence. In general, few doors of opportunity were closed to the Muslim youth, of whatever origin, who could speak and write properly; no talents of any sort ordinarily availed the youth who could not.

A second crucial division existed within the ruling elite between those who had received a modern secular education and those who had received traditional religious instruction. The resulting three elements of the society were clearly distinguished and commented upon by a contemporary, Ziya Gökalp: "In this country there are three layers of people differing from each other by civilization and education: the common people, the men educated in *medreses*, the men educated in [modern] secular schools. The first still are not freed from the effects of Far Eastern civilization; the second are still living in Eastern civilization; it is only the third group which has had some benefits from Western civilization. That means that one portion of our nation is living in an ancient, another in a medieval, and a third in a modern age. How can the life of a nation be normal with such a threefold life? How can we be a real nation without unifying this threefold education?"[5]

The ultimate response which the nation made to this demand for consensus was, of course, to give one element—those with a modern secular education—increasing power over the rest.

As has been widely noted, the history of "Westernization" or "modernization" in Turkey is in large measure the history of secular education there—of a school system which turned out more and more "modern" graduates until the balance was tipped in favor of European ways. The educational system has further been the means of transmitting a quite indigenous spirit of progress which can be distinguished

[4] This sketch relies heavily on Osman Ergin's five-volume *History of Turkish Education (Türkiye Maarif Tarihi)*, Istanbul, Osmanbey Matbaası, 1939-1943. The best discussion in English of the development of the Turkish educational system in general and the *lycée* in particular is in Richard E. Maynard, *The Lise and its Curriculum in the Turkish Educational System*, unpublished Ph.D. dissertation, Department of Education, University of Chicago, 1961. Other useful works are listed in the bibliography.

[5] Niyazi Berkes, ed., *Turkish Nationalism and Western Civilization: Selected Essays of Ziya Gökalp*, New York, 1959, p. 278.

from any concrete Western ideas. The pervasiveness of this spirit has remained correlative to the growth of the secular school system of the society.[6]

A MODERN EDUCATIONAL SYSTEM

What, we may ask, are the common features of a "modern" educational system such as the Turks have sought to establish in recent years?

In modern societies, first of all, the state accepts prime responsibility for public education, at least up to the secondary level. Minimal standards of education, such as literacy and the elementary use of numbers, are deemed necessary—and no doubt are necessary—to the modern citizen's economic, social, and political roles. Hence, general compulsory education through early adolescence becomes the rule.

Second, to ensure a supply of technically and professionally trained people, there has developed an integrated system of schools extending normally from primary to university level, and the development of these levels has to be kept in some kind of balance. Failing to attain an appropriately ordered system of this sort, an advancing society may encounter problems of alienated and unemployed intellectuals, of demanding, clerically trained white-collar classes, of half-educated technicians who waste resources, or of frustrated students denied further education.

Third, within the three-level educational pyramid, the normal or teacher-training school is generally believed of special significance, for the training and placement of a sufficient number of able teachers usually constitutes one of the greatest difficulties facing the developing nation.

Finally, if the state is going to accept these responsibilities and establish these institutions, an administrative structure adequate to coordinate them all must be created and meshed with the other administrative structures of the state. Specifically, the nation aspiring

---

[6] Indeed, it is tempting to think almost mechanistically in terms of a certain critical size or definite threshold in the production of "new Turks" before which modernizing efforts failed and after which they, at least superficially, succeeded. Nor do we want to reject such an idea out of hand, alarmed by its apparently naïve simplicity. It may well be that under certain conditions useful predictions about the development and success of a modernizing cadre could be made on the basis of the growth in size of that cadre, with a specific minimal cadre size being seen as necessary for the development of effective communications and power patterns within the cadre and between the cadre and the rest of the society.

to a modern educational system must collect tax monies to support that system and must translate those funds into buildings, textbooks, salaries, and scholarships by means of some reasonably effective administrative structure—usually in practice a ministry of education. The administration of a modern educational system itself demands a fairly complex and comprehensive political and social order. A lack of any such order doomed much educational reform in the Ottoman Empire of the nineteenth century to failure.[7]

EDUCATION PRIOR TO THE NINETEENTH CENTURY

Before the early part of the nineteenth century, the Ottoman state never accepted responsibility for the basic education of its citizens or subjects. Hence no formal system of public education then existed. The state trained some of its own military and bureaucratic officials; the clergy instructed some of its own future members; but the education of non-official, non-clerical subjects was not conceived as a public responsibility. The process of "modernization" in education involved the gradual and grudging acceptance of this responsibility by the Ottoman state.

Excluding foreign and non-Muslim establishments, three main types of school existed in the pre-nineteenth-century Ottoman Empire. These were the Palace School (*Enderun Mektebi*), the religious schools (*medrese*), and the private children's primary schools, the *sübyan* (or *sıbyan*) *mektebleri*, supported by the religious institution. The rich, moreover, made use of private tutors (*lâla*) for instructing their offspring. On the whole, the demand for a more general education hardly seems to have been urgent during the period of Ottoman decline, and no national or even approximately modern school system existed. By the nineteenth century, the instruction given in all of the traditional types of school had deteriorated. The curricula had become petrified, recruitment standards had crumbled, and the proportion of the population receiving instruction—always small—had shrunk appreciably.

INITIAL ESTABLISHMENT OF MODERN SCHOOLS TO 1869

The initiation of that secular, modern education in Turkey which first split and then eventually transformed the ruling elite is conventionally given the date of 1793-1795. At that time, after the Ottoman

---

[7] It is interesting to note that these features of a modern educational institution have their close analogues in other modern institutions, such as an army, a bureaucracy, etc.

armies had suffered repeated defeats from forces "using more advanced military tactics, a special army school was formed for instruction in the use of artillery. This," as an official Turkish description says, "was the first school that was wholly independent of the *medreses*."[8] In fact, one could as well select the opening of the naval school of mathematics in 1773, or even of the short-lived school of geometry (*Hendeshane*) in 1734, as the first institutional evidences of a change which had its historical origins stretching still further back. We need here only observe, however, that in the late eighteenth century there began that long development of a secular, modern education which remade Turkish society, and that it began in the area of military instruction, among an element already most strategically located within the power structure of Ottoman society.

For rapid modernization to occur, it is not enough that some carrying element in the society be thoroughly modernized. The location of that element in the power and communications structures of the society is also of vital importance. Scant direct influence and even scant "demonstration effect" occur if the cadre affected is one poorly placed and of meager power. Indeed, the early modernization of a pariah element may actually inhibit acceptance of modernization by majority groups. One outstanding point about the educational innovations that constituted the core of Turkish development is that they involved elements—the military and then the bureaucracy—that were already at or near the heart of the power structure of the society. The modernizing cadre did not have to work its way to power from an initially weak and peripheral position. Moreover, once converted itself, it had only one major antagonist to overcome: the religious institution. Certainly much of the relative speed of Turkish development can be comprehended in these terms.[9]

The inauguration of a few secular schools within the military establishment began a process of change of which the end result was a set of parallel educational institutions, one religious and one secular, mutually antagonistic and revealing the profound intra-elite conflict between the military and bureaucratic contingent and the religious hierarchy. These two most powerful institutions reached down deeply into the lower social orders through their own carefully protected

[8] *Education in Turkey*, New York, Turkish Information Office, n.d., p. 4.

[9] Understanding the even more rapid Japanese modernization is similarly aided by the realization that no major institutional antagonist confronted the Japanese modernizing element once that element was fully formed. See the concluding chapter.

educational systems. They were the institutions in the society which made the greatest effort to inculcate distinctive, specific, and uniform outlooks among those youths whom they recruited.

Some other consequences of the origins of modern Turkish education in the military institution are worth noting. First of all, as the avowed preservers of the state from external domination, the military, then as now, enjoyed a powerful and unimpeachable position and could push through demands which would probably have been stymied if they had sprung from any other source. Second, since the activities of a modern military establishment are varied, the educational structure which it requires is both extensive and diverse. Because the armed forces needed doctors, a military medical school was established. Because the army required veterinarians, a military veterinary school was founded. Competence in engineering was deemed essential to the modern army, and military engineering instruction was developed. By the time the needs of the army were met, an educational system was in existence which was so variously useful that it virtually cried out to be reproduced in the civil sphere. Many of the instructors in the early civil schools were military officers; the military establishment provided the nation with its initial pool of instructional talent.

In higher education, where the "modern" influences were most seminal, the sequence of events is highly revealing. Military schools were established in 1773, 1795, 1827, 1834, and 1849; then the Civil Service School (*Mülkiye*) was created; not until 1900 do we find a civilian university preparing a significant number of students for careers other than official. The same official emphasis also prevailed in early secondary education.

ATTEMPTS TO DEVELOP AN INTEGRATED SCHOOL SYSTEM: 1869-1923

In 1867, Sultan Abdülaziz visited the Paris Exposition and came away duly impressed with the glories of French culture. The following year a virtual replica of the French *lycée* was established in Istanbul and given the grand name of the Imperial School. This school lived up to that name and to the expectations of its founders. Instruction in most subjects in the school (later better known as Galatasaray) was in French, generally offered by French teachers, and of superior quality. Behind the fancy iron gate of Galatasaray, where the youth normally boarded throughout the period of his adolescence, a strong *esprit* developed. The students knew that they were destined to become the governing elite of the society—a responsibility which they not only accepted, but essentially met. Perhaps the best succinct assessment of the role of Galatasaray in Turkish political development has been given by Bernard Lewis: "The influence of the Galatasaray school on the rise of modern Turkey has been enormous. As the need for administrators, diplomats, and others with a Western education and a capacity to handle Western administrative apparatus became more and more pressing, the graduates of Galatasaray came to play a preponderant role in the politics and administration of the Ottoman Empire and, after it, of the Turkish Republic. The Imperial Ottoman Lycée had no playing fields, but not a few of the victories of modern Turkey were won in its classrooms."[10]

Not the least of the influences of Galatasaray was that it established the concept of the *lycée* in the minds of Turkish educational planners. The basic institution of secondary instruction in Turkey was patterned after the French *lycée*, and it took its place with that school, the British public school, and the German *gymnasium* as a member of the European family of intensive, academic, secondary schools for the training of an elite. It also furthered the dominant French impact on Turkish culture.

A second major reason for considering 1868-1869 a turning point in the development of the Turkish educational system is that, in the latter year, Safvet Pasha, the Minister of Public Education, promulgated a set of regulations which outlined for the first time a detailed and coherent plan for the entire Ottoman educational system. Earnestly attempting to put that plan into effect, the state introduced the broad characteristics of the Turkish educational system of today. Subsequent developments can be viewed, in substance, as elaborations of the basic scheme put forth by Safvet Pasha.

The regulations envisioned a three-level school system containing six main types of school: (1) a primary or elementary school (*sübyan*, later *ibtidaî*), having a three-year term, to be located in every village and town quarter; (2) an advanced primary school (*rüşdiye*), also having a three-year term, to be located in every town of 500 houses or more; (3) a lower and terminal secondary school (*idadî*), with a term of two to four years, to be located in every town of 1,000 houses or more; (4) an elite and university preparatory school (*sultani* or *lise*), located in every provincial capital; (5) men's and women's normal schools to be located in Istanbul; and (6) a university (*darülfünun*), located in Istanbul. Attendance at the *sübyan* was to

[10] Bernard Lewis, *The Emergence of Modern Turkey*, London, 1961, p. 120.

be compulsory throughout the nation and education at all schools through the *idadi* was to be free. There was also an important—though quiet—effort put into establishing several dozen schools for training the skilled and semi-skilled technicians needed by the state: the customs officials, dentists, railroad officials, tax collectors, policemen, etc.[11]

By the time of the War for Independence in 1919, the Turkish educational system contained, at least in rudimentary form, all the basic components of the systems of the advanced nations. The state had formally accepted the responsibility of providing at least primary education for all citizens. A network of schools actually existed at the primary, secondary, and university levels. A Ministry of Education had been formed and had gained experience in coordinating a national educational system. The burden of financing schools had been partially incorporated into the regular tax structure, and competence had been developed in translating these tax revenues into textbooks, libraries, museums, salaries, buildings, and the other material requirements of public education. Finally, the system that had been erected bore an intelligible relationship to the economic and political activities of the nation. Though the graduates of the new schools were ardently reformist, dissatisfied with defeat, with foreign occupation, and with the lack of progress in their country, they were

---

[11] A partial listing of the technical schools (excluding normal schools) established in these years would include the following:

Technical Schools Opened Between 1869 and 1923

School of Scientific Art and Architecture	1876
School of Finance	1876
Civil Medical School	1877
School of Law	1878
School of Fine Arts	1879
School of Commerce	1882
School for Civil Engineering	1884
School for the Deaf and Blind	1889
Civil Veterinary School	1889
Police School	1891
School for the Tribes	1892
Customs Officials' School	1892
School for Vaccinators	1894
Evening Courses	1908
Dental School	1909
School of Music	1910
Finance Officials' School	1910
Municipal Administrators' School	1911
Tax Collectors' School	1911
Pious Foundation Officials' School	1911
Railroad Officials' School	1915

far from a class of unemployed intellectuals incapable of being absorbed into the society which had created them. They were serving in the lower and middle ranks of the army and the bureaucracy—two of the three pillars of power in the state.

The remaining inadequacies of the system should not be glossed over. The progress in every area mentioned was severely limited though more than negligible. A strong gust of reaction might have tumbled important parts of the whole edifice. Much remained for the Kemalists to accomplish after the national struggle. Nor should we forget that the *medrese* educational system continued to exist alongside the new secular school system, just as the religious faction within the elite, though weakened, continued to wield substantial power. It had opposed and delayed most of the developments cited.

The leaders of reform were nevertheless confirmed in their confidence in the efficacy of education. Said Pasha, for example, is said to have viewed educational reform as ". . . the first prerequisite to any further improvement." The program of a rather typical contemporaneous organization, the Turkish Hearth (*Türk Ocağı,*), further reveals the faith in education and the intellectualism of the modernists. And though the Kemalists believed in diversified reforms, they too continued to place great reliance on education as an essential vehicle for modernization—a fact that explains much of the subsequent tone and technique of Turkish development.[12]

In education even more than in other fields, finally, the statist and elitist character of the Turkish modernization is revealed. Ergin's remark about Istanbul University may be extended to the entire educational movement: its origins were military and political. General public education lagged behind education for military and civil servants. By the same token, the private schools of Turks, foreigners, and minority groups in the Ottoman Empire, which we are not here discussing, are insignificant by comparison with the officially instituted schools. No important private universities, with the one exception of Robert College, are to be found in Turkey to this day. And the few private secondary schools play a smaller part in the total educational enterprise than in other approximately comparable societies.

---

[12] Said Pasha was the Grand Vezir who obtained, in 1884, the first special school tax in the Ottoman Empire. The quotation in Lewis, *op.cit.*, p. 175, is from a memorandum on proposed reforms which Said submitted to the sultan in 1880. On the program of the Turkish Hearth, see Ahmed Emin (Yalman), *Turkey in the World War*, New Haven, 1930, p. 193, and Tarık Z. Tunaya, *Türkiyede Siyasi Partiler*, Istanbul, Doğan Kardeş, 1952, pp. 380-381. The Kemalist emphasis on education permeates almost all their important statements.

Besides being statist, Turkish education was unabashedly elitist. The government leaders, including the Kemalists, conceived of transforming the society from the top down. An elaborate justification for such an educational policy was forthcoming. The concentration on secondary and higher education was supported by the "tree of heaven" (*tuba ağacı*) metaphor. The *tuba ağacı* was a tree which supposedly had its roots in heaven but which lent its delightful shade and its fruit to mankind. The expression itself became a slogan signifying that educational reform should begin not with the primary schools but with the secondary schools and universities, whence universal benefits would flow. The *lycée*, specifically, was viewed not as an institution to be opened to all,[13] but as a training school for the ruling class, whom it would prepare for their heavy responsibilities. Such a philosophy permeates the entire program of Kemalism, accounting for much of its success and for some of its failures.

EDUCATIONAL DEVELOPMENT UNDER THE REPUBLIC

The proclamation of the republic in 1923 and the abolition of the caliphate in 1924 permanently altered the power structure of Turkish society. The lone contest between the secular modernists and the religious traditionalists was decisively won by the modernists. And to consolidate their initial victory, Atatürk and his cohorts proceeded virtually to obliterate the system of religious education which had fed traditionalism, and to expand and improve the existing structure of secular, public schools. Education was still expressly viewed as the key to modernization.

In 1924, at the first opportunity, the *medreses* were abolished and all other religious schools maintained by the religious organization were taken over by the Ministry of Education. The teaching of religion in the public schools was finally discontinued in 1935, and the few remaining religious schools were allowed to lapse into desuetude. The original twenty-nine prayer leader-preacher (*İmam-Hatib*) schools set up by the republican government dwindled to two, which were in turn abolished in 1930 for lack of students. The Theological Faculty, similarly, having 284 students in 1924-1925, was instructing only 20 when it too was abandoned in 1930.[14]

The government further very positively undermined the influence

[13] Ergin, *op.cit.*, IV, 1,056-1,059.
[14] See, Maynard, *op.cit.*, pp. 71-73; Howard A. Reed, "The Faculty of Divinity at Ankara, I," *The Muslim World*, Vol. XLVI, 1956, p. 298.

of traditional religion through other educational reforms. Most important of these were the prohibition of the teaching of Arabic and Persian in the *lycées* and the introduction of the Roman alphabet, both of which measures acted to isolate the younger generation from the formal religious heritage.

The constructive accomplishments of the republic in education may be suggested by the bare statistics of national population and of school attendance for selected years from the first census under the republic in 1927 up to 1960-1961. (See Table 1.)[15] The growth of school

TABLE 1: SCHOOL ATTENDANCE AND LITERACY, 1927-1960

Year	Population	Number of Full-Time Students	Per Cent in School	Percentage of Population Literate
1927-28	13,660,275	497,300	3.7	10.6
1935-36	16,158,018	770,500	4.7	20.4
1940-41	17,820,950	1,109,300	6.2	
1945-46	18,790,174	1,507,900	8.0	30.2
1950-51	20,947,188	1,732,200	8.3	34.6
1955-56	24,064,763	2,296,700	9.5	40.0
1960-61	27,809,831	3,396,857	12.2	40.0(?)

attendance was continuous and rather steady, the percentage of the total population in school increasing threefold during those years. And the percentage of the population which was literate increased nearly twofold during the same period, though a tapering off in the last decade is worthy of remark.

The relative amounts of attention devoted to the various levels of education, meanwhile, suggests that the *tuba ağacı* approach definitely carried over into the republican era, for the upper levels of education receive more emphasis than the lower. Table 2, using the year 1927-1928 as a base, records the relative increase in the number of students at each level and, inferentially, the relative investment of national resources in each. Among the sub-university schools, we observe, the *lycée* population was expanded most, being some 41 times larger in 1960 than in 1927. Next come the middle (*orta*) schools, expanded some 19 times. The primary schools expanded a still-not-negligible 6.7 times. This same rank or order of growth is visible at each time period.

[15] This and the following three tables are based upon the author's calculations from the relevant censuses published by the General Directorate of Statistics, Office of the Prime Ministry, Ankara. These data are sometimes also furnished in the publication cited in note 16.

TABLE 2: INDICES OF NUMBER OF STUDENTS AT VARIOUS
EDUCATIONAL LEVELS, 1923-1960

Year	Primary	Middle	Lycée	Teachers'	Trade Schools	University
1923-24	80	39	68	50	172	68
1927-28	100	100	100	100	100	100
1935-36	157	294	598	56	248	175
1945-46	316	387	1,200	331	2,090	450
1955-56	468	833	1,705	352	3,800	868
1960-61	670	1,935	4,165	395[a]	4,650	1,520
N (1927)	425,997	15,135	1,819	5,022	2,332	4,282

[a] 1958-1959

The universities appear to be expanding at about the same rate as
the middle schools, though it is questionable whether a head-count
remains a proper standard of comparison. The trade schools have
grown fastest of all, particularly in the past fifteen years when mass
education has begun in Turkey. The rate of growth of the teachers'
schools has remained relatively low, like that of the primary schools
which they supply. All in all, the relative emphases in educational
development well reflect the elitist dynamic.

In interpreting all the foregoing figures, one must keep some internal variations in mind. The development of schools generally
was much more extensive in the western and littoral areas of the country than in the eastern and interior areas. Again, the town and city
youth had much greater access to education than did the village youth.
Even the somewhat inflated figures of the Ministry of Education
reveal a spread of twenty points or more between the percentage of
young village children attending primary school and the percentage
of comparable town children in school. The Turkish National Commission on Education estimated in 1959 that about one-third of all
Turkish children of primary school age were without access to primary
education.[16] Of this one-third (and the true ratio is probably higher)
the majority reside in villages. Finally, at every age and level, fewer
girls receive education than boys. The disparity for the academic year
1960-1961 may be viewed in Table 3. The preponderance of males
increases as one ascends the educational ladder. Using the 1960-1961
data alone—and the imbalances in earlier years were greater—we see
that just under 2 out of 3 primary school students, 3 out of 4 middle
school and *lycée* students, and 4 out of 5 college students were males.

[16] *The Report of the Turkish National Commission on Education*, Istanbul, American Board Publication Department, 1961, pp. 43-44.

TABLE 3: DISTRIBUTION OF STUDENTS BY SEX, 1960-1961

Level	Boys	Girls	N
Primary	63%	37%	2,855,337
Middle	76	24	292,590
Lycée	74	26	75,625
University	80	20	65,088
Technical and Vocational	70	30	108,217

Turning briefly to the universities, we may point out that in republican years the university system in Turkey has not only grown but has achieved a large measure of autonomy. A number of new, higher-level technical schools have been opened, including the Gazi Pedagogical Institute in 1926 and the Istanbul Technical University in 1944. The *Darülfünun* in Istanbul was reorganized into the present Istanbul University in 1933. In 1925 the Ankara Law Faculty was created. When, a decade later, a Faculty of Language, History, and Geography was founded in the new capital and the old Civil Service School (*Mülkiye*), now styled the School of Political Sciences (*Siyasal Bilgiler Okulu*), was moved there from Istanbul, the advent of Ankara University was predictable. Formally established in 1946, that University includes faculties of medicine, science, theology, agriculture, and veterinary medicine along with law, letters, and political science.

The extension of the university system has accelerated in the past few years as youths at least nominally qualified under present Turkish regulations have demanded university training. In 1956, Ege University in İzmir was founded with faculties of medicine and agriculture. One year later, Atatürk University, patterned after an American land-grant college and aided by the University of Nebraska, was formally inaugurated in Erzurum. Among regional universities proposed for the future are the University of the Çukurova to be located in Adana, Selcuk University in Konya, Black Sea (*Karadeniz*) Technical University in Trabzon, Gökalp University in Diyarbakır, the home town of Ziya Gökalp, and another university to be located in Edirne in Thrace. Should such a system be erected, one can expect changes in the atmosphere of higher education in Turkey. Pressure for more research and a more empirical orientation now emanates from Middle East Technical University in Ankara, a joint Turkish and United Nations-sponsored institution that is exercising considerable influence after a faltering start.

But perhaps the most important development in higher education under the republic remains the increase in the autonomy accorded to Turkish universities. The initial grants of control made in 1923 were finally followed by the Universities Law of 1946, which granted wide independence to those institutions. They have separate budgetary appropriations, are governed to a considerable extent by their own faculties, and are free from control by the Ministry of Education except that the Minister of Education sits ex officio on the university boards, just as the university rectors and deans sit ex officio on the Educational Council. The political significance of this autonomy is very great. The universities, along with the other relatively independent national institutions developed under the Kemalists, strongly resisted the anti-democratic pressures of Menderes and Bayar in the late 1950's until those errant leaders at length overreached themselves and precipitated the coup of May 27, 1960.

Another important educational project under the republic was the establishment of the much discussed village institutes. The purposes of these were to increase the supply of village (primary) schoolteachers and to keep such teachers "down on the farm." According to the laws of 1940 and 1942 which created them, these new normal schools were to be built in selected villages by the village youths aspiring to be teachers, as part of their on-the-job training. Costs would thereby be greatly reduced and the novice teachers would not be demoralized by exposure to Stamboul or Ankara Nights.

Village primary school graduates were admitted to the institutes to obtain five or more years of education, in return for which they obligated themselves to teach for twenty years in any place which the Ministry of Education should designate. Though the graduates were only youths in their late teens or early twenties, they were supposed to provide immediate leadership in their communities for many non-educational activities. They were further expected to supplement their exceptionally meager wages by raising produce and engaging in handicrafts. It became an especially sore point later on that they were not at first accorded the right of officer status during their military service— a right accorded all *lycée* graduates simply by virtue of their educational standing.

Starting with 5,371 students in 1940, the institutes were teaching 14,000 students in 21 places within ten years. An advanced village institute was also established to train teachers for them. Then they became an object of political controversy and were abolished. They were accused of sins ranging from incompetence, through partisan support of the People's Party, to Soviet Communism. Their defenders, furthermore, were often as rigid and vehement as their opponents. The echoes of that battle are still heard in Turkish politics. Nevertheless, despite the impassioned talk of bringing the village institutes back, it would seem that time has passed them by. They tended to preserve the isolation of the village, an isolation which the evolution in transportation and communication has significantly mitigated.[17] The current expedient should be (and is, to a greater extent than ever before) to increase the attractiveness of village teaching for young people. One incentive is to offer pay differentials and another is to improve the village communications further, so as to remove the isolation felt by even a moderately well-educated man in a little Anatolian community.

In broad perspective, the village institutes were symptomatic of a gradual but momentous change in the emphasis of the continuing Turkish revolution. As an effort to bridge the second and greatest division in Turkish society—that between the educated elite and the uneducated mass—they presaged the present community development programs and other efforts to bring the peasant majority into active participation in the national political and economic life.

A third and final educational issue that has excited politicians and the public in Turkey in recent years is that of religious education. After an hiatus of fourteen years, religious instruction entered the primary schools again in 1949. At first it had to be elected and was restricted to the fourth and fifth classes of the five-year primary schools. Elections were initially not very general, possibly because of uncertainty as to the real intentions of the government. Later on, the religious course was made a part of the regular curriculum, so that, unless a child's parents specified otherwise, he received it automatically. Under such provisions about 99 per cent of the eligible children took the course.

At about the same time, the *Imam-Hatib* schools were reopened. Some seven schools were started by the new democratic administration in 1951, and these grew to sixteen by 1956. In 1948, there began agitation for a new Theological Faculty at Ankara University, which received parliamentary authorization in June of the following year. The number of Koran courses was also increased—from 9 courses

---

[17] See Frederick W. Frey, "Communications, Power, and Political Development in Turkey," in Lucian W. Pye, ed., *Communications and Political Development*, Princeton, 1963, pp. 298-326.

with 232 students in 1932, to 37 courses with 938 students in 1942, to 195 courses with 11,836 students in 1952.

The significance of the so-called religious revival in Turkish education is difficult to assess. One might propose merely that the lid which had been put on the pot was lifted at this time and that some people were surprised and alarmed to see certain parts of the stew still bubbling. The change in policy was precipitated not by a revival of religious feeling or abandonment of secularism among the elite, though there are psychological differences between the new legalistic and commercial man in Turkish politics and his military or bureaucratic predecessor. It was engendered primarily by the opening up of partisan politics and the consequent quest for votes. The religious issue was deemed a good vote-getter, and for a time it probably was. But the permanent changes which religious feeling has wrought in recent Turkish education and politics do not seem to have been great.[18]

III. The Educational System and Turkish Political Culture

Persons ranging from Mustafa Kemal himself down to very ordinary Turkish civil servants have testified to the impact of their education on their political convictions. Kemal has indicated that it was in the War College (*Harbiye*) that he first became "politically aware." Rıza Tevfik and Ali Kemal have attributed a similar awakening to the Civil Service School (*Mülkiye*). The Medical Faculty has exerted a comparable influence upon the political attitudes of its students, as men like Dr. Adnan Adıvar inform us. Negative examples also abound. The official *Histoire de la République Turque* deplores the reactionary effect of the *medreses* on their students. Halide Edib and Count Ostrorog refer to the "scholasticism" inculcated in men by the classical Islamic education of the nineteenth century. In short, there is general acknowledgment that the disparate political views of individual Turks are in large degree traceable to distinctive educational backgrounds.[19]

Nor is this influence confined to the elite. Kemal himself reminded the teachers of Turkey that the new generation would be, in a manner, their handiwork. And Lenczowski agrees that "the secret of Kemal's success may largely be attributed to the strict enforcement of educational reform. The new generation of village and high-school teachers

[18] A similar view is offered in D. A. Rustow, "Politics and Islam in Turkey, 1920-1955," in R. N. Frye, ed., *Islam and the West*, s'Gravenhage, Mouton, 1956, pp. 96-97.
[19] For further evidence see Frey, *op.cit.*, Chapter III.

constituted—with the People's Party members—a zealous cadre which spread Kemalist ideals and trained the minds of Turkish youth. Teachers became Kemal's most devoted propagandists. . . ." More recently, McClelland has suggested that the acute differences in political culture between Turkey and Iran probably have to be ascribed to the Turkish school system, since the family systems and other agencies of socialization in the two nations appear remarkably similar.[20]

There has been no ample study, unfortunately, of the political socialization that is presumed to occur in the Turkish school system. Some of the findings of a 1959 survey of the value systems of *lycée*-level students in Turkey are germane, however. We may inquire into (1) the degree of political consensus among these students; (2) the magnitude of inter-school and inter-sex differences; and (3) those influences, specifically attributable to the *lycées*, which have brought about attitudinal change.

SOME AREAS OF CONSENSUS AND LACK OF CONSENSUS

The survey indicates that Turkish young people hold many political values in common. This consensus lies in the areas which one would have predicted on the basis of the best impressionistic accounts.

One of the basic tenets of Kemal, for example, was that Turkish citizens, if only they were sufficiently determined, might make their country into the sort of nation they wanted to be—namely, a modern nation matching the West at its own game and prospering materially. And one of the items in the abbreviated F-scale used in the survey inquires precisely whether the respondent believes that "If we have sufficient will-power and determination, no difficulty can divert us from our path." The respondent could express two shades of agreement or of disagreement. More than 82 per cent of the students checked the "strongly agree" response to this question and 97 per cent selected one of the two favorable responses. Certainly the schools have thoroughly inculcated this aspect of the Kemalist message in the Turkish youth of today.

The survey in general depicts the Turkish youth as quite authoritarian. It is very doubtful, however, that they are as authoritarian as the population generally. The author's own impression is that though an immoderate amount of authoritarianism *is* present in the political culture, it tends to be counteracted by a strong sense of solidarity and

[20] David McClelland, "National Character and Economic Growth in Turkey and Iran," in Lucian W. Pye, ed., *op. cit.*, pp. 152-181.

by a growing ideological commitment to democratic forms, also inculcated by the school system.

What is the evidence for this contention? Another of the questions
the survey sought to investigate was whether the respondent gave
greater emphasis to participation *in* the government or to the benevolence *of* the government. The question was phrased as follows: "Democracy is often defined in the words of Abraham Lincoln as 'government of the people, *by* the people' and '*for* the people.' If you were
forced to do so, would you personally give greater emphasis to the
concept '*by* the people' or '*for* the people'?"[21] More than three quarters
(78 per cent) of the respondents stressed participation "*by* the
people."

This response was no doubt somewhat superficial. But widely circulated shibboleths or phrases are often of great political significance.
In stressing popular participation over benevolence as a necessary
characteristic of government—presumably a conscious departure from
the previously dominant "Papa State" (*Devlet Baba*) psychology—
the students were very possibly thinking only of voting. But the
profound commitment to elections that has swept over Turkey,
while an insufficient guarantee of democracy, is nevertheless an attitudinal change of great political moment.

The students also were asked whether they thought the good citizen
should vote in local, provincial, and national elections. The possible
responses were "No," "It makes no difference," and "Yes." That the
responses were not mechanical is revealed by the extremely plausible
distinctions among them. The elections to the provincial assembly are
undoubtedly the least important, and only 56 per cent of our respondents answered "Yes" to that part of the question. Seventy-one per
cent answered affirmatively for local elections, and 88 per cent thought
that the good citizen was obliged to vote in national elections.

Agreement was decisive on the position of Mustafa Kemal in the
pantheon of heroes. The students were asked to name the two persons,
living or dead, whom they most admired. Nearly four out of every five
named Atatürk, even though their immediate family and the entire
galaxy of the world's greats were open to them, including contemporary figures like Menderes (this was 1959) and İnönü. No other
person was mentioned by more than 10 per cent of the respondents.

[21] These conceptions were explained, respectively, as: "with the participation of
the people, either directly or through elected representatives" and "a government
which acts to further what it considers to be the best interests of the people."

The secularism of these youths is also striking. They refer most readily to the tenets of the revolution and their conceptions of modernity, very seldom to religious values and principles. In answer to an open question about what two specific things they, as parents, would try to teach their children, only 2 per cent mentioned religion. When asked to select which of seven areas of activity would give them the greatest satisfaction in life only 7 per cent named religion. Even when asked what they would do if disaster befell them, only 1.5 per cent named religion as their first recourse. Religion rated extremely low in vocational prestige (picked first by .2 per cent), and only 2.7 per cent selected a religious figure as one of the two persons most admired. Virtually the only time a pro-religious response was obtained was when they were asked directly whether they found some form of religious belief necessary to a fully mature approach to life. Just over two-thirds of the students (69 per cent) said "yes." Nearly one quarter (23 per cent) were doubtful, and another 8 per cent said "no." It must of course be borne in mind that the respondents were urban youths of a relatively high class. Even so, the inter-school and inter-sex differences were surprisingly slim, a range of 14 percentage points covering all variations in the affirmative response.

One other finding warrants special mention: namely, the relatively high degree of nationalism displayed in the answers; this became abundantly evident when the Turkish responses to the relevant questions were compared with answers to the same questions from the United States or Europe.

Unlike high-school students in some other nations, however, the youthful Turks reveal very little cynicism and alienation. More than 90 per cent felt that ability was more useful than "pull" in getting ahead in life, and nearly 80 per cent felt enthusiastic or hopeful about their personal futures. Having already risen to an educational level identifying them with the intellectual elite, they would seem to have good reason for their optimism. Nearly 7 students in 10 (69 per cent) had already passed the highest educational level reached by their fathers.

INTER-SCHOOL AND INTER-SEX DIFFERENCES

The lack of any marked inter-school differences in political attitudes appears also to attest the effectiveness of socialization in Turkey. The respondents in our sample came from five types of school: regular *lycées*, commercial *lycées*, teacher-training schools, boys' vocational

schools, and girls' vocational schools. There are some significant differences in the backgrounds of the students attracted to the several
types of school, the teacher-training schools and the boys' vocational
schools reaching further down into the social structure than the others.
Only 18 per cent of the students at the girls' vocational schools, 24 per
cent of the commercial *lycée* students, and 27 per cent of the regular
lycée students came from village stock. But in the teacher-training
schools 49 per cent of the students were from villages, and in the boys'
vocational schools 51 per cent. The students in these schools are more
likely to come from low-income homes even when they are from
the city.

Despite these very real differences in background, the answers to
most of the politically relevant questions on the survey are quite
homogeneous and the exceptions are where one would expect to find
them. Picking 15 politically significant items from the questionnaire
and grouping the schools into the 3 main categories of *lycée*, teacher-
training school, and vocational school, we find that on 10 of these 15
questions fewer than 10 percentage points separated the responses
obtained. Among these latter questions were inquiries into interest in
a political career, preference for a high-risk job, the feeling that authority is important, the expectation of deriving satisfaction from one's
career, the sense of determining one's fate, the importance of voting,
the necessity of war, and the need for religion. The 5 questions eliciting
responses differing by 14 percentage points or more between the
schools were those into residential preference (the schoolteachers were
less insistent on living in the city), the opinion that memory was more
important than reason in learning (the vocational students agreed to
this proposition far more often than the regular *lycée* students and
the teachers far less often), hostility to careers for married women
(the teachers were less hostile than the other divisions), interest in
national affairs (the regular *lycée* students were most interested, the
teachers being interested rather in local affairs), and a preference
for government *by* the people rather than *for* the people (the vocational school students exhibited least enthusiasm). Since these differences are reasonable and even to a degree predictable, the agreement
on the other matters appears real rather than illusory. A final inter-
school difference deserving comment is the relatively higher degree of
nationalism among the regular *lycée* students and the teachers.

Differences between the attitudes of the sexes are pervasive, in
line with the markedly divergent roles for boys and girls in Turkish

society. The boys are, in a word, far more political. Though about half of the students in each class of school displayed interest in a political career, the boys always expressed at least 10 percentage points more interest than the girls. The boys were always more willing to take high-risk jobs. The girls were always more anxious to live in a city. In general, the girls can be said to have been more security-conscious than the boys, though they were, of course, less hostile to careers for married women. The boys always felt more in command of their fate and possessed of a better chance for the future than the girls. The boys attached more importance to voting and were relatively more interested in national as opposed to local affairs. The girls were consistently—though only slightly—more inclined to feel that war was needless.

Rather surprisingly, no clear pattern emerged with regard to religious beliefs. In the regular *lycées* the responses of boys and girls were virtually identical. In the teacher-training schools the girls were more religious (73 per cent to 59 per cent) while in the vocational schools the boys were slightly more religious (75 per cent to 68 per cent). The same mixed pattern is repeated when we look at the other questions bearing on religion.

THE INFLUENCE OF THE LYCÉE-LEVEL SCHOOL

An analysis of the differences in attitude between the grades at the several sorts of school was undertaken to determine the probable impact of the secondary school on the political convictions of its students. We could only presume, of course, that simple maturation was not the causal factor involved and that obfuscatory third factors had not intervened.

Since the vocational schools have only a two-year term and the three types of *lycée* a three-year term, we initially eased our analytical burden by considering only the first and last years of the latter. The results indicated that first-year and last-year students did indeed have significantly different values in many instances. However, the impact of the *lycées* did not seem to be uniform. The direction of change differed among the several schools. Each control subsequently imposed, especially that of inserting the intermediate class, only made the picture more kaleidoscopic.

Though it is always possible that some further control may reduce the complexity to something simple, our inclination is to propose that the Turkish public school at the *lycée* level does not act strongly or regularly upon the political opinions of its pupils. Given the degree of uniformity that does exist, the school system at lower levels must impart the standard attitudes. It is easy (perhaps dangerously easy) to note how these conclusions square with other bits of information. The *lycée*, historically, has been the place where the prospective elite obtain civilization (*medeniyet*) and culture rather than patriotism and loyalty to the state. In school curricula under the republic, basic civics is taught in the primary and middle schools, not in the *lycées*. It is natural, therefore, that there should be considerable political consensus among students at the *lycées*, but natural also that it should have been formed prior to their matriculation there. Further research is required if we are to have a definite pronouncement on the matter.

It might be profitable to compare a previous study by Hyman and others of the values of Turkish college students (at the Political Science Faculty and Robert College) with the inquiry into the values of *lycée*-level students, since a number of questions from the former investigation were repeated in the latter.[22] Such a comparison might qualify the presumption just offered that the *lycées* have little impact on the political values of their students. Hyman comments, for example, on the relatively high proportion of Turkish college students who are willing to say that "war is sometimes a good thing." Thirty-three per cent of the students queried at the Political Science Faculty endorsed this view—a high percentage in comparison with Western college students. Of the *lycée*-level students in our sample, however, some 43 per cent endorsed it, suggesting either a higher degree of militarism in the atmosphere of the *lycée*, or (more probably in the author's view) an element of ideological recruitment of students to the Political Science Faculty. Other findings from the *lycée* study do not support the contention that "militarism" is inculcated at school or is rising among Turkish youth. We hope in the future to compare the two studies further.

IV. The Educational Backgrounds of Turkish Political Leaders

It can be argued that education is the basic social distinction in Turkish society. The historic demarcation between the elite and the masses was made largely on educational grounds. Observers from many quarters still find education to be the fundamental characteristic of the elite. Webster noted in the 1930's that "the masses just are not

---

[22] Herbert H. Hyman, Arif Payaslıoğlu and Frederick W. Frey, "The Values of Turkish College Youth," *Public Opinion Quarterly*, Vol. XXII, fall 1958, pp. 275-291.

active in what is going on: they never have been and they probably will not be during the present generation. The *effective* majority, which is found among the educated portions of the Turkish society—persons for the most part with no less than a junior high school training—is vocally and sincerely in support of the Kemalist regime and its head."

Contemporary comments from persons as diverse as Mary Gough, wife of the British archaeologist and a keen observer of Anatolian life, and Daniel Lerner, a trained social scientist, attest the continued importance of education. Searching for the basic social distinction prevailing in the coffee-house of Mut, a town in southern Turkey, Mrs. Gough finds that "probably the best rough and ready criterion is that those on the lower terrace [those with higher status] have had, at least, a secondary education." Lerner uses the results of a survey carried out in Turkey in 1950 to show that the feature chiefly distinguishing the "modern" Turk from his "transitional" and "traditional" compatriots is, again, education.[23]

Many specific examples of the political significance of educational backgrounds are available. The role of *Galatasaray Lisesi* has been mentioned. Its modern rival, the Istanbul Boys' *Lycée* (*Istanbul Erkek Lisesi*), has produced so many prominent deputies and cabinet officials in recent years that one magazine has referred to it as the "ministers' school." Detailed data on the educational backgrounds of Turkish political leaders from 1920-1957 indicate how generally the schools supply the national leaders. For present purposes, we may regard as typical "leaders" the 2,210 deputies who served in the Grand National Assembly during that period.

We observe immediately the disproportionate number of well-educated men in the aggregate group. The national representatives of a society that was itself three-quarters illiterate during the period under discussion were three-quarters of them university educated. (See Table 4.) Not only are the better-educated men more likely to be chosen deputies; they are more likely to be re-elected once chosen. Looking at the four basic levels of the Turkish school system, we see that, with one exception, parliamentary longevity increases with education. The longevity of the 3 per cent of deputies educated outside the regular school system requires particular explanations which we shall not go into here. A detailed analysis of the social backgrounds of the more durable deputies shows that they possess one or more of three

[23] Daniel Lerner, *The Passing of Traditional Society*, Glencoe, Ill., 1958.

TABLE 4: EDUCATIONAL LEVEL OF DEPUTIES, 1920-1957

Highest Educational Level Reached	Number	Percentage	Percentage (less unknowns)	Average Number of Times Elected
University	1,366	62	73	2.19
Lycée	217	10	12	1.69
Middle	197	9	10	2.06
Primary	35	2	2	1.54
Private	44	2	2	2.77
Medrese	23	1	1	2.70
None	1	—	0	—
Unknown	327	15	0	1.08
	2,210	100	100	1.98

qualifications. These are, in order of importance: intellectual status, official status, and local influence, the first two qualifications being often conjoined.

Within the ranks of the university-educated, attendance at certain specific faculties was associated with parliamentary longevity. Those faculties producing officials of one sort or another—military, bureaucratic, or educational—clearly occupied a leading position.

One fifth of the deputies possessing university educations, or 13 per cent of the total group, had attended universities abroad. Of these 43 per cent went to France, 30 per cent to Germany, 15 per cent to Switzerland, and 6 per cent to the United States. The drawing power of the United States has increased sharply in recent years, however. The historic political impact of continental European culture on Turkey, especially French and German, is strongly suggested. Familiarity with the new codes of law, bureaucratic procedures, constitutional

TABLE 5: ELECTION RATE BY TYPE OF HIGHER EDUCATION

Faculty	Mean Election Rate
Political science (civil service)	2.73
Military	2.72
Education	2.64
Literature	2.32
Agriculture	2.23
Medicine	2.10
Law	2.00
Economics	1.79
Engineering and science	1.76
Pharmacy, veterinary, and dental	1.64

schemes, and other political arrangements reinforces the impression. We have thus far been lumping together all persons who served as deputy between 1920 and 1957. But we know that the occupational character of the Grand National Assembly changed drastically over this 37-year span. We know also that the incidence of "localism" in the assembly, as measured by the proportion of deputies born within the province they represented in parliament, fluctuated significantly. Were there similar variations in the proportion of university people in the assembly?

The answer is an emphatic "no." The figures reveal that the educational make-up of the parliament displayed amazing constancy over the years, despite changes in party, clique, and political system. (See Table 6.)

TABLE 6: EDUCATIONAL LEVELS OF DEPUTIES BY ASSEMBLY

Assembly		Per Cent with University Education
I	(1920-23)	70[a]
II	(1923-27)	69
III	(1927-31)	70
IV	(1931-35)	69
V	(1935-39)	76
VI	(1939-43)	78
VII	(1943-46)	78
VIII	(1946-50)	73
IX	(1950-54)	73
X	(1954-57)	77

[a] Suggestive only, since coverage is poor.

A further evidence that intellectual status (as measured by formal education) is important to a deputy is that the more leadership he exerts, the more likely he is to have been to a university. On the basis of the principal posts and committee assignments held by each man in the Turkish government and in the political parties, we divided the deputies into top leaders, middle leaders, and back-benchers. It thereupon became evident that educational background affected not only a politician's electoral chances but also his prospect of achieving national prominence after election. The top leaders were more often university-educated than the middle group, and the middle leaders than the back-benchers. (See Table 7.) In fact, since 1927 the more influential deputies have included at least 16 per cent more persons with higher education than the less influential.

The same conditions apply when we consider cabinet ministers over the same years. The cabinet is an even more select and powerful group than our category of "top leaders" generally and includes an even higher proportion of university-educated men.

TABLE 7: DEPUTIES WITH UNIVERSITY LEVEL EDUCATION,
BY ASSEMBLY AND LEADERSHIP LEVEL
(Figures represent percentage)

Leadership Level	Assembly									
	I	II	III	IV	V	VI	VII	VIII	IX	X
Cabinet ministers	87	88	100	90	92	97	100	98	97	97
Top leaders	87	79	89	89	87	92	95	94	91	95
Middle leaders	74	75	87	86	90	94	92	91	94	92
Back-benchers	63	68	71	69	70	72	75	64	65	71
All deputies	70	69	70	69	76	78	78	73	73	77
N	161	265	332	346	443	470	492	499	494	536

The educational differences between the various political parties which dominated Turkish politics during these years were insignificant —a fact predictable from the absence of change from assembly to assembly. A few factions within the parties do betray some interesting educational backgrounds, however. Most prominent of these was the "thirty-five," a liberal group within the People's Party which opposed the policies of strong-armed Premier Recep Peker in the late 1940's and gave decisive support to the policy of opening up the political life of the country. Nearly half of the "thirty-five" were professionally involved in education, one third having taught at Turkish universities. The "new men in Turkish politics" include not only lawyers and merchants but the university professor.

V. Educational Institutions as Direct Political Actors

The educational system, as a whole and in its parts, acts directly in politics to further its special interests. In the cabinet, for instance, the Minister of Education competes with his ministerial colleagues for scarce resources. A group of political experts whose opinion was sought agreed that over the years the power position of the Ministry of Education has remained rather strong and remarkably stable. It is on a par with the Ministry of Justice—below the really powerful ministries, such as Finance, Interior, Foreign Affairs, and Defense, but above such lesser ministries as Works, Health, Agriculture, Trade, and Labor. Its share of the budget over the years has been relatively large, generally amounting to 10 or 12 per cent of the total.

Within the ministry, formal power is highly centralized. Analysis of its informal power structure—for it has and deserves the reputation of being a hive of intrigue—would demand volumes. One major source of dissension is a cleavage between Francophiles and Americanophiles, each group consisting mainly of persons educated in the nation he supports and favoring that nation's educational system. Since the two systems are very different, the clashes between the factions are frequent and furious.

Three major professional associations of teachers exist in Turkey. One is a national federation of all teachers' organizations; the second is an association of village teachers having its headquarters in Izmir; and the third, which we shall not here consider, is a very small and conservative group located in Istanbul. The national federation can be likened to the National Association of Manufacturers in the United States. It encompasses so many interests that it cannot decisively commit itself to any one of them. It now maintains a cumbersome organization enrolling from one-third to one-half of all the teachers of the country, but it is rent by a right-left split. There has long been talk, though only talk, of changing it into a real trade union.

One of the factions within the national federation is the association of village teachers—a very different body. Having a nucleus of village institute graduates, this association has profited from its relatively simple and definite aims and from its internal unity. It has profited from the supposed persecution of village institute graduates within the Ministry of Education under the former Democratic party minister, Tevfik İleri. This adversity tightened the bonds among association members. Several years ago, furthermore, the association began a drive for improved conditions for village teachers just at the time when the government decided to grant concessions to that group, and the success of this drive increased the cohesiveness of the organization.

Students have long been an active political force in Turkish society. In the eighteenth and early nineteenth centuries, riots and demonstrations by the Istanbul *medrese* students (*softa*) frequently threw the capital into turmoil. After the opening up of political life in Turkey in the late 1940's, the students, whom Atatürk had in part restrained, again became a volatile political element. Their most dramatic success was scored in their clashes with the government leading up to the "Gentle Coup" of May 1960. Subsequent student eruptions, such as the abortive coup of February 22, 1962, and the destruction of political-party and newspaper property in early October 1962, have become rather ominous, as were the wild and indiscriminate "anti-Communist" outbreaks of the post-war period and the students' role in the Istanbul riots in September 1955.

The Turkish students are organized into two main organizations: the National Turkish Students' Federation (*Türk Millî Talebe Federasyonu*) and the National Turkish Students' Union (*Millî Türk Talebe Birliği*). The former is the larger and the more active politically. Though formally neutral in politics, it tends to sympathize, voluntarily, with the People's Party. There is sometimes liaison between the TMTF and the Youth Arm of the RPP. Both student organizations attempt to make their voices heard through press conferences proclaiming how "youth" feels on issues of the day, both publish periodicals containing much political discussion, and both may, on occasion, send deputations to talk with the premier or with other government officials.

Having spoken of student activities, one can hardly avoid mentioning the very pronounced "youth culture" which pervades portions of Turkish life. Mustafa Kemal proclaimed youth "the owner and guardian of the revolution"—a fact which some segments of Turkish youth will let no one ignore. Insofar as this heady assignment is taken seriously by many responsible Turkish youths, the "youth culture" is a valuable asset to Turkey. At the same time, one occasionally finds among these self-conscious and self-important young men a chauvinism that is potentially dangerous—particularly in these critical years when a weakened government strives to lead the nation through the perilous second stage of the Turkish revolution.

Whether Turkey, using its educational system as a tool, will be able peacefully to dissolve the long-standing barrier between the elite and the masses remains to be seen. No currently emerging nation has yet solved that problem and few have even seriously confronted it. But none has made so auspicious a start as Turkey, and none has more native political talent. The task of getting back on the rails after a bad collision is nevertheless proving difficult.

CHAPTER 6

THE MASS MEDIA

~~~~~~

A. JAPAN

SHŪICHI KATŌ

~~~~~~

TODAY almost all Japanese households have radios, and half of them also have television. The total daily circulation of newspapers amounts to over 36 million among a population of upwards of 94 million. The number of cinemas was counted at 7,457 in 1960; on the average every Japanese goes to the movies once a month, or about as often as the average citizen in the United States and Canada. Virtually all equipment used by the mass media is produced in Japan, and Japanese is the universal language of them all. Most of these media, finally, are nationwide in scope. Japan possesses, in sum, a single highly centralized communication system supplying information, education, and entertainment and acting in a diversity of ways for the mass of the population.

Less than a lifetime ago there was no radio, television, or cinema; there were not even bestsellers or magazines of wide circulation. There were only newspapers which, it was estimated, fewer than 0.2 per cent of the people read. The mass media constitute one of the truly dramatic innovations in Japan today.

The history of Japan since 1868 is characterized by social and political changes which may collectively be called a process of "modernization": these include establishment of a strong central government with an efficient bureaucratic system, industrialization through the introduction of Western technology, the rapid building up of national armed forces, and the development of mass education. Attending these developments was the rise, in particular, of the daily newspaper.

The first Japanese daily was published in 1870.[1] Since then daily journals have evolved from the polemical papers of political parties in early years to commercial newspapers supplying information and

---

[1] The *Yokohama Mainichi*. A short history of Japanese newspapers can be found in Ono Hideo, *Shimbun no rekishi* (A History of Newspapers), Tokyo, 1961.

entertainment. In the total period of more than ninety years the character of the readership has also changed: in the beginning, circulation was confined to a rather small number of ex-samurai in the towns; it was then extended to the rapidly growing middle class, and finally to almost the entire population, both urban and rural. The government meanwhile adopted a variety of different attitudes toward the newspapers: it encouraged their founding; then imposed strict censorship and police control; then adopted a more liberal attitude, if not *de jure*, at least *de facto*; then, in the era of military domination, exerted direct control over all means of expressing opinion; then reverted to complete *laissez-faire*; and finally has made rather sophisticated attempts to manipulate the masses through the mass media.

This essay will consider the development of the newspapers and other mass media in Japan during the period from 1870 to 1960, with particular reference to the interaction between the mass media and national political agencies. Some facts about the number of readers (and of the audience for radio and television broadcasts) are a necessary background.

I. The Mass Media and Their Public

We do not know the precise daily circulation of all newspapers in each year. The figures estimated by Mr. Uchikawa Yoshimi of Tokyo University[2] include, however, a total circulation in 1875 of 53,000; in 1924 of 6¼ million; in 1959 of over 36 million. There was a constant and rapid increase in circulation throughout the period except during the newsprint shortage of the last war. If we take into consideration the population increase during the same period, the rise in the number of readers is still remarkable. About 1 person in 600 normally obtained a daily paper in 1875; about 1 in 30 in 1904; 1 in 10 in 1924; 1 in 5 in 1945; 1 in 2½ in 1959. We may observe first that the rise from 1 in 600 to 1 in 30 suggests an important change in newspaper readership. The years from 1870 to around 1904 form a period during which the newspaper grew into a very general mass medium for one group of the population. Second, we observe that the newspapers became rapidly more popular until the 1920's, after which their rate of growth slowed down somewhat. The 1920's were a kind of transition period. During the First World War and the fol-

[2] Uchikawa Yoshimi, "Shimbun dokusha no hensen" (Changes in Newspaper Readership), *Shimbun Kenkyū*, No. 120, July 1961, p. 19.

lowing decade, Japanese industry expanded, the labor problem became serious for the first time, and a white-collar class emerged in the big cities as an important element in the society. At this time, moreover, two important media other than the daily papers were added: the cinema and radio. One can mark the end of the first period by the Russo-Japanese War (1905) and of the second by the First World War (1918).

Radio broadcasting in Japan developed mostly between the two world wars, radio sets registered in 1941 already reaching 6.6 million, while television became popular much later (7,600 sets in 1953, 1 million in 1958, 10 million in 1962). Television, perhaps the most persuasive of all mass media, is hence, in Japan, a phenomenon exclusively of the 1950's. The Pacific War was over in 1945, the Occupation in 1952. After that a tremendous industrial growth occurred which affected the national way of life both urban and rural. Perhaps 1952 initiates a fourth period in the history of the mass media in Japan.

Of the four periods distinguished, then, the first extends from the founding of the first daily paper in 1870 to the end of the Russo-Japanese War in 1905; the second from 1905 to the end of the First World War in 1918; the third from 1918 to the end of the American Occupation in 1952; and the fourth from 1952 to the present.

The thirty-five-year period after 1870 is punctuated by the revision of the Newspaper Law in 1883. Until then journalism, at least in Tokyo, was dominated by the newspapers representing the opposition political parties. Those papers, called "party papers," were vehicles of political opinion rather than of information or entertainment. The language used was traditional and literary—very far from the spoken language at that time—and circulation was limited. Uchikawa rightly suggests that most of the readers were ex-samurai who were accustomed to an elevated language.

Tokyo was the political center; Osaka the great center of commercial activity. While the party papers were flourishing in Tokyo, another type of paper appeared in Osaka—the "small papers." Although the circulation of each of these individually was less than that of the typical party papers, there were many of them in Osaka, and a few appeared in Tokyo. The small papers offered, not political information or debate, but the gossip in the street and other entertainment such as illustrated novels. Using the common spoken language, they circulated among persons having nothing to do with the party papers, such as the merchants in the big towns and the frequenters of the restaurants and geisha houses.

These distinct classes of newspapers co-existed until 1883, when most of the party papers disappeared as a result of pressure which the government exerted upon freedom of expression by means of the revised Newspaper Law. In that year, 16 newspapers ceased to exist in Tokyo, 4 in Osaka, 27 in all other parts of the country. In the following year, the strongest and most active opposition party, the Liberal Party, disintegrated. After 1883 a new type of newspaper appeared in Tokyo, of which typical examples are the *Nippon* edited by Kuga Katsunan, and the *Kokumin,* edited by Tokutomi Iichirō and founded in 1889 and 1890 respectively. These newspapers, which in the last decade of the nineteenth century to some extent filled the role of the party papers, were active in political debate, though not directly affiliated with any political party. Since they sought to lead public opinion, they addressed themselves not only to the ex-samurai but to a wider middle-class, which was then becoming politically conscious in Tokyo.

In Osaka, meanwhile, the small papers were also changing. Recent additions to the genre were supplementing with solid information the gossip and entertainment in which they had formerly specialized. The most conspicuous example of these is the *Asahi.* The *Osaka Asahi* started early in 1879 with a circulation of 3,000, then moved to Tokyo and, as the *Tokyo Asahi,* reached a circulation of 6,000. In the late nineteenth century, the *Asahi* explored the possibility of fusing the journalism of Tokyo and Osaka, combining political information with entertainment and news.

In the next twenty years, there was an extraordinary expansion of middle-class readership in the cities and of commercial newspapers patterned after the *Asahi.*[3] Throughout the second and third periods —from 1905 to 1952, that is—the circulation of the commercial newspapers further increased until not the middle-class only but the mass population in the urban areas became readers of daily papers.

Before the First World War, the commercial newspapers monop- olized, in a manner, the attention of the urban middle-class; the

[3] Ryū Shintarō explains the tremendous success of the commercial papers like the *Asahi* by this kind of combination of characteristics of the party papers and the small papers: political information in Tokyo and entertaining elements in Osaka. See Ryū Shintarō: *Nihon ni okeru taishū-shimbun* (Mass Newspapers in Japan), *Shimbun 100-nen shi kankōkai,* Tokyo, 1961.

films and radios were yet to come. Between the two world wars, the urban population as a whole was addressed by three major mass communication media: the commercial daily newspapers, the radio, and the films. The circulation of all newspapers jumped from 6¼ million in 1924 to more than 14 million in 1945; the radio sets from 350,000 in 1926 to over 6½ million in 1941; the total annual public for films reached 250 million in the year 1934. There had come into being, at least in urban areas, a mass society appealed to by a highly developed system of mass communication media.

It was between the two wars, incidentally, that the three major dailies became so firmly established that they are still able to monopolize the newspaper market. The *Asahi,* the *Mainichi,* and the *Yomiuri* sold in 1962 more than half of all the daily newspapers in Japan; the three major local papers, the *Hokkaidō Shimbun, Chūnichi,* and the *Nishi Nippon,* only about 10 per cent together. Such is the disposition toward monopoly among the mass communication media in present-day Japan.

The major happening in the period following the Occupation is, of course, the advent of television. There were 7,600 receivers in 1953 and over 10 million in 1962. This persuasive new medium is doing much to break down the barrier between the urban and rural societies—hastening a process engendered by the land-reform program which was put into effect immediately after the Second World War and by the economic growth in the 1950's which has substantially increased the incomes of most farm families. Nor are the readers of newspapers any longer limited to the urban population; they include the bulk of the rural populace as well. By means of new techniques such as instantaneous facsimile printing, the three big papers are trying at present to win over the readers of the local papers in Hokkaidō and in Kyūshū. The general consolidation of communication media is still continuing. The nation as a whole is falling increasingly under the powerful influence of three giant papers, one semi-governmental broadcasting corporation (the NHK), a few private broadcasting companies, and two film companies. Today a teenage singer can enjoy throughout the country a degree of attention accorded, as recently as 1950, only to the Royal Family. The difference between the village and the cities is quickly disappearing: both are adopting the same entertainment, fashions, and patterns of consumption; sooner or later they will probably adopt the same patterns of voting too. The continuing concentration of the population in the cities, on the one hand, and a highly centralized network of mass communications, on the other, will probably in the end approximate the political attitudes of the entire Japanese people to that of the city-dwellers at present.

II. The Mass Media and the Government

With the advent of the Meiji era, the government encouraged the publication of newspapers as it encouraged many other industries and institutions. The Mitsubishi shipping company was then subsidized and protected by the government; the first railway, the nationwide mail system, and later the first broadcasting corporation were all founded and run, directly or indirectly, by the government. The first daily paper, founded in Yokohama in 1870, was encouraged by the governor of Kanagawa Prefecture (of which Yokohama was the capital city); the first Tokyo daily was published in 1872 by Etō Shimpei, an influential figure in Meiji political circles; an irregular leaflet-like paper was created in 1871 by Kido Kōin himself, who was a councillor to the Meiji government. The Meiji reformers involved some radically new political ideas which had to be communicated to subordinates in the political movement, to the rank and file of civil servants, and to influential people in the villages. The newspapers were necessary instruments of government policy, at least until the establishment of a more direct and powerful instrument of political control, the police.

In the 1870's, the tide of the Freedom and Popular Rights Movement (*Jiyū Minken Undō*) arose under the leadership of Itagaki Taisuke. The new movement used the newspapers to demand general elections for a national parliament. Other intellectuals, like Narushima Ryūhoku, a servant of the Tokugawa regime, who had not been accorded a position in the Meiji regime, took up journalism as a means of opposing the government. Shortly after the appearance of the opposition journals, the government was confronted with widespread feelings of dissatisfaction and the excess, from the point of view of Meiji leaders, of a liberalism which was inspired by French and Anglo-American political thought and which, as was said, "does not fit in the glorious tradition of Imperial Japan." The government quickly met the situation by imposing censorship and police control on all public expression of opinion.

The revised Newspaper Law of 1875 and the attendant Law for the Control of Criticism of Civil Servants prescribed fines and imprisonment for all critics of government policy and the civil service.

In the following year a further addition to the Newspaper Law enabled the Minister of Internal Affairs to suspend or forbid the publication of newspapers. In 1875 Fukuzawa Yukichi ceased publication of his *Meiroku Zasshi,* which had played an important role in informing the people of liberal ideas in the early years of the Meiji period. Suehiro Techō, another leader of liberal opinion, was fined and imprisoned for one month in the same year for discussing the revised Newspaper Law in an editorial in the *Tokyo Akebono.* Narushima Ryūhoku, who was himself imprisoned as the editorialist of the *Chōya,* wrote that twenty other journalists, all of them from the papers of the Freedom and Popular Rights Movement, were in prison with him. In March of 1876 there were 30 journalists in prison and 3 opposition papers were forbidden to publish.

The first Diet was to be formed in 1890. In the late 1870's and early 1880's the activities of the political parties became very animated. The major parties at the beginning of the 1880's were the *Teiseitō,* the *Kaishintō,* and the *Jiyūtō,* all of which were running newspapers linked to their political beliefs. The bureaucratic government's attitude toward the several papers was described by Ono Hideo: "The government was giving an active support to the newspapers linked with the *Teiseitō,* while it was threatening the papers of the *Jiyūtō* and *Kaishintō* and the neutral papers by forbidding their publication and at the same time trying to buy them up." In the further revision of the Newspaper Law in April of 1883, the government extended the responsibility for all articles to the writer, the man in charge of printing, the publisher, the proprietor of the paper, and the editor in chief, and gave to the local administration the right to determine the legality of the articles. The new law was put into force. In 1884 the *Jiyūtō* was dissolved and almost all party papers disappeared.

In 1887 partisans of the dissolved *Jiyūtō* attempted a last protest to the government, demanding freedom of assembly, association, and opinion. The government responded by the Law for the Maintenance of Order and banished from the Tokyo area some 400 people who had participated in the protest movement, including Nakae Chōmin, Ozaki Yukio, and Hoshi Tōru, all influential liberals and partisan journalists. Thereafter, the first government of Itō Hirobumi liberalized the Newspaper Law slightly, depriving local administrations of the power to forbid publication.

In 1889 the Constitution was proclaimed. Article 29 guaranteed to Japanese subjects "the liberty of speech, writing, publication, public meetings and associations, within the limits of law." This clause did not, however, abolish either the Newspaper Law or other laws restricting the freedom of assembly and of the press. Moreover, the Constitution enabled the administration to issue imperial edicts as it needed and to prevent the publication of opinion or information unfavorable to the government. In fact, the government continued to suppress liberal opinion as before. In twenty-one instances in the period from 1888 to 1895, the Meiji government forbade the distribution of liberal newspapers published in the Japanese language by Japanese emigrants to the West Coast of the United States.[4] The second government of Itō Hirobumi suspended the publication of newspapers 87 times in the last five months of 1892, 87 times in 1893, 56 times in the first five months of 1894, and 222 times in the last ten months of 1895. It was chiefly the *Nippon* which suffered the suspensions in 1895, the editor Kuga Katsunan having protested Japanese seizure of Chinese territory after the Sino-Japanese War.

In 1905 the peace treaty with Tsarist Russia aroused further widespread dissatisfaction among the Japanese population. In downtown Tokyo people assembled in the streets and attacked and set fire to the Hibiya police station. By means of an "emergency imperial edict," the government suppressed mention of this incident and any criticism of the government's stand on the peace treaty. In 1909 the government once again revised the Newspaper Law to give the Minister of Internal Affairs regular control over newspapers.

Despite the restrictions on freedom of expression imposed by the Newspaper Law, by the imperial edict, and later by the notorious Peace Preservation Law, commercial newspapers continued to fight for the cause of liberalism against the authoritarian power of the government.

In 1912 when the Saionji cabinet refused the army's demand to create two additional divisions, the army withdrew its representative in the cabinet and thus forced Saionji to resign. The *genrō* then picked Prince Katsura to succeed Saionji. Liberal members of parliament, such as Ozaki Yukio and Inukai Tsuyoshi, protested to the Katsura cabinet and demanded that the head of the majority political party be appointed prime minister. Many newspapers, like the *Asahi*, the *Manchō*, and the *Jiji*, supported this demand, arguing that the Consti-

---

[4] Ebihara Hachirō: *Kaigai hōji shimbun zasshi shi* (A History of Overseas Vernacular Newspapers and Magazines), Tokyo, Gakuji Shoin, 1936.

tution envisaged a government run by the majority party. They did not, however, succeed in bringing this end about.

The first government to be headed by a career politician was formed in 1918 by Hara Kei, the president of the *Seiyūkai*, the majority party of the time. He attained his position after a popular movement known as the *Kome Sōdō* or Rice Riots had forced the Terauchi cabinet to resign. The *Kome Sōdō* were brought about by a sharp rise in the price of rice, the staple food of the Japanese. This in turn was supposed to have been due to the hoarding of rice by speculators anticipating the Siberian Intervention. The people attacked the storehouses of the rice merchants and money lenders in an unorganized spontaneous insurrection. According to police figures, at least 700,000 persons were involved and the disorders continued for a month all over Japan. The government of Terauchi used the police force and then the army to put down the insurrection, and forbade journalists to publish any accounts of these events.

The journalists of the *Asahi*, the *Mainichi*, and certain other papers thereupon held a meeting of protest in Osaka and passed a resolution accusing the Terauchi government of violating the freedom of the press. A young journalist of the *Asahi* was accused by the authorities of violating the Newspaper Law, one short phrase published in that paper being said to have instigated the "revolution." At the same time, by a supposed coincidence most gratifying to the government, an extreme rightist organization, the *Rōnin Kai*, personally threatened Murayama, the president of the *Asahi*. The *Asahi* compromised with the *Rōnin Kai*, retiring certain liberal-radicals such as Torii Sosen, Hasegawa Nyozekan, Ōyama Ikuo, and Maruyama Kanji. But Terauchi, the army general and prime minister, resigned; Hara, head of the *Seiyūkai* Party, succeeded him.

Until the end of the First World War, the education of the people in the ways of liberal democracy was carried out in good part by the commercial newspapers, whose circulation was constantly increasing. The papers succeeded so well that in the next decade liberal tendencies finally became predominant, at least in the press itself, and led in 1925 to the adoption of universal manhood suffrage.

The 1920's are generally known as the period of "Taishō Democracy," during which there occurred a number of the "liberal hours" of modern Japanese history. The party governments in the 1920's were not themselves wholly devoted to the liberal cause, nor did they cease to control the press. The governments formed by political parties in Japan have never tried seriously to fight the traditional political power of the emperor, the nobility, the bureaucrats, or the army; they have sought, rather, to compromise with the political establishment and with public opinion as expressed for the most part by the press. The foreign policies and the administrative practices of the government were nevertheless liberalized to a degree. Japan was involved in the League of Nations and in the Washington naval disarmament agreement. After the war, Western fashions were widely introduced —from short skirts for women to surrealism in poetry, from Kropotkin to Marx. Most of these Western fashions did not find an appropriate social or cultural ground in the Japan of the 1920's but one of them did—namely, Marxism. The economic expansion during the war permitted, for the first time in Japanese history, the emergence of a true proletarian class; there were also depressions, unemployment, and attendant misery, testifying to the close link between Japan's industrialized economy and that of the rest of the world. The economic catastrophe appeared to be explained in the most consistent way—and in a way appealing to popular emotions—by the theory of Marxism. The governments of the time seem to have been aware of the persuasiveness of Marxist ideology. They elaborated legal means of suppressing Marxists and other popular opposition movements. It was in the 1920's, in the years of the "Taishō Democracy" indeed, that the "Special Higher Police" (*Tokubetsu Kōtō Keisatsu* or *Tokkō*) was created and that, as we have noted, the Peace Preservation Law was issued. These two formidable instruments were to be used by the military governments in the 1930's to crush all opposition to the "sacred war" on the Chinese continent and later in the whole Pacific area. In short, being aware of the seriousness of the labor problem, the leaders of the political parties in power during the 1920's made a quick and effective move against the left; but they took almost no precautions against the right, apparently unaware of the coming danger of ultra-nationalistic militarism.

In 1931 the army started the war against China which continued for almost fifteen years and spread in its later stages to the whole Pacific. At the beginning of that war, the army officers threatened to use military force against the newspapers and intimidated all liberal opinion. The *Asahi* was one of the first targets of the rightist officers of the 1936 rebellion in Tokyo. The government, which became more and more militaristic and nationalistic, suppressed first Communist writers and scholars, then the social democrats who were

245

themselves opposing the Communists, and finally all leaders of liberal opinion. In 1938, when Professor Kawai Eijirō was expelled from his university and denounced by the government because of his book *A Criticism of Fascism* and other works, a spokesman for the Ministry of Justice blandly explained that liberal ideas were dangerous because they tended toward Communism.[5] By the end of the 1930's, virtually all opinion in any way critical of the government's militaristic policy in China had been silenced. A set of repressive laws and regulations was put into effect, principal among these being the National General Mobilization Law of 1937, giving the government more freedom to issue imperial edicts.

The National General Mobilization Law, however, was only one evidence of the wartime government's attitude toward the mass media. The government further sought to use those media to secure active public support. A massive movement was started after 1937, the National Spiritual Mobilization Movement, which concerned itself with the Japanese way of life, recommending frugality ("Luxury is our enemy"), discipline, and patriotism with definitely xenophobic overtones. As a part of this movement the army sent writers to the Chinese front to report to the nation on the sacredness of the war and the bravery of the soldiers of the emperor. One of those writers, Ishikawa Tatsuzō, described the war as he had seen it, namely, as a rather disgusting business of killing and perhaps of being killed. His novel *Living Soldiers* was suppressed. But of course most writers either did not write what they had seen or did not choose to see the reality of war. The same was true for thousands of press correspondents sent to the battlefields. Through "Spiritual Mobilization," the newspapers were made increasingly militaristic and inevitably less objective. In fact there was much active and spontaneous support of the war on the part of the mass media, though it was true that the leaders of the press did not always agree with the authorities or collaborate wholeheartedly with the army. Differing from political leaders in tactics rather than in aims, the newspapermen were not effectively independent. Furuno Inosuke, president of the Dōmei News agency, collaborated wholly with the war leaders. Ōgata Taketora, vice-president of *Asahi*, became minister of the Koiso cabinet in 1944; Shōriki Matsutarō, president of the *Yomiuri*, became advisor to the same cabinet. The mass media in

[5] Tōyama Shigeki et al., *Shōwa shi* (A History of the Shōwa Period), Tokyo, Iwanami, 1959.

general became part of the anonymous machine of the state which the "Spiritual Mobilization" of the nation was controlling.

As institutions, the media became increasingly centralized under the pressure of the war. The rapid growth of the three giant papers, *Asahi, Mainichi,* and *Yomiuri,* during the 1930's was due partly to the emergence of a kind of "mass culture" in urban areas and partly to the expense of covering the wide Chinese front, an expense which only the big newspapers could afford. The government in its turn sought to centralize all means of disseminating information so that it could control them better. Radio broadcasting was already centralized, the only nationwide network being maintained by the *Nihon Hōsō Kyōkai* (NHK). As for the newspapers, the many national and local papers were organized in two ways. First, the central news agency *Dōmei Tsūshin* was set up in 1936 to supply the newspapers with information from abroad, notably war information. Newspapers were obliged to rely on the *Dōmei* for foreign news unless, like the three giant papers, they could afford to send their own correspondents to the Chinese front and elsewhere. Though failing to limit the number of newspapers, the government succeeded in 1940 in organizing the Association of Japanese Newspapers (*Nihon Shimbun Renmei*), which was reorganized in 1942 into the Society of Japanese Newspapers (*Nihon Shimbun Kai*). The executive committee of the association, consisting of representatives of the major papers, of the government information office, and of the Police Section of the Ministry of Internal Affairs, promoted the collaboration of all newspapers with the government and encouraged self-imposed "discipline" in publication of news about the war and national policies. Membership was not obligatory, but the association was the central organ for assigning newsprint to each newspaper. Hence all newspapers were in reality obliged to participate.

The control of paper supplies was a powerful instrument in the government's hands for controlling the daily papers and also the book publishing houses. Publishing houses which issued "anti-national-policy" books could not get paper supplies for further publication. This kind of pressure worked better than censorship itself in mobilizing support for the official line.

From the beginning of the Pacific War in 1941 until its end in 1945, the entire mass media supported the government by suppressing objective information and opposition opinion. Then came the Occupation. The Occupation destroyed the *Dōmei* as a centralized news source,

247

and the *Nihon Shimbun Kai* as the central organization for control of the press. The tie between the press and the government was dissolved, and the opposition was encouraged to express its opinions openly. All this meant freedom of expression within the framework of the press code issued by the Supreme Commander and the censorship imposed by the Occupation forces.

It was after 1952, the last year of the American Occupation, that the Japanese mass media became wholly free—for the first time in their history—from any direct control by any political power. It was precisely from this time on, however, that a certain pressure from big business began to be exerted on journalists. The end of the era of political pressure coincided roughly with the beginning of pressure from private commercial circles.

III. The Mass Media and Business

The mass media in Japan today themselves constitute a large private enterprise. It is hence natural that they should become linked with the "collective interests" of business—for instance, on the matter of labor contracts. On the other hand, the mass media as agencies of public service should be, and are, different from other private enterprises. They must reflect not only the interests of big business but also those of the public at large. These two functions of the mass media, as private businesses and as public-service institutions, need to be held in balance, and therein lies one of the principal problems of the mass media today.

The big Japanese newspapers have three characteristics. First, by an exceptional article of commercial law, the shareholders of newspaper companies are limited to employees and persons otherwise directly concerned with the companies so that concentrated industrial wealth does not directly influence the policies of the papers. The shares of the *Asahi* were and are largely owned by the people working for the *Asahi*; those of the *Yomiuri* have been owned chiefly by Shōriki Matsutarō and his staff; the *Mainichi* has, since 1941, excluded most financing from the giant industries such as Mitsui, Mitsubishi, Kuhara, and Ōji Paper Mill, and has followed the same policy as the *Asahi* and the *Yomiuri*.[6]

Second, in most cases, the relatively small capital provided by shareholders is supplemented by rather large sums of money from the

[6] Nitta Uichirō, "Mass Communication no keizaiteki kiban" (The Economic Foundations of Mass Communications), *Mass Communication to seiji keizai* (Mass Communication Kōza, Vol. 2), Tokyo, Kawade-shobo, 1955.

banks, amounting normally to over 70 per cent of the total capital.[7] In this respect newspapers fall into the general pattern of Japanese enterprises. The importance of financing from the banks, however, is not necessarily reflected in the content of the newspapers. One can point, at least, to no serious direct influence by the banks on the editorial opinions of the big newspapers.

Third, Japanese newspapers rely much more on the sale of papers for their income than on advertising. Since the Second World War advertising income has rarely been higher than 40 per cent of the total income of the 15 major papers—a figure much lower than for American and even British papers. Hence there is strong competition for sales in a limited market.[8]

The monopolization of the market by the three nationwide papers is largely due to the system of selling over which they preside: each paper has its own network of distributors all over the country. Every morning, and every evening, papers are delivered to the doors of subscribers, even in the remote villages in the mountains, by the local distribution office of the newspaper. A few large local newspapers have similar distribution systems in their regions. Being unable to afford any such system, small newspapers cannot dream of competing in circulation with the large ones. Competition is strenuous among the three giants and a few large local papers, however, for daily newspapers are distributed to over one-third of the total population. The newspaper as an enterprise is necessarily highly sensitive to any suggestions from its local distributors for increasing sales. Sensationalism and murder cases and entertainment are likely to be recommended, or detailed reports of baseball games. Because one cannot do everything at the same time, if one finds out too much about baseball, he will not find out enough about Cuba. Precisely at the height of their power and prosperity, we note, the mass media work toward political apathy and ignorance among the public. Political affairs are regarded with indifference, or, what is perhaps worse still, with little outpourings of "patriotic" emotion.

But the suggestions from the distribution branches are not confined to recommending murder cases and baseball games; they extend to the treatment of current social and political issues. First, the more sensationally that situations are presented, the more copies of the paper will be sold. The possibility of war is always more sensational than the possibility of maintaining the peace. Second, the newer the

[7] *Ibid.*
[8] *Ibid.*

information, the better the sales, though the latest political moves are not in fact more important than developments which have been taking place over periods of years. Third, the more fully one confirms current public opinion, the more easily one can sell his own opinions. If the public does not like Mr. Kishi Nobusuke, one had better criticize Mr. Kishi, for the sake of commercial expediency. Because the mass media have condemned Mr. Kishi, the public will dislike him more. The prejudices of the commercial mass media have a snowball effect. The wind blows to the right, and the newspapers make it blow farther to the right. The wind blows to the left, and they accentuate the reaction.

Parenthetically, in Japan after the Second World War, newspapers were supposed to supply only "objective" and "neutral" and "fair" information. This expectation is not necessarily true even of democracies. In France, for example, *Figaro* is regarded as a conservative paper, and *Humanité* as on the extreme left. No one seriously believes that the information they provide is "objective" or "neutral" or without political bias, though many people might agree that *Monde* is a comparatively neutral paper. "Neutrality" and "objectivity" are attributes of only some of the French mass media. Somewhat the same situation obtains in England. In Japan, however, "objectivity" is supposed to be a general characteristic of all newspapers.

In practice, the big Japanese newspapers have almost always tended to regard themselves as "objective" and "neutral" when they have taken a central position between two opposing opinions. If we call two major opposing opinions L and R, and if we suppose L shifts to the left on certain issues, we can see that, according to a simple arithmetical rule, the middle position will also shift to the left. If R shifts to the right, the middle position also shifts to the right. At any given moment the editorials of the big papers are consciously "moderate" and "objective," yet they shift with the currents of opinion. The snowball effect which the mass media have upon changing public opinion is caused by commercial demands upon them, but is sanctioned by the putative "objectivity" of the press. In sum, the mass media tends to emphasize majority opinions and minimize minority opinions. Hence follows a conformity of political opinion among the public.[9]

[9] Kato Shūichi: "Nihon no shimbun. Gaikoku no shimbun" (Newspapers in Japan. Newspapers Abroad), *Asahi Journal*, July 1962.

So much for the newspapers. Commercial broadcasting differs from newspaper journalism in that advertising is almost its sole financial resource. The industries which pay for advertising exert, of course, a good deal of influence on the programs. They can buy any program they like—which is usually a popular one—and ignore any program they do not like. Obviously the popular programs are more or less alike and the overall programming of all the various broadcasting stations is almost indistinguishable. Commercialism here results in conformity at a very low level of taste and intelligence. Oya Soichi, one very well-known critic of current affairs, has called it, with pardonable exaggeration, the "idiotization of the nation." And no one would deny that at least some aspects of the commercial radio and television broadcasting business are exactly that. An entertainment program meeting the lowest common denominator of taste is politically neutral, and the industries sponsor almost exclusively that kind of program. Most commercial broadcast stations can freely interchange their news commentators, for example, among programs having a diversity of sponsors.

Some commercial and industrial leaders have not been quite satisfied with this situation, however, and have tried to gain direct control over the mass media to insure that they will reflect the opinions of big business. There is widely believed to be regular cooperation among business leaders who hold key positions in commercial broadcast companies and in some newspapers. This group is supposed to forge a general policy for big business toward the mass media. Mizuno Shigeo, for instance, the head of a large paper mill company (*Kokusaku Parupu*), also serves as the president of the *Fuji* Television, *Bunka* Broadcasting, and the *Sankei* newspaper. A key position in the firm of Nippon Television is held by an official of one of the two giant steel companies (Nagano Shigeo of *Fuji Seitetsu*); the president of Radio Tokyo (Adachi Tadashi) is the president of the Japanese Chamber of Commerce and Industry (*Shōkō Kaigi Sho*). It is clear that certain big industrialists are exerting a direct influence on some of the important mass media.[10] These media may be expected to hold conservative points of view on most political issues, and to forsake from time to time the "neutrality" and "objectivity" embraced by most large Japanese newspapers.

[10] Nagashima Matao, *Gendai no shimbun*, Kyoto, 1959.

IV. Paradoxical Role of the Mass Media in the
Process of Political Modernization

We have noted the steady increase of the public for newspapers and later for radio and television. This public, which originally consisted of a small number of intellectuals, came to comprehend the middle class in the cities, generally, then the masses in the cities, and finally the masses both urban and rural.

The attitude of the government toward the mass media also changed radically during the ninety-year period we have considered: from encouragement to suppression, from suppression to active organization under state control, and finally to total acceptance of the freedom of the press. When the government at length ceased to exert pressure on these media, competitive commercialism began to influence both the content and the manner of mass communication, and a direct link between the mass media and the big industries was formed.

At the very beginning, encouraged by the government, the newspapers undertook the political education of a limited public. When the opposition parties founded journals in which to carry on their political contests with the government, journalism became the arena in which the nation was trained in political thought and discussion. The role played by the press was again educational. Then came the period of the commercial newspapers, which enlarged their public quickly and supplied more and more detailed information about political matters. The press then became primarily informative rather than educational. But one of the necessary instruments of a modern state had come into being.

It seems to the writer that up to this time the mass media, and particularly the daily papers, hastened the process of political modernization, even as they were also beneficiaries of that process. Then, if one identifies modernity with popular enlightenment, they exerted a regressive influence. Nor, after the war, did they resume a lastingly benign role. Most recently, the Japanese mass media have developed into partial monopolies, a large part of the mass communication industry being concentrated in the hands of a few big newspapers and radio-television stations. A second characteristic of current mass communications in Japan is a heightened commercial competition among those enterprises, which has affected both the class of matter in the newspapers and the programs of radio and television. A third characteristic is the principle of political neutralism espoused by the big newspapers.

The concentration of control of the mass media in the hands of a few large enterprises tends to produce conformity in public opinion, which is enhanced by commercial pressures and justified by the principles of "objectivity" or "neutrality" of the press. Commercialism involves entertaining and flattering the masses. This tends to inhibit the development of political awareness and leads to political apathy on the part of the people.

The Japanese press and mass media at large are by profession neither for one government nor against it; generally speaking, they have been faithful to the principle of neutrality since the end of the Second World War. In fact even in the 1930's, while collaborating with the military regime, most newspapers had clung to at least remnants of objectivity or neutrality. Since the end of the war, however, the ideology of the government has shifted slowly but steadily to the right, while the ideology of the opposition has remained relatively constant. Consequently the middle position has shifted to the right and the "objective" papers have followed it —not in spite of their neutralist principles but because of them. A conspicuous exception to this rule was the press's stand against the Kishi government on the matter of the ratification of the revised security pact in 1960. For a short time the press, like the overwhelming mass of the people, was on the side of the opposition. But it was not slow in returning to its previous position—midway between the government and the opposition.[11]

Finally, while the mass media in postwar Japan are critical of both the government and the opposition on many particular issues, they are not critical of the general direction of Japanese national politics. Insofar as the government remains in contact with the masses, national political trends coincide more or less with the general inclination of the majority of the Japanese people. And, in most cases, the mass media tend to emphasize the political opinions of the majority and minimize those of minorities.

Whatever political modernity may be, mass conformity in public opinion, political apathy, and the minimizing of minority views

[11] Akiyama Kiyoshi: "Shimbun wa tenkō no jikaku o motsuka?" (Are the Newspapers Aware of the Conversion?), *Shisō no Kagaku*, July 1962.

hardly represent conditions envisaged as desirable by liberal or democratic thought. The role of the mass media in the political modernization of Japan has thus been paradoxical: they were originally a *sine qua non* of that process, but now they threaten the very ideals which a modern and democratic Japan hopes to attain.

B. TURKEY

KEMAL H. KARPAT

I. Traditionalist Elite Philosophy and the Modern Mass Media

The introduction of mass media in Turkey during the nineteenth century accelerated the development of political consciousness, involved diverse sections of the public in the process of modernization, and brought the exclusive and aristocratic Ottoman philosophy into collision with the individualistic liberal views of the West.

The Ottoman rulers, concerned primarily with the survival of the ruling institutions, had had little interest in developing an inquiring spirit among their subjects. "The Art of Printing," Sir Paul Rycaut observed in the late seventeenth century, "is absolutely prohibited amongst them [Ottoman Turks], because it may give a beginning of the subtlety of learning which is inconsistent with as well as dangerous to the grossness of their government, and a means to deprive many of their livelihood."[1] The deliberateness of this policy becomes manifest when one considers that the Jews had been allowed to introduce a press as early as 1493/1494 upon the condition of not printing Turkish and Arabic books, that Apkar of Sivas had introduced an Armenian press in 1567, and Nicomedus Metaxas a Greek press in 1627. The non-Muslim minorities were free to sharpen their minds as long as they kept their place as second-class subjects and paid taxes. But the Muslim, it was reasoned, had his Koran, where all truths, first and last, were already spelled out. Raising ignorance and servility to the status of virtues for the subjects, the ruler was then able to define his own exercise of power as a unique art, which he had grasped through his own superior ability and was now willing to discharge as a favor to the people.

When egalitarian ideas began to filter through from eighteenth-century France, the alarm of Turkish rulers was intensified. Ahmed Âtif Efendi, the *reisül küttap*, found the works of Voltaire, Rousseau, and other heretics consisting of "insults and vilification against the pure prophets and great kings, of the removal and abolition of

[1] Sir Paul Rycaut, *The History of the Present State of the Ottoman Empire*, London, 1686, p. 59.

255

all religion, and of allusions to the sweetness of equality and republicanism, all expressed in easily *intelligible words and phrases, in the form of mockery, in the language of the common people*" (author's italics). The authors of such sedition had a "rebellious declaration which they called 'The Rights of Man' translated into all languages and published it in all parts, and strove to incite the common people of the nations and religions to rebel against the kings to whom they were subject."[2] The reports of Mehmed Said Hâlet Efendi, Ottoman ambassador to Paris (1802-1806), said much the same thing.

Yet the government itself had eventually to introduce the printing press in an effort to match the political and military power of the West. It must be remembered that as mere instruments these and all other means of mass communication are politically neutral. They enable reformers and conservatives alike to mobilize public opinion in support of their ideas. In a backward country they nevertheless contribute to change. In order to survive, the mass media had to seek large groups of readers. In Turkey—in fact if not quite inevitably— they created new symbols and images taken from Western political thought, simplified the written language, bringing it closer to the vernacular of the commoner. Though Ottoman conservatives successfully used the printing press, books, and, to a lesser extent newspapers, to generalize traditional concepts of society and government and so to resist innovation, there lurked in the media themselves a new potentiality for expressing and disseminating criticism of the Ottoman way of life.

The Ottoman way of life, as fully codified in the nineteenth century, represented a body of ethical customs embodied in a society putatively unique and wholly superior to anything which Western ethics or social organizations could attain. But underneath the most triumphant Ottoman assertions, one could perceive a protective instinct, rejecting self-analysis, introspection, and all mental inquiry. One perceives further the hard political fact that, in an absolute state, only the strong, possibly the future masters, can criticize the rulers and get away with it. A violent critic will convey the idea of his strength and attract support; the party subjected to such criticism will seek to eliminate it merely to dispel the idea of weakness. These

[2] The quotations are from Ahmed Cevdet Paşa, *Tarih-i Cevdet*, VI, 311, as translated by Bernard Lewis, *The Emergence of Modern Turkey*, London, 1961, pp. 65-66.

perennial facts have been visible throughout the political life of Turkey; most recently we have the example of Menderes, whose stern action against the press was justified by his desire to prove the government's authority.

But let us—not to be prejudicial—acknowledge the need of truth in the conservative view of the mass media as well as in the liberal. By enabling a more complete commerce between political leaders and the populace, these media can—to the great benefit of a nation like Turkey—make for stability and ideological unity, just as, by facilitating criticism, they can make for fluidity and necessary change.

II. The Emergence of the Press and Its Role in Modernization

The system of oral communication by means of which facts and ideas had thitherto been disseminated among the general public found its first weak challenge in Ibrahim Müteferrika's printing press introduced in 1727. Müteferrika perhaps took advantage of an interest in fine arts and in color developed during this period and possibly also cherished some nascent desire to rival the West. He was not allowed to print religious books, for they would cease to be sacred if printed, and some 90,000 calligraphers would also be deprived of their living. In all, his press printed 17 books, usually 500 or 1,000 copies of each, and, though the *ulema* hampered the distribution even of those, he appears to have awakened some interest in geography and science; one book, *Usul ül-hikem fi nizam ül-umen*, further contained some information on Western governments. The printing shop closed in 1742 and, reopening in 1784, printed only textbooks for the military engineering school. In 1796 a new printing shop was opened. Yet the number of books printed in all shops until 1830 perhaps numbered no more than one hundred.

The popularization of the printing press and its use for political purposes came after the establishment of the first Turkish newspaper, the *Takvim-i Vekayi* (Calendar of Events) in 1831, well after the French had established the *Gazette Française de Constantinople* (1797) and other papers. The *Takvim*, which in issues of about 5,000 copies served the government in communicating with its administrative centers, gradually came to be published regularly. Its successors were first *Resmî Ceride* and then *Resmî Gazete* (Official Gazette), which still survives.

The first real newspaper *Ceride-i Havadis* (News Gazette) was published by William Churchill, an Englishman, in 1843. Churchill's paper was a commercial enterprise, though it would probably have collapsed without government subsidies. The staff, which was Turkish—the owner did not speak the native tongue—soon turned its offices into a meeting place for the dissatisfied intelligentsia of the day; its editor, Ali Âli, a poet in his own right, had been rejected by the Porte, and Hafız Müşfik Efendi, another writer, had been denied appointment to a high job in the Foreign Office. The *Ceride-i Havadis,* finding few readers at first, gained in circulation during the Crimean war, but its literary translations and news and discussion of the Western parliamentary system interested only a handful of people in all.

Turkish journalism is more commonly said to have started with *Tercüman-i Ahval* (Interpreter of Events) in 1860, national bigotry depriving Churchill of a place in Turkish cultural history. Unlike Churchill's newspaper, which sought chiefly to spread news, the *Tercüman* sought to express opinions and educate the citizenry: "The people living in a social body," wrote Şinasi Efendi in the foreword, "being charged with so many legal obligations . . . have (also) the right to express their opinion as part of their general vested rights. . . . If this statement needs a proof it suffices to point to the political newspapers of nations whose minds have been enlightened by the force of education."[3] It was just such ideas which the sultan and *reisülküttap* Âtıf Efendi had denounced so strongly a few decades earlier.

The moving spirit of the *Tercüman-i Ahval* was İbrahim Şinasi, the son of an officer, who had received a sound training in Western languages and culture in France. Şinasi's first editorial discussed the European custom of reading political articles and mentioned some current foreign affairs. His second criticized the Turkish educational system and demanded its adjustment to practical purposes. Other editorials dealt with industry, trade, and agriculture and demanded change in these fields. The general news was often interspersed with interpretations. Simple information on items of popular interest like the price of food was also supplied. The literary installment of the paper later had a counterpart in many Turkish papers.

Tercüman soon engaged in polemics with Churchill, who had raised the number of weekly issues of his newspaper from two to five to meet the competition and had condescendingly criticized his

[3] Şinasi, *Makaleler, Külliyat IV,* ed. Fevziye Abdullah Tansel, Ankara, 1960, p. 15.

adversary's printing faults. *Tercüman* tartly characterized Churchill as a Christian-foreigner daring to criticize an indigenous newspaper, and scolded his Turkish staff for their venality and want of patriotism.

Şinasi soon parted company with the owner of his paper, and proceeded, in 1862, to publish *Tasvir-i Efkâr* (Mirror of Opinion), which appeared twice a week. According to his foreword to *Tasvir*, newspapers were designed to make known thoughts of a civilized people about its interests and problems, and he duly published discussions of the natural law, of constitutionalism and representation, of finance, taxation, trade and agriculture, and of political and social changes in the West. He further promoted the simplification of the written language to make it accessible to the commoner. The circulation of *Tasvir* rose to 24,000 copies, a record for the period and a sign of popular interest in innovation. His approach to modernization was logical, objective, internally consistent, and duly cognizant of ideal and spiritual values. His wisdom might have attracted admiration at any time in Turkish history and his linguistic reforms helped to open up communication between the intelligentsia and the masses.

A number of related developments fostered the growth of the press. A new school system was established in 1830, a Translation Bureau in 1833, a Ministry of Education in 1847, the "Society of Knowledge" in 1851, and the "Ottoman Scientific Society" in 1860. Moreover, a postal system adopted in 1834, a railroad built in 1856, and a telegraph system introduced in 1855 provided the material conditions necessary for newspapers. Between 1850 and 1883 the number of printing presses in Istanbul rose from nine—only two of them private—to 54.

In 1865, five years after the introduction of *Tercüman-i Ahval*, the press in Istanbul comprised four dailies and five other periodicals.[4] In 1866 three new political newspapers, *Muhbir* (Informer), *Vatan* (Fatherland), and *Ayniyye-i Vatan* (Fatherland Mirror) were introduced and in 1867 yet another four.

The press began to take positions on current affairs. *Muhbir*, for example, in which Ali Suavi was writing, criticized the government's

---

[4] There existed also the reviews *Ceride-i Askeriye* (Military Gazette), 1863, *Ruzname-i Ceride-i Havadis* (Calendar of News Gazette), 1864, a supplement to Churchill's paper, and *Takvim-i Ticaret* (Calendar of Trade), 1865. Of the existing five periodicals, one dealt with medicine, one with military matters, and the others, including *Mecmua-i Fünun*, with general subjects.

surrender of the Belgrade fortress and foreign interference in the Porte. By the mid-sixties, the press's anti-government attitude was clear, as was the government's attitude towards a free press. In 1857-1858, the government issued the first comprehensive printing regulation, to be followed in 1867 by the infamous press ordinance of Âli Pasha. The government had been alarmed for a number of years by the unorthodox political ideas trickling into Ottoman society. The cautious ruling elite had begun to print and distribute among the population some of the classical political works on Islam and government. Some of the traditionalist books were specific attacks on Western ideas, the *Tanzir-i Telemak*, for instance, being a rebuttal of the Abbé Fénelon's *Télémaque*.

Living up to the government's ill opinion of them, members of the press became active in the first revolutionary organization in 1865, which two years later was organized abroad as the Young Ottoman Society. The organization's goals were a representative and constitutional government, and the replacement of the reactionary Âli and Fuad Pashas. Among its founders were Namık Kemal, who had become the editor of *Tasvir-i Efkâr* after Şinasi fled abroad in 1865, and Refik Bey, the former owner of *Mirat*, another political newspaper. The group was joined later by Ali Suavi, the publisher of *Muhbir*. Eventually the members of this society were arrested or sent into exile. Abroad, Ali Suavi republished *Muhbir* in London, and then *Ulum* (Sciences) in Paris; Namık Kemal and Ziya Pasha published *Hürriyet* (Freedom) in 1868; the leftist revolutionary Young Ottoman, Mehmed Bey, published *Ittihad* (Union) and later *Inkilâb* (Reform), and eventually in 1871 joined the Paris Commune. These papers, though united against the oppressive rule at home, variously embraced populist-Islamist-nationalism, revolutionary socialism, and a special brand of elite Ottoman nationalism.

When the Young Ottomans began drifting back in 1870-1871, after the death of their chief enemy, Âli Pasha, they found at home a fairly well-developed press. Between 1867-1871 not less than twenty periodicals publishing news had appeared on the market, including journals such as *Hadika* (Garden), *Basiret* (Insight), and *Terakki* (Progress). Within this period also, humorous magazines and papers expressed some sharp political criticism in the form of satire, jokes, and humorous stories. The humorous newspaper *Hayal* (Illusion), of Teodor Kasab, was closed because of a cartoon representing a man with tied hands and feet with a caption taken from the constitution "the press is free within legal limits." After the Young Ottomans' return home, Namık Kemal emerged as the model and example for Turkish journalists. His most mature activity as journalist and political thinker started with the publication of *İbret* in 1872, wherein he embraced the duty of "giving to the public information about political matters and the progress of civilization." Public opinion, in Namık Kemal's view, consisted in political morality, or the sum total of feelings for freedom, justice, and country among all members of the national community. It was every man's privilege to have thoughts and ideas, and express them.

Namık Kemal, like most of the Young Ottomans, conceived of a government whose aims and interests were synonymous with those of the entire social body, but was hardly aware of the actual relations between society and government in the Western world which they took as a model. The intelligentsia regarded European civilization as an innovation created by skill and ingenuity rather than as a product of social forces. The concept of progress as social evolution was hardly detectable among them. Often they judged Western institutions in the light of their own bureaucratic background and aspirations. So Namık Kemal conceived of the English parliament as the means whereby public opinion could resist government power in an atmosphere of civility and order to the end that a really strong and effective government might emerge. But "the presence of such a strong government," wrote Kemal in amazement, "is visible only through the policemen charged to maintain public order . . . while the people of such a rich country tend to their shops and work until evening like paid servants."[5]

But the admiration felt towards the West was sporadic. There was suppressed anger that the Ottomans had failed in their westward drive, and continued cultivation of the proud and heroic spirit appropriate to conquerors. If foreign-language newspapers in Istanbul or Europe criticized Turkey even in the mildest fashion, the local press would leap to the opposite position and depict all sultans and ministers as flowing with humanity. Namık Kemal himself could dismiss as insignificant the material backwardness of the empire and take pride in its moral and spiritual superiority. The democratic and egalitarian ideas of Europe, in particular, were fervently condemned as undermining Ottoman social hierarchy and bureaucratic supremacy, for the

<hr/>

[5] For quotations see *İbret*, June 13, 1872, October 28, 1872; *Diyojen*, August 21, 1872; *İbret*, January 22, 1879.

far from democratic intelligentsia saw progress as possible only while they retained the helm.

While the Turkish press struggled to catch a breath of freedom, the foreign press enjoyed in good part the immunity and privileges granted by the capitulations. Though offensively condescending, foreign newspapers remained relatively objective, were courteous to the government (which subsidized many of them), and adopted an ironic and impersonal style which contrasted with the emotionalism of the Turkish press. The total number of Turkish newspapers and periodicals published in 1872 amounted only to 9, while foreign language journals numbered 30.[6] For though, between 1862-1870, a total of 38 Turkish newspapers and 10 reviews were published, few of these except for professional reviews had much continuity. During the following decade (1871-1882) the same situation obtained.

When the government decreed the institution, at public expense, of printing presses in the provincial capitals, there also developed a provincial press. The statistics of 1874 mention 24 papers published in the provinces. This press, though following the lead of the capital city, expressed the townsmen's practical outlook and discussed agriculture and trade, thereby incurring the scorn of the journals in Istanbul.

Yet journalism was hardly a widely respected profession, even in the capital. Too many journalists appear to have been seeking either government jobs or the glory of martyrdom at the hands of the bureaucracy. They were popularly considered subversives, or libertines who spent their days in the drinking bouts of the European section of Istanbul. Permission to own a newspaper was granted to Ottomans by the Ministry of Education, to foreigners by the Ministry of Foreign Affairs. Responsibility for press offenses rested with the director of the publication and the author; press violations were judged by administrative authorities.

A newspaper cost one piaster (four cents) per copy, or from ten to fifteen dollars yearly, this high price reflecting in part the cost of tax stamps. Average circulation was a few thousand, though *Basiret* is supposed to have reached a daily circulation of 30,000 copies in 1876.

At any rate, within a decade and a half after the publication of the *Tercüman-i Ahval*, the Ottoman Empire had developed a small

[6] Paul Fesch, *Constantinople Aux Derniers Jours d'Abdul Hamid*, Paris, 1907, pp. 34ff.; Ubicini et Courteille, *État Présent de l'Empire Ottoman*, Paris, 1876, pp. 165ff.

press. Namık Kemal could boast with at least some justification in 1873 that "if the Ottomans have a literary language ... and if people have become aware of the existence of civilization in the world and acquired an opinion about ... the policy of the state, that has happened through the press. . . . If political education were given to everyone for years, that would not have helped public opinion as much as the newspapers."[7] The press had by then established permanent roots in a politically rich soil.

III. The Political Impact of Press and Literature

The second phase of press development in the Ottoman Empire, in 1870-1908, was characterized by the growing influence of the newspaper both among the masses and in government circles. The successful efforts of the press to disseminate ideas unpopular with the government and to instigate mass reaction led the government to impose severe press controls, forcing political journalists to go abroad, while the intelligentsia at home educated the public in the social and scientific aspects of modernization. But the increasing knowledge of Western achievements coupled with additional military defeats further undermined the sense of superiority surviving from the days of glory. The resulting sense of frustration infected the masses. Increasingly aware of the power of public opinion, the press began to relate current problems to people's daily lives. Political suasion gradually ceased to involve only abstract ideas and began to concern concrete policy. The newspapers lamented the widespread poverty, the decrease of population, and the corruption of the bureaucracy, and to conclude that drastic action was called for.

By 1875-1876 the populace began to demonstrate on the streets of Istanbul, demanding the removal of corrupt officials. This was in fact a demonstration against the sultan himself, and eventually Sultan Abdülaziz was replaced by Murad V. The journalists in exile were recalled amid great popular joy and hope.

The two-chamber Ottoman parliament established in 1876 represented chiefly the upper middle classes. The deputies asked characteristically for administrative reforms and for economic progress, whereas in matters connected with social mores and customs they were archconservatives. Yet they were good enough pragmatists to give priority to the satisfaction of actual national needs, regardless of cultural effects.

It is symbolic that the House of Deputies gave high priority to

[7] *İbret*, January 15, 1873.

a press bill which the government had introduced with the purpose of securing control over the newspapers. The deputies were grateful to the press for having contributed to progress, and were unwilling to impose restrictions on it. "Wherever the press is free there is progress," declared Vasilaki Efendi, "but those who saw this bill when it came to us thought that this was not a press bill but a penal code. There is nothing in it but jail punishment and fines. We have a penal code. If they (journalists) write something wrong then that law should be used. The press should be free. Everybody is amazed by America's progress. That is a new country. Those who wonder do not know that when two Americans are found together there is a printing press and a newspaper next to them."[8]

Some conservative deputies, reflecting elite philosophy, censured the humorous magazines, in particular, for their appeal to man's rebellious nature and for working against the supremacy of the mind, but even these found defenders. Solidi Efendi declared that "the need for humorous magazines is known and accepted. The humorous magazines were invented before the serious ones. If humor and comedy are abolished we shall have nothing to combat evil with. The humorous magazines are accomplishing something which the serious ones cannot."[9]

The law as eventually passed was stripped of its restrictive provisions, and this angered the sultan so much that he never enforced it. Indeed Abdülhamid II (1876-1909), who succeeded Murad V in dubious circumstances, prorogued the parliament, and suspended the entire constitution until July 1908.

Abdülhamid was keenly aware of the public influence of newspapers, and at first cultivated friendly relations with journalists for his own purposes. Gradually, however, he abolished the freedom of the press, believing, as Paul Fesch has reported, that most journalists were republicans at heart.[10] During his rule, to paraphrase Fesch, the empire had newspapers but no press. The journals were filled with official communications and anything published abroad in praise of the sultan or the Turks generally. By 1891 the total metropolitan press had fallen to 6 dailies, 2 weeklies, and a few periodicals; the foreign

[8] The verbatim records of the debates on the press bill together with other relevant documents appeared in *Takvim-i Vekayi*, Nos. 1903-1913 of 1877. These are reproduced verbatim also by Server İskit, *Türkiyede Matbuat Rejimleri*, Istanbul, 1939.
[9] *Ibid.*
[10] Fesch, *op.cit.*, p. 50.

language press then amounted to 27 dailies and periodicals. By 1908, only 3 Turkish dailies (supported by the government) had survived: *Ikdam* (Perseverance), circ. 15,000, *Sabah* (Morning), circ. 12,000, and *Tercüman-i Hakikat* (Interpreter of Truth), circ. 2,000—and about 10 periodicals. The circulation of the foreign language press then numbered about 18,000 Greek, 11,000 Armenian, 1,400 Spanish-Jewish, and 20,000 French and English.

Abdülhamid, nonetheless, expanded the educational system, made serious attempts to train the bureaucracy, instituted administrative controls, and paid closer attention to trade and crafts. All in all, he tried to promote material advances while conserving the established order. During the first fifteen years of his rule more than 4,000 books were published, 1,000 dealing with the religious and cultural concerns of the Muslim people, about 1,000 with literature, and about 1,000 with professional matters; the rest comprised textbooks, laws, and regulations. The classics of Islam were translated and disseminated.

More popular than these orthodox Islamic writings were stories depicting the exploits of Muslims against the Christians, many of which had survived among the masses as part of their folklore. The epics of Battal Gazi, Zal Rüstem, Saladin, and other legendary Muslim heroes (written in the Sufi style) were apparently avidly read. Supplementing such legends were a spate of popular love and adventure stories, some original and some deriving from Arab and Persian sources, and some quite profane. Such publications perpetuated among the lower classes the images and symbols of the traditionalist era. The monarchs or leaders were described as dedicated to religious goals (the spread of Islam), their extraordinary abilities extolled, and their charisma celebrated in an atmosphere of fairy tale and fatalism.

The intellectual event having the most far-reaching political effects, however, was undoubtedly the development of a modern literature in the latter part of the nineteenth century. The Turkish press had from the first devoted considerable space to translations and original literary works. The translations consisted of plays, novels, and the political writings of Voltaire, Rousseau, Hugo, and others, practically all published in installments in newspapers. The original works were often written by the journalists themselves. Journalism, literature, and politics hence became identified with each other. Şinasi, Namık Kemal, Ziya Paşa, Muallim Naci, Tevfik Fikret, Ahmed Midhat, Ali Suavi, Mizancı Murad, and Ahmed Rasim, all of them active in one way or other in journalism and politics, were also the founders of modern Turkish literature.

The concurrent development of a bourgeoisie and a landed gentry and of a new bureaucratic order produced the social cross currents which have preoccupied Turkish men of letters ever since. Ahmed Midhat (1844-1912) may be regarded as typical of the literary journalists who surveyed this social scene.

Ahmed Midhat was preoccupied with the rising middle classes and their moral standards. The new generation, he found, had rejected the ancient moral code and adopted new views on family life, and was indulging in a variety of frivolous pursuits. He was critical of the idle sons of the new rich, who in the search for pleasure had lost their own cultural identity and were doomed to end tragically in the hands of soubrettes and pleasure-house owners. With the same nostalgia, he described the inevitable downfall of the large household, and criticized with much earnestness the surviving effects of slavery and Janissary philosophy, the condition of women, the many consequences of social change.

General education for both sexes was his central theme. In political matters he is thought to have been conservative. Accepting material changes as unavoidable, nonetheless, he tended to believe that these should take place within the framework of generally accepted institutions; he appeared to hold that if the social body reached maturity by internal or organic processes, among which education loomed large, it would change in accordance with its real needs. Consequently, he directed all his efforts towards advancing the course of education. His two-hundred-odd works, written on subjects ranging from linguistics to astronomy, from history to medicine, sought to impart knowledge.

Throughout the process of modernization, literature served as a political and social laboratory where new ideas were concretely tried out. The governments undertook political reforms without much regard for society's capacity to absorb them, but literature conceived more consistent and natural relationships between events, people, and ideas, and eventually brought into focus the individual's role in the process of change. Perhaps the essence of modernization in the Middle East in fact consists of the individual's passage from a state of blind obedience to an active and creative role in the process of change. The Turkish writers of 1870 and 1880, though recording social change, hardly ascribed any significant social role to individuals. The succeeding generation began to look into the causes of change and discovered the individual to be a passive and powerless subject. For instance, the heroes of Halid Ziya Uşaklıgil, who was writing at the turn of the century, were idealists who sought status in newly created occupations, like writing and journalism, but were defeated by the merciless new society and its representatives. Later, in Ömer Seyfeddin (1886-1920), the human being, usually from the middle classes, begins to assume an active role in the process of change and to identify himself with a cause, even though he is more interested in personal aggrandizement than in ideas. The writers after the 1920's placed the individual in a social context and made him the spokesman for a social group and ideology. The literary evolution reflects the social and political awakening of the lower classes. Journalism and literature flourishing together at once contributed to and recorded this awakening.

IV. The Mass Media in the Service of Nationalism and Political Parties

The rise of the Young Turks to power marked a turning point in Turkish political history. The spirit of nationalism became fully articulate. A new bureaucratic middle class acquired power, displacing the bourgeoisie formed in 1870-1908 on the basis of economic success. The moralizing of Ahmed Midhat seemed outmoded alongside the authoritarian, secularist, and positivist views of the intelligentsia in power. Some members of this intelligentsia belonged to the high Ottoman families, most emerged from the middle classes by way of the schools which Abdülhamid had established for his own purposes.

In the half century before 1908, the minimum conditions necessary for modern communications media had been established. Under the Young Turks the press became directly associated with the emerging political parties or with a rather well-defined view of the nascent centralized national state.

During the period of their exile, members of the Young Turk movement had themselves published no less than 100 newspapers and reviews in France, England, Switzerland, Egypt, Greece, and Rumania. Several of these had clear-cut ideological positions: *Meşveret* (Consultation, 1895) of Ahmed Rıza Bey, probably the most influential, promoted positivism and nationalism; other papers were pro-Islamist, Westernist-liberal, and social democratic. Since the political debate in this press took place abroad, however, and was only distantly known of in Turkey proper, the year 1908 brought a sudden influx of ideas somewhat remote from the realities of the Ottoman society.

From 1908 until about 1912, when the Young Turks began to be oppressive, the press expanded quickly. One year after the revolution, according to some incomplete statistics, the total number of newspapers and periodicals published in the Ottoman Empire amounted to not less than 350. In 1911 there were 9 Turkish dailies published in Istanbul as well as 21 non-Turkish papers. In the provinces a year later there were 113 Turkish newspapers, 115 Arabic. In 1911 again, there appeared in Istanbul alone 32 magazines of various sorts. In 1913 the periodicals in all Ottoman dominions numbered 389, of which 161 were in Turkish, 118 in Arabic.

The new newspapers were profoundly political, with each political party or group striving to publish its own organ. The controlling Union and Progress group published *Tanin* (Voice, of Hüseyin Cahid Yalçın) and *Şura-yı Ümmet*. The Democrat Party, an opposition party of İbrahim Temo, published no less than four papers. Other groups, such as *Fedakâran-ı Millet* (Volunteers for the Nation), *Ahali* (People's Party), and *Ittihad-ı Muhammedi* (Muslim Alliance), had papers of their own.[11]

The Union and Progress, vexed by opposition criticism, advised its country branches to publish propaganda material supplied by the party in order to correct the wrong impression created by the opposition. The names of some of the resulting newspapers—*Silâh* (Weapon), *Süngü* (Bayonet), *Kurşun* (Bullet), *Bıçak* (Knife), and *Bomba* (Bomb)—are a fair index of their attitudes. It was in fact with such weapons that the Unionists curbed the opposition press, three members of which were assassinated in public.

The papers inherited from Abdülhamid's period, *Ikdam, Sabah,* and *Tercüman-ı Hakikat,* strove to remain independent, but they also soon moved into the opposition camp. The many humorous publications, such as *Kalem* and *Püsküllü Belâ*, stimulated interest in political activity by publishing suggestive cartoons or ridiculing their enemies. The bulk of the press, siding with the opposition, quickly increased their circulation. The circulation of the pro-government *Tanin,* which was 7,000 before 1909, went down to 4,000 before rising to 14,000 and 18,000 during war years. The opposition *Ikdam* attained a circulation of 26,000, and on special occasions (the Italian War) of as much as 50,000 before it declined in popularity.

[11] See *Ayın Tarihi,* Nos. 41-45, 1927; 51-53, 1928, for publications of the Young Turk period.

The newspaper began to reach the lower urban groups. Then the public, used to a docile press in the past and accustomed to revere their government, began to view the militant newspapers as a possible threat to organized society. When disorders developed, the citizen blamed the press, although in fact it had merely brought to the surface conflicts lying beneath the old society's nonchalant calm.

Truly ideological reviews providing intellectual leadership for the political struggle appeared in this period. Nationalism, which hoped to turn the multi-national Ottoman Empire into a cohesive national state, was promoted by *Türk Yurdu* (Turkish Homeland) and other periodicals. *Sirat-i Müstakim* (Bridge of Righteousness), among still others, was pro-Islamist. The Westernists published *Ictihad*, which appears to have influenced Atatürk, and the socialists published *İştirak* (Participation), which had the popular motto *biri yer, digeri bakar, kavga bundan çıkar* (fighting results when one eats and the other only looks). The first test of the influence exercised by the press on public opinion was provided by *Volkan* (Volcano), the newspaper of the conservative *Ittihad-i Muhammedi* (Muslim Alliance). Its fiery criticism of the secularist tendencies of the Union and Progress party let to the reactionary, popular upheaval of 1909.

The Union and Progress government used the upheaval as a pretext to institute a press law, copied after the French Press Law of 1881. The very function of the press, it was held, imposed obligations on it, and these had to be defined by the government. During the First World War the press dwindled to a few newspapers and reviews of limited political significance. Though at the end of the war there was a sudden outburst of political and press activity in Istanbul, this was of little political consequence, since it was Anatolia which became the center for Mustafa Kemal's movement of National Liberation.

The Young Turk era had served, nevertheless, as a period of political training and experience. Liberal ideas, borrowed from the West, were debated in the press, tried, and for the most part found unworkable. Then, when the Balkan War in 1913 ended in the loss of territories "sown with the bones of ancestors and nurtured with their blood," there was a reaction against the West and an infusion of Turkish nationalism, which became the main theme in the modern-minded press.

Nationalism, whatever its causes, had certain populist tendencies. In order to build a national state it was necessary to develop new cultural bonds among the whole population. Among the long-forgotten masses of Anatolia, the "real Turk" was happily discovered, unaware that his language and customs, if not his person, were about to become a political asset. The intelligentsia was urged to learn the history, folklore, and traditions of the Turkish masses, and in return teach them the rudiments of civilization. Reviews like *Halka Doğru* (Toward the People), born from this preoccupation with national culture, diverted public interest towards the lower social groups. They also exposed these groups to nationalist ideas, though not at first offering to ameliorate the actual circumstances of their lives.

V. The National Sovereignty and the Press

Mustafa Kemal's movement had, then, a populist orientation. It was based on the idea that national sovereignty was rooted in the popular will. It had also social goals, for Mustafa Kemal's first government came forth as the *halk hükûmeti* (people's government), promising to find a remedy to economic and social ills and put an end to bureaucratic oppressions.

Mustafa Kemal remained in contact with Istanbul newspapers, some of which had earlier informed the public of the purposes of his movement. The *Müdafaa-i Hukuk Cemiyetleri* (Associations for the Defense of Rights), also, which carried out the election of the National Assembly in 1920, incorporated branches of the Union and Progress Party; these in turn controlled the local press and were able to have numbers of papers declare for the nationalists.

Mustafa Kemal used all communication media intensively to win over the public. "Indoctrination and information," in his view, "was very important, as important as the question of the army, and even more important than the army."[12] In 1920 a General Directorate of Press and Information was established to direct communication and propaganda along with the Turkish news agency, *Anadolu Ajansı*, established in the same year. The latter issued news bulletins and printed pamphlets and books for distribution at home and abroad.

In view of widespread illiteracy, oral communication played a significant part in winning over the Anatolian population, some well-known people, such as Ziya Gökalp, being sent to "work among people" and convert them to the nationalist cause. Pamphlets and brochures, moreover, including epics in the folk style glorifying the

---

[12] *Atatürk 'ün Söylev ve Demeçleri*, 3 vols., Istanbul, 1945-1954, i, 124.

movement and Mustafa Kemal, were printed and distributed to be read to the public in towns and villages.

The Ankara and Istanbul governments engaged in a war of pamphlets. When a *fetva* of the sultan's condemned Kemal to death, the nationalists printed an answering *fetva*, endorsed by 152 muftis in Anatolia and distributed it in towns and villages. Not only did the local press in Anatolia declare for the nationalists; newspapers published in towns which had never had a press spontaneously opposed foreign occupation and urged popular resistance to it. Perhaps for the first time in Turkish history the press was deliberately mobilizing public opinion without any pressure from above. In Adana, the local *Yeni Adana* (New Adana) opposed the French occupation even before Mustafa Kemal's action started; closed by the French, it was published secretly and smuggled into the occupied territories. In Balıkesir, Giresun, and Kastamonu nationalist papers spontaneously arose. Numbers of journalists, some of them bringing their own printing presses, came to Ankara and actively supported Mustafa Kemal. During the War of Liberation there further appeared, in Istanbul, Eskişehir, and Ankara, the first systematic socialist publications, which also gave Kemal their support. And, on September 14, 1919, the nationalist government began to publish its own newspaper *İrade-i Milliye* (National Will), which, under the subsequent titles of *Hakimiyet-i Milliye* (National Sovereignty) and *Ulus* (Nation) remained for years the spokesman for the government and the Republican People's Party. This press itself initiated economic, social, and administrative ideas which became incorporated in the republican government's policy, and many of its publishers and editors, with the exception of the socialists, came to occupy high positions in the republic.

With the victory of nationalist forces and the abolition of the sultanate in 1922, most of the remaining papers, including the hitherto ambiguous Istanbul press, came to Mustafa Kemal's side. Nevertheless, opposition developed upon the abolition of the Caliphate in 1924. *İkdam, Tanin,* and *Tevhid-i Efkâr* were then brought to court for supporting the Caliph. The establishment of the Progressive Party in 1924, though by friends of Mustafa Kemal, and with the avowed purpose of preventing the new regime from succumbing to authoritarianism, created a new wave of opposition, in the press and in popular sentiment. The Kurdish revolt in 1925 provided the occasion for a *Takrir-i Sükûn Kanunu* (Law on Maintenance of Order), which gave the government powers to suspend newspapers and try journalists who disturbed social peace.[13]

This law, though applied with considerable leniency, marked the beginning of an era of imposed reforms and of limited interest in complex social and religious issues which had earlier engaged the press. With the consolidation of the republican regime in 1923-1925, one creative period for the mass media was over, and they began to serve primarily the end of cultural education.

VI. Modernization, Political Indoctrination, and Mass Media in the Republic

The republican leaders were fully conscious of the impact of the press and other mass media and introduced new means, such as the radio, to indoctrinate the public. The press itself was organized in a government-sponsored association. Book publishing, aided by the spread of literacy and the introduction of the Latin alphabet, acquainted the masses with the modern social and political ideas of the West and destroyed the literacy monopoly of the higher classes. Religious publications gradually disappeared. Newspapers improved qualitatively but failed to gain in circulation mainly because of restrictions imposed on political news and debates. The total number of newspapers published in Ankara and Istanbul in 1923-1930 amounted only to between 20 and 30.

The discipline imposed on the press did not prevail for long, especially among the older generation of newsmen, who still regarded the press chiefly as a political forum. When the opposition Liberal Party of Fethi Okyar was established in 1930, the new papers *Yarın* (Tomorrow) of Arif Oruç and *Son Posta* (Last Mail) and a few smaller newspapers sided with that party. Even after the Liberal Party was suppressed, the criticism did not end; for it was not the regime itself that was criticized but the new ruling class and the economic and social failures hidden behind the progressive façade of republicanism and modernism.

At this juncture—in 1931—a new press bill was passed, of which the preamble stated that the press was a "powerful means to . . . serve the progress of science and of public opinion," and had a useful role in the political, social, and ethical life of a country. The report of

[13] For memoirs of these trials see Ahmet Enim Yalman, *Turkey in My Time*, Norman, Okla., 1956, pp. 155ff.

the Judiciary and Internal Affairs Committee nevertheless accused the press of abusing its freedom, undermining the society's "moral" and social foundations, and harming the prestige of individual persons.[14] Ever since 1908, in the committee's view, it had created social dangers and jeopardized government authority. The deputies further accused the leftist section of the press, ironically enough, of religious and reactionary intrigues. These papers had in fact demanded an enforcement of women's rights, censured the lavish expenditure of public funds for unproductive purposes, and attacked a number of deputies, the new rising bureaucratic middle class, for accumulating personal wealth by virtue of public position.

These deputies in turn accused the journalists of rebelliousness and even of treason. But the government declared through İnönü, the prime minister, that the first measure of freedom in a country was the right to criticize the government. Political progress in a country, according to İnönü, depended on regarding criticism as part of the governmental process and not as a means for destroying authority. It was impossible, he said, "to presume the existence of a government by the people without a press . . . yet if freedom of the press is not properly used it quickens the downfall of a country. . . . We are forced to reconcile these two contradictions . . . freedom of the press shall be preserved but shall not harm the country."[15] The law passed as a result of these deliberations (No. 1881 of July 29, 1931), was nevertheless stringent, and, as amended in 1932, 1933, 1934, 1935, 1938, and 1940, it became one of the most undemocratic laws in the republic. The promotion of Marxism or other deviant doctrines became relegated to publications like *Kadro* and *Yeni Türk*, which were primarily nationalist and appealing to the intelligentsia.

The press continued to expand, though at a slow pace. In 1935 there were in Turkey a total of 243 publications of which 38 were dailies (22 in Istanbul, 6 in İzmir, and 2 in Ankara). The government, still dissatisfied with the performance of newspapers, continued to ask for closer "cooperation" between the Press and Publication Directorate and the press itself, and to define the "educational" function of newspapers in accordance with the republic's reformist principles.

The popularization of the mass media in Turkey was stimulated

---

[14] *Büyük Millet Meclisi Zabıt Ceridesi*, session 4, 33rd meeting, vol. 3, pp. 3ff.
[15] *Ibid.* (The speech may also be found reproduced verbatim in İskit, *Matbuat Rejimleri*, pp. 423-430, quotation p. 427.)

by the activities of the *Halk Evleri* (People's Houses),[16] established in 1931-1932, with the purpose of spreading the nationalist-secularist ideology to the masses, of bringing the intellectuals and villagers together, of developing a national culture, and of raising the general cultural standards. From 1932 to 1951, a total of 478 of these were founded in the towns. Each house was bound by statute to undertake studies in the folklore, history, and social conditions of the people in its area, these to be published in reviews or books. The chief review was *Ülkü* (Ideal) published in Ankara by the General Secretariat of the Republican People's Party. Meanwhile a group of militant leftist-*étatist* Republicans, seeking to prepare the ground for future reforms, published the competing review *Kadro*. Both reviews were distributed for a time to the People's Houses libraries, but *Kadro* was required to cease publication in 1934.

Following the model of *Ülkü*, no less than 55 reviews were published throughout the country, of which 12 enjoyed rather long careers. These reviews included firsthand anthropological and sociological observations and interpreted the reforms in a pragmatic and popular spirit. Their style, with some exception, was simple and direct. Their circulation was limited (*Ülkü*'s was about 30,000); the printing was poor and the political matter inert. Nevertheless, they popularized the new script in the towns and provided experience for future writers and journalists.

The People's Houses also published a series of books on politics (upholding the regime), history, folklore, practical occupations, and hygiene, and deposited these, together with national newspapers and other material, in the People's Houses libraries open to the general public. By 1940 a total of 366 such libraries with 462,817 books had been established; in 1941, 612,766 people attended 267 of these.

The number of books published in general also very naturally rose. The individual books and pamphlets registered between 1928-1938 numbered 16,603, of which 7,445 were published by the government and 8,618 by private firms. The translation of literary works, chiefly Western classics, was greatly accelerated between 1930 and 1948. By 1948 the Ministry of Education had translated some 560 foreign books, published them in editions of about 5,000 copies, and offered

---

[16] The information on the People's Houses derives from a monograph prepared at the Center for Middle Eastern Studies at Harvard. See also my article "The People's Houses of Turkey: Establishment and Growth," *Middle East Journal*, Vol. xvii, Nos. 1-2, spring 1963, pp. 55-67, and the article in *Bustan* cited in the bibliography.

them for sale at a low price. Private printing firms meanwhile undertook translations according to popular taste. A Sherlock Holmes series numbered 83 booklets by 1948, a Nat Pinkerton series 180. Such material has tended to displace in part the native popular stories.

The radio played a more singleminded part than the press in the process of modernization and nationalist indoctrination. The first radio broadcasting station in Turkey was put into operation in 1927 in Istanbul by a private firm under government supervision. In 1936, upon the expiration of the contract with the concessionary firm, the government decided to build a new station in Ankara, which it put into operation in 1938 under the direction of the Press Directorate. The radio was, in the view of the government, an extremely potent force; printing "remained like hieroglyphs compared to the radio."[17] With the introduction of the radio, the concept of direct mass communication became more clearly defined in the leaders' minds.

Radio broadcasts diffused both the political principles of the new regime and cultural expressions of modernization such as Western music, plays, and speeches. There were regular news broadcasts four times a day, including the very popular *radio gazetesi* (radio journal) which summarized the news. A second popular program was *Evin Saati* (Home Hour), which broadcast information on home economics. A *Ziraat Takvimi Saati* (Calendar Hour on Agriculture) was widely appreciated in villages. In 1942 some 60 per cent of the programs consisted of music, about 35 per cent of speeches and cultural discussions.

Despite the interest with which the population greeted the introduction of the radio, sets themselves remained a luxury available only to a few. The total number of sets rose from 5,000 in 1927 to more than 100,000 in 1942; yet the number of sets per thousand people was still only 4.1, which compared quite unfavorably even with (for instance) Bulgaria's 12.8 per thousand, not to speak of Sweden's 217.8 per thousand. Half of the existing sets were concentrated in Istanbul and Ankara. The owners in 1942 included professional men and government officials (a little over 40 per cent), businessmen (a little over 30 per cent), and workers and peasants (10 per cent).[18] Radio ownership required (as it still does) a special license, the revenue from which more than meets cost of operation of the state radio.

[17] *Radyo*, December 15, 1941.
[18] For all these figures see *ibid.*, September 15, January 15, October 15, 1942.

The cultural mobilization of the masses was further enhanced by the emergence of a local press. This has followed its own line of development since the 1860's, interpreting national news and policies in the light of local opinion and needs. In Anatolia there developed a rather important local press and book publishing business. In Konya alone, for example, there were published 11 newspapers and 5 reviews between 1867 and 1923, and 11 newspapers and 19 reviews between 1923 and 1949. In Erzurum the first newspaper *Envar-i Şarkiye* (Eastern Lights) was published in 1866, and lasted until the founding of the republic. Like many other provincial papers, it was printed bilingually in Turkish and Armenian.

The local press related the ideas of the government to the facts of life in the provinces with a view to securing practical results. Modernization was viewed not as ideological but as material achievement. An article in a Konya paper of the 1930's, for example, discussing the prime minister's statement on village development, noted that modest iron ploughs might achieve better results than tractors, for they could be bought cheaply and adapted easily to any kind of soil. Other articles discussed town planning, tourism, and other practical matters, which the city intelligentsia might have dismissed, like Namık Kemal in his time, as the trivial preoccupations of a provincial mind. The Konya press again, discussing the contrast between actual life and books concluded: "Books may have a relation to life, but books are not life. Before everything else one needs the schooling given by life. . . . Books and life. How far are they from each other, how beautifully they deceive each other." Such a comment coming from Konya, the cradle of conservatism and a stronghold of the *ulema*, indicated the profound changes taking place in the minds of town dwellers.

An example of a village newspaper, virtually the only one, is furnished by *Güzelordu*. This newspaper, published for twenty-five years in the republic, first used a wooden printing plant fabricated locally and manned by natives. It attained a circulation of 700-800 copies which sold in 53 villages in the surrounding area. Although supporting the ruling Republican Party, it remained, by virtue of its sober view of life, a truly independent publication. On one occasion it advised impoverished young women who had *alafranga* (French fashion) hairdoes that, "since we are adopting European habits, we should adopt before everything else the European's principle of working instead of their manners." The governor interpreted this criticism as opposition to modernization and wanted to bring the paper before the court. But the villagers regarded the newspaper as a friend, especially after it was instrumental in delaying a construction project in an area infested with malaria mosquitoes: several workers had died during the construction but the officials in charge still continued the work, for they wanted to report an achievement to their superiors. It further exposed a crooked method for dividing inheritance (*iskat*), by which some religious men were robbing the peasants. The villagers liked in particular the straightforward style of *Güzelordu*, or its habit, as the editor put it, of "calling the iron, iron and the coal, coal."

The paper supported a multi-party system and espoused freedom of press as essential for the "progress of social groups." It also had definite views on foreign affairs, condemning the Second World War and Hitler and Mussolini who had started it.

So, in general, the intelligentsia regarded modernization ideologically, and stood ready to impose "advanced" modes of behavior by force, if necessary, while they themselves kept the helm. The peasant found, on the other hand, that a forceful cultural modernization upset his value system without changing his life for the better. He did not reject authority; he actually asked for it, but insisted that it serve his own welfare. When the interests of the lower orders found political expression, the multi-party system emerged which deprived the intelligentsia of power and established the hitherto obedient citizen as the arbiter of national policy. The expanded communication media brought new ideas to the lower classes and rendered them conscious of their relation to the government and to the social groups behind the government. And when the gulf that separated the mass from the elite became a disparity in social status and economic privilege rather than in political consciousness, it could no longer be automatically maintained by the political process.

V. The Mass Media and Multi-Party Life

The establishment of a multi-party system in 1945/1946 marked the turning point in Turkey's internal politics.[19] And the political activity of the time—like that in Japan at the turn of the century—provided a suitable ground for the rapid development of mass media. The first truly mass newspapers appeared in this period and their circulation climbed rapidly.

The liberalization began with the Republican Party's decision to

[19] See Kemal H. Karpat, *Turkey's Politics, The Transition to a Multi-Party System*, Princeton, 1959.

allow the establishment of opposition parties as necessitated by post-war international conditions. The press heralded the news, and two newspapers, the liberal *Vatan* (Homeland) of Ahmed Emin Yalman and the socialist *Tan* (Dawn) of Zekeriya Sertel, joined the nascent opposition at once, defining the conditions necessary to a democratic regime and calling for the amendment of such anti-democratic laws as the press law. *Tan,* adopting a pro-Soviet attitude and envisaging the forthcoming political system as inevitably leftist, aroused the anxiety of the ruling circles and its plant was eventually destroyed during an anti-leftist student demonstration. *Vatan* was spared and soon other newspapers joined with it in an increasingly vehement opposition.

The press law was liberalized and the government-controlled Press Union abolished, to be replaced in 1946 by a voluntary association, *Gazeteciler Cemiyeti* (Newspapersmen's Association). The Press Directorate, reorganized in 1949, became a purely technical bureau facilitating the labors of journalists.

The Democratic Party was established on January 7, 1946. The press, which had already mobilized public opinion against the government, at once gave that party full support. The citizen found that political news directly affected his life, and became interested in it. Intellectuals wrote endless articles on the theory and practice of democracy. Even the government-sponsored *Tercüme* (Translation) dedicated its November 1946 issue to democracy and translated relevant passages from Western writers.

The number of periodicals rose steadily: from a national total of 154 in 1945, it became 983 in 1952, and 1,573 (472 dailies) in 1961. See Table 1.

The power of the press began to be felt when the governor of İzmir closed *Yeni Ekonomi* (New Economy) in 1946 for reporting an automobile accident caused by his son, but was unable in the face of popular demands to keep it from republishing. Again, Recep Peker, the prime minister, on one night in December of 1946, suppressed six leftist publications, two political parties, and practically all the trade unions. But the press reported and printed the militant speeches of the opposition, even in the face of jail sentences for the offending journalists. The moderates in his own party thereupon turned against him and he eventually had to resign.

The Democratic Party won the elections of 1950, thanks to an overwhelming press support, and the assumption of power by this party

hrough victory at the polls taught the citizens a far-reaching lesson.
'or the first time in Turkish history a government was changed
hrough free elections; the citizen became suddenly conscious of the
>ower of his opinion; press conferences and letters to the editor have

TABLE 1. NEWSPAPERS, BOOKS, AND PERIODICALS PUBLISHED
IN TURKEY, 1928-1961*

		NEWSPAPERS		BOOKS	PERIODICALS
'ear	Dailies	Non-dailies	Total	Total	Total
928-33	—	—	—	6,297	—
934	46	92	138	1,530	206
935	49	78	127	1,741	222
936	46	87	133	2,106	191
937	46	91	137	2,512	203
938	46	95	141	2,731	199
939	46	71	117	2,831	178
940	60	63	132	2,370	158
941	52	67	119	2,339	148
942	62	62	124	2,104	127
943	61	63	124	2,804	142
944	73	86	159	3,072	258
945	75	79	154	2,621	287
946	89	105	194	2,730	332
947	227	95	322	2,436	379
948	109	299	408	2,322	408
949	105	315	420	2,461	449
950	131	346	477	2,400	—
951	150	334	484	2,197	—
952	333	650	983	2,447	—
953	—	—	—	3,266	—
954	—	—	—	3,585	—
955	278	509	787	3,250	—
956	363	443	806	3,080	—
957	420	465	885	2,630	—
958	194	590	784	3,925	—
959	478	377	855	4,124	—
960	506	1,152	1,658	4,195	—
961	472	1,101	1,573	4,357	—

* Adapted from statistical data supplied by Mr. Türker Acaroğlu, of the Printing
and Engraving Office in Istanbul.

become customary since. The immediate task of the press was to
transform itself from a militant weapon of political education into a
means of information, since henceforth political changes were to take
place through the election mechanism.

The "independent" newspapers shortly became most influential,
an "independent" newspaper normally being one not associated
formally with a political party but generally critical of the government

and able to exploit the innumerable social needs of the public. The circulation of such papers drops immediately if they become associated with a party. *Vatan*, for instance, reached high circulation while in opposition in 1946-1950, lost readers when Ahmed Emin Yalman continued to support the Democrats even after their victory, gained readers again when he turned against the Democratic Party government in 1954. According to the same law, *Ulus*, the Republican Party newspaper, reached a peak circulation of 60,000 copies (about half that of the "independent" *Cumhuriyet*) in 1959-1960, when the party was engaged in a struggle for life with the government. After the military coup of 1960, when the Republican Party gained influence in the government, it lost readers steadily until today it sells below 15,000 copies. *Zafer* (Victory), the newspaper of the Democratic Party, also reached a circulation of about 60,000 copies as an opposition organ in 1947-1950, but lost virtually its entire readership thereafter

The total circulation of daily newspapers in Turkey, incidentally has continued to rise: from some 1,060,000 copies in 1956 to 1,411,429 in 1960.[20]

The Democratic Party government passed a liberal press law (No 5568 of July 15, 1950) in gratitude for press support received during the years in opposition. But the regime of freedom did not last long The Democrats' economic policy, abuses in handling public funds favoritism in giving contracts, and other derelictions began to be criticized in 1953, whereupon the government adopted a series of amendments abridging freedom of the press and leaving journalists at the mercy of the authorities.

The issue which started Menderes on his downward path was the controversy over the journalists' right in libel cases to produce evidence in court against government personnel accused of abuses. In denying this right the Democrats were in effect excluding public opinion from the determinations of government. During the following years, in 1955-1960, the Democrats tried to subdue the press by a diversity of means and ended by jailing journalists and closing newspapers.[21]

All these restrictions proved fruitless. The press had moral support at home and abroad and would not bow to the government's will. The public had grown used to a free press, and the press itself still could inform the public of its position by mixing innuendo with news. Failing

[20] *Türkiyede Çıkan Gazete ve Mecmualar*, 1961, p. 5.
[21] For a detailed study of the struggle between the press and the government see Kemal H. Karpat, "The Turkish Elections of 1957," *Western Political Quarterly* Vol. XIV, June 1961, pp. 436-459.

to control the press through existing laws, the Democrats formed, in April of 1960, an inquiry committee with absolute powers to investigate and suppress any publications and to arrest newsmen deemed dangerous to the national security. But the committee's inquisitorial methods failed. An underground press developed overnight. Thousands of pamphlets denouncing the government and reproducing the speeches of the opposition leaders were printed illegally and distributed to the public.

Another major dispute between the government and the opposition arose over the use of the state radio, which during the years from 1946-1950 had become gradually non-partisan in somewhat the manner of the BBC. But, after 1955, the Democrats claimed that the radio *belonged* to the government, Menderes declaring that the government needed it to "address directly our beloved nation. . . . We see," he said, "that almost all newspapers are working on behalf of the opposition. . . . They use every available means to interpret events in favor of the opposition. . . . Our speaking on the radio from time to time, may be considered an answer to them. This means that we have taken a step to establish a balance."[22] The number of radios had risen by then to perhaps four million sets, so that the balance was fully redressed.

The military take-over on May 27, 1960 opened a new phase in the development of mass media in Turkey. The press was liberalized, the jailed newsmen freed and feted as revolutionary heroes. Publications of every hue appeared to express their political opinions and publicize the backlog of social and economic problems. The military government passed a fairly liberal press law, and some members of the junta pledged to end the monopoly of the press by a few families and to provide social justice for the miserably ill-paid newspapermen. The publishers of some Istanbul dailies protested the law, but their employees, in a very novel example of organized class warfare, demonstrated in its behalf.

The military government maintained in general a rather liberal attitude towards the press, though it occasionally arrested and prosecuted newsmen, either for irresponsible reporting or for too telling criticism. Freedom of the press—guaranteed also by the new constitution—seemed to have come to stay. And the press itself, conscious of past errors, has sought to impose self-control through a code of ethics (*Basın Yasası*) signed by all major newspapers.

[22] *Zafer*, January 22, 1960.

The radio has become neutral again, and broadcasts objective news, cultural programs, and announcements. Then newspapers have had leisure to pursue technical excellence in reporting and printing. Newly prominent columnists are interpreting current events according to their personal bent. A moderate class of readers, though interested in politics, prefers objective newspapers that provide news and miscellaneous information rather than polemics alone. *Hürriyet* (Freedom), which has achieved a uniquely high circulation of 250,000-300,000 copies, appeals to this group by its succinct and non-controversial review of current events, pictures, and reading material of general interest. It has so been able to thrive under the Democrats, the military, and the present administration. The recent growth of *Milliyet*'s popularity (circulation ca. 200,000), due to its social democratic writings, is a sign, however, of growing political consciousness.

VI. Conclusion

The government introduced the modern media in order to enhance its own authority but opposed all attempts to utilize them for divergent purposes. The ensuing struggle to assure freedom of communication became a part of the fight for democracy generally and left the media little leisure to develop high professional standards.

Since the media were utilized to spread information about Western ways of life and political systems, the newspapers in particular were highly doctrinal. They envisaged the desired *civilization* or *modernization* first as consisting chiefly of political changes. Then they broadened their purview to include social and economic reforms. By the same token, they appealed first to the enlightened urban groups, then to lower social strata, and finally to the villages. The radio found its way into villages much faster than the printed word, but the newspaper is still the most influential single instrument of political education.

Current trends in the evolution of newspapers and radio, and of journalism as a profession, are approximating the mass media in Turkey to their counterparts in Europe, though not obliterating national peculiarities.

As a social force, the several media have in local instances supported tradition and even reaction. But, considered in their totality they have very decisively made for a heightened political consciousness and for political, economic, and social democracy.

CHAPTER 7

THE CIVIL BUREAUCRACY

A. JAPAN

MASAMICHI INOKI

WHEN we apply to Japan the yardstick of "political modernization," we become aware that the development of the state along "modern" lines was notably uneven and that this imbalance or inconstancy was one of its essential characteristics. The role of the civil bureaucracy in the whole process is hence best considered chronologically.

I. Civil Bureaucracy during the Tokugawa Period

The Tokugawa shogunate is often termed a centralized feudalism, but the phrase itself contains a contradiction. The shogunate was absolute in proportion to the shogun's own military supremacy. For the shogun, a kind of generalissimo, subdued the country by military force and proceeded to rule it by means of a military establishment composed of vassals of several grades and of enfeoffed nobles. But in the 1630's, a generation after the Battle of Sekigahara (1600), the civil branch of the bureaucracy (*yakukata*)—in charge of administration, finance, justice, and so forth—began to assume a more important role in government than the holders of military offices (*bankata*).

Let us first consider the highest civil offices in the central government. The chief minister (*tairō*) and the senior and junior councillors were chosen from among the ranks of the *fudai daimyō*, namely, the holders of fiefs who had declared their allegiance to the Tokugawa cause before the crucial Battle of Sekigahara. The chief minister was selected from one of four *fudai daimyō* families: Doi, Sakai, Hotta, and Ii. The post was not regularly filled, only eight chief ministers being appointed throughout the entire 265 years of the Tokugawa period. Senior councillors (*rōju*), of whom there were five or six at a time, were *fudai daimyō* who were lords of castles. They staffed the central administrative office (*goyobeya*) and collectively determined major state policies. The junior councillors, numbering three to five, were picked from among the *fudai daimyō* who had no castles. They also served in the central administrative office and supervised the shogun's direct vassals (*hatamoto*).

The monopoly of key posts by a limited number of *fudai daimyō* led naturally to the danger of encroachment on the shogun's own power. To avoid such encroachment, the office of *sobayōnin* was established in the days of Tsunayoshi (1680-1709). The occupants of this office, who were recruited from the ranks of low-grade shogunal vassals (*kenin*) and owed their appointments directly to the shogun, gained an increasingly important voice in state affairs. These officers collectively, from chief minister down to *sobayōnin*, constituted the chief political leaders of Tokugawa Japan.

The civil bureaucracy in the strict sense of the term began with the offices of *ōmetsuke* and *metsuke*. *Ōmetsuke*, of whom there were usually four or five, were chosen from among the shogun's immediate vassals and were responsible, under the senior councillors, for the supervision of the daimyo. In the event of misconduct by a daimyo, they both charged and prosecuted him. *Metsuke* to the number of sixteen, who were also selected from among the immediate vassals of the shogun, were responsible, under the junior councillors, for supervising the members of their own class and, if need arose, for prosecuting them.

No less important than *ōmetsuke* and *metsuke* were the three classes of *bugyō*: *jisha bugyō*, *kanjō bugyō*, and *Edo-machi bugyō*. All were chosen from the shogunal vassals and received special stipends for their services. The four *jisha bugyō* controlled the Buddhist temples and Shinto shrines and the monks and priests serving them. They were also in charge of lawsuits instituted beyond the borders of the eight provinces of Kantō. The four *kanjō bugyō* were in charge of civil government, finance, and justice in territories under the direct jurisdiction of the shogunate and of legal actions brought within the provinces of Kantō. The two *Edo-machi bugyō* controlled civil government, the police and lawsuits within the capital city of Edo, except in those Edo estates held by samurai, temples, and shrines.

Of these three classes of *bugyō*, the *kanjō bugyō* had especially important duties. They controlled the entire financial resources of the shogunate, traditionally estimated to yield about five million *koku* of rice per year. The office of the *kanjō bugyō* was divided into two sections: a public affairs section in charge of police and justice, and a general affairs section in charge of finance, transportation, and agricultural policy. Of these two sections, the latter became increasingly important with the passage of time. It had six bureaus, each of which was administered by a chief, accountants, deputy accountants, and apprentices. This office also supervised the activities of four major (*gundai*) and forty or fifty minor (*daikan*) governors. Below these governors again were functionaries called *tezuke* or *tedai*.

At the bottom of the bureaucratic pyramid were semi-public officials or squires, called *nanushi* (*shōya* in the Kansai area), who represented their respective villages. They were assisted by *kumigashira* (unit leaders) in the performance of their duties. Both *nanushi* and *kumigashira* were chosen from among village notables.

There was also another office called *hyakushodai*. Holders of this post supervised *nanushi* and *kumigashira*. Peasant households were assigned to five-family units called *goningumi*, and all members of such units were held collectively responsible for the payment of the land tax and for the maintenance of public order. Thus, in Tokugawa times, the control of villages by local notables provided an ultimate basis for the whole bureaucratic machinery of the shogunate.

Next, let us examine more briefly the bureaucratic structure of the separate fiefs into which most of Tokugawa Japan was divided. The development of a civil bureaucracy was somewhat delayed in those fiefs which permitted their vassals to live permanently on their estates. But, generally speaking, as the vassals were forced by economic pressure from their lord to reside in the castle town, a civil bureaucracy like that of the shogunate came into being. The civil services required of the fiefs were, of course, relatively small in scope compared to those of the shogunate, which had to supply the needs of over five thousand high-grade and over seventeen thousand low-grade vassals as well as of countless peasants. The daimyo also made use of rule by local notables in the village as a basis for their bureaucratic machinery.

Administrative service in the Tokugawa period, whether in the territories of the shogun or in those of the daimyo, was in a general way patrimonial. Bureaucrats were not, however, recruited from among either foreigners or slaves. Offices normally had to be filled by persons of a specified feudal family rank, though, among candidates of the same rank, scholastic records at the fief school carried weight. As Fukuzawa Yukichi points out in his *Kyuhanjō* (Conditions in a Former Fief), the status distance between *jōshi* (high-grade samurai) and *kashi* (low-grade samurai) was such that promotion from the latter to the former status was truly exceptional. Legitimate marriages between *jōshi* and *kashi* families were impossible, and it is said that even adultery was not committed across that line.[1]

At length, however, the gradual inroads of a monetary economy and the increasing economic difficulties of the samurai in the castle towns began to break down the old hierarchy. It became possible to purchase the status of a low-class vassal. Also, while members of the *jōshi* class absorbed themselves in the study of the somewhat rarefied Confucian classics, members of the *kashi* class competent in mathematics and business came to fill offices which were important in substance if not in name. The institution of adoption offered one means whereby the hereditary hierarchy could be reconciled with a sort of merit system based on ability.

We may therefore say that a process of modernization was covertly going on within the status-based and patrimonial bureaucracy of the Tokugawa period. But this was modernization by stealth and by loopholes. The limitations of a fixed hierarchy could not be completely eliminated by devices like adoption. Appointments to office, promotions and dismissals were made at the discretion of superiors. The powers and responsibilities of offices were poorly defined, and there was a great deal of room for inefficiency, imbalance, and the personal interpretation of official duties.

When four American warships under the command of Commodore Matthew C. Perry arrived at Uraga in 1853, the Tokugawa shogunate was faced with a crisis. In order to cope with the situation, the government was compelled to recruit talented personnel for important offices by supplementing the principle of ascription with that of demonstrable merit. In such fields as diplomacy, military science, and Western studies in particular, new offices were created, such as the Office of Foreign Affairs (*Gaikoku Bugyō*), the Institute of Naval Sciences (*Kaigun Denshujo*), and the Office for the Study of Barbarian Books (*Bansho Torishirabesho*), and were filled with men of relatively low social status, such as Kawaji Toshiaki, Iwase Tadanari, Hori Toshihiro, Inoue Masanao, Egawa Eiryu, and Katsu Yoshikuni. Particularly noteworthy is the fact that the most important positions in the Office for the Study of Barbarian Books, set up in 1856, were occupied by an elite drawn from different fiefs. The appointment of subjects of individual fiefs to offices in the shogunal government implied the collapse of traditional lord-vassal relationships. In this process we find

---

[1] *Fukuzawa Yukichi Zenshū* (Collected Works of Fukuzawa Yukichi), Tokyo, 1960, VII, 266.

the origins of an "intellectual aristocracy" which figured prominently in the transition from the Tokugawa to the Meiji regime.

It should also be noted that Confucianism, which remained the state ideology throughout the Tokugawa period, placed allegiance to one's lord above filial piety and emphasized the supremacy of public over private loyalties. Thus, in the face of the national crisis precipitated by Commodore Perry, the loyalty owed to the lords of particular fiefs came to be transformed into loyalty to the emperor as the symbol of the country as a whole. Yoshida Shoin, for example, preached the virtues of feudal loyalty until the year 1853; after that he became aware of the need for a unified national government capable of dealing with an external crisis. The ideological foundations of a modern bureaucracy were laid during the fifteen years between Perry's arrival in 1853 and the Restoration in 1868. The voluntary secession from the fiefs of many revolutionary patriots (*shishi*) shortly before the Meiji Restoration were foretokens of the service shortly to be rendered to the single central government of a unified nation.

II. The Civil Bureaucracy in the New Meiji Government

The Meiji Restoration at once destroyed an old political power, the Tokugawa shogunate, and created a new one, the Meiji government. In the destruction of the old regime, the so-called *shishi* or loyalist revolutionaries—mainly from the Mito, Satsuma, and Chōshū clans—played a decisive role. Their slogan was the battle cry of *sonnō jōi* ("revere the Emperor and expel the foreign barbarians"). But this slogan was shortly transmuted into the forward-looking summons *fukoku kyōhei* ("make the Country rich and powerful"). The most fervent supporters of *fukoku kyōhei* were a new generation of intellectuals of the lower samurai class, all of whom had studied Western learning, either abroad or at Japanese schools. The new Meiji government was brought into being, as it was shortly to be staffed, by an intellectual aristocracy.

The formation of this "intellectual aristocracy" was made possible by the highly developed systems of social communication at the end of the Tokugawa period, which enabled the elite in different fiefs to learn about and from each other. The schools that the shogunate had set up after Perry's visit to promote Western studies contributed greatly to its emergence. The government scholarship program launched in 1870 had further permitted the ablest students from the several fiefs—three from large fiefs, two from medium-sized, and one from small—to study together at the university (at first the *Kaiseijo* in Edo and later the Imperial University of Tokyo). The purpose of this program was to facilitate the recruitment of an intellectual aristocracy—a higher bureaucracy devoted to national rather than personal or parochial interests.

It is appropriate here to point out that the Confucian element in Tokugawa education favored the formation of just such an enlightened bureaucracy as in fact arose. Confucianism as practiced in Japan taught unselfish devotion to public authority (*messhi hōkō*). After Perry's arrival in 1853, the loyalties thereby cultivated were dedicated to bringing the nation into military and economic parity with the Western powers, and to establishing the national unity essential to this end. It was realistically acknowledged, at the same time, that the nation needed talents and abilities as well as loyalty. The spiritual motive force of modern Japan was provided by a combination of national loyalty, symbolized by loyalty to the emperor, and respect for achievement. Professor Bellah's work on *Tokugawa Religion* provides a commentary on this thesis.

The nucleus of the new intellectual aristocracy was composed of young civil servants who gathered at the Finance Ministry from 1869 to 1871. The most outstanding among them were:

Yuri Kimimasa: Of lower samurai origin, from the Fukui fief, he studied foreign trade in Nagasaki and acquired a knowledge of finance and banking.

Okubo Toshimichi: Of lower samurai origin, from the Satsuma fief, he lived abroad from Nov. 1871 to May 1873.

Okuma Shigenobu: Of lower samurai origin, from the Saga fief, he studied Western science at the Dutch Academy in Nagasaki.

Itō Hirobumi: Of peasant origin, from the Chōshū fief, he was adopted by a lower samurai family and went to England for study in 1863.

Inoue Kaoru: Of lower samurai origin, from the Chōshū fief, he went to England to study in 1863.

Shibuzawa Eiichi: Of rich farmer origin, from the Province of Musashi, he was made a vassal of the shogun and accompanied Tokugawa Akitake, younger brother of Tokugawa Yoshinobu, to France, where they studied from 1865 to 1868.

Matsukata Masayoshi: Of lower samurai origin, from the Satsuma fief, he studied Western science in Nagasaki.

Maejima Hisoka: A samurai of the Takada fief, he studied medicine in Edo, entered the Ministry of Finance in 1869, and went abroad in 1870.

Civil servants like these men occupied the higher positions in the first modern bureaucracy in Japan. Many of them came from the Satsuma and Chōshū fiefs—quite understandably in view of the decisive role played by those fiefs in overthrowing the old regime. Of 372 civil bureaucrats appointed to important posts in the Meiji government from 1868 to 1872, 51 or 13.7 per cent came from Satsuma and 35 or 9.4 per cent from Chōshū. Again, of 602 civil bureaucrats who held important governmental posts in 1874, 52 or 8.6 per cent came from Satsuma and 69 or 11.4 per cent from Chōshū.[2] The total Satsuma and Chōshū complement at this time hardly exceeded twenty per cent of the higher posts, however. And the leading light in the civil bureaucracy was Okuma Shigenobu, from the Saga fief, who directed the Ministry of Finance until 1881 and brought to it both an expert knowledge of public finance and diplomatic ability. The early modern bureaucracy also included a considerable number of men who had been born peasants and of former vassals of the shogun and of other daimyo. These early bureaucrats had in common a respect for Western learning which most of them had studied, and a lively sense of the need to convert Japan into a rich and powerful state.

The major steps in their program for the building of such a rich and powerful state included the abolition of the feudal system, hereditary servitude, and restraints on travel and choice of occupation; the consolidation of local, provincial, and national governments and their monetary functions; and the establishment of universal education and military conscription. These reforms were without exception planned and carried out by these early modern bureaucrats. They paved the way for the political modernization of Japan.

III. The Civil Bureaucracy as a Modernizing Oligarchy

From 1868 to 1881 the new Meiji government affected many reforms in governmental organization. In the beginning, court nobles and daimyo monopolized the most prestigious offices of state, but selection by birth was soon replaced by a merit system. By 1874 the aristocracy had largely been removed from high public office. In 1885, when the *Dajōkan* (Grand Ministry) system was replaced by the cabinet system, the last remnants of a fixed and traditional system of selection disappeared. At this time also, a clear distinction was made between the imperial household and the administrative departments of state, and Itō Hirobumi, a commoner by birth, became prime minister.

In 1881, however, a series of political upheavals had led to the

---

[2] Compiled from unpublished data of Professor Sakata Yoshio.

ouster of Okuma Shigenobu from the government and to a growing monopolization of key posts by the Satsuma and Chōshū factions. That year marked the point at which the relatively open structure of an intellectual aristocracy began to be transformed into the closed structure of a bureaucratic oligarchy. This post-1881 oligarchy continued, to be sure, to profess its devotion to general national interests, but, in reality, it tended more and more to pursue self-interest in the name of the national interest. A new type of ascription based upon Satsuma or Chōshū origins superseded the standards of achievement and ability of the early post-Restoration years, which had themselves replaced the earlier ascriptive practices of the Tokugawa period.

The new government had for some time been under fire from both right and left. The opposition from the right came from elements of the samurai class which repined at the loss of feudal privileges. This dissatisfaction led ultimately to the Satsuma Rebellion of 1877. The opposition on the left demanded a more representative form of government and sought that end by sponsoring petitions and by establishing, in 1874, Japan's first political party. The Meiji government replied to the first of these attacks through the Conscription Ordinance of 1873, whereby it consolidated its military power and its ability to cope with possible rebellions, and to the second through the Imperial Rescript on Constitutional Government of April 1875, wherein it promised gradual progress toward constitutional government through the establishment of a legislative organ (the Genrōin) and a judicial organ (the Daishinin). In March of 1884 there was further established a Bureau for the Investigation of Public Institutes, led by Itō Hirobumi, which was charged with the drafting of a constitution. Over the five-year period from 1884 to the promulgation of the Constitution in 1889, the oligarchs of the Meiji government sought to consolidate their own vested interests and privileges and to subvert the democratic aspirations represented by the popular rights movement.

To begin with, in July of 1884, a new Peerage Ordinance declared that, in addition to former daimyo and court nobles, one hundred leaders of the Meiji Restoration were ennobled as a reward for services. Of these, twenty-nine were from the Satsuma fief and twenty-three from the Chōshū. This measure was designed to unite the old aristocracy of court nobles and daimyo and the new oligarchy of Restoration leaders in a House of Peers which would be strong enough to offset the influence of the proposed popularly elected House of Representatives. The establishment of this peerage represented the determination of the Meiji bureaucrats to maintain their position as a privileged class and to direct the political course of the nation along lines compatible with their own collective interest. The former revolutionaries of the Restoration Period had become a political and social aristocracy as well as a "modernizing" bureaucracy.

The establishment of the cabinet system in 1885 produced a government resting on a balance of power among fief-based factions: the first cabinet was composed of four members from Satsuma, four from Chōshū, one from Tosa, and one Tokugawa vassal. The first prime minister, however, Itō Hirobumi, stated that in the future civil bureaucrats would be recruited by examination. In July of 1887, Imperial Ordinance No. 37 set forth rules governing civil service examinations for probationers and apprentices and divided the service into higher and lower branches with separate examinations.

Two years later, Article Nineteen of the Meiji Constitution declared: "Japanese subjects may, according to qualifications determined by laws or ordinances, be appointed to civil or military or any other public offices equally." Thus everyone was constitutionally guaranteed the right to become a civil or military official, regardless of family origin, if he met the standards of certain examinations. In 1893 the Civil Service Appointment Ordinance (*Bunkan Ninyōrei*) and the Regulations Pertaining to Civil Service Examinations (*Bunkan Shiken Kisoku*) were promulgated and the criteria for the appointment of higher and lower officials were finally made definite. Still the highest ranks of officials (*Chokunin*) continued to be selected by "free appointment." The Matsukata Cabinet of 1896, for example, appointed many "Progressive Party" members to positions as vice-minister, bureau chief, and prefectural governor. The appointments of the Okuma-Itagaki Cabinet established in June of 1898 were even more partisan.

It was under these circumstances that Yamagata Aritomo, a leading figure in both the civil and military bureaucracies, decided that the machinery of state needed to be protected from party influences. In March of 1899, he introduced a sweeping amendment to the Civil Service Appointment Ordinance which prohibited "free appointments" to civil service posts except in the case of those very high officials who were personally appointed by the emperor (*shinninkan*), and a few special posts. At the same time, the Ordinance on the Status of Civil Officials (*Bunkan Bungenrei*) and the Ordinance on the Discipline of Civil Officials (*Bunkan Chōkairei*) were promulgated, guaranteeing the status of civil bureaucrats. Since these imperial ordinances were instituted through the Privy Council, they could be changed only with the approval of that oligarchically controlled body. Thus any democratic reform of the civil bureaucracy was made impossible. The regulation of the bureaucracy by imperial ordinance rather than by law was evidence of the oligarchy's plan to establish the bureaucracy as a privileged class of "servants of the Emperor," a conception quite different from that underlying most Western civil service. Itō makes clear in his *Commentaries on the Constitution* that both the establishment of public offices and the appointment of persons to them are imperial prerogatives.

With the issuance of the Ordinance on Grades and Salaries of Higher Civil Officials (*Kōtōkan Kantō Hōkyūrei*) in 1886 and of the Pension Ordinance (*Onkyūrei*) in 1889, a modern civil bureaucracy was established in Japan. At the same time, there was established for all bureaucrats a privileged position beyond the control of political parties or the Imperial Diet. In practice, the system of recruiting civil bureaucrats by examinations assured that graduates of Tokyo Imperial University—and especially its Law Department—would dominate the bureaucratic establishment.

IV. Constitutional Government and the Civil Bureaucracy

In 1881 the government had publicly committed itself to the establishment of an Imperial Diet by 1890. In pursuance of this promise, Itō Hirobumi was sent to Germany and Austria in March of 1882 to investigate European constitutional systems. He attended lectures by Rudolf von Gneist and Albert Mosse in Berlin and studied under Lorenz von Stein in Vienna. The views of these men reinforced Itō's conviction that the imperial prerogatives should be strengthened at the expense of parliament. This view was also supported in Japan by Hermann Roessler, the legal adviser to the Meiji government. To consolidate the position of the bureaucracy by strengthening the imperial prerogative perfectly suited the interests and ideology of the Restoration leaders. Inoue's Grand General Plan of 1881 (*Daikōryō*), drafted by order of Iwakura, had been in this regard a prototype of the Meiji Constitution. And when, in 1883, Itō embarked upon the actual drafting of the constitution, Inoue Kowashi, Itō Miyoji, and Kaneko Kentaro, as well as the government's two legal advisers, Hermann Roessler and Albert Mosse, were among his principal aides.

The Constitution of 1889 sought to reconcile imperial prerogatives, equivalent in practice to bureaucratic prerogatives, with the principle of popular representation by introducing a Bismarckian concept of constitutionalism. It soon became apparent, however, that this constitution, though designed to strengthen imperial prerogatives at the expense of popular power, in fact instituted a government unable to function except under party cabinets commanding a majority in the Imperial Diet. Finally, in June of 1898, the Itō Cabinet recognized that it could no longer carry on the government's business without the support of a working majority in the lower house of the Diet. When Itō resigned his office under these circumstances, no other elder statesman (*genrō*) was willing to assume the responsibility of forming a new cabinet. It was at this time that the Okuma-Itagaki Coalition Cabinet became the first semi-party government in the history of modern Japan. Its life was brief, but it did lead to the establishment of a new political party, the Seiyūkai, of which Itō accepted the presidency. This event, which marks the beginning of the transition from non-party (*chōzen naikaku*) to party governments in Japan, led to the gradual emergence of a two-party system involving the Seiyūkai and the Kenseikai (later Minseitō). From 1924 to 1932, these two parties formed cabinets alternately. Thus the Meiji Constitution, despite the intention of its authors, eventually sanctioned a constitutionalism tending towards the British type. The victory of Dr. Minobe's "organ theory of the Emperor" in the famous controversy between two professors of constitutional law at Tokyo Imperial University, Minobe and Uesugi, was a theoretical manifestation of this shift.

But this shift in constitutional practice was in part counteracted by a simultaneous transformation of the leadership of the two parties. For many bureaucrats joined the two parties and held high offices in them, including, with few subsequent exceptions, the presidency of both. The power of the bureaucrats in Japanese party politics is shown by the fact that of thirty-four persons who have formed cabinets in the twentieth century, only five—Prince Saionji Kimmochi, Prince Konoe Fumimaro, Katayama Tetsu, Hatoyama Ichiro, and Ishibashi Tanzan—have had no bureaucratic background, either civil or military.

V. The Civil Bureaucracy and Modernization

Bureaucratic leadership has played a leading part in the modernization of Japan. Within the present century, for example, they have devised a long series of social welfare measures, of which the Factory

Law of 1911 was foremost. Braving strong opposition from Japanese capitalists and managers, the civil officials of the Ministry of Agriculture and Commerce and the Ministry of Home Affairs further succeeded in enacting such supplementary legislation as the Employment Service Law (1921), the Health Insurance Law (1922), and the Minimum Age for Factory Worker's Law (1923). These measures were later reinforced by the Regulations on Factory-Attached Dormitories (1927), the Law for Prohibition of All-Night Labor by Women and Children (1929), the Workers' Disaster Relief Law (1931), and the Retirement Reserve Fund and Retirement Allowance Law (1936) —all of them drafted and enacted on bureaucratic initiative. It should further be noted that the agrarian reform legislation enacted after World War II was projected at that time by progressive officials in the Agriculture and Forestry Ministry, such as Tohata Shiro, Wada Hiroo, and Saito Makoto.

There is no doubt that the civil bureaucracy of pre-war Japan contributed to significant advances. Yet changes of certain kinds it steadfastly resisted. The Japanese civil bureaucracy remained patrimonial in nature and spirit from early Meiji times until the Second World War. The Japanese bureaucrat was a paternalistic type of modernizer who had little love for spontaneous popular initiative.[3] The more aggressive the leadership exercised by the civil bureaucracy became, the more passive the mass of the people tended to become. Since it is often argued that German bureaucracy is as paternalistic as Japanese, we might consider the fate, in Japan, of the German tradition of *Schöffengericht*, a system under which laymen participate in trials along with professional judges. During the Meiji period, Japan imported the judicial system of Germany in toto, but failed to adopt this system of lay participation. Later a jury system of the Anglo-American type was briefly introduced, but fell into disuse before it produced any significant results.

Secondly, we must take into account some inflexible attitudes within the civil bureaucracy itself. The leaders of the bureaucracy accepted the principle of achievement in place of ascription, but the civil service examination itself was gradually made the basis for ascriptive selection. The flagrant discrimination against lower-ranking

---

[3] An eloquent protest by a liberal civil servant against the conservative paternalism of the bureaucracy can be found in a series of articles in the *Asahi Shimbun*, written by the late Professor Kawai Eijirō in 1919 when he resigned from the Ministry of Agriculture, Trade, and Industry. See Kawai Eijirō, *Denki to tsuisō* (Reflections and Reminiscences), Tokyo, 1948, p. 24.

bureaucrats and the favoritism shown those who had passed the higher civil service examinations effectively prevented any flexibility in personnel administration and established distinctions as harshly asserted as those between the upper- and lower-ranking samurai of the Tokugawa period. Herein lay the principal cause of the radicalism exhibited by the unions of government and public service employees after the end of World War II. It is true that educational backgrounds play an important part also in the hierarchies of private corporations but, because the principle of achievement is there more freely acknowledged, the unions are relatively moderate, whereas government and public service employees tend to support either the Communist party or the pro-communist factions of the Socialist party.

Despite the presence of such regressive elements within the civil bureaucracy, it remained far more sensitive to the need for change than its military counterpart—probably because the content of the education provided by Tokyo Imperial University and other civilian institutions was more progressive than that offered by the Military Academy and the War College.

VI. The Social Origins of the Civil Bureaucracy

We have already seen that most progressive bureaucrats of the new Meiji government were of lower samurai origin. Reference has also been made to the high proportion from the former Satsuma and Chōshū fiefs. When recruitment by examination was introduced in the 1880's, a great many high bureaucratic posts came to be occupied by graduates of Tokyo Imperial University. That university had come into being in 1877 through a merger of two institutions founded under the Tokugawa shogunate, the Tokyo Kaisei School and the Tokyo Medical School. Later, under the Imperial University Ordinance of 1886, it was reconstituted as the first imperial university, consisting of the five colleges of law, medicine, engineering, literature, and natural science. When a new imperial university was established in Kyoto in 1897, the original institution came to be called Tokyo Imperial University. Since it was originally designed as a training school for civil bureaucrats, it very naturally supplied a preponderance of successful candidates for high bureaucratic posts from the 1890's on. In order to secure a diploma from Tokyo University, however, one had to be able to afford six years of schooling—three of higher, or preparatory, school and three of university work. Tokyo University

students were confined in fact if not by statute to the sons of upper-
and upper-middle class families (of civil bureaucrats, military officers,
landlords, rich farmers, businessmen, and industrialists), except for
a very small number of students holding scholarships provided by
former feudal lords and other rich people. With the establishment of
an Imperial University at Kyoto and others in Tōhoku, Kyūshū, and
Hokkaidō, and with the growth of the preparatory schools, the class
origins of students became somewhat more diverse in time. Until
1945, nevertheless, when scholarship opportunities were greatly extended, it was difficult for youths of humble parentage to study at
imperial universities and hence to pass the higher civil service examination.

We might examine the data on the composition of the higher civil
service given in the 1937 *Jinji Kōshinroku* (Who's Who). Of the
42,699 Japanese listed in it, 1,377 (3 per cent) were civil servants and
584 (1.4 per cent) were judicial officials. If one adds the two categories, the total is 1,961 (4.4 per cent). Of the civil servants, 358
(26.4 per cent) were of samurai (*shizoku*) origin and 17 (1.2 per
cent) were of noble (*kazoku*) origin. Although these proportions are
higher than the ratios of such families to the total population, we
nevertheless observe that 72.4 per cent of the civil servants were
commoners (*heimin*). Of the 584 judicial officials, those of samurai
origin numbered 142 (24.3 per cent), or about the same proportion
as of civil officials. There were no judicial officials of noble origin.

When we examine the academic backgrounds of these same civil
and judicial officials, we come upon much more significant bases of
discrimination. See Table 1.

TABLE 1: ACADEMIC BACKGROUND

	Total	Tokyo Univ. Graduates (%)		Kyoto Univ. Graduates (%)		Others (%)	
Civil officials	1,377	1,007	73.6	124	9.0	246	17.9
Judicial officials	584	290	49.7	108	18.5	186	31.7
Total	1,961	1,297	66.1	232	11.8	432	22.0

Tokyo University graduates account for 73.6 per cent of the higher
civil servants and 49.7 per cent of the judicial officials. Kyoto University graduates rank second, but supply less than one-eighth as many
civil servants in all. And, symptomatically, no Kyoto University

graduate ever became bureau chief in the extremely important Ministry of Finance until Ikeda Hayato, the present prime minister of Japan, was appointed bureau chief in 1940. Of the 1,264 higher civil officials currently in office in 1937, 930 were Tokyo graduates, and 588 of these were graduates of the Law Department. The latter figure, corresponding to 46.5 per cent of all the officials listed, bespeaks the tremendously important role played by the Law Department of Tokyo University in training Japanese bureaucrats.

An investigation into the occupations of the fathers of these same civil and judicial officials would have revealed even more about the social structure of the Japanese higher bureaucracy, but proved impossible to undertake. A few significant facts are available, however: 138 (10 per cent) of the civil servants and 70 (12.0 per cent) of the judicial officials were adopted children, adoption being one of the traditional means in Japan by which an education is made available to the talented sons of poor families. On the other hand, 344 (25.0 per cent) of the civil servants and 98 (16.8 per cent) of the judicial officials listed in the *Jinji Kōshinroku* have relatives listed in the same book. This suggests that a large proportion of the civil servants in particular come from upper-class families and have superior opportunities to marry members of upper-class families.

"A study of the Social Origins and the Career Patterns of the Higher Civil Servants in the Japanese Foreign Service, 1948," by Professor Hiroshi Mannari, provides us with further information on the social origins of bureaucrats. Classifying the native places of Foreign Ministry officials who were serving in the United States and Canada in November of 1952, this study found that 9.7 per cent of them came from rural communities (usually with a population of less than 10,000), 9.7 per cent from towns (usually with a population of less than 30,000), 19.4 per cent from cities with a population of less than 500,000, 19.4 per cent from cities with a population of more than one million, and 41.8 per cent from Tokyo. This last figure is most impressive, since the population of Tokyo at that time constituted less than 10 per cent of the nation. Again, a classification of the fathers of these officials reveals that the semi-skilled workers among them numbered only 3.6 per cent; skilled workers, 3.6 per cent; farm owners, 7.1 per cent; clerical and other such white-collar workers, 3.6 per cent; managerial (owner), 10.7 per cent; managerial (executive), 21.4 per cent; public officials, 35.7 per cent; and professions, 14.3 per cent.

These limited samples decisively indicate that civil service in Japan is in a manner hereditary. Professors James Abegglen and Hiroshi Mannari have computed, in their article "Leaders of Modern Japan," that the children of government officials have 58.5 times as many chances to attain eminence as the average Japanese, their chances of becoming political leaders, cultural leaders, and business leaders being, respectively, 95, 50, and 45 times greater than the average.

The civil bureaucracy so constituted has of late years, however, been compelled to enter into open political competition to maintain its hold on the highest posts of all. Of the 48 bureaucrats who were promoted to ministerial posts in the twenty-one-year period from the Katō Cabinet (1924) to Japan's surrender (1945), only 9 became ministers by way of service in the Diet, while the remaining 39 were appointed directly from bureaucratic positions. The most important portfolios, especially, such as Finance, Foreign Affairs, Home Affairs, and Justice, were occupied by bureaucrats who were made ministers directly. But, after the post-war constitutional revision made the National Diet the highest organ of state power, it became extremely difficult for non-Diet members to enter the ministry. Hence, many outstanding bureaucrats nowadays become candidates for the National Diet.

The postwar House of Representatives includes such former officials of the Finance Ministry as O. Kaya, H. Ikeda, K. Aichi, R. Hashimoto, U. Noda, K. Uyeki, T. Uchida, M. Chira, Y. Kurogane, H. Fukuda, and S. Maeo. The House of Councillors includes such former Finance Ministry officials as J. Tsushima, K. Aoki, H. Sakomizu, S. Kiuchi, S. Shiomi, K. Miyazawa, M. Takahashi, S. Sugiyama, and C. Kamibayashi. Of these men, Kaya, Aoki, and Tsushima became ministers during the war; Ikeda, Aichi, Hashimoto, Noda, and Maeo entered the Cabinet after the war.

About twenty members of the present National Diet now have Foreign Ministry backgrounds, prominent among these being S. Yoshida and H. Ashida. The former Ministry of Home Affairs has produced about fifty postwar Dietmen. If we add officials of the former Commerce and Industry, Agriculture and Forestry, Transportation, Communication, and Education Ministries, ex-bureaucrats in the Diet make up about 20 per cent of the two houses. And the overwhelming majority of the most influential Diet members—Cabinet ministers, ex-Cabinet ministers and party leaders—are former civil bureaucrats.

VII. Democratization of the Civil Bureaucracy after the Second World War

In spite of its modernization in the late 1880's of the last century, the Japanese civil bureaucracy retained traits of patrimonialism down to 1945. Personal allegiance to the emperor was strongly emphasized. Professor Bellah is probably correct in claiming that the motive force which brought about the modernization of Japan was a collective drive toward personal achievement combined with a common national loyalty. In the 1880's an efficient and reliable bureaucracy was in fact built up through a combination of the principle of achievement (recruitment by open examinations) with that of particularism (personal allegiance to the emperor).

When Japan entered a semi-totalitarian period after 1932, the patrimonial traits of the civil bureaucracy were revived. Prominent civil servants in the ministries of Trade and Commerce, Finance, Home Affairs, Agriculture and Forestry, and Foreign Affairs, cooperated with the semi-Fascist generals and colonels in ruling the state and carrying on the campaign on the continent. They were known, flatteringly enough, as "progressive bureaucrats" (*kakushin kanryō*). Then, after the surrender of the armed forces in August of 1945, the civil bureaucracy cooperated smoothly with the United States Army of Occupation. But at length, in November of 1946, the new democratic constitution was promulgated, of which Article 15 declared: "The people have the inalienable right to choose their public officials and to dismiss them. All public officials are servants of the whole community and not of any group thereof. . . ." In accordance with this principle, a new civil service law was enacted in 1947. The very fact of this law was remarkable, since until that time all regulations concerning the civil bureaucracy had been established by imperial ordinance and placed beyond the reach of parliamentary controls. The establishment of a Bureau of Personnel Affairs and the introduction of a position classification system contributed further to the democratization of the civil service.

In the last thirteen years the bureaucracy has been infiltrated by the ruling conservative party. On the one hand, more and more high civil servants are contributing to the technical expertise of the Liberal-Democratic Party by serving in the Diet after their retirement from office. On the other, the leaders of the conservative party are seeking to gain control of the civil bureaucracy through partisan promotions and demotions of high civil servants. Thus there is a tendency toward the fusion of high civil servants and leaders of the conservative party. This tendency both threatens the neutrality of the civil bureaucracy, which is a *sine qua non* of parliamentary democracy, and makes careers in the civil service less attractive to able university graduates. Because of the amazingly high rate of economic growth in Japan during the last ten years, furthermore, the ablest graduates of first-class universities have come to prefer jobs in big business to civil service posts. The high prestige of the civil servant is steadily declining, the managers of big business being now viewed as the true elite of society. This change in the allocation of intellectual resources is a function of the transition of Japan from an authoritarian and bureaucratic state to a capitalist democracy.

B. TURKEY

RICHARD L. CHAMBERS

I. Bureaucracy and Reform

During the greater part of the past two centuries, Turkey has been ruled by a civilian government with brief though significant interludes of military predominance. Civil bureaucracies must, therefore, have been intimately associated with the changes which transformed the "traditional" Ottoman Empire of the late eighteenth century into the "modern" Turkish Republic. Let us inquire into the nature of that association.

The Turkish civil bureaucracy has been both an *object* and an *agent* of political modernization. It was an object because political modernization required new practices of personnel recruitment and training; a reorientation of the perspectives, values, and loyalties of the bureaucrats; and a radical revision of the bureaucratic structure of the state. In the end, a relatively "modern" civil service emerged as one of the clear manifestations of the changed condition of Turkey.

It was an agent of political modernization in that civil servants were themselves numbered among the Turkish modernizers. From the ranks of the civil bureaucracy came many of the early advocates of political reform, and other civil bureaucrats executed the policies formulated by these leaders. Under the republic, Presidents Atatürk and İnönü, though not themselves from the civil bureaucracy, entrusted much of their reform program to that group.

There have been two basic periods in Turkey's evolution into a modern nation state, the first of which may be said to begin in 1789, and the second in 1919.

The first phase of modernization in any society is normally characterized by "the development of individual aspects of modernization at a time when political authority is exercised by groups not fully committed to modernization," while the second "results from political decisions which allow a general modernization of society, taken either by the existing government or as a result of revolution."[1] In Turkey, the early phases of change were in a manner defensive, since they

---

[1] Quotations taken from a statement on "Comparative Modernization: Some Generalizations," drawn up by the seminar on Problems in Modern World History at Princeton University, spring term, 1957.

were effected to preserve the authority of the traditional ruling elite; the changes after 1919 were effected in a genuinely progressive spirit.

The time between 1789 and 1919 may itself be subdivided into rather distinct periods. The first of these is 1789-1839, the period of defensive imperial reform under Selim III and Mahmud II. The Tanzimat era, 1839-1878, brought bureaucrats to the fore as leaders of further defensive reforms imposed from above. The reforming pashas suffered a setback in 1878, and between that year and 1908 Abdülhamid II's absolutism forced the increasingly liberal reform movement to go underground or into exile and thus to become revolutionary. The Young Turk Revolution in 1908 signaled the triumph of the new generation of liberal reformers, young army officers, and intellectuals and the acceleration of the modernizing program until it was disrupted by war and the dismemberment of the Ottoman Empire.

The second phase, from 1919 to the present, could also be subdivided. The most obvious subdivisions would be the Atatürk era, which ended with his death in 1938, the continuation of Republican Party rule under Ismet İnönü, the transition from one-party to multi-party government between 1945 and 1950, the Menderes-Bayar decade, and the emergence of the Second Turkish Republic in the aftermath of the 1960 revolution.

II. Some Aspects of Eighteenth-Century Ottoman Government

CAREERS (TARİKS) OR INSTITUTIONS

Since first proposed in his book, *The Government of the Ottoman Empire in the Time of Suleiman the Magnificent* (Cambridge, Mass., 1913), Albert H. Lybyer's analysis and terminology have been widely used by Western scholars in describing the traditional Ottoman governmental structure. Lybyer distinguished two fundamental units which he called the "ruling institution" and the "Moslem institution." The former, he found, comprised the sultan's household and the military and administrative establishments, and was served almost exclusively by non-Muslims having the status of slaves of the sultan. The latter institution, served by free-born Muslims, included the religious, educational, and legal-judicial officials of the empire, together with certain associated groups such as the *eşraf* (descendants of the Prophet Muhammad) and the dervishes. The reputation of this thesis was enhanced when it was accepted by the British orientalists, H. A. R. Gibb and Harold Bowen, who added, however, that ". . .

by the eighteenth century the whole system of a slave-manned Ruling Institution had been swept away."[2]

For the purposes of this study it seems desirable to consider not two but at least three institutions as having existed prior to and during the initial phase of Turkish modernization. Apart from the sultan and his household, the ruling institution is divisible into a bureaucratic and a military branch; the Muslim institution is definable as the ecclesiastical arm of the Ottoman state structure. The emphasis placed by Lybyer, Gibb, and Bowen on religious backgrounds alone tends to obscure such basic career lines.[3] The three basic institutions or careers (*tariks*) may be designated as (1) bureaucratic (*mülkiye*), (2) military (*askeriye*), and (3) ecclesiastical (*ilmiye*).

THE CIVIL BUREAUCRACY

On the eve of modernization, career lines were rather sharply drawn. There was a tendency, already discernible in the early seventeenth century and becoming wholly apparent in the eighteenth, for careers if not offices to become hereditary. It would appear to have been unusual and rather difficult for a son to enter a career other than that of his father, so that each institution was largely self-perpetuating although not necessarily closed to newcomers.

Places in the civil service were filled by young men first brought into one of the numerous bureaus (*kalems*) as unpaid apprentices. When a son followed the career of his father, this initial step was easily taken. The next best expedient for the aspiring bureaucrat was to enjoy the patronage of a relative or someone else of importance in the institution. Establishing *intisab* or patronage—a form of what we might call "pull"—became increasingly important once the apprentice attained the status of a full-fledged scribe (*kâtib*) in his bureau. The favor of a higher official appears to have been more important than merit or seniority. Without it a young official was likely to remain in the subordinate scribal ranks; with it he might hope to become chief of his bureau and thus gain entry into the broad upper echelon of the bureaucracy. Patronage could be fickle, however, since the client could share in the disgrace of his patron if the latter fell into disfavor.

---

[2] H. A. R. Gibb and Harold Bowen, *Islamic Society and the West*, London, 1950-1957, Vol. I, Part 1, p. 44.

[3] A critical examination of the thesis appears in Norman Itzkowitz, "Eighteenth Century Ottoman Realities," *Studia Islamica*, 1962, pp. 73-94.

Moves from one bureau or section to another were rare among underlings, more frequent among officials advancing to higher rank. Some positions were better springboards than others. The greatest opportunity lay in the central administration headed by the *reis efendi* (or *reisülküttab*) as against the financial administration under the *defterdar*. Within the central administration some bureau headships offered more opportunity for future advancement than others. From one of these positions one might move up to become *reis efendi* and sometimes from there to the grand vezirate or to the post of provincial governor (*vali*). Promotion from within the ranks of the professional bureaucrats to the highest positions—from *efendi* to pasha rank—was rare before the eighteenth century but had become frequent by Tanzimat times.[4]

In sum, it can be said of the civil bureaucracy just prior to modernization that recruitment was by patronage and apprenticeship; that there was a tendency, short of absolute, towards hereditary career lines; that training, apart from the literacy which was a *sine qua non* for entry into the scribal ranks, consisted chiefly of practical experience in the bureaus; that promotion was based largely though not exclusively on patronage; and that, though movement between bureaus was restricted largely to the broad upper level, it was important for one aspiring to the pasha rank to become a bureau chief under the *reis efendi*. It should be added that the ruling elite, of which the bureaucracy accounted for a sizable part, was drawn predominantly from Rumelia (the European provinces) and especially from the capital city, Istanbul.

III. The Civil Bureaucracy as Object of Political Modernization

RECRUITMENT, TRAINING, AND PROMOTION

Recruitment and training became central problems as the bureaucracy was modernized. It was not difficult to attract candidates for government service, for, despite low and irregular pay, a bureaucratic career conferred high prestige, and a series of reforms provided extraordinary security of tenure. If anything, there were too many bureaucrats but too few really able ones.

Ahmed Cevdet Pasha, a leading Ottoman scholar and political figure of the nineteenth century, wrote in a memorandum prepared for the Grand Vezir in 1872: "If we are still deficient as regards judicial

---

[4] For the preceding description of "Eighteenth Century Ottoman Realities" the author is indebted to N. Itzkowitz's study cited in note 3.

officials, we are even more deficient as regards executive officials, and are growing daily more so. It is an urgent necessity to expand the *mülkiye* school in accordance with the time and situation, to rearrange the programme of studies correspondingly, to employ its graduates progressively in important posts, and thus to train competent administrative officials. Our immediate obligation is to take care to choose and employ those who are already fairly experienced and thus put the state administration on the right path. If we give up finding jobs for men, and instead make it our policy to find men for jobs, then it is certain that within a short time officials capable of administering the country will emerge. . . ."[5]

Attempts to remedy some of the deficiencies to which Cevdet Pasha referred had already been made, but apparently without significant results. Mahmud II had begun a major overhaul of Ottoman bureaucratic machinery in the early decades of the nineteenth century and had sought to provide the necessary personnel for it.

His policy of uprooting privilege and destroying the power of entrenched individuals was implemented by means of a series of regulations which began to be issued in the 1830's. New titles, precedence, and tables of rank were announced for the civil service; and, significantly, they were awarded to offices rather than to men. Other laws gave the office-holders a security of tenure approaching immunity to dismissal. Designed to improve morale and efficiency in the service, these in fact enhanced the security of office-holders more than their efficiency.

The same sultan set up a Translation Chamber (*Tercüme odası*) in the Sublime Porte (*Bab-ı Âli*) in 1833 to fill the government's need for interpreters, a need which arose when the Greek dragomans of the Porte fell suspect and were dismissed during the revolt in the Morea. Mahmud and his successors also opened several new schools to provide training for bureaucratic careers. Among these were the *Mekteb-i Maarif-i Adliye* (1838); the *Valide Mektebi* or *Darülmaarif* (1849); the *Mekteb-i Eklam* or *Mahrec-i Eklam* (1862), superseded in 1876 by the *Mekteb-i Fünun-i Mülkiye*; and the *Mekteb-i Osmani*. All of these were in Istanbul except the last, which was maintained in Paris by the Ottoman government from 1855 to 1874.

The two most important schools for the training of Turkish bureaucrats were, however, the famous Galatasaray *Lycée* (*Mekteb-i Sul-*

[5] Translated and quoted by Bernard Lewis, *The Emergence of Modern Turkey*, London, 1961, p. 368.

tani) and the Civil Service School (*Mekteb-i Mülkiye*) mentioned by Cevdet Pasha. Galatasaray was founded by imperial decree in 1868. According to M. de Salve, the Frenchman who was appointed its director, Galatasaray was projected as a model *lycée* with a twofold objective: to introduce a new secondary level of instruction given in a foreign language (French), and to amalgamate the various nationalities of the empire as a step toward giving all subjects an equal opportunity to hold public office. With the advantage of their French-style education, Galatasaray graduates played a role in the modernization of Turkey out of all proportion to their numbers.

The Civil Service School has held a central place in the training of Turkish civil servants since its founding in 1859. It at first drew its students from qualified scribes already in the government bureaus and prepared them for service as provincial administrative officials. In 1877, in accordance with the recommendations of Cevdet Pasha, the school was reorganized and expanded, and the curriculum modernized. Even during the period of Abdülhamid's despotism, the Civil Service School continued to be a center of intellectual activity. After a brief lapse during World War I, it was reopened in 1918, renamed the School of Political Sciences (*Siyasal Bilgiler Okulu*) in 1934, relocated in Ankara in 1936, and attached to Ankara University as the Faculty of Political Sciences in 1950. Throughout the school's history, a majority of its graduates have been the sons of bureaucrats; it has hence served to perpetuate the traditional tendency toward fixed career lines.

Primarily on the initiative of this Faculty, an Institute of Public Administration was set up in Ankara in 1953 by the Turkish government with the assistance of the United Nations. A working group had been sent to Turkey in the previous year by the Public Administration Division of the United Nations' Technical Assistance Administration to assess the strengths and weaknesses of Turkish administration and to make appropriate recommendations.[6]

Among other things, the working group found a problem of over-staffing aggravated by the overlapping of functions. This problem was inherited when the Turkish Republic fell heir to the proliferating bureaucracy of an empire many times its size. As new bureaus

---

[6] On this Institute and for the report of the working group, see United Nations Technical Assistance Programme, "Institute of Public Administration in Turkey," New York, 1954, and United Nations Secretariat, Technical Assistance Administration, "Report of the Working Group on the Institute for Public Administration for Turkey and the Middle East," New York, 1953.

had been added, obsolete ones had been retained, especially during the nineteenth century, when Turkey had sought to make herself over into a modern centralized state. The republic had had to accommodate this legacy from the Ottoman past, while its own economic program of *étatism* further expanded government functions and added still more names to the civil register. A phenomenally large proportion of the educated elite in Turkey has therefore continued, as in the past, to hold government jobs. With the increased educational opportunities which have accompanied modernization, the civil service and the elite class generally have expanded their social base, though without ceasing to be in good part hereditary and self-perpetuating. The loss of most of Turkey in Europe and the transfer of the Turkish capital from Istanbul to Ankara have nevertheless served to enlarge the Anatolian element in the class.

The United Nations working group commented favorably on the acceptance in Turkey of the principle of competitive entry to the civil service. It went on, however, to detail faults in the application of the principle. With each department, sometimes even each service, doing its own recruiting, examinations are too numerous and are unequal in quality. Furthermore, competition for personnel among the departments and services can lead to untoward results, especially since the competitive examination system does not extend to all civil service posts. Some posts may be offered only to persons having "vocational training," for example, though what constitutes "vocational training" is not spelled out. In addition, some branches of the service award scholarships for study in educational institutions and commit themselves to providing jobs for the scholarship holders, with or without examination. Though this scholarship program has served to expand the social base of bureaucratic personnel, it offers opportunities for favoritism and patronage.

Apprenticeship and practical training in government bureaus has declined perceptibly. The working group suggested that the trend toward requiring formal academic training and theoretical and legal expertise had actually gone too far and recommended that the new institute stress the practical aspects of public administration. One of the problems growing out of the insistence on academic diplomas and degrees is that initial salaries and status depend more on the person involved than on the job. There has been introduced a modern variation on the Ottoman theme of the priority of persons over posts.

For persons already in the bureaucracy, it has been noted, promotion once was more likely to result from patronage than from merit or seniority. Patronage remained extremely important throughout the first phase of modernization. Even then, however, it was being challenged.

In the 1790's Sultan Selim III set up permanent diplomatic establishments in London, Vienna, Berlin, and Paris, and issued instructions that the ambassadors and their staffs familiarize themselves with the institutions, languages, arts, and sciences of the countries to which they were assigned. Closed after Selim's deposition in 1807, the embassies were reactivated by Mahmud II in 1834. And, in 1833, Mahmud had set up the Translation Chamber in the Sublime Porte. It is hardly a coincidence that a majority of the modernizing bureaucrats who rose to eminence and made policy during the Tanzimat had previously served in the embassies or in the Translation Chamber or both. From the 1830's onward, a knowledge of Europe and, more specifically, of a European language (usually French) became one of the most valuable assets for an aspiring bureaucrat. The mid-twentieth-century salary scale for civil servants still entitled officials with the knowledge of an appropriate foreign language to a starting wage five levels above those without it.

There is, however, a difference between linguistic accomplishment as a factor in promotion and as a determinant of initial salary. While the laws standardizing salary ranks and regularizing promotions have reduced the incidence of patronage and bribery, they have brought a rigidity to the system which has worked against the modern concepts of merit reward and initiative advancement. Patronage in Ottoman times had not always been an evil. Often a young man became the client of a prominent official precisely because he showed promise. Through a combination of his own ability and the influence of his patron he could rise rapidly to positions of responsibility without meeting strict seniority requirements.

The laws affecting administrative personnel enacted in the 1920's put two obstacles in the way of vertical mobility. By making seniority the basis for advancement, they fixed mobility at a slow pace. And by creating an educational caste system in the bureaucracy, they placed impassable barriers in the path of promotion. A candidate's admission to the bureaucratic ranks and his initial grade were determined by his educational qualifications, and he could not hope to attain the higher offices without a university degree. It might be generalized that initially salary and status depend more on the person involved than on the job; thereafter, within the limits imposed by the educational caste system, seniority outweighs all other considerations.

It should further be pointed out that, in the nineteenth century, low and irregular salaries and a superfluity of men over jobs encouraged bribery and the abuse of the patronage system. Cevdet Pasha recognized the ultimate effects of an inadequate pay scale when he said: "The servants of the state should be superior to the mass of the people in ability and competence. But if there is no recompense, outstanding persons among the population will have no inclination to the service of the state, and will choose other professions, leaving only mediocrities to carry on the business of the state. These, lacking all prestige in the eyes of the people, will be quite unable to administer men who are in fact their superiors."[7]

Only recently, however, has this last problem reached such proportions as to cause real concern. Although the bureaucracy of the republic is assured of regular pay, the salary scale has remained low, and purchasing power has been reduced by mounting inflation. Meanwhile, careers in engineering, law, medicine, journalism, banking, and business have become increasingly respectable and profitable and have begun to lure members of the elite away from the civil service. No longer does government service possess an almost unchallenged appeal.

OUTLOOK, VALUES, AND LOYALTIES

This decline in the desirability of a civil service career in recent years has attended the gradual change which modernization has brought about in the Turkish bureaucrat's outlook, values, and loyalties. Personal and religious values and loyalties have in general given way to impersonal and secular values, though certain of the older attitudes and sentiments persist.

In the traditional Ottoman Empire personal relationships were extremely important. It was the individual leader, the hero, who commanded respect and obedience. The relatively small ruling elite, concentrated in the imperial capital and the urban administrative centers, was to a considerable extent inbred, although new blood did continue to enter it. Members of this elite were united by a common language and culture, by intermarriage, and by common personal association. The system of patronage was an evidence of these ties.

Members of the ruling cadre called themselves Ottomans (*Osman-*

[7] B. Lewis, p. 383.

lılar); namely, subjects of the sultan who was descended from Osman. The state which they served was *Memalik-i Osmaniye* (the Lands of the Ottoman Dynasty). Even the language spoken by this urban elite was called Ottoman (*Osmanlıca*) to distinguish it from the vulgar tongue of the peasant Turk (*kaba Türkçe*).

Values were rooted in a long-established Islamic tradition. The few members of the ruling elite who were not Muslims were not esteemed as true Ottomans, for they were not obligated to serve both the Ottoman state and the Islamic religion and to live according to the Ottoman cultural tradition. The "first generation Ottoman" was quickly drawn into the web of an elaborate protocol governing personal relationships and supporting traditional values, and his sons normally found a place in the ruling elite. A newcomer to the Ottoman group profited from living in an urban center—particularly in Istanbul, the fountain-head of Ottoman society. Here his chances of establishing a connection with an Ottoman house, becoming acquainted with the Ottoman cultural tradition, and acquiring the education qualifying him for inclusion in the ruling elite were greatest. It was not unheard of to find there a general or top bureaucrat whose father had been cook, gardener, or doorman in an Ottoman household.

The reverses suffered by the empire in the seventeenth and eighteenth centuries tended, if anything, to make the Ottomans even more conservative. They defined admissible change as a process of ridding themselves of those deviations from the "classical" or "ideal" norm which were, as they contended, at the root of the empire's troubles. A deep-seated feeling of cultural superiority, an ignorance of Western Europe, and a prevailing fatalism implicit in the oft-used expression *inşallah* (if God wills) reinforced their conservative tendencies and dulled their vision.

Only gradually did modern ideas begin to slip through this self-imposed iron curtain. The first major breakthrough came when Selim III, at the expense of his throne and ultimately his life, succeeded in planting the seeds of modernism in a small nucleus of young military men and bureaucrats. Under Mahmud II these seeds began to grow. Military and administrative reform, the new education provided for army officers and government officials, and the reactivation of the Ottoman embassies in Western capitals brought increasing numbers of civil and military officers into contact with Europe, though only rarely conferring, as yet, a full knowledge and understanding of the West.

The new ideas, though at first superficially held, made inroads on traditional social obligations and moral standards. Lip service was too often paid to whatever novelties might prove of immediate advantage to the bureaucrat in the fierce competition for sinecures. The breakdown of traditional values and loyalties without adequate replacement led at first to corruption and venality more widespread than under the old regime.

Prolonged exposure to modern ideas and values, however, led to a more genuine and more general understanding of them. And the bankruptcy of the old order was dramatized by the disintegration of the Ottoman Empire under the stress of revolutions and wars in the first decades of this century. Under the leadership of Atatürk, a profoundly modernized elite led Turkey into the second stage of rapid political change.

This group, a large part of which is still in government service, has set the tone for modern Turkey. The impersonal and secular values and loyalties of a modern society are beginning fully to prevail. The most striking example of this development is the emergence of an intense nationalism. Today a Turk is still, almost by definition, a Muslim; but his "Turkishness" comes first, especially if he belongs to the educated upper class of the cities. The members of this class are no longer Ottomans serving a dynasty and a religion, speaking a distinctive language, and bound to a traditional way of life; they are Turks, citizens of a Turkish nation-state, speaking a common Turkish language, and sharing in a common secular culture. The ideas of popular sovereignty and of representative constitutional government also appear to have taken root, despite recent reverses and disappointments; and although one still hears *inşallah* repeated incessantly in Turkey today, the old resignation to the inevitable has given way at least among the elite to the modern concepts of progress.

An orientation toward the future, new values, and new loyalties have quite made over the modern Turkish bureaucrat. Possessing sufficient knowledge and ability and a sense of dedication to his task, he is widely acknowledged to be honest and as efficient as the excessively centralized system will allow him to be. Slowly but surely he is coming to think of himself not as an official (*memur*) representing the state authority but as a public servant with a primary responsibility to the citizens of the nation. His new view of himself, combined with his awareness that other civilian careers now rival his own in prestige and surpass it in economic rewards, has made him more courteous in his dealings with the public and more sensitive to public criticism. It is indicative of the continuing gap between the ruling elite, as represented by the bureaucrats, and the still backward peasant masses that the latter have largely failed to perceive this change in the bureaucrat's conception of himself and his career. The peasant retains much of his old suspicion of the bureaucracy.

THE BUREAUCRATIC STRUCTURE: CENTRALIZATION, EXPANSION, AND SPECIALIZATION

1. Eighteenth-century conditions. Not only the civil servant himself but the bureaucratic apparatus has been made over. On the eve of political modernization the once-splendid governmental structure of the Ottoman Empire was in an advanced state of decay. The reasons for this breakdown of central authority—rooted in the political decadence of Turkey in the seventeenth and eighteenth centuries—are beyond the scope of this paper, but a few general observations on conditions prevailing at the end of the eighteenth century will provide a useful point of departure.

The authority of the government in Istanbul over the provinces decreased in approximate proportion to the remoteness of the province from the capital. Rebellious pashas and provincial notables had hence been able to create virtually independent principalities for themselves and to divert the provincial revenues sorely needed by an empire under intermittent attack from without.

The military, particularly the celebrated Janissary corps, had become an entrenched interest group with its influence increasing as its combat efficiency diminished. Unruly, unpredictable except as defender of its own prerogatives, it posed a threat to stable and orderly government.

The ecclesiastical institution, represented by the Muslim theologians (*ulema*) headed by the Grand Mufti (*şeyhülislam*), held a monopoly on education and on the administration of justice under the religious law (*şeriat*). Together with the dervish orders, the *ulema* corps was a powerful force in shaping public opinion. Bektaşi dervish influence was especially strong in the military. If there was anything approaching a hereditary aristocracy in the Ottoman Empire, it was to be found among the "Great Mollas" in the upper echelons of the *ulema* hierarchy. Like the military, the ecclesiastical institution was a law unto itself, and a jealous guardian of its own privilege.

Finally, there was the civil bureaucracy centered around the Grand Vezir and his subordinates in the Sublime Porte in Istanbul. Under the succession of weak sultans which succeeded Süleyman the Magnificent, Ottoman government had been carried on largely by the bureaucrats of the Porte with the Grand Vezir emerging as "acting head of state." The power of the Grand Vezir was nevertheless insecure. He was subject to the whim of the sultan, who was, in turn, the victim or instrument of the intrigues of competing factions working in and through the palace. The ranks of the civil bureaucracy reflected at once the prestige and the insecurity of its chief. This institution, too, was anxious to maintain its position of strength, acquired as it were by default, and to resist encroachments from the palace and from the rival military and ecclesiastical institutions.

We have observed that Selim III's attempts to put the Ottoman house in order ended in defeat and deposition but that Mahmud II was more successful. Mahmud sought to restore the authority of the sultan over his empire by breaking down the power of entrenched interest groups and replacing their institutions with new ones of his own. He pursued that end by centralizing and modernizing the machinery of government and at the same time extending its operations. Bureaucratic centralization and the expansion of the bureaucrat's sphere of activity thereafter constantly attended all efforts to modernize the Turkish polity.

2. *Provincial administrative reforms.* Provincial administration supplies many examples of these generalizations. Mahmud began by forcibly restoring the central government's authority over the provinces and appointing governors who were dependent on the capital. Before his death he had brought to heel, by military force when necessary, all of the rebellious pashas and other notables except for Muhammad Ali of Egypt. Only the intervention of the European powers had prevented the crushing of the rebellion in the Morea and the retention of this segment of Greece in the empire.

Mahmud next undertook a census of the male population, and a land survey to determine the financial assets of his realm. (These and other similarities in their programs have caused Mahmud to be called the Peter the Great of Turkey.) In the same year, 1831, he abolished the military fiefs (*tımars*)—the major remaining vestige of the feudal system in the provinces.

Although Mahmud had reasserted his authority over the provinces, no major overhaul of the machinery of provincial government had been made, and the collection of provincial revenues depended still on a system of tax-farming (*iltizam*). The latter evil was abolished by

313

the great reform edict (*Hatt-ı Hümayun* of *Gülhane*) which marked the beginning of the Tanzimat in 1839, but was reinstated two years later when Reşid Pasha, author of the early Tanzimat reforms, was dismissed from office. The second great reform edict of the Tanzimat period (*Islahat Fermanı* or *Hatt-ı Hümayun* of 1856) again outlawed tax-farming; it nevertheless remained for the Young Turk government in the period of World War I to rid Turkey of the last traces of this system.

In the meantime a fundamental reorganization of the administrative structure of the provinces had exercised the bureaucrats at Istanbul. Just after Mahmud's death and the announcement of the Tanzimat in 1839, an entirely new system of centralized provincial administration, resembling in many respects the French system of prefectures and *départements*, was set up on the initiative of Reşit Pasha. Most of his innovations fell into disuse, however, in the reaction which followed his dismissal. Various compromises between centralized and decentralized administration followed, leaving in their wake confusion and discontent.

A number of inspection teams were sent to the provinces in the mid-nineteenth century, and a special commission under the chairmanship of Cevdet Pasha examined their reports and made recommendations. In pursuance of these, the new Law of Vilayets was issued in 1864 by the Grand Vezir Fuad Pasha. The essence of the new code was the regrouping of the old provinces into larger units headed by officers carefully chosen on the basis of experience and ability. The influence of the French model is to be seen in the hierarchy of twenty-seven vilayets governed by *valis*, each divided into *sancaks* under *mutasarrıfs*, these in turn composed of *kazas* headed by *kaymakams*, and the *kazas* divided into *nahiyes* under *müdürs* and villages with elected *muhtars*. There were administrative councils at the top three levels in which the local population, Muslim and non-Muslim, were represented. Although the *vali* was given considerable power and the system as a whole signified a compromise between the principles of centralization and decentralization, on the whole the Law of Vilayets tended to strengthen the central authority.

Cevdet Pasha objected that the new law imposed an inappropriate uniformity on an empire made up of provinces as diverse in race, geography, historical background, and otherwise as was the Ottoman. He preferred a basic and consistent provincial policy, either of centralization or decentralization, implemented by a clearer delineation of the duties and responsibility of officials and salaries sufficient to attract men of superior quality to staff the necessary offices. Although his other points were well taken, his fears do not appear to have been borne out, for Midhat Pasha applied the new law with success in two regions as different as the Danubian Vilayet and the Vilayet of Baghdad.

The new system, with some modifications based on experiments with it in selected "pilot" provinces, was gradually extended to the rest of the empire. The law of 1864, with its emphasis on centralization, remained the basis for provincial government until 1913, even though the constitution of 1876 stipulated that provincial administration should be in accordance with the principle of decentralization and the separation of administrative, judicial, and military powers.

When the constitution was restored after the Young Turk Revolution of 1908, the obvious disparity between the law and the constitution became a subject of concern. By 1913, the drift toward authoritarian, centralized government was well advanced and was reflected in the new vilayet law finally accepted in that year. This made a bow to the principles set forth in the constitution while, in fact, retaining the principle of centralization; it so endowed the vilayet government with two identities. The province was, on the one hand, a part of the central political structure under the jurisdiction of the Ministry of the Interior; on the other hand, it was viewed as being a decentralized administrative unit having a corporate legal personality. This law is significant, both as the basis for Turkish provincial government and as a noteworthy milestone in the substitution of modern legal concepts —in this instance, the concept of the corporate legal person—for the traditional Islamic precepts of law.

The principles of provincial administration laid down in the imperial constitution of 1876 and in the vilayet law of 1913 were reaffirmed by the constitution of 1924 and by a new vilayet law passed in 1929, although the "Fundamental Law" of 1921 had made alterations in nomenclature. These acknowledged that the new republic of Turkey was only a fraction of the size of the prewar Ottoman Empire by abolishing the large vilayet unit and giving that title to the old *sancak*. The present breakdown is thus: Vilayet, *kaza*, *nahiye*, and village. The *vali* and the *kaymakam*, his subordinate on the *kaza* level, are central government officials appointed by the Ministry of the Interior. Candidates may be university graduates and must have had two years of experience in a provincial government office followed by a six months' course in the Ministry in Ankara before they become eligible for the lower of the two posts. From that position they may move up to the office of *vali*. On the *nahiye* level, the *müdür* is also an official of the central government, but he need have only a lycée diploma and is therefore cut off from the *kaymakam* and *vali* ranks by the educational caste system. The *muhtar* of the village, though elected by the villagers, is, in effect, a bureaucrat representing the Ankara government and executing directives relayed down through the administrative hierarchy.

Despite the concessions to local authority, therefore—despite the elected councils on all levels except that of the *kaza*, the corporate legal personality of the vilayet and (since 1924) of the village, and the budget for each vilayet passed upon and audited by its own council—the present system of provincial administration remains rather tightly controlled by the Ministry of the Interior.

3. Civil vs. military bureaucracy. Moving back in time to the late eighteenth century, we pick up a second thread in the movement toward political centralization in the attempts of Selim and Mahmud to subordinate the military institution to civilian authority. The failure of Selim to replace the Janissaries with a modern military establishment was made good by Mahmud. By abolishing the Janissaries in 1826 and crushing the Bektaşi dervish order associated with it, Mahmud removed the most powerful deterrent to change. His next move was to assure civilian control over the new military force in the process of its creation. This he did by creating the office of *serasker* (commander of the army), which became the nucleus of the future civilian War Ministry. Through it the civil bureaucracy was able to contain the power of the military until the Young Turk Revolution.

The revolution named, which was a military *coup d'état* led by young army officers of liberal bent, ended the conservative absolutism of Abdülhamid II and restored the Constitution of 1876. The new civilian government failed, however, to halt the internal deterioration of the empire. The power of the military increased again, for Turkey was continuously at war in the decade after 1911. And the militaristic tradition of Germany—a nation which, in the preceding twenty-five years had been trade partner, military advisor, creditor, concessionaire, and finally ally—was exerting an influence. It is small wonder that the Young Turk government gradually moved in the direction of a military dictatorship.

In the chaos following World War I, the civil bureaucracy was slow to line up on the side of the nationalist cause. It was chiefly the military, under the leadership of Atatürk, who rallied the Turks of Anatolia in the struggle for national independence. Only as the success of that cause became apparent did the bulk of the bureaucracy fall in step with the new government established at Ankara. Once the War for Independence was won and the republic had been proclaimed, however, Atatürk opted in favor of a civilian government. Both he and his successor, İnönü, confirmed the principle of civil rule by putting off their uniforms and serving as civilian presidents, and by establishing the tradition of a non-political military establishment.

In undertaking to create a modern nation-state, Atatürk sought first to rally the partially modernized ruling elite inherited from the Ottoman Empire. He lavished particular attention on the civilian bureaucracy, which was to be an instrument for modernizing the peasant masses. As he and İnönü after him won increasing support among the bureaucrats, the principle of civilian supremacy acquired the force of a tradition. Though challenged in 1960, that tradition remained strong enough to force from the military a promise to restore civilian rule—a promise of which the Second Turkish Republic is the fulfillment.

4. Civil vs. ecclesiastical bureaucracy. In the constitution of the Second Republic, Turkey is declared to be a secular state, therein following one of the basic principles laid down by Atatürk for the First Republic. The final separation of religion from politics was the culmination of the century-long efforts of Turkish modernizers to limit the influence of the conservative ecclesiastical institution and reduce its capacity to resist change.

The destruction of the Janissaries and their replacement by a military establishment loyal to Mahmud had deprived the Muslim religious hierarchy of its traditional military ally against the sultan and his civilian bureaucracy. Without the "men of the sword" to support it, the ecclesiastical institution was helpless to preserve its privilege and power. Mahmud's first step was to curtail its administrative and financial autonomy. By giving the Grand Mufti an official residence which served also as his office, and by recognizing him and his staff as a government department (known as *bab-ı meşihat*), Mahmud extended his system of bureaucratic centralization to the religious hierarchy and reduced its chief to the status of a government officeholder. He further weakened the *ulema* by putting the administration of *evkaf* (the charitable foundations or endowments which constituted the chief repository of ecclesiastical economic power) in the

317

hands of a government department created for that purpose. The practical effect of this was to make the religious institution economically dependent upon the government. An attendant result was the diversion of *evkaf* funds to state uses.

In the nineteenth century the bureaucrats increasingly infringed on two other former monopolies of the *ulema*: education and the administration of justice. Schools established by the state for the training of army officers and civil servants were the beginnings of a system of secular public education under the supervision of a Ministry of Education. The religious hierarchy's monopoly in the field of law was broken when law codes based on European models and administered by a Ministry of Justice were introduced in the mid-nineteenth century to compete with the Islamic law.

The ecclesiastical institution, as such, disappeared along with the Ottoman Empire in the epic years following the First World War. The office of Grand Mufti was abolished and two new offices—a Presidency for Religious Affairs attached to the office of the prime minister and a Directorate of *Evkaf*—were created. All dervish orders were banned. The last Muslim strongholds in education—the *medreses* (theological schools)—were closed. All Muslim religious law was at length wholly replaced by European legal codes. Judges, teachers, and religious functionaries, traditionally drawn only from the *ulema*, have become government employees. The net effect is that the religious institution has been suppressed and its functions and personnel absorbed into those of the expanding civil bureaucracy.

5. *Modernizing the central administration.* So far we have observed three changes taking place in the organization of the Turkish state: (1) the authority of the central government over the provinces was extended and regularized; (2) the military institution, itself bureaucratized, was largely divorced from politics and subordinated to a government manned by civilians; and (3) the religious institution was so thoroughly subsumed into the civil bureaucracy that it ceased to exist as a separate entity. The common denominator in all these changes was bureaucratic centralization of political authority; the principal beneficiary of all was the central administration.

By about 1830, Turkey's Peter the Great had consolidated his hold over the provinces, the army, and the *ulema* and was ready to undertake the formidable task of reconstructing the central administration itself. This core of the civil service was also a repository of entrenched privilege and a potential source of obstruction to any program of reform; it sought positively to prevent any diminution of the power it had accumulated under a long line of weak sultans, and, because of its incompetence and inefficiency, was a clog upon progress of any sort. Mahmud's aim was so to reorganize the bureaucracy as to make it both more amenable to the imperial will and more efficient. No doubt he was concerned as well with showing his European critics that a new day of progress and change had dawned in the empire, and some of his reforms were only superficial changes in appearance and nomenclature; but others cut deeply into the fabric of the traditional institution. Sometimes what appeared to be a surface change entailed in fact a radical departure from the old order.

The Sublime Porte, since the seventeenth century the official seat of the Grand Vezir just outside the walls of the sultan's palace, was the heart of the central bureaucracy. Clustered together here were the offices and bureaus of the principal administrative officials. This citadel of bureaucratic tradition was Mahmud's first target. Characteristic of his tactics was his elevation, in 1835, of two of the Grand Vezir's chief assistants to the new rank of minister and the constitution of their departments as separate ministries although they remained in their old quarters and continued to perform their old functions. The *kâhya* became the Minister of Civil Affairs and the *reis efendi* the Minister of Foreign Affairs. The former was renamed Minister of the Interior in 1837, at which time the *defterdar*'s office became the Ministry of Finance. Even the title Grand Vezir was set aside for a time in favor of Prime Minister; so renamed, the vezir presided over the newly established Council of Ministers.

A number of other councils were set up in the following years. Most were composed of a small but prominent group of bureaucrats charged with planning and carrying out specific reforms. There were, for example, the Council for Public Education, the Fiscal Council, the Council for Military Affairs, and the High Council for Judicial Ordinances. The last of these was especially important due to the legislative and quasi-judicial functions which it was in effect granted by the Tanzimat edict of 1839. In the first year of the Crimean War, the High Council of Judicial Ordinances was divided, one part being called the High Council of the Tanzimat and the other retaining the original designation. The latter was reorganized once more in 1868 to create the Divan of Judicial Ordinances and the Council of State

(*Şura-yı Devlet*). Resembling the French *Conseil d'État*, the Turkish Council of State has continued throughout the imperial and republican eras to serve as a high court of appeal in administrative cases.

These bodies illustrate two changes which took place within the bureaucracy as it was reorganized. The first was the introduction of new bureaucratic organs to replace the old. Old bureaus were not merely given new names; a government administered by powerful individuals ensconced in their traditional posts was yielding to one based on groups which the sovereign could mold and manipulate. Secondly, the names of these councils are a reminder of the new fields which the bureaucratic institution was incorporating into its jurisdiction. Both changes signify the concentration of political power in a central bureaucracy theoretically responsible to the ruler.

These same changes are perceptible in the proliferation of ministries in the century following the establishment of the Council of Ministers. The government's concern with improving the commercial and agricultural sectors of the Turkish economy led to the creation of a Ministry of Works in 1839. Police functions were removed from the province of the commander of the army (*serasker*) and entrusted first to a Ministry of Police, later to the Ministry of Interior. The department of the *serasker* was permanently renamed the Ministry of War in 1908.

The Council for Public Education created in 1841 became a ministry in 1856, and in the Public Education Regulation of 1869 the education of the general public was officially recognized for the first time as a task for the state to perform. This invasion of the domain of the theologians was followed ten years later by the establishment of a Ministry of Justice to take over the direction of the new secular courts and judiciary. Before the end of the empire, a Ministry of the Navy, of Post, Telephone and Telegraph, and of Food were added; and a Ministry of Trade and Agriculture, separate from the Ministry of Works, was formed.

The Cabinet of the Grand National Assembly and later, of the republic, included eleven ministers: Foreign Affairs, Interior, National Defense (replacing the Army and Navy ministers), Economy, Justice, Finance, Public Works, Health and Social Welfare, Education, the Chief of the General Staff (dropped from the cabinet in 1924), and Religious and *Evkaf* Affairs (replacing the Grand Mufti and *Evkaf* Minister, also dropped in 1924). A ministry of Population Exchange and Settlement (1923-1924) was in charge of implementing the Lausanne Agreement with Greece; a separate navy department was briefly restored in 1924-1928. The expansion of government economic functions led to a periodic regrouping and expansion: Commerce (1924-1928 and again 1939-1948), Agriculture (1924), Customs and Monopolies (1931), Communications and Transport (1939), Labor (1946), State Enterprises (1949).

It is impossible in this study to trace the development of each of the various new councils and ministries created in the revisions of the central bureaucracy, but we can consider in some detail the evolution of Mahmud's Council of Ministers (*Meclis-i Hass* or *Meclis-i Vükela*). It has been compared both to the old Imperial Divan (*Divan-ı Hümayun*) and to a European cabinet. Actually it was like neither one in the beginning. The Imperial Divan had dispensed justice and was empowered to make appointments; the Council of Ministers did neither. It was different from a European cabinet in that all of its members were appointees of the sultan; it was not recognized as having a corporate existence; and the principle of collective responsibility was totally alien to it.

What, then, was it? It was a consultative body composed of the heads of administrative departments appointed by the sultan which met twice weekly at the Sublime Porte under the chairmanship of the Grand Vezir. It appears that at first the ministers did little more than discuss current problems, but as the Council increased in membership with the establishment of new ministries, it also increased in importance. Under such strong Grand Vezirs as Âli, Fuad, and Midhat Pashas in the latter Tanzimat period, it was a powerful and moderately effective organ of government.

The Council of Ministers was formally recognized in the constitution of 1876. The sultan appointed the Grand Vezir and the Grand Mufti and nominated the remaining ministers by decree. Responsibility rested with each individual minister. After the restoration of the constitution in 1908, the Grand Vezir was given the right to nominate all ministers except the Grand Mufti. Further constitutional reforms in 1909 introduced for the first time the European concept of the collective responsibility of the ministers for government policy. The exact relationship between Sultan, Council of Ministers, and Parliament was never satisfactorily spelled out.

In the Atatürk republic, the Prime Minister was appointed by the President from among the members of the Grand National Assembly. The other ministers, also members of the Assembly, were chosen by the Prime Minister with the approval of the President and presented in a body to the Assembly. The Council of Ministers was collectively responsible for the general policy of the government. In addition, each minister was individually responsible for matters within his sphere of authority, including the conduct of his subordinates. No major changes in this organization were made in the constitution promulgated in 1961.

At the head of the central government in twentieth-century Turkey stands the Council of Ministers made up of politicians. Administrative officers themselves are, in theory, non-political and are excluded from seats in parliament. They may, however, stand for election on condition that they resign their administrative posts if elected. A deputy may also re-enter the civil service following his retirement from parliament and may count his period in the legislature for purposes of seniority. The result is that while all ministers must be members of the Grand National Assembly, a substantial number of ministers, as well as of other deputies, have held civil service posts before entering politics. There is also a goodly number of bureaucrats with political experience. The power given to the bureaucracy by the participation of its members in parliament can readily be appreciated and will be commented upon at greater length below.

The brevity of the tenure of ministers in many cases has kept them from becoming fully conversant with the day-to-day routine of their departments. They have in consequence left many of the actual decisions, at least in current non-political matters, to bureaucratic assistants. Otherwise, an excessive centralization without sufficient provision for coordination and a too-rigid application of the laws governing the civil service have kept much authority and responsibility from being delegated. This deficiency is aggravated by the financial accountability of individual officials. Initiative is thereby stifled. Horizontal mobility is also reduced by the over-centralization within departments and the lack of communication between departments as well as by the tendency of superiors to oppose the transfer of their subordinates to different services or departments.

Another weakness in the mid-twentieth century Turkish administrative machinery is the lack of central agencies to coordinate the work of the different departments and services. There is, for example, no central personnel agency to set standards for civil service examinations and for recruitment and training policies. Hence personnel practices are decades behind those of the more modern Western states.

V. The Civil Bureaucracy as Agent of Political Modernization

ACTIVE LEADERSHIP

Political modernization has served both to centralize the Turkish bureaucratic institution and to extend the range of its jurisdiction beyond any previous limits. A vast expansion of its apparatus and personnel has occurred since it consisted of Mahmud's frock-coated fez-topped *efendis* and pashas crowded together in the Sublime Porte. The modern civil service now encompasses the bureaucrats of the central and provincial administrations, the entire corps of judicial, religious, and academic officials and functionaries, and the executives and employees of state banks and industries, and of the other financial or commercial enterprises which are products of *étatisme*. It takes in, indeed, a major portion of the educated political elite of modern Turkey.

The enlightenment now rather generally diffused throughout this group may be traced to very small beginnings some century and a half ago. Sultan Selim III, with whom this survey begins, was very nearly alone in his desire for reform, and that was his undoing. He was unable to stand alone against the combined forces of reaction until he could bring a cadre of supporters into being. Mahmud II was more fortunate, having from the first the support of a small corps of new style army officers and bureaucrats. He set about enlarging and strengthening both groups, while eliminating or rendering impotent the chief antagonists of change.

During Mahmud's reign the civil bureaucracy which he had renovated emerged as the dominant modernizing element in the state. He himself subordinated the military to bureaucratic control to frustrate any attempt by the new army to challenge imperial authority as had the Janissaries. Civil officials gained much credit by securing through diplomacy a settlement with the rebellious Muhammad Ali, *vali* of Egypt, which the military had been unable to achieve by force of arms. During the last century of the empire's existence, military weakness forced the sultans to rely heavily upon diplomatic skills to keep their empire alive. It forced them to depend, in particular, on bureaucrats with European experience and a knowledge of Western languages.

Such bureaucratic leaders as Reşid, Fuad, Âli, and Midhat Pashas dominated the Tanzimat era of defensive modernization which followed the death of the forceful Mahmud. With weak successors occupying the throne, the bureaucrats were able to use their power as deputies of the sovereign authority to further their own class interests at the expense of rivals. Reforms in the politically crucial arenas of law and education enabled them to invade the former preserves of the theologians. Further bureaucratization of the military and the stripping from it of police functions helped to keep this major rival subordinate. Bureaucrats further benefited from the reform edicts guaranteeing to Ottoman subjects inviolability of person and property and from regulations increasing job security in the civil service. The Ottoman Constitution of 1876 and the parliamentary movement which climaxed the bureaucrat-dominated Tanzimat period represented, among other things, this group's ill-starred attempt to curb the power of its most dangerous rival of all, the sultan.

THE DILEMMA OF POLITICAL LEADERSHIP

During the second half of the nineteenth century, the old bureaucratic leaders of reform found themselves on the horns of a dilemma. The changes which had been wrought in the political structure of Turkey—changes they had helped to effect—had swept away the traditional checks on the personal power of the sultan without creating new ones. Even the most competent and strong-willed Grand Vezir was incapable of successfully opposing a determined sultan, as was shown in Midhat Pasha's contest with Abdülhamid II. The absence of effective restraints and the availability of modern instruments of communication and control made possible an absolutism far more complete than any previously known in pre-modern Turkey.

On the other hand, modernization had brought with it something more than new uniforms, weapons, titles, techniques, and technology; it had brought new ideas. Among the young bureaucrats, army officers and intellectuals who had learned European languages and received Western-style educations, ideas such as nationalism, constitutionalism, representative government, democracy, and progress began to find enthusiastic acceptance. First, the New Ottomans (*Yeni Osmanlılar*) of the 1860-1870's, many of them from the lower ranks of the civil bureaucracy, and somewhat later, the Young Turks, were converts to these new ideas.

The bureaucratic reformers were caught between two fires which they had fed if not actually kindled. On the one hand was the sultan representing absolutism and supported by the forces of conservatism and reaction; on the other were the young liberals calling for genuine constitutional democracy. The political center is often an awkward spot to be in, particularly during times of crisis and emergency. The bureaucratic reformers lost the position of leadership they had intermittently held for some half century, first to Abdülhamid and his conservative allies, then to the Young Turk army officers and intellectuals, and finally to Atatürk and the politicians.

BUREAUCRATS AND POLITICIANS

The loss of political dominance did not deprive the civil bureaucrats of any opportunity to effect change, but it made them a more passive instrument of it. No more Reşids or Midhats came from among them. Leadership was increasingly provided by military officers. The military provided the revolutionary force necessary to end Abdülhamid's despotism, and the military element in the Young Turk movement came forward again in the critical years after 1910 when civilian parliamentary leadership faltered. The Young Turk military regime could not save Ottoman Turkey from sharing in the humiliating defeat of her ally, Germany, in World War I; but it was a military officer coming through that war with an unblemished record who then led the Turks in a successful struggle for independence.

Mustafa Kemal Atatürk created out of the ruins of the Ottoman Empire a new Turkish nation-state. Once his victory over domestic and foreign opposition was assured, he found growing support for his policies among the bureaucrats and made of the civil service an instrument for implementing them. The bureaucratic class constituted, of course, along with the military officer corps, the major reservoir of talent available to him. Civil and military officials were the largest group among the deputies to the Grand National Assembly throughout the one-party period, and they accounted for more than one-half of the principal parliamentary leaders and cabinet ministers. As late as the mid-1950's men of bureaucratic background occupied nearly twenty per cent of all ministerial posts, being second in numbers only to lawyers.

An astonishing uniformity in education is to be observed among these men. Fifty-two per cent of the former bureaucrats in the Grand National Assembly for whom such information is available attended the Faculty of Political Sciences of Ankara University (formerly the Civil Service School). Another twenty-three per cent had studied in the Law Faculty. These same faculties were the training ground for from fifty to seventy-five per cent of the cabinet ministers of the First Turkish Republic. Their graduates still dominate those higher echelons of the civil service which are filled chiefly by promotion from the ranks. In the provincial administrative apparatus, graduates of these faculties have a virtual monopoly on high office, accounting for ninety-nine per cent of all provincial governors (*vali's*) and ninety-five per cent of all sub-governors (*kaymakam's*). The Ministry of Interior, which commands this centralized internal administration, is the preferred ministry for bureaucrats who have political ambitions.[8]

At least until 1950, therefore, there was considerable community of social, educational, and occupational background among parliamentary deputies and cabinet ministers on the one hand and the upper levels of the civil bureaucracy on the other. Though Atatürk and İnönü themselves were formerly military officers, their immediate subordinates were very often former bureaucrats. Together with members of such other official or quasi-official groups as retired army officers, local administrators, university professors, and public school teachers, members of the judiciary, government physicians, and the employees of government economic enterprises, these men dominated Turkish politics. Until 1950, there existed a sort of closed corporation of professional public servants who, acting as politicians, passed laws which they and their colleagues administered as bureaucrats.

The multi-party system brought about changes in the social and occupational complexion of political leadership. As Turkey continued her social and economic advance, the private sector of the economy attracted increasing numbers of her educated elite. The competition among political parties for popular support after World War II revealed this fact. In the free elections of 1950, lawyers, businessmen, private physicians, journalists, engineers, landowners, and farmers won parliamentary seats previously held by public officials. The lower ranks of political leadership were affected most directly, but even the higher ranks were to some degree invaded.

Long held in check by the bureaucratic one-party regime, social and economic demands began to be articulated. The promises made to win votes raised popular expectations. When the Democratic Party found it impossible to fulfill these promises, criticism mounted. Neither concessions nor repressive measures were able to silence the swelling voices of opposition. And on May 27, 1960, a military *coup d'état* brought an end to the First Turkish Republic.

[8] For further information on the social background of parliamentary deputies, see Frederick W. Frey, *The Turkish Political Elite*, Cambridge, Mass., 1964.

In the new Second Republic, rapid social and economic development is required to meet urgent expectations. Whether the necessary advances are consonant with political democracy is an unanswered question. It is nevertheless certain that only the educated elite has the requisite experience and ability to operate the complex political machinery—democratic or authoritarian—by means of which the task must be accomplished. The role of civil bureaucrats in the modernization process will remain at least proportionate to their quantitative and qualitative strength within the national elite, though this strength will itself diminish as the elite becomes larger and occupationally more diversified. So long as government is the agency for modernization, the bureaucracy will occupy a uniquely advantageous position for influencing the process of change.

CHAPTER 8

THE MILITARY

~~~~~~

A. JAPAN[1]

ROGER F. HACKETT

~~~~~~

ALL political systems have been shaped in part by military considerations. The measures adopted by nations to meet internal and external dangers have been intimately related to the political structure of the community; in turn, the manner in which force has been organized and controlled has vitally affected the political system. Military developments, furthermore, have stimulated economic and technological changes and have channeled social change. Sir Lewis Namier has boldly said that "the social history of nations is largely moulded by the forms and development of their armed forces."[2] His statement hardly seems an exaggeration when we consider how the building of a modern military force influenced the political and social development of Japan. The leaders who sought to make Japan a modern nation confronted the overriding problem of national security. Among the Meiji government's earliest important decisions, therefore, was to build a modern army and navy, and the measures adopted to raise, equip, train, and manage military forces affected all aspects of Japan's transition into a modern state.

To understand the prominence of the military in recent Japanese history, we must remember that, in the less than one hundred years from the end of Tokugawa rule in 1868, Japan has fought four major wars and many lesser engagements. For roughly a third of that period, military forces have been involved in maintaining internal order or protecting national interest from real or imagined external threats. Prior to 1945, furthermore, a succession of military victories had earned for Japan the status of a great power. It is hardly to be wondered at that military leaders and considerations have had great influence on the conduct of state affairs even during times of peace.

[1] The author would like to express his appreciation to the Carnegie Corporation of New York City for assistance received in connection with the preparation of this essay.
[2] Quoted by Herbert Butterfield in "Sir Lewis Namier as Historian," *Listener*, May 18, 1961, p. 873.

This essay attempts to assess the role of the military in the political development of Japan. It seeks to examine how the growth of the modern military system affected the political process and how and why the military bureaucracy achieved its marked advantage in the political relationships between civil and military authority. It gives primary attention to the earlier years of the modernization process, and to the army as the branch of service most active in politics. Sections are devoted to: the legacy of a military tradition, the external impetus to military and political change, the military reforms in relation to political unification and the modernizing consequences of these reforms, the character of the military bureaucracy, and the intrusion of the military in politics.

I. The Military Legacy

The military enjoyed from the beginning the superior position traditionally accorded the warrior class. Throughout the Japanese feudal period (1185-1868) the military houses, ruling in the name of the emperor, held ultimate authority over the nation. The record of seven centuries of military dominance has few parallels.

The privileged position of the samurai class was asserted during the Tokugawa period (1603-1868) by laws and by Confucian ideology. The founder of the Tokugawa system had decreed that "the samurai are the masters of the four classes. Agriculturists, artisans, and merchants may not behave in a rude manner towards samurai."[3] In return, the samurai were to practice self-discipline and austerity, and to give loyal service to their lord, thereby fulfilling the "way" prescribed for them. The Confucian scholar Yamaga Sokō (1622-1685) exhorted them specifically to subordinate personal gain to moral uprightness and to loyal duty to the lord. He taught that "the samurai dispenses with the business of the farmer, artisan, and merchant and confines himself to practicing the Way; should there be someone in the three classes of the common people who transgresses against these moral principles, the samurai summarily punishes him and thus upholds proper moral principles in the land."[4]

Because the samurai was also exhorted to become cultivated in letters and to combine military skills with classical learning, he also represented an intellectual elite. From this class emerged the leaders who initiated the Restoration movement and the innovations which

[3] James Murdoch, *A History of Japan*, London, 1926, III, 802.
[4] Wm. Theodore de Bary, ed., *Sources of the Japanese Tradition*, New York, 1958, p. 399.

transformed Japan. There are many writers who, while not denying the importance of the samurai class in ending the feudal regime, emphasize the thrust for change provided by the peasantry and the merchant class. The most convincing interpretations, however, continue to stress the central role of the samurai and treat the contributions of peasants and merchants as marginal. Furthermore, without overlooking the economic difficulties and resulting discontent of the samurai class at the end of the Tokugawa era, these interpretations affirm the vitality of the traditional order which enabled samurai to react with vigor to the external pressure exerted by the Western challenge and provide leadership in building a modern nation.[5]

The prestige traditionally belonging to the samurai class was transferred to the modern military. Soldiers and sailors of the armed forces have enjoyed and inherited a tradition which earned them popular respect throughout most of Japan's modern history. And the legacy of the past was powerfully reinforced by dramatic military victories which brought international prestige to the nation, won admiration for military leaders, and sustained the popular esteem for military service.

Other features of the feudal society fostered the development of a modern military system. The natural hierarchy of pre-Restoration society was like the stratification in a military organization. One might even more specifically propose that the two essentially closed hierarchies of the samurai and commoners answered to the officer corps and the enlisted ranks. In fact, in the early years of the modern army, ex-samurai status almost automatically converted into a commission. Finally, the officer corps, like the upper level of the feudal society, bore responsibilities for instructing the rank and file, and inspiring loyalty to the existing system.

It is manifest, therefore, that the character of the traditional society, far from inhibiting innovation, contributed positively to the formation of a modern military establishment. There was no sudden switch from a "traditional" to a "modern" model, but rather a constant interplay between the features of the past and the reforms of the present. It was possible to link certain traditional features to the aims of modernization. Perhaps this is nowhere better illustrated than in the modern use of the samurai's ideology. Loyalty, courage, bravery, and other virtues of the samurai were identified in the Meiji period

---

[5] For example, Albert Craig, *Chōshū in the Meiji Restoration*, Cambridge, 1961, and Marius Jansen, *Sakamoto Ryōma and the Meiji Restoration*, Princeton, 1961.

as necessary for the discipline and morale of the modern fighting unit. Thus the new leaders of Japan were able to unite virtues and inherited habits of thought with an urge for innovation and progress. It is clear that certain factors in the traditional society were utilized to reinforce the process of modernization.

II. The Impetus to Military Change

The legacy of military leadership also helped Japan to confront the international realities of the nineteenth century. Military men could quickly realize that without warships and guns comparable to those of the Westerners the orders issued by the Tokugawa government to drive away the officious vessels of Russia, Britain, and the United States were meaningless. The Japanese could comprehend the military superiority of the West more quickly than other Asian nations in part because the nation was ruled by a military class.

The military ideas and weapons of Europe had been introduced into Japan before Perry's arrival. The Tokugawa government had been purchasing guns and mortars from the Dutch since the seventeenth century, and a few officials had studied Western books on military science. As early as 1840 one Nagasaki official succeeded in training in the Western style two infantry companies and an artillery battery. But Perry's forceful advent stimulated greater efforts.

In the 1860's both the Tokugawa government and the most powerful feudal domains (han) undertook further to modernize their military forces. The former purchased foreign vessels, employed Dutch naval instructors, and engaged French officers to train infantry, cavalry, and artillery units. The strongest western han, such as Tosa, Chōshū, and Satsuma, improved organized rifle units trained in Western battle tactics. In Tosa, a people's militia was organized as a Western-style unit. In Chōshū, auxiliary rifle units were formed by peasants trained in the use of modern weapons and led by samurai; in 1865 the han army itself was reorganized, equipped with Western rifles, and trained in the modern manner. These measures were opposed by traditionalists who felt it degrading for samurai to engage in drills, replace their swords with rifles, and adopt modern dress, but within the councils of the more advanced han and among the leaders of the Tokugawa government, there was general understanding of the need to adopt the newer weapons and techniques.

The internal struggle between the shogunate and anti-Tokugawa forces calling for a restoration of imperial authority vindicated the superiority of the Western military technology. The triumph of Chōshū's modernized army over the more obsolete army of the shogun in 1866, and the victory of combined Chōshū-Satsuma troops over Tokugawa forces in 1868 demonstrated the success of the military reforms undertaken by the great western *han*. The military forces of these *han* provided the main support for the new regime. The leaders of the new government were the commanders of the superior military forces in the civil war.

Once in power, the Meiji leaders were determined to build a unified, strong, and prosperous nation. In practice this meant centralizing authority under a national government with sufficient military power to maintain domestic order and preserve the nation's security. The new leaders' concept of international politics was an extension of their view of the national order of competing independent *han*. Because military modernization had improved the competitive position of certain *han*, they realized the need for national military reforms to enable Japan to compete in the international arena. This easy projection to the national level of concepts that had proved necessary and successful at the local level helps to explain the success of the far-reaching political and military innovations in the Meiji period.

III. The Army and Unification

A "modern" nation usually has a political system with a single center of authority controlling or at least influencing the economic, political, and social conditions of the people. The transition in Japan from the feudalism of the Tokugawa era in which political authority was divided among numerous fiefs to a modern polity with power in the hands of the central government was a major part of the process of political modernization. Essentially it was a process of moving authority away from many centers of political prestige to a single center of national political, economic, and military responsibility. In this process, political and military unification were interdependent. Genuine political unity required the sanction of force, but effective military unity required political integration. Also, the distribution of political power in the Meiji government was influenced by the military, and the character of the military structure was influenced, in turn, by the role of specific *han* in the Restoration.

At the time of the formation of the Meiji government, the nation had no army, the government relying on the *han* forces that had defeated the Tokugawa armies. There was hence no specifically national power available for sustaining the national authority. Though the restoration of the emperor had been accomplished in 1868 and the feudal lords had voluntarily turned over their land registers in the following year, the political power of the fiefs was still little impaired. The ex-daimyo still ruled their autonomous realms as governors and retained, for example, the right to levy taxes and raise armies. The Meiji leaders nevertheless believed that feudal autonomy would have to give way to a central government and that without a central army political unity would remain a myth. During the year 1868, they took steps toward forming a central military organization. A guard unit composed of contingents from several *han* and totaling some four hundred men was organized under a court bureau. By the end of 1868 all fiefs were ordered to limit the size of their armies and contribute to the expenses of a national officers' training school in Kyoto.

Unification of the feudal armies, which continued to be resisted for a time, implied the adoption of some single Western model. In October 1870 the Council of State ordered that "since in the regular government forces the navy is to adopt the English system and the army the French system, each *han* army should first change its organization and adopt the French system."[6] The French model was selected because a French military mission had been present in Japan and partly because those responsible for planning the national army had studied the French military system.

At length, in April of 1871, the *Goshimpei* or Imperial Guard was formed. This division of 10,000 men, made up of modern infantry and artillery units from Chōshū, Satsuma, and Tosa, became the first significant military force under the direct command of the emperor. Its organization provided the opportunity to liquidate the fiefs, and thereby take a major step toward centralizing authority. In August of 1871, feudal autonomy was ended by imperial order and political, military, and fiscal authority became the exclusive property of the Tokyo government. This series of developments illustrates how, in the early years of Meiji, the civil decisions of the nation builders were involved with the military. During the first decade of the new regime the army provided a police power to protect the new government against opposition and to enforce political change. The political leaders

6 Quoted in Matsushita Yoshio, *Chōheirei seitaishi* (History of the Enactment of the Conscription Law), Tokyo, 1943, p. 41.

realized that radical political changes could not run ahead of the government's power to enforce its viewpoint.

The second major development in the process of unifying Japan was the institution of universal military service. No reform contributed more to unifying and stabilizing the young state. The introduction of conscription proved more difficult than doing away with the fiefs. The 1869 orders reorganizing and standardizing *han* armies included the phrase that "only samurai and foot soldiers may be selected for the soldiers."[7] The Imperial Guard, though supporting the measures ending the feudal order, remained a force of samurai from three *han* and so preserved something of a *han* identity. Only after the abolition of the *han* did a feasible opportunity for putting universal conscription into effect arise.

Six months after the fiefs were abolished, high officials in the Military Department proposed a number of measures for increasing the nation's military strength: the construction of warships and an expanded coastal defense system, the development of a military academy, arsenals, and storage depots for arms and ammunition. The heart of the proposal, however, was the plea for a system of universal military training. "Although standing armies vary with each country," the proposal read, "even such small countries as Belgium and the Netherlands have at least 45,000 regular [troops] and . . . all European countries have reserves."[8] The proposal went on to say: "The establishment of a permanent force is our most urgent task and should not be delayed a single day. Courageous, healthy youth should be selected from each area in proportion to its size and trained and drilled in Western tactics and used in any emergency. . . . By settling on this national system now, all males who have reached twenty years of age and are healthy and without home problems would be called to service and be organized into units, regardless of whether they be samurai or commoners, and sent home after one year's service. . . . By doing this we will develop a means of defense."

The authors of the memorial further emphasized the importance of a trained military reserve for external defense: "The immediate concern of the military department is with domestic affairs while external matters are of future significance. Upon reflection, however, these are aspects of a single problem. That is to say, if adequate

[7] *Ibid.*, p. 40.
[8] The proposal is quoted in Watanabe Ikujirō, *Jimbutsu: kindai Nihon gunjishi* (Biographical History of the Modern Japanese Military), Tokyo, 1937, pp. 135-140.

preparations are made against the outside world, there will be no cause for anxiety over internal matters. At present our military strength, aside from the Imperial Guard established merely to protect the palace and emperor, includes only the troops of the four garrisons numbering twenty battalions. These are assigned to maintain internal security not external defense . . . but with the significant changes resulting from the dissolution of the *han* armies and the collection of weapons, circumstances are appropriate for determining a policy for external defense."

These recommendations became the basis of the conscription law which went into effect, after vigorous debate, in January of 1873. The law provided for seven years of military service for males over twenty-three in the regular army and four years in the reserves. Certain exemptions were allowed: for example, to the heads of household and to criminals. The law further stipulated that those who proved superior in basic training would be transferred to the elite Imperial Guard division. In subsequent revisions of the conscription law, the period of reserve service, active and inactive, was made longer, and the categories of exemption were gradually reduced.

Conscription represented a means both for solidifying the authority of the government and for enhancing the national security. Further, though the Imperial Rescript announcing universal military service recalled the ancient Japanese past when there was no distinction between soldiers and peasants, the insistence on the equal obligation of all males was inspired largely by Western practices. Declaring that "samurai are no longer the samurai of former times and commoners no longer the commoners of the past," the Council of State proclaimed that "all are now equal in the empire and without distinction in their duty to serve the nation."[9]

The new system of conscription was at first resented both by those newly included in it and by those who ceased to enjoy exclusive military status. Peasant uprisings ensued and ex-samurai reaction threatened to destroy the system before it was firmly rooted. Within ten years of the Restoration, however, all overt resistance to the conscription law was overcome. The quelling of the Satsuma Rebellion in 1877 demonstrated that the imperial regime could depend upon a conscript army for its security.

[9] Quoted in Tokutomi Iichirō, *Kōshaku Yamagata Aritomo den* (Biography of Prince Yamagata Aritomo), Tokyo, 1933, II, 195-196.

IV. The Consequences of Military Reforms

The modern Japanese army was an agent of change as well as an instrument of unity. The national army sought to emulate the training, armament, and organization of Western military forces. The nation further imitated the West in the many activities required to support a modern army.

The establishment of institutions in support of the military arm of the nation had important political consequences. Military service constituted a certain involvement in political process. Does not the obligation of military duty presume also some political rights? The spokesman of the anti-government political rights movement so believed. Some of them declared in 1877 that "a just military system requires that the method of recruitment be in accord with the forms of government; that a despotic government must not impose conscription requiring a 'blood tax' of the people unless it adopts a constitutional system."[10] In fact, by 1890, the obligation of military service for qualified males was accompanied by the right to vote for males over twenty-five who met certain property qualifications. In the course of time the grounds for exemption from military service were narrowed and the franchise was broadened. Through both activities an increasing number of citizens became participants in the public life of the nation.

Universal conscription eventually required a centralized financial support for the services, an armaments industry, and an ideology inspiring loyalty and discipline. These were all developments which influenced the process of political unification and modernization. The emergence of a corps of trained professional officers to manage the army was, in itself, an exemplification of the modernizing process. It led to the development of a professional and functionally specialized bureaucracy of a highly modern sort.

Perhaps more significantly still, conscription demanded education, broadly defined. The army supplied whatever instruction was necessary to enable recruits to read simple orders, identify the names of weapons, and comprehend elementary arithmetic. This was no minor problem. Even in 1910, at the end of the Meiji period, it was reported that, of 439,266 men examined for military service, 25,971 were illiterate. For the 1908-1910 period about four per cent of the first class

[10] Quoted by Fujita Tsuguo in Guntai to jiyū (The Military and Liberty), Tokyo, 1953, p. 146.

336

conscripts were classified as illiterates.[11] But many young men also studied hard before entering the army in order not to delay their progress through the ranks.[12] Conscription was viewed as an integral part of the national educational process by the author of the conscription act. He had said: "If boys enter grammar school at six, high school at thirteen and graduate at nineteen, after which, from their twentieth year, they spend a few years as soldiers, in the end all will become soldiers and no one will be without education. In due course, the nation will become a great civil and military university. . . . "[13]

The army further founded a variety of specialized technical schools. These included a medical school, a veterinary school, a paymaster school, and training institutes for military tailors, surveyors, telegraphers, and so forth. By 1893 there were more than 16 such schools instructing over 2,600 students.[14] In addition, military schools for officers which had existed in several *han* were replaced after the Restoration by a central government military school. By 1870 over 400 cadets were receiving instruction there. In 1875 a single military academy (*shikan gakkō*) was established, the top graduates of which were sent abroad for study; in 1880 there were 44 officers studying in Europe. The selection of candidates for these schools was based chiefly on education and capacity.

Another major development in military training was the opening of a War College in 1883 under the jurisdiction of the Chief of the General Staff. Promising candidates with some experience in the field took preliminary examinations at divisional headquarters after being recommended by regimental commanders. Those who survived the first round of examinations in subjects such as tactics, weapons, topography, communications, and military organization became eligible for final examinations at the General Staff College. Some fifty of these passing the latter test were finally selected each year. For graduates of the War College the way was open to the highest rank and the most powerful positions. Both in this competition and in the army promotion system generally, intellectual promise and actual performance were major considerations in advancement.

[11] Gotaro Ogawa, *The Conscription System in Japan*, New York, 1921, pp. 144-145.

[12] Sato Naosuke, "Nihon no kindaika ni okeru chōhei seido to gumbu" (Conscription System and the Military in the Modernization of Japan), *Sophia*, Vol. VI, No. 1, Spring, 1957, p. 29.

[13] Matsushita, *Chōheirei*, p. 121.

[14] Okuma Shigenobu, ed., *Fifty Years of New Japan*, London, 1909, I, 209.

Perhaps the most important educational function of the new army was the propagation of a national ideology. The beliefs instilled in the thousands of new recruits each year to give cohesion to the modern army formed also the basis of official popular ideology: duty and loyalty to the emperor, the spirit of courage and sacrifice. Army training inculcated the "Japanese spirit," a compound of the traditional samurai ethic and imperial nationalism. In the handbook of each soldier from 1872 on were entered the "Soldier's Rules," of which the first read: "The army is established for the purpose of executing the will of the emperor, to strengthen the foundations of the country and protect the people and the nation. Thus, those who become soldiers must make loyalty to the emperor their guiding principle."[15] Six years later, after the most serious opposition to the government had been defeated and a mutiny within the ranks of the Imperial Guard itself quelled, the War Minister issued the "Admonition to Soldiers," decrying spiritual weakness in the military and declaring that the three guiding ideals of all military personnel must be loyalty, bravery, and obedience. In 1882 the emperor issued the celebrated Rescript to Soldiers and Sailors defining the moral qualities of the military man (loyalty, valor) and the values he should cultivate (propriety, righteousness, and simplicity.)[16] These were the same values that permeated all Japanese society: a national ethos subsuming the virtues of the traditional warrior class but with duty to lord now elevated to loyalty to the emperor, who was the symbol of the united nation.

The attainments of the army in reducing illiteracy, teaching specialized skills and knowledge, and promoting a national ideology served the interests of political modernization in at least two ways. First, a growing number of Japanese acquired technical skills and insights into life beyond their native villages. The experiences of all soldiers better equipped them to adjust to the evolving modern economic and political systems. Second, by inculcating discipline, obedience, and devotion to the emperor, the army helped to gain support for the central government and its aims. Conscription was a powerful force for turning the parochial loyalties of the people into a generalized patriotic feeling for the nation as a whole.

[15] Quoted in Tokutomi, *Yamagata den,* II, 764.
[16] The text of the rescript is frequently reprinted, e.g., Arthur Tiedemann, *Modern Japan,* New York, 1955, pp. 107-112.

V. The Structure of the Military Bureaucracy

A feature in the development of modern Japan which meets one measure of a modern polity was the evolution of more complex governmental forms. An important part of the evolving machinery of government was the military administration. As the army grew in size, and its tasks became more varied, the military bureaucracy became of necessity larger, more complex, and more highly specialized. Administrative reforms were continually devised to answer the needs of growing specialization within the military.

In the first uncertain years following the 1868 Restoration the government was several times reorganized, and in each administration there was an office charged with responsibility for the military. At first it was called the Navy and Army Affairs Section (*Kairiku Gummuka*), then the Office of Military Defense (*Gumbō Jimukyoku*), and then as one of seven major divisions in the administrative organization of June 1868 it was named the Department of Military Affairs (*Gummukan*). In August 1869, it was renamed the War Department (*Hyōbushō*), only to be divided into separate army and navy departments in 1872. Thus, in the first five years of the Meiji government the agency administering the military underwent constant reorganization. The most important development was the eventual separation of the army and navy administration into independent and equal departments of the government.

The next major step in the evolution of the military bureaucracy was the separation of the staff and command authority from administrative functions. Responsibility for plans and operations had resided in the Staff Bureau of the War Ministry. Then in 1878, under German influence, the Staff Bureau was elevated into a separate General Staff Headquarters (*Sambō Hombu*), no longer subordinate to the Ministry. The General Staff, under a Chief and an Assistant Chief, had jurisdiction over the staff sections of the various army commands and was fully responsible for strategy and plans. This reform had far-reaching political consequences, for the order establishing the General Staff stipulated that, as major adviser to the emperor on military policy and strategy, the Chief of the General Staff was independent of the War Minister and superior to him. This effectively removed the command function from any political checks which might be applied through the cabinet. Indeed, one reason for making the General Staff independent of the War Ministry and placing the Chief of Staff under the direct command of the emperor was to free decisions relating to national defense and strategy from any interference by the civil government.

The third development was the granting of independent authority to the agency responsible for training and inspection. In 1879, an autonomous Board of Supervision was established within the army for overseeing military education and training. The chief of this board, later (1898) reorganized as the Board of Military Education, came to be known as the Inspector General of Military Education and possessed authority approximating that of the War Minister and the Chief of the General Staff. Thereafter the War Minister, responsible for military administration, the Chief of the General Staff, directly responsible under the emperor for military strategy and the training of staff officers, and the Inspector General of Military Education formed a powerful triumvirate known as the "Big Three" of the army.

It is evident that the military bureaucracy was not a unified administrative command, and the division of power within it encouraged rivalries between sections of the military apparatus. Until after World War I, however, a few commanding personalities, successively occupying different posts in the army, effectively coordinated the several functions of the military bureaucracy. For example, Yamagata Aritomo, the dominant military figure of the first half century of modern Japanese history, served for six years as War Minister and six as Chief of Staff, in addition to occupying political posts of importance. General Oyama Iwao served eight years as Chief of Staff and almost seven years as War Minister. A later high-ranking general, Sugiyama Gen, served as head of the Military Affairs Bureau of the War Ministry (1928), Vice-Minister of War (1930-1932), Vice-Chief of Staff (1934-1936), Inspector General of Education (1936-1937), War Minister (1937-1938), Chief of Staff (1940-1944), and War Minister again (1944-1945). Although this fluidity at the top level did not prevent factionalism, it minimized the possibility of generals dividing the segments of the military administration into personal fiefdoms.

The changing structure of the military bureaucracy affected the political process in many ways. When the Chiefs of Staff were not responsible to cabinet ministers, an area of decision vital to the welfare and security of the state was isolated from civil authority. In this situation the War Minister played a difficult double role: as a member of the army hierarchy he was bound to represent the policy advocated

340

by the army; as a member of the cabinet he was bound by certain legal and constitutional principles. If the policies he advocated on behalf of the army did not prevail in the cabinet, he was compelled either to espouse the decisions of the ministers, thereby arousing the opposition of the army, or to resign from the cabinet, thereby disrupting the government. If, as less frequently happened, he should favor policies other than those advocated by the Chief of Staff, he ran the risk of reducing his authority within the army.

VI. Composition of the Military Bureaucracy

As is frequently the case, the real line of authority within the military was informally determined by the influence of certain individuals and groups rather than by the formal structure of the bureaucracy. A leading feature of the military bureaucracy was factionalism. This had initially inhered in the composition of the Restoration forces which ushered in a new Japan. The victors were a coalition of the most powerful western *han* and a few court nobles, and, after the Restoration was proclaimed, each gained a representation in government councils roughly commensurate with his contribution to the Restoration movement. As the two most important *han*, Satsuma and Chōshū tended to dominate the new government, though the nominal heads of the newly created departments were imperial princes or nobles of the court. The highest ranks of the military were filled by Chōshū, Satsuma, Hizen, and Tosa clansmen.

The army in particular continued to bear the marks of its origin. Of the 18 men attaining the rank of general in the first ten years of Meiji, 8 were from Satsuma and 5 from Chōshū.[17] The proportions were altered somewhat by the rebellion led by Satsuma in 1877, so that of 22 generals in 1879, 7 were from Satsuma and 6 from Chōshū. Satsuma officers remained among the highest ranks in the army administration and among the most celebrated field commanders, but did not dominate that service as they did the navy. If we examine the list of full generals down to 1926 we discover that, of the total of 72, 7 were princes of the blood; of the remaining 65, 16 (or 30 per cent) were from Chōshū. During the same period, there were 40 full admirals, of whom 3 were imperial princes and 16 (or 44 per cent of the remainder) were from Satsuma.[18]

[17] Matsushita Yoshio, *Nihon gunsei to seiji* (Japanese Military and Politics), Tokyo, 1960, p. 147.
[18] *Ibid.*, p. 48.

Growing Chōshū influence in the army was due in good part to the position of Yamagata Aritomo, the senior Chōshū general, who was War Minister from 1872, when the army and navy were placed under separate departments, until 1878, when he became the first Chief of Staff. He was the acknowledged leader in the inauguration of conscription and, all in all, the guiding light of the army in the first decades of its development. Yamagata was Prime Minister twice, Home Minister and Justice Minister in two cabinets, for years the president of the Privy Council, and, from Itō's death in 1909 until his own in 1922, the leading elder statesman of the realm. Throughout his long service he retained his active military status. Since he was a proud Chōshū clansman, it is logical that a Chōshū faction should have come to dominate the army leadership.

Though this faction was not unchallenged, the able officers who followed after Yamagata kept Chōshū influence in the army secure. The mantle was passed from Yamagata to Katsura Tarō to Terauchi Masatake to Tanaka Giichi. From 1898 to 1911 three Chōshū generals in succession (Katsura, Kodama Gentarō, and Terauchi) served as War Minister, Terauchi himself for nine of those fourteen years. During his long tenure 6 full generals retired but not one of them was a Chōshū officer; of 45 officers with the rank of lieutenant general during the same period, 10 were from Chōshū, and 4 of these were merit promotions.

The term military clique (*gumbatsu*) refers to those ambitious soldiers who have historically used the military establishment to influence national policy. Such men were inclined to form factions to gain control of the key positions within the army. These included, in addition to the "Big Three" posts, the offices in the Military Affairs Bureau of the War Ministry, those of Vice-Minister of War and Vice-Chief of Staff, and such lesser posts as Commanding General of the Korean, Formosan, or Kwantung Garrisons.

One can distinguish three generations of leaders among the "political soldiers" after the Restoration. The first generation, down to the turn of the century, was dominated by generals from Chōshū, led by Yamagata. Though more Satsuma than Chōshū generals in fact served as War Minister during those years, Oyama, who was principal among them, was not politically minded and often deferred to the opinions of his own subordinates. For more than half the time, from the establishment of the General Staff in 1878 to 1900, two apolitical imperial princes held the post of Chief of Staff. It was hence possible for Yamagata and his Chōshū faction to control policies and personnel of the army throughout this period. Nor was there then any conflict within the army over national military objectives, such as appeared in the 1930's.

In the second generation, from 1900 to World War I, the appointees and protégés of Yamagata maintained the Chōshū hegemony. Generals Katsura and Terauchi, the most representative of these, were competent officers and able politicians (both became prime ministers). They favored fellow Chōshū officers for high military positions, although educational background and training became increasingly important qualifications.

Among the third generation of military leaders, from World War I to the 1945 surrender, the principal basis for the formation of factions was the military education of the officer. After 1912 the Chiefs of Staff and War Ministers were graduates of the military academy and the War College, and owed their appointments principally to their academic standing at the War College, only secondarily to regional affiliation. The growing professionalization of the army corps made this development inevitable. In the 1930's, however, intra-army feuds arose between the *rikudai batsu* (War College graduates) and the *muten gumi* (those without the War College graduation emblem). Academic achievement rather than regional association became vital. Most of the soldier-politicians of the 1930's and 1940's had outstanding records in the military schools.

The economic and social stresses of the inter-war years became further sources of factionalism. Factions—such as those named the Imperial Way, Control, Purification, and Young Officers[19]—had different prescriptions for Japan's foreign and domestic problems. All of them nevertheless sought greater army control over national and international policy, and all strove to control the key posts of the army as a first step toward their objectives. The rivalry between these factions and the irreconcilability of their views and practices were major causes of the aggressive militarism of the period.

VII. The Army in Politics

A fundamental characteristic of Japanese politics during the modern period, then, was the constant intrusion of the military in the affairs of the nation. All efforts to maintain a clear separation between

[19] See James B. Crowley's "Japanese Army Factionalism in the 1930's," *Journal of Asian Studies*, Vol. XXI, No. 3, May 1962, pp. 309-326.

military and civil authority failed. These efforts were, in the first instance, sincere enough. The Meiji leaders reacted against the feudal past in which both civil and military authority were held by the shogun, and discerned that one feature of a modern nation was a separation between civil and military functions. Kido Kōin, for example, one of the most influential leaders of the Restoration, voiced alarm when he discovered that Saigo Takamori, a leading councillor in the Meiji government, was being appointed commander-in-chief of the army. "If I were to single out for praise the fundamental virtue in the government of the enlightened countries of the Occident," he wrote, "it would be the established distinction between the duties of the civil and the military."[20]

Those responsible for the military organization of the country, furthermore, were genuinely convinced that discipline within the armed forces would be undermined if military personnel entered into politics. Discipline problems and even, in 1878, a mutiny had arisen from the involvement of soldiers in the political currents of the times. In the "Admonition to Soldiers," issued by the army in 1878, soldiers were warned against "questioning imperial policies, expressing private opinions on important laws, or criticizing the published regulations of the government."[21] Two years later, the government's "Regulations for Public Meetings and Associations" prohibited soldiers on active service or in the first or second reserves from attending political meetings and joining political organizations. The "Rescript to Soldiers and Sailors" of 1882 warned soldiers "neither be led astray by current opinions nor meddle in politics but with single heart fulfill your essential duty to loyalty." Other regulations forbade military personnel from voting and from standing for election; involvement in politics became a criminal offense under Army and Navy Penal Laws.

Paradoxically, however, the separation of the military from politics has perhaps itself been a basic cause for the emergence of factions within the army. The military's pledge not to "meddle in politics" lent itself to casuistry. When generals were accused by politicians of violating their rules against such meddling, they retorted that they

[20] Quoted in Umetani Noboru "Waga kuni ni okeru heisei bunri (tosuiken no dokuritsu) no tokushusei" (The Special Characteristics of the Military Separation in Our Nation [The Independence of the Supreme Command]), *Nihon Rekishi*, 135, September 1959, p. 8.

[21] Quoted by Matsushita Yoshio in *Meiji gunsei shiron* (Historical Essays on the Meiji Military System), Tokyo, 1956, I, 500.

were merely fulfilling their duty to safeguard the nation's security. Since the line dividing purely military from exclusively political matters could never be drawn precisely, political acts could be undertaken under the guise of military necessity. In such instances, political or public pressure proved ineffective in limiting the political forays of military leaders. If such pressure developed, generals could always retreat behind the theoretical wall between civil and military authority.

In the last analysis, the legal independence of the military from civil authority encouraged the army to assume a dominant role in politics. Upon the establishment of the General Staff system in 1878, the military responsibilities of the state, referred to as the "supreme command" authority, became the prerogative solely of the emperor and his military advisers. The articles in the Meiji Constitution of 1889 which defined the emperor's military role further stipulated that he "has the supreme command" (Article 11) and "determines the organization and peace standing of the armed forces" (Article 12). The ordinance on the organization of the cabinet, issued in the same year, said that "matters pertaining to military strategy and military command" will be reported directly to the emperor. In practice, the emperor's "supreme command" power meant that virtually all functions of the army were divorced from civil authority. When the cabinet did deliberate upon issues such as mobilization, conscription, and national defense policy, it was never sure when the military ministries might invoke the principle of the independence of the supreme command.

The military could limit or prevent civil interference in military matters by another practice: the custom of only active generals and admirals serving as service ministers in the cabinet. The principle of military men representing their services in the cabinet was established early in Meiji history, and an ordinance of 1900 added a rank and active duty qualification. In 1913 the active duty requirement was dropped so that reserve or retired officers might serve, but in 1936 it was reinstated at the behest of the military. Thus until the end of World War II civilian service ministers were excluded and, even though reserve officers were eligible for a short period, all service ministers were in practice selected from the ranks of the active senior officers of the services.

The requirement of active duty status for the War Minister gave him, as we have noted, a dual position. He was one of three principal army officials, the others being the Chief of Staff and the Inspector

345

General of Military Education; in the cabinet he was a civilian functionary. As an active officer, he was responsive to army decisions, even decisions in which he may have had a minority voice. Since he was designated War Minister by the army high command, the army might withdraw its support from him or fail to recommend anyone for the office in the first place, thereby causing cabinets to fall or not to be formed in the first place. This virtual veto power was demonstrated in 1912 when the War Minister submitted his resignation directly to the throne following the refusal of the cabinet to approve the army's request for additional divisions. Since the army refused to designate a new War Minister, the cabinet was forced to resign notwithstanding its command of a clear majority in the Diet. Again, in 1914, Premier-designate Kiyoura Keigo was unable to form a cabinet because the navy, having failed to extract the promise of an expanded budget, refused to nominate a navy minister.

The laws and practices governing civil-military relations ended by depriving civil officials of a voice in military affairs but admitting the military into civil government. The number of civil posts held by generals and admirals was disproportionately large. From the inauguration of the cabinet system in 1885 to the surrender in 1945 there were 43 cabinets headed by 30 different prime ministers. Of these 30, 15 were military leaders—9 generals and 6 admirals—and they led 19 governments for 29 years and 3 months, or virtually half of the sixty-year period. Out of the 490 posts in the 43 cabinets 86 represented the military portfolios, which were always held by ranking officers; and of the 404 civilian posts, 115 were occupied by generals and admirals. In sum, from 1885 to 1945, about 28 per cent of all the civilian ministries were under military men (41 of 112 during Meiji, down to 12 of 127 during Taishō, and up again to 62 of 165 in the Shōwa period prior to surrender). The Home Minister in 11 of the 43 cabinets, and the Foreign Minister in 14, was either a general or an admiral. The Finance Ministry was the sole civil department not under a military man during this same period.

The concentration of military men in the individual cabinets will serve to indicate the principal periods of military domination. In the first Itō government (1885-1888) under the new cabinet system, 6 of 10 ministers were military men (4 generals and 2 admirals). In the second cabinet, under Kuroda Kiyotaka (1888-1889), the proportion has risen to 7 of 10. While the number of ministries under generals or admirals thereafter declined, the balance did not tip in favor of civilians until 1898. In the cabinets of the late 1930's and especially the war cabinets of Tojo the balance again favored military men.[22] These data suggest in a general way the influence resting with the military even in civil affairs. For the military men representing civil departments in the cabinet, though differing among themselves, did possess a common background and were sympathetically aware of the stake of the military in all national affairs.

In extenuation of the military, it must be noted that the officer corps constituted a principal reservoir of talent. In the Meiji period the military elite were members of that social class which preserved traditions of learning. We may note that of the 269 generals whose biographies appear in the standard nine-volume dictionary, *Dai jimmei jiten*, 1937-1941, the social origins of 137 are listed, and of these, 117 were of samurai background and 8 were sons of nobles, daimyo, or from the imperial family. Later, the examination system in the military academies placed a premium on intelligence and academic proficiency, and the position of the military in society was such as to attract a high calibre of student.

Deriving originally from a privileged caste and continuing to enjoy a privileged position, the military did much to shape national policy. Their definition of national security, and of what was required to defend it, became part of the policy of every government. There was, hence, over the years, a steady increase in the size of the army and navy and in the military budget.

Paradoxically, victorious wars stimulated this trend. Despite unvarying success, the military were usually able to persuade the government that the nation's strength was inadequate to meet the international test. The national goal, it must be remembered, was equality with the Western powers, and this goal was pursued at the high-water mark of Western imperialism. In the late nineteenth and early twentieth centuries East Asia was an arena for the international contest for power. This being the case, it is not surprising that the army's view of national and international politics often prevailed. Even the political parties, although opposed to the military on grounds of its excessive political power, supported a foreign policy requiring a powerful military force.

It is possible to distinguish four periods in the army's political activity. In the first, from 1868 to 1878, there was no clear distinction between the military, political, and economic aspects of the national

<hr/>

[22] Matsushita, *Nihon gunsei to seiji*, pp. 172-174.

need for strength and unity. Raising a conscript army was one of many reforms changing the institutional structure of the country. During this period military authority was sometimes exercised by civil ministers, as when Home Minister Ōkubo was given military authority to subdue an uprising in 1874, and Prince Arisugawa, not then a military official, received orders to direct government forces in suppressing the Satsuma Rebellion. (The Prince did receive military rank before the fighting ended, and thereafter occupied high positions in the military bureaucracy.)

One basis for this unity was the similarity in the background of the Restoration leaders. These "old comrades" all inherited a tradition placing executive power in the hands of the military class. There were no major differences in the education and backgrounds of Itagaki Taisuke, Itō Hirobumi, and Yamagata Aritomo which explain why the first should form an anti-government political party, the second emerge as a civil leader of the government, and the third exercise military sway. It was a matter of special experience, inclination, and even chance. Only after 1878, when the last threat to the infant government had been subdued and the radically new institutions had developed roots, did the Meiji leaders begin thinking of themselves as belonging to either the civil or military branch of the government or (exceptionally) to a political opposition.

In the second period of the army's participation in politics, from 1878 to 1912, the command of the army passed to the "new comrades," the second generation of modern military leaders, and the new political framework, supported by laws and ordinances, became fixed. There was then a clear differentiation between civil and military authority and a separation of command and administrative functions within the armed forces. The independence of military authority was reinforced by military regulations against political activities, by provisions in the constitution, and by the rule that only active officers could become the military ministers. The one point at which military decisions were vigorously disputed by civil authority was in determining the need for increased appropriations. The national budget required the Diet's approval and the military request for ever higher appropriations was often resisted. But, in the end, the contest proved to be uneven, the forces in the Diet failing to match the power in the hands of the bureaucracy.

The army's political power was somewhat curbed during the third period, from 1912 to 1930. Military forces were then reduced for the first time, the arbitrary political conduct of the military (as in the constitutional crisis of 1912-1913) was deeply resented, and the area of civil authority was expanded. The governorships of Korea and Formosa were opened to civil bureaucrats during that period and the qualifications of the service ministers were changed to allow reserve or retired officers to serve. In Formosa *bona fide* civil servants became governors, and in the cabinet a civilian prime minister (Hara Kei) temporarily assumed the responsibilities of a service minister (Navy Minister Katō Tomosaburō). During the same period international agreements emerging from several meetings such as the Washington Conference and the London Naval Conference placed limitations on Japan's armed forces. The limitations agreed upon in London in 1930 and accepted by the Japanese government against strong opposition within the navy were part of a chain of events provoking the military to resume its interference in politics.

In the fourth and final period, from 1930 to defeat in 1945, the army reached the height of its political power. Economic problems at home and military aggression abroad led, through a period of violent crises, to the relinquishment of authority by the civil government. The military's disdain for civil authority, the sympathy of a growing segment of the armed forces for the views of extremists, and the disruption by factional rivalry of orderly process in the army and navy foreshadowed military totalitarianism. Young officer groups forced the hands of their superiors by inciting incidents abroad or by terroristic acts at home, and at length the military took over and decided to go to war.

The generation of generals then leading the army, many of them talented "technicians" of the military machine but narrow in their political vision, included "uniformed politicians" bent on reasserting political power. The army began to duplicate civil functions and to strengthen its ties with the population at large. Its press bureau flooded the country with pro-military pamphlets. It used the existing veteran's association, which was a compulsory and therefore a semi-governmental organization, as an instrument. These techniques for winning popular support and uniting the nation, and its sponsorship of the technical and educational advances required by a rapidly changing military technology, gave a modernizing flavor to some of the army's activities in the 1930's. Yet militarism also had its regressive consequences. The officers dominating the government imposed limitations on popular political activities and obstructed social change. The army, which could impose change quickly and efficiently, could with equal competence prohibit it. Finally, the ambitions of military leaders led to a disastrous war which retarded, temporarily at least, further national development.

VIII. Conclusion

We have observed that the relationship between the military and the political system was determined, first, by the historic position of the military class and by the subsequent successes of the modern army; second, by the recognition that national security required revolutionary military reforms; third, by the intimate connection between the processes of unifying the nation politically and those of centralizing military power; and, fourth, by the independent position given the military in the political structure. Civilian authority over military affairs was never established. On the contrary, the military took an active and often decisive part in civil political decisions.

Many of the measures adopted in the interests of building up and maintaining an adequate military force contributed to national characteristics which we should call modern. Universal military service helped to reduce class lines, to promote social mobility based on performance, to raise the level of general and technical education, to diffuse what was borrowed from abroad, and to broaden the experience and outlook of rural conscripts. It further imparted a sense of involvement in national affairs and a heightened feeling of identification with the state. It is unlikely that any conscript passed through military service, particularly in the Meiji era, without gaining a stronger orientation to the advantages of superior performance and achievements, without acquiring some new skills, or without being exposed to an ideology tending to strengthen nationalism. He undoubtedly gained new attitudes and behavior patterns which were conducive to modernization. In these senses, the military did serve as an agent of political modernization.

Of equal interest are the clues which the Japanese military experience gives to the role of military systems in general in the political modernization process. The creation of a national army to preserve, protect, and promote the national interest requires centralized control, and the institution of centralized control has made all modern armies national armies. Second, universal conscription provides a strategic opportunity for training, educating, indoctrinating, and "nationalizing" a major section of the population of modernizing societies.

Third, the development of a professional military organization and staff, serving the increasingly specialized needs of an increasingly complex national agency, provides useful experience of more general applicability in the development of a modern administrative apparatus. Finally, the very tensions between a military bureaucracy and the political system, though unsatisfactorily resolved in the Japanese case, are characteristic of a nation seeking to keep abreast of political change.

B. TURKEY

DANKWART A. RUSTOW

I. Political Modernization and the Turkish Military Tradition

The political modernization of Turkey occurred for the most part under military aegis. The "New Order" proclaimed by Sultan Selim III (1789-1807) when he first undertook a program of Westernization consisted in the creation of a new army. The final victory of constitutional and representative principles came in 1908, as the result of a threatened military rebellion. A decade later, Mustafa Kemal (Atatürk) and other generals transformed the Ottoman Empire into a modern nation-state. Thus, for nearly two hundred years, the soldier has been Turkey's foremost modernizer.

The prominent role of soldiers in Turkish society was not, however, ushered in by Selim's new troops with their *alla franca* goosestep. Throughout recorded Turkish history, military service has been accepted as the noblest episode in a man's career, and professional soldiers have enjoyed the most profound esteem. Selim himself, in devoting his chief attention to military matters, was reverting to the example of the Ottoman soldier-sultans and, beyond that, resuming the tradition of the frontier warriors, or *gazis*, who founded the Ottoman state along the Selcuk-Byzantine border in the late thirteenth century and spread its rule through Anatolia and the Balkan peninsula in the two centuries following. The *gazis* themselves had blended the heritage of their Turkish ancestors in Central Asia with that of their Muslim spiritual ancestors who, within a century of the death of Muhammad, conquered a vast empire in Asia, Africa, and Europe.

Islam, for all its tolerance of other faiths and its syncretism in belief and practice, is in its origins the most martial of major world religions. Its scripture promises to true believers power and prosperity on earth as well as eternal bliss in the hereafter. Its theology anticipates the spread of the true faith by conquest as well as by conversion and extols death in that enterprise as the most direct path to paradise. Its legal doctrine divides the world into the House of Islam and the House of War, conceding no more than temporary truces between the Muslim commonwealth and its infidel neighbors. Appropriately, the earliest Islamic rulers were known not only as caliphs, or successors (to Muhammad in his temporal functions), but also as commanders of the faithful. Yet, unlike the early caliphs, whose realm began to break up within a few generations, the Ottoman sultans developed a system of administration more extensive and efficient than any the Mediterranean world had known since Roman days. At the time of its maximum extent, in the late sixteenth century, the empire stretched from Algiers to the Caspian and from Hungary to Aden.

The most palpable symptom of Ottoman decline was the series of almost uninterrupted defeats at the hands of the Habsburg and Romanov empires—from the failure of the second siege of Vienna (1683) to the loss of Hungary (1699) and the northern Black Sea coast (1774-1783). For centuries the truth of their religion, the prowess of their sword, and the justice of their rule had given the Ottomans a sturdy sense of superiority over Europe. Now adversity forced them to recognize that, at least in the arts of war, Muslim Turks must learn from the despised infidel.

II. Military Reform and Foreign Relations:
Defensive Modernization

Ottoman modernization at first took the form of a piecemeal program of which the conscious aim was not acceptance but rejection of modern Europe. Yet by a compelling logic the program slowly spread. The army could not be reformed in isolation from the rest of the body politic. The new soldiery needed officers schooled in mathematics, French, and geography, and army surgeons with *alla franca* medical training. Military conscription required a tightening of administration in the provinces, where powerful vassals ruled in increasing defiance of the sultan. The costs of the new army and administration had to be borne by systematic taxation. An entire new school system was instituted to prepare the future officers, administrators, and tax collectors for their tasks. The schools required more money—and yet more schools for the training of teachers. The change in reformist nomenclature reflects the expansion of the program. Selim III's edicts of 1793 creating his new troops were called the *Nizam-ı Cedid* (New Order), in the singular intransitive form. When his third successor, Abdülmecid, in 1839 issued his promises of administrative reform and civic equality, the program was named *Tanzimat-ı Hayriye* (Beneficent Orderings), in the plural transitive.

353

The woof and warp of social interdependence would very likely have spread the reform movement throughout the fabric even if the mid-eighteenth-century reverses had remained an isolated impetus. But worse defeats were to follow; and it is a remarkable proof of the Ottoman elite's receptivity to innovation that, some conservatives aside, it took these as signals for further intensive reform rather than as tokens that the original program of adaptation had failed. In sober fact some of the later reverses were clearly aggravated by the maladjustments attending reform—as in Serbia, where the first movement for Balkan Christian autonomy profited from the seesaw struggle between the sultan and his local vassals. The destruction of the Janissaries in 1826 provides an even more striking illustration. The empire was denuded of troops except for the still embryonic new army, and was thereby directly exposed to the military and diplomatic calamities of 1827-1833, which forced the sultan, in the Treaty of Hünkâr İskelesi, to put himself under the protection of the czar.

Meanwhile, European military strength increased at a brisk pace, forcing the Ottomans to pursue a rapidly moving goal. At a time when European instructors were laboriously teaching Selim's new troops the rudiments of artillery, Carnot's *levée en masse* increased the manpower scale of military operations tenfold. In the late eighteenth century the Ottoman Empire would have done well, after a century of defeat, to hold its own against Austria-Hungary. By the second half of the nineteenth the Habsburg Empire was itself lapsing into a secondary power. With the progress of colonial conquest in Southern Asia and Africa, moreover, only the Ottoman Empire and Iran at one end of Asia and China and Japan at the other remained to tempt the further imperial ambitions of Europe. While the Ottomans in the eighteenth century had had to cope only with their immediate Austrian and Russian neighbors, Bonaparte's occupation of Egypt (1798-1801) and the destruction of his fleet by Nelson at Abukir inaugurated the nineteenth-century pattern of great powers, near and far, fighting out their conflicts in the Near East. Known, in the czar's condescending phrase, as the "Sick Man" of Europe, the Ottoman Empire survived by virtue not of its own strength but of the rivalries among its presumptive heirs.

In the First World War the Ottoman Empire put into the field the strongest, best-organized, and best-equipped armies in its history. In warding off the landings at Gallipoli in 1915, they prevented a juncture of the Western Allies with Russia and thereby hastened the czarist collapse. In the War of 1919-1922 the decimated Turkish armies won a hard-earned victory over the Greek invasion forces and thereby secured independence for a much-reduced Turkish national state. Yet, despite these exploits, Turkey's *relative* military strength continued its steady decline. Whereas the Ottoman Empire in the eighteenth century still was a formidable antagonist for Russia or for any single European power, Turkey today is no more than a makeweight in the global military contest between the Western and Soviet blocs. Concurrently, the focus of Turkish modernization has shifted from military concerns to political, economic, and social—although the role of the army in the revolution of 1960-1961 testifies to the continued importance of the military in that total process.

The changing configuration of power in which Turkey had to find a place was reflected in the changing sources of her military assistance. In its eighteenth-century military reforms, the Ottoman Empire relied largely on individual European converts. Thus Comte de Bonneval (1675-1742), an adventurous Frenchman, entered the Ottoman service in 1729, embraced Islam, organized the first Turkish artillery, and appropriately became known as Humbaracı Ahmed Pasha (Ahmed Pasha the Bombardier). His work was resumed in the 1770's by a Hungarian-French artillerist, Baron de Tott. The steady trickle of converts continued until the nineteenth century, several prominent Ottoman generals and diplomats of the period being of Hungarian, Croatian, or Polish origin. Meanwhile, as the Ottoman Empire found a place in the ever-shifting constellation of European alliances, regular missions of military instructors began to appear. In 1835 Mahmud II called Hellmuth von Moltke, the later chief of the Prussian and Imperial German General Staffs. Yet an exasperated comment in one of Moltke's letters ("an army on the European model with Russian jackets, French regulations, Belgian weapons, Turkish caps, Hungarian saddles, English swords, and instructors from all nations")[1] indicates that the instruction remained polyglot and the sources of equipment various. In the late nineteenth century, General (later Field Marshal) Colmar Freiherr von der Goltz (1843-1916) —beloved and respected by a whole generation of Turkish officers— served as inspector-general of Ottoman military schools; and after the defeat in the Balkan war (1913) another German mission arrived under General O. V. K. Liman von Sanders to undertake a compre-

[1] Cited by Roderic H. Davison, *Reform in the Ottoman Empire, 1856-1876*, Princeton, 1963, p. 31.

hensive military reorganization. Liman became the first foreign officer to hold a command position in the Ottoman army. During the First World War, this precedent was widely followed: one Ottoman army group in two or three and two armies in a total of from five to nine were commanded by German generals. While these German generals had Turkish chiefs of staff, most Ottoman commanders even of regiments and battalions had German staff officers attached to them. Late in 1913 Liman had arrived at the head of a German military mission of 42 officers. By the time of the armistice of 1918, the mission had grown to 646 officers and 6,686 men; German personnel attached to other parts of the Ottoman forces brought the total to 25,400.

In the period between the World Wars there was no more foreign military assistance of this sort. Soviet support of the Turkish effort in the War of Independence, for example, was limited to several large deliveries of gold bullion and of ammunition. In the 1920's and 1930's military equipment from submarines to tanks and rifles—but still equipment only—was imported from Europe; ammunition was increasingly manufactured at Turkish armaments plants at Mamak and Kırıkkale in Central Anatolia.

Toward the end of the Second World War, however, a British Royal Air Force mission arrived to train Turkish pilots in the use of fighter aircraft. With the proclamation of the Truman Doctrine a large-scale program of American military assistance began, and by the late 1950's American-Turkish cooperation ranged all the way from the building of a string of radar stations along the Black Sea coast, missile bases, and airfields to the preparation of literacy primers for military recruits. For the period from 1947 to 1962, U.S. grants for military aid are estimated to have totalled $2,288 million.

III. The Early Impact of Military Reform

Military reform in Turkey was effected in four distinct phases, following a pattern of innovation that was to become familiar in other parts of public life. First, a new military institution was transplanted from abroad. Second, there followed a period of uneasy coexistence between the new armies and the old. Third, after nearly half a century, the old army was done away with. Fourth, in the following decades, enough indigenous personnel were trained to staff the new institution, and by this time the reform had been carried far beyond its original intent.

The major strategies for effecting cultural change were demonstrated in the military reforms, but the difficulty of attaining a concept of citizenship suitable for a modern empire became simultaneously evident. In traditional times, the Ottoman standing army had been recruited from men whose legal status was that of slaves: some had been recruited as boys from among the empire's Christian subjects and brought up as Muslims in the imperial training schools; others had been imported from abroad, mainly from the Caucasus. Some served as a standing army, others were given fiefs in return for wartime service. By the eighteenth century, the professional soldiery, the Janissaries, had become a hereditary caste supplemented in time of war by cavalry contingents which were raised locally by the sultan's landed vassals and which were often not clearly loyal to the central authority. When Mahmud II destroyed the Janissaries and dispensed with the feudal cavalry, conscription remained as the logical basis for the recruitment of the new army. The two major reform decrees of the Tanzimat period, the Hatt-ı Şerif of Gülhane (1839) and the Hatt-ı Hümayun (1856), provided a theoretical base for such conscription by promising civic equality to all subjects regardless of religion—putting into question the age-old *millet* system of denominational segregation and autonomy. Meanwhile, a decree of 1843 fixed the term of military service at five years, to be followed by seven years in the reserves.

Equality and fraternity, however, were more easily proclaimed than practiced. For centuries the Ottomans had been proud defenders of Islam, their soldierly virtues solidly anchored in religious devotion. Yet the empire, in its mid-nineteenth-century borders, included a bare majority of Muslims; just over one-third of the population spoke Turkish. If the age-old ethnic division of labor was to give way to uniform patriotic obligation, what was to replace the traditional appeal of Holy War? How were Muslims and Christians, Turks, Greeks, Arabs, Bulgarians, Kurds, Albanians, Armenians, and the other groups of the polyglot empire to be welded into a single army? Ahmed Cevdet Pasha, a mid-nineteenth-century statesman, vividly pictured the difficulty: "But in time of need, how could the Colonel of a mixed battalion stir the zeal of his soldiers? In Europe, indeed, patriotism has taken the place of religious devotion, but this happened at the end of their feudal period; their children hear the word fatherland (*vatan*) while they are still small, and so years later the call of patriotism has become effective with their soldiers. But among us, if we say the word 'fatherland' all that will come to the minds of the soldiers is their village squares. If we were to adopt the word 'fatherland' now, and if, in the course of time, it were to establish itself in men's minds and acquire the power that it has in Europe, even then it would not be as potent as religious zeal, nor could it take its place. Even that would take a long time, and in the meantime our armies would be left without spirit."[2]

In fact, no colonel ever had to march a mixed battalion of Muslims and Christians into battle. The conscription laws were supplemented with a decree permitting non-Muslims to pay a "commutation fee" (*bedel-i askerî*) in lieu of military service. In the name of religious equality, Muslims also were presently allowed to pay a *bedel*, but at a substantially higher rate. The ranks of the service were thus filled in practice with Muslims either not affluent enough to pay the *bedel* or not ingenious enough to dodge the conscription agents—mainly Turkish, Albanian, and Arab peasants. The officers consisted of Muslims, mainly Turks, who had chosen the army as a career, for the Christians eagerly availed themselves of the privilege of commutation.

The theory and practice of army recruitment directly foreshadowed ultimate political solutions. Universal military service, centralized taxation, universal education, and civic participation in politics are among the principal hallmarks of the modern nation-state. In modernizing the Ottoman Empire, the sultans and statesmen of the Tanzimat period preached civic equality regardless of religious and ethnic distinctions. The new civil service included, along with its solid majority of Turks, some Albanians, Arabs, and other Muslims, and even a few non-Muslims. Representatives of all major nationality groups sat in the parliaments of 1877 and 1908 (although the Turks were vastly overrepresented), and within the constitutionalist exile movement of the years in between, Turks, Arabs, and Armenians tentatively fraternized. In the modernized army, by contrast, the religious lines were clearly drawn: service in the army was a universal obligation and privilege, but only for Muslims and mainly for Turks. The secession of Christian nationalities had begun in the days of Selim III; by the end of the century it was well-nigh complete, even the widely dispersed Armenians having declared for separatism. In the years between 1908 and the First World War, the loyalty of all remaining non-Turks was severely strained by the rapid political mobilization

[2] Cited from Cevdet's *Maruzat* by Bernard Lewis, *The Emergence of Modern Turkey*, London, 1961, p. 332.

of urban strata throughout the empire and by disputes over such matters as the choice of language for the schools and the selection of personnel for government service. The Albanian secession of 1912 and the Arab Revolt of 1916 spelled the doom of the multi-national empire. The nationality principle, suggested by the composition of the conscript army of the Tanzimat period, was accepted on all sides by the end of the World War and therefore furnished the basis for the empire's successor states.

The most important single contribution of the early military reforms to political modernization turned out to be the establishment, during the reigns of Selim III, Mahmud II, and Abdülmecid, of a set of officers' training-schools: a naval school (1773), an artillery school (1793), a military medical school (1826), and an army officers' school (1834) supplemented later by a general staff college (1849). Later, civilian schools also were founded and by the end of the nineteenth century these higher schools had produced a new elite of officers and officials to whom Europeanizing reform was no longer an occasional expedient for preserving tradition but an instrument for transforming tradition itself. Modernization, starting out as the command of an autocrat, had become the project of ministers and at last the fervent mission of a new social class. In laying the foundation for military reform, the sultans, like the sorcerer's apprentice, had released a process which became increasingly autonomous and which they eventually became unable to control. In 1922 the heirs of Selim III's new army deposed his cousin's grandson and brought in a coroner's verdict on the Ottoman state and sultanate.

The mid-nineteenth-century reforms were carried out largely by diplomats and officials self-taught in the ways of the West. Many of the men of Tanzimat were trained in the Translation Room (the embryonic Foreign Office at the Sublime Porte), in the early embassies to Paris and London, or in the reformed vilayet administrations; a few came from the *ilmiye* class, the traditional religious establishment. The Tanzimat sought ministerial reform within an autocracy by means of decrees and codes, a tightened administration, an expanded education. The reformers' source of power was their access to the sultan's ear. By mid-century there were the first stirrings of what may properly be called public opinion within upper-class Istanbul society amid a bustle of new literary and journalistic activity. The loose and unorganized movement known as the New Ottomans—the men who prepared the double political *coup d'état* of 1876 and fashioned the constitution of that year—grew out of this environment. In the next generation, the political constellation shifted. Abdül-hamid II (1876-1909) continued many of the reforms of his predecessors, such as the extension of public works (especially telegraphs and railways), expansion of higher education, and European-style training for the armed forces. (It was during his reign that von der Goltz Pasha served as inspector-general of Ottoman military schools.) But he did his best to stamp out the constitutionalist movement by adjourning the new parliament *sine die* and banishing Midhat Pasha, chief author of the 1876 constitution, and the sultan's vague Pan-Islamism replaced the Parisian dandy manners of the Tanzimat period. In this atmosphere, the officers' training schools increasingly became the seedbeds of constitutionalist sentiment.

The military schools admitted young Muslim men from all parts of the country and from some adjacent regions and subjected them to rigorous training in mathematics, French, and history, as well as in strategy and tactics. Both in the schools and in the officer corps promotion depended far less on favoritism and intrigue than in the civilian bureaucracy. An army career thus combined the advantages of Westernized training with those of merit advancement and high social mobility. The cohesiveness and *esprit de corps* among the cadets and within the officers' corps furnished an essential prerequisite of political organization.

The first secret political society directed against Abdülhamid's autocracy was founded in 1889 under the name of "Progress and Union" by a handful of students at the military medical school. Within a few years, the movement was totally stamped out in Turkey by the sultan's secret police. But Abdülhamid's practice of exiling political suspects could not eradicate the growing political dissatisfaction. Young cadets banished to Fezzan in the Libyan desert became even more firmly dedicated to revolutionary ideas. Others joined the growing exile movement in Cairo, Geneva, or Paris (known to Europeans as Jeunes Turcs) and smuggled their subversive newspapers back to Istanbul via the extraterritorial mail services of the European consulates. By the turn of the century, dissatisfaction in the military schools was again rife. Young officers assigned to fight Balkan nationalist insurgents in Macedonia and disloyal vassals on the Arabian peninsula could observe at first hand the dynastic empire's weakness and the political advantages of a nationalist spirit and organization. In 1906 a group of officers and civilians in Salonica founded the secret Ottoman Society of Liberty, and a group of officers in Damascus formed a society named Fatherland and Liberty. The next year the two groups merged and declared their affiliation with the exile movement in Paris and Geneva. The name of the consolidated opposition, the Ottoman Society for Progress and Union, was later changed to the Society for Union and Progress or, as commonly translated, the Committee of Union and Progress. While Salonica remained the headquarters and officers of regimental rank provided the core of the movement, other branches were founded in towns throughout Macedonia and new adherents were recruited among school teachers, telegraph clerks, and junior administrators. The movement grew so strong that a few demonstrative acts of defiance—the formation of armed bands in the hills, the assassination of a general sent to suppress the discontent, and a strategically timed flood of telegrams—sufficed to force Abdülhamid to reproclaim the constitution on the twenty-fourth of July 1908.

Though there had been many revolts and depositions throughout Ottoman history, these had grown out of dynastic quarrels, palace intrigue, or insurrection by provincial governors. In 1908 a major political revolution was accomplished for the first time by popular pressure spearheaded by a party organization within which the military played a leading role.

IV. Three Periods of Military Involvement in Twentieth-Century Politics

The Young Turk period of 1908-1918 was the first of three major waves of military involvement in Turkish politics in this century. It was to be followed by the nationalist revolution of 1919-1923 and the revolution of 1960-1961. Before attempting to analyze the factors that prompted soldiers successively to enter the political arena and then to withdraw, let us briefly survey the salient events of each period.

THE YOUNG TURK PERIOD, 1908-1918

The revolution of 1908 required little if any overt military action. The telegrams which poured into Abdülhamid's Yıldız palace in July 1908 from civilian and military groups in Macedonia threatened that the crown prince would be proclaimed ruler unless the 1876 constitution was restored. To anguished inquiries from the palace concerning the local strength of the Union and Progress movement, the commanding general in Salonica replied, "Sire, I swear that apart from Your Majesty's most obedient servant, there is no one left here who is not a Young Turk."[3] Within a few days, Abdülhamid reproclaimed the constitution and scheduled the first parliamentary elections in thirty years.

The Society of Union and Progress, despite its easy and resounding victory, at first remained in the background. The most unpopular of the sultan's ministers were dismissed and his network of spies disbanded. But the government was carried on by cabinets composed of the customary assortment of aging officials, now responsible to a popularly elected legislature. The following months were a period of intense political activity in the capital. The press, unaccustomed to its newly won freedom, adopted a tone of petulance and vituperation. Stirred up by *medrese* students who denounced the constitution as a Frankish machination to abolish Islamic custom, the Albanian soldiers of the Istanbul garrison mutinied on April 13, 1909, calling out "We Want the Holy Law." (According to the Julian calendar then in effect and to accepted canons of euphemism, the uprising became known as the "Thirty-First of March Incident.") The terrified officers of the garrison and the Union and Progress majority of parliament hid in their homes or fled the city, while the leaderless soldiery roamed the streets and cowed the rump parliament.

This time, the Macedonian army intervened more energetically. Within a week, volunteer contingents of an "Army of Deliverance" (*Hareket Ordusu*, literally Action Army) were on the march. When these troops entered the capital, the mutineers quietly returned to their barracks with a promise of amnesty. Abdülhamid, alleged on slender evidence to have instigated or condoned the Thirty-First of March Incident, was deposed by the full parliament. A few days later, he was exiled—insult upon injury—to Salonica, the stronghold of his Young Turk antagonists.

For the next three years, the Young Turks reigned supreme under the pliable Sultan Mehmed V Reşad (1909-1918). They occupied crucial posts in the cabinet, amended the constitution so as to transform the checks-and-balance system into one of legislative supremacy, and secured very nearly a clean sweep in the "Big Stick" elections of 1912. Meanwhile, however, a serious rift had appeared within the constitutionalist movement. As over against the Union and Progress

---

[3] Quoted in *Belleten*, Vol. 23, 1959, p. 311.

group, which advocated administrative centralization and tended increasingly to equate Ottomanism with Turkish nationalism, there arose a "liberal" opposition, with vaguely federalist tendencies that appealed strongly to Albanian and Arab leaders. Thwarted in its parliamentary and electoral efforts, the opposition proceeded to turn upon the Unionists the very weapons of military conspiracy by which the Unionists had come to power. Once again a rebellious group took to the hills in Macedonia, calling itself the Savior Officers (*Hâlaskâr Zabıtan*), while their anonymous spokesmen in the capital threatened the Unionist speaker of the house with "the supreme penalty" for his "nefarious" and "dissolute" activities, unless he at once dissolved the "clubhouse and theater" over which he presided.[4] Once again the government resigned (July 1912) without risking a showdown. The cabinets of veteran generals and officials which succeeded ruled without parliament for the next six months.

Turkey's disastrous defeat in the First Balkan war enabled the Unionists to recapture power—this time by an audacious raid on the government offices in which the minister of war was shot dead and Kâmil Pasha, the 80-year old Grand Vezir, forced to write out his resignation. The raid, known as the Sublime Porte Incident (January 23, 1913), was undertaken by a handful of young officers led by Enver, who had taken one of the first armed bands to the hills in 1908. It proceeded to install a Unionist party cabinet under Mahmud Şevket Pasha, the commander of the Action Army of 1909. When Mahmud Şevket was assassinated a few months later, the Unionists launched upon a program of repression far more vigorous than that of 1909. The sultan was forced to sign the death sentence of his niece's husband, who, in a public trial, had been found guilty of complicity in the assassination. Other prominent anti-Unionists were banished or went into exile. Parliamentary elections were held, after a two-year interval, in 1914, and once again the Union and Progress Party carried all but a few non-Turkish seats. Wartime economic regulations greatly strengthened the political power of the Unionists, among whom Enver as minister of war and Talât as party secretary and Grand Vezir held the most prominent positions. No serious challenge arose to the Unionist regime until the defeat of 1918 spelled the collapse of its grandiose war policy and prompted the resignation and flight of its leaders.

---

[4] Cited in Tarık Z. Tunaya, *Türkiyede Siyasi Partiler*, Istanbul, 1952, p. 229.

THE NATIONALIST REVOLUTION, 1919-1923

In the months after October 1918, the sultan's government increasingly committed itself to a policy of collaborating with the victorious powers and to accepting gradual occupation under the conveniently vague provisions of the armistice. By contrast the general staff and the field commanders of the decimated army—whether acting in concert or by individual initiative—did their best to delay the demobilization of troops and the surrender of arms. The departing Unionist leaders, moreover, had encouraged the formation of nationalist resistance groups, especially in peripheral provincial centers such as Edirne, İzmir, Adana, Trabzon, Kars, and Erzurum, which were threatened by enemy occupation and annexation.

The coordination of these efforts was the work of Mustafa Kemal Pasha (later known as Atatürk), who, after fruitless endeavors to form a nationalist government in Istanbul, had secured the post of army inspector with wide administrative powers in Northeast Anatolia. Although he was forced to resign from the army in July 1919 to avoid recall to Istanbul under Allied pressure, Kemal used his two months' head start to prepare two nationalist congresses, at Erzurum and Sıvas, where the scattered resistance societies joined in a nation-wide "Anatolian and Rumelian Society for the Defense of Rights." When the Allied armies completed their occupation of the capital, the nationalists called a Grand National Assembly in Ankara (April 1920), whose executive committee, chaired by Mustafa Kemal, claimed to rule the country in the name of the captive sultan.

For two and a half years thereafter, Turkey had two rival governments. After a futile attempt to stamp out the Anatolian "rebellion," the sultan's cabinet resigned itself to a shadow existence under Allied occupation in Istanbul. The humiliating treaty of Sèvres, which it signed in August 1920, proved stillborn and was soon disregarded by the victors themselves. The Anatolian nationalists, who had rebuilt the army with the covert support of the general staff in Istanbul, established full control over the civilian administration in Anatolia during the summer of 1920. In the fall and winter of 1920, they defeated the Armenians in the northeast and drove the French back into Syria. Then, in the campaigns of 1921 and 1922, they concentrated their forces against the Greeks in the east. Earlier, the regular army had quelled a mutiny by Çerkes Edhem, who, together with his guerrilla forces, deserted to the Greek lines. By 1921, Mustafa

Kemal's government concluded a treaty of friendship with the Soviets and gained *de facto* recognition in Europe. The armistice of Mudanya (October 1922) and the peace treaty of Lausanne (July 1923) confirmed the nationalists' victory in the hard-fought war. The nationalist program of Erzurum and Sıvas, calling for independence within the 1918 armistice lines, had become the basis of Turkey's political future.

Having asserted the independence of Turkey from foreign powers, Kemal and his followers proceeded to clarify and consolidate the internal form of government. The sultanate was declared defunct (1922), a republic proclaimed (1923), the caliphate abolished (1924), and a representative constitution enacted (1924). These measures, together with the introduction of European dress, law codes, calendar, measures, and letters (1925-1928), provided the legal framework for a Westernized nation-state.

Meanwhile, the formation of an organized opposition, the Progressive Republican Party (1924-1925), gave rise to the young republic's first serious internal crisis. Among the leaders were Rauf (Orbay), a naval hero of the Balkan War and Kemal's closest political ally in 1919-1920, and Generals Ali Fuad (Cebesoy) and Kâzim Karabekir, organizers of the nationalist western and eastern fronts—the most prominent early leaders, in short, of the War of Independence, who resented Kemal's drift toward personal rule and their own diminished role in public affairs. By contrast, Kemal had the firm support of two leaders who had joined him somewhat later: İsmet (İnönü), the victorious commander of the western front in 1920-1922, and Fevzi (Çakmak), nationalist chief of staff. Even before the formation of the Progressives, Kemal had forced all politician-generals to choose between their legislative mandates and their army commands. Later, the outbreak of a conservative rebellion in the Kurdish east supplied a convenient pretext for abolishing the opposition party. In 1926 the ex-Progressive members of the assembly were tried for high treason in connection with an attempt on Kemal's life—although Karabekir, Cebesoy, and other ex-generals were released after a month's detention, apparently upon strong pressure from the army.

For the next two decades, the Turkish Republic pursued its program of modernization in law, culture, economy, and education under the civilian auspices of the Republican People's Party. Many of the national leaders had military backgrounds—foremost Kemal Atatürk himself (president until his death in 1938), and İsmet İnönü (prime minister, 1923-1925 and 1925-1937, president 1938-1950). But after the War of Independence Atatürk was seen only once in uniform—during an acute foreign policy crisis—and İnönü never; İnönü in 1927 applied for his retirement from the army. This withdrawal of the military from politics was facilitated by the advent of a period of peace of unprecedented duration. Turkey had been continuously at war at the beginning of the century: there had been insurrections on the Balkans and in Yemen from 1900, the Italian war in Libya in 1911-1912, the Balkan Wars in 1912-1913, the First World War from 1914 to 1918, and the War of Independence from 1919 to 1922. By contrast, the republic, since its proclamation four decades ago has not been involved in any war.

THE REVOLUTION OF 1960-1961

The principle of strict separation of the military from politics had long been accepted when President İnönü, in the wake of the democratic victory of 1945, decided to allow the formation of opposition parties. The Republican People's Party cabinet of 1948 was the first, in fact, to include no politicians of military background. Total civilian rule was even more firmly assured by the landslide election victory of the Democratic Party in 1950, which brought to power President Celâl Bayar and Premier Adnan Menderes.

Gradually, however, the internal political situation after 1950 deteriorated to the point where the armed forces reentered politics once again. The Democrats' control of the government was confirmed in the elections of 1954 and 1957, though this last time with a declining margin. But government pressure upon the opposition became increasingly heavy-handed, while the strains imposed by Menderes' over-ambitious program of economic expansion led to widespread discontent in the towns. The more precarious Menderes' position became, the sterner his measures of repression. In the spring of 1960, the Democratic majority in the assembly set up a "committee of investigation" with summary and unconstitutional judicial powers clearly aimed at stamping out all political opposition.

It was the Menderes government itself, however, which brought the army back into politics after more than three decades of civilian rule. As early as in 1955, martial law had been declared in Istanbul, Ankara, and İzmir in the wake of anti-Greek riots; these demonstrations, originally designed to strengthen the Menderes government's case in the Cyprus negotiations, had quickly deteriorated into an orgy of destruction. In the spring of 1959 the government deliberately instigated riots in Western cities (Uşak, Manisa, İzmir), and in Istanbul, wherever ex-President İnönü was campaigning during an extensive tour. The intention apparently was to cause İnönü's death in what could be made to appear a "spontaneous outburst of popular indignation." Since the Ankara authorities did not trust the police alone to handle these disorders, army contingents were ordered to stand by. Early in April, 1960, İnönü's train was stopped, when he was on his way to a meeting in Kayseri, by soldiers acting under orders from Ankara; and later that month troops were used to quell anti-government demonstrations by students and faculty at Istanbul and Ankara universities.

Menderes had for several years attempted systematically to fill the highest military posts with officers amenable to his political directives. But the army's *esprit de corps* proved too strong to admit of effective infiltration from the top. The army resented the government's attempts to blame it for the Istanbul riots of 1955 and when an enterprising reserve officer, eager to ingratiate himself with Democratic authorities, reported on an anti-government plot among officers of the Istanbul garrison in 1957, the army's reaction was an overt indication of a rift between the government and the military establishment. The court martial that looked into the charges of high treason took the unprecedented step of making its proceedings public "because the army's honor had been impugned." The defendants denied the existence of any plot at all, one of them adding haughtily, "This is not Syria." In the end, it was the informer and not his intended victims who were sentenced.

In the next three years, such indications multiplied even though the anti-government plotters used more caution. In the various incidents of the spring of 1959, phone calls from anonymous army officers warned the Republican People's Party leaders of the government's machinations against them. In April of 1960, the soldiers ordered to detain İnönü on his trip to Kayseri filed through the railroad car to kiss the pasha's hand. Shortly afterward, General Cemal Gürsel resigned as commander of land forces with a pointed appeal to the army not to become entangled in politics. In the tense days of May 1960, Bayar's anxious query to a private of the presidential guard whether the troops would defend him against popular attack elicited the deadpan reply, "Yes, if our officer commands us to do so." When an American reporter questioned an opposition deputy concerning

Menderes' claim that the army was on his side, he was told "Menderes may have the generals, but we have everyone from colonel down." In the midst of the strict martial law curfew, the cadets of the Ankara War College marched through town in a silent, defiant demonstration; according to newspaper reports, the commanding general "implored" the cadets to return to their billets—an uncharacteristic blandishment in a professional army accustomed to the order "Turn about, march!"

The climax came on May 27, 1960, when army contingents arrested President Bayar, Premier Menderes, and other cabinet members in a series of coordinated pre-dawn moves, and placed most of the Democratic members of the assembly under arrest in the course of the next few days. A junta of thirty-eight officers under the chairmanship of General Gürsel took over the government as the "Committee of National Unity," promised a speedy return to civilian rule under a new constitution, and prepared a mass trial of members of the deposed regime for their violations of the constitution and other political crimes.

The regime of the Committee of National Unity faced a number of unanticipated difficulties, the soldiers proving inexpert in the unfamiliar political arena. Solicitude for legal procedure delayed the preparation and conduct of the trials at Yassıada, and yet, when the death and prison sentences against the Democratic leaders were handed down in the fall of 1961, even their legal validity remained doubtful, to say nothing of their political wisdom. The elaborate charges of corruption and sexual libertinism, no matter how shocking to the frugal and puritan officer corps, were received with indifference or even admiration among the peasant masses, while the continuing economic crisis diverted dissatisfaction from the previous to the present government. The constitutional theory embraced by the junta, moreover, involved an internal contradiction: the coup was justified by the Menderes regime's subversion of the 1924 Constitution; yet the remedy proposed was not a return to that constitution but its replacement by a new document providing better safeguards of personal liberty and a superior system of checks and balances. And the drafting of the new constitution occasioned prolonged wrangling among the lawyers (and, later, the anti-Menderes politicians) to whom the committee entrusted the task.

Meanwhile, a split became apparent within the junta itself. A faction of fourteen officers headed by Colonel Türkeş, which was reported to favor radical social reform under continued military dictatorship, was ousted in November 1960, and its members assigned as "counsellors" to remote embassies. Prior to this victory of the moderates, the abrupt dismissal of 147 professors had threatened to alienate the universities, which had been among the regime's staunchest civilian allies. Finally the rise to political power of officers mostly holding ranks beneath that of colonel caused strains within the military hierarchy and brought about a mass retirement of high-ranking officers.

At length, a new constitution for the Second Turkish Republic was adopted in the summer of 1961, and was ratified by popular referendum. A new bicameral assembly was chosen in elections that were free —except for bans on discussing the legality of the 1960 revolution and the Yassıada trials—and Cemal Gürsel doffed his uniform and assumed elective office as president of the republic. But the system of proportional representation adopted for the lower house led to an uneasy balance of four minority parties—İnönü's Republican People's Party, the Republican Peasant-Nation Party, and two newcomers (the Justice and New Turkey parties), which had rather obviously sought to capture the orphaned Democratic vote. While the coalition regime under Premier İnönü began to tackle the problems of economic development, there were ominous clamors—on the one hand for speedy rehabilitation of the convicted Democrats and on the other for renewed military intervention.

V. The Soldiers and the Political Stage

The preceding account of the revolutions of 1908-1918, 1919-1923, and 1960-1961 may provide the background for some generalizations concerning the role of the military in politics during the present century.

ENTER THE SOLDIERS

The intervention of an army in politics by coup or revolution is never a sudden, isolated occurrence.[5] Commonly it follows upon a period of internal unrest in which the civil authorities have themselves come to rely on armed force. Abdülhamid's losing battle against guerrillas on the Balkans and rebels in Yemen helped to set the stage for the 1908 revolution. In the late 1950's, as we have seen, Menderes

[5] Some of the following remarks parallel or even paraphrase my observations on the dynamics of military politics in the Middle East as a whole. See my article on "The Military in Middle Eastern Society and Politics," in *The Military in the Middle East*, ed. Sydney N. Fisher, Columbus, Ohio, 1963.

was using the army as a tool of repression. The army officers, as a result, suffered a conflict of conscience. Their professional training and their Kemalist tradition demanded obedience to civilian authority. But their civilian superiors were gradually undermining the ethos of the Atatürk reforms, violating the constitution which the soldiers were duty-bound to uphold—and were using the army as a tool in that enterprise. Gürsel's parting advice to the army in April 1960 echoed Atatürk's precept of military abstention from politics. But in fact the army by then had no choice. If it obeyed the orders issuing from Menderes, it would be in politics on his behalf; if it refused, it would be even more deeply in politics against him. Choosing the second alternative as the lesser evil, it could invoke the peroration of the *Six-Day Speech* in which Atatürk justified his fight against the sultan's government in 1919-1922—a text that every army officer and other educated Turk commits to memory in his grade-school days: "Conditions may be yet more grievous and yet more dangerous; for, inside the country, the men in power may be caught in heedlessness and error and even treason. Those in power may even unite their personal interests with the political aims of the conquerors. The nation, devastated and indigent, may have fallen into poverty and dire need. O Turkish child of the future! Even under these conditions and circumstances your duty is to save the Turkish independence and Republic! The required strength you will find in the noble blood that is coursing through your veins!"[6]

Atatürk's indictment of the Ottoman regime, significantly, came five years after that government had ceased to exist. The Kemalist revolution of 1919-1923 was unique because its avowed target at the time was not an internal foe but an external one—not the sultan whom Kemal in 1920 solemnly vowed to uphold, but the foreign armies poised to proceed from victory to occupation, partition, and annexation. Throughout the War of Independence Kemal was careful to disguise or obscure his differences with the sultan,[7] to create new

[6] *Nutuk*, 1934 edn., ii, 337.

[7] Only once, in a rare fit of choler (when the Istanbul government in the fall of 1919 held up his telegrams to the sultan, whom he hoped to sway to his side), did Kemal briefly and partly drop the mask: "You are preventing the nation from addressing the sultan. Scoundrels, criminals!" he fulminated in a cable to the interior minister. "Together with the enemies you engage in treacherous schemes against the nation. I did not doubt that you were incapable of appreciating the nation's power and will. But I did not wish to believe that you would resort to treacherous and butcherous actions against fatherland and nation. Get some sense into your heads. . . . When being taken in by empty promises and selling your consciences to

institutions pragmatically one at a time, and to delay a showdown until the external victory should be won and the existence of the new state a visible fact. The fight against the Greek and other invaders preserved and reinforced national unity; an overt rebellion against the sultan would have disrupted it. The army's avoidance of blatant partisanship enormously facilitated its subsequent withdrawal from the political stage.

As we have been reminded by the experience of the Arab countries after the Palestine War of 1948, military coups often result from an army's frustration over external defeat. In Turkey, the Sublime Porte Incident of January 1913 clearly fits this pattern. In the First Balkan War in the fall of 1912, the Ottoman Empire had lost most of its remaining European possessions, and Enver and his Unionist backers justified their coup by the charge that the government of the aging Kâmil Pasha was not fulfilling the national desire for the recapture of the ancient Ottoman capital of Edirne. The Kemalist revolution began in 1919 when the nation had suffered an even more decisive defeat and was anticipating dismemberment by European powers. A somewhat similar anticipation had strengthened the hand of the revolutionaries of 1908, the British-Russian rapprochement of 1907-1908 having aroused fears that those powers would deprive the empire of Macedonia.[8]

In broader perspective, a military revolution is likely to result from a growing disparity—in social background, cultural ethos, and political purpose—between the civilian government and the military. Significantly, in the period of Turkish history dealt with, such a cleavage was brought about or accentuated by a shift in the political course not of the military but of the civilians. The Janissaries constituted a conservative force against the innovations of Selim and

---

foreigners . . . harmful to our fatherland and our nation, keep in mind the accounting which the nation will exact from you. When you learn of the fate of the persons and the forces on which you rely [Kemal had just thwarted a forcible attempt to seize him and his associates at the Sıvas Congress] do not forget to compare it with your own future fate." (*Ibid.*, i, 94.) The future fate of the hapless recipient of this outburst turned out to be that he was put (along with Çerkes Edhem, Damad Ferid, and Ali Galib, who tried to capture Kemal at Sıvas) on the list of 150 persons exempted from the political amnesty provisions of the Treaty of Lausanne and died in exile.

[8] E. E. Ramsaur, in the best assessment to date of the origins of the 1908 revolution (*The Young Turks, Prelude to the Revolution of 1908*, Princeton, 1957, p. 133), holds that this "factor . . . has probably been somewhat overemphasized" by earlier authors. He stresses instead the conspirators' fear of discovery by the sultan. The two considerations are not, however, mutually exclusive.

Mahmud. The officer corps of the late nineteenth century continued the modernizing and constitutionalist tradition of the Tanzimat and of Midhat Pasha; it was Abdülhamid's Pan-Islamic and autocratic policies which departed from that tradition. In 1918-1919 Sultan Mehmed VI Vahideddin switched to a policy of collaboration with Britain and other Allies and brought anti-Unionist politicians back from exile or retirement, whereas Kemal continued to pursue, on a modest and realistic scale, the nationalist wartime policy of the Union and Progress. In 1960 the army stood up for the constitutionalist and democratic traditions initiated respectively by Atatürk and İnönü but undermined by the civilian Menderes. Minor causes of friction in each instance exacerbated relations between the army and the civil authority: the chronic arrears of military pay before 1908, the arrest and deportation of military leaders by Ottoman and Allied authorities in Istanbul in 1919, the political reshuffles in top military ranks in the 1950's.

Finally, military intervention in politics tends to be precipitated by the clogging of civil channels of political change. The repression of opposition sentiment by Abdülhamid at the beginning of the century and by Menderes fifty years later left the military as the only available weapon against the regime. In 1919, the need for military leadership was even more urgent: only the army could muster the secrecy and speed, the cohesion and physical force required for effective nationalist action against the sultan and the Allies. In all three periods, Turkish officers and civilian sympathizers could ask (as Colonel Nasser did in 1952), "If the army does not do this job, who will?"[9]

Within this framework of similarity, the means by which the army seized power offer a fair degree of variety. The 1908 revolution, triggered by threats over the wires from Macedonia to the capital, was the type of coup which Latin Americans, with their ample opportunities for classification, have come to call a *telegráfico*. In the following years the army intervened in politics in a variety of ways: in 1909 there was a mutiny in the capital suppressed by means of improvised units of the regular army; in 1912, an abortive campaign of guerrilla action and political threats by the Savior Officers; and in the Sublime Porte incident of 1913 a successful *coup de main* against the government offices—*ein Leutnant und zehn Mann*, in the classic German phrase. In 1919, nationalist resistance was coordinated by the inspector of one of the three armies into which Ottoman forces

[9] Gamal Abdul Nasser, *Egypt's Liberation*, Washington, 1955, p. 27.

were grouped after the armistice—openly supported by one and later several neighboring army corps and secretly abetted by the war ministry and general staff. Since political-military action was initiated by the highest commanders, no violence was required for the seizure of power. Discipline within the armed forces was fully maintained, and this facilitated the subsequent transfer to new civilian institutions. The 1960 revolution followed the grammar of mid-twentieth-century coups: coordinated seizure of cabinet members and of the radio stations, occupation of the major cities, and the triumphant breakfast communiqué to an agreeably surprised populace.

THE SOLDIERS ON STAGE

The performance of the regimes so variously installed itself varied widely. The Young Turks of 1908 and 1913 hastened rather than reversed that disintegration of the Ottoman Empire of which they complained. Their attempt to extend the parliamentary elections of 1908 to Bosnia and Herzegovina prompted Austria formally to annex that region after thirty years of military occupation; and, within a week, Bulgaria had proclaimed its annexation of East Rumelia and its independence, and Greece its annexation of Crete. Administrative reforms in the Balkan and Arab peninsulas further helped crystallize secessionist tendencies. The Albanians, resenting the disarmament of hillside tribesmen and the expansion of a school system with a Turkish curriculum, declared their independence in 1912. A few years later, efforts to bring the Hijaz under closer administrative control clashed with the political ambitions of Sharif Husayn, the guardian of the Holy Cities, who conspired with the British in Egypt and with Arab nationalists in Damascus in proclaiming his "Revolt in the Desert" in 1916. Meanwhile the Italian attack of 1911 led to the loss of Libya, and the Balkan War to the loss of most of the empire's remaining European possessions. Despite the Young Turk propaganda accompanying the Sublime Porte Incident, it was the Mahmud Şevket government which formally yielded Edirne in the subsequent peace treaty. Only the fortuitous quarrel among the victorious Balkan allies that resulted in the Second Balkan War from June to September 1913 enabled the Ottomans to recapture that city and to establish Turkey's present frontier on the Maritsa.

Enver's secret German alliance of 1914 precipitated the final calamity. His order to shell the Russian Black Sea ports, which propelled Turkey into the World War, came six weeks after German hopes for an early victory had been decisively checked at the Marne. Aside from some isolated victories such as the capture of Townshend's army at Ctesiphon and the successful defense of the Dardanelles, the Turkish phase of the war turned into a dreary sequence of failure, retreat, and defeat. Enver consistently confused political propaganda and personal vainglory with strategic calculation. The ill-prepared move to encircle the Russians in the winter of 1914-1915, which Enver personally directed at the head of 90,000 of the best Ottoman troops in the icy Armenian mountains, resulted in 80,000 casualties. Instead of husbanding his remaining manpower, he launched a series of "Pan-Islamic" attacks on Egypt in 1914 and 1915; sent seven of his best divisions to faraway fronts in Galicia, Romania, and Macedonia to prove to the Germans and Austrians his worth as an ally; refused, again in the name of Islam, to withdraw the exposed garrison of Medina in 1917-1918 to the steadily receding Syrian front;[10] and in 1918, amid blasts of "Pan-Turkish" propaganda, dispatched a large army into the Transcaucasian military vacuum when the Ottoman armies in Iraq and Syria were crumbling under Allied attack.

Compared to this grandiloquent ineptitude, Kemal's campaigns in the War of Independence stand out as a supreme achievement of military genius. Even more remarkable than his battlefield victories was his determination to scale down the ambitions of the nationalist movement to the strategically and politically feasible—to cast aside dreams of Pan-Islamic or Pan-Turkish glory for the manageable though still difficult task of building a Turkish nation state in Anatolia.

It is tempting to attribute this difference in performance to striking and profound traits of personality: Enver, the flamboyant, diminutive hero of the revolution who spellbound Istanbul theater audiences by jumping on stage in the grand finale of a patriotic melodrama to mete out justice to the villains,[11] the parvenu who married the sultan's niece and promoted his brother from major to lieutenant general, the easy prey to flattery who returned from the festive dinners of Berlin a lifelong Germanophile, the opportunist who left his assigned battle station to be the first to march into Edirne but fled his country in the dark of night after leading it into ruinous defeat, the quixotic

---

[10] Fahreddin (Türkkan), the corps commander at Medina, was so thoroughly isolated that word of the armistice did not reach him for over two months. He capitulated with 12 battalions on January 10, 1919.

[11] See Charles Roden Buxton, *Turkey in Revolution*, London, 1909, pp. 16ff. On Enver's career as a whole, see my article "Enwer Pasha," *Encyclopaedia of Islam*, rev. edn., Vol. 2, Leiden 1963.

dreamer, finally, who concluded among Turkestani bandits the me-
teoric career begun among Balkan *komitadjis*; and—in sharpest contrast—Mustafa Kemal, the tall soldier of calm professional bearing,
diffident and taciturn, moody and pensive behind his steel-grey eyes,
an energetic battlefield "leader that delighted in responsibility," a
"splendid general"[12] at his best in extreme adversity, as during the defense of the Dardanelles, the Syrian defeat of 1918, which he converted from rout to orderly retreat, and finally the period of reviving
a decimated army and a demoralized populace for the nationalist defense of Anatolia. A close personal acquaintance of both Enver and
Kemal, Falih Rıfkı Atay, has aptly proposed that Enver, after a battle such as Kemal won over the Greeks on the Sakarya, would have
thrown away victory and national independence itself by marching off
to the conquest of Syria or Macedonia.[13]

But such a juxtaposition of personal characteristics in fact only
dramatizes the problem to be resolved. Enver and Mustafa Kemal
were exact contemporaries. Enver graduated from the staff college
at 21, Kemal two years later at 23. At the time of the 1908 revolution, Enver was a major, Kemal a senior captain, and both had taken
part in the secret political activities of the Young Turk movement.
In 1911-1912 both volunteered for assignments in Libya; and both
served as military attachés, Enver in Berlin in 1909-1911, Kemal in
Sofia in 1913-1914. Each of them, moreover, at the time of his rise
to power, was surrounded by personages like himself—Enver by men
of pride and high courage like Cemal, Hafız Hakkı, and his uncle
Halil (Kut), Kemal by circumspect and tenacious officers like Orbay,
Cebesoy, and Karabekir—who might have taken their places in their
absence. Why was it that a man like Enver rose to power in the moribund multinational empire of 1908 and a man like Kemal after the
collapse of 1918?

The historical situation clearly exercised a subtle and decisive se-
lectivity. The empire of 1908 was a loose dynastic structure with a
population half Muslim and half Christian and only two-fifths Turkish. The political program of the Young Turks, which envisaged
welding this congeries into a modern nation-state, posed a task that
would have exceeded Kemal's powers as well as Enver's. Yet the

---

[12] In the judgment of General Liman, his superior at the Dardanelles and in
Syria and an observer notably sparing with praise of his Turkish colleagues (O.V.K.
Liman von Sanders, *Five Years in Turkey*, Annapolis, 1927, pp. 85, 264).
[13] Atay, *Zeytindağı*, 3rd edn., Istanbul, 1943. The author was chief journalistic
spokesman for Cemal Pasha in Syria and for Kemal in the 1920's.

Young Turk leaders could not have been expected, any more than Winston Churchill, to preside over the dissolution of their empire; nor would their followers have tolerated such a course. A desperate situation called for desperate leadership. The visions of future glory —the romantic illusions of Pan-Turkism or Pan-Islam—wished away the flaws of the existing empire. Yet by their very lack of realism the Young Turks hastened the Ottoman collapse and forced a way out of the historic impasse. There then remained the grimly realistic task of reconstruction within a greatly reduced but nationally more homogeneous territory—a task for which Kemal was prepared by temperament and the populace by the experience of overwhelming defeat.

In their more purposeful intervals the Young Turks themselves had prepared a groundwork for the national resurgence of the early 1920's. Under their aegis, major issues of social and cultural policy were debated with seriousness and imagination in the rapidly proliferating daily and weekly press, so that the only task required of Kemal a decade later was to pick a single feasible program out of the turmoil of existing ideas. (It has often been noted that Kemal's reform program was forecast almost item by item in the utopia described by the Young Turk publicist Abdullah Cevdet in 1912.) The extension of Union and Progress Party activity to all major towns of the empire, furthermore, made possible the Defense of Rights and People's Party movements later on. And the Young Turk guerrilla activities on the Balkans before 1908, in Western Thrace in 1913, and in Libya and the Caucasus in 1914-1918 provided experienced personnel for the War of Independence when all of Anatolia had become an irredenta. In short, the Young Turks' resounding failures hastened the dismantling of the ramshackle empire; their quiet accomplishments laid the foundation for the new national structure.

During the period of nationalist reconstruction, the populace quickly became politically active. To draw one illustration from many, Kemal at the time of an impending cabinet change early in March of 1920 asked all his followers in Anatolia to wire the sultan and the House of Representatives to press for the appointment of a pro-nationalist government. Within the next three days, 217 cables were received by the House alone, from Defense of Rights Societies, army commanders, muftis, teachers, and town councils throughout Anatolia;[14] on the second day the desired cabinet was formed. When Sir Andrew Ryan, the

---

[14] They are reprinted in *Meclis-i Mebusan Zabıt Ceridesi*, Dördüncü Devre-i İntihabiye, pp. 253-291 (appendix to minutes of session of March 6, 1920).

British government's last accredited representative to the sultan, cleared out his office in 1923, he regretfully discarded a heap of such telegrams and letters, kept in what he aptly called the "*vox populi* sack."[15]

To evaluate the performance of General Gürsel's National Unity Committee of 1960-1961 in similar terms is premature. Its immediate goal—the overthrow of Menderes' oppressive government—was achieved within a few hours before dawn, and the promised return to constitutional and civilian rule within seventeen months. But the Menderes government, by stirring the peasant population into greater political activity, had helped bring into the open age-old differences between the urban population and the rural and had shifted elective power to a stratum little concerned over constitutional niceties. The success of the Second Republic will depend, politically, on the feasibility of cabinet government under proportional representation and, socially and culturally, on the gradual closing of this urban-rural gap. And its success or failure will determine whether the military, having assumed the role of constitutional guardians in 1960-1961 and being urged by certain impatient officers to become authoritarian social reformers as well, will remain on the sidelines or will again become politically involved.

EXEUNT SOLDIERS (QUOUSQUE TANDEM?)

The performance of the military in politics and their subsequent withdrawal depend in large part upon the relations which they establish with civilian groups. In 1908 and 1919 these relations were intimate from the start: The Society of Union and Progress originated as a civilian-military conspiracy, and the Kemalist movement consisted of a wide civilian base of Defense of Right Societies (themselves largely a Union-and-Progress legacy) crowned with a military apex. The National Unity Committee of 1960, by contrast, was a purely military group. Widespread discontent with Menderes among educated persons provided enthusiastic initial support for the revolution. In fact, the military conspirators, after some years of preparation, were impelled to act when university riots had brought the issue to a head. But İnönü, as leader of the opposition People's Party, had staunchly refused from democratic principle to participate in the coup or to be brought to power by means of it; and the law professors whom the junta hastily shepherded to Ankara on the morrow of the revolu-

[15] Sir Andrew Ryan, *The Last of the Dragomans*, London, 1951, p. 226.

tion proved inexpert in the ways of practical politics. Only with the appointment of a constituent assembly and a civilian cabinet in the winter of 1960-1961 did the military regime create for itself a firmer civilian base.

Both the 1908 and 1960 coups proceeded upon what may be called the one-shot theory of military intervention. Both times the military began by pursuing limited, specific political ends without any intent to install themselves in permanent power. The 1908 revolutionaries at first succeeded; the constitution they wished to restore had been written thirty-two years before and had even been hypocritically reprinted in Abdülhamid's government almanac in each succeeding year. But the single shot, as it turned out, had had to be followed by what we might call boosters—in 1909 and 1913. In 1908 the military stayed in their barracks; the civilian Unionists threw themselves into the election campaign, though entering the cabinet in sizable numbers only after the "Thirty-First of March" of 1909. From 1908 to 1913 nevertheless, military action or the threat of it became the only means of producing governmental change; the first coup had created a "breeder reactor" of revolutionary action. Not until the Sublime Porte Incident of 1913 did the leaders of the new conspiracy assume positions of official power. The 1960 revolutionaries insisted from the start on a new constitution and were somewhat surprised that the learned jurists were unable to produce one from their desk drawers or at least contrive one within a month. As a result, the return to civilian rule, which the junta had promised within a few months, was delayed over a year. In the interval, the proponents of such a restoration had won a narrow victory over those who had shifted to advocacy of prolonged military rule. In 1919, Mustafa Kemal saw a long and fundamental task ahead—a task of which the military facet was to secure national independence and the civil facet to create a new state. Significantly, the responsible performance of this long-range task made possible a quicker withdrawal of the military from the political stage than did the piecemeal interventions of 1908-1919.[16]

Although unfinished business is likely to keep the military in power longer than they first intended, military rule in a modern state engenders its own pressures for the separation of political affairs from

[16] John Marlowe makes a corresponding observation on the British military intervention in Egypt in 1882—which was meant to be temporary but took seventy years to liquidate. A "permanent" occupation, he suggests, could have terminated sooner. (*A History of Modern Egypt and Anglo-Egyptian Relations*, New York, 1954, p. 253.)

military. It is virtually impossible for military officers to remain in command of their battalions and regiments while running a cabinet ministry or party organization. Soon after the 1908 revolution, the Union and Progress movement explicitly required its party inspectors to resign their military commissions. The splits that are likely to arise among the revolutionary soldiery provide further pressure for a separation. In 1911-1912, for example, there was a contest for party leadership between Ali Fethi (Okyar), who had just retired as a lieutenant colonel, and Talât, supported by Enver and other officers. One senses in the proposals of this period for military abstention from politics an underlying desire of each faction to exclude its rivals from the arena. Turkey's first sweeping law forbidding the participation of the military in politics (which went so far as to deprive soldiers and officers on active duty of their franchise) was passed by the Unionists in response to the abortive Savior Officers' uprising of 1912. Early in 1914, Enver presided over a purge of elderly generals whose ineptitude had contributed to the Balkan War defeat—and many of these were to reappear as members of the Istanbul governments of 1919-1922.

During the Young Turk period, also, the military were placed firmly under the constitutional control of the legislature. One of the most serious clashes between Abdülhamid and the new parliament of 1908 occurred when the sultan claimed the privilege of personally selecting the two service ministers. The parliamentary majority insisted that the army and navy ministers must be nominated by the Grand Vezir and thereby kept subject to the cabinet's collective responsibility to the legislature. While the two military posts in the cabinet were in fact filled by former officers for several more decades, these served in a political capacity and were above the military command structure rather than within it. We may recall the sharply contrasting issue of the Japanese constitutional crisis of 1913. From 1908 to 1924 the Turkish war minister was the superior of the chief of the general staff; after 1924 the two were in roughly coordinate positions. Turkey in the Young Turk years hence conformed more closely than Japan to Western constitutional principles. And if she also experienced more *coups d'état* and other forms of military interference, we might observe that Japanese officers, who could calmly dictate to the civilian cabinet, had no need—as did Enver's band in 1913—to shoot its members.

In the Kemalist revolution, many developments contributed to the

379

eventual separation of military from civilian affairs. Kemal's close associate, Hüseyin Rauf (Orbay) had resigned from the navy in the spring of 1919 to preserve his political freedom of action in Anatolia. Somewhat later, the Istanbul military authorities, as part of their secret cooperation with the nationalist movement, strictly forbade the formation of any societies among officers—a move directed against such groups as the "Military Guardian Society" (*Nigehban Cem'iyet-i Askeriyesi*) and the "Red Dagger Society" (*Kızıl Hançer Cem'iyeti*) which were supporting the collaborationist tendencies of Istanbul politicians.

"In July 1919, Kemal, having exhausted all subterfuge in resisting the Istanbul government's orders to return to the capital, had announced his resignation from the army. He forthrightly stated that he had found that to continue his beloved military career would hinder him in his service to the nation, and that he therefore would continue the struggle 'in the bosom of the nation as an individual fighter for the cause.' The immediate practical effect of this step was only slight: both Kâzım Karabekir, whom Istanbul had designated as his replacement, and other commanders continued to follow his directives; and soon the Erzurum and Sıvas congresses, by making Kemal the head of their Representative Committee, placed him in effect, at the head of a provisional nationalist government. But the moral significance of Kemal's decision was immense. It testified to his conviction that an army career was not an end in itself, but must at every point be subordinated to wider considerations of service to the nation; and that a time might come when political and military functions could not legitimately or effectively be combined in the same person.

"Somewhat later, in December 1920, the arrogance and insubordination of Çerkes Edhem, commander of the nationalists' irregular cavalry, precipitated a showdown with the regular army. The result was the complete integration of these guerrilla forces into the army's more disciplined command structure. Edhem's subsequent treason did much to destroy the legend of the *komitadji*—half bandit and half national hero—which the early Kemalists had inherited from the Macedonian Young Turk movement and which, while its spell lasted, blurred any dividing line between civilian and military authority.

"The Grand National Assembly of 1920-1923 included a large number of higher officers on active duty, but in practice they were kept fully occupied at the front or at headquarters in Ankara. Kemal's energies, on the other hand, were largely devoted to careful maneuvering in the proud, faction-ridden, and intractable Assembly. Only during the critical phases of the military contest with Greece did Kemal, at the Assembly's insistence, assume personal direction of operations, and the cautious legislators in each case renewed his powers as Commander in Chief for only three months."[17]

Finally, during the formation of the Progressive Republican Party of 1924, Kemal (as we have seen) forced men like Ali Fuad (Cebesoy) and Kâzım Karabekir to choose between their military commands and parliamentary seats, and obtained passage of a law barring the candidacy of any officers not resigning their commissions two months or more before election.

In 1960-1961, the anomaly of majors and lieutenant-colonels on the National Unity Committee issuing, in their political capacity, orders to officers of higher rank gave rise to considerable friction. Two remedies were devised. First, the National Unity Committee announced the retirement of most generals on active service and of a majority of the colonels. Second, the 1961 constitution gave ex-officio senate seats to the members of the committee, who had meanwhile relinquished their military commands. This sorting out of functions did not, however, remove the threat of interference in politics by officers who remained at their military posts—as witness the buzzing of the capital by the air force in the summer of 1961 in protest against the threatened removal of its chief and the abortive cadets' coups of February 1962 and May 1963.

The separation of military and civilian functions in 1923-1924 was sanctioned by a basic agreement among the highest ranking and most prestigious military leaders, of whom two severed their formal connection with the army to assume the highest civilian governmental posts and the third retained unhampered control of the military establishment. Kemal, voted the title of *gazi* (victor) after the decisive battle on the Sakarya (September 1921), became president; İsmet, the victor of İnönü, premier; and Fevzi Çakmak, chief of staff from 1921 to 1944. The military undertook to remain aloof from politics; in return, the chief of staff under a law of March 1924 gave up his cabinet membership and acquired immunity from direct parliamentary control. The withdrawal of the military from politics was achieved in sum by command of General Headquarters in return for a reciprocal withdrawal of politicians from military affairs.

[17] Quoted from my article on "The Army and the Founding of the Turkish Republic," *World Politics*, Vol. XI, No. 4, July 1959, pp. 546f.

The arrangement was recommended by the sobering experience of the Young Turk period and especially of Enver's wartime regime, which had made advancement in the army contingent on political intrigue, subordinated strategy to ideological romanticism, and laid the civil administration open to constant interference by military personnel; these policies had led at once to bureaucratic corruption and military defeat. Kemal was presumably reflecting upon this experience in a part of his *Six-Day Speech* of 1927 wherein he reviewed his differences eight years earlier with the nationalist commander in Thrace:

"Commanders, while thinking of and carrying out the duties and requirements of the army, must beware of letting their minds be influenced by political considerations. They must not forget that there are other officials whose duty it is to think of the requirements of the political side.

"While leading the children of the fatherland and the material means of the country that have been entrusted to their orders against the enemy and toward death, commanders must think of only one thing—to perform and fulfill the patriotic duty that the nation expects from them with gunfire, with bayonet, and in death. Military duty can only be performed in this spirit and conviction. With talk and politicking a soldier's duty cannot be done. . . ."[18]

The memory of the defeat of 1914-1918 and the victory of 1919-1923 lent cogency to this plea. No less essential to the early retirement of the army from politics was Kemal's longstanding ability, exemplified by the founding of the People's Party, to create a potent civilian instrument for the formulation of national policy. In Turkey as elsewhere it has been the weakness of civilian institutions which has brought the military onto the political stage. The experiences of 1908, 1919, and 1960 all indicate that their withdrawal from that stage depends not on the sincerity with which they espouse the "one-shot theory" of intervention but on their ability to find remedies for the weaknesses in civil government. In the absence of such remedies, they may temporarily leave the scene, but they can be expected to remain hovering in the wings. Clemenceau once said that warfare was too important a matter to be left to the generals. If the political stalemate that characterized the first year of the Second Republic should continue, Turkish generals and colonels may again decide that statecraft is too crucial a matter to be left to politicians.

[18] *Nutuk, op.cit.*, ii, 43.

VI. The Military in the Modern Social and Cultural Setting

The most important steps toward modernization that Turkey took under military leadership were the definition of the territorial limits within which national integration was to take place and the induction of new social classes into the political process. The very failure of the Young Turks to hold the weakened empire together sped the process of territorial redefinition, just as their self-contradictory ideological posturing—Pan-Islamic, Pan-Turkish, Ottoman, Western, or Nationalistic—accentuated the fundamental issues. During the Young Turk period, also, daily journalism, political rallies, and party organization in the major towns became accepted features of political life. The administration was reorganized and a tighter central control imposed—although for the time being this control was one-sidedly partisan. Wartime exigencies led to a first systematic attempt at government regulation of the economy to cope with the opposite pressures of military procurement and civilian needs in the face of rising prices. Partisan favoritism in the award of economic contracts brought about transfers of commercial enterprise from non-Muslim to Muslim Turkish hands. Political and economic changes thus were creating, in the capital and in the provincial centers, a new political class made up of army officers, teachers, journalists, civil servants, and entrepreneurs.

The contributions of the Atatürk period to political modernization were immense and crucial. In the War of Independence the state, once dynastic, multi-national, and religious, was rebuilt upon nationalist, secular, and republican lines. A decade of warfare (1911–1922) gave to the peasant recruit some vision of political entities beyond his narrow village horizon. Defense of the homeland provided for the first time in Turkish history a task around which all social classes could rally. The more progressive elements in the urban-educated class fought for fatherland and nation (*vatan ve millet*), the more conservative leaders and the peasantry rallied around faith and dynasty (*din ve devlet*); but everyone somehow rallied and fought. The resulting social and national unity was reflected in the first National Assembly of 1920, which represented a wider social and ideological spectrum than any other, Ottoman or republican, until at least 1950. Victory on the battlefield over European foes, moreover, provided self-assurance that facilitated the wholesale acceptance of European ways.

The republican period brought a consolidation of the political elite within the Republican People's party. During the 1920's, military officers who had accompanied Kemal into civilian life played an important role within the executive and legislative branches of government. In the 1930's there was a gradual shift toward younger bureaucrats trained in the European fashion in the early Kemalist period. In the 1940's, physicians, lawyers, businessmen, and others from outside the narrow government circle became more prominent in civic affairs. The peasants, upon the reestablishment of dictatorial control in the 1920's, largely relapsed into their former passivity. Only with the intensive agricultural development since the 1940's did prosperous peasants in the countryside, and the ex-peasants migrating to the cities, become very directly involved in the political process.

That energetic military leadership was essential to national survival in the War of Independence is obvious. Only the army among all agencies of leadership then available could have established unity inside the country and redefined national goals. Only a victorious military hero could have imposed the territorial self-limitation of the National Pact of 1919-1920. The rapidity of legal and cultural reforms in the 1920's and 1930's also reflects the decisiveness of a militarily trained leadership. The converse of this energy and impatience was a predilection for legal fiat and a relative unconcern with the execution and the popular acceptance of the reforms. (It was this lag between formal proclamation and popular acceptance which was to haunt Turkey during the competitive political period of the 1950's and which required the renewed intervention of the military in 1960.) In economic affairs, there was a similar preoccupation with autarky, with transport, and with industrialization in strategically safe rather than economically profitable locations.

The military in the 1960's are caught between two conflicting roles, one envisaged for them by men like Cemal Gürsel, the other by men like Alparslan Türkeş. In the first view, the Turkish people are considered, on balance, mature enough to govern themselves by democratic processes, the military needing to step in only briefly, as in 1960, when democracy is threatened. In the second view, dynamic and authoritarian leadership is required to secure social justice, mass education, and economic development; since bickering politicians are incapable of such leadership, the military must provide it. Kemalist tradition and principles can be invoked in support either of military self-abnegation or of authoritarian reform. The choice between these depends largely on a complex and intuitive assessment of social realities and prospects.

Even during periods when the military had withdrawn from the central political stage, as from 1923 to 1960, indirect military influence was palpable throughout the political system. The principal political leaders of the War of Independence and the First Republic were men of military background—Presidents Atatürk and İnönü, prime ministers İnönü, Fethi Okyar, and Refik Saydam, party secretary Recep Peker. Well into the 1940's the ministers of defense were regularly drawn from among ex-officers, as were very frequently also the ministers of public works, communication, and interior. In the early 1920's, many corps and division commanders doubled as provincial governors, and during extensive periods of martial law (in Kürdistan after 1925, in Istanbul during the Second World War, and in major cities after the 1955 riots) civilian administration was taken over by the armed forces. After 1924, moreover, the chief of the general staff was removed from the cabinet and thus from ministerial control. As we have seen, this independence of the military establishment from political control was the price for the withdrawal of the military from the rest of the political scene.

Together with the political activities of officers and ex-officers, universal military training has exercised a pervasive modernizing influence. Of all low-income countries in the world today Turkey has one of the most comprehensive conscription systems. Though the period of military duty was reduced from five years in the mid-nineteenth century to two and more recently one and a half years,[19] the effectiveness of the draft has been concomitantly increased. And for the average Turkish boy in the Anatolian village, the call to military service provides a first occasion for coming into contact with the outside world, and acquiring at least some breadth of outlook. Service in the army, moreover, constitutes a common experience for the entire male population of Turkey.

The officer corps, as we saw, provided a national channel of merit advancement. During the nineteenth century, the military academy became a place where impecunious youngsters could prepare for a career giving access to the highest positions in society. There is, however, one important limitation upon such advancement. Limited opportunities in primary education have sharply restricted access to all

[19] The term of service was fixed at three years by a law of January 21, 1942, at two years on July 12, 1950 (see Gotthard Jäschke, *Die Türkei in den Jahren 1942-1951*, Wiesbaden, 1955, pp. 2, 125).

professions, including the military. The years of "middle school" (*orta okul*) and high school (*lise*) still remain the major social divide. The village or small-town parents who can send their boy to twelve years of school have given him the means of entering the upper class. For the brighter *lise* graduates, government scholarships cover room and board for four years of undergraduate university education—repayable by a fixed number of years of public service as judge, teacher, army officer, or government official of some sort. Two years of service are usually demanded for each year of scholarship aid. In recent years, moreover, there have been increasing opportunities in private enterprises, which, on behalf of the able young graduate, will sometimes repay the government in cash. But the village parents who rely on their young son for help in the fields, or have no means of sending him to the faraway town where the school is located, will see him remain in their own lowly condition. Beyond the *lise* barrier, there is considerable social mobility; on its hither side, little or none as yet.

The army hierarchy itself reflects this basic class division. The officers are gentlemen, members of the urban educated class. The recruits are peasant boys subject to barked commands without back talk. The seating arrangements in the public conveyances of Istanbul symbolize this traditional caste system. All uniformed personnel are entitled to reduced fares. But in street cars and ferry boats, officers ride in the upholstered and spacious first class, whereas the non-commissioned ranks must herd together on the wooden and often vermin-infested benches of the second class.[20]

The latest wave of cultural change under military auspices—that initiated by the post-war U.S. aid program—is beginning to affect these traditional patterns. Whereas the reforms of Selim III and Mahmud II gave the new officer corps access to Western learning, the current program of military service gives a measure of modern technological training to the privates as well. Conversely, there are foretokens of a reduction in the social status of the officer corps. Prestigious opportunities in such fields as engineering and business compete increasingly with an army career. And whereas earnings in private enterprise keep in step with inflation or ahead of it, the fixed salaries of officers, as of other public servants, have steadily declined in purchasing power. Upon American advice, the armed forces have further adopted regulations allowing qualified sergeants to enter the

[20] Buses, however, have only a single class—and these provide the only public transportation in Ankara and other major cities, and since the 1950's have replaced the street cars of Istanbul.

officer corps.[21] Though little use has as yet been made of this opportunity, it is an augury of the future.

Nowhere are the rapid changes in mid-twentieth-century Turkish culture as sharply reflected as in the experience of the army recruit. Back in the village, the ideals of manly courage and martial valor are inculcated in him at a tender age. "A future pasha!" is a common compliment to the mother of a new-born male. "A soldier doesn't cry," the tearful toddler is admonished. Circumcision, commonly administered without anesthesia at age seven or nine, is considered an early test of courage for the future soldier. And a threat that "The Moskovs will get you" keeps the rebellious youngster in line. Once in the army, the recruit is transferred abruptly from the technology of the stick-plow and the ox-cart to that of the jeep, the automatic rifle, and the armored car. Nor is this training limited to military and technical skills. Since the late 1950's fully half the recruits have been given intensive courses in reading and writing (devised in part by an American technical assistance team), in arithmetic, and in social studies. A *New York Times* correspondent reported the following colloquy in one of the first literacy classes:

"What will you be if you do not learn to read and write?" asked the teacher.

"Privates," chorused the class.

"And what will you become if you study hard and learn your lessons?" pursued the teacher.

"Corporals and sergeants," the class answered enthusiastically.[22]

The technological training given by the army further supports recent efforts at farm mechanization and rural development. The enterprising draftee returning to his village may become the founder of the first mechanical repair shop or garage.

The Turkish army represents at one and the same time an element of historical continuity and a dynamic modernizing force. Its tradition, as we have seen, goes back to Osman, the Prophet Muhammad and the Central Asian nomads, as well as to Selim III, the Tanzimat, the Young Turks and the formative period of the present Turkish

---

[21] There had been occasional promotion from the ranks until Abdülhamid's time. Şemsi Pasha, for example, whose assassination in Manastir set off the 1908 Revolution, had risen from the ranks. But under the training system taken over from Germany in the late nineteenth century, the military schools and the Staff College provided the only entry into the officer corps.

[22] Quoted by Daniel Lerner and Richard D. Robinson, "Swords and Ploughshares: The Turkish Army as a Modernizing Force," *World Politics*, Vol. 13, No. 1, October 1960, p. 36.

nation-state. The armed forces were the most important single legacy which the Ottoman Empire bequeathed to the Turkish Republic. (For example, fully 93 per cent of the empire's general staff officers continued their service in Turkey, and only 7 per cent in the other successor states.[23]) By virtue of that fact, Mustafa Kemal's efforts to build up a new nation had an incalculable advantage over parallel efforts in Syria and Iraq. Atatürk's individual reputation as a radical cultural innovator is amply justified. Yet his combined role as military leader, state builder, and chief educator fitted perfectly into the great Ottoman tradition of Mehmed II and Süleyman I.

The continuing disparity between town and country which the social upheaval of the 1950's has brought to the fore pervades the entire culture including the military establishment; and, since 1960, the army has again assumed the obligation of dealing with the political perplexities attending cultural change. The future of both army and society depend largely on a resolution of the differences between villager and townsman which are in a general way the differences between tradition and modernity.

[23] By contrast, the republic inherited only 85% of the empire's trained civil servants. These figures are based on the summaries of careers of the alumni of the General Staff College and of the Civil Service School contained respectively in Muharrem Mazlum (İskora), *Erkaniharbiye Mektebi ve Harp Akademisi Tarihçesi*, Istanbul, 1930, and Ali Çankaya, *Mülkiye Tarihi ve Mülkiyeliler*, 2 vols., Ankara, 1954. I am indebted for the relevant calculations to Mrs. Krystyna Smays Samurovich. Details will appear in my forthcoming study of twentieth-century Turkish politics.

CHAPTER 9

POLITICAL LEADERSHIP AND POLITICAL PARTIES

~~~~~~

A. JAPAN

NOBUTAKA IKE

~~~~~~

I. Parties and Modernization

THOUGH politics itself is as old as man, political parties are of relatively recent vintage. Even in the Western world, they date back only some hundred and fifty years, and in Asia they make their appearance still later. The late emergence is to be explained by their debt to the idea of democracy. Today enough nations have either achieved a degree of democracy or had to deal with democracy in some way, so that parties have become a characteristic feature of government. It is hard to imagine a truly "modern" government, even a totalitarian one, operating without political parties.

Before we enter into a discussion of the role of parties in political modernization, it might be useful to set down what appear to be their salient characteristics. First of all, they are groups of persons united for the purpose of getting their leaders into positions of influence in the government. Second, although those who acquire office obtain material rewards, the party as a whole at least purports to embrace policies which will promote the interest of the public at large. Third, parties are not ephemeral or ad hoc organizations; they are relatively stable and enduring. Fourth, at least in democratic regimes, they open their membership to the public, and must solicit and obtain support from important sectors of the public if they are to fulfill their aims. Finally, they are quite often coalitions rather than monolithic organizations, and this feature sometimes enables them to effect compromises among conflicting interests in the society.

If these are their attributes, then certain conditions must be met before they can come into being. In many of the older societies of Asia, most of the people were peasant farmers, and social organization rested on kinship and other immediate personal relationships. In such societies, the recruitment of political leaders was governed by consideration of caste or class. Eligibility for office was usually inherited, the bonds of unity within the ruling class hence being partly familial. The duties of the peasants to their government consisted chiefly of paying taxes and providing free labor. Although, in the villages, the daily operation of government was often in the hands of local leaders, the notion that peasants might have some say in selecting provincial or national officials or in determining the policies these men should pursue was not entertained.

Everywhere modernization has produced far-reaching changes in the traditional social and political structure. First of all, the relationship between the elite and the subject population has been modified. The elite group itself has been reconstituted, the principle having been adopted, at least in theory, that political careers should be "open to talent." In modern states, membership in the government elite is acquired through competition rather than conferred by birth.

Second, subjects have become transformed into "citizens." In premodern agrarian societies, ordinary persons were never expected to involve themselves in political concerns extending beyond the boundaries of their own villages. The citizens of modern states, by contrast, are expected precisely to become so involved. Even though the average man may still not actively participate in national decisions, the duties of citizenship now require him to be interested in national politics and well-informed concerning it.

Third, modernization has invariably transformed the economic system. Agriculture has given way to commerce and industry. The peasant, or his offspring, have forsaken the villages in which they were born and migrated to the cities. Economic specialization and regional differentiation have created well-defined interest groups, which have sought expression through political organization. The result is political conflict which must be resolved somehow if the body politic is not to be torn asunder.

It is precisely in these areas—the recruitment of leaders, political mobilization, and the accommodation of disparate interests—that political parties play a crucial role. Once political leadership ceases to be hereditary, there must be some other arrangement for deciding who should occupy the positions of power; one instrument of such decision is the political party. The party can also relate individual citizens to the political system, at once providing an arena for political action and reaching the less active citizens through political education and propaganda. Finally, political parties can often serve as a means of bringing about accommodation among competing interest groups. It is evident that political parties are a "modern" phenomenon and provide, indeed, a kind of index of political modernity.

II. The Origin of Japanese Parties

THE HISTORICAL MILIEU

There appear to be no prototypes of political parties in Japanese history. Parties represented an innovation, coming into being, first, as a direct result of Western influences, and, second, in response to the program of modernization carried forward by the Meiji government. Hence parties were quite clearly products of their milieu, and it is perhaps useful at the outset to state, in summary fashion, the principal historical developments affecting party growth.

(1) According to tradition, the aim of government was to achieve and maintain social harmony throughout the land. Persons forming groups for the purpose of political action—even for submitting, let us say, a petition to the authorities to redress a grievance—were likely to be treated harshly, on the ground that they were a divisive influence and disturbed that harmony. In the early Meiji period, however, many of the stringent regulations of the Tokugawa regime were relaxed. Accordingly, when a small group of intellectuals who had studied Western governments, either at first hand or in literary sources, decided to establish in their own country organizations resembling the political parties of the West, they were not considered to be engaging in an illegal enterprise. They nevertheless aroused a certain hostility because, in the face of a tradition that prized harmony, they seemed to be promoting political division. Initially, then, parties had the problem of establishing their moral right to exist; although they now have a rather long history, it is still not certain that they have fully convinced everyone of their legitimate place in the political system.

(2) The decision of the Meiji elite to modernize the country rested on a desire for national prestige and power. The desire to make Japan a potent force in the international community was shared, moreover, by many persons and groups outside the ruling circles. There was little disagreement over the purpose of modernization between the elite in control of the central government and political outsiders such as the "local" elite to be discussed later.

(3) There were, however, certain occasions for disagreement, both *within* the elite, and *between* the elite and other parts of the population.

391

(a) A fundamental problem within the elite was the fate of the samurai as a privileged warrior class. Toward the end of the Tokugawa period, the samurai had suffered economic deprivation, partly because of the near bankruptcy of their patrons, the feudal nobility. The situation worsened under the new Meiji government. The new regime, although controlled by men of samurai origin, decided to liquidate the samurai class. Being dedicated to a far-reaching program of modernization, the Meiji government could not afford to divert sorely needed funds to the maintenance of any large unproductive class; moreover, a class of hereditary warriors trained in the art of swordsmanship was something of an anachronism in an era in which conscript armies had come into being. To facilitate the transition of the samurai to the status of commoners, the state first provided them with pensions, and later commuted these pensions into lump sums. In most cases, however, such aid was inadequate, and although some samurai managed to find careers in the new government, in the armed forces, in the professions, or in commerce, many of them suffered both economic and psychological hardships. On several occasions, groups of disaffected samurai openly rebelled against the government. When in 1877 the government armies put down the last and most serious of these rebellions—the Satsuma rebellion—the attempts to oppose the new regime by force came to an end.

A second conflict within the elite arose from competition for high office. The Restoration had been achieved by a coalition of young samurai leaders from four feudal principalities—Satsuma, Chōshū, Tosa, and Hizen. As might be expected, the important positions in the new government came to be monopolized by men from these areas; and the preponderance of power was wielded by a small group from Satsuma and Chōshū. The growth of a Satsuma-Chōshū clique led to growing dissatisfaction among men from the lesser areas, especially Tosa. Such dissatisfaction eventually found expression in the formation of political societies dedicated to changing the political structure of the country.

(b) The struggle between the elite and the non-elite had several sources. First of all, there were the questions of who would bear the cost of modernization and who would reap its benefits. Since modernization in Japan was financed largely by the internal resources of the nation, agriculture was compelled to bear, at least in the beginning, a disproportionately heavy burden. The peasants found the government taxing their land at a high rate but conferring no comparable benefits upon them, a good part of their money being used to build industries in the towns and cities.

A second source of resentment was military conscription. Modernization entailed the development of a new army and navy conscripted from the male population at large. Although the samurai class before the Restoration had considered military service a privilege, the sons of a peasant were not gratified by the forcible extension of that privilege to themselves.

A third issue was related to the methods by which the central government carried out its program of modernization. As in many developing areas today, the government was impatient for results and abhorred the time-consuming processes of consultation, deliberation, and compromise. The members of the government class were often dictatorial and arbitrary, therefore, and aroused the resentment of the general public.

(4) The resentment deriving from official arrogance, economic deprivation, and other sources found expression in a national movement for political liberty and a legislative assembly. Since these fundamental issues bore upon the structure of government and were of crucial importance to the entire future course of Japanese politics, they were heatedly discussed. It was clear to almost everyone that the traditional governmental structure was inadequate to the requirements of a modern nation and that Japan was in as serious need of political modernization as of military and economic. Given the national mood of the times, which was receptive to everything Western, and given also the power yielded by Great Britain in world affairs, it was natural that Japanese intellectuals first turned to the British parliamentary model.

In the 1860's and 1870's Japanese students of British government had at best a superficial understanding of the inner workings of British politics, but they were all aware of the existence of that parliamentary assembly wherein laws were discussed and enacted. The concept of an assembly was further appealing because it promised to resolve certain problems inherent in coalition movements, dispelling fears, in particular, that one or two members of the coalition might dominate the others. If Japan had a national assembly in which the various classes and factions were represented, the problem of unity might be solved. In 1868, therefore, shortly after it came into existence, the Meiji government promulgated the well-known "Charter Oath of Five Articles." This was a document proclaiming in the name of the em-

393

peror that "assemblies shall be widely convoked and all measures shall be decided by open discussion." Shortly thereafter a bicameral assembly was formed, but it soon proved unworkable. In subsequent years, a variety of other assemblies were created at local and prefectural levels. These assemblies, though never acquiring much power, kept alive the principle that governmental policies should be "decided by open discussion."

POLITICAL SOCIETIES IN TOSA

One of the first political societies in Japan was the Patriotic Public Party (*Aikoku Kōtō*) established in Kōchi Prefecture in January 1873. It is interesting that the founders of this society used the terms "patriotic" and "public." Because of the traditional antipathy toward "factions," they apparently felt it necessary to proclaim to the general public and to the authorities that they were establishing a "public party" and not a secret clique, a patriotic and not a subversive organization. Indeed, in their declaration of principles, they further stressed that they "loved their monarch and they loved their country." A somewhat later society, also formed in Kōchi, was the Achieving One's Aim Society (*Risshisha*), which eventually became nationally known. The members of these two societies, incidentally, were almost all ex-samurai.

The leader of both was Itagaki Taisuke, a prominent samurai from Tosa. He had participated in the Restoration movement against the Tokugawa forces and had subsequently been given a post as councillor in the new government. He seems to have resented the growing power of the Satsuma-Chōshū clique, however, for he resigned from the government in 1875 when a split occurred within the elite over the issue of war with Korea. After resigning, Itagaki returned to his native province, Tosa (now called Kōchi Prefecture), and, gathering other disaffected samurai around him, formed the political societies named. Using these organizations as a basis, he and his associates next submitted a memorial to the central government urging it to honor its commitment to establish a national assembly. The memorial charged that a few officials in the government were guilty of making arbitrary decisions, and it went on to argue that the creation of a popularly elected assembly would help to unite the government and the people, and would thereby strengthen the nation. The government responded to the memorial with the argument that the time was not ripe for such an assembly. Itagaki's efforts hence fell short of their immediate aims.

But the memorial did have certain effects. It made the creation of a representative assembly a national issue, and thereby stimulated the formation of other political societies. What started out as a local movement among disaffected ex-samurai eventually assumed national proportions, involving, as time went on, fewer and fewer samurai and more and more of those rural leaders who constituted a "local elite" in their areas. In the next section we shall take a look at developments in rural Fukushima prefecture.

THE CASE OF FUKUSHIMA PREFECTURE

Fukushima Prefecture lies in northern Japan, rather remote from Tosa, the birthplace of Japanese parties; but it, too, perhaps stimulated by the example of Tosa, felt the stirrings of political ferment. Initially the Fukushima movement owed a great deal to the leadership of one man, Kōno Hironaka (Banshū), who was later to achieve a national political reputation. Kōno was born into a *gōshi* or "country samurai" family, which had become rather successful in business, purveying dry goods and wholesale fish and brewing sake. As a young man, Kōno participated in the Restoration movement on the imperial side, and was later appointed to a minor post in a local government. In the 1870's he became exposed to Western political thought, particularly the writings of John Stuart Mill, which apparently encouraged him to form political societies in his native prefecture.

Very few of Kōno's associates in these enterprises were members of the samurai class. In the main, the leaders of the Fukushima political societies and parties came, like Kōno himself, from prominent local families. These families typically owned either farmland or small-scale business enterprises, such as silk factories or both. Their scions were what Duverger has called "notabilities" and we have here the beginnings of what he would call caucus parties.

Of course not all locally prominent families joined these political societies. As among the samurai elite nationally, divisions sometimes occurred within the ranks of the local elite. What caused such splits is not altogether clear. We do know that a few locally prominent families tended to monopolize positions of leadership in their communities, and one may speculate that other families, perhaps just rising to prominence, chose to lead or support the newly created societies.

395

These brief remarks will serve as a preface for the consideration of the *Sekiyosha,* the first society formed in Fukushima by Kōno. The head-quarters of the *Sekiyosha* were located in the village of Ishikawa in Ishikawa-gun. All of its officers, including Kōno, who was named president, were commoners. It boasted a membership of about 200, most of them peasants who lived in the area.[1]

The declaration of principles which the society immediately made public is noteworthy in several respects. First of all, it contains the assertion that heaven has endowed man with certain immutable and eternal gifts, namely, vigor, self-reliance, and liberty.

Second, it argues that governments come into being only when there is first a people, and that the people create government in order to achieve tranquillity. This idea, which appears to have been borrowed from Rousseau's concept of the social contract, was a denial of the accepted view that, in Japan, the ancestors of the imperial family had appeared first and that their descendants had become their subjects. In short, the declaration argued for popular sovereignty and against imperial sovereignty.

Third, the founders of the *Sekiyosha* argued that a government which denied political freedom sapped the energies of the people and weakened the international position of the nation as a whole. Two examples were cited. China, though a large and ancient empire, could not even raise itself to the level of a small European power and the Chinese people had lost their spirit as a result of misgovernment. In England, on the other hand, the leaders heeded public opinion, were not tyrannical, and paid attention to what the people desired. And England had flourished. "Is this not because political freedom is not restricted and the people are enterprising and energetic, and they bear the burdens of state and love and protect the state?"

The statement went on to suggest that when the Japanese government and people were united because of the freedom of the latter, then there would be no difficulty in achieving equality with foreign countries.[2] It is evident that, in its view of ultimate national goals—the strengthening of the Japanese nation and the attainment of equality with the West—the *Sekiyosha* was in agreement with the Meiji elite. The authors of the document, indeed, took pains to emphasize that they

[1] Kichinosuke Shoji, *Nihon Seisha Seitō Hattatsushi* (History of the Development of Political Societies and Parties in Japan), Tokyo, 1959, p. 7.

[2] The document is reprinted in its entirety in *Kōno Banshū Den* (Biography of Kōno Banshū) issued by Kōno Banshū Den Hensankai, Vol. 1, Tokyo, 1924, pp. 243-247.

were patriots and not traitors. Fortunately, they were able to cite the "Charter Oath" to show that they were merely carrying out the imperial will. "We the people must do everything to respond to these [i.e., the provisions of the Oath] by taking them seriously."

In addition to the statement of principles, the *Sekiyosha* also made public the rules governing its internal organization. These too contained noteworthy features. Membership was open to all irrespective of wealth, and all members enjoyed equal rights. The president and other officers were to be elected. Members were forbidden to join other societies based on similar principles. Two semi-annual meetings were scheduled, and special meetings could be called. No meetings could be held unless at least half of the members were present. Resolutions to be voted on in these meetings could be presented not only by the president and by special committees, but by individual members and even by non-members. Membership dues were set at one yen a year, plus 25 sen (one hundredth of a yen) to be assessed at the regularly scheduled general and special meetings.[3] Since we do not know how the society was actually run, we cannot judge the degree of democracy that in fact characterized its proceedings, but it would appear that its founders at least formally intended it to be a democratic organization. Within a few years, furthermore, a number of political organizations patterned on the *Sekiyosha* were formed in the prefecture.

THE FORMATION OF PARTIES

Political societies were founded at about this time in a number of other prefectures, and a logical outgrowth of these was a national organization dedicated to coordinating and guiding the work of the local units. The framework of such an organization was set up in 1879 and 1880, by leaders chiefly from the Tosa group, at a series of conventions held in Osaka under the sponsorship of the safely designated Patriotic Association (*Aikokusha*). The fourth convention of this organization, in March 1880, was attended by 114 delegates purporting to represent some 87,000 people in 2 urban and 22 rural prefectures.

The association laid the groundwork for Japan's first political party, the Liberal Party (*Jiyūtō*), established in 1881. Itagaki, of Tosa, was elected president, and the party issued a statement indicating that it

---

[3] Tetsuo Takahashi, *Fukushima Jiyū Minken Undōshi* (The Movement for Liberty and Popular Rights in Fukushima), Tokyo, 1954, pp. 33-36.

would carry on the struggle for popular rights. The party platform, if it may be called that, consisted of four short articles, calling for the expansion of the people's freedom and the protection and preservation of their rights, the promotion of national progress and the popular welfare, the achievement of equality among all Japanese, and the creation of constitutional government in Japan.

Before long a second party was organized in the form of the Constitutional Progressive Party (*Rikken Kaishintō*). Unlike the Liberal Party, which drew most of its support from rural areas, the Progressive Party was urban, its supporters consisting chiefly of intellectuals, ex-government officials, and businessmen. A third party made its appearance at about the same time, the Constitutional Imperial Party (*Rikken Teiseitō*), the interesting feature of which was that it was a government-sponsored party. The government's response to the formation of political associations had heretofore been to intimidate or repress them, but it was now experimenting with the tactics of rivalling them and depriving the opposition of its monopoly of partisan activity.

III. Functions of Political Parties

Political societies and parties performed at least two important functions during the 1870's and 1880's. The first of these was political education; the second, related to it, was to serve as a means for relating the people to the political process.

POLITICAL EDUCATION

The parties were able to attract to their cause some of the leading intellectuals of the times. Since this was a period when virtually the entire nation was engaged in a gigantic effort to absorb elements of Western civilization, it was natural that intellectuals should have devoted their energies to the study of Western thought. Hosts of translations of the works of well-known Western political theorists were published, as well as commentaries on them. Many ideas originating in the West—those of natural rights and popular sovereignty, for example—found their way into the pronouncements and programs of the political associations. The parties and the intellectuals associated with them provided an important channel for the importation of Western thought in the middle of the Meiji era.

The parties did not stop with importation, but contributed significantly to diffusing the new and often heady ideas among the people generally. Almost all of them organized political lectures and discussion groups. Contemporary accounts indicate that their leaders and theorists often travelled to nearby villages to address local residents assembled for the occasion. Sometimes speakers were brought from more distant points, Itagaki, for example, undertaking a number of extensive speaking tours.

The Meiji government took a jaundiced view of such activities, on the ground that they tended to incite the populace and undermine the social order. Accordingly it issued decrees designed to regulate public assembly and the press. Those wishing to sponsor meetings or lectures were required to obtain a permit three days in advance, and uniformed policemen were sent to the meetings themselves, with instructions to disband them if subversive sentiments were uttered.

According to a police report, the number of political lectures held in Fukushima Prefecture alone between January and August 1882 came to 36, of which 16 were ordered disbanded. Altogether 201 speakers were involved.[4] No nationwide figures on such lectures appear to be available, but the fragments of evidence suggest that the total number must have run into the hundreds or even the thousands during the decades of the 1870's and 1880's.

The spoken word, which is particularly effective where the literacy rate is low, was augmented by the printed word. The concept of a newspaper, as of many other things, was imported from the West in the early Meiji period. The first newspapers were principally government-sponsored papers designed to inform the public of the laws and decrees which were being issued in great numbers; but before long private publishers entered the field. In the 1870's newspapers began to be published even in the outlying towns and rural communities, and some of these were not so much commercial ventures as party organs. As might be expected, political opinion provided the main fare of the latter publications.

A third instrument for diffusing new ideas was the party-sponsored school for young men. Kōno, for example, established one in Fukushima Prefecture and invited two teachers from Tosa. They used Rousseau's *Social Contract*, and works by Mill and Spencer as textbooks; according to one account, "when they had time between their studies, (the students) were encouraged to make speeches and engage in debate as part of their training, and the nurturing of the spirit of constitutional self-government was made the first principle.[5]

4 Shoji, *op.cit.*, p. 174.
5 *Adachi Kenseishi* (Constitutional History of Adachi), issued by Adachi Kenseishi Hensankai, Tokyo, 1933, p. 37.

399

POLITICAL MOBILIZATION

A crude index of the penetration of new ideas and of the effectiveness of the parties in mobilizing public sentiment against the government was provided by the nationwide circulation of a petition to the Meiji government to summon a national legislative assembly. The decision to undertake this national campaign was made at the fourth convention of the Patriotic Association in Osaka, in March 1880. The convention also changed the name of the sponsoring organization itself to the Association for the Petitioning for a National Assembly (*Kokkai Kisei Dōmeikai*).

Comprehensive data on this campaign are currently not available, but fragmentary information on specific areas suggests that leaders of political societies played an important role in collecting signatures. In the county of Yama-gun in Fukushima Prefecture, 225 signatures were collected in 20 villages. But 52 per cent of these were obtained in only two villages: 64 in Yoneoka, and 53 in Miyakawa.[6] Two prominent leaders of local political societies lived in these villages, Miura Noboruku in Yoneoka and Hara Heizō in Miyakawa. One surmises that these two leaders were responsible for the disproportionately large number of signatures in their own villages.

In persuading peasants to sign the petition, the appeal was sometimes made not to abstract principles of political liberty but to specific issues, like taxation. The following excerpt from a contemporary police report provides us with a first-hand account: "In studying the situation in various areas, one is struck by the fact that there are one or two agitators who are the instigators, and the arguments they use to persuade the people are indeed unsound. In brief they say that they are endeavoring to get established a national assembly and that all people who are independent should hereby get together. After all, a national assembly is something which has been actually established in civilized countries and is an extremely worthy institution. Therefore, if a national assembly is established, it will not permit the government to waste money, and hence there is no question that national taxes will thereby be reduced. The ignorant people do not know what a national assembly is, but are pleased at the prospect of reduced taxes. The more intelligent people have already signed the petition, and they imagine themselves as already being members of the assembly and possessed of the right to participate in government. Many are eagerly

---

[6] Based on data in Shoji, *op.cit.*, pp. 151-154.

signing petitions and already several tens of thousands of names have been recorded on the petition."[7]

An inducement in the same category as lower taxes was supposed exemption from military service. Rumors were spread in one village in Okayama Prefecture that anyone joining the Achieving One's Aim Society would be exempt from the twin evils of taxes and conscription; and as a result groups of villagers chose a representative and sent him off to Kōchi.[8]

By organizing a nationwide campaign and using some of the tactics described above, the leaders of the Association for the Petitioning for a National Assembly were able to compile an impressive list of names of persons supporting the creation of a national assembly. Armed with such a list, a delegation tried to present a petition to the government, only to be rebuffed. The immediate contest between the government and political opposition was won by the former; but events were to prove that the partisan activities had not been wholly in vain. In following years, the government announced that a parliament would be established under a constitution to be granted in 1889.

The political structure created by the constitutiton of 1889 was a constitutional monarchy with an Imperial Diet consisting of a House of Peers and a House of Representatives chosen by a severely restricted electorate. Real power in the government was exercised by non-parliamentary forces—the bureaucracy, the military, and elder statesmen—in the name of the Emperor; the scope of action allowed the elected House of Representatives was very limited. Nevertheless, the lower house did thereafter exist as a part of the government and was able to question the wisdom of government policies and in some degree to obstruct, in the name of public opinion, those of which it disapproved.

IV. Parties and Political Leadership

In the early decades of the Meiji era, as mentioned earlier, power was exercised by a relatively small group of men, most of them of samurai origin and most of them coming from southwestern Japan. It was under their leadership that Japan was transformed into a modern state.

A noteworthy feature of this elite group was that one looks in vain among them for the equivalent of a Sun Yat-sen, a Sukarno, a Nehru,

[7] Quoted in Seichu Naito, "Kokkai Kaisetsu Undō no Hatten Kōzō" (The Development and Structure of the Movement for the Establishment of a National Assembly), *Keizai Ronsō*, Vol. LXXX, No. 2, August 1957, p. 32.
[8] *Ibid.*, p. 34.

or an Atatürk. Whereas in many of the developing nations today, modernization is proceeding under the guidance of charismatic leaders, in nineteenth-century Japan there appeared no one endowed with a magnetic personality and capable of attracting a mass following. The typical political leader was, and even today remains, the strong, silent man, skilled in quiet maneuvering and manipulating persons more effectively than verbal symbols.

At least two explanations for the absence of charismatic leaders may be advanced. Modernization in many parts of Asia today was either preceded or accompanied by the destruction of the traditional bases of authority, and the people have turned toward a magnetic leader in order to supply the lost sense of communal security and identity. In Japan, however, the modernization process conserved many traditional values and forms of social organization; hence there was less need for a charismatic leader. The second is that a peculiar virtue came to be vested in the Meiji emperor through the development of an emperor cult, and this formal and, as it were, institutional charisma inhibited the emergence of charismatic persons who might rival it.

It is clear, in any case, that though the members of the Meiji elite had their internal differences, they were united in their hostility toward the early parties and in their determination to thwart the claims of party leaders to a share of power. In combatting the parties they made good use of the doctrine of imperial sovereignty, as it came to be embodied in the constitution. According to this view, the emperor, in whom sovereignty resided, was virtuous and all-wise and his will more truly reflected the nation's will than any determination which might be reached by means of the ballot box.

Hence in the beginning the political elite sought to ignore the existence of political parties and to carry on the business of governing without consulting party leaders. The result, as might be expected, was a certain amount of political turbulence. In the first sessions of the Imperial Diet in the early 1890's, the parties, placed in a position of opposition to the government, refused to vote appropriations bills and generally took an obstructionist tack. Before long, some of the politically perceptive members of the elite concluded that since the parties had influence in parliament, it made more sense to work with them, preferably by means of securing important party posts, than to resist them wholly. In 1900, therefore, Itō Hirobumi, a prominent member of the elite, himself assumed the presidency of a new party, the Association of Political Friends.

The parties also changed their tactics. Behind this shift in party positions were several important considerations. First of all, the constitutional structure was such that the government held all of the important cards, so to speak; if the parties wished to share in material rewards, such as offices, government contracts, expenditures for public works, subsidies, and so on, it was incumbent on them to cultivate good relations with the government.

A second, and perhaps even more important reason, appears to have been related to the very structure of the parties. As already indicated, the parties began as small rural societies formed around one or two local leaders. The parties were in a sense national federations of such societies and hence were loosely organized and possessed little in the way of a solid organization.

Moreover, the party leaders who acted as spokesmen for the parties on national issues were generally of two types in the early period. The first type consisted of ex-officials (Itagaki is a good example) who had given up their positions within the government for one reason or another. In terms of their ideological orientation these were quite often not so different from the elite in power, and were indeed enticed back into the government from time to time, leaving the party on such occasions bereft of proper leadership. The second type was represented by men like Kōno Hironaka, who began as local leaders and then used local organizations to parlay themselves into positions of national prominence. Once such men attained following and stature they, too, found it more expedient to work with the government than to oppose it consistently.

There also appears to have occurred a gradual change in the relationship of the party leadership to the rank-and-file as the years went by. Although the parties remained loosely organized, determination of party policy became concentrated in the hands of their national leaders.[9] This development is attributable in part to the increasing cost of political campaigns; as the electorate was gradually expanded party expenses increased, and it became necessary to turn to persons, often with bureaucratic backgrounds, who enjoyed access to the businessmen and corporations able to fill party coffers. And, as the parties became bureaucratic and party policy making centralized, it became easier for the government to achieve accommodations with them.

The increasing centralization of party policy-making no doubt

[9] Yasushi Toriumi, "Shoki Gikai ni okeru Jiyūtō no Kōzō to Kinō" (Structure and Function of the Jiyūtō in the Early Diet Sessions), *Rekishigaku Kenkyū*, No. 255, July 1961, pp. 16-29.

worked at times to the disadvantage of the local leaders who headed the constituent societies. But some sort of accommodation seems to have been attained between the party leadership and those local leaders whom Professors Scalapino and Masumi have called the "pure politicians."[10] In the early years of the Imperial Diet a great many of the latter secured seats in the House of Representatives, after having gained experience in village, town, or prefectural assemblies. This was possible because the tax qualification so restricted the franchise that one could be elected with as few as a thousand votes. Under the circumstances, campaigning consisted largely of calls on relatives and personal or professional associates, and probably involved no large expense. As the number of voters grew, and campaigning became more expensive, fewer and fewer "pure politicians" could afford to run for national office.[11] Many local figures must then have given up their ambitions of becoming small frogs in a big pond and contented themselves with service in prefectural assemblies.

The latter course yielded some material advantages. Though the prefectural governors were appointees of the central government, they were often, at least by the 1920's, members of one or the other of the conservative parties and provided local politicians with access to the national parties. Perhaps more important, local leaders were usually able to get their share of funds for public works and government contracts by working in the prefectural assemblies, so that, to promote local economic interests, they did not need to seek seats in the House of Representatives.

In the pre-war period, then, parties were assigned a minor role in the political process. They were able to provide only limited access to the political elite. Especially in the 1930's, most of the political leaders came from the military or from the bureaucracy. On the eve of World War II, the parties disappeared, being amalgamated into a single organization known as the Imperial Rule Assistance Association.

Among the reforms decreed by the Allied Occupation after the end of World War II were changes in the constitutional structure. The demobilization of the armed forces removed the military as a political force, and their place came to some extent to be filled by

[10] Robert Scalapino and Junnosuke Masumi, *Parties and Politics in Contemporary Japan*, Berkeley and Los Angeles, 1962, pp. 11ff.

[11] Oka, Yoshitake, ed., *Gendai Nihon Seiji Katei* (The Political Process in Contemporary Japan), Tokyo, 1958, p. 330, contains a table showing the historical decline in the number of ex-prefectural assemblymen elected to the House of Representatives.

the parties. In the new institutional structure described by the constitution of 1947, the power of the National Diet was greatly enhanced. There was, moreover, the constitutional requirement that at least half of the cabinet ministers had to be drawn from the Diet. In practice most of them have been drawn from that body. Cabinet rank cannot, as in the pre-war era, be obtained by bureaucrats directly. Many politically ambitious bureaucrats have consequently resigned from the civil service and sought seats in the Diet, with the endorsement of the conservative Liberal Democratic party. There has been a further recent tendency for these ex-bureaucrats to take over the more important party posts. In recent years, the political parties have become active in the recruitment of the political elite, but the dominant conservative party has itself come increasingly under the control of ex-bureaucrats rather than of professional politicians who have worked their way up by winning local and national elections.

V. Parties and Political Participation

The single act which contributes most to a sense of popular participation in politics is voting. That is true, at least, when the citizen is given an opportunity to state a preference among genuinely competing candidates, and when his action, combined with the actions of many other of his fellow voters, indeed determines who will hold public office. In Japan, as has been indicated, the vote was first limited to those adult males who had paid a specified sum in direct taxes; this requirement severely restricted the number of voters. Most government personnel, moreover, even at the local level, were appointed rather than elected. But over the years the property qualification was gradually lowered, so that more and more persons joined the ranks of eligible voters. The following table shows the expansion of the electorate:

EXPANSION OF THE ELECTORATE

Year	No. of Qualified Voters
1912	1,503,650
1920	3,069,787
1928	12,409,078
1936	14,303,780
1947	40,907,493
1955	49,235,375
1960	56,554,475

Source: *Japan Statistical Yearbook*, 1949 ed., and R. Scalapino and J. Masumi, *Parties and Politics in Contemporary Japan*, p. 157.

We see that unusually large expansions of the electorate occurred in 1928 and again in 1947. These resulted from the enactment of universal manhood suffrage in 1925 and the granting of the franchise to women in 1947. It should further be noted that, in the postwar period, the number of elective offices has markedly increased so that the people have more opportunities to exercise their franchise than before.

When noting the expansion of the electorate, however, one should be aware that the parties have not always sought to bring more people into the electoral process. After the end of the First World War there was agitation by intellectuals, students, journalists, and others for abolishing the tax qualification for voting, but most party leaders were less than enthusiastic supporters of that proposal. Some even argued that universal manhood suffrage would break down the system of social classes and lead to instability. Even the socialists who would presumably have benefitted from the extension of the vote to the propertyless had their misgivings. At the turn of the century, Japanese Socialists had placed great faith in the parliamentary system, arguing that, if the poor could send their own representatives to the Diet, all Socialist aims could be attained through legislation. But before long they became disillusioned with parliamentary process. By the 1920's many leaders of the left had become convinced that a grand extension of the vote would only blunt the revolutionary edge of their movement, and were favoring instead such techniques of "direct action" as the general strike. When, despite the misgivings of both right and left, universal manhood suffrage was enacted in 1925, a number of so-called proletarian parties did make their appearance, but won under five per cent of the popular vote in the general election of 1928.

Although by the 1920's political parties had become strong enough to form cabinets occasionally, they had not become a wholly integral part of the political structure. It will be recalled that the concept of a party was something borrowed from the West. During their formative years, the parties had to work within an alien and even hostile setting. Even after decades of existence they were exercising no very immediate power. They were unable, therefore, to exhibit or even to develop a lively sense of political responsibility. More often than not, they appeared to the public as symbols of factional strife and corruption.

There was also the problem of the means by which the Imperial Diet arrived at decisions. The traditional method of decision-making in the villages—and that which was therefore most familiar to a great many people—was the formation of consensus without open debate or a visible split between majority and minority. To the public generally, the principle of majority rule as used in the Diet seemed strange and even outlandish.

It is hence not altogether surprising that the parties failed to survive the crisis ushered in by the Great Depression of the early 1930's. Japan's response to the strains imposed on the social system by the economic crisis was increased meddling in politics by the military, especially the army. High government posts were increasingly taken over by professional officers, and the tone of government came to be set by the military. There is some evidence that in their drive to gain power, the military used the association of reservists to mobilize grassroots support. Because of universal conscription, virtually every able-bodied male served in the armed forces and, upon release, was enrolled in the reservists' association in his city, town, or hamlet. The local branches of the reservists' association were customarily led by members of locally prominent families, usually of landlord families. These were often the same families that provided the grass-roots support for the political parties; and it may well be that the use of the reservists' organization by the military in this period deprived parties of local support and left them further weakened. In any event, the parties were not able to impede the military in their drive to control the government and were forced to dissolve.

The Allied Occupation produced significant changes in the institutional framework within which parties were to work, but it did not modify in any startling way the relationship of the average citizen to the parties. Neither the conservative nor the socialist parties have yet succeeded in building substantial local organizations of faithful members and workers. The conservatives rely heavily on local notables and political bosses, while the socialists, especially the left-wing factions, make use of the labor unions, both for votes and for funds. Recent surveys of voter attitudes, moreover, show the voters swayed by personalities rather than by issues or party labels.

Partisan allegiances cannot quickly be built up. Recent studies suggest that, in the United States, these are likely to be determined early in life through socialization processes within the family. In the absence of comparable data for Japan, it would be unwise to make categorical statements, but the average Japanese family perhaps provides little equivalent political socialization. The political education of the individual citizen appears to be left to such other agencies as the peer group in the school.

Japanese parties, furthermore, are characterized by a high degree of factionalism. Professors Scalapino and Masumi note that, within them, "factional interest tends to take precedence over party interest and, one is tempted to say, over the public interest as well."[12] Party leadership becomes unstable when party leaders are chosen only after in-fighting within the group. Factionalism also impedes the development of clear-cut partisan positions on urgent issues, and, for this reason also, makes them less effective as instruments of government.

Finally, the parties bear a sometimes unhealthy relationship to interest groups. A characteristic feature of modernization is that it leads to occupational and economic specialization. This specialization in turn encourages the growth of interest groups and of their organizational agencies, such as farmers' cooperatives, chambers of commerce, and labor unions. From time to time these organizations will ask the government for subsidies, tax relief, preferential legislation, and other favors. In many cases the demands being made on government by various groups will conflict, and one of the important functions of parties is to bring about accommodation among these demands.

Japanese parties undoubtedly effect many such accommodations, but they have failed so far to resolve one of the great issues engendered by modernization: the conflict between capital and labor. In the 1920's the existing parties were either unwilling or unable to cope with the growth of a working class, so that labor came to depend on its own political organization, namely the Socialist Party.

Today the conservative Liberal Democratic Party, drawing votes from rural areas and financed by business, controls the government, while the Socialist Party, backed by organized labor and unorganized intellectuals, forms the opposition. Between the government and the opposition there is little communication, to say nothing of an accommodating spirit.

In short, Japanese political parties leave something to be desired as instruments of popular participation in politics and of accommodation among diverse interest groups. In many spheres of activity, for example in the diverse uses of electronics, Japan has achieved a high level of modernity; but in politics, "traditional" forms of behavior and organization persist. The public does not seek to be involved in politics or to be represented in the high councils of government; the exist-

[12] Scalapino and Masumi, *op.cit.*, p. 19.

ing political organizations, such as parties, have not kept pace with the industrial and technological urges toward modernization. One measure of this gap is the periodic eruption of violence in politics, in the form either of political assassination or of mass demonstrations and riots, like those occasioned by President Eisenhower's proposed visit to Japan in 1960.

VI. Conclusion

We began with the notion that party development provides a kind of index of modernization. What results are obtained if we apply this measurement to Japanese political history during the last hundred years? It is evident that, viewed in the long perspective, parties have come to play an increasingly important role in the political process. The curve of partisan activity, though far from regular, has in a very general way tended to move upward, and with an accelerating pace since 1945.

On the other hand, if we were to place Japanese parties against some ideal democratic standard of party function, we should conclude that they fall far short. Certainly prior to 1945 they failed in performance of certain vital functions, namely, the recruitment of the political leaders and the provision of means for popular participation in government. Even today they exhibit the force of long tradition, and remain imperfect instruments of popular rule.[13] They served, as we have seen, as vehicles for importing and diffusing Western political thought in the Meiji era. By educating and mobilizing at least some of the people, moreover, they at least helped to shape the *form* of government which was established under the constitution of 1889. Yet that government was parliamentary in form only. And there may be some value in speculating why Japanese parties have not managed, even to this day, to bring about a government fully parliamentary in spirit as well as in form.

At the risk of oversimplifying matters, we might directly attribute this failure to deficient political leadership. In the Tokugawa period there was a social elite based on birth, the traditional warrior class. This elite supplied the reservoir from which national leaders were drawn. In the workaday process of governing, especially in the villages, the national leadership made use of rural or local elites. Members of this latter gentry were generally not of the warrior class, their claims to local eminence resting on their possession of land or other property, their superior education, and their long residence in the community.

13 *Ibid.*, Chapter v.

They did not, as in China, have access to positions in the higher reaches of government.

One of the consequences of political change in the Meiji era was to remove this disability. The parties succeeded in giving a major social group or caste some access to national office during a crucial period of transition. A good deal of actual or potential disaffection was thereby siphoned off.

Another factor making for accommodation between the national elite and the rural was the agreement between the two groups on national goals. A driving ambition of the Meiji elite was to elevate Japan to a world power. The same ambition was shared by the parties and their rural adherents. So long as the government was enhancing national prestige, as it did through victories in the Sino-Japanese war and the Russo-Japanese war, the local elites had little ground for complaint.

To the extent that the rural elite could articulate both their own needs and demands and those of the peasantry, they served as spokesmen for the total agrarian interest. The parties also came to represent the business interest—particularly after business leaders and firms began to contribute to election campaigns and party expenses generally. But in this century, notably in the 1920's, industrialization, urbanization, and the gradual growth of a working class created additional groups needing admission into the political system. The existing parties were not successful in meeting this demand, for they represented the propertied classes and were traditional in their orientation. As result, new proletarian parties, espousing Marxian principles in varying degrees, emerged to compete with the parties which they called bourgeois.

The division of the parties into two ideological camps, conservative and socialist, is keenly felt today, and materially impairs the effectiveness of parliamentary institutions. If modernization involves the creation of political instruments, including parties, that can gain popular acceptance by accommodating the simultaneous demands made by diverse political interests, Japan has not yet attained a full measure of political modernization.

B. TURKEY

ARİF T. PAYASLIOĞLU

"Political modernization" entails change in political institutions. More significantly, it entails changes in the structure of the political forces which vitalize the institutions. Among these forces, political leaders and parties are the most important.

The emergence of a political leadership out of party organizations is itself a modern phenomenon. At least in Turkey, the original nucleus of party organization underwent a long process of development before any such leadership came into being. We shall here specifically ask what changes have occurred in the socio-political basis of leadership during this process, how party organizations have developed, and what the policies and methods of political leaders and parties have been. Recurring phenomena and the direction or general trend of development will be given special attention.

I. Socio-Political Basis of Leadership

As explained by Professor İnalcik, there were four traditional forces which competed for power during the decline of the Ottoman Empire. These were the Ottoman dynasty, a semi-feudal landed aristocracy, the religious dignitaries, and the Janissaries. The early reforms were the result of the struggle among these internal forces in the face of increasing pressure from abroad. During the first half of the nineteenth century three sultans—Selim III, Mahmud II, and Abdülmecid—emerged as reformers. Except for Abdülmecid, who had a Western-style education, these men did not differ from their predecessors in educational background or in the manner of their accession to power. But through their efforts to eliminate the rival forces they contributed to a number of changes, including the creation of new rivals. By the mid-nineteenth century the Janissaries were completely destroyed and, except for Muhammad Ali of Egypt, the semi-feudal landlords, the rebellious provincial administrators, and powerful religious dignitaries were brought to heel. In their place three new forces appeared on the political scene: the reformed administration, the new army, and a small Western-oriented intellectual elite. From the mid-nineteenth century until recent times, these three agencies have supplied almost all the political leadership either directly or by means of party organization. For our purposes the most significant is the new elite, which has been instrumental in establishing and developing political parties.

It did not take long for the ruling dynasty to realize that the new forces which it had helped to create could pose as serious a threat to their power as those they had eliminated. One of the sultans, Abdülhamid II, very ably kept them under control for about thirty years. But after the revolution of 1908 the Ottoman dynasty itself lost significance as a major political force. In 1922 it was abolished as a political institution by the nationalist revolutionary government, and two years later its religious functions were discontinued, the caliphate being abolished and all members of the dynasty exiled.

The religious groups and local landlords ceasing to compete directly for power tried to influence politics by forming parties and occasionally by fomenting open rebellion, as in various local revolts during the War of Independence and the Kurdish revolts in 1925 and 1937. In general the local landlords and religious groups were allied in reaction to the reforms.

The reformed bureaucracy initially produced some very able statesmen whose policies profoundly influenced the course of development. Among these the names of Reşid, Âli, Fuad, and Midhat Pashas are prominent. Except for Fuad Pasha, all these men came from humble families and had little formal education. They were trained in civil service, however, had lived or traveled in Europe, and were cognizant of Western political institutions and ideas. On the basis of their talents, they climbed the bureaucratic ladder and served in ministerial positions. But after 1908 the impact of bureaucracy as a political force declined and the military took the lead. From then on, men trained in administration have in most cases risen to power through political parties.

Since the 1908 revolution, as Professor Rustow has shown, the army has continued to play a major role in politics. On three occasions it actually assumed control of the country. But each of these periods was significantly shorter than the previous one. In general, since the beginning of the twentieth century, the major forces on the political arena have been the military and the parties, the latter coming increasingly to the fore. Even those leaders who entered politics by way of the army's intervention have almost all joined political parties later.

It may be concluded that, since the inauguration of the first reforms, political leadership has been provided either directly or indirectly by formal official institutions of the state. These institutions have been increasingly open to the members of various social strata. The ascriptive elements in recruitment have been minimized, and a chance given to able and well-educated people of modest social background to enter government service. But it was soon obvious that the bureaucracy and the military could not themselves assure the political participation of the masses, all competing to express interests, or provide all the necessary leaders for a modern state. A group of intellectuals therefore attempted to establish a rudimentary party organization in 1865. Since then parties have gradually become the major organization for political action.

II. The Development of Party Organization and Structure

The basic social structure of the Ottoman Empire is described in Professor İnalcik's essay. It is clear that there was a sharp distinction between the ruling elite (which included the court, the army, the bureaucracy, and the religious dignitaries) and the ruled population (re'aya), which embraced the totality of subjects. One of the most significant divisions within the ruled population was on the basis of language and religion, three broad categories, being discernible: the Muslim Turks, the non-Muslim minorities, and the Muslim ethnic groups, which, like the Turks, were called Ottomans.

The non-Muslim ethnic groups living under Ottoman rule were economically rather well off, in contact with Western ideas, and protected by the Great Powers in various ways. Early in the nineteenth century they started organizing revolutionary societies and guerrilla groups with the aim of gaining national independence. These activities, continuing until the end of World War I, resulted in the formation of several independent states in the Balkan peninsula. The non-Turkish Muslim groups, most of which eventually came under the rule of imperialistic powers, were not regarded as faithful either by the caliph or by the Muslim Turks. Those non-Turkish elements, Muslim or non-Muslim, which remained within the shrinking empire either continued their independent agitation or tried to infiltrate Turkish political organizations for their own purposes. Some joined with the Young Turks in their struggle for a liberal system of government, though with disappointing results. Gradually they were eliminated through wars, massacres, migrations, and population exchange.

The activities and the eventual fate of the ethnic groups have had some important effects on Turkish politics. First, Turkish political activists learned from their example such revolutionary conspiratorial tactics as secret political organization and guerrilla action. Secondly, the Ottoman administration was forced to grant equal rights to minorities, thus establishing legally the idea of the rights of all citizens. At length the emphasis in the national political ideology gradually shifted from Ottomanism to nationalism and Turkism and from Islamism to secularism.

At to the Turkish elements of the empire, their economic status, their educational level, and their place of residence all affected their political behavior. Istanbul, as the most advanced city in Turkey, was the natural seat of the first significant political movement. The earliest reforms contributed to the emergence of a small Western-oriented elite, the members of which were urban, relatively well-educated people whose economic status depended mostly on the wealth of their family and on their own professions. In 1865 persons from among this group established a secret political organization of about 250 members, the Association of the New Ottomans, with the aim of achieving a constitutional monarchy. This movement represented three important firsts in Ottoman history: it was the first political organization; it aimed for the first time to achieve a drastic change in the political institutions of the empire; for the first time, a political group seemed to agree that not only Western technology and science but also Western political institutions and values had to be adopted to counter European superiority.

The New Ottomans disseminated their ideas in poems, plays, and newspaper articles. In these works attempts to reconcile constitutionalism and freedom with traditional Islamic law were apparent. But there were also some hints of secularism—some conscious separation of political interest from religious. This naïve and chiefly literary experience was the earliest anticipation of today's partisan activity.

The Association of the New Ottomans was disbanded in 1872, but its impact was considerable. The growing belief in intellectual circles that a constitutional system of government was necessary for the salvation of the empire brought about, together with some violent events, the first Constitution in 1876. The words of Midhat Pasha, the chief architect of the constitution, reflect what was expected from it: "The Ottoman state being a part of the European community, it has to follow the same methods that they use in order to be on an equal footing with its neighbours in the way of progress; and since a constitu-

tional system is one of the basic conditions of the advancement of nations, I hereby proclaim the adoption of this system of government
within the framework of religious law (*şeriat*) and our national customs."[1]

This constitution established a species of constitutional monarchy.
But the House of Deputies, convening twice, lasted only about eleven
months. No partisan activity emerged either at the elections or in the
parliament. Except for a small group of intellectuals, the great majority of the population remained completely indifferent. When some
deputies became critical of the sultan's ministers, the sultan dissolved
the House until 1908, when new elections were held. The intervening
period forms the "thirty-one years of absolutism" of Sultan Abdülhamid II.

The sultan's absolutism provoked the opposition which is usually
referred to as the "Young Turk" movement. From 1889 on, about
twenty secret political organizations were formed with the aim of
ending Abdülhamid's despotism and restoring the constitution. Many
leaders of the movement, being forced to live in exile in foreign
capitals, were strongly influenced by Western liberal ideas. And the
Young Turks generally believed that freedom and constitutionalism
were the ultimate remedy for the ills of the rapidly declining empire.[2]

The movement started among the students of the new higher schools
—chiefly the military schools—and soon spread. Later, journalists,
members of the local nobility, non-Muslim elements, and, towards
1908, many army officers became active in it. Significant attempts
were made to coordinate and centralize the activities of the constituent groups at two meetings held in Paris. Though divergences in
views were very great, all present agreed on the purposes of restoring
the constitution and putting an end to the despotic rule of Sultan
Abdülhamid II. One of the constituent associations, the Ottoman
Union and Progress Society (*Osmanlı İttihad ve Terakki Cemiyeti*),
gained an ascendant power when it was joined by army officers. The
continued intimidations of the sultan, aggravated by both internal and
external circumstances, resulted in the revolt of the army in Mace-

---

[1] Excerpt from Imperial Rescript drafted by Midhat Pasha for the sultan's proclamation of the constitution. Recai G. Okandan, *Amme Hukukumuzun Ana Hatları*
(Outline of our Public Law), Istanbul, 1957, p. 138, also Victor Bérard, *La Révolu-
tion Turque*, Paris, 1909, p. 93.

[2] Tarık Z. Tunaya, *Türkiye'de Siyasî Partiler (1859-1952)*, Istanbul, 1952,
pp. 117, 123, 126, 128, 129, 143-144, 146, 153, 155.

donia, whereupon, in 1908, Abdülhamid restored the constitution. This time there was widespread popular interest in politics, especially among the many persons believing that freedom and constitutionalism would solve all problems. The restoration of the constitution brought many hitherto secret associations into the open as political parties. Yet most of these proved ephemeral. The whole period was dominated by one party, the Union and Progress.

In its origin this association was a quite heterogeneous secret revolutionary society, united by a common interest in ending Abdülhamid's despotic rule. After the restoration of the constitution the association had difficulty transforming itself into a coherent party organization. Though possessing an imposing majority in the parliament and a good representation of the Council of Ministers, it remained technically a private society until 1913; during that period its parliamentary contingent was called the party. But a regulation approved at the 1913 convention declared the association as a whole a political party. According to this regulation, the central organization of the party consisted of a general council chaired by a president, a central committee under a secretary general, and a central office which dealt with matters concerning the parliamentary group. The most powerful of these organs was the central committee, which still preserved a secret nature. The field organization of the party consisted in local branches in the towns, some clubs, and occasional conventions.

After a brief period of relative freedom, the constitutional regime deteriorated rapidly. The religious reactionary forces became increasingly active, until finally their agitation led to a mutiny in the Istanbul garrison. When the mutiny was put down, some of the political organizations allegedly inciting this incident were abolished. In the face of growing opposition, the Union and Progress resorted to highhanded methods, whereupon an increasing number of dissidents left its ranks to form parties of their own. Gradually these other political organizations and interests formed a common-front opposition, this time with the purpose of ending the despotism of the Union and Progress. This tense situation was resolved in 1913, when Enver, the outspoken leader of the Union and Progress, raided the Sublime Porte and established himself and his party in power until the end of World War I.

After 1908 popular responsiveness to political problems and issues was increased by the activities of the press and of political organizations, and by such regular political happenings as elections and parliamentary debates. The constitutional system did not in fact work well: elections were indirect and rigged, there was repression and violence, the army was infected with politics, and the final destruction of the empire was at hand. Yet socio-political changes occurring during those years paved the way for later developments. The limitation of the sultan's authority became a fact and his prestige declined, as did that of the aristocratic administrators of the Sublime Porte. Turkish elements, increasingly aware that they had to rely on themselves for survival, were comforted and encouraged by idealistic nationalists. Some experience was gained in party organization and parliamentary methods. Had these and other changes not taken place, it would have been far more difficult for Mustafa Kemal and his associates to create the new Turkey.

After the collapse of the Ottoman Empire at the end of the World War I, political activity took two forms. In Istanbul several small parties appeared, seeking to save what was left of the empire. In Anatolia a movement for national defense was born: "Associations for the Defense of Rights" were established in many localities to protest the occupation and to secure national independence if possible, and after 1919 these organizations were combined into the Association for the Defense of Rights of Anatolia and Rumelia, under the leadership of Mustafa Kemal. The goals of the association, as codified in a conference held in 1919, are called the National Pact. Local officials, army officers, and provincial notables all participated in this conference. Although any connection with the Union and Progress Party was denied by the nationalists and all merely partisan activities condemned, many of the local Defense of Rights committees were no more than transformed branches of the Union and Progress Party. Of the 337 deputies in the first National Assembly, nearly 100 came from the Istanbul parliament, which was dominated by Unionists.[3]

According to the National Pact, the movement proposed to save the Ottoman state, with its sultan-caliph, and the constitution. But it is probable that from the beginning Mustafa Kemal had in mind a completely new Turkish state and was biding his time, for he was soon working toward a secular state with a homogeneous population and with political institutions similar to those of Western nations.

Atatürk was by far the most important leader who ruled the country dictatorially under a republican regime. After his death in 1938 İsmet İnönü, one of his closest lieutenants, took over and pursued

[3] Tunaya, op.cit., pp. 410, 474, 480, 482.

the same general policies until 1945. Both these leaders were dependent on a party which Atatürk founded, the Republican People's Party. This organization, first created within the National Assembly during the War of Independence, was initially a parliamentary group designed to assure Kemal a majority in the face of opposition from reactionaries, conservatives, and personal rivals. The executive board of the group, however, elected by the membership, according to its internal regulations, formed also the central organ of the Association for the Defense of the Rights of Anatolia and Rumelia. Once a decision was reached within the group, the minority was obligated to comply with it under penalty of expulsion. Finally, the executive board members were permitted to succeed themselves in the semi-annual elections. The aim of the group was to achieve the goals indicated in the National Pact and to determine the organization of the state within the framework of the Constitution of 1921.

By these means the foundations of a future party were established, for in the first instance, the parliamentary group was linked with a countrywide organization. Second, voting discipline was secured. Third, permanence in leadership was made possible. Finally, the group pledged itself to be an instrument of political change. This was the apparatus which led to the evolution of the first major party of the republic, the Republican People's Party.

This party served to recruit and organize persons loyal to Atatürk and his policies, to educate people in politics and disseminate the reforms, and to preserve the appearances of a parliamentary regime and prepare the ground for future democratic developments. It remained the overwhelmingly dominant party until 1945, though probably not by prior intention. It has been remarked that the Kemalist one-party system developed empirically and its ideology came later.[4] A brief analysis of these happenings may serve to clarify some underlying features of political change in Turkey and of the role of Turkish parties.

During the struggle for independence, the nationalist movement despite its heterogeneous character, was united by a common desire to save the country. But as Mustafa Kemal's power grew and he began to introduce drastic changes, dissent and opposition became apparent. He and his group introduced Western forms, institutions, and sets of mind as rapidly and uncompromisingly as possible. The reactionaries,

---

[4] Maurice Duverger, *De la Dictature*, Paris, 1961, p. 124, and Paul Gentizon, *Mustapha Kemal ou l'Orient en Marche*, Paris, 1928, p. 45.

of course, radically opposed such innovations. The Communists at first supported Mustafa Kemal, along with Soviet Russia; later, as Soviet policy toward the Turkish revolution changed, the attitude of the internal Communists changed accordingly. Extreme right- and left-wing political views were not tolerantly received, and organizations holding these views were later outlawed. Two opposing groups remained, conservatives and Westernizers. In the conservative view the masses could not accept drastic reforms, and many traditional institutions and values, especially including religion, needed to be preserved for sake of the spiritual health of society. Reforms should therefore be implemented slowly, and there should be a compromise between Western institutions and indigenous.

Mustafa Kemal seemed eager to gratify the moderate conservatives within the forms of a Western form of parliamentarism. The first test came with the establishment of an opposition party by some of the dissenters from his own People's Party. The leaders of the new party, the Progressive Republican Party, were heroes of the War of Independence, such as Rauf and, Âli Fuad, Refet, Kâzim Karabekir Pashas. Some of them had expressed concern at the abolition of the sultanate and opposed the abrogation of the caliphate. Yet there was nothing in the program of their party which suggested a revival of these institutions. Seeming to be chiefly opposed to the personal power of Mustafa Kemal, they professed a devotion to freedom and asked tolerance for religious beliefs and practices.

A few months after the establishment of this party, the Kurds in the eastern region of the country revolted against the government, hoping to restore the caliphate and perhaps to form an independent state. The government soon crushed the revolt, but its already tense relations with the opposition deteriorated further. For the government believed it had discovered some connection between the Progressive Party and the rebellious Kurds. Hence it abolished the party on the basis of a law giving extraordinary powers to the executive.

From then on, Mustafa Kemal's authority increased and his party became the only one in the National Assembly. Another experiment with a multi-party system, which is usually cited as an evidence of Atatürk's devotion to democracy, occurred in 1930. The new party, the Republican Free (Liberal) Party, was established with the permission of Mustafa Kemal, and he encouraged many of his friends to join it. Its leader, Fethi (Okyar), was a former member of the People's Party and a former ambassador in Paris. In a letter to Mustafa Kemal, he inquired whether the establishment of a new party which would compete with the party in power would meet with his approval. Mustafa Kemal promptly replied that he had always been a believer in free debates in the National Assembly and would therefore consider a new party as one of the supports of the republican regime. But he emphasized that parties could act only within the provisions of secularism.

As soon as Fethi began political tours in Anatolia, it became clear that many persons were dissatisfied with the government's secularist and economically progressive policies and were intending to use the new party as an instrument of reaction. The party then came under attack in the National Assembly, and Fethi thought that it would be wise to disband the organization. Though he and some of his associates were sincere in their belief in a liberal democracy, it was in fact impossible to sustain a party such as he envisaged in the face of pressure from reactionaries and conservatives. After the abolition of the Republican Free Party, the Republican People's Party remained the sole party until 1945.

As a political organ designed to recruit and organize the supporters of the reforms, that party has worked in a variety of ways. Closest to Atatürk was a relatively small group of leaders, his collaborators during and after the War of Independence. Several of these men were army officers such as İsmet (İnönü), Kâzım Karabekir, Ali Fuad (Cebesoy), Refet (Bele), Rauf (Orbay), Receb (Peker). Others were administrators and intellectuals. As we have seen, dissensions and rivalries among them were not infrequent. On the whole, however, they supported the new regime and some later emerged as leaders. The party regularly introduced into the National Assembly those who seemed talented and willing to support the reforms.

The party also made some efforts to reach the lower strata of society. One such effort was the establishment of the People's Houses and People's Rooms, which were intended to educate the peasants. The People's Rooms were located in towns and villages, and by 1950 there were over 4,000 of them. Women and youth branches were also formed, and these became more significant after the extension in 1934 of the franchise to women. But on the whole very large segments of the population remained aloof from politics. Even the symbolic introduction into the National Assembly of an illiterate peasant woman as deputy brought hardly an echo from the villagers. The customary membership of the party consisted of administrators, intellectuals, retired or resigned military men, professional and businessmen, country notables, and rich farmers. A good many persons joined the party out of interest or fear.

During the period from 1927 to 1938 there were some vague attempts to transform the party into the more rigid type customary in one-party regimes. At the 1927 party convention Mustafa Kemal was made the permanent leader of the party, and it was decided that the administrators of all social, political, economic, and cultural agencies as well as the village headmen could be appointed only with the approval of the party's inspectors. In 1935 the party was proclaimed to be an organization which embraced all the aspirations of all the citizens. The Minister of Interior was made the General Secretary and the provincial governors were appointed chairmen of the local party organizations. Two years later the basic principles (the "six arrows") in the party's program were introduced into the text of the constitution. In 1938, after his death, Atatürk was declared "Eternal Leader" and İnönü "National Unchangeable Leader." On the whole, however, the Republican People's Party preserved the appearance of a parliamentary party, and hence the capability of liberalization. Although indirect and "guided" elections were regularly held, certain measures were debated in the National Assembly, and the party retained a parliamentary group. Very significantly indeed, the party did not impose upon its members a strict adherence to its program. Different tendencies and affiliations were allowed to develop within manageable limits. This situation facilitated the emergence of future political leaders and contributed to plurality within the unique party. Hence all the major opposition parties, including the Democratic Party, were direct emanations from the Republican People's Party.

After the death of Atatürk, İsmet İnönü became both President of the Republic and head of the party. He had been a successful commander during the War of Independence and had played an important role at the Lausanne Conference as head of the Turkish delegation. As Atatürk's closest associate, he was his almost constant premier. Under Atatürk he faithfully carried out the reform movement; as president he successfully kept Turkey out of the Second World War. After the war he made the dramatic decision to initiate a multi-party political system. Eleven days after V-Day in Europe İnönü promised that the principles of democracy would prevail to a greater extent than before in Turkish political and intellectual life. By the time the National Assembly convened in November 1945 he had clarified his intentions: "The democratic character (of the regime) has been preserved during the whole period of the republic. Dictatorship has never been accepted and always considered as harmful to, and unworthy of, the Turkish nation. . . . Our only deficiency has been the lack of a party opposing the party in power."[5]

Although the first party to emerge, the National Resurgence Party (*Millî Kalkınma Partisi*) was established during the summer of 1945 by a wealthy industrialist, the major opposition party, the Democratic Party, was officially founded in January 1946. The four founders of this party, Celâl Bayar, Adnan Menderes, Fuad Köprülü and Refik Koraltan, were former members of the People's Party. Celâl Bayar, who was born near Bursa of immigrant parents, had received his education in a private French school, and had worked in a foreign bank. Later he joined the Union and Progress, served as a guerrilla leader during the War of Independence, and held various ministerial posts. He was prime minister when Atatürk died. Generally he and İnönü have been represented as bitter rivals. Adnan Menderes (1899-1961) was the son of a rich landowning family in Western Anatolia, and was educated at an American college and Ankara Law School. He joined the People's Party and was elected deputy in 1931. Until the foundation of the Democratic Party he had been an obscure figure. Fuad Köprülü, a university professor of literature and history, had not much prior experience in politics. Refik Koraltan received a law-school education in Istanbul, started his career as an administrator, and served as a deputy in the National Assembly almost continuously after the establishment of the republic. He had been one of the strongest and most determined supporters of Atatürk and his reforms. It may be observed that none of these men had a military background.

The disposition of Menderes and Koraltan to forsake the People's Party first became apparent in May 1945, when they opposed a land reform law. In June all four submitted to the party group a proposal demanding a more democratic system. This proposal was rejected and the four were either expelled from the party or resigned from it to form the Democratic Party.

A few months after its establishment, the Democratic Party organization in the country began to develop very rapidly, being supported very strongly by the press and by the people. Soon relations between this party and the Republican People's Party became strained. On several occasions it appeared that the government would abolish

[5] *Ulus* (Republican People Party's Ankara daily), November 2, 1945.

the Democratic Party or that the Democrats rebel against the government. But the government, by amending or abolishing those laws which threatened the opposition, cleared the way for the peaceable development of a multi-party system. The Democratic Party's strength grew at an accelerated pace. Finally, after honest and direct elections in 1950, the Democrats came to power with a sweeping majority.

Although more than twenty political parties were established after 1945, only few were able to survive. The major role in transforming the one-party regime into a multi-party democratic system was played by the two largest parties. The Democratic Party, in particular, has been instrumental in introducing the masses to politics. The percentage of voters in the elections has been very high. The establishment of local party organizations, the visits of politicians to small towns and villages, open air party meetings, and the relatively free atmosphere of expression have contributed to arousing the common people to their own political importance and their stake in governments. The pressure of public officials and security forces on villagers and humble citizens has been relaxed.

Beside the common people, some important interest groups have gained political power. The dual structure of the society in many areas has given country notables and rich landowners the opportunity of interposing themselves between the government and the peasants. Parties, being aware of this situation, tend to rely on these persons especially in their local organizations. Signs of land reform and personal rivalries among themselves encouraged many of these local leaders to support the Democratic Party. The commercial and industrial class and many professional people also supported the Democrats. At the beginning this seemed to be natural, for the Democratic Party, although professing a liberal economic policy, was more articulate in its protests than in its positive recommendations. Later, when the policies of Democratic Party governments favored chiefly big landowners, the commercial and industrial class, and the liberal professions at the expense of salaried people and wage earners, class consciousness and class interest began to be more powerfully voiced in Turkish politics.

From 1946 on, the power struggle between the parties forced them both to extend their local organizations to every corner of the country, including thousands of villages. In general there is a great simi-

From 1946 on, the power struggle between the parties forced them because they are addressing themselves to the same sectors of the population and partly because of the limitations imposed by the laws on partisan activity. The local organization of each is adapted to the administrative subdivisions of the country: province, sub-province, town, and village. After the revolution of 1961, however, local party branches below sub-province level were abolished on the ground that they have destroyed peaceful relations among the people. Though the local organization's most important function was to have been the nomination of the candidates, this function has usually in fact been controlled by the parties' national headquarters. An unofficial function, on the other hand, the protection of party members or sympathizers before the public authorities, has been all too vigorously performed. This function has strengthened the position of local notables and, degenerating into partisan warfare, has destroyed the careers of many public officials. The central party structure usually provides for an annual convention, a parliamentary group, an executive committee, a leader, and a disciplinary commission. The most powerful single force has almost always been the party leader.

Accompanying the party organization has been the relentless effort of the parties to infiltrate associations and institutions of every sort. Politically motivated changes in the high military ranks, transfers of the provincial and sub-provincial administrators before and after every general election, and partisan appointments to governmental agencies have become common practices. Student organizations, labor unions, bar associations, and chambers of commerce and industry have become the targets of infiltration.

Faced with inflation and other economic difficulties, the leaders of the Democratic Party began to take restrictive measures and, especially after the 1954 elections, to intimidate the growing opposition. These measures, becoming tighter when the government was forced to reverse its inflationary economic policy in 1958, gradually alienated the most articulate elements in the society such as civil servants, army officers, university professors, students, and journalists. Finally, deviating from well-established tradition, the leaders of the Democratic Party used troops against the opposition and against demonstrating students. Despite İsmet İnönü's warnings and the demonstration of the cadets of the War College, Menderes did not modify his extreme measures. On May 27, 1960, as a result of a coup engineered largely by young army officers, the Democratic Party and its leaders were ousted from power.

After the coup a thirty-eight-man junta established itself in power

424

under the name of the National Unity Committee, and military rule officially continued until the election of October 15, 1961.

During this period the parties and their leaders concentrated on obtaining an early return to a normal democratic regime. They tried to dissuade the junta from embarking on haphazard reforms and from succumbing to the temptation to prolong its rule. Although they failed to gain some particular points, they were successful in general.

Soon after the coup—but contrary, it would seem, to their original purpose—the junta felt compelled to abolish the Democratic Party. This party still commanded very large support in the country, and its members did not believe there was sufficient justification for the violent overthrow of their leaders. In the vacuum created when that organization ceased to exist, two parties, the Republican People's Party and the Republican Peasant National Party (a former minor party called the Nation Party), remained on the scene. Although party activity was officially prohibited until the new constitution had been voted upon, it was apparent that the People's Party was playing a role behind the scenes. While embittered Democrats became more antagonistic towards him and his party, İnönü enjoyed high prestige and the respect of the armed forces and the junta. About a month after the coup he warned the military rulers and the nation that early elections were urgently required.

In the eyes of the former Democrats he and his party were responsible for the coup and were regarded as partners of the junta. The leaders of the People's Party, for their part, perceived that the growing discontent with the National Unity Committee might reduce their own electoral strength. It is probable that the People's Party leadership played an important part in the dramatic arrest and deportation of the so-called radical members of the junta on November 13, 1960. But even after the victory of the moderates in the committee, pressures on the junta continued, and finally a Constituent Assembly was convened at the beginning of 1961 to prepare a new constitution.

After this constitution was written, the ban on partisan activity was lifted for the referendum campaign. There was an immediate rush for the votes of the former Democrats, who, though deprived of their leaders, were preserving their solidarity. Eventually two new parties emerged, the Justice Party and the New Turkey Party. The leader of the former is Ragıp Gumüspala, a general who was among the officers put on compulsory retirement by the National Unity Committee. The New Turkey Party's leader, Ekrem Alican, is a business-

425

man who received his education in the Ankara School of Political Sciences. He had been a member of the Democratic Party until 1955, when he joined dissenters from it to form the Freedom Party. He had also served for a time as Minister of Finance in the Council of Ministers after the coup.

The Justice and the New Turkey parties tried to rally the former Democrats, as did the Republican Peasant National Party. To please this group all three parties took a cool attitude toward the May 27 Revolution and played on feelings of hostility towards the People's Party.

On October 15, 1961, less than a month after the former leaders and deputies of the Democratic Party were sentenced to heavy penalties, general elections were held on a proportional representation basis. The outcome of the elections precipitated another crisis, for it meant that parties hostile to the May 27 Revolution could capture power. The commanders of the armed forces intervened, and negotiations between them and the party leaders resulted in the formation of a coalition government comprising the People's and the Justice Parties. General Gürsel, the former leader of the junta, was elected President and İnönü became prime minister. The alliance of two hostile parties in government was, of course, awkward and fragile, but it was probably the only alternative to continued military rule. This coalition lasted only about six months. When it collapsed, a new coalition was formed between the Republican People's Party, the New Turkey Party, the independents, and a faction of the Republican Peasant Party. The most urgent task for the parties and their leaders now seems to be the realization of socio-economic development under a democratic regime. The impression is that both democracy and a rapid improvement in living conditions have become aspirations of the majority of the population. The question is how to satisfy demands which at times come into conflict. Underlying this conflict is the old struggle between the conservatives and reformers, which revived after the May 27 Revolution. Many intellectuals are convinced that all the present parties represent vested privileges and will never undertake the necessary radical reforms. They believe that democracy and economic development can coexist only if new leaders and parties arise to fight for the underprivileged masses. Inspired by these opinions and encouraged by the new constitution, a Socialist party, the Turkish Labor Party, was recently established with the participation of some intellectuals and union leaders. It remains to be seen whether parties and leaders will be able both to preserve the political peace and to achieve rapid economic development.

III. Patterns of Political Action

On the basis of the foregoing account, we may generalize concerning the development of party organization and leadership in Turkey over the past century.

THE CYCLICAL NATURE OF POLITICAL DEVELOPMENT

One basic characteristic of the process of political modernization in Turkey has been its cyclical nature. Whenever a major change has occurred in political institutions and leadership, a period of relative freedom has been followed by a period of repression. These cycles may be analyzed in the following manner. Certain groups or their leaders demand changes in the exercise of power or in political institutions. They are resisted by those in power and begin to be oppressed. In the face of this oppression a more general and heterogeneous opposition arises and seeks to eliminate the oppressors. Once they succeed, one group among them captures power. This group and its leaders almost immediately face opposition in turn. They face reactionary forces defending the old system; and they face disaffection, either personal or ideological, among their former allies. After a period of relative tolerance and freedom, the new leaders, who usually lack both a well-defined positive philosophy and practical experience in government, become nervous in the face of criticism and then restless and intolerant. The first target for attack is usually the reactionary opposition, the second the liberal opposition. As repressive measures become more stringent, the opposition grows stronger. In the face of this oppression, the elements in opposition, usually reinforced by dissenters from the group in power, join forces to eliminate the oppressors, and a new cycle begins.

Obviously this simple scheme is far from being exactly applicable in all cases. Nevertheless, the following general cycles may be identified:

First cycle: (a) the New Ottoman movement, beginning in about 1865, demands constitutional monarchy; (b) the constitution is put into effect, 1876-1878; (c) Abdülhamid II suspends the constitution and rules as despot, 1878-1908.

Second cycle: (a) The Young Turk movement, beginning around 1889, seeks to end the despotic rule of Abdülhamid II and to restore the constitution; (b) the constitution is restored, 1908-1913; (c)

Enver seizes power and the dictatorial rule of the Union and Progress prevails, 1913-1918.

Third cycle: (a) Mustafa Kemal and the nationalists struggle for a republican regime, 1920-1923; (b) the republican regime is established 1923-1930; (c) Mustafa Kemal and İnönü preside over a one-party regime, 1930-1945.

Fourth cycle: (a) Agitation to end one-party rule and establish a democratic multi-party system begins in 1945; (b) multi-party system prevails 1946-1954; (c) multi-party system declines as the Democratic Party leaders become increasingly autocratic.

Fifth cycle: (a) Reaction sets in against the dictatorial measures of the Democrats, 1957-1960; (b) Democratic regime established by a new constitution, 1961 to present.

Underlying these recurring cycles are certain persistent and more or less constant trends.

THE INTENSIFICATION AND EXPANSION OF PARTY ACTIVITY

In general, political activity has spread from the leaders to the followers, from the elite to the masses, and from the capital cities to the towns and villages. It has also become less and less intermittent as the period of relative freedom in each successive cycle has lengthened. This concentric spread of political activity and party organization may be attributed to the long-term socio-economic development of the nation as well as to the cumulative effect of the lengthening periods of relative freedom.

Since the socio-economic condition of the urban population and of the elite groups especially has been very high in comparison to that of other segments of the population, it was natural that effective leadership should come from the urban elite. The New Ottoman and Young Turk movements were hence born in Istanbul and spread only to a few other relatively well-developed cities of the empire. The first political party or movement to have a significant network of local branches was the Union and Progress. Although this network never covered even all the major cities or penetrated below the sub-province (*sancak*) level, it later greatly facilitated the establishment of local Defense of Rights committees during the national independence movement. The Republican People's Party did penetrate to the small towns and villages but was not successful in stimulating peasant participation. The Democratic Party at length rallied the support of the masses on

428

an unprecedented scale, the local population sometimes spontaneously forming branches of that party.

That advances in education, the communication system, transportation, and general economic conditions have played an important part in this development is undeniable. However, it is also deeply affected by qualitative changes in political practice during the successive periods of relative freedom. During the first constitutional period the House of Deputies convened twice and lasted only about eleven months. The deputies were not elected by the people but nominated by the provincial councils. Under these circumstances the emergence of party activity either in the parliament or at the electoral centers could hardly be expected. The second constitutional period was at first more conducive to party activity, and several parties were in fact established. But the atmosphere of relative freedom lasted only a few years, during which the regime endured wars, coups, and conspiracies. Under the republic the period of freedom was lengthened, though still overshadowed by Mustafa Kemal and constrained by the need for forced reforms. Given the conditions in the country, a competitive multi-party system could not flourish. Compared with these earlier phases of political development, the last two decades have been far more conducive to comprehensive political activity and organization. For the first time in Turkish history elections were direct, the practice of voting was greatly extended and the laws and regulations threatening the freedom of political activity were gradually eliminated. The leaders no longer had to force people into political activity but merely organized the eager and enthusiastic masses.

THE CHANGING EMPHASES OF PARTY ACTIVITY

The policies of the political parties and their leaders may be seen as reflecting their answers to the questions: What are the problems of the country? How should these problems be solved? How should the political leadership work toward the necessary solutions?

During the first phase of the reform movement, the problem identified was that of balancing Western superiority. This problem was later translated into the more urgent one of saving the country. Finally, after the establishment of the new Turkey, the problem might have been stated, "How can this country be elevated to the level of contemporary civilization?"

It was first believed that the West was superior only in the techniques and weapons of warfare it possessed and that the internal

429

troubles of the nation were due to simple mismanagement. The policies of the early leaders were therefore pragmatic, and limited mainly to the administrative and military reform.

When it became evident that the limited reforms fell short of fulfilling their goals, the reformers turned their attention to the traditional political institutions of the empire. From then on, constitutional government and the classical rights of citizens became desiderata, which were sought first in constitutional theocratic monarchy, then in a secularist republic with a single party, and finally in a democratic multi-party state.

Before Mustafa Kemal, social and economic problems were secondary concerns, the advances achieved in these areas being in part byproducts of political modernization. After the one-party regime was established and the drastic secularizing reforms of Kemal were underway, social and economic problems gradually attracted attention for their own sake. But the formulation of these problems and of tentative solutions long remained vague and incoherent. In fact, until 1931, the Republican People's Party had no systematic socio-economic program. Of the Six Arrows finally representing the principles of the party, only the first three—Republicanism, Populism, and Nationalism—were included in its program in 1927; the three others—Secularism, Etatism, and Reformism—were added in 1931. What these principles mean, how they stand in relation to each other, and how they should be implemented are still being debated, but even the extreme left and right today find elements in them which they interpret in their own way and freely embrace.

The policies and program of the Democratic Party were equally pragmatic. That party began by demanding democracy, free elections, and a vague "economic liberalism"; once in power, and profiting from a good harvest and quite generous foreign aid, they made economic development a slogan.

This lack of coherent policies is not hard to explain. As we noted earlier, the parties and their leaders in each period concentrated their attention on ending a despotic rule and capturing power rather than on constructive future programs. The Young Turks, for example, at their second conference in Paris, could agree on hardly anything except putting an end to the rule of Abdülhamid II. Mustafa Kemal knew from the beginning that he wanted to defeat the foreign invaders and create a new Turkish state. But the nine-point declaration issued for the first election after his victory announced only that a party would be formed and its program prepared later. The Democrats, at least while they were in opposition, in fact met inquiries about their special policies by saying, "Let us get freedom first and the rest will come of itself." Finally, the parties arising after the 1960 Revolution preoccupied themselves almost solely with seeking the votes of the former Democrats.

Until recent years, furthermore, hardly any sustained public discussion of social and economic problems has occurred. It has therefore been difficult to bring such problems to the attention of the people and to formulate programs in the light of all attitudes and interests. This situation has been due partly to the restrictions upon the establishment of parties and upon political propaganda. Only in 1948, for example, did the High Court of Appeals rule that the formation of a Socialist party would not constitute a criminal offense. It has also been fashionable of late to label ideas, persons, and parties as leftist or Communist, and so to insinuate their treachery. Almost all political leaders and parties have at one time or another been accused of Communist inclinations or associations. Under those conditions, politicians will avoid controversial issues and fail to enunciate strict and well-defined policies.

During virtually the whole process of development, furthermore, the leaders have taken a paternalistic attitude toward the people, believing or at least asserting that their policies were for the benefit of the people even though the people themselves could not wholly understand them.

Their views of themselves as men bringing enlightenment and progress to the people explain in part their tendency to stay in power indefinitely and their intolerance of opposition. In over a century only one political leader, İsmet İnönü, has left office by his own choice, and even he was under heavy internal and external pressure to step down. The leaders' lively sense of their mission and of their own extraordinary talents has further been supported by traditional popular conceptions. A cycle is established in which a worshipful populace tends to create a charismatic-authoritarian leader, while the leader in turn half-willfully demands that he be so regarded.

In point of fact, all modern Turkish leaders have had conflicting roles or duties forced upon them. They have had simultaneously to face the two types of opposition traditionally conceived as conservative-religious and modernist-secularist, the former wanting less change and the latter more.

431

In the early periods the reforming sultans were seeking to change an order of things of which they themselves were symbols. During the Reformation (Tanzimat) era the strength of the reactionary resistance on the one hand and the urgency of the need for reform on the other forced the sultans to seek the help of enlightened and able administrators. But, again as the prestige and power of these men grew, their demands for further reform threatened the sultan's own status and power. The embarrassment of the sultans was evidenced in their successive dismissal and reappointment of the same men to the highest positions. The administrators, meanwhile, had on the one hand to persuade the sultans to initiate cautious reforms and on the other hand to defend themselves from intellectuals who wanted more drastic changes.

When the heirs to these intellectuals assumed power in 1908, they were very naturally expected to adapt themselves to the constitutional system of which they had been the protagonists. But this meant, in practice, that they were expected to carry out reforms and overcome the resistance of reactionary elements while respecting the rules of parliamentary monarchy—and all this in a period of international crisis and internal disorder. The political experience both of the leaders themselves and of the nation proved wholly inadequate. It developed that political freedom worked in favor of the conservatives; the population, generally lacking cohesion and largely apathetic, constituted no true citizenry. The leaders then reverted to oppressive and authoritarian policies.

Atatürk set his face decisively against the old order. His carefully planned and ruthlessly executed reforms have changed the face of Turkey. Yet he too had to play a conflicting role; he was the champion of a republican regime, but had to resort to dictatorial methods to force his reforms upon the nation. Working with a single political party, and keeping the army and the bureaucracy out of politics, he preserved the concepts and some of the appearances of a parliamentary regime, while overriding conservative opposition.

His successor, İnönü, inaugurated the multi-party regime and has since been its defender. He has nevertheless remained in the eyes of many people a former autocrat maneuvering to perpetuate his rule under a democratic system which he has been compelled to accept; in the opinion of others he has been unhappily forced to compromise both Atatürk's reforms and those of the May 27 Revolution for the sake of a superficial and theoretical democracy.

The leaders brought to power by the multi-party system were subjected to a somewhat similar tension. They aroused demands for a standard of living which the resources of the country were inadequate to supply. They were forced in the end to modify their reforms and resort to inflation; when opposition began to grow rapidly, these former apologists for democracy resorted to anti-democratic measures that finally led to a military coup.

If earlier periods of modern Turkish history could be characterized as the "political awakening," the present period may be called the "social awakening" of the people. This awakening, of course, is only beginning. The task of the leaders is more arduous and more complicated than ever. They are now expected to remove the legacy of bitterness resulting from the coup, to promote rapid socio-economic development, to keep right- and left-wing extremists under control and yet to carry out their tasks within a very sensitive and complex democratic system. Their success will be determined by the skill with which they can reconcile the competing claims of stability and of change.

CHAPTER 10

CONCLUSION

ROBERT E. WARD AND DANKWART A. RUSTOW

THE preceding chapters have provided a rich store of data and analyses relating to eight different facets of the political modernization of Japan and Turkey. They have also demonstrated the tremendous complexity and interrelatedness of the processes involved. In every case, political modernization is depicted as mingling with a far larger stream of development that also contains economic, technological, social, and psychological components. It is almost as difficult to distinguish and describe separately the specifically political content and transformations of this larger stream of modernization as it would be to trace the waters of a single tributary amid the whirls and eddies of a swiftly flowing river. Yet, when we take the long view of modernization—as with the lower and the upper reaches of our river—there is little doubt that it represents a distinguishable stage of many national histories. Whatever the uncertainties about beginning dates and particular defining qualities, there are massive differences between those stages of a particular society's history which we crudely characterize as "traditional" and those which we somewhat hesitantly and self-consciously proclaim to be "modern."

This distinction between the "modern" and the "traditional" is our starting point, and we have in the introduction attempted to describe what we believe to be the defining characteristics of a "modern" society and a "modern" political system. The intervening chapters have provided a great deal of information about the numerous ways in which the traditional is giving way to the modern in both Japan and Turkey. Our present task is not to reformulate these findings, but to examine them from a somewhat different viewpoint. We are primarily interested in two questions. First, how does the process of political modernization in Japan compare with that in Turkey and what accounts for the differences between the two? Second, what light do these detailed analyses of the Japanese and Turkish experiences shed on the theoretical and methodological problems posed by studies of political modernization in general?

434

The preceding chapters make it quite clear that, in all respects defined in the introduction as critical to political modernity, both Japan and Turkey have been developing along generally parallel lines. Their political systems have been acquiring a larger component of modern characteristics, partly by the addition of new institutions and attitudes which supplant the traditional ones and partly by the infusion of new content into existing institutions and the refocusing of traditional attitudes. This similar course of change creates the possibility of comparing the process of political modernization in the two countries. It also raises, however, a prior problem of considerable importance.

If we are to compare the political modernization of Japan with that of Turkey, at what point of time shall we initiate the comparison? Are there functionally equivalent periods in the political histories of the two countries? In particular, what years may be said to constitute the critical period which, for purposes of economic development, W. W. Rostow characterizes as the time of "take-off"? More specifically, if one identifies the twenty-two years from 1868 to roughly 1890 as a really seminal time in the development of the modern Japanese political system—a political "take-off" period—then what is the functionally equivalent period in Turkish political development?

In the years 1868 to 1890 the leadership groups in Japanese politics irrevocably committed themselves and their country to a set of political actions and institutions that had profoundly revolutionary consequences for the subsequent development of Japan. These were the years when the traditional political institutions of Japan were finally found inadequate to the society's needs, when a new national identity for Japan began to be established and a more modern mixture of attitudes, behavior patterns, and institutions was introduced. Traditional attitudes and institutions were not thereby suddenly eliminated from the society, but the dominant commitment of the Japanese government —and, increasingly, of the people as well—became the political and economic modernization of the nation. Where should one look for a roughly equivalent period in Turkish political history?

There are several possibilities. Some might look as far back as the reign of Selim III (1789-1807) or that of his successor, Mahmud II (1808-1839); others might regard the Edict of Gülhane of 1839 as marking some such political watershed. From the standpoint of a durable and definitive commitment to the tasks of political modernization, however, the Young Turk Revolution of 1908 seems a more valid starting point and—somewhat less certainly—the completion of

435

the first great wave of political and social reforms about 1928 a useful terminal date for this early take-off period. It was with the 1908 Revolution that the Young Turks turned their backs on their long-disintegrating traditional Ottoman heritage; it was in these two decades that Young Turks and Kemalists salvaged and constructed from the wreckage of the empire the new nation-state of Turkey. These were the years when the national identity of modern Turkey was defined, a new and revolutionary leadership established in power, and the country itself irrevocably committed to a broad course of development which was distinctively modern. We suggest, therefore, that in a rough and general fashion, the twenty-year period from 1908 to 1928 may be viewed as functionally equivalent in the history of political modernization in Turkey to the twenty-two-year period from 1868 to 1890 in Japan.

If this suggestion is accepted, it might further be supposed that as of 1963 Turkey's position on a scale or continuum drawn to provide some rough cross-national measurement of stages of political modernization would be appreciably behind Japan's. Indeed, one might expect something approximating a forty-year gap between the performance characteristics of the two polities. Unfortunately, in the absence of quantifiable measures of such characteristics of political modernity as structural differentiation, rationality of decision making, or degree of popular political involvement, no very precise or direct confirmation of such a hypothesis is possible. But, viewed in qualitative terms, the findings of the preceding chapters would support such a hypothesis. In most respects political modernization, and the modernization process in general, does seem both to start later and—once launched—to make somewhat slower progress in Turkey than in Japan. In fact, in a number of instances, the gap seems to be more than forty years.

Some degree of indirect support for this hypothesis may be derived from the indicators of general socio-economic modernization. For example, if one takes the following indicators of modernity for Japan as of 1920 and for Turkey as of 1960—thus building a forty-year spread into the comparison—it will be seen that in most cases the Japanese performance still surpassed that of Turkey.

In all instances save expectation of life, the Japanese figures of 1920 indicate significantly more modern rates of performance than do those of Turkey forty years later. It seems highly probable that most other indexes of this sort would show comparable variations.

436

	JAPAN 1920	TURKEY 1960
Percentage of population in communities of 20,000 or more	23.1%	18.2%
Expectation of life at age 0		
Males	42.06	46.00[1]
Females	43.20	50.41[1]
Percentage of eligible school children enrolled	98.8%[2]	42.0%[3]
University students per 1,000 of population	39	2.3
Daily general interest newspaper circulation per 1,000 inhabitants	107[4]	45
Distribution of labor force		
Primary industries	53%	68%
Secondary industries	21%	14%
Tertiary industries	26%	17%

[1] In 1950-1951   [2] In 1918   [3] In 1959   [4] In 1924

This poses two questions: Why did the process of intensive modernization start so much earlier in Japan than in Turkey, and why did it develop at a more rapid rate?

It seems to us that two different sets of factors must be taken into account in attempting a reply to these questions. The first consists of those factors which are predetermined to such an extent as to be wholly or largely beyond the control of the leaders of the modernizing society concerned. Such factors would be the country's geographic location and geopolitical circumstances, the question of the timing of massive foreign impacts of a modernizing sort with respect to the course of domestic development, and the nature of the country's particular cultural heritage. These are "given" qualities of a particularly inflexible sort with which the leaders of Japan and Turkey simply had to deal during their respective take-off periods. The second set consists of factors which permit leadership an appreciably greater degree of discretion and control. This is still far from complete control, but it is sufficient to distinguish these factors from those in the first category.

When we examine the Japanese and Turkish experiences in terms of these two sets of factors, many of the basic reasons for Japan's earlier start and more rapid progress in political modernization become apparent. Let us consider first the relative positions of the two societies with respect to geography, timing, and cultural heritage—the first or relatively inflexible set of factors. What did these contribute to a process of early and rapid political modernization in Japan that they denied to or withheld from Turkey?

There is, first, the role of geography in facilitating the definition,

437

establishment, and operations of a nation-state. In our historic experience with the rise of contemporary political systems, the vehicle for effecting the change from traditional to modern characteristics has been the nation-state. This was certainly so for both Japan and Turkey. Yet their cases well illustrate the profound consequences of widely differing geographic and geopolitical circumstances on the nation-building process.

Japan was an island kingdom of remarkably homogeneous racial, religious, and linguistic composition; of an ancient tradition of unity vis-à-vis outsiders; and of naturally delimited frontiers. More favorable environmental conditions for the development of a modern nation-state are hard to envisage. Nineteenth-century Turkey, on the other hand, was an empire stretching over parts of three continents; lacking racial, linguistic, and religious homogeneity; precariously compounded of a motley assortment of peoples with separate and competitive traditions and aspirations; and possessed of few natural boundaries. A more refractory set of ingredients for a modern nation-state is difficult to conceive. It was necessary for the Ottoman Empire to disintegrate even further, for more of the non-Muslim and non-Turkish peoples to gain their independence, and for the imperial scale of the Ottoman tradition, values, and aspirations to be replaced by their specifically Turkish analogues before a modern and much smaller Turkish national state could emerge. Geography was of minor help or significance in this process. Turkey's new national frontiers were in large part delimited in terms of historic or political factors, including the accidents of the armistice of 1918, rather than of geography.

Geography affected the nation-building process in these states in still another way. Japan and Turkey both represent instances of what Cyril Black terms "defensive modernization." Their principal incentive to modernize came not from within their own societies but from the outside and primarily from their realization of the need to acquire sufficient national stability and strength to protect themselves against political and economic encroachments by the earlier developing states of the West. For them, modernization and nation building were essential to national security. Under these circumstances, it is instructive to examine the geopolitical positions of Japan and Turkey vis-à-vis the impact of Western imperialism.

The islands of Japan lay at the end of the trail of Western imperialist expansion. Except for the limited and relatively inconsequential contacts of the Christian century (1542 to ca. 1640), they were not seriously exposed to Western influence or threats prior to 1854. Thereafter, they were subject to some "imperialist exploitation," primarily economic in character, but this never resulted in outright warfare with the West on a national scale (prior to 1904) or in Japan's reduction to colonial status. Seen in historical perspective, these were circumstances very favorable to modernization and nation building in Japan. The country was spared the experiences of conquest and colonial status, but was still exposed to a grave enough danger to induce a pervasive sense of national crisis among both its leaders and people. The threat was never so imminent or overwhelming as to produce apathy or despair; instead, it was of a scale and duration conducive to the encouragement of patriotism, discipline, and self-sacrifice among the people, and energy, dedication, and a sense of the priority of national over parochial needs and interests among the leadership. In these terms the initial impact of Western culture and imperialism upon Japan in modern times was most unusual. It stimulated political integration rather than disintegration and touched off a truly spectacular process of defensive modernization. One is tempted to assign a significant share of the credit for theses unusual consequences to geography. Had Japan been situated on the main path of imperialist expansion across Asia rather than at its most distant terminus, it is doubtful that the results for nation building and modernization would have been quite so constructive.

The Turkish experience documents this point rather well. While the Ottoman Empire stood firm, Western imperial expansion was largely deflected across the oceans. Yet the Ottomans, from their very beginnings, were in continuous contact with European military power. Their empire lay at the crossroads of three continents. The most direct routes to India and the Far East ran through these territories. A persuasive case could be made for the claim that the Near East throughout recorded history has been the most invaded region of the globe and Japan among the least.[1] The consequences of such a geographical

[1] Quincy Wright has tabulated the participation by fifteen leading states in "wars of modern civilization" from 1430 to 1941. He distinguishes 278 such wars, of which Turkey took part in 43 and Japan in only 9. In frequency of participation, Turkey ranks sixth and Japan last. (Britain leads the list with 78, followed by France, Spain, Russia, and Austria in that order. See Q. Wright, *A Study of War*, Chicago, 1942, I, 650.) A similar calculation establishes the even more striking fact that Turkey, from 1450 to 1900, was at war for an average of 30.5 out of every 50 years—being outranked only by Spain with 33.5 years per half-century (vol. I, p. 653). The Ottoman Empire, since the late fifteenth century, was only four times at peace for more than fifteen years (1590-1610, 1718-1735, 1739-1768, 1878-1897).

situation for nation building and modernization in Turkey are clear. Although she never completely lost her statehood or national identity, Turkey was for centuries the object of Western attacks and ambitions. Toward the end of this process, although Turkey had not been reduced to colonial status, she had, like China, become a sort of "hyper-colony"—exploited by all, the responsibility of none. The impact of the West upon Turkey was thus of two sorts. During the Ottoman period it was politically disintegrative in the highest degree, and the process of defensive modernization to which it gave rise was weak, intermittent, and inadequate to the country's needs. But, once the decision was taken to abandon the empire and to build a nation-state on Turkish foundations, the West provided the appropriate models for action and Western exhaustion after the First World War played a major role in allowing Turkey's limited victory in the War of Independence of 1919-1922. The role of geography was important. Turkey was situated in the direct line of Western imperialist expansion.

The timing of the outside impact is a second factor over which the leaders of modernizing states have little control. The crucial questions are: Does this impact hit the recipient country at a point of dynastic decline, domestic strife, and political weakness or at a period of some strength and prosperity? How resilient and how integrated is the affected political system at the moment of impact? Domestic circumstances of this sort made a great deal of difference in the respective experiences of Japan and Turkey. To an important extent, it was the timing of Western impact with respect to the course of autonomous developments within these two states that was responsible. This is apt to be the case in most instances of defensive modernization.

In Turkey, the impact of the West was relatively gradual and cumulative in effect. Substantial parts of the Ottoman Empire lay in southeastern Europe and political, military, and economic contacts with Western Europe developed since at least the fourteenth century. From the eighteenth century, however, the discrepancy between Ottoman and Western power and development grew rapidly and their relationships entered what might be described as an almost "semi-colonial" stage. The political impact of the West during this period was catastrophic for the Ottoman Empire, which lost the greater part of its territories and, ultimately, its imperial status and form of government as well. From the standpoint of the timing of modernization, therefore, the critical aspects of the Turkish experience are the coincidence of the Western impact with an advanced stage of political weakness and

disintegration, and the great duration of the period required to produce an effective political reorganization on national lines.

Compared to this, the timing of the impact of the West on Japan
was more favorable, although its political consequences were also
deeply subversive to the established order. If one excepts the Dutch
influence (which was of relatively minor significance), the impact of
Europeans on Japan in modern times came at a point when the country
had been systematically isolated from most foreign contacts for upwards
of two hundred years. During this period Japan had been ruled by
as centralized and effective a government as she had ever known.
Opposition to this government was growing within Japan, but no
process of political decline and disintegration comparable to the Ottoman experience had yet set in. Instead, the advent of the Western
threat and influence after 1854 served as a catalyst for local disaffection
and facilitated a political revolt and the emergence of new forms of
government which would not otherwise have been possible in so
brief a space of time. The critical stages of the process from initial
impact to a definitive reorganization of political power took place in
the thirty-six years between 1854 and 1890. Thus there is a surgical
quality to the Japanese experience as opposed to the Turkish—a brief
and violent impact followed by rapid reintegration and recovery. It
seems quite doubtful that this would have been the case had the vectors
of Western impact and autonomous local development met at some
other point in Japanese history. For Turkey, the beneficial aspects of
this "shock therapy" can first be seen in the War of Independence in
1919-1922. Territorial ambitions, under Kemal's resolute leadership,
were reduced to a feasible national scale. Victory over Greece, only
half-heartedly supported by the weary Western allies, gave a positive
impetus to Westernization in contrast to the ambiguous effect of earlier
centuries of defeat. The matter of timing was of great importance to
the course of both Japanese and Turkish political development, and it
was a factor over which the countries' leaders could exercise little
control.

The cultural heritage of the two countries was another such "given"
factor in the modernization of Japan and Turkey. The leaders to a
large extent inherited the circumstances and raw materials with which
they had to work in their attempts to modernize both countries. Some
sets of inherited or traditional institutions, attitudes, and values are
more amenable to modernization than others. Indeed, with vision and
intelligent management, some of the institutions and values of tradi-

tional societies can be so manipulated that they will reinforce rather than oppose the course of modernizing change. To the extent that this is possible, factors in this category are amenable to leadership exploitation, but the initial presence or absence of particular institutions and values within a culture is a fixed quality—the product of history rather than leadership. In the present instance, the Japanese cultural heritage seems to have been considerably more adaptable than was the Turkish.

In both cases a large proportion of the modern component in Japanese and Turkish society was borrowed from abroad and superimposed upon a pre-existing native base. The Western element in what was borrowed assayed very high. Under these circumstances, the established attitude of these societies toward cultural borrowing as such becomes of major importance. The Japanese were used to borrowing on a massive scale. Their script; many of their literary, artistic, and architectural genres and styles; Buddhist and Confucian thought and institutions; and many aspects of their political, legal, economic, and social systems had been initially borrowed from China and subsequently naturalized in Japan. To the Japanese, cultural borrowing was a familiar and profitable experience which carried with it no lasting stigma of inferiority or indignity. As a consequence they quite readily recognized the practical superiority of Western technology and many Western institutions and were able to borrow and assimilate them with a minimum of delay and cultural shock. This greatly facilitated the modernization of Japan.

In the Turkish case, however, cultural borrowing from the West came much harder. The Ottomans, to be sure, had borrowed their religion, script, and literary forms from the Arabs and Persians much as Japan had from China. But by the sixteenth century they had conquered the Arabs, and had come to consider themselves the chief exponents and defenders of Islam. Thus they were accustomed to look down on other societies as their cultural and religious inferiors. Added to this was their ancient tradition of armed strife with the European powers and the subordinate social roles normally played by their own Christian populations. It is not easy to borrow from peoples and cultures that are very different from one's own and that are held to be both hostile and inferior in basic values. The very success of the Ottomans in conquering and administering a far-flung empire in the fifteenth and sixteenth centuries (the largest and most durable in the Mediterranean region since Roman times) delayed their adaptation to later adverse circumstances. Consequently, the psychological adjustments essential to modernization have taken much longer in Turkey than in Japan.

Many other aspects of cultural heritage, besides attitudes toward borrowing, have also been of importance in the modernization of Japan and Turkey. Considerations of space preclude the mention of any but a few of the most important. High among these is the role of religion in the two societies. Some would claim that secularization has been the single greatest problem of the modern Turkish state. Islam, in its original conception, embraces theology, ethics, law and government, polity and society. Once the traditional Ottoman concept of Faith and Dynasty proved inadequate for survival, religion became a powerful obstacle to modernizing change. The absence of a comparably entrenched and potent religious adversary made an enormous difference in the problem which confronted the leaders of modernization in Japan. While it is true that the Japanese emperor—like the Ottoman sultan-caliph—combined roles of both temporal and spiritual leadership, these functions were largely symbolic and fictional. Above all, there existed in Japan no predominant organized religion of national scope with a powerful hold on both the religious and socio-political loyalties of the people, and no corporate clerical body comparable to the *ulema*. The primary concerns of Buddhism were other-worldly, while Confucianism was more philosophy than religion and of very limited appeal. Shinto did not yet exist as an organized national faith with strong political content. Japan was thus spared the problems of disentanglement of religion and politics and of secularization which have so seriously beset the endeavors of Turkey and many other societies to modernize their political systems.

The relative adaptability of traditional institutions and attitudes to the imperatives of economic development is a second aspect of the cultural heritage of Japan and Turkey that seems of major importance to the subsequent course of political modernization. In both societies, trade and commerce were traditionally held in low esteem. In Japan the merchants stood on the lowest rung of the four-class status system, while in Turkey these aspects of economic activity were left almost exclusively to Greeks, Armenians, Jews, and other non-Turkish elements. Only the bearing of arms, religion, government, or agriculture were considered to be proper employments for a Turk. In this sense, neither heritage seemed well adapted to modern economic organization and the desperate needs of both states for rapid economic development. But the Japanese disabilities were far less serious than the Turkish. At least the merchants of Tokugawa times were Japanese, and, in fact, their actual status, influence, and accomplishments were far greater than is usually recognized. With recruits and assistance from the samurai and the rural gentry in particular, they were able after the Restoration to staff the economic roles of the new society with notable efficiency. In Turkey, the process of replacing the minority elements in control of industry and commerce by Turks has begun rather recently; up to the time of the early republic non-Turkish elements still dominated the scene. The economic aspects of the modernization process have in general tended to lag behind others in Turkey, and a major reason for this is to be found in the limiting nature of the Turkish cultural heritage in this respect.

There are numerous other aspects of cultural heritage which condition the political modernization of Japan and Turkey, but perhaps these will suffice to establish our general point. The pace and achievements of the modernization process in all societies are determined in an important and partially unalterable degree by the nature of a society's cultural heritage at the take-off period. At the same time, some types of cultural heritage are notably more amenable to modernization than are others.

Let us turn next to a consideration of the second major group of factors explaining the earlier and more rapid modernization of Japan —the factors more amenable to control or influence by leadership. It should be made clear at the outset that the distinction here envisaged between factors more and less subject to leadership control is strictly one of degree. Leaders everywhere must work with the materials presented to them by the existing conditions of their society and people. The limits within which they can act effectively and produce significant social changes are thus very seriously conditioned by the society's heritage. Even so, however, this seems to leave an appreciable area wherein the play of leadership is important and where the factors involved are more subject to influence or control than are the aspects of geography, timing, and previous historical experience which have just been discussed.

Important among the more flexible factors which can contribute to the process of rapid and effective political modernization is tradition itself. No society is wholly modern; all represent a mixture of modern and traditional elements. It has often been thought that these elements stood in basic opposition to each other, and that there was implicit in the social process some force which would ultimately lead to the purgation of traditional "survivals," leaving as a residue the purely "modern" society. The preceding chapters amply document the falsity of such a thesis, at least where Japan is concerned, showing that the role of traditional attitudes and institutions in the modernization process has often been symbiotic rather than antagonistic. Thus, having in mind, first, this dual traditional and modern quality of contemporary societies and, second, the supportive role which tradition can play in the modernization process, we can identify a quality of "reinforcing dualism" within at least some modernizing experiences.

There are many instances of "reinforcing dualism" in the Japanese case. The most conspicuous, perhaps, is the political role of the emperor. Here is an institution which is not only traditional but archaic. Yet when faced with the problem of constituting a modern nation-state in Japan, it was possible for the Meiji leadership to exhume this ancient institution, imbue it with a quite new content and a much higher degree of visibility and status, and emerge with an extraordinarily effective symbol and instrument of national unity, discipline, and sacrifice. This may well be one of the classic instances of the systematic and purposeful exploitation of a traditional political institution for the achievement of modernizing goals. Somewhat comparable use was made of state shinto, the samurai ethic, and the traditional forms of hierarchical social organization as a means of maximizing order, obedience, and discipline in the difficult early stages of the new society. It also proved possible to derive an important part of the professional bureaucracy from the former fiefs. The types of training and the values provided there were not too different from those required by the new government. Similarly, in the economic field, the maintenance of small traditionally organized units of production alongside the most modern factories seems to have contributed to the rapid and effective economic development of the country. The conclusion is that, in Japan's case, many elements of the traditional society could be converted into supports for the process of political modernization. The result was added impetus of a sort conducive to modernization.

The Turkish experience was less favorable in this respect. The attitudes toward the past and its symbols were at best ambivalent throughout the modernization process. The sultan, unlike the Japanese emperor, was an actual ruler. Hence, one way or the other, he was bound to be involved quite directly and personally in the modernization process: he could not be manipulated as a convenient and adaptable symbol. Selim III and Mahmud II were direct leaders in the early phase of modernization—which to them meant administrative centralization at home and strengthened defense abroad. There were other sultans, notably Abdülmecid (1839-1861) and Mehmed V Reşad (1909-1918), who were content to let their ministers carry on without interference, and in 1876 the bureaucrats of the capital demonstrated their skill and power by engineering two depositions. Perhaps, if this trend had continued, the sultanate might have evolved from aristocracy into a neutral point of reference for representative government, as did the British monarchy from Queen Anne to Queen Victoria. But a tradition of autonomous parliamentary institutions was totally lacking, and the accidents of succession brought to the throne headstrong and suspicious monarchs such as Abdülhamid (1876-1909) and Mehmed VI Vahideddin (1918-1922), who were bent on reasserting full monarchic power and who sharply opposed the representative-populist trend of modernization. Vahideddin's collaboration with the victorious powers after 1918 exacerbated the contrast and precipitated the break. The sultanate-caliphate, in the eyes of the leading modernizers, had become the quintessence of backwardness and reaction.

Similarly, the major thrust of Islam and of its clergy came to be (and to be considered) adverse to modernization. In the mid-nineteenth century, some *ulema* had joined the "liberal" protest against bureaucratic centralization. In the War of Independence, religious sentiment and symbolism greatly reinforced national unity and resistance. Both during the Young Turk period and in the 1920's there were some attempts to reform the religious establishment in a modernizing spirit. Finally, in the 1950's there was vague talk of Islamic revival and an Islamic-modern synthesis. But the majority of the *ulema* clearly were conservative and deeply opposed to Frankish, infidel innovation. And any opponent of modernization could easily appeal to the religious-conservative sentiment of the lower classes—witness the 1909 counter-revolution, the anti-nationalist proclamations of the *şeyhülislâm* in 1920, and the Kurdish rebellion of 1925. As a result, the most ardent Turkish modernizers of the last century, while disclaiming opposition to religion as such, have been imbued with implacable hostility to the Islamic establishment and its tradition. Meanwhile, the legal and cultural reforms of the Kemalist period, and particularly the alphabet change of 1928, have torn open a gulf between modern life and religious tradition which it would be difficult or impossible to close. To a limited extent, Kemal's role as victor (*gazi*) and

soldier-ruler-educator harked back to old Ottoman symbols and traditions. But against the sultan himself and the religious establishment,
the modernizers were in the end impelled to make a frontal attack
that precluded any possibility of reinforcing dualism.

It would seem, therefore, that a considerably larger proportion of
the traditional Japanese heritage was capable of conversion and exploitation for modernizing purposes than was the case in Turkey.
This is doubtless an element of some importance in explaining the
differential performance of the two societies.

A second type of basic advantage enjoyed by Japan in the modernization process relates to what Lucian Pye has termed the "crisis of
identity." In the non-Western world traditional societies usually lack
any very strong or well-defined sense of national identity. This is
particularly true at the popular or mass level, where some combination
of family, clan, caste, religious, or communal identifications is apt to
be the only one considered as truly important or meaningful. The transition to a modern form of political organization, however, requires
the partial replacement of such parochial identifications and loyalties
by some sense of identification with and allegiance to the nation.
Essentially what is involved is the creation of a form and scale of
political organization appropriate to dealing with the problems of
modern life on both the domestic and international scene. Up to the
present at least, the nation-state has proved to be the only effective
answer to this problem. Thus most developing societies are at the
outset confronted with this overriding problem of how to pull together
all the atomized "little societies" of their traditional period into some
minimal semblance of nationhood. In this sense they are seeking a new
form of integration, in effect a new and national personality—hence
the "crisis of identity." This must be met and solved in at least
temporarily viable terms before a society can advance far along the
path of political modernization.

The problems confronting Ottoman Turkey in this respect are obvious. In a political sense, her inherited form of organization was
dynastic-imperial and her empire was steadily disintegrating under
both internal and external pressures. Some new and more stable form
of political organization had to be found. In terms of boundaries and
peoples to be included, a variety of solutions to this problem were
possible. The normal tendency was to define the new form in the most
expansive and inclusive terms thought to be militarily defensible.
Consequently, it took a long time and much experimentation with

other and more grandiose schemes—including Pan-Islam and Pan-Turkism—before the Turks became desperate enough to settle for the boundaries of their present state. This point was not finally reached until the War of Independence. As a consequence, Turkey did not really face or resolve the basic territorial aspect of her crisis of identity until at least 1919 or even 1922. Between 1912 and 1923, the secession of non-Turkish Muslims such as the Albanians and Arabs, the decimation of the Armenians, the defeat of the empire itself, and the population exchange with Greece had reduced the nationality problem to manageable dimensions. Nonetheless, the Kurdish minority remained as a challenge to national unity into the 1930's. And there still remained the massive problem of superseding parochial village loyalties with national identifications in the minds and hearts of the Turkish people. This attempt continues in the present.

Japan was exceptionally fortunate in this respect. During the early modernizing period, there was never any serious doubt as to where her major boundaries lay. They were naturally defined by the sea. Her population was racially homogeneous; the same language—with some dialectical differences—was spoken throughout the islands; religion was not a divisive factor; and there was a tradition of national unity and identity extending back at least twelve hundred years. The major elements of a new national identification were already at hand. The Meiji leadership had only to assemble them and give them a new formulation and heightened emphasis. This was a task calling for great insight and skill, but it was in no sense comparable to the problem confronting Ottoman and Turkish leadership. Japan's crisis of identity was relatively mild.

Much the same might be said of a second kind of crisis which confronts almost all emerging nations—the crisis of security. It has already been pointed out that the modernization process in non-Western societies has been characteristically defensive. That is to say that its prime impulsion has been the defense of their territory, sovereignty, institutions, or economy against real or fancied encroachments by more developed societies—usually Western ones. The struggle of colonial peoples for independence is but a special case of this crisis of security. Once having gained independence, they are, if anything, apt to be even more harassed than others by fears that some aspect of their national security is in jeopardy. In practically all cases, concern for security is a major, if not dominant, factor in determining the policies and actions of developing societies, particularly in their earlier stages. The modern-

448

ization process is, therefore, normally initiated and accompanied by fear projected on a national scale. Whether or not this is in fact justified is considerably less important than that it is felt.

In this respect, too, the experiences of Japan and Turkey have been markedly different. The modernization of Japan was undoubtedly propelled by fear. The leaders of Japan were quite adequately informed about the march of Western imperialism across Asia and the fate of the countries which had succumbed in the process. Edge was added to this fear by the circumstances under which Japan was forced to resume intercourse with the Western powers and by the types of pressure and exploitation which she subsequently experienced at their hands. One constantly has the feeling, in reading about the early stages of modernization in Japan, that the Meiji leadership habitually acted with a fearful eye cocked over its shoulder at the menacing foreigners. Despite this, however, the period during which Japan was seriously concerned about Western threats to her national security was brief. For most purposes it had ended by 1890. And even before that, actual foreign encroachments were largely economic in nature and not too critical in effect. The wars in which Japan was involved came at a later point in her course of development and were of her own choosing. And, with the exception of the last one, they were relatively brief and uniformly resulted in Japanese victories. Their general effect was undoubtedly favorable to the course of modernization.

The Turkish case was different. Foreign pressure was fairly continuous after the end of the seventeenth century and involved a number of major military campaigns against the Ottomans, in the course of which large portions of the empire were lost. In addition to this, Western support and encouragement were constantly extended to the efforts of the subject peoples to establish their independence of Turkish control. At later periods there was also frequent Western intervention in the purely domestic affairs of the Ottoman government and economy. Even after the Revolution of 1908 Turkey was involved in no fewer than four wars with European states. And it was only with her victory over Greece and the Treaty of Lausanne in 1923 that Turkey finally achieved a reasonable degree of national security. Thus her crisis of security was both far more prolonged and far more serious than that of Japan.

In terms of the consequences of such experiences for the process of modernization, one is tempted to conclude that a moderate, manageable, and not-too-prolonged threat to national security is apt to provide a useful stimulus, as in the case of Japan, but that a threat of truly desperate dimensions, such as that confronting Turkey, is apt to focus a country's attention and total resources on the immediate imperatives of self-defense and thus to prevent, delay, or otherwise seriously complicate the drive towards modernization.

Something should also be said about the differential qualities of the Turkish and Japanese leaders and their followers in this attempt to explain the course and pace of political modernization in the two countries. It seems useful to treat these factors in tandem since in practice they operate with a high degree of interdependence. Where the element of leadership is concerned, we are obviously dealing with two quite different varieties of the species. The Turkish variety springs from a cult of the hero as warrior, statesman, and educator—a belief in the great man and his ability to mold the course of history. This is reflected in many sources ranging from the folk tales told to children to the pattern of officer training in the armed forces. In modern times Kemal Atatürk is a prototype of this ideal. The consequences politically are an emphasis upon a highly personal brand of leadership and decision making associated with highly personalized and hierarchical patterns on the part of the followers at lower levels.

The Japanese variety of leadership is quite different. One of the most salient characteristics of modern Japanese history is the almost total absence of "great men" who stand head and shoulders above their colleagues. Even what was widely termed Japanese Fascism notably failed to produce a leader. Political leadership in Japan is a collegial phenomenon and the patterns of decision making associated with it are consensual rather than personal. The Japanese simply are more comfortable with committee types of political organization and procedure. The functioning of the entire system reminds one strongly of the qualities widely attributed in this country to the "organization man."

Although divergent in these respects, there are also ways in which the roles played by leadership in the political modernization of Japan and Turkey have been similar. If one leaves aside issues of style in political leadership, the general development of leadership patterns in the two countries has not been dissimilar. In Japan after 1868 and in Turkey after 1908 there was an extended and very critical period when leadership was of a generalized character. This is to say that specialization into sharply defined categories of civil, military, economic, domestic, foreign, and other types of leadership, with separate individuals or groups taking a leading role and responsibility in each, had not yet set in. The Meiji leadership, the Young Turks, and the Kemalists were to a remarkable extent jacks-of-all-trades. They dealt with problems and provided leadership in an across-the-board fashion that may be characteristic of the critical early stages of intensive modernization.

This first generation of leadership proved astonishingly durable in both countries. In Japan, for example, the *genrō* continued to provide a source of ultimate political leadership and decision making until after the First World War. In Turkey, Kemal Atatürk played a similar and even more active role until his death in 1938. But in both cases a continuing erosion of the generalized quality of this leadership is apparent. The facets and demands of the modernization process are too numerous and too technical to admit of the continuance of truly generalized leadership. Except in its early and, so to speak, revolutionary stages, no individual leader or really small leadership group has either the span of control or the technical knowledge to keep abreast of expanding national needs and activities. Specialization of leadership becomes cumulatively more necessary.

At this point some dilution of the earlier leadership situation is necessary on grounds of specialization. It also seems to become more probable in terms of rising domestic political competition. The dynamics and complexity of the political situation make it advisable to expand the membership of the leadership circle beyond its earlier and narrower limits. For example, the second generation of military officers are apt to be more specialized and professionalized in their interests and competence than the politico-military leaders of the first period. Given the critical importance of this group to the preservation of domestic political stability as well as national security, however, it is difficult and even dangerous to seek to exclude them from the inner circles of leadership. The same sort of argument frequently applies in slightly different terms to economic and financial leadership and to the leaders of groups of growing or established political importance. The strategy and demands of stabilizing and constructively modernizing a polity are certain to be markedly different from those appropriate to the more revolutionary needs of establishing that polity in the first place. This applies to leadership needs as well as other categories. Japan and Turkey were extraordinarily fortunate in having leadership groups that combined both revolutionary and constructive talents and who were thus able to bridge effectively what can be a most difficult gap. Even so, however, both groups soon found it necessary to admit other elements to an increasing role in national political leadership. The reasons were partly political and partly a result of the country's growing need for more specialized talents.

Both Japan and Turkey were also fortunate in being able to solve or postpone serious issues over who should provide political leadership during the early stages of their modernization process. This is a problem which can have the most serious adverse consequences for modernizing politics. They need a measure of political stability sufficient to permit the allocation of a maximum amount of time, talent, and resources to the manifold tasks of modernization. Nothing can be more distracting than a prolonged crisis over political leadership.

Japan managed first to delay such a crisis until 1877 and then to face and solve it in the Satsuma Rebellion within the space of some seven months. Thereafter, the ultimate ascendancy of the Meiji leadership, although gradually diluted, was not seriously challenged until after the First World War. This gave Japan an extended period of time during which she did not have to divert any serious portion of her energies or time to squabbles over political leadership but could concentrate on the solution of less glamorous but more constructive problems.

In Turkey, there was intense rivalry for leadership from the beginning of the modernization process in the late eighteenth century down to the 1908 Revolution, and this constitutes one important reason for the considerable delay intervening in Turkey between the first reform impulses and the final adoption of an all-embracing program. At first the conflict was one between reformers and conservatives: sultan vs. Janissaries and âyan. Later it became one among rival groups pursuing competing reform policies: Tanzimat ministers vs. New Ottomans, Abdülhamid vs. Young Turks. The prolonged crises of 1807-1808 and 1876-1878 testify to the intensity of these conflicts. From 1908 to 1950, on the other hand, there was a remarkable continuity of leadership. The early Kemalists, for example, were mostly Young Turks of secondary rank who took the lead with a modified program of modernization after the first rank of leaders were forced to step down. Yet the political turmoil of the years from 1908 to 1913 and the existence of two rival governments from 1919 to 1922 indicate that the Young Turks and Kemalists had to overcome major opposition. From the establishment of the republic in 1923, however, leadership was unified, and it was during this period that the most intensive progress was made. Only with the advent of the multi-party system after 1945 did Turkey enter a phase of rivalry among more differentiated leadership groups.

A further aspect of the question of political leadership in Japan and Turkey that deserves comment is the role of the military. Kemal Atatürk was a career military officer. The Meiji leaders were practically all samurai by birth and training and thus shared in an ancient military tradition. Furthermore, as the modernization process continued in both countries, the military continued to play an important and conspicuous role. This frequently included outright political leadership. Thus the military element is prominent in the political modernization of both countries. In the early stages at least, there is reason for believing that the military training and skills of the top political leadership were useful, if not indispensable. Both countries faced threats to their integrity and security from abroad, while at home their most urgent task was the establishment of a stable and secure national government. The answers to both these problems were in important part military and revolved about the creation of strong, loyal, and modernized armed forces. This was one type of problem with which Kemal and the Meiji leaders were well equipped to deal.

In both countries the role of military factors in the modernization process was by no means confined to matters of leadership. The contributions of the conscription systems were also numerous and important. These systems took conscripts from the villages, often taught them to read and write or provided them with training in modern trades and specialties, introduced them to city life and other parts of their countries, and served as a major means of building bridges between traditional village society and the new attitudes and institutions of the modernizing state. The armed forces were themselves a modernizing force and experience in a variety of ways, the consequences of which were in both cases society-wide.

At a somewhat lower level of leadership, the roles played by the higher officials of the professional bureaucracies were also of great importance in the political modernization of Japan and Turkey. Both societies enjoyed a special advantage in this respect. They had long been sovereign and independent and had been forced to develop a group of specialists charged with the conduct of national administration. Their experiences differed from the former colonial societies where the imperial power had usually replaced whatever high-level

453

national administrative group may have existed by members of its own bureaucratic service.

One is also impressed by the relative depth and sophistication of the Japanese and Turkish experiences with the staffing and operation of their higher administrative services. These were professionalized and specialized bodies which developed gradually over a period of several centuries. There were schools or specialized types of training and education which prepared men for entrance to administrative offices. In both societies means were developed at astonishingly early dates to recognize talent and apply standards of ability and achievement rather than of birth and status to the selection and advancement of higher officials. Professional bureaucratic careers came to be recognized, as did areas of specialization within the bureaucracy. As a consequence, from a standpoint of administrative staffing and leadership both Japan and Turkey were better equipped to face the problems of modernization than were most developing societies. In a working sense, the role of the higher bureaucracy is apt to be critical in determining the pace and degree of success which such societies can achieve. The experience of Japan and Turkey reinforces this conclusion.

Where the followers are concerned, the two national situations are quite different. In this case, however, the difference resides largely in the relative values and skills which the two populations brought to the tasks of modernization. It is hard to speak with much assurance about the distribution of values related to modernization among two national populations, but it is certainly not irrelevant that the Japanese of the 1868-1890 period were a remarkably disciplined, hardworking, and frugal people. It also seems important—especially from the standpoint of economic development—that they possessed a strong sense of craftsmanship, which was notably lacking among Ottoman Turks.

Of greater political importance, perhaps, was the low level of the political expectations harbored by the bulk of the Japanese population at this time. In 1890 most people still did not expect to play any significant role in the political process. Voting, civil rights, and responsible government were unfamiliar and exotic concepts, and practically no one looked to government as the proper source of social security, equal opportunity, or guaranteed prosperity. In this sense timing was again of assistance to the Japanese. It is considerably easier to demand discipline, sacrifice, and saving of a people who regard government as something done to them by their betters for reasons which are none of their business, than of a people who are beginning to question the correctness of such traditional attitudes in the name of democracy and the social service state. One suspects that the Japanese leadership of 1868-1890 enjoyed appreciably more freedom of action in this sense than did the Turkish leadership from 1908 to 1928.

There were also more concrete ways in which the practical skills of the Japanese followers were better adapted to the needs of modernization than were those of the Turkish. In this respect, nothing is more striking than the extent of literacy in Japan on the eve of the Restoration. R. P. Dore estimates that perhaps forty to fifty per cent of all Japanese boys and fifteen per cent of the girls were receiving formal schooling outside the home. When one considers the essentiality of an effective national communication system, of the ability to read and write, and of mass public education to all aspects of the modernization process, the truly remarkable nature of such a claim for Japan during the 1860's becomes clear. This was a level of performance matched in very few European states at a comparable stage of development and is not too different from Turkish performance in the 1950's.

It is interesting to note also the different approaches adopted to the problem of public education by Japan and Turkey. The former chose at the outset to concentrate the bulk of her educational expenditures in the field of mass elementary education. Large-scale concern with secondary and higher education came later and was based upon prior accomplishments at the elementary level. Turkey chose at first to stress more elitist and selective types of education which emphasized the role of the *lycée* and higher education at the expense of mass popular education. More recently, however, the emphasis has shifted more in the direction of Japanese practice. The evidence of these two cases alone is not sufficient to warrant generalizations as to the possible superiority of the one educational strategy to the other, but there may be some presumption in favor of the Japanese.

Viewed in retrospect, therefore, it would seem that these linked phenomena of leaders and followers had something to do with the earlier start and more rapid progress of political modernization in Japan. The specific contribution of a different variety of leadership to this result is elusive. One might guess that the collegial Japanese type was more productive of leadership in depth, more hospitable to diversity of opinion and approach, and thus more pragmatic and flexible in practice. But conclusive evidence is lacking. The case of its followers is clearer. Japan did enjoy definite advantages over Turkey, where the attitudes and values and the skills of her population in general were concerned. The matter of differential levels of literacy is particularly notable here. But this should not lead to an under-valuing of the relevance to the process of political modernization of more intangible characteristics such as discipline, diligence, frugality, and a sense of craftsmanship. The importance of these qualities to the rapid and successful modernization of Japan is probably not best demonstrated through the Turkish comparison. The case would be far clearer if it juxtaposed the Japanese circumstances in these respects to those of several developing societies in Southeast Asia.

Similarly, the Turkish experience might be considerably clarified by comparison with neighboring Arab societies. While Turkish patterns of political leadership have been less effective than Japanese, they clearly surpass those prevalent among the Arabs. The tendency toward personalism, rhetoric, and hero worship, derived from a common Near Eastern and Islamic heritage, is equally present. But examples of successful political leadership are few among the Arabs. One of Mustafa Kemal's most cogent arguments in rallying the Anatolian Turks to national resistance in the War of Independence was that a people accustomed to political rule for six and one half centuries could not willingly submit to colonial subjection. In the Arab countries, by contrast, the memories of imperial rule by the early caliphs were distant; that early empire itself, moreover, had begun to disintegrate within a few generations of its founding. From the sixteenth century to the twentieth, most Arabs had been ruled by the Ottomans and there had been no independent Arab government except in distant Morocco. It is not unrelated to this lack of a vital Arab political tradition that no Arab country by the middle of the twentieth century had developed a nation-wide party organization with local branches comparable in scope, durability, and unity with the Republican People's Party (1923 ff.), the Defense of Rights Association (1919-1923), or even the earlier Union and Progress Movement (1908-1918). In a broader comparative perspective, it thus appears probable that, in respect to political leadership, Japan and Turkey do not represent opposite extremes among modernizing countries. While Japan may well be one end of the spectrum, Turkey is somewhere in the middle, and, very likely, the upper-middle ranges.

In the light of the findings in several of the earlier chapters, it would also seem appropriate to identify a crisis of economic develop-

ment which afflicts all developing societies and has profound importance for their political modernization. Here, too, Japan enjoyed
major advantages. In a comparative sense, it seems that in Japan
during the early take-off period relatively equal importance was attached to both economic and political modernization. The sources of
the Restoration itself were primarily political, but very soon thereafter
one finds the Meiji leadership embarking on far-reaching endeavors
to modernize major sectors of the economy and devoting a large
proportion of the national revenues to these efforts. As a result, the
two sequences of change—political and economic—proceeded more or
less in tandem during the critical early years. The consequences were
favorable for political modernization. Economic development was conducive to the expansion of the new government's power and span of
control, to the early acquisition of a sense of national security and
self-assurance vis-à-vis foreign threats, and to the diversification and
expansion of the ranks of the essentially politico-military elite which
initially ruled the new Japan. Perhaps most important of all, however,
was the contribution of economic development to the sense of dynamism and progress which came to characterize the Japanese state
during the 1890's. In large part this was based upon obvious and
rapid improvements in economic plant and productive capacity, but
it also had a foundation in slowly rising living standards and an
expanding number of jobs for the rapidly increasing population. In
a practical as well as a spiritual sense, therefore, the growing success
of development in the economic sphere provided grounds for a growing sense of popular and elite identification with the process of modernization as a whole. It provided some payoff for most of those concerned, as well as tangible evidence that the new ways were working
and that all of the upsetting changes attendant upon modernization
were worth the price. These were products of great importance in
the political sphere.

Economic development in Turkey was seriously delayed by external and internal political factors. The capitulations, by which citizens of European powers and other local protégés could carry on
business outside the country's territorial jurisdiction, were abolished
as late as 1914. From 1881 to the World War, even the collection
of major government revenues was in foreign hands through the institution of the Dette Publique. Tariff sovereignty was not recovered
until five years after the Treaty of Lausanne. The political modernization period of 1908-1928 coincided with a transfer of some major

businesses and most cash-crop land from non-Muslim to Turkish hands. But a concerted attack on problems of economic development did not come until the *étatist* program of the 1930's and the Menderes period of the 1950's.

The internal reason for this delay was not simply the one-sided military training of the Young Turk and Kemalist leadership or the traditional Ottoman disdain for trade and industry. Rather, it was the purposeful (if not necessarily conscious) precedence accorded to the "crisis of identity." Where the Young Turks had tried to tackle the problems of security, identity, and modernization helter-skelter all at once, Kemal clearly sensed the need for priorities. Major issues were tackled one at a time: military defense (1919-1922), the institutions of a new state (1923-1924), and legal and cultural reforms (1924-1928). Economics was added only to the end of this list. After the *étatist* decade of the 1930's, the mobilization of manpower in World War II (without corresponding industrial effort), and the decision in 1945-1950 to move from authoritarian to democratic politics further delayed concerted attention to agricultural and industrial development. While 1908 in Turkey may be considered the analogue in political modernization to 1868 in Japan, the greater complexity of the political issues resulted in a further time-shift whereby the analogue of Japan's decades of economic development from 1870 to 1890 comes in Turkey, at best, in the 1950's and 1960's.

A further way of analyzing the differential performance of Japan and Turkey with respect to political modernization is to be found in the field of popular relationships to the political system. We would suggest that there are at least three dimensions to this relationship which are of importance—integration, penetration, and participation. By integration we mean the degree to which a population accepts and, when necessary, supports the nation-state within whose boundaries it resides. Integration may be regarded as an index of popular nationalist identification. Penetration, on the other hand, is an index of politicization. It refers to the extent to which different elements and cross-sections of a total national population are in some manner aware of, interested in, and involved with (in manners other than those treated as "participation") the political process. A category of this sort is suggested because of the prevalence and importance of the phenomenon of massive political apathy in traditional and early modernizing societies and the restricted and largely elitist nature of the resultant political process. Motion away from such a condition is an important part of the process of political modernization. Finally, participation is a measure of positive political activity which refers primarily to the extent to which a total national population possesses and exercises the suffrage or is involved in interest group action. The three categories are, of course, related and interactive and find their common denominator in political attitudes and behavior at the most inclusive popular level.

If one looks at the experiences of Japan and Turkey in terms of these three related categories, it will once more be seen that Japan has probably had fewer and less serious problems to solve. National integration raised few difficulties. During the political take-off period there were groups that were bitterly opposed to the new distribution of political power and to the policies of the ruling group, but integration in a national sense was not seriously in question. It was taken for granted that "Japan" as then defined was the proper—indeed, the natural—organizational form in which the people should collectively confront their problems, and they shortly acquired strong nationalist identification with the new form of the Japanese state.

A high integration quotient of this sort, of course, connotes a certain amount of penetration—of a specialized and restricted sort, at least. In a larger sense, however, the general politicization of the masses came more slowly in Japan. It seems to have progressed by layers, affecting the literate and more politically sensitive urban and rural upper and middle classes first and penetrating to the urban poor and the lower peasantry last of all. The speed and intensity of penetration seems to have been partially a function of improvements in the communication system, partially of the spread of new ideas about the relations of citizens to government, and partially of the position in which particular individuals and groups stood with respect to contemporary governmental policies, actions, or supports. At the lower and most numerous levels of the population, progress was slow. Very sizeable segments of the total population had been effectively politicized by the end of World War I, but one suspects that the ranks of the urban and rural lower classes were not massively penetrated and involved until the late 1930's in connection with the government's campaign for total national and "spiritual" mobilization.

Participation, in the sense of expansion of the suffrage at least, is more precisely measurable. In a legal sense, there was no national electorate in Japan until the enactment of the Meiji Constitution and its attendant basic laws in 1890. At that time 1.13 per cent of the total population was enfranchised. By 1924 this figure had increased only to 5.61 per cent. The advent, first, of universal manhood suffrage in 1925 and, second, of universal adult suffrage in 1946 expanded these figures to 19.98 per cent and 48.65 per cent respectively. Thereafter, the lowering of the age qualification resulted in the enfranchisement of 60.46 per cent of the entire Japanese population by 1960. Viewed in isolation, this may not seem to be a very rapid change but, considered in both time perspective and in relation to the records of most Western states, it is certainly not slow. The expansion of interest group participation is harder to measure. In any massive sense, it doubtless lagged behind expansion of the suffrage. In fact, it has become a normal and general facet of the political process only since World War II.

In Turkey, two of these three political processes—integration and penetration—came later, and evolved more slowly and unevenly. In the Ottoman Empire, Muslims were in a minority until the eighteenth century and Turks until the Balkan Wars. Europeans had always used the words "Turk" and "Turkey" for the Ottomans and their empire, and the Ottoman political exiles of the mid- and late nineteenth century were naturally known as "Young Turks." In the empire itself, however, the very word "Turk" was used until the beginning of the present century as a condescending designation for the unlettered peasantry of Anatolia. It was not until the loss of the Balkan-Christian population in 1912-1913 that a substantial portion of the Ottoman elite shifted to a Turkish national consciousness. Even the "National Pact" of 1919-1920, which defined the territorial aspirations of the Kemalist resistance movement and the later boundaries of the republic, studiously avoided the controversial term "Turk," referring instead to the "Ottoman-Muslim" population. "Turk" and "Turkey" have thus been used consistently in official parlance only since 1923. The ambiguity of the word *millet*, which once meant religion or religious denomination but then became the equivalent of "nation," contributed to the confusion. To this day, an Anatolian villager is as likely to say that his nation is "Islam" as that it is "Turkish"; and a member of the Istanbul Christian or Jewish minority groups, while readily conceding that he is a Turkish citizen, will hotly deny being a "Turk." Integration has thus come slowly in Turkey.

Penetration—or expansion of the human scope of politics—was equally slow. Measures such as universal conscription and taxation, while proclaimed in Tanzimat days, did not become effective until the time of the First World War. A uniform secular system of law was adopted only in the 1920's. Universal public education, decreed during the same period, still remains to be carried into practice in the remote villages. Indeed, this gap of half a century or more between legislative enactment and administrative execution is characteristic of the entire process of Turkish modernization and contrasts sharply with the prompter and more purposeful performance typical of Japan.

Political participation in Turkey, on the other hand, developed more rapidly—albeit unevenly—than in Japan. The Constitution of 1876 envisaged manhood suffrage, although the first parliament was prorogued in 1878 before it had a chance to enact an electoral law. The law of 1909 formalized manhood suffrage. Yet in the "big stick" elections of the Young Turk period, there was little effective choice and in those of the Republican period until 1945 there was only a single list. In 1934, the franchise was extended to women; in 1945, the two-degree system was replaced by direct elections; but only with the elections of the 1950's and of 1961 did voting in fact become universal, participation consistently exceeding the 80 per cent mark. Political activity in journalism, speech making, and associational life has gone through periodic cycles of efflorescence and repression. It reached successive peaks in 1876-1877, 1908-1912, 1918-1920, 1945-1960 and since 1961. Down to the Young Turk period, it was largely limited to Istanbul and a dozen or so other major cities; in the Republican one-party period it extended to the small towns; and only with the transition to a multi-party system in the late 1940's did it reach into the villages. In fact, the greater instability of Turkish parties in contrast to Japan may be attributed to the relative lag of integration and penetration behind participation—although further evidence and, very likely, a systematic comparison of more than two countries would be required to establish this thesis more securely.

Finally, in this listing of factors which seem to relate to an explanation of the differential performance of Japan and Turkey with respect to political modernization, it is possible to identify a crisis of output and distribution. This has two aspects. It can be viewed, first, as a problem of allocating political power and political roles among the populace. With what degree of efficiency has the leadership stabilized the domestic contest for power, directed it into non-revolutionary channels, and distributed offices of authority or prestige? Efficiency in such a context is judged in terms of general acceptance and con-

461

sequences for the viability of the system. Or, second, it can be viewed as a problem of political performance. Is the political system producing "goods" or "values" of a type and in a volume adequate at least for the maintenance of systemic viability? There are for every polity minimal levels of performance below which it cannot fall and still avoid disintegration, revolution, or some other form of drastic systemic change. These levels fluctuate with time and varying national circumstances. There may also be corresponding maximal systemic tolerances for innovation and change, the exceeding of which may bring about similar adverse results. These, too, are subject to change. The consequence of acceptable levels of performance in both the power allocation and output functions of a political system is the maintenance of some viable degree of systemic stability. This crisis of output and distribution is of particular importance in the early period of political take-off when a developing society with limited resources and tolerances is confronted simultaneously with so many other desperate challenges, but it continues to play a major role throughout the life of the polity.

Japan has met this continuing crisis rather well. In the critical early stages from 1868 to 1890, her leadership managed to meet and cope decisively with several serious challenges to the existing allocation of power and leadership roles. With the putting down of the Satsuma Rebellion in 1877, however, a quite cohesive leadership group was established which managed to maintain its solidarity until the end of the century. During this period there were, of course, numerous instances of dissent from the role allocations dictated by this leadership, but they were all handled without serious disruptive consequences for the system.

Where performance was concerned, the leadership was greatly benefited by the low levels of expectation characteristic of most of the Japanese population at this time. Thus it was not necessary until much later—after 1945 in fact—for government to produce broad popular participation, general social security, a high level of political and civil rights, or a consumers' economy. The people in general simply were not yet conditioned to such levels of political expectation. Yet, as their expectations did gradually rise as a result of education and the successes of the new state, the governmental output of such "goods" rose too, and the people by and large, if not really satisfied with their share of the output, at least did not become alienated from the system on a critical scale. Thus throughout the years after 1868 the Japanese leadership was continuously able to perform at levels which were acceptable in terms of current popular expectations and thus to avoid major challenges to or disruptions of the political system.

In Turkey, popular expectations from the political system, well into the Republican period, were political rather than economic. The Young Turk leadership aroused expectations of individual and national political expression among a polyglot population that aggravated internal conflict. The release of powerful centrifugal forces, including the Albanian (1911-1912) and Arab (1916-1918) secession movements, hastened the disintegration of the empire and made a mockery of the dreams of national strength and imperial glory so dear to the Young Turk orators and their audiences. Atatürk's major achievement was the deliberate scaling down of territorial ambitions which for the first time laid a basis for internal unity and relative external strength within these more modest limits. Aspirations for economic improvement were held down by the one-party system of 1923-1945. With the advent of competitive party politics, a sudden wave of economic expectation swept the countryside, and once again performance lagged behind aspiration. The economic dislocations of Menderes' ill-planned expansion program hit with special force the urban population, who also were most sensitive to his mounting measures of political repression. The Second Republic thus has inherited a thoroughly aroused participant population with an unprecedented awareness of economic needs and expectations of government performance. To harmonize the potentially conflicting group and class demands upon governmental output, and to raise total output to commensurate levels, will require more ingenuity, wisdom, and firmness than most governments of Turkey have shown in the past.

As one reviews in this manner the basic factors which affected the modernizing experiences of Japan and Turkey—particularly during the critical early stage of political modernization—it becomes apparent that we are dealing with two very different societies. Japan in the 1860's was a homogeneous society with a common language and culture, no serious religious antagonisms, some sense of national identity, a stratified and quite immobile pattern of social organization based upon a loyal and diligent peasantry, a surprisingly high level of elite and popular education, and a reasonably efficient system of authoritarian government often described as centralized feudalism. On the other hand, Turkey, as recently as 1908, was still a diffuse, polyethnic, and multi-lingual society with little or no sense of national identity, a more fluid class structure, a very low level of literacy and secular education, and a system of despotic government struggling with diminishing success to preserve an empire which had been steadily disintegrating for upwards of two hundred years. These are major differences that confer an important measure of distinctiveness on the modernization process in both states.

But should one stop with such a finding? Is there not more to the story than a chronicle of uniquenesses? Without denying either their scale or importance, is it not possible to plumb somewhat deeper beneath the surface in a search for the shared substratum of experience that logic and probability indicate should underlie the process of political modernization in all societies—assuming, of course, that our conception of political modernization is valid?

The problem is where and how to search for this shared substratum. Ideally speaking, it would be most convenient if we could validly identify some underlying process of unilinear evolution. In such a typology, the development of all societies from their "traditional" to their "modern" phases would be progressive and uniform, and we might ultimately expect to be able to trace with some assurance and precision the structural adaptations and mechanisms of change leading from "lower" to "higher" levels. Unfortunately, we have little evidence to support so optimistic a finding. Indeed, given the presently open-ended and evolving quality of the very concept of modernity, it is by no means certain that any patterns of modernizing change which we can identify as probable in terms of the present standards and requisites of a modern performance will be equally probable with respect to the "modernity" of the twenty-first century. In terms of our data, therefore, it would seem necessary to discard or, at least, to suspend judgment upon schemes based on unilinear evolution.

It would be almost equally satisfying if we were able to identify several different but valid patterns of political modernization, that is to substitute a multi-linear for a unilinear evolutionary model. And, on the face of it, this seems a more promising and practicable undertaking. But, unfortunately, our present study is based upon the experience of only two countries and, hence, is not well adapted to the elucidation of a model which might well turn out to have more than two components. A larger sample would be required for the fruitful pursuit of the multi-linear hypothesis. If this is the case, then what sort of theorizing will the available evidence support in this search for the shared substratum which we think underlies the process of political modernization in Japan and Turkey? The answer which our data suggest might be called "the problem-focused approach."

It seemed possible to us in the light of the preceding chapters to draw up a typology of major problems or crises which confronted Japan and Turkey in the course of efforts to modernize their political systems. This is what we have attempted to do in the earlier part of this chapter. All of the problems identified were shared by both countries and were of critical importance to the success of their undertaking. They had to be solved in some way if a modern political system was to be established and maintained. It seems possible, therefore, that these problems or crises are generic to the process of political modernization and that their identification, even if partial and tentative, may represent a useful step in a continuing attempt to understand and describe this process in more precise terms. It may be helpful if we briefly recapitulate our findings.

The problems which a country confronts in setting out to modernize its political system seem to us to be of two main types: (1) those which are set or predetermined in such a manner as to be wholly or largely beyond the control of the leaders of the modernizing society, and (2) those which are amenable to some significant degree of influence or control by these leaders. Examples of the former can largely be subsumed under the following three headings:

(1) Geopolitical problems.
(2) Problems of timing of external stimuli for change.
(3) Problems relating to the nature of a society's traditional heritage.

These are the "givens," the problems with which a society standing on the brink of its "take-off" stage is inexorably confronted by its geographic circumstances and location, by the temporal relationship which its take-off stage and activities bear to the developmental cycle and activities of other impinging societies, and by the nature of its particular cultural heritage.

The second category consists of somewhat more flexible problems with respect to which a society's leaders can exercise an appreciably greater degree of discretion and control. These seem to us to fall into the following major categories:

(1) The exploitability of traditional institutions, attitudes, and behavior patterns for modernizing purposes ("reinforcing dualism").

(2) The crisis of identity.

(3) The crisis of security.

(4) Problems of leadership and followership.

(5) The crisis of economic development.

(6) Problems of popular relationship to the political process.

    (a) The crisis of integration.

    (b) The crisis of penetration.

    (c) The crisis of participation.

(7) The crisis of output and distribution.

It may well be that we are slighting some additional problems of major consequence for the process of political modernization in Japan and Turkey or that an examination of additional cases would lead to the discovery of further major categories of problems, but, on the present evidence, the above ten categories seem to us to have been crucial for the political modernization of these two societies.

Their applicability to the political modernization process in other societies remains to be established. This is a problem which falls beyond the scope of our present endeavor, but it is interesting to speculate about the gross shape which such an inquiry might take.

If we view the problem in the abstract, several factors would seem to demarcate the political modernization process in Japan and Turkey from that in many other modern or modernizing societies. First, there is the matter of timing. How critical was it to the pace and to the degree of success achieved in Japan and Turkey that they both underwent the critical early stages of the modernizing process in times that were different from the present in many important respects? In the late nineteenth and early twentieth centuries a state's fortunes and feasible courses of action were less seriously affected and determined by uncontrolled external forces than is the case today. A greater measure of national isolation was feasible, and this provided more ample grounds for intra-national decision making and maneuver. The leaders of Japan and Turkey may have enjoyed substantially more latitude in determining the success or failure of their modernization programs than is today available to their counterparts elsewhere. If so, what effect would this have upon the types of problems which characterize ongoing processes of political modernization? Would the above list remain valid, or would it require amendment?

466

Second, there is the question of colonial status. Neither Japan nor Turkey were subject to foreign imperialist control. Both succeeded in maintaining at least technical sovereignty and independence. But many of today's modernizing states are working from a different background—a background that includes a long period of colonial subjugation to some major power. We have not really faced the question of the relationship between colonial status and political modernization. Presumably the former does not preclude a substantial amount of development supportive of the modernization process. But does such status significantly alter the utility or fruitfulness of the above set of factors and crises as an instrument for analyzing the political development of such ex-colonial societies?

A third factor that would have to be taken into account might be termed the "state of the models." We do not really understand very well the effect that the pre-existence of models of a "modern society" has on the goals and actions of societies beginning to modernize at later dates. England is often spoken of as the first "modern" society. Yet it achieved this condition without the aid of any pre-existing model. Like Topsy, English society just grew, and one day the consequences were identified as "modern." For a long time, the standards set by the accidents of English history—somewhat elaborated by analogous Western European and American developments—stood alone as models of what a "modern" society should be like. But, more recently, this happy circumstance has been drastically altered. Today there is also a Russian Communist model of political modernity, and there may shortly be a somewhat different Chinese Communist one as well. One may also speak of a Japanese model. All of these, to be sure, share certain characteristics, but they also differ in a number of important respects.

Thus a society embarking upon modernizing efforts during the latter half of the twentieth century has a variety of models to influence its goals and tactics. These are in some respects mutually incompatible. Such a society is, therefore, modernizing in circumstances which differ markedly in this respect at least from those in which Japan and Turkey launched ostensibly comparable endeavors. How important is this difference, and does it require alterations in our present list of basic problems of modernization?

Finally, we cannot help but be curious about the results of an attempt to apply this same list of factors and crises affecting the political modernization of Japan and Turkey to an analysis of the same process in England, France, or the United States—or, for that matter, in Canada or Australia. If this concept of political modernization has validity and utility for research purposes, why should it be restricted solely to the cases of late-developing societies? Does the list describe the main problems encountered at earlier stages of history by the major Western societies or does it require amendment?

None of these are questions which can be faced here. But they should at least be posed for serious consideration by others interested in exploring the research utility of this concept of political modernization or of refining our insights into this whole problem of political development. Further attempts at the comparative investigation of the modernizing experiences of other polities—perhaps selected with some of the above questions in mind—would be very helpful in determining the validity and utility of this entire line of approach.

BIBLIOGRAPHY

JAPAN

~.~

GENERAL

Beardsley, Richard K., John W. Hall and Robert E. Ward, *Village Japan*, Chicago, 1959. A detailed interdisciplinary study of village life in postwar Japan.

Benedict, Ruth F., *The Chrysanthemum and the Sword*, Boston, 1946. A provocative but overstated attempt to analyze the structure of Japanese "national character."

Borton, Hugh, *Japan's Modern Century*, New York, 1955. A good general history which stresses political developments since the mid-nineteenth century.

Brown, Delmer M., *Nationalism in Japan*, Berkeley, 1955. The standard work on this subject.

Burks, Ardath W., *The Government of Japan*, New York, 1961. A recent and good survey of postwar Japanese politics.

Dore, R. P., *City Life in Japan*, Berkeley, 1958. An excellent sociological analysis of life in a section of postwar Tokyo.

Ike Nobutaka, *Japanese Politics: an Introductory Survey*, New York, 1957. A good brief introduction to contemporary Japanese politics.

Japan, Ministry of Education, Japan UNESCO Committee, *Japan: its Land, People, and Culture*, Tokyo, 1958. An encyclopedic compendium of information about all aspects of Japanese culture.

Kawai Kazuo, *Japan's American Interlude*, Chicago, 1960. A brief but excellent study of the Allied Occupation of Japan from 1945 to 1952.

Maki, John M., *Government and Politics in Japan*, New York, 1962. A study of the democratization of postwar politics in Japan.

McLaren, Walter W., *A Political History of Japan during the Meiji Era, 1867-1912*, London, 1916. A detailed and useful account of political structure and history during these years.

Quigley, Harold S., *Japanese Government and Politics, an Introductory Survey*, New York, 1932. The standard prewar text on the subject.

———— and John Turner, *The New Japan: Government and Politics*, Minneapolis, 1956. A good standard treatment of the structure and operations of government in postwar Japan.

Reischauer, Edwin O., *The United States and Japan*, rev. ed., Cambridge, Mass., 1957. An excellent brief introduction to Japanese history and institutions.

———— *Japan, Past and Present*, rev. ed., New York 1956. A brief and good general survey of Japanese history.

Reischauer, Robert K., *Japan: Government-Politics*, New York, 1939. An excellent short study of prewar Japanese politics.

Yanaga Chitoshi, *Japanese People and Politics*, New York, 1956. A detailed account of postwar Japanese political institutions.

469

———— *Japan since Perry*, New York, 1949. A very detailed general history—with political emphasis—of Japan since 1854.

TRADITIONAL SOCIETY

Beasley, William G. *Select Documents on Japanese Foreign Policy, 1853-1868*, London 1955. A documentary collection focussed on the fall of the Tokugawa Shogunate.

Bellah, Robert N. *Tokugawa Religion*, Glencoe 1957. An analysis of the relationship between values and modernization in Japan.

Craig, Albert, *Chōshū in the Meiji Restoration*. Cambridge 1961. A study of the role of the Chōshū clan in the Restoration Movement.

de Bary, William T. *Sources of the Japanese Tradition*. New York, 1958. A well-selected collection of translations, with commentary, illustrating many aspects of Japanese culture.

Hall, John W. *Tanuma Okitsugu, 1719-1788, Forerunner of Modern Japan*. Cambridge, 1955. A biographical study of a high Tokugawa official.

———— "The Castle Town and Japan's Modern Urbanization," *Far Eastern Quarterly* XV, No. 1 (1955), pp. 37-56. A study of castle towns as progenitors of the modern city in Japan.

———— "The Confucian Teacher in Tokugawa Japan" *in* David S. Nivison and Arthur F. Wright (eds.), *Confucianism in Action*. Stanford 1959, pp. 268-301. An examination of the role of Confucian scholars in the Tokugawa Period.

Jansen, Marius B. *Sakamoto Ryōma*. Princeton 1961. An analysis of the Restoration Movement seen through the career of a prominent participant.

Murdoch, James H. and Yamagata Isoh, *A History of Japan*, London, 1949, 3 volumes. A detailed, and primarily political, general history of Japan.

Norman, E. H. *Japan's Emergence as a Modern State*. New York, 1946. One of the first socio-economic interpretations of the Restoration.

Reischauer, Edwin O. and Fairbank, John K. *East Asia, the Great Tradition*, Boston 1960. One of the best general treatments of premodern Japanese and East Asian history.

Sakata Yoshio and Hall, John W. "The Motivation of Political Leadership in the Meiji Restoration," *Journal of Asian Studies*, Vol. XVI, No. 1 (1956) pp. 31-50.

Sansom, Sir George B. *The Western World and Japan*. New York, 1950. An analysis of the Western impact on Japan from 1600-1894.

———— *History of Japan to 1334*, Stanford, 1958 and *History of Japan from 1334 to 1615*, Stanford, 1960. The first two of a projected three volume study. These constitute the most definitive of the English-language treatments of pre-Restoration Japanese history.

———— *Japan: A Short Cultural History*, 2nd rev. ed., New York, 1952. The best of the shorter studies of Japanese cultural and political history.

Smith, Thomas C. *The Agrarian Origins of Modern Japan*. Stanford, 1959. An examination of social and economic changes in rural Japan before the Restoration.

BIBLIOGRAPHY

——— "Japan's Aristocratic Revolution," *Yale Review*, September 1961. An analysis of the social characteristics of Restoration leadership.

ENVIRONMENTAL AND FOREIGN CONTRIBUTIONS

Ike Nobutaka, *The Beginning of Political Democracy in Japan*, Baltimore, 1950. A significant monographic study of the early influences of Western political systems and ideas upon Japan.

Kosaka Masaaki (ed.), David Abosch (trans.), *Japanese Thought in the Meiji Era*, Tokyo, 1958. This work, along with other volumes of the Centenary Culture Council Series, is especially useful for the new and detailed data which it presents.

Nitobe Inazo and others, *Western Influences in Modern Japan*, Chicago, 1931. An uneven but interesting collection of essays by various Japanese authorities on the influence of Westernism upon many aspects of Japanese life.

Okuma Shigenobu (ed.), *Fifty Years of New Japan*, 2 vols., London, 1910. A number of prominent Japanese leaders discuss the source-springs of modern Japan, and in the process, reveal much about their own values and concepts.

Sansom, G. B., *The Western World and Japan*, New York, 1950. An historical cultural study of interaction between Japan and the Western world by one of the foremost scholars of Japanese history.

Schwantes, Robert S., *Japanese and Americans*, New York, 1955. An excellent general study of Japanese-American interaction from the nineteenth to the mid-twentieth century.

ECONOMIC MODERNIZATION

Allen, G. C., *A Short Economic History of Modern Japan*, 2nd edit. London, 1962. The best brief account in English.

Dore, R. F., *Land Reform in Japan*, New York, 1959. Appraisal of the postwar Occupation reform.

Economic Planning Agency, *Economic Survey of Japan*, Tokyo, 1956-, annual. Growth and structural changes from year to year.

Economic Planning Agency, *Kokumin Shotoku Hakusho (White Paper on National Income)*, Tokyo, 1962. Summarizes official statistics covering 1930-60.

Kawai Kazuo, *Japan's American Interlude*, Chicago, 1960. Account of the postwar Allied occupation.

Levine, Solomon B., *Industrial Relations in Postwar Japan*, Urbana, 1958. Rise of trade unionism.

Lockwood, William W., *The Economic Development of Japan, Growth and Structural Change, 1868-1938*, Princeton, 1954. Broad study of economic modernization.

Ministry of Education, *Education in Japan*, Tokyo, 1961. A summary of postwar developments.

Nihon Gaikō Gakkai, *Taiheiyō Sensō Gen-in Ron [On the Cause of the Pacific War]*. Tokyo, 1953. Essays on the origins of World War II by leading Japanese scholars.

Ohkawa Kazushi, and others, *The Growth Rate of the Japanese Economy Since 1878*, Tokyo, 1957. The standard work in this field.

Prime Minister's Office, Statistics Bureau, *Nihon Tōkei Nenkan* [*Japan Statistical Yearbook*], Tokyo, 1949-. The most inclusive yearbook published in Japanese and English, and continuing the pre-war series of the Cabinet Bureau of Statistics, *Nihon Teikoku Tōkei Nenkan*.

Rosovsky, Henry, *Capital Formation in Japan, 1868-1940*, Glencoe, 1961. Authoritative pioneering study.

Scalapino, Robert A., *Democracy and the Party Movement in Prewar Japan*, Berkeley, 1953.

Scalapino, Robert A., and Masumi Junnosuke, *Parties and Politics in Contemporary Japan*, Berkeley, 1962. This volume, and the one preceding, describe the evolution of party politics.

United Nations, *Economic Survey of Asia and the Far East*, Bangkok, 1947-, annual. Japanese economic developments reviewed in a comparative Asian setting.

EDUCATION

Aizawa Akira, *Kyōiku Hyakunen-shi-dan* [*Chats on a Hundred Years of Educational History*], Tokyo, 1953. Valuable, if undocumented, gossip concerning, chiefly, the formation of educational policy. By a long-lived journalist who specialized in educational matters.

Hall, R. K., *Kokutai no Hongi: Cardinal Principles of the National Entity of Japan*, Cambridge, Mass., 1949. A translation of a wartime civics text.

Hall, R. K., *Shūshin: The Ethics of a Defeated Nation*, New York, 1949. A translation of extracts from the ethics text-books in use in junior and middle schools.

Inokawa Kiyoshi and Kawai Akira, *Nihon Kyōiku Undōshi* [*A History of Educational Movements in Japan*], two vols. Tokyo, 1960-61. A left-wing history of educational associations and pressure groups with emphasis on the post-war teachers union.

Karasawa Tomitarō, *Kyōkasho no Rekishi* [*A History of Text-books*], 2 vols., Tokyo, 1956. A general survey of contents, publishing, control systems, etc.

Karasawa Tomitarō, *Kyōshi no Rekishi* [*A History of Teaching*], Tokyo, 1955. A general history of the teaching profession.

Keenlyside, H. L. and Thomas, A. F., *History of Japanese Education and Present Educational System*, Tokyo, 1937. A general survey of the educational system in the thirties.

Kikuchi, D., *Japanese Education*, London, 1909. The official view of late Meiji education, its purposes and performance. A series of lectures for a London audience.

Mombushō (Japan: Ministry of Education), *Nempō* [*Annual Report*], Tokyo, 1873-. A basic source, replete with statistical information, reports of inspectors, etc. Substantial English summaries were prepared for the earlier reports and for most post-war years.

———, Kyōkushi Hensankai (Committee on educational history) *Meiji ikō kyōiku seido hattatsushi* [*A History of the Development of Education since the*

Beginning of the Meiji Period], 12 vols., Tokyo, 1938. A digest of the annual reports, plus some additional material, for the period of 1868-1932.

Mombushō (Japan: Ministry of Education), *Kyōiku Hachijūnenshi* [*Eighty Years of Japanese Education*], Tokyo, 1954. Another official history, more concisely digested.

Noma Kyōiku Kenkyūkai, *Kindai Nihon Kyōiku Seidō Shiryō* [*Materials on the Modern Japanese Educational System*], 35 vols., Tokyo, 1956-59. For the period since 1932. Admirably detailed.

Shimizu Yoshihiro, *Shiken* [*Examinations*], Tokyo, 1957. A first attempt at a sociological analysis of the process of educational selection. Historical section sketchy.

MASS MEDIA

Ebihara Hachiro, *Kaigai Hōji Shimbun Zasshi Shi* [*A History of Japanese Newspapers and Periodicals Published Abroad*], Tokyo, 1936. An excellent study of newspapers and periodicals in the Japanese language published by Japanese on the West Coast of the United States in the early Meiji period.

Hanazono Kamesada, *The Development of Japanese Journalism*, Osaka, 1924. A history of Japanese journalism in English. A rather detailed description of the 1920s but not much information about early history.

Hidaka Rokurō et al., *Mass Communication to Seiji-Keizai* [*Mass Communication, Politics, and Economics*], Tokyo, 1955. A quite informative book about the finances of Japanese journalism and its relation to the government.

Iwasaki Tōru, *Eiga Shi* [*A History of Motion Pictures*], Tokyo, 1961. A historical description of Japanese films and their directors from the beginning to date.

Katō Shuichi, "Nihon no Shimbun, Gaikoku no Shimbun" [*Japanese Newspapers —Foreign Newspapers*], *Asahi Journal*, June 17, 1962. A study of the characteristics of Japanese newspapers since 1960.

Nagashima Matao, *Gendai no Shimbun* [*Contemporary Newspapers*], Tokyo, 1959. A study of Japanese newspapers between the second World War and 1960.

Ono Hideo, *Shimbun no Rekishi* [*A History of Newspapers*], Tokyo, 1961. A general history of journalism which covers the period from the mid-19th century to the present.

Shimbun Kyōkai, *Nihon Shimbun Hyaku-nen Shi* [*A Centenary History of Japanese Newspapers*], Tokyo, 1961. Useful information about small local newspapers all over Japan. Very incomplete as a general history of journalism.

Uchikawa Yoshimi, "Shimbun Dokusha no Hensen" [*Changes in Newspaper Readership*]. *Shimbun Kenkyū*, No. 120, July, 1961. The most important historical survey of estimated circulation of the dailies as well as of the social characteristics of the reading public.

Wittemore, Edward P., *The Press in Japan—A Case Study*, Columbia, South Carolina, 1961. A study of the attitude of Japanese newspapers toward the anti-Security Pact demonstrations in Tokyo in 1960.

473

THE CIVIL BUREAUCRACY

Bellah, R. N., *Tokugawa Religion* (Glencoe, Ill., 1957). An analysis of the modernization of Japan according to Talcott Parson's theory of action.

Hoshi Hajime, *Kanrigaku Tekiyō* [*Essentials of the Civil Bureaucracy*], Tokyo, 1924. A legal history with special reference to the civil bureaucracies of Japan, China, and the western world.

Ishida Takeshi, *Kindai Nihon Seiji Kōzō no Kenkyū* [*Studies on the Political Structure of Japan*]. Six essays on the political structure of Japan with special reference to bureaucratic rule.

Ishii Ryōsuke, *Hōsei Hen* [*Legal History*], in *Meiji Bunkashi*, Tokyo, 1954. A legal history of the period 1868-1912.

Inada Masatsugu, *Meiji Kempō Seiritsushi* [*Birth of the Meiji Constitution*], Tokyo, 1960-62, 2 vols. The most reliable history of the Meiji Constitution.

Kimura Motokazu, *Kanryō oyobi Kanryō Soshiki* [*Civil Servants and Civil Bureaucracy*], Tokyo, 1960, in *Keizai Shutaisei Kōza* Vol. 5.

Oka Yoshitake, *Kindai Nihon Seijishi* [*Political History of Modern Japan*], Tokyo, 1962, Vol. I is a political history of Japan from 1853 to 1890.

Ōshima Tarō, *Kanryōsei* [*Civil Bureaucracy*], in *Iwanami Kōza Nihon Rekishi* Vol. 7, Tokyo, 1962]. An essay on the formation of the Japanese civil bureaucracy.

Sakata Yoshio, *Meiji Ishinshi* [*History of the Meiji Restoration*], Tokyo, 1960. The most reliable history of the Meiji Restoration in one volume, with special reference to political power.

Sakata Yoshio (ed.), *Meiji Ishin no Mondaiten* [*Problems of the Meiji Restoration*], Tokyo, 1962. Six papers on political thought and behavior during the Meiji Restoration.

Sakata Yoshio, *Meiji Zenhanki no Nationalism* [*Nationalism during the First Half of the Meiji Period*], Tokyo, 1958. Eight papers on the Meiji Restoration.

Tsuji Kiyoaki, *Nihon Kanryōsei no Kenkyū* [*Studies on the Civil Bureaucracy of Japan*], Tokyo, 1952. The first scientific study of the history and social structure of the civil bureaucracy in Japan.

THE MILITARY BUREAUCRACY

Itō Masanori, *Gumbatsu kōbōshi* [*History of the Rise and Fall of the Military Clique*], Tokyo, 1957-59, 3 vols. Good survey of the fortunes of the Army and Navy from 1868 to the end of the Pacific War by an experienced journalist and critic of military affairs.

Kennedy, M. D., *The Military Side of Japanese Life*, London, 1924. Useful first-hand observations on the Japanese army prior to World War I by a trained observer.

Lory, Hillis, *Japan's Military Masters*, New York, 1943. A general account of the army in the 1930's and, as the subtitle indicates, of "The Army in Japanese Life," based on personal observations.

Matsushita Yoshio, *Meiji gunsei shiron* [*Historical Essay on the Meiji Military System*], Tokyo, 1956, 2 vols. The most comprehensive treatment of the evolution of the military system to 1912 by the dean of Japan's military historians.

————, *Chōheirei seiteishi* [*History of the Enactment of Conscription*], Tokyo, 1943. A careful analysis of the background, formulation, and execution of the conscription law.

————, *Nihon gunsei to seiji* [*The Japanese Military System and Politics*], Tokyo, 1960. Essays on some aspects of political-military relations.

Ogawa Gotarō, *Conscription System in Japan*, New York, 1921. The best study in English of the conscription system and its economic effects.

Tokutomi Ichirō, *Kōshaku Yamagata Aritomo den* [*Biography of Prince Yamagata Aritomo*], Tokyo, 1933, 3 vols. The major biography of the architect of Japan's modern army by a veteran journalist-historian. Uncritical but indispensable because of the inclusion of many private papers and documents.

Umetani Noboru, *Gunjin chokuyu seiritsushi no kenkyū.* [*Study of the History of the Enactment of the Imperial Rescript to Soldiers and Sailors*], Memoirs of the Faculty of Letters of Osaka University, No. 8. A penetrating study of the political and ideological background of this key document.

Yamagata Aritomo, "The Japanese Army," *Fifty Years of New Japan*, compiled by Count Ōkuma Shigenobu. London, 1909, Vol. 1, pp. 194-217. Brief but authoritative essay on the early development of the army.

POLITICAL LEADERSHIP AND PARTIES

Beckmann, George, *The Making of the Meiji Constitution*, Lawrence, 1957. A study of the background of the Meiji Constitution.

Ike Nobutaka, *The Beginnings of Political Democracy in Japan*, Baltimore, 1950. An analysis of the origin and early developments of political parties in Japan.

Itagaki Taisuke, *Jiyūtōshi* [*History of the Liberal Party*], 2 volumes, Tokyo, 1910. The official history of the Liberal Party by its founder and first leader.

Jiyū Minken Shisō [*Liberty and Popular Rights Thought*], in the Aoki Bunko series, Tokyo, 1957-. A Study of an early liberal movement important in the development of Japanese political parties.

Kōno Banshū Den [*Biography of Kōno Banshū*], issued by Kōno Banshū Den Hensankai, 2 volumes, Tokyo, 1924. An account of the life and career of Kōno Hironaka (1849-1923), a well known political figure from Fukushima.

Oka Yoshitake (ed.), *Gendai Nihon Seiji Katei* [*The Political Process in Contemporary Japan*], Tokyo, 1958. A collection of essays dealing in theoretically oriented terms with several aspects of domestic politics and foreign pressures thereon.

Sansom, Sir George, *The Western World and Japan*, New York, 1950. A study of the Western impact on Japan from 1600-1894.

Scalapino, Robert, *Democracy and the Party Movement in Prewar Japan*, Berke-

ley and Los Angeles, 1953. A detailed analysis of the reasons for the failure
of the party movement to achieve democracy in prewar Japan.

————, "Japan: Between Traditionalism and Democracy," in Sigmund Neumann (ed.), *Modern Political Parties*, Chicago, 1956. A general treatment of Japanese political parties.

———— and Masumi Junnosuke, *Parties and Politics in Contemporary Japan*, Berkeley and Los Angeles, 1962. The most detailed examination of parties and party politics since 1945.

Shoji Kichinosuke, *Nihon Seisha Seitō Hattatsushi* [*History of the Development of Political Societies and Parties in Japan*], Tokyo, 1959. A good standard history of Japanese political parties.

Takahashi Tetsuo, *Fukushima Jiyū Minken Undōshi* [*The Movement for Liberty and Popular Rights in Fukushima*], Tokyo, 1954. A monographic study of this early liberal movement in a northern Japanese prefecture.

BIBLIOGRAPHY

TURKEY

~~~~~~

GENERAL

Belleten [*Bulletin*], Ankara, 1937-, quarterly, Journal of the Turkish History Society.

Frye, Richard N., *Islam and the West*, The Hague, 1957. The chapters by Niyazi Berkes, Dankwart A. Rustow, and Howard A. Reed deal with modernization and Islam in Turkey.

İnal, İbnülemin Mahmud Kemal, *Osmanlı Devrinde Son Sadrıazamlar* [*The Last Grand Vezirs of the Ottoman Period*], 14 fascicles, Istanbul, 1940-53. Careful biographies, in the traditional Ottoman manner, covering the period from 1852 to 1922.

Jäschke, Gotthard, and Erich Pritsch, *Die Türkei seit dem Weltkriege: Geschichtskalender 1918-1928*, Berlin, 1929; Gotthard Jäschke, *Die Türkei in den Jahren 1935-41*, Leipzig, 1943; *Die Türkei in den Jahren 1942-1951*, Wiesbaden, 1955. Detailed chronologies, based on Turkish newspapers and official and secondary sources, of political and cultural events; a prime work of reference.

Jorga, Nicholas, *Geschichte des Osmanischen Reiches*, Vol. V, Gotha, 1913. The last volume of the Roumanian historian's general history, particularly useful for questions concerning the Balkans.

Karal, Enver Ziya, *Osmanlı tarihi*, Vols. V-VII, Ankara, 1947-1956. [*Ottoman History*] General history, covering 1789 to 1876, often topically organized, including diplomatic and domestic affairs.

Lewis, Bernard, *The Emergence of Modern Turkey*, London, 1961. Political and cultural transformations, 1850-1950, by the leading Western historian of Turkey. Good bibliography.

Lewis, Geoffrey, *Turkey*, London, 1955. A brief introduction by a British philologist.

Robinson, Richard D. *The First Turkish Republic: A Case Study in National Development*, Cambridge, Mass., 1963. A general introduction by an American economist.

Rosen, Georg, *Geschichte der Türkei . . . 1826 . . . 1856*, 2 vols., Leipzig, 1866-1867. A good general history of this period, based in part on Rosen's own experience.

Sax, Carl Ritter von, *Geschichte des Machtverfalls der Türkei . . .* , 2nd ed., Vienna, 1913. A good general history, largely political and diplomatic, covering essentially 1796 to 1913.

Thomas, Lewis V., "Turkey" in L. V. Thomas and R. N. Frye, *The United States and Turkey and Iran*, Cambridge, Mass., 1951. An interpretation of Turkish politics and society.

477

TRADITIONAL SOCIETY

Ahmed Cevdet Paşa, *Tarih-i Cevdet* [*History*], 12 vols., Istanbul, 1891. The classic Ottoman history covering the years 1774-1826 by an official court historian with access to government documents, many of which are included.

Gibb, Hamilton A. R., and Harold Bowen, *Islamic Society and the West*, 1 vol. in 2 parts, London, 1950-1957. A detailed scholarly study of Ottoman administration on the eve of modernization; no further volumes published.

İnalcık, Halil, "Osmanlı Hukukuna Giriş" ["Introduction to Ottoman Law"], *Siyasal Bilgiler Fakültesi Dergisi*, XIII-2, 102-126 (1959).

———, "Osmanlı Padişahı" ["The Ottoman Sultan"], *Ibid.*, XIII-4, 68-79 (1959).

———, *Tanzimât ve Bulgar Meselesi* [*The Tanzimât and the Bulgarian Question*], Ankara, 1943. A scholarly study emphasizing social problems.

———, "Türkiye'nin İktisadî Vaziyeti" ["Turkey's Economic Situation"], *Belleten*, XV, 629-90 (1951). Three articles dealing with the classical Ottoman period.

Kaynar, Reşat, *Mustafa Reşit Paşa ve Tanzimât*, Ankara, 1954. Especially interesting for the archival documents it reproduces.

[Koçi Bey,] *Koçi Bey Risalesi*, ed. Ali Kemali Aksüt, Istanbul, 1939. Penetrating observations on the causes of the decline of the Empire presented to the reformist Sultan Murad IV. This edition in romanized transcription is, however, not satisfactory.

Lutfi, Ahmed, *Tarih* [*History*], vols. I-VII, Istanbul, 1290-1328 A.H. The official Ottoman chronicle on the events from 1826 on.

Uluçay, M. Çağatay, *18. ve 19. asırlarda Saruhan'da Eşkıyalık ve Halk Hareketleri* [*Banditism and Popular Movements in Saruhan, in the 18th and 19th Centuries*], Istanbul, 1955. A rich collection of original documents on the rise of the *âyan* in Western Anatolia.

Uzunçarşılı İsmail Hakkı, *Alemdar Mustafa Paşa*, Istanbul, 1942. Documentary account of the rise of a famous paşa of *âyan* origin, who became the leader of the revolution of 1807.

Yaman, T. Mümtaz, "Osmanlı Imperatorluğu Mülkî İdaresinde Avrupalılaşma" ["Europeanization of the Ottoman Administration"], *İdare Mecmuasi*, nos. 138-142.

ENVIRONMENTAL AND FOREIGN CONTRIBUTIONS

Bailey, Frank E., *British Policy and the Turkish Reform Movement*, Cambridge, Mass., 1943. Deals with the mid-nineteenth century.

Davison, Roderic H., *Reform in the Ottoman Empire, 1856-1876*, Princeton, New Jersey, 1963. A scholarly study of Turkish political reform and diplomacy.

Devereux, Robert, *The First Ottoman Constitutional Period*, Baltimore, 1963. A study of the drafting and working of the Midhat Pasha constitution, 1876-1878, based on original sources.

Engelhardt, Edouard, *La Turquie et le Tanzimât*, 2 vols., Paris, 1882-1884.

Now quite outdated, yet still valuable as a survey of the Tanzimat reforms and western influences from 1826 on.

Heidborn, A., *Manuel de droit public et administratif de l'Empire ottoman*, 2 vols., Vienna, 1908-1912. A useful compilation of information on laws, justice, administration, public finance, etc.

Mardin, Şerif, *The Genesis of Young Ottoman Thought*, Princeton, New Jersey, 1962. A scholarly study of political thought and action, 1865-76.

Okandan, Recai G., *Umumî âmme hukukumuzun ana hatları*, Istanbul, 1948. [*Outline of our General Public Law*]. A detailed examination of the constitutional periods and documents of 1876 and 1908.

Ostrorog, Leon, *The Angora Reform*, London, 1927. Three brilliant lectures on the law; its bases, the Ottoman mentality and 19th century reforms, and the drastic changes of 1922 to 1926.

Tanzimât I: Yüzüncü Yıldönümü Münasebetiyle [*Tanzimât I: On the Occasion of Its Centenary*], Istanbul, 1940. A collection of essays by Turkish scholars on various aspects of the Tanzimat reform era.

Temperley, Harold, *England and the Near East: The Crimea*, London, 1936. Well-written and scholarly examination of the Eastern Question, especially Anglo-Turkish relations, 1808-1853, with sections on Ottoman reforms.

Ziemke, Kurt, *Die neue Türkei: politische Entwicklung, 1914-1929*, Stuttgart, 1930. A good political study of these years, with much on the international relations in the period from 1918 to 1923.

EDUCATION

de Salve, M., "Education in Turkey," *Circulars of Information of the U.S. Bureau of Education*, No. 3-1875, Washington, Government Printing Office, 1875, pp. 237-252. An interesting, contemporary impression of Turkish education in the late 19th century by the first director of the Galatasaray Lycée.

Ergin, Osman, *Türkiye Maarif Tarihi* [*History of Turkish Education*], 5 vols., Istanbul, 1939-1943. Though discursive and in need of editing, this is the indispensable basic source on the development of the Turkish educational system.

Hyman, Herbert H., Arif Payaslıoğlu, and Frederick W. Frey, "The Values of Turkish College Youth," *Public Opinion Quarterly*, Vol. XXII, Fall, 1959, pp. 275-91. A comparative survey of certain values of students at the Political Science Faculty in Ankara and Robert College in Istanbul.

Kirby, Fay, *Türkiye'de Köy Enstitüleri* [*The Village Institutes in Turkey*], Ankara, 1962. The most detailed investigation to date of the short and happy life of the Village Institutes.

Kuran, Ahmet Bedevi, *Harbiye Mektebinde Hürriyet Mücadelesi* [*The Struggle for Freedom in the War College*], Istanbul, n.d. A highly personal, suggestive recollection of the role of the War College in the struggle for political development in Turkey, especially during the Second Constitutional Period.

Maynard, Richard E., *The Lise and its Curriculum in the Turkish Educational*

System, unpublished Ph.D. dissertation, Department of Education, University of Chicago, 1961. Broader than its title indicates, heavily based on Ergin, this is the best general survey in English of the development and character of the Turkish educational system.

Millî Eğitimle İlgili Söylev ve Demeçler [*Remarks and Speeches Regarding National Education*], 3 vols., Ankara, 1946. A collection of the remarks and speeches related to education of prominent Turkish political leaders.

Oğuzkan, Turhan, *Adult Education in Turkey*, Educational Studies and Documents, No. XIV, Paris: UNESCO, 1955. A carefully prepared short study that includes some useful general comments and data.

Publications of the Test ve Araştırma Bürosu, Maarif Vekâleti [Test and Research Bureau, Ministry of Education], Ankara, Turkey. A series of several dozen publications presenting valuable statistical data, unobtainable elsewhere and based on original research, concerning the Turkish educational system.

Reed, Howard A., "The Faculty of Divinity at Ankara," *The Muslim World*, Vol. XLVI, October 1956, pp. 295-312, and Vol. XLVII, January 1957, pp. 22-35. Provides valuable information and interpretation on religious education in Turkey.

The Report of the Turkish National Commission on Education, Istanbul: American Board Publication Department, 1961. An important report by a National Commission on Education set up by the Turkish Ministry of Education, supported by the Ford Foundation, to "examine the educational situation in Turkey" and in selected other countries—one of which, interestingly enough, was Japan.

Türkiye Cumhuriyeti Maarifi, 1923-1943 [*Education System of the Turkish Republic, 1923-1943*], Ankara, 1944. An official resume of educational developments under the Republic.

MASS MEDIA

Balkanlı, Remzi, *Mukayeseli Basın ve Propaganda* [*Comparative Press and Propaganda*], Ankara, 1961. An extensive legal study with occasional illuminative court decisions.

Banoğlu, Niyazi Ahmet, *Basın Tarihimizin Kara ve Ak Günleri* [*Dark and Bright Days of Our Press History*], Istanbul, 1960. Includes some documents on press during the reign of Abdülhamid II.

Birinci Basın Kongresi [*The First Press Congress*], Istanbul, 1936. Minutes and discussion of a press convention which expressed the government view on press.

Candar, Avni, *Bibliğrafya, Halk Evleri Neşriyati* [*Bibliography, People's Houses Publications*], 2 vols., Ankara, 1939, 1941.

Fesch, Paul, *Constantinople Aux Derniers Jours d'Abdul Hamid*, Paris, 1907. Includes one chapter on the press with some critical analysis.

Gerçek, Selim Nüzhet, *Türk Matbaacılığı* [*Turkish Printing*], Istanbul, 1939. A valuable work based on first hand sources.

————, *Türk Gazeteciliği* [*Turkish Journalism*], Istanbul, 1931. A source book on the early phase of journalism.

İskit, Server R., *Türkiyede Matbuat Rejimleri* [*Press Regimes in Turkey*], Istanbul, 1939. The most comprehensive history of press with verbatim records of debates on press laws and development.

————, *Türkiyede Neşriyat Hareketlerine Bir Bakış* [*A Look at Press Movements in Turkey*], Istanbul, 1939. A biographical study of the press bureau chiefs with a brief synthesis on press history.

————, *Hususî Ilk Türkçe Gazetemiz "Tercumanı Ahval" ve Agâh Efendi* [*Our First Private Turkish Newspaper "Tercümanı Ahval" and Agâh Efendi*], Ankara, 1937. A brief biographical study of one of the first Turkish newsmen.

Karpat, Kemal H., "Social Themes in Contemporary Turkish Literature," *Middle East Journal*, 2 parts, Winter and Spring 1960, pp. 29-44, 153-168. A study of social and political currents in Turkish literature along with its evolution.

————, "Die Geschichte der ideologischen Strömungen seit der Begründung der Türkischen Republik: Der Populismus und seine Vertreter," *Bustan*, January 1962, pp. 17-26. A study of political thought and publications.

Köden, Bilal, *Güzel Ordu Gazetesinin 25 Yıllık Hikayesi* [*The 25-Year Story of the Newspaper Güzelordu*], Ordu, 1955. An original account of the story of a local newspaper with excellent sidelights on political problems arising from modernization.

Legarde, Louis de, "Notes sur les journaux Français de Smyrne à l'epoque de Mahmoud," *Journal Asiatique*, vol. 238, 1950, pp. 103-144. A good study of French press in İzmir at this early stage.

Lerner, Daniel, *The Passing of Traditional Society*, Glencoe, 1958. Includes an analysis of the modernizing role of mass media in Turkey.

Mardin, Şerif, "Some Notes on an Early Phase in the Modernization of Communication in Turkey," *Comparative Studies in Society and History*, Vol. III, April 1961, pp. 250-271. An interpretive study of communication in the light of Deutsch's theory of nationalism.

Müftüoğlu, Hakkı, and Başak Gültekin, *Basın Yayın ve Turizm Mevzuatı* [*Laws on Press, Publications, and Tourism*], Istanbul, 1958. A useful guide for legal studies and press history.

Önder, Mehmet, *Konya Matbuatı Tarihi* [*History of the Press of Konya*], Konya, 1949. A brief but informative study based on the content of some local newspapers.

Özön, Mustafa Nihat, *Namık Kemal ve İbret Gazetesi* [*Namik Kemal and İbret Newspaper*], Istanbul, 1938. An original study of Namık Kemal's career as journalist and the content of his articles.

Perin, Cevdet, *Tanzimat Edebiyatında Fransiz Tesiri* [*French Influence on the Literature of the Tanzimat*], Istanbul, 1946. A study of the translations in the early stage of literary and intellectual modernization.

Tanpınar, Ahmet Hamdi, *XIX Asır Türk Edebiyatı Tarihi* [*History of 19th Century Turkish Literature*], Istanbul, 1956. Excellent accounts of journalism and literature with interpretations.

Tokgöz, Ahmet İhsan, *Matbuat Hatıralarım* [*My Memoirs of Journalism*], 2 vols., Istanbul, 1930. An excellent account by one of the veteran newsmen covering several decades of press activity.

Tütengil, Cavit Orhan, *Diyarbakir Basını Tarihi Üzerinde Notlar* [*Notes on the History of the Press in Diyarbakir*], Istanbul, 1954. A short descriptive study.

————, *Türkiyede Bölge Basını ve Diyarbakir Gazeteciligi* [*Regional Press in Turkey and the Diyarbakir Press*], Istanbul, 1962. As above.

Ülken, Hilmi Ziya, *Uyanış Devrinde Tercümenin Rolü* [*The Role of Translation in the Awakening Period*], Istanbul, 1935. An interpretive study of translation in cultural modernization and intellectual mobility.

[Yalman,] Ahmed Emin, *The Development of Modern Turkey as Measured by Its Press*, New York, 1914. The only study in English, based partly on Fesch, covering the history of the press. Original in the part dealing with the Young Turk period, 1908-1914.

ECONOMIC MODERNIZATION

Bonné, Alfred, *State and Economics in the Middle East*, London, 1948. Includes a general account of 19th century economic conditions.

Grunwald, Kurt and Joachim O. Ronell, *Industrialization in the Middle East*, New York, 1960.

Hershlag, Zvi Yehuda, *Turkey, An Economy in Transition*, The Hague, 1958. The best general study, by an Israeli economist.

International Bank for Reconstruction and Development, *The Economy in Turkey; An Analysis and Recommendations for a Development Program*, Baltimore, 1951. More sympathetic to the state's role than Thornburg.

Kerwin, Robert W., "Etatism in Turkey," in Hugh G. J. Aitken, ed., *The State and Economic Growth*, New York, 1959. Brief historical account and critical appraisal by a former U.S. foreign service officer.

Mordtmann, A.D., *Stambul und das moderne Türkenthum*, II, Leipzig, 1877. Includes a description of economic conditions.

Sousa, Nasim, *The Capitulary Regime of Turkey: Its History, Origin and Nature*, Johns Hopkins University Studies in Historical and Political Sciences, Baltimore, 1933. A scholarly study.

Thornburg, Max Weston, et al., *Turkey: An Economic Appraisal*, New York, 1949. Study for the Twentieth Century Fund, highly critical of etatist tradition.

[Yalman,] Ahmed Emin, *Turkey in the World War* in the Turkish Series of Shotwell, James T. (ed.), *Economic and Social History of the World War*, New Haven, 1930. A general survey of the Young Turk period, with some information on economic conditions and policy.

THE CIVIL BUREAUCRACY

Ankara Üniversitesi Siyasal Bilgiler Fakültesi Dergisi [*Review of the Faculty of Political Sciences of Ankara University*], Ankara, 1953-, quarterly. Articles on political science including Turkish government and administration.

Birkhead, Guthrie S., and Fahir Armaoğlu, *Graduates of the Faculty of Political*

Sciences, University of Ankara, 1946-1955, Ankara, 1957. Survey of social origins, post-graduation employment, job satisfaction, etc.

Çankaya, Mücellitoğlu Ali, *Mülkiye Tarihi ve Mülkiyeliler [History of the
Civil Service School and Its Graduates],* 2 vols., Ankara, 1954. Vol. I consists of a history of the Civil Service School and Vol. II contains short biographies of its graduates from 1859 to 1949.

Frey, Frederick W., and Arif T. Payaslıoğlu, "Babalarının mensup olduğu mes-
lekler bakımından Siyasal Bilgiler Fakültesi öğrencileri üzerine bir inceleme"
["Students of the Faculty of Political Sciences: A Trend Analysis of the
Occupational Backgrounds of their Fathers"], *Ankara Üniversitesi Siyasal
Bilgiler Fakültesi Dergisi,* Vol. XIII, No. 3, September 1958, pp. 225-243.

Gorvine, Albert, and Arif T. Payaslıoğlu, "The Administrative Career Service in
Turkish Provincial Government," *International Review of Administrative
Sciences,* Vol. XXIII (1957), pp. 467-474. Recruitment, training, promotion, etc., in the modern Turkish provincial administration with emphasis on the career nature of the service. Includes a brief historical survey
of Turkish civil bureaucracy.

İdare Dergisi [Administrative Review] Ankara, 1927- , monthly. Appeared as
İdare until 1945. Contains laws and executive orders as well as articles on
public administration.

İller ve Belediyeler Dergisi [Provincial and Municipal Review], Ankara, 1945- ,
monthly. Articles on various aspects of Turkish provincial and municipal
administration. Final issue of each year includes a chronology of significant
events concerning local government.

Kingsbury, Joseph B., and Tahir Aktan, *The Public Service in Turkey: Organization, Recruitment and Training,* Brussels, 1955. A brief survey of Turkish
civil bureaucracy in the mid-twentieth century.

Matthews, A. T. J., *Emergent Turkish Administrators: A Study of the Vocational
and Social Attitudes of Junior and Potential Administrators,* Ankara, 1955.
Based on a survey of 270 students of the Political Sciences and Law Faculties
of Ankara University and of the Public Administration Institute for Turkey
and the Middle East.

Orhun, Hayri, *Türkiye'de Devlet Memurlarının Hukukî Rejimi [The Legal
Status of State Officials in Turkey],* Istanbul, 1946. Surveys the legal position of Turkish civil bureaucrats under Empire and Republic with regard
to recruitment, training, promotion, disciplinary action, salaries, etc.

Presthus, Robert V., and Sevda Erem, *Statistical Analysis in Comparative Administration: The Turkish Conseil d'Etat,* Ithaca, New York, 1958. A
statistical picture of the activities of the Turkish supreme administrative
court based on sample cases selected from decisions rendered, 1947-54.

Sturm, Albert L., and Cemal Mıhçıoğlu, *Bibliography on Public Administration
in Turkey 1928-1957, Selective and Annotated,* Ankara, 1959. The most
complete bibliography available on the subject. Some titles of lasting historical value published prior to 1928 are included.

THE MILITARY

Allen, W. E. D., and Paul Muratoff, *Caucasian Battlefields 1828-1917,* Cambridge, England, 1953. A scholarly military history of the Russian-Turkish frontier with significant political sidelights.

Bıyıklıoğlu, Tevfik, *Atatürk Anadoluda* [*Atatürk in Anatolia*], Ankara, 1959. Military and political organization, 1919-1921, by a former staff colonel and secretary to Atatürk.

——, *Trakya'da Millî Mücadele* [*The National Struggle in Thrace*], 2 vols., Ankara, 1955-56. Scholarly, richly documented from original sources; mainly on the 1919-1921 period.

Cebesoy, Ali Fuat, *Millî Mücadele Hatıraları* [*Memoirs of the National Struggle*], vol. I, Istanbul, 1953. By the commander of the Western front in 1919; detached and documented, an important supplement to Atatürk's *Nutuk*.

[Cemal, Ahmed,] *Memories of a Turkish Statesman 1913-1919* by Djemal Pasha. Apologia of the Young Turk leader.

Fisher, Sydney Nettleton, ed., *The Military in the Middle East: Problems in Society and Government*, Columbus, Ohio, 1963. See the chapters by D. A. Rustow on the Middle East in general and by S. N. Fisher on Turkey.

Harp Tarihi Vesikalari Dergisi [*Journal of Documents of Military History*] Ankara, 1952- , quarterly. Telegraphic correspondence of military and political leaders in the War of Independence in facsimile and romanized transcription. A rich primary source.

Karabekir, Kâzım, *İstiklâl Harbimiz* [*Our War of Independence*], İstanbul, 1960. The long suppressed memoirs of the commander of the Eastern front; with many documents and some sharp polemics.

Larcher, Maurice, *La guerre turque dans la guerre mondiale*, Paris, 1926. The most authoritative account of the Ottoman war effort, by a French officer, based on Turkish general staff sources.

Mühlmann, Carl, *Das deutsch-türkische Waffenbündnis im Weltkriege*, Leipzig, 1940. By an officer on Liman's mission, based on German military archives.

Rustow, Dankwart A., "The Army and the Founding of the Turkish Republic," *World Politics*, XI, 4, July 1959, pp. 513-52. Military politics of the War of Independence, based on published Turkish and foreign sources.

Weiker, Walter F., *The Turkish Revolution 1960-61: Some Aspects of Military Politics*, Washington, D.C., 1963. A scholarly examination of the Committee of National Unity and its policies.

POLITICAL LEADERSHIP AND PARTIES

[Atatürk,] Mustafa Kemal, *Nutuk* [*Speech*]. (The 3 vol. edn., Ankara, 1934, in romanized Turkish, has an index of names and subjects. The English translation [*A Speech Delivered by Ghazi Mustapha Kemal*, Leipzig, 1929] is inadequate.) Kemal's famous *Six-Day Speech* of 1927, a richly documented account of his leadership in the War of Independence; a source of prime importance, though not unbiased.

Frey, Frederick W., *The Turkish Political Elite*, Cambridge, Mass., 1964. A penetrating analysis of the power structure of the First Republic based on a careful examination of the social and occupational background of National Assembly members.

Gökalp, Ziya, *Turkish Nationalism and Western Civilization*, tr. and ed. Niyazi Berkes, London, 1959. Selections from a leading Young Turk writer.

Heyd, Uriel, *Turkish Nationalism*, London, 1950. An examination of Gökalp's thought.

Karpat, Kemal H., *Turkey's Politics: The Transition to a Multiparty System*, Princeton, 1959. A detailed study, based on original sources, of the period after 1946.

Ramsaur, Ernest Edmondson, Jr., *The Young Turks: Prelude to the Revolution of 1908*, Princeton, N.J., 1957. The most reliable examination of the political antecedents of the revolution.

Rustow, Dankwart A., "Turkey's Second Try at Democracy," *Yale Review*, Vol. LII, No. 4, Summer 1963, pp. 518-538. An analysis of the aftermath of the 1960 revolution.

Tunaya, Tarık Zafer, *Türkiyede Siyasî Partiler 1859-1952* [*Political Parties in Turkey 1859-1952*], Istanbul, 1952. A rich compilation of party documents with lists of leaders and an interpretive commentary by a Turkish political scientist.

Us, Hakkı Tarık, *Meclisi Mebusan 1293-1877*, 2 vols., Istanbul, 1940-1954. Reprint of the proceedings of the first Ottoman Legislature.

CONTRIBUTORS

RICHARD L. CHAMBERS is Instructor in Turkish Language and Civilization in the Department of Oriental Languages and Civilizations at the University of Chicago and is a member of that university's Committee on Near Eastern and African Studies. His research has been devoted primarily to the history of the Ottoman reform movement. He was educated at the University of Alabama, Georgetown, and Princeton and has also studied in Turkey, Egypt, and Germany. Before coming to Chicago, he was on the faculty of St. Lawrence University, Canton, New York.

RODERIC H. DAVISON is Professor of History and Chairman of the department at the George Washington University, and a member of the editorial advisory board of the *Middle East Journal*. He is author of *Reform in the Ottoman Empire, 1856-1876*, and of *The Near and Middle East: An Introduction to History and Bibliography*, as well as contributor to *The Diplomats, 1919-1939* (ed. G. A. Craig and F. Gilbert). His articles have appeared in numerous scholarly journals and symposia. He has taught at Princeton, Johns Hopkins, and Harvard. His areas of specialization are European diplomatic history and Near Eastern history.

R. P. DORE is Reader in Sociology with special reference to the Far East at the London School of Economics and Political Science, London University. He was educated at the School of Oriental and African Studies, London University, and has previously taught at that School and at the University of British Columbia. He is author of *City Life in Japan* and *Land Reform in Japan*, and of *Education in Tokugawa Japan*, now in press.

FREDERICK W. FREY is Associate Professor of Political Science at the Massachusetts Institute of Technology and a member of the senior staff of its Center for International Studies. He was a Rhodes Scholar and did his graduate work at Princeton University. From 1957 to 1959, he did research in Turkey under a Ford Foreign Area Training Fellowship, and has returned to Turkey to engage in research three times thereafter. A consultant to the Agency for International Development, he is the author of the *Turkish Political Elite* and several articles on Turkey in symposia and academic journals.

ROGER F. HACKETT is Associate Professor of History at the University of Michigan and a member of the Center for Japanese Studies of the same university. He was formerly editor of the *Journal of Asian Studies* and is co-author of *A Global History of Man*. His research has centered on key figures in the development of Japan's modern army and he has published articles on two of these personalities: Yamagata Aritomo and Nishi Amane. He was born in Japan, educated at Carleton College, Harvard University, and Tokyo University, and he taught at Northwestern University before assuming his present post at the University of Michigan.

JOHN WHITNEY HALL is a A. Whitney Griswold Professor of History at Yale University, chairman of the Yale Council on East Asian Studies, and chairman of the Conference on Modern Japan of the Association for Asian Studies. He is author of *Tanuma Okitsugu, Forerunner of Modern Japan*; *Japanese History, A Guide to Japanese Research and Reference Materials*; co-author of *Village Japan*; and author of the forthcoming *The Evolution of Government in Japan, 600-1600*. He has contributed articles to numerous professional journals. Professor Hall was born and raised in Japan and educated at Amherst College and Harvard University. Before going to Yale he taught for many years at the University of Michigan.

NOBUTAKA IKE is Professor of Political Science at Stanford University. He is the author of *The Beginnings of Political Democracy in Japan*, and *Japanese Politics*. He is also a contributor to *Major Governments of Asia*. He has written numerous articles in professional journals on Japanese political affairs. He was educated at the University of Washington and Johns Hopkins University.

HALİL İNALCIK is Professor of Ottoman History and of the History of Turkish Institutions at the University of Ankara, and a member of the Turkish Historical Society. He is author of *The Tanzimat and the Bulgarian Question*, *Studies on the Reign of Mehmed the Conqueror*, *The Ottoman Register of Albania of 1431* (all in Turkish) and of many articles on Ottoman history and institutions in scholarly journals in Turkey and abroad. He was educated in Turkey and spent two years on research at the British Museum and the Public Record Office, London. He has also been a visiting associate professor at Columbia University and a research fellow at Harvard University.

MASAMICHI INOKI is Professor of Political Science at Kyoto University, and a member of the South-East Asian Studies Center at the same University. He is the author of *The Political Theory of Dictatorship* (in Japanese) and of several books on communism and national socialism. He also contributed the chapter on "Maoism and Leninism" to *Unity and Contradiction* (ed. by Dr. Kurt London). Professor Inoki was educated at Tokyo University and also studied in Germany.

KEMAL H. KARPAT is with the Department of Government, Graduate School of Arts and Science at New York University. Earlier, he was a staff member of the United Nations, Chairman of the Public Administration Department at Middle East Technical University in Ankara, and Associate Professor of Political Science at Montana University. Dr. Karpat has also been a research Fellow at Harvard University and recipient of an SSRC grant. He is the author of *Turkey's Politics* and of articles in American, European, and Turkish journals. He received his education at the Universities of Istanbul and Washington (Seattle) and New York University and is a member of the Istanbul Bar Association.

SHŪICHI KATŌ was educated at Tokyo University and is now Professor of Asian Studies at the University of British Columbia. He is co-editor of *Kindai Nihon Shisō-shi Kōza* and author of some dozen books on Japanese culture and social problems. He has lectured at Yale, Princeton, the University of Michigan, the *Wiener Rundfunk* in Austria, and at the *Association Franco-Japonaise* in France.

WILLIAM W. LOCKWOOD is Professor of Politics and International Affairs at Princeton University. He is author of *The Economic Development of Japan*, and editor of a forthcoming volume on *The State and Economic Enterprise in Japan*. He has long been a specialist in Far Eastern affairs and once was Assistant Chief, Division of Japanese and Korean Economic Affairs, Department of State. During 1963-1964 he was President of the Association of Asian Studies. Born in China, he received his education at DePauw and Harvard Universities.

ARİF T. PAYASLIOĞLU is Dean of the Faculty of Administrative Sciences and Associate Professor of Political Science at the Middle East Technical University in Ankara. He is the author of two books on political parties and voting behavior (both in Turkish) and several articles published in Turkey and abroad. He was educated in Turkey, in France, and in the United States. Before joining the Middle East Technical University he worked at the University of Ankara, at the Institute of Public Administration (Ankara), and at the State Planning Organization of Turkey.

DANKWART A. RUSTOW is Professor of International Social Forces at Columbia University, a member of the Board of Governors of the Middle East Institute (Washington, D.C.), and a consultant to the U.S. Department of State. He is author of *The Politics of Compromise* and *Politics and Westernization in the Near East*, co-author of *The Politics of the Developing Areas* (edited by G. A. Almond and J. S. Coleman), and a contributor to the *Encyclopaedia of Islam* and to many professional journals and symposia published in this country and abroad. He was educated in his native Germany, in Turkey, and in the United States. Before joining the Columbia faculty he was associated with the Program in Near Eastern Studies of Princeton University. He has also taught at Heidelberg and Yale and more recently has served on the senior staff of the Brookings Institution.

ROBERT A. SCALAPINO is Professor of Political Science at the University of California, Berkeley; Editor of the *Asian Survey*; and member of the Executive Board of the Institute of International Studies. He has served as consultant to the Ford and Rockefeller Foundations and to the Rand Corporation. His writings on Japan include *Democracy and the Party Movement in Pre-War Japan, Parties and Politics in Contemporary Japan* (with Junnosuke Masumi), and numerous other symposia contributions and articles. Professor Scalapino has lectured in many Japanese universities as well as in other institutions in the Far East.

PETER F. SUGAR is Associate Professor of History at the University of Washington. He is the author of *Industrialization of Bosnia-Hercegovina, 1878-1918* and a contributor to numerous professional journals. Professor Sugar has lived in Turkey for over five years. He was educated at the City College of New York and at Princeton University.

ROBERT E. WARD is Professor of Political Science at the University of Michigan, an associate of the Center for Japanese Studies at the same university, and a member of the Social Science Research Council's Committee on Comparative Politics. He is co-editor and a co-author of *Modern Political Systems: Asia* and *Modern Political Systems: Europe* and of *Village Japan*. He is a contributor to numerous professional journals and symposia. Professor Ward has studied and worked extensively in Japan and is a specialist in East Asian politics. He was educated at Stanford and the University of California (Berkeley).

INDEX

Note: J = Japan, Japanese; T = Turkey, Turkish

Abdülaziz, 155, 213, 263
Abdülhamid II, 95, 99-100, 113, 152, 156, 158-59, 173, 264-65, 267-68, 302, 306, 316, 324-25, 360-62, 369, 372, 378-79, 387n., 412, 415-16, 427, 430, 446, 452
Abdullah Cevdet, 376
Abdülmecid, 62, 94, 96, 353, 359, 411, 446
Abdurrahman Şeref, 103n.
Abe Isō, 184
Abegglen, James C., 203n., 298
Abosch, David, 73n.
absolutism: J, 121; T, 151
Acaroğlu, Türker, 279
Action Army (T, 1909), 362-63
Adıvar, Abdülhak Adnan, 106n., 223
ağa's, 48, 59-60, 63
agriculture, 87, 125; *see also* land tenure, peasants
ahi, 46
Ahmed Vefik Pasha, 105, 111, 114-15
Aitken, Hugh G. J., 168n.
Aizawa Akira, 190n., 191n., 192n.
Akçura, Yusuf, 114
Akiyama Kiyoshi, 253n.
Albania, 373, 448, 463
Alemdar Mustafa Pasha, 51
Âli, Ali, 258
Ali Cemali, 43
Ali Galib, 371n.
Ali Kemal, 223
Âli Pasha, 55, 95, 98, 103, 113, 260, 321, 323, 412
Ali Suavi, 259-60, 265
Alican, Ekrem, 425
Almond, Gabriel, 10n.
Anadolu Ajansı, 270
anarchism, in J, 184
Anderson, C. Arnold, 206n.
Angell, George W., Jr., 208n.
Ankara, battle (1402), 149
Apkar of Sivas, 255
Arabs: influence on T, 442; leadership among, 456; secession from Ottoman T, 373
Arahata Kanson, 184
Araki Manshō, 14
Arisugawa, Prince, 348
Armenians, 448

armistice: Mudros (1918), 161, 364-65, 373; Mudanya (1922), 365
Asahi, 239-40, 243-49
Asahi Shimbun-sha, 123n.
Asakawa Kan'ichi, 14, 32n.
Asano, Lord, of Hiroshima, 34
askerî, 44
Asō Makato, 202n.
Asoka Mehta, 137
associations in J (*see also* parties in J): for Petitioning a National Assembly, 400-01; parent-teacher, 143; patriotic, 126, 129, 133, 397, 400; reservists, 407; Society of J Newspapers, 247-48; Society of New Men, 185; veterans, 349
associations in T: Defense of Rights (*see* parties in T; learned, 259; military, 362-63, 372, 379-80; Newspapermen's, 278; religious, 268-69; students, 235; teachers, 234; Turkish Hearth, 216; youth, 235
Atatürk, Mustafa Kemal, 63, 101, 108, 110, 151-52, 161-64, 167, 169-71, 174, 217, 223-25, 234-35, 269-71, 301-02, 311, 317, 321, 325-26, 352, 364-66, 370-72, 374-78, 380-85, 388, 402, 417-22, 428-30, 432, 441, 446, 450, 451, 453, 456, 458, 463
Ata'ullah, Şeyhülislâm, 50-51
Atay, Falih Rıfkı, 375
Âtıf Efendi, Ahmed, 106, 255, 258
Austria (Habsburg Empire), 6, 97, 99-100, 109, 353, 373
authoritarianism: in J, 124, 393-94; in T, 62, 161-63, 169, 224
âyan, 45-54, 59-61, 63, 452

Baghdad, 46
Bailey, F. E., 57n.
Bakufu, *see* shogun
baku-han system, 20-27, 34
banking: in J, 129; in T, 165-68
Barker, Ernest, 5n.
de Bary, Wm. Theodore, 30n., 329n.
başıbozuk, 60
Battal Gazi, 265
Baumann, 112
Bayar, Celâl, 172, 174, 221, 302, 366-68, 422
Beckman, George M., 81n.
Bele, Refet, 419-20
Belgrade, 46